"Fellow citizens,
we cannot escape history."

—Abraham Lincoln, 1862

ALCATRAZ

A Definitive History
of the Penitentiary Years

Michael Esslinger

OCEANVIEW PUBLISHING

SAN FRANCISCO, CALIFORNIA

Ocean View Publishing
P.O. Box 222317
Carmel, CA 93922
www.alcatrazhistory.com
e-mail: coastbooks@aol.com

Third Edition 2006

ISBN: 0-9704614-0-2

Library of Congress Card Number: 00-109107

Esslinger, Michael 1965–

No biographies within this reference have been authorized by those persons named or associated.

Cover Design by James Zach
Book Design and Composition by John Reinhardt Book Design
Original Illustrations by Phil Hall, Mira Kamada, and Phil Bergen

Cover Photo by Jack Hollingsworth (Getty Images)
Back Photo by Julie R. Esslinger
Back Portrait by Jun Cong (J.C. Art Studio, SF)
Back Text: Patrick O'Conner / Stephen Mills

The paper used in this publication meets the minimum requirements of the American National Standard for Information Sciences-Permanence of Paper for Printed Library Materials, and Archival Preservation.

Printed in the United States of America.

Phil Bergen at Alcatraz
1995
90th
Birthday

"Lieutenant Bergen was a tall, square jawed, handsome man who looked as if he could have been the hero of every Saturday movie serial ever made. He had cool direct eyes and a natural fearlessness. On Alcatraz, he was a "high-risk" guard. He was a daredevil who thought nothing of plunging head-first into danger. In addition he was a deadly shot."

This is how Clark Howard described Philip Bergen in his novel *Six Against the Rock*. Bergen is also depicted in Thomas E. Gaddis' classic novel *Birdman of Alcatraz*, and he appears in numerous other books and films. When I asked Bergen which character depiction he found most accurate, he simply replied: "*Well . . . the birds were very well written don't you think?*"

Philip R. Bergen, former Captain of the Guards at Alcatraz, spent sixteen years working and living on the island, raising both his daughters on "The Rock." I had spent nearly two years conducting exhaustive research, and I was quite pleased to hand him what I considered to be the final version of this book. A few weeks later I called Phil to get his opinion of the content, and to see if he had any last minute recommendations. He stated in a very matter-of-fact tone: "*Sure, rewrite the whole thing or make sure that it is marked 'fiction.'*"

Over the next eighteen months I recommenced my long journey, heading back to the archives, cross checking references against archival records, conducting additional interviews, attending lectures, and even going out with County staff (in the rain and mud), to verify the unmarked burial sites of a few deceased inmates. Thus while Bergen did not have any formalized connection to my book, his mark remains obvious. Even when the perspectives presented were not favorable to him personally, he pushed me to become an objective listener, and then to document what I had heard, rather than interpreting the facts. That was the theme of his contribution, and with that said, it has been a long and extraordinary journey.

Well into his nineties, Phil Bergen remained an Alcatraz aficionado. I attended several Alcatraz reunions, and would watch in amazement as Phil rattled off names of people he hadn't seen in over fifty years. His ability to recount specific events and their chronologies was phenomenal. Phil Bergen represents only one of the many voices of those that lived the Alcatraz experience—but his was a very prominent and authoritative voice. Getting to know Phil was a rare privilege, and I feel blessed that he was able to read and comment on all but the final two chapters. Although he has passed, his voice has not been silenced.

Thank you Phil, for helping me see Alcatraz through your eyes, and leaving behind a remarkable legacy.

Phil Bergen at Alcatraz, 1995

Acknowledgments

Alcatraz may well continue to stand as a symbol of confinement and isolation, but the scope of my research and the influence of those who have contributed were, simply stated, not. They encircled the globe, from across the United States to as far away as Holland, and these people have helped me to define the framework upon which to build. I once came across a quotation from the Dalai Lama, who stated in his great wisdom that sharing knowledge is the path to immortality. As it may, I will be forever grateful to the following immortals:

First and foremost, Joseph V. Sanchez, Archivist at the National Archives, was an enthusiastic supporter, and always went above and beyond to help me navigate through the endless maze of files and records. Michael Frusch and Rosemary Kennedy also extended their support, and always came through on my short-notice requests. John Martini, historian, writer, and masterful researcher, was a phenomenal resource on a multitude of levels. His passion for exploring history, his willingness to share new discoveries, and his careful attention to detail have made my work so much more intriguing. In addition he is the author of one of my favorite books, *Fortress Alcatraz*, which remains "the" landmark reference on the military years. I would also like to take this opportunity to thank the late Erwin Thompson, whom I never had the chance to meet, but whose mammoth reference entitled *Alcatraz—The Rock* was key to my studies.

Kim Sulik at the National Park Archives suffered through my never-ending requests for material, and was always a kind spirit. Susan Ewing Haley was also instrumental in offering advice and direction regarding materials in the early stages of my research. Sam Daniel at the Library of Congress helped me to locate some hard-to-find photographs from a variety of sources. Bill Kooiman and Irene Stuchura at the San Francisco Maritime Museum were extremely obliging in allowing me to repeatedly set up camp in their offices, to explore materials. Chuck Stucker, another skilled historian and former resident of Alcatraz, proved to be one of my most exceptional resources. Chuck's passion to preserve the history and perspectives of those who called Alcatraz home will undoubtedly be celebrated by future historians who are tasked to chronicle this chapter of America's history. Pat Akre and Susan Goldstein, Archivists at the San Francisco Library, were also very gracious in helping me with my photograph inquires. Thanks also to my good friends at the Monterey and Carmel Library for helping me in my early California research, and likewise to my good friends at the National Steinbeck Center for their support and sound advice. I must also mention Loretta Thompson and Yolanda Talamonte of Hartnell College, who helped me transcribe numerous documents.

Herbert Hart was one of the pioneers in collecting information on the military years, and he allowed me to use quotations and photographs from his 1969 Report to the San Francisco Mayor's Office. Tom Paiva was kind enough to let me use his wonderful portrait of Phil Bergen for the dedication. Vernel Crittendon and Lieutenant Pat Blanson at San Quentin State Prison both proved to be excellent resources in helping me to locate materials and information on Warden Johnston. Another unique source was Frank Keaton at Keaton's Mortuary. Keaton's handled the body of Sam Shockley following his execution, and Frank directed me to a variety of repositories, to help verify burial records for various inmates. Unfortunately, much of this information was left on the cutting room floor, and didn't make it into the final reference. Frank was also helpful in providing unique insight into many of the subjects covered in this reference.

The late Jim Quillen was another wonderful source to whom I owe very special thanks. He recounted for me his numerous experiences while incarcerated at Alcatraz, and offered me his first hand memories of the 1946 events, which he witnessed while incarcerated in D Block. I came to admire his honesty and his willingness to revive some very unpleasant memories. Willie Radkay and the late Dale Stamphill also provided valuable assistance in understanding the challenges of confinement at Alcatraz. Former inmates Darwin Coon and Glenn "Nate" Williams are likewise two people whom I greatly admire, and I am grateful for their contributions. Former President Ronald Reagan awarded Williams the President's Action Award, and Glenn is without question one of nicest and most inspirational people I have ever met. A true Christian and a great storyteller in his own right, Darwin Coon has dedicated himself to openly sharing his experiences, and giving back to society. He has offered the public a rare gift by capturing the interest of youths who are intrigued by Alcatraz, and educating them about the consequences of crime. Lorna Joy Williams, Marti Newell, Renée Keith, Tom O'Donnell, Linda Gray, Joe Holt (also a good friend from my Apollo research), Nielen Dickens, Kathy O'Brien, Wendy Swee, all deserve a special thank you for helping share stories and documents.

It would be difficult to adequately thank former Alcatraz Correctional Officers Cliff Fish and Phil Bergen for the extensive time they spent painstakingly reviewing my manuscript, giving direction, and making appropriate corrections. Both provided extensive commentary on various aspects of the prison and its history, and they made this project an extraordinarily special experience. Both men passed away during the final stages of publication, and I will forever remain grateful having had the opportunity to get to know them. I would also especially like to thank Shelly Roby of Michael Hoff Productions and the Discovery Channel for inviting me to tag along during the filming of Cliff's first visit back to Alcatraz since he left in 1962. This was a very special privilege, and I feel extremely honored to have been included in the endeavor to capture this wonderful moment in history.

I also wish to thank Ronald Paolini and Don Graffe of the Marin County Department of Parks and Open Space, who were very helpful in the search for and identification of Miran Thompson's unmarked burial site. Don deserves special mention, since he helped personally in the tedious search, and even when the rains hit, he didn't mind getting a little soiled while excavating mud. Anne Diestel of the Bureau of Prisons provided me with some excellent photographs and other materials. A.G. Sevinga offered expertise and knowledge, corresponding from Holland. He offered numerous suggestions on the manuscript, and was always a prodigious source of guidance.

Thanks also goes to my family at AMR, with whom I've worked side by side for nearly two decades. To each of them, my appreciation for their unwavering friendship and support—I salute them all. A special thank you goes to Alcatraz Ranger John Cantwell, and to the volunteers and staff members at Alcatraz. These men and women always took time to accommodate my requests and answer my questions, and always approached the island's historical past in a balanced and dignified fashion. They are the key conservators of this important history.

I would also like to thank the various officers who risked their employment by covertly snapping photos of the prison, notably George DeVincenzi, and many others. Without them, much of the history would have been lost. There were many others I met at Alcatraz who suffered through my endless questions and requests for clarification—I thank them for their contribution. Jolene Babyak, who wrote "the" book on Robert Stroud and the Morris-Anglin escape, offered a perfect stranger some early advice on locating a few specific Stroud photos. Ernest Lageson, who wrote two exceptional books on the 1946 events, helped me to locate a few key photographs that remained elusive until our meeting at Alcatraz. Brad Sears, the owner of the launch *Warden Johnston*, shared his photos and information on the history of this San Francisco seafaring icon. I applaud his relentless efforts to save this important historical treasure. Mario Gomes, Curator of the Al Capone Museum, was also a wonderful help in locating unpublished photos of Al Capone. Stan Hamilton of the National Press Club was supportive, and offered some early tips on researching Machine Gun Kelly.

Kathryn Marusak, Bruce Hagen, and Jamie Schoonover all provided guidance on the manuscript through its various stages of development. The first drafts were so large that we joked about entitling the book "*The Brick.*" Thanks to their careful surgical guidance, the book will now fit on a bookshelf. Lucy Boling, the true wizard behind the curtain, was a master in the final editing stages, and was always honest yet gentle in her advice on changes in structure and content. John Reinhardt, the extraordinary designer, has contributed with infinite patience. He engaged in the process years before the design concepts ever started. Kathleen Strattan made me feel in good hands during the indexing phase. Phil Hall and Mira Kamada are the skillful creators of this book's wonderful illustrations, and I feel lucky to have collaborated with them.

Lastly, I'm very lucky to have the opportunity to say publicly to the special people in my life how much they mean to me. Words can't express my gratitude to my mother and father, who have always shown full support in all of my interests. This in itself could be the subject of another book. From my youngest years they encouraged my small adventures, and allowed me to explore a variety of places on my own—something that is sadly no longer possible in today's world. Whether it was by dropping me a off at a movie studio in Hollywood, or by letting me explore Alcatraz, they always encouraged me, and their love and trust have blessed me with a most gifted life. My beautiful wife Julie deserves the greatest thanks for always believing in me over the past ten years—I love you, and in the next ten years let me show you a whole new world. To Forrest and Brandon, the two little men who make my world, may you both do great things (and I don't mean becoming great Jedi Fighters). Love also to my terrier and companion Luck (and Spark too).

And finally, to my late friend Michael Lundeen, my best friend—God speed . . .

Thank you all,
MICHAEL ESSLINGER

Contents

Foreword

I can still vividly remember that crisp September day in 1958. I stepped from the prison launch, the *Warden Johnston*, straining to get a good view of my new surroundings. The cold steel shackles chafed against my skin as I walked through the gates and into a world kept secret from the public. It was a somber feeling, trying to come to grips with the idea that I had been branded as one of the nation's most incorrigible inmates in the Federal prison system. I had been a bank robber, and I was now collecting the wages of my sin. After entrance processing I was strip-searched, then permitted a brief shower and escorted to my new home— a diminutive five-by-nine-foot cell. As I lay back on my hard bunk, I realized that this was it . . . I had finally reached the end of line . . . ALCATRAZ.

I lived under the strict routine of America's most infamous prison, and faced head-on the relentless pressures of existence within my cramped and tiny cell. I became well versed in the cloak-and-dagger underground of Alcatraz, a silent code known only to the inmates. Not everyone was able to come to terms with the stressful and unrelenting regimen. Some responded by committing suicide, and others with explosive surges of deadly violence. Meanwhile, the painful landscape of freedom was spread before us, just out of reach across the bay. The sights and sounds were a continuous reminder of everything we had lost. On some occasions while we were locked in our cells, an eerie quiet would pass over the men. Distant feminine laughter would resonate from a passing tour boat through an open barred window. The voices would quickly fade into the backdrop of seagulls and slow time, and the men would be left with only their thoughts and their memories.

I personally knew many of the famous and not-so-famous inmates who served time on The Rock. I helped my friends John Anglin and Frankie Morris to acquire some of the essential tools that they used in their famed escape attempt (later portrayed in the motion picture *Escape from Alcatraz* starring Clint Eastwood), and I would dream like so many others of someday making my own escape.

A long time has passed since I last heard the frequent clashing of steel gates, and the prison guards calling out their counts. Even still, I remain a marked man. One cannot survive such a profound experience and expect to emerge unaffected. When Alcatraz finally closed in 1963,

I was one of the last inmates to step off the island, and it was then that I started my long journey back to freedom. In 1972, after serving nearly fifteen years in the Federal prison system, I made my way back into society with a newfound spirit and outlook. I earned my way to a respectable career, was a proud foster parent to ninety-four beautiful children, and wrote a successful book entitled *Alcatraz—The True End of the Line*.

I think you will enjoy reading Michael's book. Through meticulous research, he has captured the experience of Alcatraz with an authentic voice. It is a skillful blend of history and character study, and a compelling portrait of America's most notorious prison.

Over the years, I have returned to the island on various occasions to share my experiences with inquisitive visitors. I sometimes return to my old cell, and think of that young man lying on his bunk, dreaming of this day. As Richard Nixon once said: ". . . only if you have been in the deepest valley can you ever know how magnificent it is to be on the highest mountain . . ."

DARWIN E. COON, AZ-1422
Former Inmate, Alcatraz Federal Penitentiary
Author—*Alcatraz, The True End of the Line*

Introduction

My first introduction to Alcatraz came at a very young age, during a visit to San Francisco with my parents in the late 1970's. Just as thousands of others had done before me, I peered in wonderment from across the Bay at the small and forbidding island known as "The Rock." I had seen the books that lined the sidewalks of Fisherman's Wharf, illustrated with faces of hardened convicts and vintage photographs, all indicating that the island prison was a kind of living hell. My parents were generous enough to purchase a few of these books for me, and I was destined to immerse myself in them over the next few weeks. Even as we walked along the pier, I sneaked a few quick peeks into my shopping bag, hoping to catch brief glimpses of the inmates and prison photos. I knew that there were no longer any prisoners residing on the island, but to a young and curious mind, there was still something intriguing and mysterious about it all.

After reading my books from cover to cover, I began plotting my first visit to the island. I had prepared for my excursion by studying the various escape attempts, the lives of former inmates such as Al Capone and Machine Gun Kelly, and the chilling personal accounts of these and others that that were said to be the "rogues of society." During the first years when the island was open to the public, Park Service employees guided all of the visitor tours. As we hiked up the steep path to the cellhouse, I remember the stillness of the surroundings, broken only by the occasional screeches of passing seagulls. The misted smell of the ocean was thick and almost tropic. As the ranger guided us past the dimly lit cells, I lagged behind, blending into the shadows, absorbed by the incredible history of the abandoned prison.

The highlight of my trip was meeting a former inmate who had come to the island to talk with visitors, and to describe the twenty years during which he had lived on The Rock as inmate #AZ-714. Clarence Carnes had been involved in a disastrous attempt at armed robbery at only fifteen years of age. When a gas station attendant challenged Carnes and fought to disarm him, the young delinquent pulled the trigger, and changed his life's destiny in a matter of only seconds. Carnes was ultimately convicted of first-degree murder, and he arrived on Alcatraz at the young age of eighteen. One year later he participated in what would be considered the island's most significant and catastrophic escape attempt, which would ultimately result in five tragic deaths. For his role in the escape and the murder of a correctional officer by a co-conspirator, Carnes received an additional ninety-nine years, which were added to the life sentence he was already serving. He would therefore spend the great majority of his life in prison. Seeing Carnes in person, I was amazed at how much he had changed since the mug shot photos were taken on his arrival at Alcatraz. His hard looks had evolved into soft rounded features, and he certainly didn't resemble the cold-blooded criminal that I had read about. It was interesting to hear him describe in chilling detail his recollections of the famous aborted escape attempt of 1946.

A few hours later, after the boat had delivered our group back to the boarding pier, I noticed Carnes sitting at a street vendor's booth signing books. I tried to muster the courage to introduce myself, and ask him a few questions about the '46 events. But just as I approached him, he got up, motioned to the vendor that he was hungry, and started walking away. Keeping a safe distance, I followed him through Fisherman's Wharf, finally arriving at a food concession stand. Carnes purchased a hot dog and soft drink and walked over to the telescopes located at the end of Pier 45, which advertised a close-up view of Alcatraz Island for only ten cents. He dropped a dime in the first telescope and looked through it for about a minute. Noticing me, he turned and motioned to the telescope, inviting me to have a look. He said that if I looked quickly, I might be able to catch a glimpse of a group walking down the stairs from the recreation yard. Knowing his past, I cautiously accepted the invitation, and watched him carefully as I positioned myself at the telescope. Eventually I was able to navigate through the scenery with the eyepiece, and Carnes started walking away, gazing casually at the island every few seconds. I finally got the courage to approach him and introduce myself. I explained that I had learned who he was from two books I had read about the prison. He graciously shook my hand, and allowed me to ask some unskilled questions about his long habitation on Alcatraz and the events of 1946. Our dialog remained fairly superficial, until a woman approached Carnes, interrupting the conversation.

The woman told Carnes that she had been a young girl during the 1946 escape attempt, and that her father had brought her to Aquatic Park, where many of the correctional officers' families had gathered to watch the events unfolding from the mainland. She explained that she had been terrified, seeing the flashes of light and hearing the thunderous guns. She told Carnes that she had hugged her father's steel thermos, praying that it would block any bullets fired by the inmates, and she described how that same fear remained in her thoughts every time she looked at the island. She jokingly commented that after the '46 riot, she was annoyed at having to give up her bed to masses of visiting relatives. They all had come to hear at firsthand her father's description of what he had witnessed from the mainland. They were all hoping to catch a glimpse through binoculars of a guard on the yard wall catwalk, or perhaps even the faint figure of an inmate.

The conversation then progressed to Carnes' thoughts on being out of prison. He commented that when he was inside, he constantly thought and read about what people were doing on the outside, but once he got out, he couldn't stop thinking about his friends on the inside, and what they were doing. He said that the most difficult years of his life had been spent on Alcatraz, and that even now it consumed much of his daily thoughts. The woman made a parting comment that I still remember today. She offered to him that although they had followed different paths, and had lived their lives on opposite sides of the prison's wall, they were both still haunted by memories of Alcatraz. Carnes nodded and smiled at her, then walked off, disappearing into the crowd of tourists along the pier. It would be several decades before I realized that it was during my conversation with Carnes that I began to write this book.

Each year over one million tourists board the island's ferry to visit what was once considered the toughest Federal prison in America. Today, Alcatraz is one of the biggest tourist magnets and most famous landmarks of San Francisco. The island's mystique, which has been created primarily through books and motion pictures, continues to lure people from all over the world to see firsthand where America housed its most notorious criminals. Cramped cells, rigid discipline, and unrelenting routine were the Alcatraz trademarks, and it became known as the final stop for the nation's most incorrigible prisoners. On any given day thousands of visitors can be found wandering the island, and taking in its unique history. The cellhouse, now abandoned by the criminals who were once housed there, still bears the marks of the events to which the walls once bore witness. It is a journey into a dim piece of American history, and few walk away fully comprehending. The clichéd expression "*if these walls could talk*" is taken to a deeper level.

Even today, decades after the prison's closure, the name Alcatraz still evokes a variety of dark, forbidding images for many. In the decades of the prison's active years, people would stroll the shorelines of San Francisco, weaving their own mental images of the horrors that lurked behind the concrete walls and fencing. In some ways, Alcatraz became almost two distinct entities—the prison and the myth. In many cases, the Alcatraz that people still imagine was a cruel and vile chamber of horrors, and to some former inmates, this may seem a valid perception of that environment. One such case was illustrated in an informal meeting between the late former inmate Jim Quillen and myself, in August of 1997, in the kitchen basement of Alcatraz. Forty years earlier Quillen and a few fellow inmates had plotted an escape in this same area. During our brief conversation, Quillen confided to me that returning to the main cellhouse had been a painful and difficult journey. It was obvious that decades later, he was still troubled by the many experiences he had endured on Alcatraz.

In my approach to assembling the information presented here, there has been no attempt to minimize the allegations of brutality, though the facts often argue the opposite. I am bringing forward a more factual and balanced view through the eyes of those who lived and worked on the island, both inmates and officers. This book is intended to reflect a blend of perspectives, researched and derived from a variety of sources. The historical framework comes from both published and unpublished archive materials, supplemented by extensive interviews with a multitude of former inmates as well as correctional officers and their families. Statements of historical and technical fact are as precise as I could make them, given the resources at my disposal. Errors doubtlessly remain, as there are simply too many sources with contrasting perspectives to consider. I have made every attempt to verify information against archival record and the knowledge of those involved. Nevertheless, there is certainly some information included in this text that is reported as fact, but has most likely been embellished over the years. I don't necessarily believe that anyone has intentionally set out to falsify history, but when source information is derived primarily from personal memory, details become impure with time, and thus historical interpretation tends to fall into the trap of extrapolation, rather than adhering to essential fact.

During the initial phases of my research, I received a letter from former Alcatraz inmate Willie Radkay, who wrote in part: "*Nobody wants to print the facts, even if it comes direct from the source himself. Artistic license is used to alter true incidents and events, and even the language used by the cons, whose jargons weren't spoken in church circles.*" This statement emerged as a common theme of discussions and interviews with former guards and inmates alike. In communicating this history, I felt it was important for the reader to understand that I am aware of the limitations of recollection and memory. I have chosen to maintain the integrity of the source material, and to reconstruct events based on period documentation, unless the original sources contain obvious errors. This may challenge the opinions of many who are versed in the history of Alcatraz.

Too often in historical works, writers have filtered events in a fashion that they felt would better acclimatize their readers to the subject matter. Often as a result, the characters of individuals and the sense of place are lost. One of my favorite examples of "image softening" is the famous portrait of General George Washington crossing the Delaware in 1776, by Emanuel Gottlieb Leutze. Most people would probably prefer to believe that Washington stood stately and commanding in the prow of the boat, a model of dignified leadership before his men. But as historian Kenneth Davis later revealed, the truth was much different from this romanticized image. When documenting his experiences with Washington, General Harry Knox made an entry in his journal commenting that on this historical occasion, Washington poked him with the tip of his boot, remarking: "*Move your fat ass Harry, and not too fast or you'll swamp the boat.*"

Another example of historical coloring involves our perceptions of the early days of space travel. Following the return of the Apollo 12 Astronauts from the second lunar landing mission, the crewmen were televised in a worldwide broadcast with President Richard M. Nixon via telephone. While awaiting the President's arrival, the crew sat idly as television cameras focused on the planetary explorers, trapped behind the glass window of their quarantine trailer. As the world watched, Mission Commander Pete Conrad cupped his hand over the telephone receiver, turned way from the camera, and whispered a comment to Command Module Pilot Richard Gordon. The public would never hear his remark, which was later revealed to have been: *"See Dick, I told you if you stuck with me you'd be farting through silk."* I never met George Washington, but I did get to know Pete Conrad extremely well, and humor was a hallmark of his personality. He was a brilliant astronaut, but he never let an opportunity for a joking comment pass him. I had heard this story before meeting him, and it helped me to shape a more accurate image of his personality. But I've always wished that I had read more such stories when I was in school, rather than the carefully woven images that my textbooks always seem to provide.

With all of this in mind, the greatest weakness of *Alcatraz — A Definitive History of the Penitentiary Years* also remains its principal strength. I felt it was important to capture the essence of the island's history, but at the same time to ensure the integrity of the archival records. Above all, I had to resist the temptation to venture too deeply into the states of mind or the thought processes of the individuals involved, or to replace plain fact with entertaining narrative. The voices of Alcatraz are numerous, and one simply cannot understand the complex history of the island by looking solely at any exclusive source. In my process of researching specific events, when the source materials provided little or no information, I turned to the excellent works that are listed in the bibliography to verify the chronology. These works have served to preserve the history of Alcatraz to the present day. It should also be noted that the bibliographic references provided herein serve as a comprehensive map for those whose interests require a more expanded research base. *Alcatraz—A Definitive History* is intended as a source reference, rather than a conclusive text. The history of Alcatraz is a fascinating window into one of the richest, and debatably one of the darkest aspects of America's history. I hope that this book will inspire you to read further on the subject, and will help you to hear for yourself the many voices of Alcatraz, and their fascinating stories.

MICHAEL ESSLINGER

History of Alcatraz

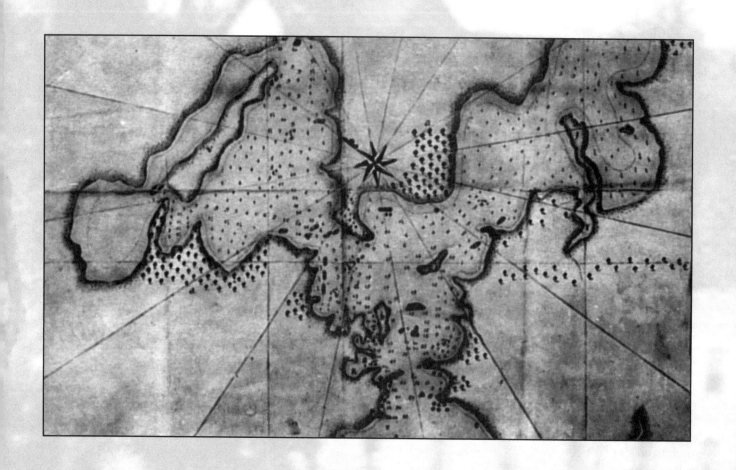

Discovery and Exploration

FOR CENTURIES the Bay of San Francisco lay hidden to passing ships, due to a unique illusion created by a small island that is known today as Alcatraz. This island, which is positioned at the center of the bay and three miles inland from the Pacific Ocean, was indistinctly visible from the misty coastline. The rocky formations draped with gloomy vegetation blended in with the soft features of the East Bay Hills, screening the mouth of the harbor.

In 1542 Antonio de Mendoza, the Viceroy of New Spain, commissioned a Spaniard named Juan Rodriguez Cabrillo to explore the northern reaches of the colony's west coast. Following the discovery of America by Christopher Columbus in 1492, a steady stream of explorers had charted expeditions to the New World in search of gold, and to claim territory for their rulers. Mendoza was lured by their tales of magnificent wealth in this unexplored territory, with coastlines said to be rich with pearls, and interiors abundant with precious gold. The main purpose of the expedition, however, would be to seek out the legendary waterway called the Strait of Anián, known to English explorers as the Northwest Passage. For centuries, voyagers had dreamed of a westward route to Asia through the waters of North America, but their expeditions had often ended in disaster.

There is little known about Cabrillo's early life, and the factual traces that remain are debated by historians. It is believed that he was born in Portugal between 1498 and 1500, and spent most of his life in military service. Historical records in the Spanish archives maintain that in 1520, Cabrillo accompanied Panfilo de Naravaez in an unsuccessful attack against Hernán Cortés, the conqueror of Mexico's Aztec Empire—though this is disputed by equal numbers who believe that Cabrillo fought along-

A survey map from the 1800's showing Alcatraz Island set against the background of the East Bay Hills. This unique topography masked the small island and the San Francisco Bay from early explorers.

Spanish Explorer Juan Rodriguez Cabrillo.

A vintage engraving made in 1740 by a Benedictine Monk, depicting early seafaring explorers.

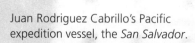

Juan Rodriguez Cabrillo's Pacific expedition vessel, the *San Salvador*.

side Cortés. Some references suggest that Cabrillo himself served as Governor of Guatemala, and was one of the conquerors of the Central American region including Nicaragua and El Salvador.

Many historians believe that Cabrillo's interest in exploring the northern coast originated with Cortés. In 1522 Cortés had built a shipyard at Zacatula on the Pacific coast of Mexico, as a base from which to send out expeditions to chart the Pacific. Building the ships proved problematic, and by the time they had managed to produce seaworthy vessels in 1526, the King of Spain ordered them sent to the South Pacific. Cabrillo was destined to command one of history's most daring voyages of discovery, and to become the first European ever to explore the Californian coast.

On June 27, 1542, Cabrillo departed from Navidad (known today as Acapulco) in a small sailing vessel christened the *San Salvador*, accompanied by a support vessel named the *Victoria*. His ships were equipped with modern weapons of the era — cannons, swords, and crossbows — and loaded with massive food rations. The *San Salvador* was also loaded with trade goods, as the explorers hoped to return from their voyages bearing treasure. Cabrillo was instructed by Mendoza to maintain records regarding which trade goods proved most popular, for the benefit of future expeditions.

Blessed with strong and steady winds, they journeyed north along the North American coastline, staking claim to prominent territories along the way. Cabrillo and his crew of nearly one hundred men made few stops to explore the interior of his newfound claims, which were known as Alta California.

The expedition resulted in extensive charting of the Pacific coastline, but it also conveyed a myriad of mapping inaccuracies. The explorers aboard the *San Salvador* sailed past Monterey and the San Francisco Bay without even noticing them. Although Cabrillo was noted as a distinguished navigator, references indicate that his course-plotting logs erred by one to two degrees of latitude. This was likely the result of an inaccurately calibrated compass. Navigation was further complicated by inclement weather, which did not allow for reliable sextant readings. Several months into the voyage the crew would also endure violent storms, as described on November 11, 1542 in a post summation ship's log written by a scribe:

> The weather from south-southeast worsened so much with rain in the southwest, and darkness, that they could not have a palm of sail and were forced to run with a close-reefed piece of sail on the foremast, with much work all night, and on Sunday the weather grew so much worse that day and night were ruined, and it continued until Monday at midday. The storm was as violent as any could be in Spain, and on Saturday night the ships lost sight of each other.

Storms were often demoralizing to the ship's crew. Severe weather also meant slower progress, and if the conditions grew harsh enough, they could easily prove fatal to the ship and its crew. November storms forced the *San Salvador* back out to sea, and she became separated from her companion vessel. Nevertheless, Cabrillo decided to continue his voyage north.

After exploring as far as the Russian River in Northern California, the expedition turned south, as Cabrillo had decided not to voyage any further unaccompanied. On his way back he would again miss sighting the inlet to the San Francisco Bay, probably due to fog or the masking illusion of Alcatraz. Cabrillo found his companion ship anchored near Santa Cruz. While his crew repaired damages from the storm, Cabrillo briefly explored the Monterey Bay territories. After the necessary repairs had been completed, both ships sailed southward along the coast.

Cabrillo's return voyage led the explorers to San Miguel Island in the Santa Barbara Channel. Here the expedition was further complicated when Cabrillo met an untimely death from a severe leg injury. One of Cabrillo's men, Francisco de Vargas, described how several crewmen were ambushed by natives while filling drinking urns with fresh water. Cabrillo led a rescue party, and severely injured his leg when jumping from the small shore boat. Vargas wrote: "one foot struck a rocky ledge, and he splintered a shinbone." Weeks later the open fracture became severely infected, and gangrene set in. Cabrillo would die shortly thereafter on January 3, 1543. He had given final orders to Senior Navigator Bargolomé Ferrelo to resume the expedition, taking a northern course.

After burying Cabrillo on the Channel Islands, Ferrelo took charge of the expedition, and continued the exploratory voyage north. He decided to push further than was originally planned, charting the coastline up through the northwest regions of Oregon. The ships rounded

Cape Mendocino, finally reaching what is now known as the Rogue River in Oregon. With rations running low and huge winter storms inhibiting the visibility necessary to plot their course, they turned south and made the journey back to Navidad. Only ten months after their original departure, they arrived back at their homeport on April 14, 1543, and their expedition was judged a great failure by Mendoza. The surviving crewmen were weakened by starvation, and many were seriously ill with scurvy. They had found no riches, and no mystical passage joining the great oceans.

Mendoza had the ships refitted and sent them to Peru on a trading voyage. Neither the *San Salvador* nor the *Victoria* would ever return, both falling victim to the shipworms that fed on the wooden hulls, deteriorating their structures. There is little documentation detailing Pacific coastal expeditions over the next two centuries. The crude charts from Cabrillo's voyages were published, and they served as the primary means of navigating the California coast for explorers of this period.

The earliest authenticated instance of the name California being used by explorers was in the summation ship logs of Cabrillo's expedition in 1542. But the first ever recorded use of the name was discovered in a romantic novel entitled *The Exploits of Esplandián*, written around 1500 by Garci Ordóñez de Montalvo. This work referred to an "Amazon Island" called California, and it is believed that explorers of this period were familiar with the book—which further romanticized the early exploration of these waters.

In late 1577, England's famed sea voyager Sir Francis Drake embarked on a courageous expedition, once more in hope of locating the elusive Northern Passage. He would journey to the Pacific Ocean via the Strait of Magellan with five ships, and he announced to his crew: "Whoever first descries her, shall have my chain of gold for his good news." As they ran down the Atlantic Coast of South America, storms, separations, dissension, and a near fatal encounter with natives marred their passage. Drake was forced to scrap two of his severely damaged vessels, and it would be several months before he could recommence his journey. His flagship the *Pelican* would be christened under a glorious new designation, and would henceforth be known as the *Golden Hind*.

In September of 1578, now traveling with only three ships, Drake sailed through the deadly Strait of Magellan, emerging dangerously into terrific Pacific thunderstorms. For two months the ships endured horrendous weather, unable either to sail out of the storms or to stay clear of the treacherous coastline. The ships were scattered, and the smallest, the *Marigold*, went down with her entire crew. The *Elizabeth* found herself in the Strait once again, and turned back for England. The *Golden Hind* had drifted far to the south, ultimately sailing around the end of the South American continent, and then plotting a northward course.

After stopping to make repairs off the coast of Southern Mexico, the *Golden Hind* sailed out of Spanish waters in April of 1579, and continued north along the California coastline. After nearly one and a half years of this journey, Drake was forced to bring the *Golden Hind* close to

Renowned English sea voyager Sir Francis Drake.

shore for key repairs. The *Hind* was a small, one-hundred-ton vessel carrying over thirty tons of Spanish treasure, which had been acquired through pirating raids, and consisted mostly of gold and silver. The repairs required were so extensive that on June 17, 1579, Drake set up camp in an area south of Point Reyes California, now officially named Drake's Bay. While waiting for the work to be completed, Drake spent five weeks exploring the interior region of the Marin coastline — yet he too failed to notice the inlet leading into the Bay of San Francisco, perhaps due to fog and inclement weather. Centuries later, historians are still passionately debating over Drake's western voyage. The discoveries made on his North American expedition are poorly documented, and only fragmentary records of them remain.

Much of Drake's five-week respite on shore was spent interacting with native people. Francis Fletcher, the chaplain of the *Hind*, maintained a detailed journal of events throughout their expedition. He described the Indians at Drake's Bay, and their brave shore landings in their canoes. They approached Drake's crew with peaceful gestures and welcoming gifts. Although there are no official records of Indians occupying the island of Alcatraz previous to its official discovery, there are some references indicating that the native Ohlone and Miwok Indians may have used the island as a fishing platform, and it is almost certain that they were the first to explore Alcatraz by canoe.

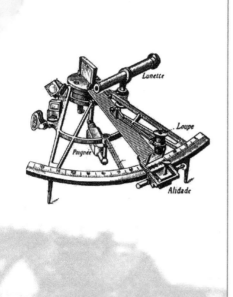

In 1595 Sebastián Rodriguez Cermeño, another explorer searching for harbors along the California coast, sailed only twenty miles from the shores of the Golden Gate — but nevertheless he too failed to detect the clandestine bay. Although the details of his voyages are often disputed, numerous descriptions illustrate how he was forced to set anchor in Drake's Bay during a heavy storm, and subsequently lost his vessel the *San Agustin*, which sank just offshore. The *San Agustin* was carrying a cargo of porcelain ware, silks, wax and other trade goods, some of which were salvaged by the shipwrecked Spanish, and left on shore when they departed in a small launch that had been used to explore the coastal regions. Cermeño would make the first recorded use of the name San Francisco, misidentifying Drake's Bay. He named the land the "Bay of San Francisco," for the founder of his order, Saint Francis. The Cermeño expedition was termed a disgrace by his government, and even his navigational charts would be considered suspect. In recent years, there have been several maritime artifacts discovered in this area that date from the same period, giving credence to modern theories of Cermeño's landing and the wreck of the *San Agustin*.

In 1602, yet another Spanish explorer would lead an expedition to this region in search of a good shipping harbor. His name was Sebastían Vizcaíno, and his exploration would result in some of the most extensive charting ever made of the northern coastline. Sailing with two vessels and a small launch for land exploration he departed Navidad, and on the sixteenth of December landed in what he termed the "deepest harbor near land to lay anchor." He named the safe harbor for his Viceroy, the Conde de Monterey, and saw it as a profitable northern frontier port. He wrote that the magnificent harbor was rich with timber for shipbuilding, and a natural paradise with abundant shelter from wind. Despite these romantic tales of a harbor in Paradise, the new Viceroy of New Spain, Marqués de Montesclaros, did not trust Vizcaíno's stories. A study written by Walton Bean, Professor of History at the University of California at Berkeley, suggests that the Viceroy's distrust of Vizcaíno was so great that the expedition's mapmaker, Martínez Palacios, was convicted of forgery and then hanged. San Francisco was destined to remain isolated and barren of formative discovery for nearly two hundred years longer.

In New Spain, Jesuit missionaries had ruled the northwestern frontier regions dating back to late 1580, under the terms decreed by their King. These missionaries established settlements along the northern Baja peninsula, which were considered to be the most structured and disciplined of all the missions in New Spain. The Jesuits maintained their dominance in Baja until around the late 1760s, when the King ordered their expulsion, under suspicion that they would attempt to fragment the Spanish government and take power for themselves. The evictions of the Jesuits were delegated to Visitor-General José de Gálvez, a special envoy of the King. His role was to conduct tribunals, and to restructure the political systems in various regions. Gálvez proposed to the King that a new governmental unit be established throughout the northwest.

Opposite: Sir Francis Drake's flagship, the *Golden Hind*.

The new structure would be called a commandancy-general, and it was intended to expand Spanish territories up into the Californias. Gálvez claimed that the Europeans were starting to populate the northern lands beyond the Californias, and would soon begin a southward migration to establish their own rule.

In late 1768, Gálvez sent Captain Gaspar de Portolá on what he termed a "sacred expedition," to establish colonies in the Californias. Father Junípero Serra, a Catholic missionary, would accompany him to sanctify and establish the holy missions. Serra had been born in the village of Petra on the island of Majorca in 1713, the son of a poor farmer. His given name was Miguel, but he chose Junípero as his religious designation, naming himself for the closest companion of Saint Francis. Serra became a Professor of Philosophy at the University of Majorca, but left in his mid thirties to pursue a more meaningful life as a foreign missionary. In Walton Bean's fascinating interpretive history, the author described Serra:

"Through his life he was a vigorous, hard-driving man, never turning back from a task he had begun, always demanding the full measure from others as well as himself. In physical stature, Serra was short, not more than 5 feet 2 or 3 inches in height, but in courage and determination, he was a giant."

Father Junípero Serra.

Serra's role in the colonization of California was most significant. He inspired the settler communities with missionary sermons that communicated divine principles and ethics. He would also establish the first Missions in San Diego (on July 16, 1769) and Monterey (which he founded on June 3, 1770, originally at what is known today as the Royal Presidio Chapel, and then relocated to a site in Carmel in 1771, naming it Mission San Carlos Borromeo del Rio Carmelo). Father Serra died in 1784, and is buried in the Basilica at the Mission in Carmel.

There were three vessels that made the sacred voyage to California. The *San Carlos* would serve as the flagship, with Portolá commanding from her helm. The other ships, the *San Jose* and *San Antonio*, were filled with livestock and other goods to be used in establishing the colonies. These vessels transported some of the furniture and other artifacts from Portolá's expedition that still remain at the Carmel Mission. The condition of the ships was less than adequate, and they took on large amounts of water through their leaky hulls. The *San Jose* went down, taking with her all of her crew, who were believed to have been stricken with scurvy as well. The crews of the other vessels were also sick, and the expedition would lose nearly half of its total number of nearly three hundred men. The expeditions into Monterey and north to San Francisco would have to be continued by land.

The first overland expedition failed to locate the Port at Monterey. It is suspected that Vizcaíno's romanticized description may have been misleading, and caused the frontiersmen to press too far northward in

A period engraving of Mission San Carlos Borromeo del Rio Carmelo, founded in 1770.

search of a site for their future mission. By the time the crew arrived in the area that is today known as Berkeley, they had already realized that they had overshot their destination. Many of the men had fallen ill during the exhausting expedition, with several documented as having severe diarrhea, and others stricken with scurvy. Portolá himself was described as being ill with "sickness of the intestines," and with rations low, the expedition settled for a brief period to allow the men time to rest.

On Tuesday October 31, 1769, Portolá's party made the first official references to the discovery of San Francisco. In excerpts from the logs of Portolá and Miguel Costansó, the expedition's engineer and cosmographer, the historic moment is described:

"We traveled two hours of very bad road up over a very high mountain. We stopped upon the height and the sergeant with eight soldiers were dispatched to explore, as some farallones, and a point of land, and a bight had been seen. Here we stayed for four days to explore. The pioneers set out, and we afterward followed along with the packtrain and the rest of the people at eleven o'clock in the forenoon. From the summit we descended a large bay lying to the northwest under a point of land reaching far out to sea, over which there had been much disputing the evening before whether it was an island or no, it having been impossible then, because of some horizon-mist covering it, to make it out as clearly as we did now. Out beyond, about to the west-northwest with respect to our position, and a bit to the southwest from the point could be seen seven white farallones of differing sizes and looking back along the north side of the bay there were abrupt white bluffs made out more toward the north, while turning around toward the northeast, the mouth

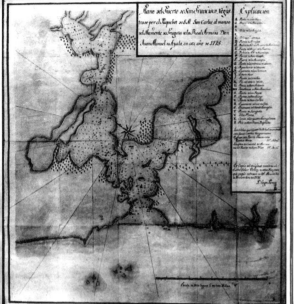

(Left) A map of San Francisco Harbor sketched in 1772 by Father Juan Crespi. This map accompanied the diary of his overland expedition with Gaspar de Portolá. Earlier Spanish maps mislabeled Yerba Buena Island as Alcatraz.

(Right) An original survey chart drawn in 1775 by José Cañizares, the First Pilot of the vessel *San Carlos*. This detailed chart of San Francisco Harbor was surveyed from a small boat during a forty-five-day expedition.

of the inlet was discovered that seemed to reach inland. At the sight of these marks we turned to the Cabrera Bueno's sailing directions, and it seemed to us out of all doubt that we were looking upon was the Harbor of San Francisco, and so persuaded that Monterrey Harbor lay behind us."

Father Crespi who was present on the expedition wrote:

"All Saint's day and All Soul's day. The two of us said mass here, and on All Saint's day after Mass by the governor's order Sergeant Ortega set out with eight soliders to scout for three days' march, wherefore we remained here until the 3rd, when they arrived back at night from scouting. At this place there are limitless very lush brambles, many rose patches, and all kinds of lush plants, very plentiful. Shortly after we here there came over to the camp a good sized village of very well behaved friendly natives (Indians), most of them well bearded and brought us a great many large dark-colored tamales, very rich, which the soldiers say are very good and would go well in a pipiánfricassee. There must be many villages all about this rich harbor, for we have seen many smoke [columns] from here; mussels are also very plentiful here, and very large, and the soldiers have brought back a great deal of them. Many deer have been seen upon the hills here. Bear tracks and droppings have been seen here. Our sick men have been improving everyday and are now all riding on horseback, thank the Lord Who has granted them this relief."

On November 2, 1769, Portolá's party climbed the eastern side of Sweeny Ridge and documented the large waterways that led to an open ocean. Yet despite their astonishing discovery of the San Francisco Bay, Portolá was convinced that he had failed in the objectives of his mission. He turned his expedition south to retrace his steps back to San Diego, arriving safely on January 24, 1770.

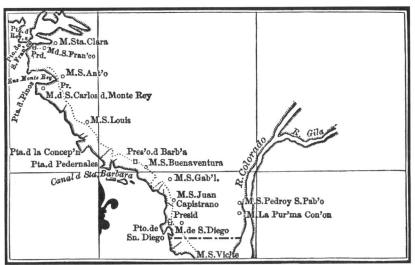

(Left) A map of the Pacific Coastline, drawn in 1787.

(Below) This United States Survey Map from 1851 illustrates how Alcatraz Island masked San Francisco Harbor. The combined factors of the near perfect positioning of Alcatraz across the mouth of the bay, the textured blending of the East Bay Hills, and the frequently foggy weather conditions may have hidden the Golden Gate from explorers for several centuries.

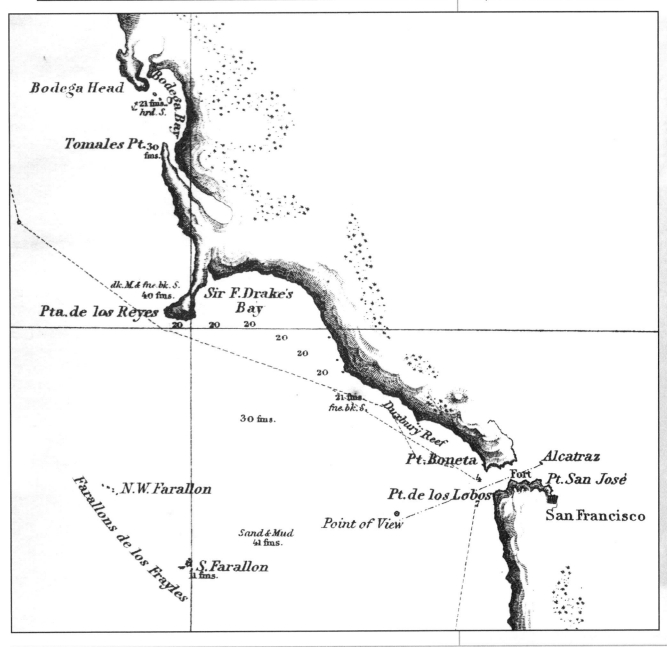

Six years after Portolá's discovery of San Francisco by land, and in the same period when Thomas Jefferson and Benjamin Franklin were completing the first draft of the Declaration of Independence in the new America, Juan Manual de Ayala, a young Spanish naval lieutenant, commanded the *San Carlos* on a voyage to chart the waters of the San Francisco Bay.

After so many explorers had sailed right past it in their search for safe harbors, Ayala would be the first to log the discovery of the island of Alcatraz in 1775. Here is an excerpt from the ship's log of the *San Carlos*:

August 11, 1775: The boat was launched and I set out to search for better anchorage for the ship. I went out toward the island I named de los Angeles (Angel Island), which is the largest in this harbor, in search of proper moorings for making water and wood; and though I found some good ones, I rather preferred to pass onward in search of another island, which when I reached it proved so arid and steep there was not even a boat-harbor there; I named this island La Isla de los Alcatrazes (Island of the Pelicans) because of their being so plentiful there. After this I attempted to reach the SW shore at the mouth of the of the inlet running to the SE, in order to examine a bight, but neither wind or current allowing it, I returned aboard the San Carlos at 5:30 p.m.

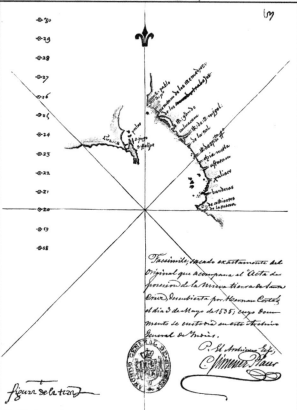

Nevertheless, the Spanish maps of the bay waters would mislabel the names and locations of Alcatraz and Yerba Buena. It would not be until 1826, when British Naval Captain Frederick Beechey secured permission to survey the San Francisco Bay and surrounding waters, that the names would be properly assigned. There also is still considerable speculation as to why the bay went undiscovered for so long, despite a series of explorations that sailed in close proximity to the inlet. A United States Survey Map from 1851 indicated that the Farallon Islands might have played a role in the deception. This survey suggests that the Farallons may have influenced explorers to stay clear of the coastline, since they indicated hidden reefs lying close by, which could have kept the mariners sailing in deeper waters far from shore. Along with the near perfect positioning of Alcatraz across the mouth of the bay, and the textured blending of the East Bay Hills, this may have been what kept the Golden Gate from discovery for several centuries.

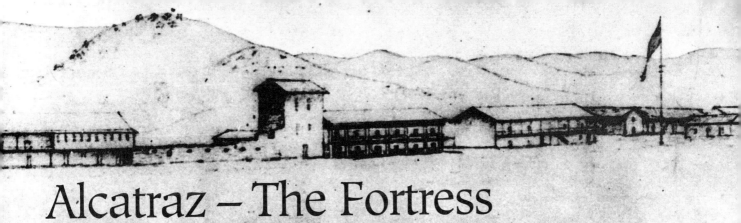

Alcatraz – The Fortress

WHEN THE TERRITORIES of Mexico were granted their independence from Spain in 1822, the Mexican Government inherited the land title for California. Despite the development potentials of Monterey and San Francisco, the government's focus remained on developing the lowlands within the southern regions of California.

On May 13, 1846, when relations dissolved between the United States and Mexico, the U.S. Congress officially declared war against its southern neighbor. In June of 1846, John Charles Frémont and Kit Carson led an attack to seize a Mexican garrison in Sonoma, and declared California's independence from Mexico. In their victory, they raised a makeshift flag with the claim seal entitled in bold print, "The *California Republic.*" The flag was made from white cotton sheeting fabric, with a broad strip of red flannel and a woven California Grizzly Bear, representing power and strength. The flag was later officially adopted by the territory, and is flown today as the state flag of California. Frémont also took Colonel Mariano Vallejo, one of the most respected Mexican military officers, as a prisoner. This event would go down in history as the "*Bear Flag Revolt.*"

Frémont and Carson continued their migration south, ultimately engaging in another attack, and taking the Mexican Fort in San Francisco. They again raised their flag, announcing the independence of the newly founded republic. Soon two United States warships arrived in San Francisco, and announced to Frémont and his men that the territories were now under martial law, and that California was under jurisdiction of the United States. The Stars and Stripes were then raised over the flag of the California Republic. In another of his more notable acts, Frémont would also take credit for naming the Golden Gate. As he wrote in a personal memoir, he would christen the grand entrance to the bay "*Chrysopylae, or Golden Gate*" for the same reason that the harbor of Constantinople was called "*Chryoceros, or Golden Horn.*"

Several years prior to the war, Mexico had passed legislation allowing governors to grant coastal land titles to Mexican citizens who would agree to develop the land. On June 8, 1846, the last Mexican Governor of California, Pio Pico, granted the title for Alcatraz to Julian Workman, a Mexican national. Workman had petitioned Pico for use of the island, stating that "*Alcatraces, or Bird Island, has never been inhabited by any*

John Charles Frémont, the disputed first governor of California, purchased Alcatraz Island for a mere $5,000 in 1846. As a military officer, Frémont recognized the strategic importance of the barren island as a potential site for military fortifications.

(Top of page) A period sketch of the Mexican garrison in Sonoma, California, where Frémont and Carlson led a rebellion to declare California's independence from Mexico. This was the historic location of the "*Bear Flag Revolt*" of 1846, and the site of the first raising of the California Flag.

The earliest known photograph of Alcatraz, taken in 1853 from Nob Hill. This picture shows the island's original topography, with soft desolate features, prior to any development or habitation.

person, nor used for any purpose," and seeking the right to develop the land. Alcatraz was granted to Workman "*under the sole condition that he cause to be established as soon as possible a light, which may give protection on dark nights to the ships and smaller vessels which may pass there.*" It is also documented that Workman never visited the island, and never made any attempt to establish a lighthouse as he had agreed. In 1846, his son-in-law Francis Temple sold the island to John Charles Frémont, "*in the terms of a bond for the purchase money in my official capacity as governor of California,*" for the price of $5,000. The property was eventually conveyed to Palmer Cook & Company, but the money was never paid to Temple.

United States Commodore Robert F. Stockton, a grandson of one the signers of the *Declaration of Independence*, eventually appointed Frémont, a man with strong political ambitions, as California's Governor. However the U.S. Government disputed Frémont's appointment, and later formally ruled that he did not have the authority to make purchases of land as an agent of the United States. Palmer Cook & Company eventually sued the U.S. Government, but they lost their case. The government insisted that even if the land had been rightfully purchased by Frémont, he had made the purchase under the name of the United States Government, and therefore had no right to claim it. Frémont would later be court-martialed in Washington D.C., and his unauthorized purchase claims contributed to the trial verdict.

Despite these conflicts, Frémont did make the important observation that Alcatraz was strategically positioned to be a premier military fortification for the protection of San Francisco. Shortly after the signing of the peace treaty with Mexico in February of 1848, the U.S. Military took notice of The Rock and its strategic value as a military fortress. First Lieutenant William Horace Warner, of the Corps of Topographical Engineers, had begun conducting geological surveys on Alcatraz a year earlier in May of 1847. Warner was stationed out of Monterey under the command of Brigadier General Stephen Watts Kearny, who had been in the forefront of the dispute over Stockton's appointment of Frémont as Governor.

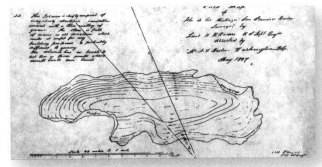

Lieutenant William Warner's 1847 Survey Map of Alcatraz.

The Gold Rush

The California Gold Rush is remembered as an extraordinary episode in San Francisco's colorful history, and it also influenced the government to find the means of protecting its land claims from other powers. On a cold and crisp morning on January 24, 1848, mill carpenter James Marshall walked down a steep path to a river clearing where his crew was building a mill for John Sutter. Marshall wrote of what followed:

> One morning in January—it was a clear, cold morning, I shall never forget that morning—as I was taking my usual walk along the river after shutting off the water, my eye was caught with the glimpse of something shining in the bottom of the ditch. There was about a foot of water running then. I reached my hand down and picked it up. It made my heart thump, for I was certain it was gold!

The tiny nuggets that Marshall had found that morning in Coloma, California had little value—their total worth was less than fifty cents. But Marshall's discovery would change the entire history of California. Marshall's find at Sutter's Mill stirred little excitement from local newspapers, and it was a Coloma general store owner named Sam Brannan who would become the mastermind behind the gold frenzy. Marshall told Sam about his find, and soon Brannan had collected several nuggets that he gathered into a small medicine bottle. Riding a horse into San Francisco along Montgomery Street, he shouted at the patrons announcing his gold find in the American River. In January of 1848 the entire population of San Francisco was less than four hundred, but by the following year the populace would explode to over thirty thousand, and Brannan would become exceptionally wealthy from selling mining equipment to the new settlers.

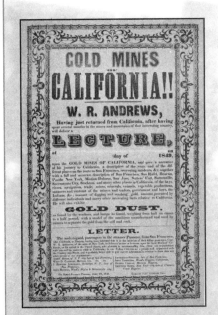

The discovery of gold in Coloma California in 1848 caused a world-wide frenzy, and families from around the globe journeyed to the region with dreams of striking it rich. The population of San Francisco surged from four hundred in 1848 to thirty thousand by late 1849.

(Above) San Francisco depicted in 1851, with settler camps and a thriving harbor, as viewed from Telegraph Hill (also visible is Yerba Buena Island).

(Right) An 1860 illustration showing the fast-growing city of San Francisco, with romanticized vistas of European architecture and a developing urban culture.

As word spread around the globe of abundant riches in California, the United States Government would evoke security measures to protect its land and mineral resources from seizure by other countries. San Francisco developed into a principle port of U.S. commerce, second only to New York's grand harbor. The incentive to safeguard San Francisco using the United States Military had now become a key priority. A commission was appointed to select sites for military fortifications, and Alcatraz seemed to be a strategic gift from nature.

By 1849, the Port of San Francisco had become tremendously active. Establishing a lighthouse became an immediate priority, to help ships navigate into the new western shipping harbor. Since the military had not yet begun development of the island into the promising military

A bird's-eye view of the City of San Francisco, rendered in 1868. Alcatraz Island is clearly visible towards the entrance of the bay, and a dense crowd of vessels has congregated at the city's eastern crest.

(Below left) Alcatraz was the site of the first lighthouse on the Pacific Coast, which commenced operation on June 1, 1854. The structure featured a Cape-Cod-style two-story cottage with a central light tower. The optical lens concentrated the luminance from the flame of a whale-oil lamp into a powerful beacon that could be seen from nearly twenty nautical miles out at sea. The small signpost visible next to the planter indicates that this building also served as a post office.

(Below right) A full view of the original lighthouse, surrounded by the fort's arsenal of cannonballs. A close study shows what appear to be children and their mother (left) sitting atop the pile of fifteen-inch cannon balls, each of which weighed over four hundred pounds. Also visible (far left) is the post headquarters.

fortress that it would become, the construction of the first western lighthouse was contracted to a Baltimore firm. The crew arrived in San Francisco on January 29, 1853, and immediately began work. The design was for a Cape Cod style two-story cottage with a central light tower, and the fifty-foot lighthouse was to be painted white with black trim. The fixed third-order lens did not arrive until October of 1853, and budget problems would delay its installation until June 1, 1854. A fog bell would be added in 1856, after it became clear that frequent fog layers often rendered the light ineffective. The original fog bell had to be rung by hand, but later versions were equipped with a clockwork mechanism that automatically struck the bell at prescribed intervals. As the city of San Francisco continued to grow, a new flashing fourth-order lens was installed, which aided mariners in distinguishing the lighthouse from the city lights.

On November 1, 1850, a joint Army-Navy military commission presented a report detailing a military defense plan to guard San Francisco from unfriendly powers. Their report stated: *"The first consideration in*

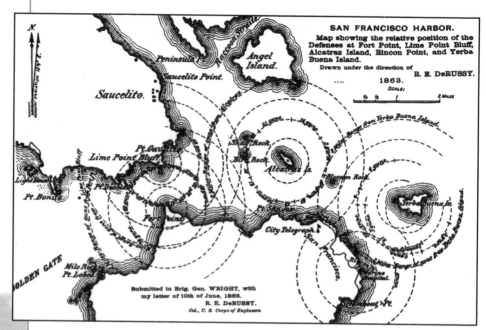

An early San Francisco defense map drawn in 1863 shows cannon firing ranges from various strategic locations. As the port and city of San Francisco continued to flourish, the military established a concentrated system of fortifications to protect the prosperous settlement. Clearly visible is the triangular defense pattern, which was anchored by the strategically located Alcatraz. Hostile ships entering the harbor would first come under fire from both Lime Point and Fort Point, and would eventually progress into the operative firing range of all three positions. It was an effective and lethal schematic.

conjunction with defense would be to prevent the passage of hostile vessels through the channel of entrance." This would be achieved by creating two lines of defense. The report continued: "The outer one at the Golden Gate to consist of a fortress at Fort Point of one hundred and fifteen guns and a battery of one hundred guns directly opposite on Lime Point; the inner to consist of a fortress at Alcatraz with batteries at Black Point (now Fort Mason), and Angel Island." The aim was to create a gauntlet of cross fire, which could pour down a continuous barrage of shot and shell all the way from Point Lobos to Telegraph Hill, a distance of about seven and a half miles—which no vessel of the day could survive. In its report, the commission urged immediate development of the fortresses to solidify the authority and protection of the infant U.S. territory.

By 1851, the United States had started preparing detailed plans for the three new forts and batteries. The Pacific Army of Engineers arrived at Alcatraz in the winter of 1853, and began to finalize specific plans for the development. Construction at Alcatraz would commence in 1854, with a $500,000 appropriation from the U.S. Congress. In his first report to Washington, Major John L. Smith gave a description of his initial surveys, writing: "The island of Alcatraces is a mass of rock with a very thin layer crust of soil and bird manure on the surface." Construction at Alcatraz would commence only months later. First Lieutenant Zealous Bates Tower had been assigned to manage the building of the fortress at Alcatraz, along with his assistant, Second Lieutenant Frederick Prime. The topography of fine-grained sandstone proved to offer more challenges than was originally predicted. Tower would report:

The island is rougher than I anticipated, very rough, steep, and broken on the Eastern Portion of the North West Battery and where the three gun battery is designed to be placed . . . The sandstone composing the island is very friable; even where hardened on the surface it can be cut with a hatchet. Wrought iron spikes can be driven into the rock without much trouble... During the month of October, I expect to finish all of the temporary buildings required

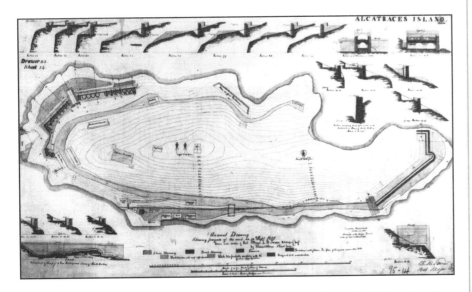

for the rapid progress of the work, including water tanks, to build the wharf, to prepare the road at least as far as the guardhouse and to make good progress on the ditch of the South Battery.

The task of converting The Rock into a sound fortress entailed a series of hardships for the labor crews. On July 9, 1857, when three men were excavating the cliff between the wharf and the guardhouse, they unleashed a massive landslide. Two of the men, Daniel Pewter and Jacob Unger, were fatally trapped under the loose debris, and the other worker escaped with serious injuries. They would become the first ever fatalities on Alcatraz. During the construction, it was found that the rock mineral proved to be too frail to be used in the fortification, and this necessitated the importation of stone from as far away as China. Granite of the type that was ordinarily used as ballast on ships was also apparently employed in the construction. Masons used a high grade of brick, set in heavy concrete forms to create a dense shield of armor against enemy ammunitions. Construction crews also dug well-concealed tunnels that offered safe storage for cannon powder and other munitions. There were specialized furnaces designed to heat incendiary shells, which would be fatal toward fire-prone wooden ship hulls.

(Above) An 1870 Eadweard Muybridge photograph of "*Pirate's Cove*," which is located on the western side of Alcatraz. This photograph illustrates the island's primitive terrain, which discouraged boat landings. Much of the current geographical contours are the result of blasting and reshaping efforts by the early Army Engineers.

(Below) A 19th-century woodcut engraving from William Cullen Bryant's 1872 publication "*Picturesque America*," showing an early portrayal of Alcatraz as a military fortress.

Second Lieutenant James Birdseye McPherson took command of the fortification construction in January of 1858. In personal letters he implied regret for his post assignment, indicating that the conditions on Alcatraz were cold and miserable. Nevertheless, he proved to be an effective commander at the fort. He would later advance through the ranks, and was eventually killed during the Civil War, in the Battle of Atlanta.

On December 31, 1857, 2nd Lt. James Birdseye McPherson was assigned to Alcatraz to continue supervision of the final construction activities. McPherson lived on the island full-time, and in several letters he implied that he disliked his assignment. In one of these he wrote:

> I often think of my position one year ago, and instinctively draw a comparison between it and my present one. Candor compels me to state that in everything appertaining to the social amenities of life the "Pea Patch" [Fort Delaware] is preferable to Alcatraz — though I am determined to make the best of the matter, looking forward joyfully to the time when I can return to the Atlantic States.

Regardless of his personal bias, McPherson was a dedicated commander and an effective taskmaster. He kept his men focused on their orders, and accomplished his objectives at Fort Alcatraz. During an inspection report filed in January of 1859, J. K. F. Mansfield wrote the following:

> I this afternoon inspected the fortifications on Alcatrazes Island in this harbor, and have to report the result to the general chief as follows:
>
>> This work has been under the superintendence of 2dLieut. James B. McPherson of the Corps of Engineers since the 1st of January 1858 when he relieved Brevet Major Z.B. Tower of the Corps of Engineers who commenced this work. This work from the beginning has been extremely well conducted, and managed by most faithful and meritorious officers. The progress has been great under the difficulties to be encountered in a new country, at the time the work was commenced.
>> At first it was difficult to obtain suitable building materials. New stone is had at various places. Excellent granite comes from Folsom on the American River, for both coping and walls. Granite for coping is had at Monterey. Blue calcarious hard stone is had in this harbor from Angel Island. Brick is in the greatest abundance, and excellent quality from Sacramento. Lime from Diablo via San Joaquin River. Water from Sausalito on the Main, and cement from New York, and all at constructively reasonable rates.

McPherson left Alcatraz in late 1859, and died following an attack by the Confederate Army during the Battle of Atlanta in July of 1864.

After several years of laborious construction and several armament expansions, Alcatraz was established as the United States' western symbol of military strength. The fort boasted over a half mile of masonry walls

Eadweard Muybridge, one of the great pioneers of photography, shot an extensive series of stereoscopic views of life at the military fortifications on Alcatraz. His photos would endure to become the primary pictorial documentation of the military occupation of the island.

This photo series from 1870 illustrates the massive armaments at the fort. Featured are the long-range cannons, ordinance, and massive 36,000-pound, 15-inch Rodman guns, which were capable of sinking enormous hostile ships at a distance of three miles.

The Citadel

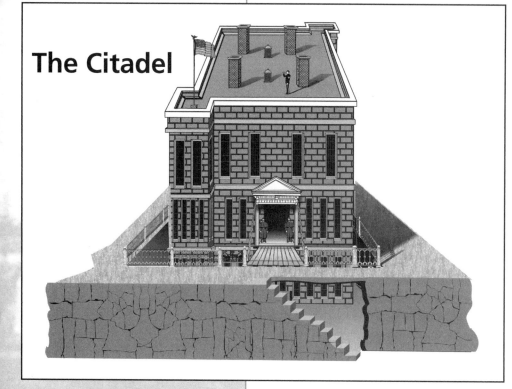

Alcatraz Island circa 1860.

Battery Rosencrans
Battery Halleck
North Caponier
Battery Mansfield
NCO Housing
Defensive Wall
Prison
Guard House
Battery Stevens
Quarter Master Stores
Boat House
Citadel
Garden
Dock
Lighthouse
Engineers Barracks
Bakery
Bowling Alley
Temporary Barracks
Battery Prime
South Caponier
Battery McClellan
Fog Bell

made of dense brick and sandstone, which surrounded the island, and in some sections stood over thirty feet tall. The new military fortress featured long-range iron cannons and four massive 36,000-pound, 15-inch Rodman guns, which were capable of sinking mammoth hostile ships three miles away. The guns of Alcatraz could fire 6,949 pounds of iron shot in one barrage. At the island's peak of military supremacy, which came at the end of the Civil War, the fortress had 129 cannons lining the perimeter, capable of firing fifteen-inch cannon balls weighing over four hundred pounds, to a distance of nearly three miles.

On January 24, 1859, Army Inspector General J. K. F. Mansfield examined the fortifications and reported: *"The workmanship as well as plans for the defenses are excellent."* The island dock was also guarded by massive cannons and protected arsenals. The sallyport entrance had a moat like a medieval castle that could only be crossed by drawbridge, and it was arrayed with powerful weaponry aimed at the only access pathway. At the island's summit was a three-story brick Citadel for soldiers, offering a full 360° view of the island. The Citadel was designed as self-sustaining defensive barrack of four-foot-thick brick construction, with multiple rifle slits in every wall to allow soldiers to fire upon a potential enemy landing party. Adjacent to the Citadel was an underground cistern that could sustain the soldiers with a liberal water

(Left) Alcatraz Island photographed from North Point in 1865.

supply for several months. The island's jagged rocky perimeter offered no natural landing points for invading enemies.

The first military command, Company "H" of the Third Artillery, assumed its post on December 30, 1859, with Captain Joseph Stewart as the first commanding officer. In May of the same year, Company "H" was ordered to Carson Valley, Nevada, to quell a disturbance among the Pah Ute and Shoshone Indians, and various other units would assume stations at Fortress Alcatraz. During this same year, the Army would bring the first military prisoners to be confined at Alcatraz.

As is illustrated by these 1870 photographs, the gardens situated next to the Citadel flourished in the rich soil ferried over from Angel Island. These opulent beds were meticulously nurtured by the officers and their families. The formal gardens featured beautiful panoramic vistas of the Bay, and they were a popular gathering place for residents.

(Right) An engraving from 1883, depicting the original fortification buildings.

(Below) The original elevation and section plans for the Citadel. This building was designed as a self-sustaining defensive barrack of four-foot-thick brick construction, with multiple rifle slits in each wall to allow soldiers to fire upon enemy landing parties. There were no cannons or heavy armory mounted inside the building. The fortress was to be defended by infantry soldiers with musket rifles, and was accessed by crossing a small drawbridge over a dry moat. The original plans included iron shutters, and large water cisterns to help sustain soldiers for long periods of siege.

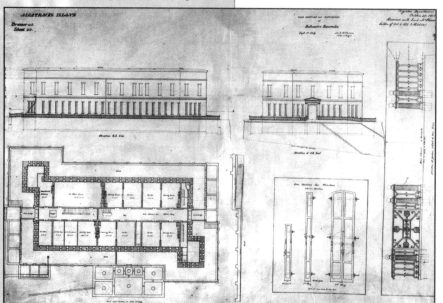

April 12, 1861 marked the official start of the American Civil War between the Northern and Southern States. On April 25th, General Edwin Sumner assumed command of Alcatraz, and prepared for war against the Confederate forces. However, many military advisors remained concerned that the Civil War might create vulnerabilities to watchful foreign powers. Sumner therefore issued orders to fire upon any vessel that flew the Confederate flag or advanced aggressively. Sumner proposed to station 400 men at Alcatraz, and to provide ample provisions of food and water to sustain the fort for at least six months. However, the fort would only briefly house a staff of this size in 1862.

On October 1, 1863, a suspicious vessel entered the San Francisco Harbor and approached the Raccoon Straights. Typically a Revenue Service cutter would greet all vessels entering the Golden Gate, but on this fateful day, the cutter had been assigned to assist a Russian vessel that had run

(Right) General Edwin Sumner

(Below right) The Citadel in 1893 following the Civil War. With no threat of impending attack, the building was converted into apartments for married officers. Cannonballs lined the perimeter as decorative border pieces, and the lawn area where a tennis court can be seen here was once the storage area for ordinance.

The pathway known as "Officers' Row" as it appeared in 1883. These Victorian-style homes were built in 1881, and were reserved for the post's ranking officers. This photograph was taken from the Citadel grounds, with the descending stairway in the right foreground. Cannonballs are clearly visible as decorative borders along the path.

(Above) A 1902 photograph showing the pathway leading up to "Officers' Row." Note the brick Citadel building in the upper right corner.

(Below) The caption from the original print reads: "Smoothbore, buried muzzle-first serves as a traffic bumper on the uphill turn." Comparison of the 1902 image to the modern-day photo taken nearly one hundred years later illustrates the changes in architecture and landscape. In the earlier photograph, note the Hospital and Lower Prison on the downhill roadway. Visible in the modern-day photo is the 250,000-gallon water tower built in 1939, and the Spanish-Mission-style chapel, which was later converted into bachelor quarters for Federal prison officers.

aground. The Commanding Officer at Alcatraz, William A. Winder, had been instructed to confront any vessel that was not registered for entry. His officer reported the sighting of a heavily armed ship being towed by several pilot boats. There was no wind, and the ship's flag was folded vertically with her colors indiscernible. Winder later reported:

> I deemed it my duty to bring to her and ascertain her reason of admittance to the harbor. I therefore fired a blank charge, which apparently not attracting her attention. I directed a gun to be loaded with an empty shell and to be fired 200 or 300 yards ahead of her.

The ship seemed to return fire, but it was ultimately determined to be firing a salute. Alcatraz then responded with a twenty-one-gun salute, and it is documented that Fort Point commenced firing also, to join in the salute. The approaching vessel was eventually identified as Her Majesty's ship the *Sutlej*, the flagship of Rear Admiral John Kingdome. The Admiral was not impressed by the welcome he had received, and several months later correspondence was still being exchanged, in which the Military was accused of a careless action.

Though in its entire history as a military installation, the fortress had fired only one 400-pound cannon round, and had missed, nevertheless the island lived up to its self-proclaimed status as an icon of U.S. military power. But within a few decades the island's role as a military fortress would start to fade away, and its defenses would become obsolete by the standards of more modern weaponry.

The "*Great Sham Battle*" of July 3, 1876 was meant to celebrate America's centennial, and to provide the citizens of San Francisco with a grandiose display of military prowess. With one stationary and one floating target (an old Navy schooner), the Bay of San Francisco resonated with the massive barrage of firing weaponry. But despite the awesome power of the 15-inch Rodman Cannons firing in sequence from Alcatraz, the idly floating target (carrying tons of explosives, and with its hull soaked in coal oil) effortlessly evaded the bombardment. To avoid further embarrassment, a young soldier finally was launched under cover of the billowing smoke to set fire to the vessel.

The Casting of a New Prison Concept

The punishment of criminals has existed as a social force throughout the history of mankind, and the earliest records offer horrific tales of rat-infested dungeons and the use of barbaric torture devices. Before offenders were sentenced to serve time in confinement, they were publicly tormented both physically and mentally. One of the most common means of punishment in past centuries was to lock the convicted criminal into a pillory device for public display. Use of the pillory can be traced back to a remote period in English history, as early as the twelfth century. Throughout the history of this device, the prominent display of a pillory represented a firm presence of law and order within a community, and it remained as a popular mode of punishment even in more modern society. There were several other forms of discipline that were equally barbaric, such as public lashing and mutilation, as well as a variety of other means of degradation. Public executions were also frequent, and hanging or fatal stoning were the common form of punishment for sadistic crimes.

Prisons have been documented to exist for several centuries, but until the 1700's they were grim places that served only for transitory confinement while prisoners were awaiting trial or punishment. The conditions in these jails were horrendous, with open sewers and diseased rodents that scurried across dirt floors on which the men were forced to sleep without bedding. But after the American Revolution, the newly formed

Eastern State Penitentiary in Philadelphia, Pennsylvania was the world's first true penitentiary. Eastern State opened in 1829, and was designed to inspire penitence in the criminals incarcerated there. The idea was to reform criminals through a Quaker-inspired system of strict isolation, which would allow for deep thought and remorse. It was from this philosophy of spiritual penitence that the term "*penitentiary*" was born. The medieval castle-like structure was intended to present a forbidding and haunted facade.

Military soldiers in formation at the dock in 1902. The brick bombproof barracks are visible in the background. The predicted attacks by the Confederacy during the Civil War never materialized, and the original casements, which accommodated two tiers of mounted cannons, were eventually fully converted into permanent barracks. The wooden structure on top was added only as temporary quarters for enlisted soldiers.

A broken device similar in appearance to a Pillory was found in a storage area on Alcatraz, indicating possible use of this device during the island's early history as a military prison.

United States sought to reform those who violated public laws. The Pennsylvania Quakers initially introduced the concept of reforming criminals through time spent under confinement. The Quakers built a small prison, which was comprised of sixteen individual and fully isolated cells. This new concept was intended to achieve reform by forcing criminals to serve out their entire sentence in complete isolation and silence. The criminals were left only with a Bible, and the reformers believed that this would help them to achieve penance. It was from this practice that the word "*penitentiary*" was cast into a modern era.

As a prison, Alcatraz would become a modernized and less barbaric form of the pillory. From its humble beginnings as a small military jail, it would eventually silence the most feared public adversaries, in the interest of maintaining the good order of society. It became both an icon and a societal pillar, a symbol of firm justice for America's worst offenders.

(Above) A crisp photograph from 1893, showing the interior of the temporary wooden barracks. Visible are the gun racks and the neatly made bunks on both the upper and lower levels. The barracks were always immaculate and kept in perfect order.

(Above) Another view of the temporary wooden structure set atop the unfinished bombproof barracks in 1893. Note the neatly trimmed decorative planters set in front of the First Sergeant's dwelling and the other cottage, which served as a barbershop.

(Below) A contemporary view of the corridor located behind the bombproof barracks, known as "China Alley."

The Early Years
as a Military Prison

IN AUGUST OF 1861 the U.S. Military began sending Civil War prisoners to Alcatraz Island, which seemed perfect for this purpose because of its natural isolation. At this point the island had no prison facilities, and prisoners were housed in a large damp cell located in the basement of the Guardhouse. Living conditions for the inmates were grim. Their jail was a crude structure, similar in many ways to a medieval dungeon, and accessible only through a fortified ceiling hatch via a small ladder. The primitive cell was unheated, and it accommodated approximately fifteen soldiers. There was no plumbing, and the inmates were forced to use buckets to relieve themselves. By day the prisoners were assigned to exhausting hard-labor details, and by night they were generally forced to sleep in cramped conditions, side by side on the ground. In a 1969 military history report to the San Francisco Mayor's Office, Herbert M. Hart described some of the problems that the commanders at Alcatraz were faced with in 1862. He wrote:

> The problem of prisoners was a pressing one from the early days of the war as pointed out on September 10, 1862, by Captain William A. Winder. He wrote to department headquarters that the ". . . caponiere at the entrance of the fortification, defending approach from the wharf,

A period photograph of the sallyport entrance. The support beams along the ceiling include both the base floor of the library and the distant passage is situated under the lower prison cellblock. At least one historical reference indicates that the gunroom on the immediate left was used as a dungeon cell for troublesome prisoners who were housed in the original jail, which was accessible through a hatch panel on the floor of the guardhouse.

(Right) An exterior view of the entrance leading to the Lower Prison in 1902. The blacksmith shop is seen on the right.

(Far Right) A modern view of the sallyport entrance as it appears exactly 100 years later.

A 1903 photograph showing the blacksmith shop, the tool house under the wooden stairs, the library situated above the guardhouse, and an open latrine suspended over the water's edge on wharf pilings. The *"Overseer's Squad Room"* (seen here with the door ajar) is located on the upper floor above the sallyport entrance. Also visible is an armed sentry standing ready at the edge of the catwalk in the foreground.

is occupied by the guard and prisoners; the latter being so numerous they entirely fill the casemate on the right of the entrance, rendering it necessary that the guard should occupy the one on the left. For this reason the howitzers intended for the defense have never been mounted, nor can they until some other arrangement is made for the care of the prisoners."

Despite these difficulties, the military realized the potential of Alcatraz as an escape-proof prison for hard-core offenders. The first twenty arrivals were from Fort Point, and during the next year over a hundred more prisoners would be ferried to Alcatraz. In April of 1865 President Abraham Lincoln issued an executive order providing discretionary jurisdiction to arrest public activists for the Confederacy. Numerous sympathizers were arrested and sent to Alcatraz as punishment, and several of these offenders were prominent citizens and politicians.

As the role of Alcatraz began to evolve, the island's defensive systems would eventually be redesigned. Major George Mendell from the Army Corps of Engineers filed a report that showcased flaws in the design of the original fortification. He illustrated that if cannon shot were to strike any of the stone or brick structures, the post could suffer extensive casualties from the shard debris that would violently rain down on the soldiers. He submitted a new design that eliminated all exposed brick and rock, replacing it with sand and earthworks. The new plan would allow for better absorption of the powerful explosive debris, and would thus effectively reduce casualties among the soldiers. Using inmate labor, crews leveled many of the brick structures, and packed soft soil ferried from Angel Island in front of the gun placements.

A 19th-century photograph showing the Lower Prison (to the right of the Sallyport and Guardhouse, with six visible skylights), and the Mess Hall (situated at the lower right, with four visible skylights). The small narrow building to the left of the Mess Hall was the prisoners' bathhouse.

In 1868, the Department Commander officially designated Alcatraz as a place of confinement for prisoners serving long sentences. In the same year, the Spanish-American War elevated the prisoner population from a mere twenty-six men to over four hundred and fifty. It wasn't long before overcrowding and increasing demand gave cause to build a two-story brick jail structure with individual cells, and construction of this edifice was completed in 1867. The confinement conditions for inmates still left much to desired, as there was no ventilation system and the men would still be required to sleep on hard wooden pallets. A report submitted by the Assistant Surgeon General in 1870 described in detail the facilities at Alcatraz:

A rooftop view of the Lower Prison with an armed sentry patrolling his post, taken in 1893. The brick building on which the soldier is standing was the original jail, built in 1867. Following the completion of the larger three-story wooden prison structure, the brick building was converted into a guardhouse. The small wooden pinnacle was a bell tower. The bell was housed behind the grill, and was used for signaling escapes and other emergencies.

The buildings consist of a citadel, two brick barrack buildings for troops, and three prison buildings on the summit of the island, and the laundresses' quarters, blacksmith and carpenter's workshop, two boathouses, coal and wood house, and bowling alley and theater for the men, most of which are situated on the eastern face of the cliff.

The citadel, of brick, is 200 by 100 feet, and is two stories high above the basement, with bastion fronts facing the northwest and southeast. It is well ventilated by the main hall passages and windows. It is used as officers' quarters, hospital, and quartermaster and subsistence offices and storerooms. The set for each officer consists of two large and comfortable rooms, with kitchen and dining room attached, and water—closets and bathrooms. The rooms set apart for hospital use comprises of a dispensary, and two wards, a kitchen, and an adjoining mess room, a store-room, bathroom,

A circa-1902 view looking east toward the Lower Prison. The hospital can be seen on the right.

and a water-closet. The wards are each 35 by 26 by 17 feet, well floored and ceiled, and are furnished each with ten beds and bedside tables, chairs, dumbwaiter, closet, and a washstand. They are warmed by coal grates, lighted and ventilated by side windows. Air space per bed, 1,547 cubic feet; area, 91 feet. . . .

The prison rooms are three buildings, ventilated by skylights and warmed by stoves in the main hall. They are arranged in two tiers (in one three), with galleries for the upper tiers. Ventilators are placed over the door of each cell, and air tubes in the walls. One building contains fourteen single and two double cells; the second has forty-five cells, and the third forty-eight single and four double cells. The average size is 8 ½ by 6 by 3½ feet, giving an airspace to each of 161 cubic feet. Adjoining these buildings are the kitchens and mess-rooms for the troops and prisoners, and the bakery for the post.

During the same decade, the military adopted the practice of sending what they termed as *troublesome Native Americans* to the post at Alcatraz. The first documented case of an American Indian incarcerated on Alcatraz was Paiute Tom, who arrived on June 5, 1873. There is no formal documentation providing a history of his prison time on The Rock, but it is recorded that he was fatally shot by a guard only two days after his arrival, presumably while attempting to escape. Four months later, two Modoc Indians named Barncho and Sloluck were transferred to Alcatraz following an attack on peace commissioners during the Modoc War in Northern California. Barncho died of scrofula at Alcatraz on May 28, 1875, and he was buried on Angel Island and later moved to the Golden Gate National Cemetery. Sloluck was eventually transferred to Fort Leavenworth in February of 1878, having endured the longest prison term on Alcatraz of any Native American soldier. Several others would be arrested and sent to serve time at the prison, though some of them had not been convicted or sentenced for any specific crimes, but were held at Alcatraz for *safekeeping.* Among others who were sentenced to

A photograph of the Prison Hospital taken in 1893 from the rooftop of the Lower Prison. Note the finely crafted lattice skirt covering the base of the structure, and the detail of the Lower Prison skylight on the right.

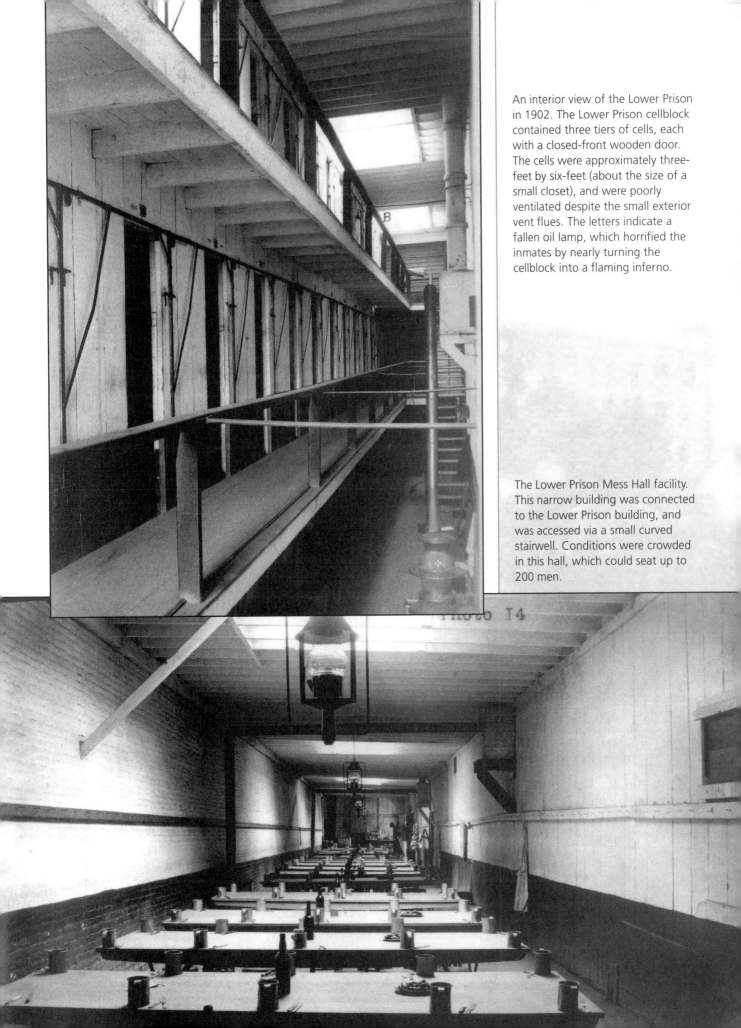

An interior view of the Lower Prison in 1902. The Lower Prison cellblock contained three tiers of cells, each with a closed-front wooden door. The cells were approximately three-feet by six-feet (about the size of a small closet), and were poorly ventilated despite the small exterior vent flues. The letters indicate a fallen oil lamp, which horrified the inmates by nearly turning the cellblock into a flaming inferno.

The Lower Prison Mess Hall facility. This narrow building was connected to the Lower Prison building, and was accessed via a small curved stairwell. Conditions were crowded in this hall, which could seat up to 200 men.

serve time at The Rock were two privates from the Company "A" Indian scouts. These soldiers had been involved in the mutiny at Cibicu Creek, Arizona Territory on August 30, 1881, in which Captain E. C. Hentig and six privates from the Sixth Cavalry were killed. Five Indian Scouts who mutinied at San Carlos, Arizona Territory in June 1887 were also imprisoned on the island, as were several Indian chiefs, most notably Kae-te-na, a Chiricahua Apache and a friend of the famed Chief Geronimo.

In January of 1895 nineteen Hopi Indians were sent to Alcatraz from northern Arizona. The Hopi tribe had been involved in serious land disputes with the U.S. Government, and had refused to allow their children to attend government schools. Intense pressure had been levied on the Hopi people to "*Americanize*" by adopting governmental education for their children. However, the Hopi tribes fiercely opposed sending their children to distant schools to learn the trade skills of the white culture. References indicate that the school facilities were mostly inadequate to accommodate large numbers of children, and that potential outbreaks of disease were a concern. The Hopi used the tactic of passive resistance, making commitments to send their children, but never following through. The government grew increasingly frustrated with their defiance, and began using its troops to intimidate the Hopi villages. When the Hopi continued to resist, the government representatives finally imposed force, and arrested "*the headmen who are responsible for the children not being sent to school.*" During the course of their imprisonment at Alcatraz the Indians were brought to the mainland to tour San Francisco schools,

A group of Hopi Indian prisoners posing in front of the original lighthouse in 1895. These Arizona Indians spent nine months on Alcatraz for refusing to establish a community farming system, and for keeping their children out of governmentally established schools. They are seen here wearing second-hand military uniforms.

in hopes that they would become interested in formalized education. They were released in September of 1895, after agreeing not to interfere with the "*plans of government for the civilization and education of its Indian wards.*"

In April of 1900, Alcatraz was temporarily used as a makeshift health resort for soldiers returning from the Philippine Islands with tropical contagious diseases. Many of these men had returned with severe dysentery, and they were initially sent to the General Hospital at the Presidio. While convalescing, the men were actually organized into military companies, and "*Convalescent Company Number Two*" was sent to Alcatraz.

As the prison population had continued to grow at Alcatraz, a temporary wooden cellhouse had been constructed on the parade ground. The cells in the wooden prison were small enclosures with the appearance of horse stables. There were 113 cells, and the average air space per man was only 161 cubic feet. The cells had an average size of 8¼ x 6 x 3¼ feet, only a little

larger than a standard closet. The wooden cellhouse was inadequate and unsafe for housing a large prison population. A medical report of the era described the following conditions:

> Sanitary defects of the prison are especially apparent. The ventilation of the buildings is very faulty. The corridors, kitchen, and mess rooms are disagreeably drafty . . . The prisoner when locked up for the night is virtually boxed in for so many hours . . . The means available for solitary confinement are such as have long been discarded in the better class of civilian penal establishments.

In 1902, a lantern fire inside the wooden prison almost turned catastrophic. A quick-thinking guard immediately smothered the fire using water and sand, but the inmates remained terrified of the potential dangers. They knew that

(Left) The only known photograph of the interior of the Upper Prison, circa 1902. The Upper Prison complexes could accommodate 307 prisoners in total, with two-tiered cellblocks. Close examination of this damaged photograph reveals several cells containing family pictures, and a stairwell with no safety railings.

(Above) Army prisoners seen working in the Upper Prison against the stockade wall, breaking rock into gravel in 1910.

(Left) Another 1910 photograph showing army prisoners breaking rock with small hammers, while kept under close guard by an armed sentry. This view is looking east toward the future site of the powerhouse.

(Below, left) A rare photograph of garrison soldiers congregating at the island dock, taken on August 12, 1904. One of the Upper Prison buildings is partially visible at the top left.

(Below) A 1910 photograph of the Alcatraz Morgue. The Morgue was not used during the years in which the island served as a Federal penitentiary.

Alcatraz in 1907.

if another fire should start, they would be trapped inside a wooden inferno, and understandably they feared being burned alive.

By 1904, inmate labor had been harnessed to modernize the prison at Alcatraz. The inmate population was moved to the upper prison, which now had the capacity to safely accommodate 307 men, and the lower prison was converted to a work area for inmates, housing the laundry and other small workshops. By 1905 the inmate population had grown to over 270 inmates, and convict labor was being used to demolish several of the old building structures and begin new construction. In April of 1906, following the catastrophic San Francisco earthquake, which completely destroyed the city's jail facilities, 176 civilian prisoners were temporarily transferred to the island for safe confinement.

A panoramic photograph showing the massive fires and destruction that followed the San Francisco Earthquake of 1906.

THE EARLY YEARS AS A MILITARY PRISON   45

U.S. Disciplinary Barracks

On March 21, 1907, Alcatraz was officially designated as the Pacific Branch of the United States Military Prison, and the Third and Fourth Companies of the U.S. Military Prison Guard were established there as a permanent garrison. Trained sentries would supervise all prisoner activities, and it was during this period that the rigid routine of Alcatraz would begin to emerge. By the turn of the century, the military prison on the island had grown so large that it obscured the lighthouse. Work on a new lighthouse began in 1909, and soon the tower would soar into the sky at a height of eighty-four feet. Electricity powered the light, as well as the fog sirens at the north and south ends of the island. The new keeper's house was adjacent to the quarters of the Warden and the prison doctor, at the top of the main roadway.

In 1909 Major Reuben Turner, a military construction engineer from the 29th Infantry, designed and supervised an ambitious building project. He created a fully enclosed building that incorporated the main prison, hospital, kitchen, mess hall, library, shower rooms and auditorium—all encapsulated within a single cement superstructure. The top floors of the old Citadel were destroyed and a large new cellhouse was constructed, literally on top of the solid masonry structure of the old defensive barracks. The cellhouse was the largest steel-reinforced concrete structure in the world at the time of its construction, and it was designed to hold six hundred inmates. Each inmate could oc-

The original lighthouse would be replaced in 1909 by an eighty-four-foot concrete tower, which loomed over the newer concrete prison. This photograph shows the new lighthouse under construction.

The original prison blueprints by Major Reuben Turner, a military construction engineer from the 29th Infantry. Turner's escape-proof design featured a fully enclosed building that incorporated the main prison, hospital, kitchen, mess hall, library, shower rooms and auditorium — all encapsulated within a single steel-reinforced cement superstructure.

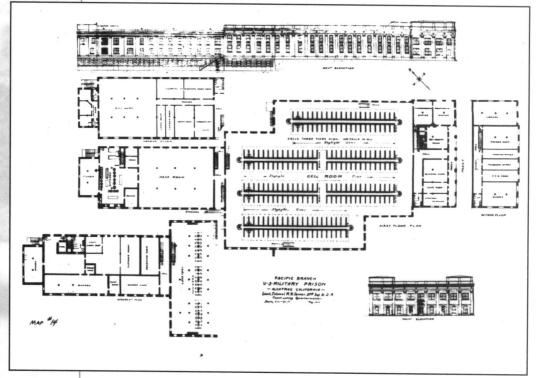

cupy a private cell, with a forced air ventilation system and cold running water. A convict labor force with a meager $250,000 budget would be tasked to build the entire cement complex, which would be completed in 1912. By the late 1920's the three-story structure was nearly at full capacity.

(Above four photos) Construction photographs of the main prison taken in roughly 1909–1910.

(Right) The Alcatraz Military Prison cellhouse was completed in 1912. This was the largest steel-reinforced concrete structure in the world at the time of its construction, and it was designed to house six hundred inmates. The new military super-prison opened on February 6, 1912.

Alcatraz was the Army's first long-term prison, and it was beginning to build its reputation as a tough detention facility by exposing the inmates to severe and harsh confinement conditions and iron-handed discipline. The prisoners were divided into three classes based on their conduct and the crimes they had committed, and each class held distinct levels of privilege. The system was described in a manual of *Alcatraz Rules and Regulations* from 1914:

CLASSIFICATION OF PRISONERS:

General Prisoners will be received in first class with exceptions made by the Commandant only. Third class men will be promoted to second-class and second-class men to first class after two and one half months excellent conduct respectively. Promotions, paroles, and re-

(Top) The main corridor of Alcatraz, known as "*Broadway.*" This 1912 photograph looks toward the east end of the cellhouse. The cell door lock mechanisms were controlled by simple swing arm levers (seen on the left). Also note the absence of the Gun Gallery, as compared to later photographs from the Federal prison period.

(Middle) A view of the ramps leading to the prison auditorium and administration wing. These ramps and spiral staircases were removed from the refurbished cellblocks in 1934.

(Bottom, left) A photograph showing the original D Block during the final construction phase in March of 1911. Note the dirt floor prior to cementing, the flat steel bars, and the group of open swing-out doors on the second tier.

(Below) A military prison sentry patrolling A Block in 1932.

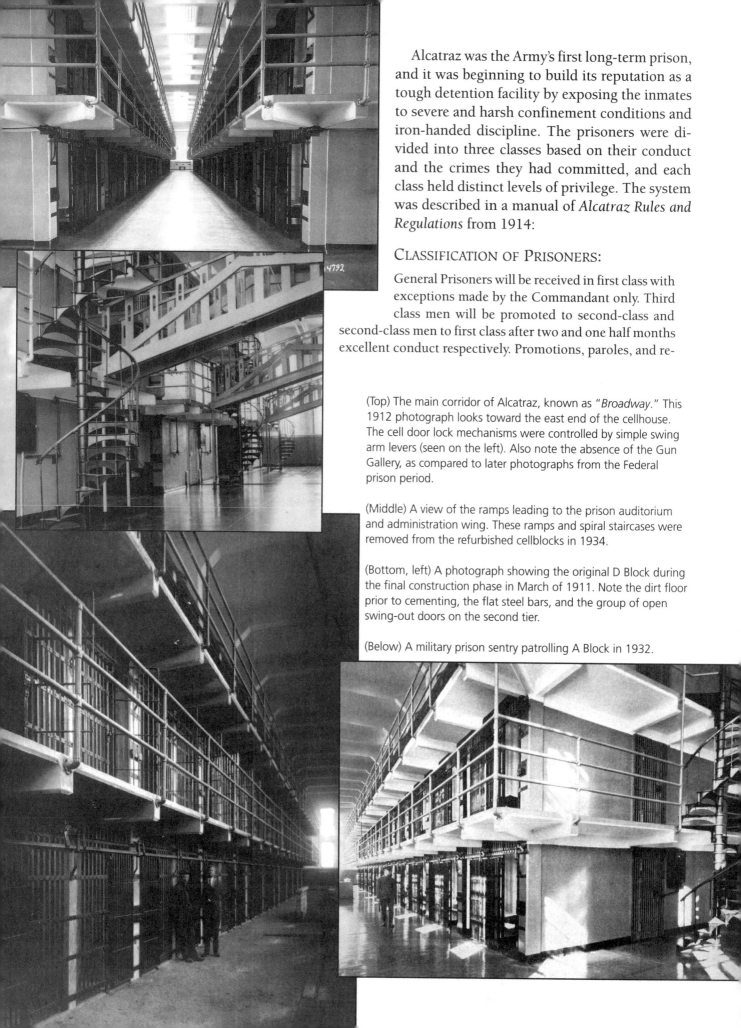

ductions will be made by the Commandant only. Promotion Order will be issued on the 15th of each month. Any first class prisoner may be paroled (under 943 A.R.) after serving half of his sentence. . . . Class will be designated by a cloth badge 2½ inches by ½ inch, white, red, and yellow for first, second and third class respectively, on a brown cloth patch 3½ by 1½ inches which will be sewed on a sleeve of right arm above cuff. Paroled prisoners will be designated by a white triangular cloth badge 1½ inches to a side which will be sewed on the sleeve directly above the class badge.

An early photograph of the new Mess Hall during the military period.

The quarters, mess tables and benches in the Assembly Room of disciples will be separated from those of other general prisoners by an aisle. There will be no correspondence between such prisoners. Similarly the Quarters and Mess tables of enlisted prisoners will be separated from all general prisoners by an aisle.

PRIVILEGES:

Third class prisoners will enjoy the letter and tobacco privilege only. Segregated prisoners and 2nd class prisoners will enjoy letter and tobacco privileges in addition the library privilege once a week and entertainment privilege once a week, by detachment, as segregated. The second-class men making a separate detachment. First class prisoners will in addition enjoy the privilege of closed but unlocked door to individual quarters, between Reveille and Tattoo… The disciples will in addition have the privilege of open doors from Reveille to Tattoo, talking in quarters and visiting in day room.

The "Torture Cages" that were installed at Alcatraz during World War I as seen in a San Francisco Examiner illustration. In later years an inmate work crew cleaning out a storage area located a broken pillory device. One of the inmates recalled a guard jokingly referring to it as an "Alcatraz Life Preserver."

Prisoners who violated the rules faced harsh disciplinary measures. In addition to losing their earned class rankings, violators were assigned other punishments including but not limited to hard labor details, wearing a twenty-four pound ball and ankle chain, and solitary lock-downs with a highly restricted bread and water diet. In his book entitled *Alcatraz 1868–1963*, author John Goodwin referred to the use of disciplinary cages that were merely twelve inches deep and twenty-three inches wide, thus *"forcing anyone locked inside to remain standing throughout his confinement."* The cages were used specifically for inmates termed as *"conscientious objectors."* These were men who had objected to military service during World War I, based on religious or political beliefs. The National Civic Liberty Bureau claimed that several of these inmates were confined in the disciplinary cages for ten-day stretches, and that upon being released they would collapse to the floor. Prison officials, however, claimed that the cages were to be used only in the most extreme cases.

AREA CLOSED! for your safety

A 1918 photograph of the Alcatraz Medical Unit Staff. During this era, the prison maintained an advanced medical center that included full surgical, dental, and laboratory facilities.

The average age of law-offending soldiers was twenty-four years, and they were generally serving short-term sentences for desertion or lesser crimes. However, it wasn't uncommon to find soldiers serving longer sentences for the more serious crimes of insubordination, assault, larceny and murder. One interesting element of the military order was that prisoner's cells could be used only for sleeping, unless the prisoner was in lock-down status. All inmates were prohibited from visiting their cells during the day. Inmates with first or second class rankings were allowed to go anywhere about the prison grounds, excepting the guards' quarters on the upper levels.

Despite stringent rules and harsh standards for those convicted of thuggish crimes, Alcatraz primarily functioned in a minimum-security capacity. The types of work assignments given to inmates varied depending on the prisoner, their assigned prison class, and how responsible they were. Many prisoners worked as general servants, who cooked, cleaned, and attended to household chores for island families. In many cases select prisoners were entrusted to care for children who lived on the island. Alcatraz was also home to several Chinese families who were employed as staff servants, and they represented the majority of the island's civilian population.

During this period, the lack of strict focus in the minimum-security environment worked to the advantage of some inmates who hoped to make a break for freedom. Most prisoners never made it to the mainland, and they usually turned back to be rescued. Those who were not missed and failed to turn back would eventually tire and drown. The prison did not start to utilize trained military prison guards until 1907, and up to that point inmates were usually guarded by young garrison soldiers, which sometimes provided seasoned prisoners with valuable opportunities. For this reason, there were numerous escapes during the military period.

In August of 1898, four young soldiers serving time for minor crimes escaped from the prison library, and stole a rowboat that was tied under the wharf. The inmates ultimately reached the mainland, but not before

(Opposite page) A view of A Block as it appears today. Also visible is the entrance to the basement or "dungeon" cells as prisoners referred to them.

(Opposite page, inset) A modern view of the flat steel bars from the military era. Note the primitive lock bar mechanism.

Colonel G. Maury Crallé.

one of them had been wounded by a garrison soldier who was on guard at the military wharf. The inmates were able to paddle a considerable distance out, when one of them missed a stroke, and the splash attracted the sentry's attention. The soldier opened fire on the inmates and hit one of them, who dropped into the bottom of the boat, moaning in pain. Another of the inmates stood up in the boat and shouted to the sentry soldier, *"Don't shoot any more. Don't you see we've got no oars? We surrender."* The sentry stopped firing, and briefly left his post to get assistance. Having succeeded with their clever ruse, the prisoners quickly pulled out their oars and rowed towards the mainland. A prison break alarm was sounded, and the island's five-oared boat was launched. The guards gave chase, but in spite of their best efforts, the prisoners got away. In another incident in 1884, two inmates stole a boat and rowed against the currents to the Marin shores. A sentry spotted the escapees but did not shoot, and the inmates made a successful getaway.

In June of 1900 two inmates worked themselves through a chimney, and using a large section of lumber as a float, they attempted to swim to the mainland. However, they got caught in a whirlpool and remained clinging to the log until they were rescued. In one example of remarkable ingenuity, four prisoners attempted to use a large butter vat as a boat, and struggled to paddle the unstable vessel to the San Francisco shore. They were promptly captured when the currents proved too fierce. Other escape attempts involved forgeries of orders, disguises, and cutting of bars. Several shooting deaths also resulted from attempted prison breaks. Each of these attempts displayed a certain amount of courage and desperation, coupled with the ingenuity born of constant contemplation under long years in confinement. The theme of the desire to escape was continuously evident throughout the prison's history.

One of the more interesting escape-related incidents occurred in the fall of 1926, when a crowd of inmates allegedly plotted a mass prison break. Colonel G. Maury Crallé had recently taken over as Commandant of the Disciplinary Barracks, when rumors began to circulate among the military guards about the mammoth plot. The alleged plan was for all of the inmates who were at work outside of the cellhouse perimeter to rush on signal toward the water's edge, and swim for San Francisco. From the prisoners' viewpoint, the scheme had considerable merit, but Colonel Crallé made the decision to address the inmates before they could attempt any such action. He called all of the inmates working on the labor details into the parade ground area, and stood with his back to San Francisco. None of the officers were armed, and Crallé spoke to the men in a soft tone. He explained that he had been made aware of their intent to escape, and he expressed his opinion of such a foolish strategy. *"GO AHEAD, SWIM!"* he challenged the men, giving no indication that he would attempt to stop those who tried. He dared the men to make a run for the water, and assured them that there would be no pursuit. However, he did calmly mention the "hungry sharks" that would surely attack the large groups of swimmers . . . and without incident, the inmates went back to work.

Perhaps one of the best descriptions of the Military Prison was written in a presentation entitled *Definition and Operation* by Major W. R. Stewart in 1930. Stewart wrote in part:

The mission of the United States Disciplinary Barracks is two-fold. First, rehabilitative, and second, punitive. Punishment by confinement at hard labor is not the paramount aim of such institutions. The reclamation of the convicted soldier for the Army and society is of equal importance… The Pacific Branch of the United States Disciplinary Barracks is located on Alcatraz Island in San Francisco Bay. Here, on this little island, some 600 soldiers are expiating their crimes. Their sentences range from six months to life imprisonment. Approximately 10 percent of them are serving sentences of ten years or more. Over one-third have been sentenced for military offenses, the remainder for misdemeanors and felonies.

The prisoners at this institution are subjected to a firm, impartial discipline. Misconduct and misbehavior result in punishment, good conduct is rewarded. The punishments are not cruel but consist of forfeiture of good conduct time, loss of privileges, and solitary confinement for a limited period. The punishment is made to fit the offense and for minor infractions of rules may be only a reprimand or the loss of one or more entertainments. Every infraction is recorded for each prisoner and this record is considered in making work assignments and in taking action on requests for parole, clemency, or restoration.

All men in good standing—over 90% of the inmates of the institution are granted all of the privileges allowed by law. Such men are permitted to attend all entertainments, including motion pictures, boxing bouts and shows provided by theatrical organizations of San Francisco and vicinity. They are permitted to write at least two letters weekly, with writing materials and stamps furnished by the government. They are issued tobacco with liberal smoking privileges. A well-stocked library is open to them. When not at work in the daytime they are allowed the freedom of the jail yard for exercise and games. Once a week all men in good standing are permitted to have visitors. Misconduct results in the loss of all privileges for stated periods, in the most refractory cases.

The spiritual welfare of the inmates of this institution is the charge of an Army chaplain detailed for this purpose. He holds regular services, teaches Bible classes and is the friend and advisor of all. It is also his duty to provide materials for sports and to provide and supervise entertainment . . .

The living conditions at Alcatraz are not uncomfortable, to say the least. The prison proper is considered to be a model in cleanliness, orderliness, and sanitation. The entire 600 prisoners housed in one great cell room,

(Top) Military prisoners at work in the Cobbler Shop.

(Bottom) Prisoners in the Barbershop in the prison basement. Note the shaving mugs lined up along the walls. Each inmate was provided with their own shaving mug for sanitary purposes.

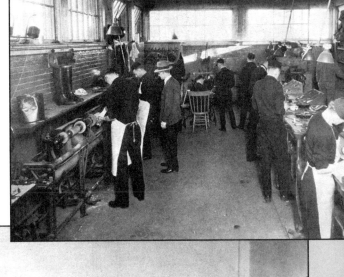

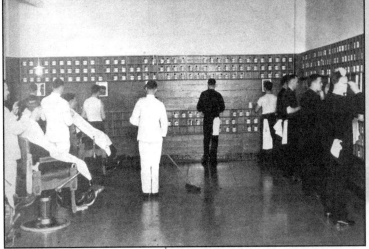

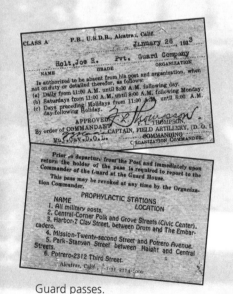

The first known aerial photograph of Alcatraz, taken by the U.S. Army in 1920.

Guard passes.

well lighted and ventilated. Each man has his own private cell, completely equipped. Every necessity is furnished to him. He wears a neat black uniform. His food is that of a soldier of the United States Army, the best fed of all the armies. The prisoner's laundry and dry cleaning are done for him. A sanitary barber-shop and baths are open to him daily. And, finally, a well-stocked storeroom is at his service from which he draws, as needed, everything from a toothbrush to a uniform.

Every opportunity possible is afforded the ambitious man for study. Illiterates must attend school daily. For others there is a night school. Many are taking correspondence courses or devoting their evenings to self-study. The prison library has a large and varied selection of technical works. Study is encouraged to the fullest extent possible.

The hours of labor, except for such men as cooks and bakers, are from 7:30 A.M. to 4:30 P.M., with one hour for the noonday meal and Saturday afternoon and Sunday off. The prisoners rise at 6 A.M. and go to bed at 9 P.M. Their work varies. Many are engaged in rock quarrying, road building construction and farming. A large number work in the prison itself as clerks, cooks and janitors. In conformity with the mission of the institution to prepare prisoners for their return to civil life by teaching them trades, a number of industries are operated for this purpose. A few of these trades are furniture making, tailoring, book making and printing. In all, there are fifty trades open to the ambitious prisoner.

Lest the picture of the prisoner's life seem too roseate let us turn to the other side of the picture. The prisoner, for long, weary months, is under a strict, never ceasing discipline, under which every lapse brings some punishment. He is cut off from all communion with his relatives and friends, except that for one hour weekly his relatives may visit him. Day after day, night after night alluring freedom spreads itself before his eyes across the narrow bay. Narrow it may be, but a gulf to the prisoners, as some of them have discovered, to their cost, in trying to escape by swimming. The city is so close that its sounds and sights are a constant reminder of the freedom that has been lost.

Fremont Older, president and editor of the *San Francisco Call Bulletin*, seemed to concur with Stewart when he visited the island during the same year. In a 1930 newspaper editorial, he described Alcatraz as one of the cleanest and best-run prisons in the world. He wrote in part:

It hasn't the atmosphere, nor the feel of a prison. It is a clean, wholesome place and the five hundred young men who are temporarily abiding there seem more like students in a training school than men convicted of crimes. Alcatraz, being an island, where escape is practically impossible, it is not necessary to have many gunmen in evidence. I saw only two or three of these strolling about with shotguns. The cells where the men sleep are the most comfortable I have ever seen. They are spotlessly clean, contain a wash stand with running water, a flushing toilet, and a spring bed with a regulation army mattress, as many as eight army blankets, if desired, and a pillow and clean pillow case. Each cell has an electric light.

The food is excellent, as good, I should think, as the average soldier's mess. There is a theatre with a show six nights in the week, a library containing twelve thousand well-selected books, and a playground for tennis and handball. The prisoners all wear a cheerful look and their behavior is excellent. Many of them are at work in the vocational department where trades are taught them. Twenty-six care for the vegetable gardens on Angel Island, and raise sufficient fresh vegetables for the entire prison.

Since January 1, 1915, up to the first of last January, 8495 men have passed through this prison. Out of that number 1609 have been restored to the colors without a black mark. Five hundred and forty paroled men should be subtracted from those figures; also ten percent should be deducted for men who didn't care to return to the army. Those who are interested in prison reform should visit the disciplinary barracks at Alcatraz.

But despite these glowing reports, the public disliked having an Army prison as a sterile focal point seated right in the middle of the beautiful San Francisco Bay. In order to soften the island's appearance, the military made arrangements to have soil from Angel Island brought over, and it was spread across the barren acreage of Alcatraz. The Army trained several prisoners as gardeners, and planted several varieties of flowers and foliage. The California Spring and Wild Flower Association made contributions of top-grade seeding, for plants ranging from rose bushes to lilies. The residents enjoyed tending their gardens, and it was said that the landscape work assignments were among the most favored by the prisoners.

Over the decades the prison's routine grew increasingly more relaxed, and recreational activities became more prevalent. In the late 1920's prisoners were permitted to build a baseball field, and even to wear their own baseball uniforms while playing. On Friday nights the Army hosted "*Alcatraz Fights*" featuring boxing matches between inmates selected from among the population of the Disciplinary Barracks. These fights were popular, and they often drew visitors from the mainland who had managed to finagle an invitation. These boxing matches became such an attraction that sold-out arena events were held at Fort Mason, sponsored by local businesses. Patrons received event programs that included business advertisements and listings of the inmates' weight classes.

In 1934 the Military decided to close the prison due to the high cost of operation, and ownership shifted to the Department of Justice. The Great Depression had become the root of a severe crime surge during the late 20's and 30's, and this gave birth to a new era of organized crime. The gangster era was in full swing, and the nation was a helpless witness to violent crime waves brought

(Below) A program cover from one of the many "*Alcatraz Fights*" events. Originally held in the prison Mess Hall, these fights became so popular that they would eventually develop into small stadium events held at Fort Mason.

(Above) A page from the "*Alcatraz Fights*" event program. Note the inmates' names and weight classes, and the various advertisers.

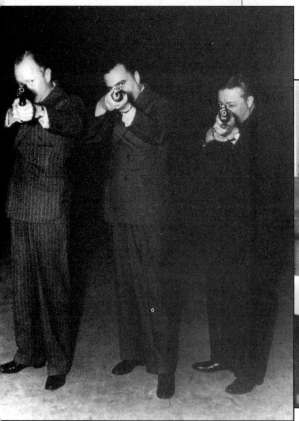

(Above) Hoover is seen above (middle) in a public campaign photograph publicizing the FBI's mission against crime.

(Above right, at desk) J. Edgar Hoover, then the Assistant Director of the Federal Bureau of Investigation, waged a public war against the American gangster.

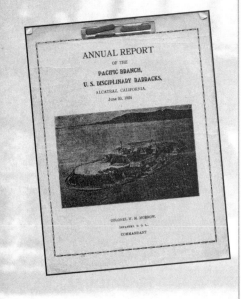

on by the twin forces of Prohibition and desperate poverty. The nation watched in fear as influential mobsters and sharply dressed "*public enemies*" exercised their considerable influence on metropolitan cities and their authorities. Law enforcement agencies were often ill-equipped to deal with the onslaught, and would frequently cower before better-armed gangs in shoot-outs and public slayings.

J. Edgar Hoover had been appointed as Assistant Director of the Federal Bureau of Investigation in 1921, and in 1924 he would take over as the Director. This was a position he would hold until his death in 1972. It has been written that Hoover exercised immense power, and was a persuasive politician. Together with Attorney General Homer Cummings, Hoover waged a public war against the American gangster, and petitioned for establishment of a "*super-prison*." Future inmates at Alcatraz would later call their home "*Hoover's Heaven*." A sentence to Alcatraz would come to be seen as the maximum penalty for crime short of execution, and it was reserved for the most violent, predatory, and relentless criminals of the era.

Alcatraz
Federal Penitentiary

> You are entitled to food, clothing, shelter and medical attention. Anything else that you get is a privilege.
>
> —ALCATRAZ INMATE REGULATIONS, RULE # 5

ALCATRAZ WOULD SOON come to play a major role in the Federal government's overdue response to organized crime. If gangsters such as Al Capone were the symbol of the nation's lawlessness, then Alcatraz would be the national symbol for punishing the lawless. In this respect, gangsters and Alcatraz were perfect foils in a common tragedy—two iconic extremes drawn together on an unavoidable collision course. Thanks to the celebrity status of the American gangster, the stage was set for the birth of a unique detention concept.

Aside from the military prison facilities, the Federal government did not establish its own penitentiaries until 1891, so it was forced to incarcerate Federally convicted inmates in state and local jails. In the late 1800's, the number of Federal prisoners housed in these institutions was quite significant. As an example, in January of 1877, twenty-nine of the fifty-two inmates confined at *Greystone*, the Alameda County Jail located in Pleasanton, California, were Federal convicts. But in 1887 the situation changed, as the U.S. Congress made it illegal for states to hire or contract out the labor of Federal prisoners housed in their institutions. Up to this point, the Federal inmates

Alcatraz Federal Penitentiary.

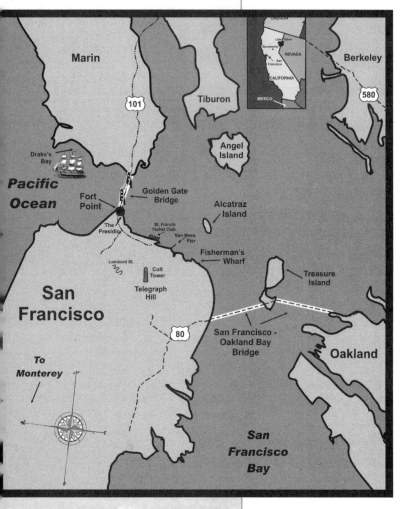

had cost the states little or nothing, since the prisons benefited financially from inmate labor. To offset operating costs after the new laws came into force, state facilities began charging daily fees for maintaining the incarceration of each inmate. In the early 1900's, these charges ran from thirty to fifty cents a day per inmate.

In 1891, Congress had authorized construction of three Federal prisons. The first of these would be Fort Leavenworth, in Kansas. Leavenworth had originally been a military fortress, and it was taken over by the Department of Justice in 1895. A second Federal prison opened in Atlanta in 1902, and the third would be a converted territorial jail on McNeil Island in Puget Sound. On May 27, 1930, Congress authorized the establishment of a Federal Bureau of Prisons within the Department of Justice:

It is hereby declared to be the policy of the Congress that the said institutions be so planned and limited in size as to facilitate the development of an integrated Federal Penal and Correctional System which will assure the proper classification and segregation of federal prisoners according to their character, the nature of the crime they have committed, their mental condition and such other factors as should be taken into consideration in providing an individualized system of discipline, care, and treatment of the persons committed to such institutions.

On October 12, 1933, the Justice Department announced plans to take over Alcatraz as a Federal Prison. Alcatraz was officially named as a Federal penitentiary on January 1, 1934, during a time of severe economic depression. As a Federal "*super-prison*," Alcatraz would serve the dual purpose of incarcerating the nation's most notorious criminals in a harsh, disciplined environment, and acting as a visible warning to the new brand of criminal, that the Federal government meant business. The Bureau established a strict policy of controlling every piece of information regarding prisoners that was released to the press. Part of the punishment for famous inmates would be never allowing them to see their names in print again. Alcatraz would serve to completely isolate the inmates from the public, and would maintain firm control of every aspect of their daily lives.

Break the rules and you go to prison, break the prison-rules and you go to Alcatraz.

The citizens of San Francisco bitterly resented the Bureau's decision to concentrate the nation's worst criminals in the middle of the scenic San Francisco Bay. Several public campaigns were led to block this transition, but all were unsuccessful. The Department of Justice called upon patriotic Americans to support the nation's war against crime through the establishment of Alcatraz. The Department also assured the residents that the prison would be designed as an escape-proof fortress, and that this would completely eliminate any threat that might be posed by escaped prisoners. The project was led by Sanford Bates, Director of the Federal Prisons, James V. Bennett, Assistant Director, and Attorney General Homer Cummings, assisted by soon-to-be Warden of Alcatraz James A. Johnston, and each of these men had a hand in the design concept. Johnston would later write in his 1949 memoir entitled *Alcatraz and the Men Who Live There*:

> I assumed office on January 2, 1934. Hour after hour, day after day, I walked back and forth, up and down and around the island, from the dock to the administration building, from the office to the powerhouse, powerhouse to the shops, shops to the barracks, into the basements, up on the roofs, across the yards, through the tunnels: I sent more suggestions to Washington.

One of the nation's foremost security experts, Robert Burge, was commissioned to design a prison that was escape-proof as well as outwardly forbidding. Burge's basic concept would be to fully restrict the movements of all inmates. No longer would prisoners have the right of entry to any part of the island. They would be restricted primarily to the main cellhouse building, and transit to the Industries would be equally controlled. The main entrance was securely designed so that anyone entering would have to pass through several gates, with access controlled by an officer stationed in the Armory. The Armory would be a control center that oversaw all movements of people leaving or entering the cellblock. The duty officer could view the sallyport area through a two-inch-thick bulletproof rectangular glass portal, and the gates were controlled electronically. The sallyport also featured electronically manipulated sliding steel plates on the gate lock mechanisms, which shielded the key slots. The Armory officer was the only person who had access to the slide panel. Once the shield was opened, the officer would need a key to open the first gate manually. There were then two more gates to pass through before entering the cellhouse. This would become the hallmark of Alcatraz: security safeguards set into layers upon layers of redundancies.

James A. Johnston, the first appointed warden of Alcatraz Federal Penitentiary.

A view of correctional officers standing inside the prison's main sallyport entrance. In the background is the main door to the prison, and of special note is the gate lock mechanism (right). The sallyport featured sliding steel plates on the gate locks, which shielded the key slots. The Armory Officer was the only person who had access to the slide panel. Once the shield was opened, the officer would use a key to unlock the gate manually.

Under the transfer agreement from the War Department to the Justice Department, Alcatraz would continue to provide laundry services to the U.S. Army, as well as several other support services. The Army transferred title of nearly all of the industry equipment, and established a long-term agreement to provide fresh water delivery, which would continue in force throughout the history of the island. The Army would finally evacuate from the island on June 19, 1934.

Earlier, in April of 1934, work began to give the prison a new face and sound security features. The Stewart Iron Works Company of Cincinnati, Ohio, was contracted by the Bureau of Prisons to install elaborate precautions that would ostensibly render Alcatraz escape-proof. The guards would have the ability to control each cell remotely, in full view of the Gallery officer. By utilizing clutch style linkages and pull levers, the guard would be able to open individual cells, or select groups of cells.

The soft squared bars were replaced with modernized tool-proof models. Electricity was routed into each cell, and all utility tunnels were cemented to eliminate the inmates' ability to enter or hide in them. Tool-proof iron window coverings would shield all areas that could be accessed by inmates. Special elevated gun galleries would traverse the cellblock perimeters, allowing guards to carry weapons while secured behind out-of-reach iron rod barriers. These galleries would allow the armed guards to oversee all inmate activities, and thus to safeguard the vulnerable officers who walked the cellhouse floors unarmed.

A view showing the main door open to allow access to the cellhouse.

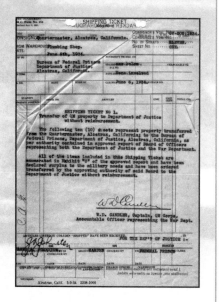

One of several documents authorizing the transfer of military property to the Bureau of Federal Prisons.

(Opposite page, bottom left and right) Gun galleries were positioned at each end of the main cellblock, allowing guards to carry weapons while secured behind iron rod barriers that were beyond the prisoners' reach. These galleries allowed the armed guards to oversee all inmate activities, and to cover the officers who walked the cellhouse floors unarmed.

SECTION A-A
LEVER AND MOUNTING REMOVED

THRU BAR   RELEASE BAR

M
N
BLOCK
(53336-10)

FRONT OF CABINET

POSITION 1 - CELL DOORS UNLOCKED WHEN OPEN
"   2 - "   "   LOCKED   "   "
"   3 - KEYHOLES OPEN
"   4 - FULL RELEASE OF CELL DOORS

M PLUNGER
N PLUNGER
N KEY
M KEY

POSITION 4
POSITION 3
POSITION 2
POSITION 1

FIGURE 3 - EMERGENCY MECHANICAL RELEASE

(Left, above, and right)
Officers could control
each cell remotely using
pull levers located at the
end of each cellblock.
The officer could open
an individual cell or a
group of cells.

ALCATRAZ FEDERAL PENITENTIARY

Special teargas canisters were installed in the ceiling of the Dining Hall, which could be remotely activated from both the Gun Gallery and the outside observation points. Guard towers were strategically positioned around the island's perimeter. A new technology allowed for the use of electromagnetic metal detectors, which were positioned outside the Dining Hall and on prison industry access paths. The prisoners would later affectionately refer to these devices as *mechanical stool pigeons.*

Metal detectors were positioned at strategic entry and exit points around the prison. Inmates would later affectionately refer to these devices as *"stool pigeons"* or *"snitch boxes,"* as they were effective in detecting hidden metal contraband. Other detection devices were also utilized throughout the prison's history to discover metallic contraband items.

DESIGNED FOR U.S. PENITENTIARY, ALCATRAZ ISLAND

Alnor TYPE 6002 FOREWARN MATTRESS FRISKER
MOBILE TYPE – 110 V. D.C.
OVERALL DIM. 14" X 14" X 50"
SIZE OF OPENING 36" X 6"

The New Cellhouse

After the 1934 renovations were complete, the new steel reinforced concrete cellhouse would contain four blocks, each housing 168 cells, with no one cell adjoined to any perimeter wall. If an inmate were able to tunnel his way through the cell wall, he would still need to find a way to escape from the cellhouse itself. There were 336 cells in B and C Blocks, and each block spanned 150 feet in length. Each tier contained twenty-eight cells that were nine feet long and five feet wide, with a ceiling height of just seven feet. There had originally been 348 cells, but twelve were removed when stairways were installed at the end of each cellblock. Two cells at the end of C Block were used as restrooms for the guard staff. The primary inmate population would only be assigned to B, C, and D Blocks, since the total number of inmates would not exceed three hundred. Inmates would typically spend anywhere from twelve to twenty-three hours a day confined in their cells. Each cell contained a cot with a sleeping mattress approximately five inches thick, blankets, a small worktable, a toilet, a sink that supplied cold fresh drinking water, and a shelf that could be used for the inmate's personal effects.

In the middle of each block was a utility corridor containing plumbing and ventilation ducts for each cell. The cross-aisle at the front of the prison was named by inmates "*Pekin' Place.*" This was the location of the visiting area, which consisted of four small bulletproof windows with small partitions. Inmates would sit here to talk with relatives and authorized guests during their visiting period. Directly across on the opposite end of the cellhouse was "*Times Square,*" so named because of a large wall-mounted clock that hung at the base of the West Gun Gallery.

The cells in A Block were generally used as special solitary confinement cells for short-term lock-up periods, when an inmate needed to be fully isolated from his fellow prisoners. Following the construction of D Block in 1941, A Block was used only in special circumstances. Several of the cells served as storage space and others were set up as small offices, with ribbon typewriters and law references for inmates who were preparing their legal cases.

Inmates later named the main corridor running between B and C Blocks "*Broadway.*" The cells along this passageway were considered the least desirable of all. Those on the bottom tier were inherently colder because of the long slick run of cement, and they were also the least private, since guards, inmates, and other personnel frequented this corridor. The newer "*fish*" were assigned to the second tier of B Block in a quarantine status for the first three months of their imprisonment on The Rock. The outer aisle to B and

A view of cells from the second tier of B Block, taken in December of 1954.

"*Broadway,*" the main prison corridor (between B and C Blocks). This contemporary photo was taken from the Mess Hall gate, looking toward the East Gun Gallery and the Visitors' Station. The cells along the flats of Broadway were the least favored by the inmate population. These cells were subject to the greatest amount of traffic and the least privacy. They received no direct sunlight, and were considerably colder than cells in other sections, since the heat radiators were located along the cellhouse interior perimeter.

(Below) This is a period view of Broadway around 1940, looking toward the West End Gun Gallery and the Mess Hall. Note the officer visible in the Gallery. New inmates were assigned to the second tier of B Block, and were quarantined in their cells for a ninety-day period. During this time they were not provided with work assignments, and were not allowed to see movies in the upstairs auditorium. They were only released from their cells for meals, recreation, religious services, and showers. Alcatraz was racially segregated, and African-American inmates were assigned to this area of the prison.

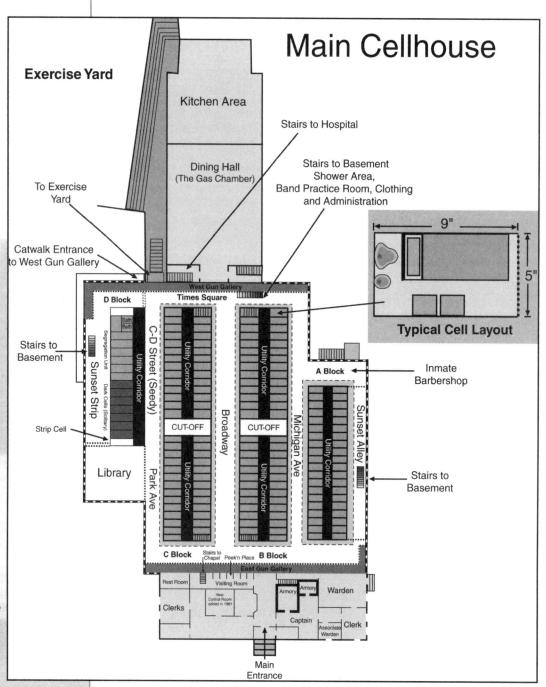

Main Cellhouse

Exercise Yard

Kitchen Area

Stairs to Hospital

Dining Hall (The Gas Chamber)

Stairs to Basement Shower Area, Band Practice Room, Clothing and Administration

To Exercise Yard

Catwalk Entrance to West Gun Gallery

9"

5"

Typical Cell Layout

West Gun Gallery

D Block

Times Square

Stairs to Basement

Segregation Unit

Sunset Strip

C-D Street (Seedy)

Utility Corridor

Utility Corridor

Utility Corridor

A Block

Inmate Barbershop

Strip Cell

Dark Cells (Solitary)

Broadway

CUT-OFF

CUT-OFF

Michigan Ave

Sunset Alley

Utility Corridor

Stairs to Basement

Library

Park Ave

Utility Corridor

Utility Corridor

Utility Corridor

C Block

Stairs to Chapel

Peek'n Place

B Block

East Gun Gallery

Rest Room

Visiting Room

Armory

Armory

Warden

Clerks

New Control Room added in 1961

Captain

Associate Warden

Clerk

Main Entrance

A series of views showing the cellhouse area known to inmates as *"Times Square."* The photograph, below right, was taken on August 20, 1934.

(Above, right) The area known to inmates as *"Seedy Street."*

(Below) Park Avenue. This was considered by inmates as the best cell location, because of its warmth and sunlight.

(Below) Block entrance, looking down *"Seedy Street"* towards *"Park Ave."*

(Above) A present-day photo showing one of the many stairwells used by inmates to access the upper tiers.

C Blocks was named "*Seedy Street*", and "*Michigan Avenue*" between the B and A Blocks. The section of C Block directly facing the library was known as "*Park Ave.*" Inmates considered this group of cells to be the best living area in the entire prison. The cells were considerably warmer, as they received some direct sunlight, and when no one was at work in the library, there was some limited privacy. The cellhouse plumbing system piped in saltwater from the Bay for the flushing of cell toilets. It was said to have permeated the cells with a foul smell that the inmates hated, and this would be the origin of Warden Johnston's nickname, "*Saltwater Johnston.*"

There were several tests performed on the new "*tool-proof*" bar structures. The new round-style bars were forged from a layered composite material, and they replaced the older flat-style bars. In tests, prison personnel utilized several hacksaw types that could be found within the prison industries. Their studies showed that sawing through the soft steel exterior of the cell bars was seemingly easy, but once the blade struck the hardened core section made from carbon steel, it could progress no further, and would quickly dull. There were other tests utilizing abrasives and piano wire, and these had limited success in making significant cuts into the bar, but all failed to saw completely through. The Stewart Iron Works Company completed the remodeling of the cell house structure and locking mechanisms in late July of 1934, and also facilitated the training all of the prison personnel.

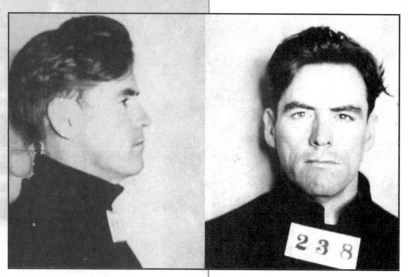

John Paul Chase, the partner of Baby Face Nelson, was convicted for the murder of an FBI Agent, and was an avid artist during his tenure at Alcatraz.

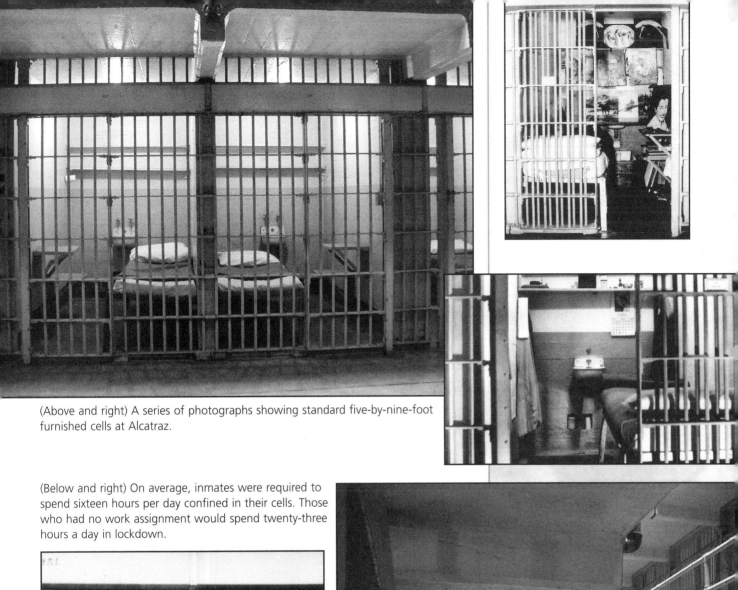

(Above and right) A series of photographs showing standard five-by-nine-foot furnished cells at Alcatraz.

(Below and right) On average, inmates were required to spend sixteen hours per day confined in their cells. Those who had no work assignment would spend twenty-three hours a day in lockdown.

Guard Towers

The prison had six watchtowers that were constructed as tactical look-outs. The *Dock Tower* was located at the north end of the dock area. The officer assigned to this post would watch for any vessels that failed to maintain a minimum 200-yard distance, and he would also be the keeper of the keys to the prison launch. The *Main Tower* was originally located on the northeast roof area of the main cellhouse. It was manned twenty-four hours a day during its seventeen years of operation, and was ultimately removed in 1951. Had it been left in place, this tower would likely have prevented the famous Morris and Anglin brothers' escape in 1962. In the early years of the prison there was also a *Powerhouse Tower* located at the northeast end of the island, adjacent to the powerhouse. It was eventually abandoned when the *Dock Tower* was rebuilt to a higher elevation. The *Model Tower* was located on the rooftop of the Model Industries Building, and was staffed only during daylight hours. The *Hill Tower* was located between the main prison yard and the prison Industries, and there was a long catwalk that ran from the recreation yard wall to the Model Shop Building. The tower was positioned to allow the officer on duty to provide assistance to officers posted at these locations. The *Road Tower* was accessed by a catwalk leading from the prison yard catwalk, and was isolated by a barbed wire cyclone gate in the middle of the walkway.

Most of the tower posts had their own toilets and running water. Nevertheless, officers considered these posts to be the worst assignments of any on the island. Former Captain of the Guard Philip Bergen, who was assigned to Alcatraz from 1939 until 1955, would later comment: "*There was nothing worse than being assigned to a tower or on the yard wall. I had that duty on a number of occasions and it was hell. Your lips and skin were always chapped from exposure, and the cold metal [of your gun] would numb your hands.*" The tower assignments were typically cold and extremely boring. Radios were considered a dangerous diversion, and were strictly prohibited. The tower officers were well armed with a variety of weapons, in a different configuration for each post. The weapons used included the Thompson submachine gun, the powerful .30-06 Springfield Rifle, the Colt .45 pistol, the gas gun, and gas grenades. Former Correctional Officer Al Bloomquist recalled his assignment to the Road Tower:

> At night, it was freezing cold and if the fog was thick enough, it had a very eerie feeling. You couldn't see anything when the night fog shrouded the island, and I can still remember hearing the deafening screech of the seagulls that would startle the hell out of you. It always made you a little nervous, especially after knowing that those desperate inmates had rushed Stites (an officer assigned to the Model Shop Tower during a 1938 escape attempt). When they finally gave me a day assignment in the industries, I can remember never being happier. I used to think that this was worse than being locked in one of those cells on the inside of the prison.

The Dock Tower.

(Above and below) The Federal Bureau of Prisons built six guard towers, which were manned by officers armed with high-powered rifles and machine guns.

Two exterior views of armed officers standing on the catwalk of the Road Tower. Guard Tower Officers stood ready to fire upon any inmate who attempted to escape, or any vessel that breached the 200-yard perimeter.

UNITED STATES
PENITENTIARY
ALCATRAZ ISLAND   AREA 12 ACRES
1½ MILES TO TRANSPORT DOCK
ONLY GOVERNMENT BOATS PERMITTED
OTHERS MUST KEEP OFF 200 YARDS
NO ONE ALLOWED ASHORE
WITHOUT A PASS

The Guard Towers were considered one of the worst post assignments by correctional officers. The towers were typically cold and boring during the long shifts, and activities such as reading or listening to a radio were prohibited.

An armed officer standing on the exterior walk of the Road Tower. Visible in the distance is the Model Shop Tower.

A photograph of the first Warden of Alcatraz, James A. Johnston. This image was produced for his book *"Prison Life is Different."* He authored several other publications, including a book on Alcatraz entitled *"Alcatraz and the Men Who Live There."*

Warden James A. Johnston 1934–1948

In November of 1933, the U.S. Attorney General chose James A. Johnston, a strict disciplinarian with a humanistic approach to reform as the new Warden of Alcatraz. Johnston came to the position with a broad-based background in business, and twelve years of experience in the California Department of Corrections. James Johnston was born in Brooklyn, New York on September 15, 1874, to Thomas and Ellen Johnston. He moved to California, and attended Sacred Heart College in San Francisco to study law. In 1905 Johnston married Ida Fulton, and the couple decided to remain in California. From 1912 until 1913, Johnston served a brief term as the Warden at Folsom Prison, on the appointment of the Governor of California. His successful term at Folsom led to another position as the Warden of San Quentin Prison, where he would remain until 1925. After leaving the prison system, Johnston became the Vice-President of the American Trust Company, and later took an appointment as a chief appraiser for the Federal Home Loan Bank Corporation.

The Department of Justice considered Johnston a *"scientific penologist,"* and he had a remarkable track record of successfully returning a high percentage of inmates to productive society. Johnston had become well known for the programs he implemented in the area of prisoner reform, and he was also a promoter of inmate rights. He abolished the wearing of striped uniforms, which he considered demeaning to the inmates, and he advocated active inmate participation in religious services. He didn't believe in chain gangs, but rather in having inmates report to a job where they were respected and rewarded for their efforts.

Nicknamed the *"Golden Rule Warden"* at San Quentin, Johnston was praised in newspaper articles for the California highways that were graded by San Quentin prisoners. Although inmates were not compensated for this work, they were rewarded with sentence reductions. Johnston also established several educational programs at San Quentin, which proved successful for a good number of inmates. He invited famous actors and actresses of the era to entertain on special occasions, including such greats as Mary Pickford and Sarah Bernhardt. Johnston

Two photographs of James A. Johnston as a young man, during his terms as Warden of Folsom Prison in 1912–1913 (left), and as Warden of San Quentin Prison from 1913–1925 (right).

purchased a motion picture projector for the inmates at San Quentin, and vaudeville companies were permitted to perform for the prisoners. But despite Johnston's humane approach to prison reform, he also carried a reputation as a strict disciplinarian. His rules of conduct were among the most rigid in the correctional system, and harsh punishments were meted out to defiant inmates. During his tenure at "Q," Johnston also oversaw the executions by hanging of several inmates.

During his time at Alcatraz, Johnston was allowed to hand-pick his correctional officers from the entire Federal prison system. Johnston's first appointment was Cecil J. Shuttleworth from St. Paul, Minnesota, who he chose as his Deputy Warden. He also appointed four lieutenants who were all well versed in the Federal prison system. They were Edward J. Miller and Paul J. Madigan (who was later to become Warden himself) from Leavenworth, Edward Starling from Atlanta, and Richard Culver from Virginia. Fifty-two other correctional officers would be transferred to Alcatraz to assume guard posts.

(Top right) James Johnston was considered an icon of San Francisco during his term as Warden of Alcatraz. He is seen here during a public fundraiser, circa 1942.

(Right and below) Johnston abolished the wearing of striped prison uniforms, which he considered demeaning to the inmates. He didn't believe in chain gangs (depicted below, with the men walking in what was termed as *Lock Step*), and he advocated having inmates report to a job where they were respected and rewarded for their efforts. Johnston held a remarkable track record of successfully returning a high percentage of inmates to productive society, by teaching them job skills that could translate to employment outside of prison.

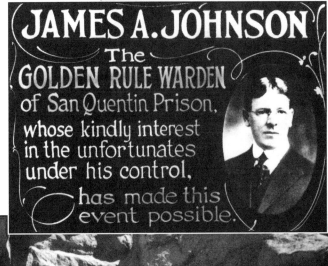

Each of the following officers transferred from Leavenworth to Alcatraz were given a promotion at the time of their transfer:

	grade	salary	Min. at which prom. made
Stucker	90.25	$2100	86 or better
Orr	89.95	$2200	86 or better
Czarkowitz	89.05	$2100	86 or better
Lindsay	87.55	$2100	" "
Owens	87.40	$2100	" "
Klein	86.80	$2100	" "

These senior officers from Lewisburg were all given promotions at the time of their transfer.

Prindle	86.45	$2100	85 or better
Bergen	88.10	$2200	85 "
Hathaway	86.25	$2100	85 "
Martensen	85.60	$2200	85

Senior officer Bert A. Burch who was transferred from Fort Leavenworth is the only one who did not receive a promotion. The 1939 promotions were based on a competitive average in that dist. of 86 or better. Mr. Burch made 85.70 and so was not promoted. He still earns $2000. He made

A letter detailing officers' salaries for their new appointments at Alcatraz.

A group photograph of the Alcatraz Federal Penitentiary Personnel, taken on June 4, 1936. Warden Johnston is seen sitting in the middle. To his left is Deputy Warden C. J. Shuttleworth, and to his right is future Deputy Warden E. J. Miller.

The Guards of Alcatraz

The guard to prisoner ratio on Alcatraz was one to three, which compared favorably with other prisons, where there could be twelve or more inmates to every guard. The Alcatraz guards were able to keep extremely close track of each inmate, thanks to the Gun Galleries at each end of the cellblocks, and the frequency of prisoner counts. Because of the small number of inmates on Alcatraz, the guards generally knew each one by name. Salaries for the correctional staff were also better than at most other penitentiaries. In 1934 the average annual salary of a correctional officer at Alcatraz was $3,162, and by the time the prison closed in 1963, salaries for officers had risen to nearly $5,000 a year. Officers at Alcatraz were provided with extensive training, and were considered to be the best in the Federal system. After being signed into service on Alcatraz, they would undergo a formalized program to help prepare them for their new position.

The guard-training curriculum was condensed into an extremely intensive four-week program. The classes covered self-defense skills, teaching aggressive Judo as well as defensive maneuvers. Officers also were expected to qualify with the various firearms used at the secure posts. They would learn how to operate the cell mechanisms, and become versed in the rules and regulations governing the prison. Furthermore, officers were trained in psychology, including role-playing techniques for de-escalating potential riot situations, and identification of unusual behavioral patterns. Inmates frequently made contraband weapons that could put the unarmed officers assigned to inmate areas at significant risk. As an additional precaution, officers would learn the language of the underground prison code, and the importance of not getting too friendly with the inmates. The officers were expected to remain firm, and to enforce the regulations to the letter.

(Above) A small group of Alcatraz officers posing in 1953. Standing on the far left is Captain of the Guard Emil Rychner.

Warden Johnston and Attorney General Sanford Bates created a set of rigid guiding principles under which the prison would operate, and the first of these was that no prisoner would be directly sentenced to Alcatraz from the courts. Instead, wardens from the various Federal penitentiaries were polled and permitted to send their most incorrigible inmates to The Rock. They chose inmates with histories of unmanageable behavior and escape attempts, but they also sent high-profile inmates who were receiving privileges because of their status and notoriety. Assistant Director of the Bureau of Prisons James V. Bennett later commented, "*In a sense, I was a talent scout for Alcatraz. One of my jobs was to review the records of all the men in the various federal prisons and decide who would be sent to the Rock.*" Inmates would be required to earn their way back to another Federal institution before they could be considered for parole. Those who sought an attorney to represent them while incarcerated at Alcatraz would have to do so by direct request to the U.S. Attorney General. All privileges would be limited, and no inmate, regardless of his public stature, would be extended special entitlements.

(Above) Alcatraz officers receiving defensive training.

(Below left) A photograph of Captain of the Guard Emil Rychner (standing), during an officer training session.

(Below right) Another training photograph with Associate Warden Arthur Dollison seated in the center.

Visitation and Inmate Rights

Inmates had to earn visitation rights, but no visits would be allowed for the first three months. The warden would have to approve all requests, and would allow only one visit a month per inmate. The visitor was required to be a spouse or blood relative, and would be allotted two hours. Visitors would not be allowed any physical contact with the inmate, so there would be no opportunity for a visitor to pass any form of contraband. They would talk through a two-inch-thick bulletproof squared porthole, via a telephone intercom that was monitored by a correctional officer. Any discussion of current events, topics specific to the prison or other inmates, or anything that could have a potential link to crime would be forbidden. An inmate who violated this rule would immediately be cut off, and the visit would be terminated. For inmates with relatives traveling from afar, the Warden would sometimes allow consecutive visits (e.g., January 31st and February 1st).

Inmates were given restricted access to the prison library, but no newspapers, radios, or other non-approved reading materials would be allowed. Mail service was considered a privilege, and all letters, both in-coming and out-going, were to be screened, censored, and typewritten. Work was also assigned as a privilege and not a right. Consideration for work assignments would be based on an inmate's conduct record.

Each prisoner was assigned his own cell, and allotted only the basic minimum necessities of life, such as food, water, clothing, and medical and dental care. Inmate Willie Radkay (who occupied a cell next to Machine Gun Kelly at Alcatraz), later indicated during an interview that

The visiting area, called *"Pekin' Place"* by inmates because they were only allowed to talk with visitors through small bulletproof glass portals. The visiting area was located next to the main prison entrance. The barred gate on the right was the access gate to the stairway leading to the prison Chapel.

(Below right) Bureau officials are seen here posing as visitors seated in the visitors' gallery. No physical contact was allowed between family visitors and inmates for any reason.

(Below left) An inmate talking with family members in the visiting area, using a hands-free intercom.

having your own cell was a great advantage over other Federal prisons. When inmates lived in separate cells, the chances of being sexually violated were reduced, and the privacy afforded was also a cherished benefit. Personal property was generally limited to a few photographs, and the cells were subject to meticulous inspections that were frequent, random, and unannounced.

The inmates' contact with the outside world was completely cut off. Convicted spy Morton Sobell stated that the rules at Alcatraz were so stringent that inmates were never allowed to explore the cellhouse on their own. They would be marched from one location to another, always in a regulated manner. The routine was unyielding, day after day, year after year. As quickly as a right was awarded for good behavior, it could be taken away for the slightest infraction. Johnston would tell the press on opening day: *The essence of Alcatraz is a maximum security prison, with minimum privileges*.

(Above left) A correctional officer sitting at the desk in the inmate visiting area.

(Above right) Conversations were monitored by prison officers, and the visit was immediately ended if an inmate violated the prison rules and regulations pertaining to visits.

Transition to a Civilian Prison

When the Military evacuated the island on June 19, 1934, they left behind thirty-two hard-edged prisoners to serve out their sentences on Alcatraz. The remaining military inmates were assigned Alcatraz numbers alphabetically, with Frank Bolt as AZ-01. These men later became resentful of being imprisoned with what the media had publicized as America's worst criminals. There was a thread of dissention among these inmates, who thought that they should be released to more lenient institutions. The first civilian to be held at Alcatraz was Frederick Grant White, who arrived on July 13, 1934 from McNeil Island. The next civilian inmate had an interesting connection to the island prison. Robert Bradford Moxon had once served at Alcatraz as a soldier. Ironically, after being discharged, he was arrested on charges of forgery and sent back to serve out his sentence on The Rock, arriving on August 2, 1934.

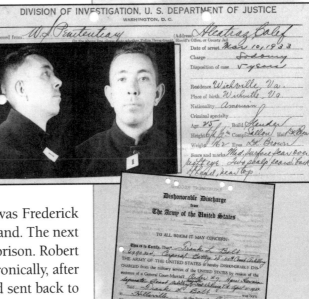

Frank L. Bolt was Alcatraz inmate #AZ-01. (Also shown) Bolt's dishonorable discharge papers from the US Army.

The first official group of fourteen Federal inmates arrived at Alcatraz from McNeil Island on August 11, 1934. Their identities were kept completely secret from an aggressive press, hungry to report on the first arrivals. Their train pulled into Oakland at 9:40 A.M., and the inmates were led in handcuffed pairs to the prison launch *General McDowell*. As the prisoners were lined up in formation along the dock, the island's residents peered down through their curtains to get a glimpse of their new neighbors. The inmates were forced to walk up to the main cellhouse

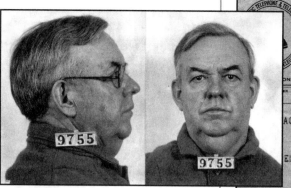

Frederick Grant White was the first civilian inmate at Alcatraz. He arrived on July 13, 1934 from McNeil Island.

(Right) A telegram to Warden Johnston, providing transfer details for inmate White.

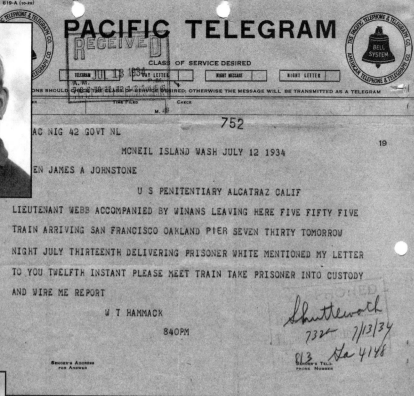

A photograph of military inmate John Miller, one of the thirty-two inmates left to finish out their sentences at Alcatraz following the prison's transition to a civilian institution. Miller's photograph illustrates one of the rare instances of leniency at the prison, which would be short-lived. Mustaches were not allowed at Alcatraz during its tenure as a Federal penitentiary.

Robert Bradford Moxon

heavily shackled, and under heavy guard. Once they arrived at the receiving area in the prison basement, they were photographed, stripped, and assigned their inmate numbers. They were then each given a medical examination, showered, and marched naked to their new cells carrying their clothes and utensils. Renowned inmate Darwin Coon recalled his first experience of arriving at Alcatraz, in his compelling personal memoir entitled *Alcatraz— The True End of the Line*:

Five or six officers were standing in front of the prison. Without ceremony, they ushered us through a solid steel door with an electric lock. Then we had to wait for a key to be lowered down so that the officer could open a barred gate in front of us. We went into a room where they removed the handcuffs and leg irons. I was so happy to get those things off I didn't care where I was. Then we were strip searched and marched naked to the showers. After that we were taken to fish row where we were each assigned a cell in an area that came to be known to us as Broadway.

The second group of fifty-three inmates arrived on August 22, 1934 from Atlanta, and the third and largest group consisting of 106 inmates came from Leavenworth on September 4, 1934. The routine for admission would essentially remain unchanged throughout the history of the prison. When the first groups arrived, Associate Warden C. J. Shuttleworth distributed a brief set of rules describing the disciplinary matrix that would govern their confinement. In this communication he also described the system that would be employed to discipline inmates who refused to abide by the rules set down by the Warden:

The U.S.A. Attorney General
The Honorable Homer S. Cummings

Dear Sir:-

I am one of the "32" soldier prisoners that was turned over to this Federal Institution June the 19th 1934, & at that time I couldn't see why we was being left here, for most of us was first time losers, & we understood that this place was to harbor nothing but the toughest kind of convict, which is "true", that is why I'm writing this letter, asking you to have me transfered, because I don't think I belong here, & I know that some of the "32" that are here with me now, are all of the same frame of mind, but I am speaking for myself for they have the same writing privileges that I have.

My record is "very good," as I haven't caused any trouble in the 5 years that I have been confined, & I'm doing my best to keep it that way. Sir, if you think that I deserve a transfer & will give me one, I will certainly appreciate it, for I sure want to get away from this place. I thank you.

Respectfully Yours

Ervie R. Walters
#28

Darwin E. Coon

(Above right) New inmates are seen here shackled in leg irons during the admissions process. They are standing in the basement hall next to the shower room.

(Below) Machine Gun Kelly under heavy guard, boarding an armored train car.

You will receive your punishment of perhaps 10 days in isolation on a restricted diet of bread and water. That practice will continue while you remain in isolation, and you will be provided with medical care if required for any illness. Isolation is a dark cell known here as the Hole. It consists of nothing but four walls, a ceiling and a floor. When you sleep, you will be provided blankets for warmth and a pillow for your head, but you may be required to do so on concrete. When a prisoner's required number of days in the hole expires, he is placed in what is known as Solitary Confinement. Here he enjoys the nighttime use of a bunk. He gets bread and water for breakfast, a noon meal the same as on the prison main line, and bread and water before he goes to bed.

When he is released from solitary he goes to his regular cell in the main prison. He will be placed in "grade." Grade will consist of the following: He will have a red tag placed on the cell plate of his door, which will indicate third grade. He may leave his cell only to go to the mess hall for scheduled meals. This will continue for three months. If he has not violated any rules for this period, he will be elevated to second grade. Now he will be able to write and receive a restricted number of letters. When he performs satisfactorily at this level, he will be promoted to first grade, where he will enjoy instatement of all normal prison privileges.

Among the first inmates to arrive were notorious gangsters Al Capone and Doc Barker (the last surviving son from the famous Ma Barker Gang), as well as George "Machine Gun" Kelly, Harvey Bailey, Roy Gardner, Floyd Hamilton (a gang member and driver for Bonnie & Clyde), and several other gangland criminals. Warden Johnston was openly concerned over the security of the new arrivals. The inmates would not even be permitted to leave the train, which would be transferred onto a floating barge and towed across the Bay. The train was diverted to Tiburon, and then ferried to Alcatraz. There was an officer stationed in each railcar, who sat inside a reinforced cage with a loaded shotgun. It was later noted that the train cars seemed horribly unstable, and many feared that they could tip and plunge the inmates into the frigid water, to meet their demise by drowning. It was also during this trek across the turbulent Bay waters that rumors of man-eating sharks and fin sightings started to circulate among the inmates.

The first groups of inmates transferred from other Federal penitentiaries were brought to the island still shackled in the train cars that had carried them across the United States. They were considered the nations' most incorrigible criminals, and no chances would be taken by off-loading the train cars on the mainland. During the transfers, newspaper reporters followed the trains across the country, with onlookers flocking to see America's worst public enemies.

Attorney General Homer S. Cummings and Warden James Johnston inspecting the staff of correctional officers during the opening of the prison in 1934. The officer standing second from the left is future Associate Warden E.J. Miller.

Warden Johnston on August 18, 1934, leading a tour for dignitaries. Pictured from left to right are San Francisco Mayor Angelo Rossi; Attorney General Homer Cummings, one of the conceptual founders of the prison; Warden Johnston; and San Francisco Police Chief William Quinn. The photograph opposite shows the group leaving the prison.

The Daily Routine

The life of the Alcatraz convict was repetitious, regimented, and monastic. Everything was done in accordance with a strict schedule, and the methodical routine cycle was unforgiving and relentless. It never varied through the years, and became a definitive model of clockwork organization. The daily schedule was established by Warden Johnston as one of his original directives in 1934, and it would remain fairly consistent throughout the prison's tenure.

DAILY ROUTINE

6:33 A.M.—Morning Gong. Prisoners arise, make beds, place all articles in prescribed order on shelf, clean washbasin and toilet, bowl, wipe off bars, sweep cell floor, fold table and seat against the wall, wash, and dress.

6:45 A.M.—Detail guards assigned for mess hall duty; they take their positions so as to watch the prisoners coming out of cells and prepare to march into the mess hall with them. The guards supervise the serving and the seating of their details, give the signal to start eating, and the signal to rise after eating.

6:50 A.M.—Second morning gong. The prisoners stand by the door facing out and remain there until the whistle signal, during which time the lieutenants and cellhouse guards of both shifts make the count. When the count is found to be correct, the lieutenant orders the cells unlocked.

6:55 A.M.—Whistle signal given by deputy warden or lieutenant; all inmates step out of their cells and stand erect facing mess hall.

Upon the second whistle, all inmates on each tier close up in single file upon the headman.

7:00 A.M.—Third whistle signal; lower right tier of Block 3 (C) and lower left tier of Block 2 (B) move forward into mess hall, each line is followed in turn by the second and the third tiers, then by the lower tier on the opposite side of their block, followed by the second and the third tiers from the same side. The Block 3 line moves into the mess hall, keeping to the left of the center of the mess; Block 2 goes forward at the same time, keeping to the right. Both lines proceed to serving the table; the right line served from the right and occupies the tables on the right; the left line to left, etc. As each man is served, he will sit erect with his hands at his sides until the whistle signal is given for the first detail to begin eating. Twenty minutes are allowed for eating. When they are finished eating the prisoners place their knives, forks, and spoons on their trays; the knife at the left, the fork in center, and the spoon on the right side of the tray. They then sit erect with their hands down at their sides, After all of the men have finished eating, a guard walks to each table to see that all utensils are in their proper place. He then returns to his position.

7:20 A.M.—Upon signal from deputy warden, the first detail in each line arises and proceeds through the rear entrance door of the cellhouse to the recreation yard. Inside detail, are those not assigned any detail, proceed to their work or cells.

7:25 A.M.—Guards and their details move out in the following order through the rear gates:

1. Laundry
2. Tailor shop
3. Cobblers
4. Model shop
5. All other shops
6. Policing, gardening, and labor details.

The guards go ahead through the rear gates and stand opposite the rear gate. There they count prisoners passing through the gate in single file and clear the count with the rear-gate guard. The detail stops at the foot of the steps on the lower level road and forms into two ranks. The guard faces them to the right and proceeds to the shops keeping himself in the rear of his detail. Upon arrival in the front of the shops, the detail halts and faces the shop entrance.

07:30 A.M.—Shop foreman counts his detail as the line enters the shop and immediately

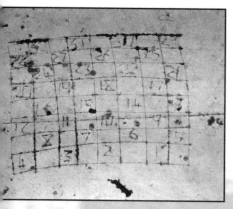

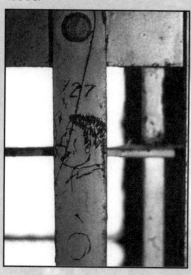

Inmate graffiti of a calendar etched on the floor of a cell, and a caricature found on a soft iron bar, drawn by inmate Olin Stevens in the late 1930's.

phones his count to the lieutenant of the watch. He also signs the count slip and turns it over to the lieutenant making his first round.

7:33 A.M.—Rear-gate guard makes up detailed count slip, phones it to the lieutenant of the watch, signs it, and proceeds with it to the lieutenant's office.

9:30 A.M.—Rest period, during which the men are allowed to smoke in places permitted, but are not allowed to congregate.

9:38 A.M.—Foreman or the guard gives whistle signal; all of the men on each floor of the shops assemble at a given point and are counted, and return immediately to work. This assembly and count is quickly done, the count is written on a slip of paper, signed by the foreman or guard, and then turned over to the lieutenant making his next round.

11:30 A.M.—Prisoners stop work and assemble in front of the shops. The foreman or the guard takes the count. The foreman phones in the count and signs the count slip, turning it over to the guard, who proceeds with the detail to the rear gate and checks his detail in with the rear-gate guard.

11:35 A.M.—In the recreation yard the mess hall line is immediately formed in the same order as in the morning. The details proceed in the same lines to the mess hall.

11:40 A.M.—Dinner routine is the same as for breakfast, except at the completion of dinner, when the details immediately proceed to the cells.

12:00 P.M.—Noon lockup cell count; the detail guards remain in front of cells until the prisoners are locked up and the count made.

12:20 P.M.—Unlock and proceed the same as before going to breakfast, except that the prisoners march in single file into the yard #3 cell-block first. Shop details again form in front of their guards.

12:25 P.M.—Details are checked out of the rear gate the same as in the morning.

12:30 P.M.—Details enter the shops and are counted by the foreman and the guard. Procedures are the same as at 07:30 hours.

2:30 P.M.—Rest period: the procedure and count are the same as in the morning.

4:15 P.M.—Work stopped with standard count procedure.

4:20 P.M.—Prisoners enter the rear gate, with count.

4:25 P.M.—Prisoners march into the mess hall, with count.

4:45 P.M.—Prisoners return to their cells.

4:50 P.M.—Final lockup.

5:00 P.M.—Standing count in the cells by both shifts of the lieutenants and the cell housemen.

8:00 P.M.—Count in the cells.

9:30 P.M.—Lights out count.

12:01 A.M.—Count by the lieutenants and the cell housemen of both shifts.

3:00 A.M.—Count in the cells.

5:00 A.M.—Count in the cells.

A total of thirteen official counts were made in a hour 24-hour period, with several other unscheduled and unofficial counts. In addition, the shop foremen made six verification counts during the scheduled workdays. Sunday and holiday routines required their own schedules, with time reserved for haircuts, showers, clothing changes, and recreation.

COUNT PROCEDURES

Warden Johnston drew up careful, detailed procedures for taking official counts and unlocking and locking cells in the morning, at noon, and at the end of the day.

1. The deputy warden is in command and gives the signals. He takes a position at the east end of the cellhouse, between blocks B and C.
2. The lieutenant of the watch takes a position at the west end of the cell house, between blocks B and C; there he receives reports of count from the guards.
3. The guards take their assigned positions, ready to take the count when the signal is given. On signal, the count is started on the south side of block B and the north side of block C.
4. As each guard completes his count he goes to the west end of the cellblock and reports ft the lieutenant. The count must be accurate and the report must be made as soon as it is ready.
5. After his report of count, each guard returns quickly to his position. Upon the whistle signal guards open the cells in the same order of movement as when taking count. Example: Guard in position 1, Block B, lower east end, opens the cells controlled by Box 1C, then proceeds quickly to opening the cells controlled by Box 7.
6. After the prisoners have stepped out of their cells, the deputy warden and the lieutenant give hand signals for locking.

PROCEDURES FOR OPENING CELL DOORS

Work Area and Yard Turnouts:

1. This will be done by tiers, taking lower tier on "C" outside, working on the same side top to top. Then, coming over to "inside" of "C", and working down to lower tier. Then proceed to "B" Block and starting on lower "inside" tier, working to the top. Then turn out other side of Block by starting on top and working down.
2. Officers operating doors will not be required to wait until line clears control box, as aisle will be covered by other officers.

3. Inmates should be let out in a steady stream, but overcrowding should be avoided. Note: East end officer must synchronize his opening with West end officer.

Main Line Dining Room Turnouts:

1. This will be done by blocks, beginning on lower tiers, either inside or outside, and working up to top tier as schedule calls for. Then proceeding to other block, beginning at the lower tier and working up to the top.
2. A weekly schedule should be prepared by cellhouse Lieutenant and Officers, verifying the turnouts as much as possible, but still beginning on the lower tiers, one block at a time.
3. Cellhouse officer will give signal when each tier is to be turned out.
4. Officers opening doors will check tiers immediately after inmates have left the tier, taking the number and locking up any inmate remaining in his cell.

Bath Turnouts:

1. Bath turnouts on Saturday mornings will be done by blocks as directed by the cellhouse Lieutenant.

Inmates were required to shave three times a week, with no exceptions. Men who refused to shave were immediately placed in solitary confinement, and they would be force-shaved with a dry razor by guard staff until they complied. No inmate was allowed to grow facial hair of any kind, including mustaches, sideburns, or beards. Each inmate was provided with a personal shaving mug, a shaving brush, and soap. The guard staff would pass out razors to a small number of inmates at a time, and then collect the blades from each person once they were finished. The inmates were allowed a three-hour window in which to shave,

Period photographs showing the shower room in the cellhouse basement, and the clothing issue station located in the same area. All new inmates were processed in this area.

84

A present-day photograph showing the basement shower area.

from 5:30 P.M. to 8:30 P.M. Prisoners in B Block were assigned to shave on Monday, Wednesday, and Friday, and C Block inmates were assigned on Tuesday, Thursday, and Saturday.

General population inmates were required to shower twice a week, and the water temperatures were fully regulated by the on-duty correctional officers. The water was kept hotter than average, to eliminate the possibility that inmates could attempt acclimatization to the temperature of the chilly Bay waters. The showers were located in the basement area, and they were considered one of the more dangerous parts of the prison. There was a large community shower room with water pipe columns suspended from the ceiling above cement basins on the basement floor. Guards stood at the doorway, controlling the flow of inmates entering and exiting the room. The inmates were marched down to the basement in their bathrobes, and once they had finished showering, they were issued new underwear, socks, tooth powder, toilet paper, hand towels, bed linen, and a handkerchief.

The Rule of Silence and Strict Regimen

In the early years of Alcatraz, Warden Johnston employed a silence policy that many inmates considered to be the most unbearable punishment of all. Prisoners were not permitted to talk to each other while confined to their cells, while walking in line formation through the cellhouse, or during inmate counts. They were only allowed to talk quietly in the Dining Room when seated; at their job assignments, as long as it didn't interfere with their work; and at other community events such as motion picture shows and church services. In the early years, inmates were harshly disciplined for even the slightest violation of the silence rule. There were exaggerated reports that several inmates went slowly insane on Alcatraz because of the "*severe order of silence.*" One inmate, a former gangster and kidnapper named Rufe Persful, took a fire ax from the

Mug shots of Rufe Persful.

prison garage while working a garbage detail and chopped off two fingers from his left hand in order to win a transfer off the island. Rumors among the inmates indicated that Persful begged fellow inmate Homer Parker, who was assigned to the same job detail, to "*finish the job*" by cutting off his right hand. In later years several other inmates used similar tactics, such as slashing their Achilles' tendons, to protest the alleged harsh confinement practices and mental harassment they said they suffered at Alcatraz.

Another alleged casualty of the silent system was thirty-six year old inmate Edward Wutke. Prior to his imprisonment at Alcatraz, Wutke was an able seaman employed on the steamship Yale. When a friendly drunken scuffle with his best friend turned into a serious fight, Wutke drew a small pocketknife and stabbed his friend in the groin area, fatally severing his femoral artery. The wounded man would bleed to death before the ship made it into port at San Diego. Wutke became panic-stricken upon realizing the gravity of his act and had to be shackled to a fixed object. Following his conviction for murder on the high seas, Wutke became withdrawn, and was sent to Alcatraz because of what officials described as a "*desperate disposition.*"

On December 27, 1934 Wutke refused to report to his work assignment, and was sent to the lower solitary unit below A Block, better known as the "*dungeon.*" He would remain in the damp, dark dungeon for eight days. Wutke made his first suicide attempt in January of 1936. He complained that he was unable to do his time "*under the present conditions,*" and indicated that the silence and harsh rules had finally become unbearable. Using a small contraband blade, he sliced a prominent vein near the elbow, and bled profusely before a guard was able to intervene. Dr. Milton Beacher, who would later write an exceptional memoir on his experiences at Alcatraz, sutured the inmate's wound and then admitted him to the hospital for an examination by the prison psychiatrist. Wutke's unsuccessful suicide attempt would only intensify his hatred of the Alcatraz regimen. He remained incorrigible, and found himself locked in solitary on at least three later occasions.

Deputy Warden E. J. Miller and Dr. Beacher were called to Wutke's cell on November 13, 1937, after the prisoner was found dead by Lieutenant Weinhold. Miller's official report read in part:

Approximately 2:40 this morning I was awakened by the telephone. Upon answering the telephone, found it was Lieutenant Weinhold stating that he believed Wutke had cut his throat in his cell and that he had notified the Doctor. Told Lieutenant Weinhold that I would be there immediately.

It was about 2:50 A.M. when we opened the cell door and Doctor Beacher entered with me into the cell. Wutke was sitting on the toilet bowl in a drooping position with his back braced against the corner of the wall. The cell was quite bloody and the sheets and blankets were full of blood.

Doctor Beacher examined the man and said that he was dead and stated that about 2:35 A.M. was approximately the time of death. The body was removed from the cell to the hospital. I then called Warden Johnston stating that the man had committed suicide and was pronounced dead by the doctor and moved to the Morgue.

I had Lieutenant Weinhold search the cell to find out what he had used and he found that Wutke had cut his throat with a small blade from a pencil sharpener fastened in the head of the safety razor.

Wutke was buried on November 17, 1937, at the Cypress Lawn Cemetery in Colma, California. Following his suicide, numerous stories were leaked to the press alleging harsh confinement practices at Alcatraz. Countless inmates believed that the unrelenting torture of strict confinement had contributed to several inmates "*going crazy.*" Over the span of the island's tenure as a Federal penitentiary, there would be a total of five inmate suicides. Some even claimed that the first escape attempt at U.S.P. Alcatraz by Joseph Bowers was actually an intentional suicide. This was never substantiated, but inmates would later assert that his mental condition had deteriorated as a direct result of the prison's conditions, because a person of "*weak mind*" could not survive there.

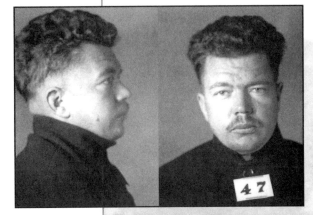

Edward Wutke—the first inmate to commit suicide at Alcatraz.

When James Bennett became the Bureau Director, he made a concerted effort to provide psychiatric services for Alcatraz inmates. He also differentiated between inmate rights and inmate privileges in the official policy of the Bureau. In correspondence to Warden Johnston, he stated: "*it is unnecessary to impose such rigorous rules.*" As a result, the silence policy was relaxed in 1937, and this would be one of the few policy changes that occurred over the prison's history. However, it should be restated that the track record of Warden Johnston demonstrated his desire to rehabilitate the inmates rather than simply to punish them. In his 1949 memoir, he described his perspective on prison discipline:

> Discipline in prisons is frequently confounded with punishment. Punishment or deprivations are sometimes necessary to hold some men in line, but the measures taken to instruct and train men are more important. Discipline is systematic training to secure submission to authority. The value of discipline is the respect it induces in individuals and the resultant good order of the group.
>
> When discussing the discipline for prisoners we should keep in mind the purpose of the prison. Alcatraz is reserved by the government for perplexing problem prisoners and organized on the basis of maximum security with every precaution taken to insure safekeeping of prisoners and to prevent the possibility of escape.
>
> Privileges are limited, supervision is strict, routine is exacting, discipline is firm, but there is no cruelty or undue harshness, and we insist upon decent regard for the humanities.

Stories of inmate suicides, accompanied by media hype based on limited information, eventually earned Alcatraz the unflattering nickname

A letter smuggled out of the prison to a San Francisco newspaper in 1935, claiming abuse and cruelty at Alcatraz.

San francisco news
San francisco Cal

Please investigate criminal cruelty practices on prisoners at Alcatraz Prison. A few of the cases are (1) Edgar Lewis, age 28, serving 3 ys sentence, kept in dungeon for a total of more than 6 wks, starved, shot in face with gas gun, beaten over head with clubs by three guards (names will be given to investigating committee). He is now insane and is kept in a cage in the hospital. No hope for his recovery. His family lives at Los Banos, Calif. They don't know about it yet. The warden naturally wont give out information that will hang himself, but if an investigation is made and the inmates are questioned you will get the evidence. Another case is Jos. Bowers also insane from same cause, but not as bad condition as Lewis. James Grave is also insane and is under mental observation. John Stadig is

(Below, top) John Stadig, one of the inmates referenced in the smuggled letter, who allegedly suffered from psychosis resulting from severe abuse.

(Below, bottom) Verrill Raap was the first inmate paroled from Alcatraz as a Federal Penitentiary. The *San Francisco Examiner* printed news stories that told of horrid conditions at Alcatraz, which were alleged by Raap.

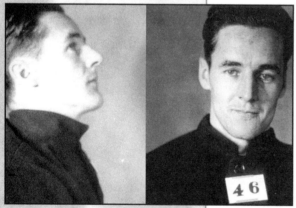

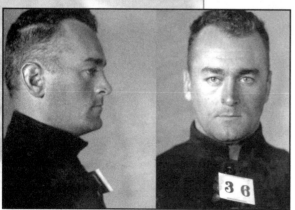

of "*Devil's Island.*" Warden Johnston succeeded in keeping the media at a distance, and this resulted in the dissemination of various misleading stories. The fact that inmates were never directly paroled from Alcatraz added to the mythology of the island. The media had a difficult time finding men who had lived on the inside, because after prisoners were released from Alcatraz, they were sent on to other prisons to finish out their sentences. When the press did manage to talk with former inmates, they usually told horrific stories about the brutalities they had experienced while incarcerated on the island. Most of these depictions were flawed, but the stories of horrid beatings, rigid disciplinary measures, and extreme isolation fueled the media's interest. In July of 1935, the *San Francisco Examiner* ran a headline article entitled "Alcatraz Silence Awful." The editorial featured an interview with an inmate who had been released for exportation. He described the tough rule of silence, stating that this was the harshest aspect of confinement at Alcatraz. He said that it created a constant pressure, with only a brief reprieve in the recreation yard on weekends. The article concluded with the inmate stating: "*It's the toughest pen I've ever seen. The hopelessness of it really gets to you. Capone feels it. Everybody does.*"

The stressful regimen of Alcatraz did indeed create a pressure-cooker environment for some of the inmates. The cellblocks were always illuminated, and there was no privacy of any kind. There was a continual sense of mistrust and suspicion among inmates and staff alike. Writer Susan Lamb offered a unique perspective in her book entitled *Alcatraz—The Rock*:

Parallel to the regimentation imposed by authority was the conformity demanded of one another by the inmates. Rival subcultures, complete with hierarchies and arcane jargon, left no one in peace. Independence and character had no chance for expression.

In Erwin T. Thompson's masterful historic reference on Alcatraz, the author quotes a letter sent to Bureau Director James V. Bennett on June 6, 1937 by Burton

RECEIVED ... Mar. 23, 1935 ...
FROM ... D-Kansas-Wichita ...
CRIME Nat. Bank Robbery. Armed-Kidnapping.
MILITARY OR CIVIL ... Civil ...
SENTENCE: ... LIFE Yrs. ... Mos. ... Days
DATE OF SENTENCE ... Mar. 23, 1935 ...
BIRTHPLACE ... Kansas ...
RELIGION ... Prot. ...
EDUCATION ... HS-4 ...
OCCUPATION ... Taxi Driver ...
MARRIED ... yes ... CHILDREN ... 1 ...
RESIDENCE ... Hutchinson, Kansas ...
HABITS ... smokes ...

DESCRIPTION:
AGE ... 22 ... BIRTHDATE ... May 20, 1912 ...
HEIGHT ... 5'11" WEIGHT ... 153 ... BUILD ... M. ...
HAIR ... Lt. Ch. ... EYES ... Lt. Hz. Yel. Blu.
COMP. ... M. ... CHIN ... Reg. ...

MARKS AND SCARS:
Faint obl. scar ½" 1st joint left index finge
front and out. Faint curved scar ¼" 2nd join
right small finger front. Irregular scar 5"
2" above right wrist front and ½ in. Obl. scar
1¼" under right side chin.

I hereby authorize the Warden of the United States Penitentiary, Leavenworth, Kansas, or his authorized representative, to open all mail matter, and express or other packages which may be directed to my address, and to sign my name as endorsement on all checks, money orders, or
bank drafts, for deposit to my credit in the Prisoners' Trust Fund as long as I am a prisoner in said institution.

Signature _Burton P. Phillips_

USPA—FLK—5-14-33—5000—4531-37

Burton Phillips

Phillips, a young convict sentenced to Alcatraz for kidnapping and robbery. Phillips wrote to Bennett claiming that the Bureau had violated his
constitutional rights by denying his request for specific legal publications. The letter read in part:

> Are you to put me in here for life, stop all my mail and deny me the right
> of legal redress by keeping me in ignorance of legal decisions? Then I
> would be better off to slit my throat, or perhaps, someone else's and
> make you hang me, ending quickly and mercifully a life which would
> otherwise be carried on tortuously year after weary year without hope or
> possibilities of legal release.
>
> I'll grant you the point that there is nothing in the Constitution to keep
> you from starving, torturing and mistreating me but it
> must be a regrettable oversight on your part to deny
> me full access to legal documents.

Los Angeles mobster and gambler
Meyer "Mickey" Cohen a famed
inmate of Alcatraz. Mickey was the
trusted friend of racketeer Benjamin
"Bugsy" Siegel.

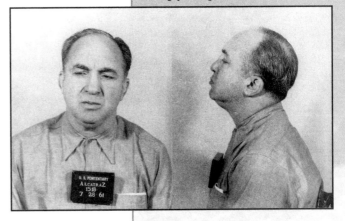

Hon. Frank Murphy   Alcatraz.
U.S. Attorney General
Dept of Justice Bldg
Washington D.C.
Sir:

We the undersigned respectfully submit this petition for the purpose of obtaining your approval in granting we inmates the privilege of subscribing for the Nation's newspapers.

We do believe that if an unbiased analysis is made with a view of determining the amount of good contributed by a newspaper as compared with the theoretical harm that is alleged both from the Institution's point of view as well as the inmate a good deal of constructive good is to be concluded.

We do further believe that at this time World History is being written and destiny molded in a manner vital to the Nation as well as to the individual.

Heretofore we have been given to understand that we inmates have been denied access to the

newspapers because of the crime news contained therein.

Incredible tho it may sound crime news to a man in this Institution is of less interest than it is to the man on the street.

There are at present in this Institution men whose Homelands, which are now the scene of the tragedy taking place in Europe and it so follows that it is a natural desire to wish to be informed of the events there taking place the same as if your Country or Home Nation where to be invaded altho we hope that the latter will never occur.

We have it is true, weekly newsmagazines but it can be readily seen that these are of necessity limited in scope, accuracy and detail, it is also obvious that mail facilities are unable to cope with the present situation.

There are circulating in this Country many conservative newspapers of unimpeachable character many of which you are no doubt personally acquainted with and can

vouch for as to their integrity and lack of sensationalism.

Doubtless these same newspapers assist you in your daily life and if contact with these newspapers were to be severed their value would be apparent.

The healthy minded person enjoys keeping pace with progress in the worlds of National and Foreign affairs with science and invention, history and civic life, industries and world markets, sports and modern trends to mention a few of the educational features to be found in the every day newspaper.

We inmates urge that we have no other means to employ in making this contact with you and wish to assure you that this petition will not be the forerunner of future attempts to petition your office with requests of this nature.

We also wish to assure you that we will deeply appreciate any consideration you may show us in regard to this request and remain

Respectfully yours,

Phillips' rage would finally flare out on September 20, 1937. Following the lunchtime meal, he and over a hundred other inmates remained in their cells, refusing to work, and announcing a general strike in protest against confinement conditions at Alcatraz. Four days later when the inmates filed into the Mess Hall, Warden Johnston stood near the line to observe the inmates. Suddenly and without warning, Phillips stepped out of the line and viciously attacked the Warden. He knocked Johnston to the floor and delivered several sharp kicks to his head and torso. Johnston was rendered unconscious, and the guards quickly tackled Phillips. Correctional Officer E. F. Chandler used his Browning automatic rifle to smash away one of the windowpanes in the Mess Hall catwalk, and aimed the rifle straight at Phillips. The other inmates took cover, and the disturbance was quickly quelled. Phillips was removed to the A Block Dungeon, and handcuffed to the bars in a standing position.

Johnston woke up on the operating table in the hospital, and he would later write that he had no recollection of the event. It is said that Phillips was taken to the dungeon where he was severely beaten and rendered unconscious, but this is not officially documented. He was then transferred to the hospital, where he was quoted as saying that he regretted not having had a weapon with which to kill the Warden. Johnston, however, did not cower after the attack. Though he had suffered several cuts and bruises to his head, face, and upper body, he reaffirmed his stature by returning to the Mess Hall, standing in the very spot where he had been attacked, and greeting the inmates who were filing in for lunch. Johnston would finally lift the rule of silence in late 1937, thus ending one of the most trying aspects of prison life on the island.

Violence among the inmates was not uncommon at Alcatraz over the entire span of its operation. Former inmate John Dekker, a Chicago born bank robber, recalled witnessing a murder that resulted from a simple dispute over a pack of cigarettes. During the island's tenure as a Federal penitentiary, eight people were murdered by inmates, five men committed suicide, and fifteen died of natural causes. The island had its own morgue, a remnant from the military period, but no autopsies were performed there. All deceased inmates were brought back to the mainland and released to the San Francisco County Coroner.

Alcatraz wanted no surprises when it came to administering discipline to prisoners. Adherence to the rules at Alcatraz was mandatory in the strictest sense, and inmates who broke the rules were subject to a level of discipline that was dictated by the severity of the offense. Due to the tales that leaked out about strict routines and harsh punishments, the public came to believe that Alcatraz was a grim place, but the reality was that the morale at Alcatraz was typically better than at most other penal institutions. Former inmate Willie Radkay commented: *"The correctional staff treated us with respect, though we rarely spoke to one another. If you minded your own business and did your own time, no one ever bothered you."* Former inmate Darwin Coon would concur with this assessment. He stated: *"If you were on the "up and up" and didn't carry any*

(Opposite page) A letter smuggled off Alcatraz to the Attorney General, requesting that inmates be allowed to read the newspaper in order to keep up with current events. This letter, considered as contraband, was signed by numerous famous inmates at Alcatraz, but it did not reach its intended destination. A mail handler found the letter in Sacramento and turned it over to the authorities.

debts towards other inmates, you would be okay." Former correctional officer Al Bloomquest recalled: *"It was really a very respectful environment. The public's idea that Alcatraz was some hellhole wasn't at all true. We ate the exact same menu as the inmates, we lived together day-to-day, and for the most part, we treated each other with dignity."* And former correctional officer Phil Bergen would write:

> The public never wanted to know the real Alcatraz. There was never any form of abuse that I ever witnessed. If an inmate struck an officer, well, that might earn someone a hard dragging to the hole. There wasn't ever a true silence rule like some of these men claim; it was essentially a quiet rule. I imagine it was a better deterrent letting people believe that it was a place straight out of a horror film, but the real Alcatraz wasn't at all like some of these guys claim. I was there for sixteen years—I know the truth. Even today after the prison has been closed for so many decades, the public just wont let go of the myths.

The Dungeons

The infamous so-called "*dungeons of Alcatraz*" were the subject of countless news stories in the early years of the prison. The dungeons or "*lower solitary*," as they were referred to in inmate files, consisted of eight cells located below A and D Blocks. These cells were primarily used in only the most serious disciplinary cases, until 1938, when the cell fronts were finally dismantled. They would also become the focal point in the famous 1940 trial of Henri Young for the murder of fellow inmate Rufus McCain (this incident is discussed in greater detail in a later chapter).

Warden Johnston would openly testify that Young and several other inmates had been confined in "*lower solitary*" for serious violations of various prison regulations. One of Young's attorneys disputed this, emphasizing his contention that inmates were thrown into the dungeons for "*trivial offenses,*" though this was never proven.

(Below) A rare photograph taken in May of 1933, showing the original configuration of the basement dungeon cells. The fronts were removed in 1939, and the cells were later used only for storage.

(Below right) The cellhouse was built on top of the military Citadel foundation. Only the first floor of the citadel remains, under the cellblock. The hallway seen here was actually the dry moat during the Civil War years. The Citadel framework is still intact, with the windows and rifle slits visible.

It was alleged that inmates were placed into the dark dungeon cells without bedding, and without any form of lighting. In Young's case, Johnston testified that the prisoner had been confined in the basement cells on at least three occasions, and was forced to sleep on the cement floors without any type of bedding or pillow. The cells had no running water or toilet, and inmates were forced to blindly use a bucket which would be emptied only once or twice a day. The cells were said to be damp and poorly ventilated. Warden Johnston described during trial testimony the *"restricted diet"* that inmates would be served during their solitary confinement:

If a prisoner is placed in solitary in the morning, after he has had his breakfast, he is furnished bread at the noonday meal, and salads and one-fourth of the evening meal from the regular main-line menu. If he is placed in solitary in the afternoon, that is after he has had his full noonday meal, then he gets only bread for the evening meal.

In all cases the second day menu consists of a breakfast of cereal, milk and coffee; the noonday meal, bread and soup; the evening meal is one fourth of the allowance from the regular main line menu leaving out the soup but feeding the salad and greens and bread and the hot drink, whether it happens to be tea or coffee.

On the third day a man in solitary receives the full dinner meal at noon, also the one quarter quantity, that is the light breakfast or cereal and milk and coffee and the light supper consisting of the salad and greens and bread and hot beverage, tea or coffee.

If an individual is continued in solitary past the third day, then the fourth day is the same as that prescribed as the second day, the fifth day the same, and the sixth day he gets a full meal again at dinner and the light breakfast and light supper, just the same as the third day.

Sometimes the menu is added to on the advice of the Chief Medical Officer, even during the earlier stages of incarceration in solitary or isolation. When a prisoner is removed from solitary and it is thought necessary to keep him in open isolation for a longer period of time, he begins his time in isolation with one full meal and two light meals each day. If he is continued in isolation for more than a week, he is given two full meals and one light meal daily. If it is decided to keep him in isolation for a long period of time, he is given three full meals a day, the same as the main line.

The inmates in solitary would also be provided with a water basin that was always kept full under the Warden's orders. Many of the inmates who testified during the Young trial, including Harold Brest, George Miller, Harmon Waley, Samuel Berlin, Burton Phillips, and James Grove, all stated that they had served stretches ranging from seven to ten days without proper meals, living strictly on small portions of bread and water.

The use of solitary confinement at Alcatraz was put on trial again in another incident that is described in the official digest from the Young trial testimony transcript. Inmate Samuel Berlin testified that on this occasion, inmate Jack Allen had rattled his cup along his cell bars to gain the attention of a correctional officer. When the officers arrived, he explained that he was sick and needed a doctor. Berlin claimed that Allen

(Top left) Alcatraz inmate Harold Brest being led to court to testify against conditions at Alcatraz.

(Middle left) George Miller

(Bottom left) Harmon Waley

Mug shots of Alcatraz inmate Jack Allen.

was reprimanded for making excessive noise, and that when he again started yelling for a doctor, he was thrown into the Hole. He was heard by other inmates pleading for blankets, and was allegedly found dead fifty-two hours later. A letter explaining his death, submitted by Chief Medical Officer Dr. George Hess to the United States Surgeon General, only seemed to complicate the matter further. Their correspondence was entered as evidence in the trial, and the defense attorneys systematically illustrated how inmate Allen had been abandoned, which was said to have contributed to his death. The letter written by Hess to the Surgeon General on January 23, 1936 proved extremely detrimental to the administration's case. It read:

I have the honor to present a resume of the case of Jack Allen, No. 211, an inmate of this institution who died on January 17, 1936.

On January 13, 1936, the above inmate named man called for the doctor. Doctor Jacobsen was on duty and responded to the call. After an examination of the patient the doctor decided that there was no acute pathology present but did give the man some medicine. He then instructed the guard on duty not to call him anymore about this case, that the patient would be all right.

At midnight the guard was changed and the retiring guard informed the new guard that the doctor did not care to be bothered anymore for this case.

At about 1:00 A.M. January 14th, the patient created a noise by groaning and was placed in isolation so that he would not disturb the rest of the inmates.

The following morning at 8:00 A.M., I saw the patient in the cellhouse and immediately had him brought to the hospital. Shortly after admitting him to the hospital I made a tentative diagnosis of a probable perforated gastric ulcer. We decided that an operation was in order and at 1:15 P.M., an exploratory operation was started. Upon entering the abdominal cavity there was found about 1 ½ quarts of free fluid and a generalized peritonitis accompanying a perforated gastric ulcer on the lesser curvature near the pylorus on the anterior surface of the stomach. A Castrorrhaphy was done and drain tube placed in the operative wound coming out.

The patient was put to bed and was given the proper postoperative treatment such as suction through the nasal tube to the stomach, glucose and saline and other supportive measures.

At 1:00 P.M., January 16th, the patient appeared to be making an uneventful recovery from the operation. By 7:00 P.M. that same day he developed signs and symptoms of pneumonia and by 11:00 P.M. the entire right lobe was consolidated. The next morning there developed an acute edema of the left chest and the patient became unconscious, remaining in this condition until he died at 1:28 P.M., January 17, 1936.

The post mortem examination had to be partial because of the uncertainly of his relatives claiming his body. I examined the abdomen through the operative wound and found that the peritonitis had practically cleared up, there was little free fluid in the abdominal cavity and no abscess formation. The omentum which was placed over the repaired ulcer was adherent and upon examination of the Castrorrhaphy it was found that repair had been successful.

The unfortunate thing is that the doctor did not recognize the condition at the first visit and although this might not have played a major part in the fatal outcome it certainly made a very bad impression on the inmate population and on others. Another unfortunate thing, for the patient, was the more or less general feeling that the man exaggerated minor complaints.

This is the first mortality at this station under the present regime. It is unfortunate that it had to happen at this time when the inmates were in a state of unrest. It seemed to be the spark that was needed by the leader to incite followers into rioting.

Berlin also testified about another inmate named Edward Bearden, who was likewise apparently left in solitary, and became mortally ill. Berlin claimed that Bearden's pleas for help went unheeded, and that he too later died. It was this type of testimony that eventually led to a conviction of involuntary manslaughter for Young, as he was judged to have suffered overly severe punishment.

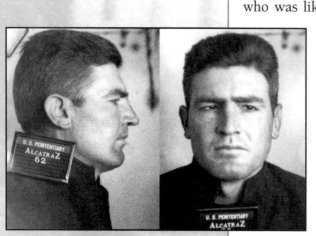

Edward Bearden

Despite the harsh allegations against Alcatraz and its treatment of prisoners, many inmates also provided positive testimony on behalf of the prison. These supporters claimed that if you followed the rules, Alcatraz was the best penitentiary in which to be incarcerated. They maintained that Warden Johnston was an advocate of inmate rights and rehabilitation, and would not tolerate any form of intentional maltreatment. It should also be noted that during this period, the bread and water "*restricted diet*" rule was common policy under the Bureau for inmates being held in solitary confinement for serious misconduct. Most other Federal institutions employed the same policy for unmanageable inmates.

Warden Johnston indicated in his personal memoir that he did not particularly like utilizing the dungeons as a form of punishment. One telling section reads:

United States Penitentiary

Alcatraz, California

Disciplinary Report

Name BERTA, Charles   No.   132

Cell 305   Employed   None   How long   11-21-4

Violation   ATTEMPTING TO ASSAULT AN OFFICER, INSOLENCE, FOUL AND ABUSIVE
             LANGUAGE DIRECTED AT AN OFFICER

              While taking a bath with a number of other inmates, the
above-named man deliberately took his time and slowed up in every way possible, so
that he would be the last one finished. When told by me to "Hurry", he (Berta)
jumped out in front of me and in the presence of the other guards and inmates,
squared off as if he wanted to fight and said in a loud tone of voice "God damn
it, if you want to fight, come on and put up your hands". I then marched the
other inmates out of the bath room and when they had gone Berta again offered to
fight not only myself but Guards Faulk and Chandler. All the time this was
taking place, Berta was very insolent and insisted on directing numerous
sarcastic remarks at the Guards and Institution in general.
                                    Report by   R. O. Culver

Date   2-2-35   1:00 P.M.   Title   Lieutenant

Punishment or action taken

        TO BE PLACED IN LOWER SOLITARY ON RESTRICTED DIET

        TO BE FOLLOWED BY PERMANENT ISOLATION

        TO BE CONTINUED IN THIRD GRADE FOR AN ADDITIONAL NINETY DAYS.

Age   32   Mental Age_____ No. of previous violations   TWO

Date   2-2-35   Deputy Warden
                                                   C.J.Shuttleworth
U.SP.A.C.F.-47

Charles Berta, considered by several correctional officers as the toughest inmate ever incarcerated at Alcatraz. He was the last inmate ever to be confined in the basement dungeon.

When we took over the island in 1934 we did not like the disciplinary cells that were inherited with the building. The Army had solitary cells on one of the top tiers (A-Block) and the dungeon cells in the basement… the brick walls of which were often damp. They [dungeons] were badly located, poorly constructed and unsafe because they were easy to dig out of and in the few instances where we did use them we had to chain the men to keep them from breaking out . . . I did not like these cells, in fact I was ashamed of them and were used only under necessity.

The last inmate to serve time in the dungeon was Charles Berta. Berta had been convicted of mail robbery and aggravated assault, and he was known as a frequent visitor to the dungeon at Alcatraz. Correctional Officer Clifford Fish remembered Berta as the toughest inmate that any of the guards would ever encounter at Alcatraz. He had previously participated in one of the most violent escape attempts ever made at Leavenworth, which resulted in the deaths of two officers. At Alcatraz, Berta held a reputation for violent outbursts toward correctional staff and fellow inmates, and in early 1938 he viciously attacked an officer. Following this incident, several officers carried Berta to the A Block basement entry for placement in isolation.

Officer Fish would later describe seeing Associate Warden Miller kick Berta down the cement stairs. When the prisoner reached the bottom, he was found to be almost completely unscathed, and he continued to resist forcefully by kicking and thrashing. Berta was handcuffed to the bars face forward in a standing position, and was left in the darkness of the dungeon for almost eight hours. The Associate Warden then came and personally removed the inmate to a standard isolation cell. Following this event, both Johnston and Miller ordered that the bars be removed from the dungeon cells, and the dungeons were banned from any future use. Officer Fish stated that he was one of the guards assigned to remove the bars using welding torches. After the cell bars were removed in 1938, the dungeons were never used again. Berta would become a model inmate, and following his direct release from Alcatraz in 1949, he owned and operated a bar on Mission Street in San Francisco.

Solitary Confinement (D Block)

In October of 1940, work began to completely refurbish the Treatment Unit, otherwise known as D Block. This area was comprised of forty-two cells which were used for varying degrees of punishment. For the most serious infractions of prison rules and regulations, inmates could be confined to the "*Strip Cell*". This cell was by all accounts the most severe punishment any human could endure. Among other discomforts, the total absence of light assured complete depravation of all peripheral senses.

(Above left) D Block as it looked in 1934, with flat soft iron bars. (Left) Inmate Earl Cox was the first prisoner to serve time in the strip cell, in 1941. (Below left) The new Treatment Unit under construction in 1941. (Below) D Block in April 1941, following a complete reconstruction. Note the closed-front solitary cells to the right. The remainder of the open-front cells were considerably larger than those in the main cellblock. The new unit, generally referred to as "Segregation," "Isolation," or the "Treatment Unit," consisted of forty-two cells.

June 1, 1941
ALCATRAZ
Cell Block "D" (completed)

The six solitary confinement cells in D Block.

Serious violators of the prison rules were locked in a pitch-black strip cell with no clothing or blankets during the day, where they could only sit or lie on cold steel flooring. There was a hole in the floor for the inmate to relieve himself, and the contents could only be flushed remotely by a guard. The maximum duration permitted for confinement in full darkness was nineteen days. At night, inmates were provided with a mattress and a set of blankets. These were removed immediately at daybreak.

The single Strip Cell, also known as the "*Oriental*," was a dark steel-encased cell with no toilet or sink. There was only a hole in the floor for the prisoner to relieve himself, and even the ability to flush the contents was controlled by a guard. Inmates were placed in the cell without clothing, and put on restricted diets. The cell had a standard set of bars with an expanded opening through which food was passed, and a solid steel outer door that remained closed, leaving the inmate in a pitch-black environment. Inmates were usually only subjected to this degree of punishment for one or two days. The cell was cold, and a sleeping mattress was only allowed after lights out at 9:30 P.M. It was considered the most invasive type of punishment for severe violations and misconduct, and was generally feared by the inmates.

The "*Hole*" was similar to the Strip Cell, and it included the five remaining dual-door cells on the bottom tier of D Block. The Hole cells contained a sink and a toilet, and were lit by a 25-watt light bulb. Inmates could spend up to nineteen days in this level of isolation, which was also considered to be a severe punishment by the general population of inmates. The mattresses were taken away during the day, and the inmate was left in a state of constant boredom and severe deprivation. Guards would sometimes open the small cover on the solid steel outer door, to admit light for inmates who were serving their time in solitary peacefully. The remaining thirty-six segregation cells were similar in design to the cells of the general population. One exception was that all of the cells in D Block had steel floors, ceilings and walls for greater security. The West Gun Gallery Officer operated the door mechanisms for the cells along the bottom tier, from a remote control panel located in the secure Gallery. The Bureau of Prisons described these facilities as follows:

> A special treatment unit called D Block, is walled off from the rest of the institution for the housing of those few prisoners who must be kept locked in their cells at all times except for certain periods of exercise in the yard. In this unit some of the cell doors are operated electronically

but are controlled by the cell house officer and the officer in the gun gallery working together. When a door is to be opened, the cell house officer pushes the appropriate button in his control box and then signals to the officer in the gallery. The latter then presses an electronic button in his control box, which opens the door.

Inmates held in segregation were allowed only one visit to the recreation yard and two showers per week, and they spent their remaining time in their cells. All meals were served in the cells, and the inmates' only means of psychological escape was through reading. Many inmates considered the city views from D Block to be an additional form of torment. Former inmate James Quillen later recounted that inmates could frequently hear sightseeing cruise boat narrators talking about the prison as they passed by. On New Year's Eve, the laughter from the shoreline Yacht Club could be heard sharply inside the inmate cells when the window vents were left open. Quillen would recall that a

(Top) An inmate's view of "The Hole."

(Above) The cold steel flooring inside the isolation and segregation cells.

(Right) Another view of D Block. Note the door access panel to the left. The cells to the immediate left are two shower stalls. Inmates held in segregation were allowed two showers and one visit to the recreation yard per week.

(Below left and right) Period diagrams showing the state-of-the-art remote-controlled door access features.

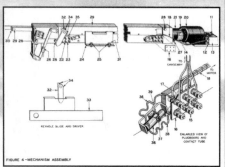

FIGURE 4 - MECHANISM ASSEMBLY

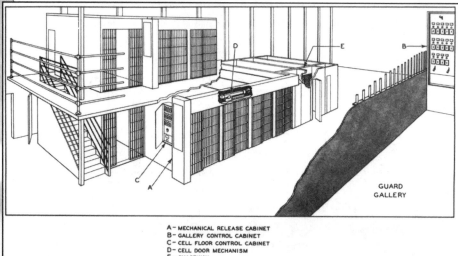

FIG. 1-CELL BLOCK LAYOUT

A – MECHANICAL RELEASE CABINET
B – GALLERY CONTROL CABINET
C – CELL FLOOR CONTROL CABINET
D – CELL DOOR MECHANISM
E – CHASEWAY

GUARD GALLERY

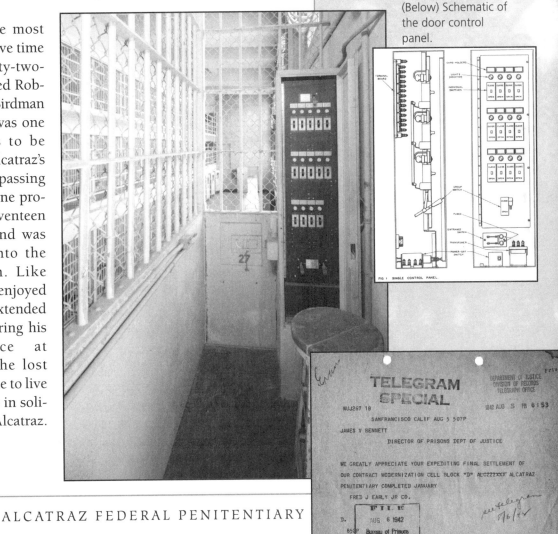

The wrap-around Gun Gallery located in D Block. Note the rounded gun ports on each tier. This photograph shows the Gun Gallery in its modern form, with the armored panels that were installed following the 1946 mass escape attempt.

(Below left) Another view from the inside the Gun Gallery shows the door control panel.

(Below) Schematic of the door control panel.

strange calm would blanket the cellblock as the inmates lay in their bunks listening to the sounds of voices. Pleasure boats would pass the island with loud peals of what sounded like feminine laughter. In many cases, the prisoners hadn't seen or heard a woman's voice during the entire period of their incarceration, except when watching movies in the prison theatre. The sounds and sights of freedom were so near, and yet so far . . .

Perhaps one of the most notable inmates to serve time in D Block was a fifty-two-year-old convict named Robert Stroud (a.k.a., the Birdman of Alcatraz). Stroud was one of the few inmates to be placed directly into Alcatraz's Segregation Unit, bypassing the standard quarantine process. Stroud spent seventeen years on Alcatraz, and was never introduced into the general population. Like Capone, Stroud had enjoyed many privileges not extended to fellow inmates during his previous residence at Leavenworth, and he lost them all when he came to live out the rest of his life in solitary confinement at Alcatraz.

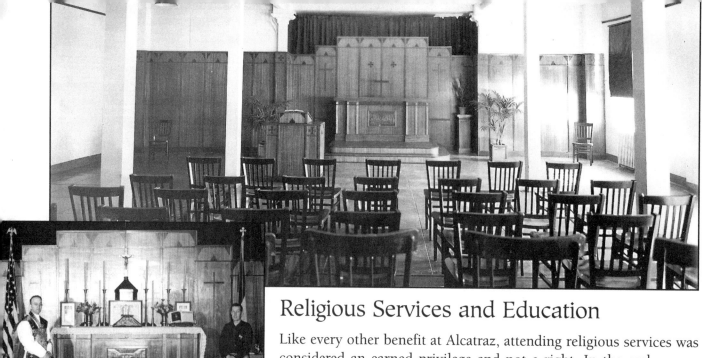

(Top right) The Alcatraz Prison Chapel, located in the upstairs auditorium. The Chapel was built almost entirely by the inmates themselves.

(Above) Father Clark (at left) standing at the altar inside the Prison Chapel.

A 1949 Easter Sunday service program from Alcatraz.

Religious Services and Education

Like every other benefit at Alcatraz, attending religious services was considered an earned privilege and not a right. In the early years, inmates who chose to attend religious services forfeited an equal amount of recreation time. The administration felt that the inmate population would attend services just to have time outside of their cell. Warden Johnston later relaxed this rule, and interestingly enough, this did not increase attendance at any of the services. The religious services were held in the upstairs auditorium, where inmates usually enjoyed watching motion pictures.

Separate services were provided for the prisoners of various denominations. The Pastor of the Calvary Presbyterian Church of San Francisco held Protestant services in the chapel on the first and third Sunday of the month. A priest from St. Anne's Church in San Francisco conducted Catholic services on the second and fourth Sunday of every month. And on some occasions, a visiting Rabbi and members of the Jewish Committee on Personal Service held Jewish services.

The chaplains, or "*Sky Pilots*" as inmates commonly referred to them, were permitted to make Saturday visits to the recreation yard with the prisoners. The Chaplain would spend his time offering personal counsel to those who sought assistance. The resident Chaplain (a position that was established in 1936) was also granted an active seat on the Classification Committee. This body was comprised of senior correctional officers, the chief medical officer, and the Warden. The committee reviewed the progress of each inmate and recommended programs to help in their rehabilitation. The most famous inmate to assume the role of altar boy was Machine Gun Kelly, and he held the position for several years. The Chaplain also assisted in facilitating and providing oversight of the educational programs for inmates. A Bureau of Prisons bulletin offered inmates various programs in which to enroll:

For those interested in really improving their time, extension courses are available through the courtesy and cooperation of The University of California, Pennsylvania State College, and the International Correspondence

A service program showing a reading led by Bonnie and Clyde's former chauffeur, Floyd Hamilton.

School. Because of space limitations and the essential restrictions of maximum custody, classroom activity is not possible. However, inmate students show keen interest in education and enroll in a variety of subjects ranging from differential calculus to foreign languages to English and engineering. Art, too, is a popular outlet; approximately twenty percent of the population do some painting in oils or in pastels. Exhibitions of their work have been displayed in the San Francisco area and in Washington, D.C.

A request to the chaplain by George "Machine Gun" Kelly to be allowed to take an elementary Spanish course.

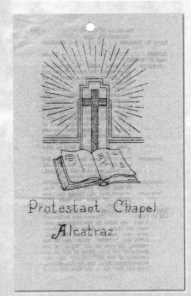

A contemporary photograph showing the entrance to the Chapel from the administration area.

The Prison Industries

Warden Johnston believed in managing Alcatraz as an institution for rehabilitation. When Johnston assumed his post as Warden in 1934, he brought with him the vision that Alcatraz would not be the final stop for any inmate. He wrote that after his tenure at Folsom and San Quentin, that if he had to manage any prison upon condition, that his choice would be only one thing, an agency for reform. Johnston wanted the inmates to develop work skills that they could carry with them to the outside. He felt the rigid structure would offer his men an advantage back in the outside world, as they would become accustomed to a hard day's work and a strong work ethic. Inmates earned their right to work by conforming to the rules and regulations of the prison. Phil Bergen later recalled:

> At Alcatraz, we always a felt a greater responsibility towards the inmates rather than simply confining them. Inmates learned skills that could be translated to meaningful employment upon their release. Many inmates took considerable pride in the quality of their work. Whether it was making furniture or cleaning an assigned area, the inmates usually did exceptional work.

In 1960 the Bureau of Prisons published an informational booklet that briefly described the operational features of Alcatraz. One of the items featured was the Prison Industries:

> Alcatraz, in common with other institutions throughout the Federal Prison System carries out a program of constructive work activity for all inmates who are physically qualified. All employment other than that needed for the maintenance of the prison is under the jurisdiction of Federal Prison Industries, Incorporated. Men assigned to the various shops receive modest wages, as well as certain reductions in sentence over and beyond that regularly awarded for proper conduct and good behavior in prison.
>
> Industrial units in operation on the island include a glove factory, rubber mat shop, clothing factory, a brush shop, and a furniture factory. The shops and factories perform contract services for the armed forces.
>
> The Alcatraz branch of Prison Industries has been awarded numerous commendations for its contribution to national defense during World War II and the fighting in Korea.

(Above) Inmates in the recreation yard lining up in single file, awaiting a count and escort to their work assignment.

(Below) Inmates lined up according to their work assignment.

A photograph series showing the Tailor and Glove Shops.

Prisoners are not forced to participate in the industrial program at Alcatraz. However, all prisoners in work status are required to work on assigned tasks. A large percentage prefer assignments in industries and usually volunteer immediately after arriving at the institution. Other than the therapeutic value offered by gainful employment in prison, the inmates are zealous to earn the wages paid and make regular contributions to their dependants or accumulate savings for use following release.

Inmates employed in the Prison Industries were also compensated by having time deducted from their sentences. The accrual rate was minimal. On average, each inmate would be awarded two days off his sentence per month. Johnston introduced a work-for-pay program that incorporated four grade levels of compensation based on trade skills. Monetary wages generally ranged from five to twelve cents per hour. By the time of the prison's closure in 1963, the top grade rate was over thirty cents per hour.

The prison at Alcatraz was kept spotlessly clean. Even the correctional staff maintained the areas that were not accessible to inmates, with exceptional pride. Cliff Fish remembers working a shift in the East Gun Gallery, and finding a small graffiti message written with a laundry marker on the second-tier wall. Correctional Officer Freeman Pepper wished to communicate his frustration with someone who had dropped a sticky substance on the gallery floor, and he wrote the following message:

> I've labored long, and labored hard, to make myself some riches. But I'll gladly pay good money, to the guy that will snitch on the son-of-a-bitch, who smeared my floor with honey.

(Below) Prisoners are seen here walking down through a metal detector on their way to their work assignment in the Industries. The small building in the foreground is the dry-cleaning plant.

The regulations at Alcatraz decreed: "*There is no commissary at Alcatraz . . . The institution supplies all your needs.*" From the beginning this rule created conflict between the administration and working inmates, especially for the prisoners serving long sentences, who had little interest in building savings accounts. Alcatraz was the only prison within the Federal system that did not allow the purchase of special toiletries, candy, or even filtered cigarettes. The administration controlled purchases by inmates, which were limited to authorized magazine subscriptions, musical instruments, and only a handful of other articles.

(Above and below) A photograph series showing the Tailor and Glove Shops.

(Right) A distant view of an inmate at work in the Cobbler Shop.

(Below) The Blacksmith Shop.

(Right) A correctional officer sitting next to office chairs built by Alcatraz inmates.

(Below) Office furniture built by prison labor at Alcatraz.

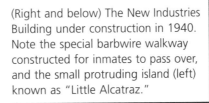

(Right and below) The New Industries Building under construction in 1940. Note the special barbwire walkway constructed for inmates to pass over, and the small protruding island (left) known as "Little Alcatraz."

(Above) A present-day view of the Prison Industries Building.

(Above) A present day view of the old Model Industries Building. Following the completion of the New Industries Building in 1941, this structure was abandoned and used only for storage.

(Left and above) Coast Guard survey photos showing the workshops following the prison's closure.

(Below left and right) The interior of the abandoned New Industries Building following the prison's closure. All that remains is the rusted equipment left from the prison.

The Prison Hospital

The hospital ward at Alcatraz was located at the west end of the prison on the second floor, directly above the Mess Hall. The Hospital was accessed via a stairwell leading to the Mess Hall entrance, and was completely isolated from the rest of the prison. A Bureau of Prisons bulletin described the medical facilities at Alcatraz in further detail:

> The U.S. Public Health Service provides medical faculties and staff for Alcatraz, as well as for other federal penitentiaries and correctional institutions. The Alcatraz Hospital, adjacent to the main cell house, is equipped with modern x-ray and physical therapy apparatus, operating theater, laboratories, and dental unit, and contains wards and individual rooms for the treatment and convalescence of inmate patients. It has been certified by the American College of Surgeons and compares favorably with the up-to-date hospitals and clinics in the free community.
>
> The medical staff includes a chief medical officer and highly trained technicians, all career personnel of the Public Health Service. Specialists from the Marine Hospital in San Francisco also are available for consultation and to augment the permanent local staff. Three San Francisco Psychiatrists are employed to counsel and treat Alcatraz inmates and they visit the island frequently in the performance of their duties. Inmates whose mental disorders indicate psychotic trends or continuing deterioration are transferred to the Medical Center at Springfield, Missouri.

There were also two designated isolation cells that were known by inmates as the "*Bug Rooms*." These small rooms for special confinement only measured approximately 8' x 8' x 10'. The interior surfaces were completely covered with ceramic tiles that were pinkish in color. The door was also covered with a matching tile surface, and light entered through fogged translucent glass tiles that were smoothly set into the walls. One of these rooms was equipped with only a hole in the floor for the patient to relieve himself. There was a small clear glass pane that would allow observation of the patient, and a small rectangle portal that was used to pass in food and medicine. The two cells were only used in the most of extreme cases of mental instability.

The Prison Hospital at Alcatraz.

(Below) A present-day view of the Operating Room.

(Below right) The X-Ray suite. Many inmates trained to become x-ray technicians, and found successful employment following their release.

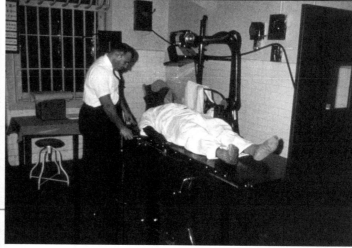

The "Bug Room." Note the ubiquitous tile surface, even on the door. The barred door resembling a cell is actually the entrance to the hospital shower.

Sick call took place after the noon meal each day. Former correctional officer Frank Heaney would indicate in his book *Inside the Walls of Alcatraz* that an estimated ten percent of the inmate population showed up every day in the sick line. Many exaggerated their illnesses in efforts to break the monotony, or asked for sleeping medications to help them deal with the stresses of confinement.

Alcatraz in War Time (1942–1945)

During World War II, Alcatraz became a prominent contributor to the war effort. This was the one period during which the inmates and administration stood together. Following the bombing of Pearl Harbor in December of 1941, the Mat Shop was quickly converted into a cargo net factory. The netting manufactured in the Industries would be used to protect the harbor from submarine attacks. The inmates would also be responsible for the maintaining the marine buoys that held the nets, and making field jackets for field soldiers. Former inmate Jim Quillen recalled when he first entered the recreation yard in 1942, the sight of inmates cheering from the bleachers as Naval ships passed the island with sailors lining the decks. The inmates' work was inspired, and they took great pride in their contribution.

As a result of the prison's contribution to the war industries, Alcatraz also became an enemy target. Fears of a Japanese attack became pronounced among the citizens of San Francisco, and Alcatraz would renew her role as a military fortress. Like their Civil War predecessors, the military strategists of the day recognized the strategic position of Alcatraz. The Military positioned three 40-mm anti-aircraft guns atop the main cellhouse and apartment building structures. Air-raid drills were performed for both inmates and island residents. Former Captain of the Guard Phil Bergen assumed the role of Air Raid Warden, in addition to his normal duties. During drills, a special siren would be sounded and Alcatraz would go into blackout mode. Every light was

World War II Soldiers from the 216th Coast Artillery Regiment manning a 40mm anti-aircraft gun positioned on top of the family apartments.

required to be doused in efforts to reduce the chances of being bombed by enemy aircraft, though the lighthouse shutdown would only be simulated. The inmates were trained to take cover beneath their cell bunks while under attack, but it became obvious that this would offer them only minimal protection. The island residents were required to retreat into shelters located in Building #64, and Phil Bergen would be tasked with inspecting the island dwellings to insure that everyone complied with the blackout regulations.

The stationing of a military unit at Alcatraz also created a unique challenge for prison officers and their families, as the young soldiers were integrated into the living arrangements of the island. They were provided access to the recreational facilities, and as a result, several romances blossomed. The young soldiers were often idolized by many of the teenage daughters of correctional officers. Bergen would later comment that several officers were not shy when it came to establishing the *"stone rules of dating their daughters."* It was an exciting period for the teenagers, as the bowling alley and dance hall became popular hangouts on weekends.

With time, it became evident that the fear of enemy attack which had inspired the establishment of a military base on Alcatraz was not entirely unfounded. After the war, it would be confirmed that Japanese submarines had patrolled the waters and plotted attacks just outside of the San Francisco harbor.

The Prison Library

The library at Alcatraz contained over 15,000 books of fiction and nonfiction. Reading was the primary pastime for all inmates, especially between the idle hours of 5:30 P.M. and 9:30 P.M. There were few activities available to the inmates while they were confined to their cells. They could write letters to family members, smoke, do artwork, play a musical instrument (if approved), work a crossword puzzle, or play a game of chess or checkers with a neighbor. In these games, each player maintained their own board and quietly called out each move to the player in the neighboring cell.

The Alcatraz Library contained over 15,000 volumes of fiction and non-fiction. Reading was the primary pastime for all inmates, especially between the idle hours of 5:30 P.M. and 9:30 P.M.

The inmates at Alcatraz were typically very well read. The average inmate in the general population would read seventy-five to a hundred books a year, not including periodicals and magazines. The reading materials at Alcatraz were heavily censored, and the subjects of sex, violence, and crime were strictly forbidden. Each inmate was provided with a full library catalog of available titles, and could submit a weekly request slip to check out books. The general population inmates were never allowed to visit the library and browse through the collection. The cellhouse orderly filled requests by manually delivering the books on a pull cart. Several notable inmates, including Al Capone and Bernard Paul Coy, held this job assignment for a brief tenure during their incarceration at Alcatraz.

The resident Chaplain, who was also responsible for the content of the reading materials, generally supervised the prison library. The prison featured its own bookbindery, and utilized a special catalog system. The library also included a music collection of nearly 1,000 records. A Federal Bureau of Prisons booklet published in 1960 described the reading habits of Alcatraz inmates:

> . . . these men read more serious literature than does the ordinary person in the community. Philosophers such as Kant, Schopenhauer, Hegel, etc., are especially popular and their books have a wide circulation. Advanced mathematics and physics texts, too, are in great demand, as are other types of literature having to do with more profound aspects of our culture. The latest magazines and periodicals are furnished and enable men to keep abreast of current events in the free community.

In his exceptional memoir *Alcatraz from the Inside*, former inmate Jim Quillen described the most popular reading materials from an inmate's perspective:

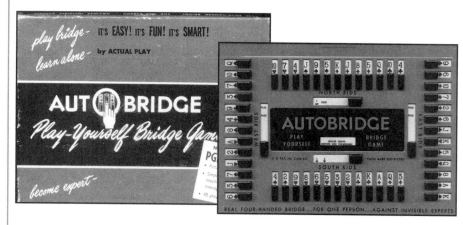

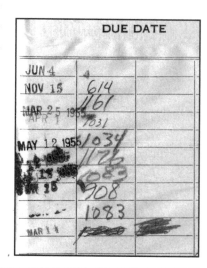

(Above right) Inmates were permitted to purchase an Autobridge gaming device, which allowed them to play the game by themselves.

(Above) The Culbertson's series on playing Bridge was in high demand among inmates, and these books were always the most requested for reading. The library stocked multiple copies of each volume.

Radio jacks were installed in the cellhouse in 1955, when for the first time inmates were allowed to choose between two radio programs, which included sports and talk shows.

Culbertson's Beginner's Book of Bridge was beyond doubt the most desired and read book in the prison's twenty-nine years of existence. When the Warden permitted "Auto Bridge" (a device where an inmate could play a game by himself) to be ordered, it was to some inmates like Christmas had happened twice in one year.

The most popular magazine subscriptions were to *Life*, *Time*, *Newsweek*, and technical publications such as *Popular Mechanics*, *Science Digest*, *Mechanics Illustrated*, and *Popular Science*. Inmates were allowed to keep three books in their cell at any one time, in addition to a Bible and a dictionary.

For twenty-one years after the opening of Alcatraz as a Federal penitentiary, reading was the primary means of passing the time until lights out at 9:30 P.M. Then on October 4, 1955, the 295 inmates at Alcatraz were given a special treat when radio jacks were installed in all of the general population cells. The cellhouse residents cheered, stomped and laughed as they listened to the Brooklyn Dodgers pull off their first and only World Series victory over their arch-nemesis, the New York Yankees. On this special occasion, the inmates were allowed a day off from work to listen to the World Series events. Two radio receivers and a reel-to-reel tape recorder were installed in the Control Center. The inmates could select a station by simply plugging their headset into the jack of their choice. The inmates were allowed to listen to radio programs from 5:30 P.M. until lights out at 9:30 P.M. every day. This proved to be the biggest morale booster ever afforded to the prisoners, though the radio jacks were not available in the hospital or in D Block. One inmate recalled:

I can remember lying on my bunk with my eyes closed, and dreaming that I was at this baseball game with my gal. I could imagine all of the sights and smells of the hotdogs and the summer breeze in the stadium. Those headphones were my escape to another world.

The Recreation Yard

The recreation yard at Alcatraz was considered a sacred place among the inmates. The yard was a cement-enclosed area with thick twenty-foot walls, and a perimeter catwalk for armed officers. The general population inmates were allowed recreation time in the yard on weekends, ordinarily a 2½-hour visit on Saturdays and Sundays. Inmates who were confined to the Treatment Unit were allowed one weekly visit, lasting only one hour. These inmates would sometimes be allowed to visit with one or two others who were also serving time in segregation.

Inmates lived for the yard. It was the only escape from the daily routine of reform. Morton Sobell, the famed co-defendant of Julius and Ethel Rosenberg, would later recount a vivid memory of country music being amplified through the recreation yard. He commented that his leisure time in the yard was almost sacred, and that he never missed a visit for the first three years of his imprisonment. He would also describe the unusual beauty of the prison's position in the San Francisco Bay in his personal memoir entitled *On Doing Time*:

> . . . standing on the top of the steps leading down to the prison yard I saw the Golden Gate in all its splendor. It was magnificent, as I absorbed the view I thought to myself, "I will never have such a magnificent view in any other prison." Prison notwithstanding, I enjoyed it until the day I left. The distant green hills, and the soaring towers of the bridge, with graceful catenary suspended between them, always lifted my spirits.

(Top right) Comparison photographs showing the recreation yard in August 1934 before the cement bleachers were constructed, and a present-day view with the bleachers. Numerous inmates enjoyed sitting high atop the cement bleachers to enjoy the beautiful panoramic scenery of the San Francisco Bay.

(Middle right) Inmates in the recreation yard playing the card game Bridge, which was the most popular pastime among the prison population. Specially marked wooden dominos were used to replace standard playing cards, since the cellulose coating was a flammable substance which could be used as an explosive. Dominos were also better suited to the prevalent wind conditions common in the San Francisco Bay.

(Below left and right) Inmates playing handball in December of 1954. Note the painted wall markings identifying the court boundaries.

(Above) The general population inmates were permitted two visits per week (on Saturday and Sunday) to the recreation yard, weather permitting. There were a variety of activities available to the inmates during their recreation period. They could play baseball, handball, or volleyball, or simply walk the yard for exercise.

(Above right) Armed officers supervised the inmates from perimeter catwalks during the weekend recreation periods.

The recreation period also offered participation in several sports, as well as card games that were played using Tonk brand Dominos in place of standard decks. Playing Bridge was the favorite pastime. Former inmate Jim Quillen stated:

> These guys were fanatical about bridge and they knew all of the conventions. The Alcatraz library stocked various Culbertson books, and they memorized them cover-to-cover. They dreamed about Bridge. It was all some of these men thought about. The expert Bridge players held a very special status amongst this circle of inmates. These men caused little trouble to the guards, and always followed the rules to the letter so they could compete.

Inmates could also play shuffleboard, handball, or softball. The prison rules differed slightly from the standard regulations, with shorter innings, and balls hit over the wall considered as an out. Fights were commonplace in the yard, whether they were initiated during line-up for the industry details or during recreation periods, the yard could be a violent place. Softball bats were favored weapons, and knives were frequently smuggled into the yard as well. With loaded machine guns and high-powered rifles, guards paced back and forth along the perimeter wall catwalks, watching over the inmates. This was a powerful reminder that stepping out of line could be fatal.

Some inmates simply took their time outdoors to connect with the outside world by walking around the yard with friends, and smelling the salt ocean air. They would occasionally watch the tour boats cruising the Bay from the yard bleachers, and sometimes they could even smell the aroma of the chocolate and coffee factories on the mainland.

(Left) A correctional officer is seen standing atop the bleachers, looking out over the recreation yard.

The Mess Hall

The dining area, or "*Gas Chamber*" as the inmate population referred to it, was considered the most dangerous section of the prison. Nearly the entire prison population (with the exception of D Block inmates) would assemble into one space, which could mean a congregation of more than 258 inmates at one time. For this reason, tableware was issued to inmates on a need only basis. This was a critical element in minimizing inmates' access to potential weapons, because sharp eating utensils and even food could be used in this way. Hot coffee could be used to incapacitate an opponent with burns, and the sharp bone from a T-bone steak could easily be used like a knife. All of the cooking and cutlery tools were kept in locked cabinets, and carefully guarded. Butcher knives were all stored in a wooden case with painted silhouettes behind the utensils, so that guards would quickly notice if anything was missing.

To maintain order, fourteen fixed teargas dispensers were permanently mounted on ceiling structure beams. The switches used to discharge the toxic gases could be remotely operated by a guard stationed on the exterior catwalk, who was able to observe all interior activities from a secure position. The Armory officer also had control of two of the dispensers in the entrance area. Former inmate Jim Quillen stated that the mere threat of "*being gassed by a screw*" seemed to have a quieting effect on most of the inmate population.

At mealtimes, inmates entered the Mess Hall and stood in a single serving line, and then seated themselves by order of their cell assignment. The men were seated side by side at bench tables, with five places set on each side. This system was replaced in 1961, and from then on small cafeteria-style tables allowed inmates to sit with whomever they

(Left) A photograph from 1950 showing inmates entering the Mess Hall, nicknamed by prisoners as the "*Gas Chamber*." Note the dual locking mechanisms on the open steel barred gate. The redundant lock system included both a remotely controlled electric mechanism and a manual key lock. It took two officers to control access in and out of the Mess Hall.

(Top) The floors at Alcatraz were always polished to a glowing shine.

(Below left) Inmates marched into the Mess Hall and lined up for their food in the order of their cell assignments.

(Below) Inmates filing past the steam tables. Prisoners were allowed to fill their trays with as much food as they wanted, but under strict orders that no waste would be permissible.

MARCH 13 1956
2 GRILLED FRANKFURTERS
1 HOT CHILI
PARSLEY POTATOES
POT FRIED SAUERKRAUT
BUTTERED CARROTS
1 MUSTARD
1 BANANA PUDDING
2 FRANKFURTER ROLLS

BREAD & TEA

(Above) The Mess Hall was considered the most dangerous section of the prison for correctional officers. The unarmed floor officers had to supervise almost the entire prison population within a single area. Eating utensils, steak bones, and steaming hot coffee were only a few of the items that could be used as makeshift weapons.

The interior of the kitchen in 1934.

(Below) An inmate working inside the bakery.

(Right top) One of the fourteen permanently fixed teargas dispensers in the Mess Hall.

(Right) A photograph of the caged exterior Gun Gallery and catwalk. The gas release panel was located inside this enclosure.

wanted, with only four places at a table. After Warden Johnston abolished the rule of silence in 1937, the inmates were allowed to talk quietly among themselves at their tables during meals. In the early years of the prison, inmates had been required to wear special pocket-less coveralls to minimize the concealment of contraband, but this rule also was later lifted. The officer positioned in the West Gun Gallery had a large rifle port that allowed him to supervise activities, and also to represent a show of force.

Quality food was considered an essential right, and the food at Alcatraz was considered the best in the entire prison system, with menus prepared under the supervision of civilian stewards. Inmates were allowed to fill their trays with as much food as they wanted, but under strict order that no waste would be permissible. They were not allowed to rise from their tables until all of the eating utensils were counted and reckoned. At the end of each meal, the utensils would be passed to the end of the table for counting by the officer on duty. Once the count was confirmed, the men would rise in unison and then walk in military formation back to their cells.

During the Christmas season, inmate Morton Sobell recalled that Bing Crosby's White Christmas was amplified throughout the cellhouse, and the Dining Hall would be decorated. After the breakfast meal on Christmas Day, the inmates would each receive a care package from the

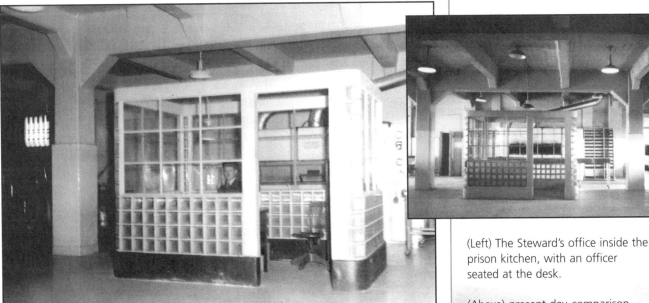

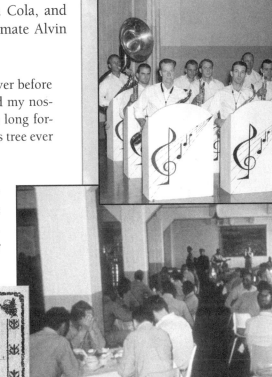

(Left) The Steward's office inside the prison kitchen, with an officer seated at the desk.

(Above) present-day comparison photograph, showing one of the ovens visible in the background.

(Below) On holidays, inmates enjoyed special menus and live music played by the prison ensemble. The inmate orchestra, known as the "Rock Islanders." This 1949 photograph shows orchestra leader Lloyd Barkdoll (front left) and John Bayless (back right), two of the many men who attempted to escape from Alcatraz.

Bureau of Prisons. In a report to the Bureau Director on December 25, 1942 it was stated that every inmate had received the following package, at a total cost of only .621 cents per inmate:

2 packages of filtered cigarettes
1 Uno Chocolate Bar and 1 Baffle Bar
3 Cellophane bags of salted peanuts
½ Lb. bag of hard candy
1 Package of Fig Newton's, 17 cookies to a package

On select holidays, the prison band would entertain the inmates. Quillen remembered that on every Fourth of July, T-bone steaks would be served along with a carbonated beverage such as Coca Cola, and apple pie for desert. In his memoir *On the Rock*, former inmate Alvin Karpis recalled the first Christmas tree at Alcatraz in 1948:

As I file into the dining hall this morning, I witness a sight never before seen inside these walls. Her soft scent, which has not aroused my nostrils for more than twelve years, reawakens strange emotions long forgotten. In the middle of the mess hall stands the first Christmas tree ever to be erected at Alcatraz.

The culinary detail was a prime work assignment for inmates. The men on this detail were allowed daily visits to the recreation yard, and were allotted daily showers if requested. It was a non-paying assignment, but inmates serving life or

(Above) The Officers' Dining Room, located upstairs and across from the prison Chapel and Auditorium.

(Below) Inmates (seen here in uniform) worked as stewards in the Officers' Dining Room.

Inmate Theodore "Blackie" Audett serving "Jailhouse Chili" in the officers' kitchen.

Warden Madigan is seen greeting an officer's family member inside the Officers' Dining Room. Inmate Theodore Audett (one of the stewards) is seen here assisting Madigan.

unusually lengthy sentences didn't seem to mind. At Alcatraz, "*lifers*" had no use for money. Inmates assigned to the culinary detail were also granted benefits that were not always available even to the correctional staff. Alvin Karpis described the access to "*unlimited food,*" commenting: "*we have our choice of the food supplies and can prepare appetizers whenever we crave them rather than being regimented to strict meal hours like the general population or the guards.*" Karpis would also claim that the kitchen detail was a haven for sexual encounters among the inmates. He indicated that the basement was a "*labyrinth of vegetable rooms, showers, freezers, and storerooms, where . . . delights are exchanged frequently and freely.*" In the best-selling classic *Escape from Alcatraz*, J. Campbell Bruce describes the acquisition of alcoholic beverages at Alcatraz:

> . . . generally the inmates had to make their own booze and the best place for such an illicit operation was the bakery in the basement beneath the kitchen. Here the yeasty aroma of a fermenting brew was so akin to that of rising dough that the making of pruno [an exotic prison homemade cocktail] went undetected for a long time . . . The recipe was simple: put raisins and other dried fruit to soak in a crock, add yeast to speed up the fermentation, and cover the crock with flour sacks. The bakers realizing they had a good thing going, drank in moderation, an aperitif before meals.

Paul Ritter was known by fellow inmates as the "Brew Master." He was said to be an expert at making alcoholic beverages.

Former inmate Darwin E. Coon was also assigned to the kitchen during his incarceration on The Rock, and he recalled some of the special meals inmates were served at Alcatraz in his memoir *Alcatraz—The True End of the Line*:

> Whenever the inmates saw the chef's meal on the menu board, they knew that they were in for a special dinner. We usually had a chef's meal about once every three months . . . Some of the really special meals that I remember were when the striped bass were running in the Bay. The officers caught them by the wheelbarrow load and wheeled them into the kitchen. The cooks cleaned and cooked them and the inmates got all the fish he could eat. We would stuff the small ones, one to two pounders, with a nice gumbo and bake them. The bigger ones were cut into steaks and fried. The bass run would last about a month and since Friday was traditionally fish day, we could have four or five of these fish meals.

Coon would also remember a group of inmates that were nicknamed the "*animals.*" These men had appalling eating habits, and would always sit at the same table in the Mess Hall. Coon recalled that when these men entered the hall, they would be booed by all of the other inmates.

Warden Edwin Burnham Swope: 1948–1955

E. B. Swope,
WARDEN.

Edwin B. Swope was appointed as the second Warden of Alcatraz in April of 1948.

On April 30, 1948, Edwin B. Swope was appointed as the new Warden of Alcatraz at fifty-nine years of age. He would replace Warden Johnston, who had reached the mandatory retirement age of seventy-four. Swope carried a tough reputation as a strict disciplinarian. When the newspapers discussed how he would approach his new position, he would comment: *"It will be different alright."* Swope was a believer in reform, and he held to the concept of creating a structured plan for inmates to follow. He was firm; he was strict; and he had his own vision of how to deal with incorrigible inmates.

Swope was born in Santa Fe, New Mexico on May 6, 1888, and he left a political career to enter the prison service. He had served as the New Mexico State Democratic Chairman, the State Land Commissioner, and later as a County Treasurer. While working as the Albuquerque City Commissioner in the 1920's, Swope became appalled at the horrific conditions in the city jail. He made the decision to take up prison work, and to help develop strict programs that would successfully reform inmates in a humane environment. During one interview with the press in April of 1948, just before taking his new assignment, Swope would be quoted as saying:

> Alcatraz is the supreme end of a criminal career. Alcatraz gets all of the rotten apples out of the barrel. If one can get a new seed to grow from those rotten apples, they're on the right track.

(Above) Swope seen here in a meeting with the Classification Committee.

(Below) Warden Swope was known as a tough taskmaster and strict disciplinarian. But despite his authoritarian reputation, he also initiated a variety of inmate reform programs. He is seen here in a meeting with staff members.

By the time Swope stepped off the prison launch onto Alcatraz, he had already served in various Warden appointments in a prison service career that spanned more than eighteen years. Swope had worked at the State Penitentiary in New Mexico, and at the Federal Penitentiaries at McNeil Island, Terre Haute, Indiana, and Englewood, Colorado. He had been credited with turning around McNeil, and he was the first choice of Bureau Director James Bennett when making his selection for Johnston's replacement.

Swope served as Warden from 1948 until 1955.

Warden Johnston proved to be a tough act to follow, and Swope made many decisions that were unpopular with the correctional officers. In one instance he removed the stools from the tower posts, and in another, he forced the officers to serve meals to inmates during a strike. A fair number of officers ultimately became resentful of Swope's leadership style. The guards usually contested his decisions and won, but Swope maintained his firm headship. Former Officer and Captain of the Guard Phil Bergen recalled:

> Swope was a tough act. I can't say that I ever liked him. He lived and died by the rules, and he didn't let the inmates get away with killing a fly, or even the officers for that matter. I can remember working in D-Block and Swope would check the "Hole" cells and make sure that the lights were left off by the officers, and the fronts closed. He wanted to make sure those men did hard time.

Warden Swope and his wife sitting in the rounded parlor of the Warden's mansion at Christmas in 1954.

Although many of his decisions were not well received, Swope also instituted several inmate programs that proved popular with the inmate population. In his first year he arranged for the inmates to see two movies per month, and loosened censorship to allow westerns and an occasional wartime film. Comedies featuring actors such as Shirley Temple and Laurel and Hardy had been the most common style of films selected by Johnston and the Chaplain. Swope also increased recreation time on weekends, and extended visitation privileges.

Released by Warner Brothers in 1937, *Alcatraz Island* was one of the first motion pictures filmed against the backdrop of the notorious prison.

Inside "The Rock"! WHERE THE MOB-MASTERS WALK THE LAST MILE!

"ALCATRAZ ISLAND"

They'd even bust out of ALCATRAZ to get to a dame like her!

ANN SHERIDAN and hundreds of others

WARNER BROS. RE-RELEASE

Warden Paul Joseph Madigan: 1955–1961

[signature] Madigan

P. J. Madigan,
Acting Warden.

Prior to his appointment as Warden, Paul Madigan had navigated his way through a variety of positions at Alcatraz. Therefore his perspective was unlike that of any of his predecessors. Madigan had originally transferred to Alcatraz from Leavenworth as a correctional officer. He was well liked by most of the correctional staff at Alcatraz, having been promoted through the ranks, and having served in various appointments including Lieutenant, Captain, and later Associate Warden. Madigan had a unique and diplomatic approach in his directorship. He possessed the skills of a soft-spoken mediator, and when necessary, he was not afraid to issue unpopular directives to both the staff and the inmate population. Madigan challenged the old regime of Alcatraz. He abolished the solitary confinement bread and water diet, and on one occasion, encouraged inmates in good standing to donate blood to the Irwin Memorial Blood Bank in San Francisco.

Paul Madigan, pictured here with his wife, advanced through the ranks at Alcatraz. He had previously held a variety of positions including Captain, Lieutenant, and Associate Warden. Madigan had a very diplomatic style of leadership with staff and inmates alike.

Madigan was also credited with preventing the 1941 escape of Joe Cretzer, Sam Shockley, Arnold Kyle, and Lloyd Barkdoll. He skillfully talked the inmates into surrendering, after he had been tied up and threatened. By the time the other officers were alerted to the escape attempt and had arrived to assist him, Madigan had already convinced the desperate inmates to give themselves up, and was escorting them up to the Treatment Unit.

Madigan carried the affectionate nickname of "*Promising Paul*," which was given to him by other officers, since he frequently made promises that would never be fulfilled. Nevertheless, Madigan was considered a great Warden by most of those who worked with him. He was a devout Catholic, and attended mass with the inmates in the prison chapel. He was also credited with adding cigars to the inmates' Christmas gift packages, and creating special holiday meals for the general population. In late 1941, following the escape attempt of Cretzer, Barkdoll, Kyle and Shockley, Madigan was promoted to the post of Associate Warden at the Terminal Island Federal Correctional Facility in Southern California. He later received another promotion, and transferred to Minnesota. He returned to serve at Alcatraz from 1955 until 1961, and then he accepted a transfer to McNeil Island. Prior to his departure, he would appoint Associate Warden Blackwell to be his successor.

(Right) A candid photo of Warden Madigan and his wife inside their home, taken by childhood resident Chuck Stucker.

Warden Olin Guy Blackwell: 1961–1963

O. G. BLACKWELL
Warden

The last Warden of Alcatraz, Olin Blackwell. Over his brief term as Warden, he relaxed numerous longstanding strict regulations, including those regarding censorship and visitation limits.

(Below left) Deputy Director of the Bureau of Prisons Fred T. Wilkinson and Alcatraz Warden Olin Blackwell on March 23, 1963, the day Alcatraz closed.

(Below right) The Warden's office, located inside the prison administration area.

Olin Blackwell would become the last Warden of Alcatraz on November 26, 1961. A former rancher from Texas, Blackwell had come to Alcatraz from Lewisburg Federal Penitentiary in Pennsylvania, where he had served as a Captain and Associate Warden. Blackwell was nicknamed "*Blackie*" and often signed his name as such, and he was only forty-six years old when he accepted the position of Warden at Alcatraz. He possessed a softer style than his predecessors in his approach, and was said to have been "*very warm, with a coy sense of humor.*" He relaxed many of the strict rules that weighed heavily on the inmates, also allowing a greater variety of radio programs, and relaxing regulations on reading and mail censorship.

During his brief appointment at Alcatraz, Blackwell was faced with a myriad of challenges. The prison was old, and was starting to show visible signs of structural problems, as well as deterioration of the primary utility systems. The lack of funding led to a reduction of staff, which left critical observation posts unmanned. Some criticized Blackwell for allowing such reductions to occur, and many believed that without them, the final two escapes at Alcatraz could have been prevented. Blackwell was generally evasive when responding to these allegations, implying that the escapes had resulted from simple human failures.

Blackwell would prepare Alcatraz for its ultimate destiny in 1963.

Family Life

Perhaps even more interesting than the prison itself were the families of the officers who resided on Alcatraz. During any given period the island was home to over fifty such families, with nearly one hundred children. The daily life of families on Alcatraz was unique, and they were not unaffected by the strict rules that governed island operations. But on reflection, those who lived and grew up on the island have mostly considered it a rare and privileged lifestyle. Despite their own isolation from society and the inherit tensions of crowded living, they found that life on Alcatraz was like residing in a small and very close-knit community. Even more interesting was the fact that there was no crime on the island, no one locked their doors, and the residents never carried their house keys. The families were kept fully isolated and fenced off from the prison, though its presence was continually evident.

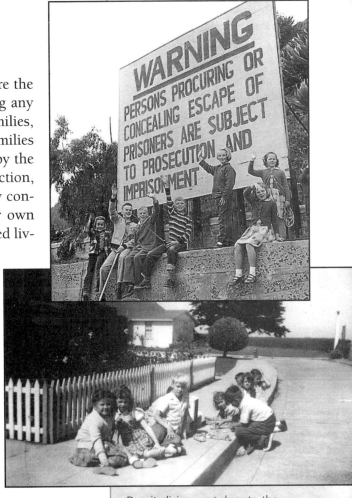

One of the most popular games for youngsters was "*guards and cons*," though toy guns and knives were strictly prohibited in any form, and the children would substitute with a banana or a stick. Wind sports were also popular. Using a jacket or sheet as a sail and wearing roller-skates, the children could sail across the parade ground when the sometimes-forceful Bay winds blew across the island. There was also a baseball diamond on the cement parade ground, as well as a standard playground area and a tennis court. Although at least one kindergarten class was held on the island, there were no schools on Alcatraz, and the children would attend classes on the mainland, traveling back and forth via the prison launch. The Alcatraz children were very popular among their teachers and classmates. Everyone was interested to hear about what life was like at Alcatraz, and teachers were always encouraging the children to give class presentations. Kathryn O'Brien lived at Alcatraz for approximately two years, and she recalled:

> I used to tease my friends and make up stories that worked to my advantage. I would tell them that Machine Gun Kelly waved good-bye to me through the bars that morning, or if one of my friends was getting picked on by a school bully, I'd warn them that I knew a lot of convicts and that they'd better watch it! Of course I didn't really ever come close to the inmates, but it really worked. My friends rarely got picked on.

Despite living next door to the nation's most notorious criminals, children found that growing up on Alcatraz was similar to being raised in any small town, with only a few exceptions. For example, the children were never allowed to play with toy guns or knives.

(Below) Officers who resided on the island considered Alcatraz the safest place to raise a family in San Francisco. One former resident commented, "*there was no crime in our neighborhood, we knew where all of the criminals were.*" Pictured here are four children posing atop one of the fortress era Rodman Cannons left on the island.

(Above and below) Family life on Alcatraz was hidden from the public until 1954, when Colliers Magazine published a series of photographs by William Woodfield depicting life behind the curtain.

Alcatraz sponsored several social clubs, including an all-girls club for teenagers called "Just Us Girls," and kids' clubs for the younger residents.

The fact that the only access to Alcatraz was by boat created special challenges for the residents. Few of the families owned automobiles, since most shopping was within walking distance of the Van Ness Pier. Fisherman's Wharf was just a short walk from the pier, which also boasted a special waiting room for residents and officers. Since navigation techniques of the era were relatively primitive, heavy fog would suspend or delay launch operations, and occasionally a family would get stranded on the mainland. In August of 1954, *Collier's Magazine* ran a feature story by Gitta Parker entitled "Children on Alcatraz," describing their unique lifestyle:

> The children and their parents occupy apartments and cottages dotting a four-acre section on the south tip of Alcatraz. Three hundred feet of distance and a barrier of steel towers, concrete walls, and armed men separate the circle of homes from the prison heights. From their windows, the happy boys and girls of Alcatraz have an unequaled view of one of the world's great panoramas: the breathtaking Golden Gate and the cities perched around the Bay. Much closer at hand, they look down to the bottom of the island and glimpse convicts loading wash from the prison laundry onto barges for delivery to nearby government installations. Otherwise, the only prisoners the children see are the three or four trustees assigned to collect garbage and tend gardens in the residential area.

Although it was uncommon, there were some unavoidable instances when a resident would come in contact with an inmate. One former resident recalled an occasion when he had thrown a ball over a link fence, and an inmate passed it back a few days later. Another remembered an incident when an inmate was tending a garden, and left a small flower bouquet with a perfectly tied ribbon made from a vine on a cement step. The families were instructed that if they should come in contact with an inmate, they were to treat him respectfully, and not engage in conversation. Kathryn O'Brien related one interesting story:

"I have a vivid memory inside our apartment located in Building #64. I can remember seeing a small group of inmates chained in handcuffs and leg irons, and were being led from the prison boat to a small bus. My brother and me watched from a window as the inmates took small steps with the chains hampering their movement, and we could hear the guards talking to them. Thinking back, I guess it was kind of scary... I had made one of those colored paper link chain ornaments that I made in crafts for our little Christmas tree. I took it off the tree and had my brother place his hands and feet through the links and marched him around the apartment like he was a convict. I can remember my dad didn't think it was too funny... You couldn't help be influenced by the prison to at least some degree. It was a constant presence. Strangely enough though, my dad never talked about it. Even after he left the job,

(Top left) A children's Sunday School class.

(Top middle) The small convenience store run by residents inside Building #64.

(Top right) Two young girls playing with their pet parakeet inside their apartment, located in Building #64. No dogs or cats were allowed as pets. The cellblock is clearly visible through the apartment window. The prison was a constant presence in the lives of both the officers and their families.

(Right) Playground equipment built for the officers' children by prison labor at Alcatraz. The cement slide was a favorite among the children, but was finally scrapped after the exposed steel at the slide's edge tore a fair share of children's clothing.

(Above) Alcatraz featured several recreational facilities for residents, including an indoor handball court, a pool hall, a two-lane bowling alley in the Officers' Club, a soda fountain often manned by off-duty guards, a gymnasium, and a dance hall for island parties.

(Right) A teenage Christmas dance held inside the Officers' Club.

he always changed the subject when people would ask him questions about Alcatraz."

Like their neighbors living "*up top*" in the cellhouse, the families were also subject to firm rules. The residents were not allowed to explore the island, and could only venture into approved non-restricted areas. No dogs or cats were allowed, and there were strict curfews. Family members were required to stay at home after 9:00 P.M. on weekdays, and after 11:00 P.M. on weekends. If anyone missed the last boat from the mainland, they would be stranded in San Francisco until morning. The families' lives were governed by the boat schedule. There was only one telephone available for island residents to use, though another was added later. There was a post office, and also a small convenience store that carried a very basic variety of household foods and supplies. Phil Bergen would comment about life at Alcatraz:

"You never had to worry about someone knocking on your door and trying to sell you a vacuum cleaner, and the parents never worried about their children when they were outside playing. We knew exactly where all of the criminals were. It was a special place to raise a family. I consider my sixteen years at Alcatraz the best years of my life."

The recreational activities available at Alcatraz were plentiful. There were ballet classes for the officers' daughters, an indoor handball court, a two-lane bowling alley in the Officers' Club, a soda fountain often manned by off-duty guards, a pool hall, a gymnasium, and a dance hall for island parties. There was a women's club, a club for the young adult girls called *Just Us Girls* (J.U.G.s), and a kids' club for the youngest residents. The most popular activities for the island families were the holiday events. There were Christmas musicals, a special Santa Claus visit, and even shows for Halloween. Special dances were held frequently for both the officers and the teenagers, and talent shows were always a town favorite. During the 1950's the Women's Club printed cookbooks that were advertised in *Sunset Magazine*. Profits from the book sales helped fund the special events. As one resident would remember: "*People would buy the cookbooks as gifts just so they could collect the Alcatraz Postmark.*"

Former resident Chuck Stucker (above left) recalled that some of his fondest memories were of fishing off Alcatraz as a child.

The unique location of Alcatraz also provided residents with a special perk that most men would envy. As former resident Chuck Stucker would recall: "*Alcatraz was the best fishing site in San Francisco.*" Stucker had many fond childhood memories of fishing with his father, who retired as a Lieutenant, and with an uncle who served as both a Captain and Associate Warden, as well as with a cousin who worked as an officer. But most unique were his memories of fishing with the Warden's wife, who also enjoyed the sport.

Several family members would also have a very rare opportunity to see behind the secret curtain that veiled the workings of the prison. Before the prison staff returned the motion pictures that were shown to the inmates every two weeks, the families would be taken in a large group into the upstairs theatre to have their turn to watch the films. While waiting in the visiting area before being led upstairs, the residents could peek through the thick bulletproof glass and get a rare glimpse into the cellhouse.

The Warden also lived on the island with his family, occupying a majestic fourteen-room Spanish-Mission style mansion that was located only a few steps from the prison entrance. The mansion had been constructed by military prisoners in 1922, and it featured a spectacular panoramic view of San Francisco, as well as its own lush garden. The furnishings were made from beautiful black walnut, which had been constructed by inmates at Leavenworth. The wardens all employed exemplary prisoners known as "*passmen*" to cook and clean at the residence, and every thirty minutes these inmates would emerge onto the front porch, where they would stand until they had been counted by an officer who could see them through a prison administration window. James V. Bennett, the Director of the Bureau of Prisons, would later write in his 1970 memoir:

Warden Johnston's home on the peak of the rock was like the pilothouse of a ship at anchor in the bay, beneath the cottony clouds. At night I would stand at the guest-room window and listen to the steel doors of the cellblocks clanging open and shut while the guards said to one another, as if they were at sea, "All's well." I spent the evening in Warden Johnston's living room before a cheerful fire in the grate. Whenever a

The Warden's fourteen-room mansion, built during the military period in 1922. It was decorated with beautiful wooden furniture made from black walnut by inmates at Fort Leavenworth.

An aerial photograph with the residential living quarters in prominent view. Note the lawn and garden perimeter of the Associate Warden and Captain of the Guard duplex (bottom center of the parade ground), and the four officers' cottages (right).

(Right) The Chief Medical Officer's residence, located next door to the Warden's mansion.

Island electrician Frank Brunner is pictured here walking from the Warden's residence in an extremely rare San Francisco snowfall.

(Below) The new apartment buildings under construction in 1941, with San Francisco and the Bay Bridge notably visible in the background.

gust of wind blew down the chimney, scattering ashes in the hearth, a white-jacketed houseman entered the room noiselessly, swept the ashes back into the fireplace, and withdrew. He must have been watching all the time.

But there were a few occasions when the cracking sound of gunfire broke the calming rustle of the ocean waves—a stark reminder that the surrounding barbwire and chain-linked fencing could not fully isolate residents from the dangers of living at the nation's most notorious prison. The sound of the wailing escape siren was a signal much feared by residents, because it could indicate that a loved one was in harm's way. At these times, families were instructed to remain inside their homes until they were notified that the island was secured and safe.

(Below) The new apartment buildings as they appeared in the 1950's

Another favored pastime at Alcatraz was gardening. When the families of the first military inhabitants of Alcatraz put down roots, they planted Victorian-style gardens that would flourish in the seaside climate. Gardening became a popular activity for many of the residents, and some of the plant life introduced by the military families in the 1800's still thrives even today. During the military years, the families held small parties in their lush, Victorian-style gardens. Gardening continued to be a popular pastime through the successive generations of Alcatraz residents. These ranged from Civil War soldier families to gangster era criminals assigned to the various work details, such as inmate Elliott Michener, who reportedly introduced many rare and unique botanical varieties to the Alcatraz landscape. Ultimately, Alcatraz would be home to nearly 145 non-native garden species, and flowers such as red-hot pokers and snapdragons carpeted the once barren rock with splendid colors. There were also beautiful rose varieties, as well as poppies and blackberries. There was even a children's garden, which Phil Bergen established adjacent to the parade ground. Many of the trees planted during the military period still prosper today in the salt-misted air.

(Top right) Gardens flourished on Alcatraz in the moist and rich ocean breeze. Gardening was one of the preferred pastimes among the island residents.

(Middle right) A childhood resident is seen here posing next to one of the neighborhood flower gardens in 1938.

(Right) The garden located in the Warden's side yard.

(Below left and right) Mug shots of inmate and prison gardener Elliott Michener. It is believed that Michener was responsible for introducing many rare and unique botanical varieties to the Alcatraz landscape.

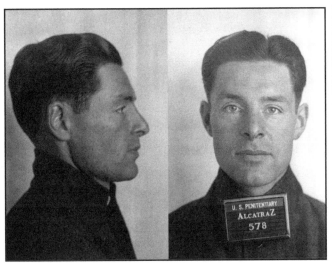

A photograph showing the prison bus and jeep bearing the Department of Justice seals. The bus was the primary mode of transportation between the cellhouse and the dock for staff and inmates.

(Below top) The *Warden Johnston* served as the island's passenger launch from 1945 to 1961.

(Below bottom) Transit by boat was the only means of access to Alcatraz.

Island Transit

For the correctional officers and their families, the only link to mainland society was by boat. Traveling to and from the island proved challenging, and during periods of inclement weather, it was frightening to hear the foghorns of larger vessels closing in, and be unable to see them. Each day the families were ferried back and forth, and this routine became an integral part of their daily lives. The residents were at the mercy of the daily boat schedule, which could be problematic at times. If they missed the boat, they would have to wait another hour for the next scheduled run. In stormy weather it could also be challenging to navigate the gangplank onto a rocking deck. Kathryn O'Brien remembers:

> I was afraid of falling into the water when the weather was stormy, and I can remember the boat officer grabbing me by the arm and helping me into the boat. The guards always made us feel safe.

In a poetic reminiscence of his travels aboard the *Warden Johnston*, former resident Robert Burrill wrote in a letter:

> The countless adventures going to and from the island are what I remember the best. Waiting in the protective staging area near the water's turbulent edge, we would first hear the bright sound of the *Warden's* horn announcing the boat's arrival. Excited, we would rise from our benches, gather up our travel bags, and button up our coats to begin the short walk to the loading dock. There ahead of us, in the choppy waters that lined the adjacent pier, we would first see the *Warden Johnston*, turning as she approached the dock. With the red and green running lights turned on, the *Warden* would slow its speed, which caused it to begin a rocking motion up and down, and then it would carefully choose its approach through tidal conditions that were challenging, and always changing.
>
> My eyes would go toward the pilot house, adorned with five wood-framed windows that looked like attentive eyes, wide open and focused on the dangerous task at hand. For an instant, the *Warden's* character would be revealed as the boat came to life. It was a bright, handsome, white-faced, wooden boat; a spirit—proud and courageous for all to witness; a bounty, a soul. Then the guard standing above the bow bridges the notion, anticipating and holding the gaffing hook on a pole with which he slowly reaches for, then skillfully mates with the hanging docking line; the second guard at the controls spins the pilot wheel and reverses the throttle, kicking up white water and a stream of smoke from the stack while easing the port side slowly, carefully into contact with the rubber tire bumper, while the first guard walks back to tie off the stern. Then the railing hinge would be swung open, signaling the passengers on board to debark. The conversations were always friendly, because everybody knew each other.

Finally it would be our turn to go down the swaying gangplank amid the cold air blowing up from the water's surface, and the odors of the sea splashing up and under the dock pilings that were textured with barnacles, black tar and the occasional starfish. Being helped on board by the strong, warm hands of a guard, following the passengers to the back of the boat, climbing down into the warm main cabin, and sitting on the beautiful wooden benches as the salt water splashed on the windows—these are the memories that stay in my mind.

The children of Alcatraz traveled to and from school everyday via the island launch.

Traveling on board the *Warden Johnston* was like a trip to Disneyland. The moans and vibrations of the engine below our feet, the rocking motion of the boat as he—or "she"—is put into gear. First she floats away from the pier, often aided by the push of a guard's foot as he hops on board. Then backward away from the dock, a change in direction, and the visual difference of a changing horizon. First away from the adjacent pier, and then the flow of the water, the wake, and a quick view of Alcatraz in the distance, as the *Johnston* completes its turning maneuvers and departs into the San Francisco Bay. Here the wind picks up, and the *Johnston* begins to pitch in a swell. Salt water sprays the windows, periodically causing the windowpane to wash out of focus. Here the trip would feel like we were running in place, not really moving—and then suddenly the island, The Rock would slide into view, and the sensation of motion would return, gliding past the large, majestic green and black rocks, the eucalyptus and bay-leafed trees, and the large black and white warning sign: "Cable Crossing Do Not Moor." Then the stockade buildings would appear, large and strong with a wide staircase leading up diagonally, and then the main guard tower. A gentle reminder that Alcatraz was indeed a prison.

During the island's initial years as a Federal penitentiary, the primary vessel for mainland access was a boat named the *McDowell*, which was approximately fifty feet in length and had a seating capacity of thirty-eight. In May of 1941, planning was commenced to build a boat specifically for Alcatraz. The new vessel was constructed by prisoners at McNeil Island Penitentiary, overseen by professional boat builders Everet Soldin and Woody Woodruff. The boat was completed and launched into service in June of 1945. The *Warden Johnston* was a sixty-five-foot wooden-framed vessel with a seventeen-foot beam, and it weighed sixty tons. This boat served as the island's passenger launch from 1945 to 1961. The *Warden Johnston* made approximately 140,000 trips during its service life. In March of 1961 the island newsletter, the "*Foghorn*," featured a heartfelt parting letter written when the *Warden Johnston* was retired from service:

(Above and below) A series of photographs showing island residents disembarking at the Van Ness Street Pier.

BOAT SCHEDULE

EFFECTIVE   OCTOBER 11,

Leaving Alcatraz

Weekly	Saturday	Sunday	Holiday
A.M.	A.M.	A.M.	A.M.
12:10	12:10	12:10	12:10
6:40	7:05	7:05	7:05
7:20	8:10	8:10	8:10
8:10	9:00	9:00	9:00
10:00	10:00	10:00	10:00
	11:00	11:00	11:00
P.M.	P.M.	P.M.	P.M.
12:45	12:45	12:45	12:45
3:20	3:20	3:20	3:20
3:55	4:55	4:55	4:55
4:40	5:40	5:40	5:40
5:10	7:00	7:00	7:00
5:40	8:45	8:45	8:45
7:00	10:00	10:00	10:00
8:45	11:15	11:15	11:15
10:00			
11:15			

(Reverse Side Leaving Ft. Mason)
USP-AZ—10-8-59—5C—P

TENTATIVE

FAREWELL TO AN OLD FRIEND

Early in the morning one summer's day in 1945, its sturdy and graceful lines glistening under its recent coating of paint, a newly commissioned launch floated from out the McNeil Island shipyards headed for Alcatraz where it was destined to spend most of its entire nautical career as a passenger boat between the Island and San Francisco. For 16 years it plied the waters of the Bay, as much a representative of the area as Coit Tower or the Ferry Building or Alcatraz, itself.

Constructed by prison inmate labor following plans drawn by Bureau draftsmen, the launch was named in honor of the late Warden James A. Johnston, the then beloved Chief Magistrate of Alcatraz.

The "Warden Johnston" was more than a vehicle of transportation, it was a way of life, the link to the outside world. It took the children to school, the sick to the hospital, housewives shopping, the light of foot dancing; it brought food, news, mail, visitors, doctors; in short, it became to the residents as indisputably a part of their lives as their toothbrushes.

It was used as a freighter by Federal Prison Industries, as a rescue boat to sailors in distress, a gunboat in search of prisoners; it was a link in the transfer and discharge of inmates; it was one of the forces around which local activities revolved.

(Left) The *Warden Johnston* following her maiden launch on June 20, 1945, in the waters of Puget Sound.

(Below) The *Warden Johnston* was specifically designed and built for ferrying residents, personnel, and inmates to and from Alcatraz. The boat was constructed by prisoners at McNeil Island Penitentiary. The *Warden* is seen here in dry dock before its launch on June 1, 1945.

Now the "Warden Johnston" is gone, a victim of the auctioneer's gavel. Even to the end she transported herself with the same dignity that identified her throughout her reign. And as she rode away from the Alcatraz docks for the last time Thursday, February 16th, the residents began to know the feeling that would be England's if she were ever to lose the "Rock of Gibralter."

A Korean War supply vessel that had been converted into a high-bowed passenger cruiser replaced the *Warden Johnston* in 1961, and was christened the *Warden Madigan*. The name was changed to the *Warden Blackwell* following the new appointment. In maintaining the continuity of the island's unique society, the warden would always remain as the central authority figure, setting the tone of life on Alcatraz not only for the prisoners and the guards, but for all of the inhabitants.

(Right) Candid views inside the prison launch in 1954.

Strikes and Protests

The inmates at Alcatraz were not always amenable to the confinement rules enforced by their keepers. During the course of the island's history as a Federal penitentiary, there were twenty-four major inmate strikes in protest of the harsh rules. Former inmate Roy Gardner would comment in his 1939 memoir entitled *Hellcatraz*:

> . . . discipline. Rigid, severe, unrelenting. Rules on Alcatraz, like the bars, are steel. Both are inflexible; neither bends.

In January of 1936, nearly one hundred and forty inmates went on strike to protest the rule of silence and the lack of privileges at Alcatraz. As inmates filed from the cellblock to their work assignments, many of them encouraged fellow convicts to help them protest by joining the strike. The tower guards came out onto the catwalks and raised their weapons toward the inmates, who walked defiantly and slowly to their assignments. The prisoners who refused to work were marched back into the cellhouse and locked down in their cells. Then one by one, the inmates were pulled from their cells and given hearings. A small percentage of them chose to return to work, but several were hostile toward the administration, and maintained their stance. The known ringleaders and vocal agitators where escorted to the dungeon cells in the basement.

The following day, kitchen workers joined the strike, forcing the prison staff to take over the kitchen. The inmates who continued their protest were fed only bread and water. Most of the prison population returned to work after only a few days on the reduced diet, but a handful continued to stand their ground. As the strike continued, a group of six inmates who had refused to take a full meal after nearly five days on bread and water were taken the hospital and force-fed with a tube. This was a traumatic experience, and all of the men eventually returned to work.

Over the years, there were several other instances of strikes and protests. When protests occurred inside the cellhouse, the inmates would throw toilet paper or anything else at hand into the cellblock corridors. The inmates would thud their steel-framed bunks onto the floor, drag their tin cups across the bars, and yell at the top of their lungs, thus creating a thunderous and resonating surge of sound. Former Correctional Officer Louis Nelson, who would later become the Warden of San Quentin, described the noise:

> It didn't happen too often, but when it did, it was fierce. It sounded similar to standing inside a stadium with the crowd yelling and stomping their feet. The first time I experienced it; I admit that it was a little intimidating. When new inmates would arrive, the rest of the population would let off a little steam and put a little fear into the new fish. It haunted the new inmates for at least a few days.

On average there would be six to ten small-scale riots in the Mess Hall per year, whenever the food quality waned. Phil Bergen recalled that on some occasions the stewards would fail to budget properly, and toward the end of the month, they would be forced to serve the same type of meal for days on end. This would provoke the inmates into protests in which they would violently overturn the tables, and pitch food all over the floor. These outbreaks would often cause the officer on the Mess Hall catwalk to punch out windowpanes and take aim at the inmates. The prisoners would then file back to their cells without any further disturbance. In the prison's entire history there were only eighteen major strikes, aside from those incidents that occurred in the Mess Hall.

Famous Inmates

WHEN ALCATRAZ OPENED as a Federal penitentiary in 1934, the operating premise was to gather the nation's worst offending criminals under one roof, in the securest possible circumstances. One important principle of this plan was to punish notorious convicts by never allowing them to see their names in print again, and thus ultimately to deglamorize the gangster mystique. The famous inmates who inhabited Alcatraz during its tenure as a Federal penitentiary included Al Capone, George "Machine Gun" Kelly, and Robert Stroud, the much-publicized *"Birdman of Alcatraz,"* who has been characterized in a number of classic books and films. These men and others like them contributed to the mythology of the famous prison, which eventually became an icon of the struggle between the forces of crime and the rule of law in the United States during one of the country's most troubled eras.

Alphonse "Scarface" Capone

Al "Scarface" Capone is a name that remains indelibly linked with the island prison of Alcatraz. This famous gangster would live to become the best-known symbol of organized crime during the Prohibition Era of the 1920's. In a biography written by Warden James Johnston in 1949, the author reminisced about the intensity of public interest surrounding Capone's imprisonment, stating that he himself was continually barraged with questions about "Big Al." Each day newspaper reporters and press agents flooded his office with phone calls, wanting to know every detail, from how Capone liked the weather on Alcatraz, to what job assignment he was currently working. Al Capone was considered the most powerful criminal figure of the era of gangsters and prohibition. But even with his wide-ranging influence and his networks of strapping hit men and corrupt politicians, he couldn't budge the strict regimen of The Rock.

Alphonse Capone was born on January 17, 1899 in Brooklyn, New York, to Gabriele and Teresina Capone. His parents had arrived only five years earlier at Ellis Island from a small village just south of Naples, Italy. They had crossed the Atlantic

(Opposite page) The concept of using Alcatraz as a maximum-security penitentiary was developed in the 1930's as a response to gangster violence.

(Left) Alphonse "Scarface" Capone.

(Below) Al Capone's Alcatraz mug shot, taken August 22, 1934.

Johnny Torrio.

seeking a life of promise, hoping to raise their children in a value-driven society. But America was suffering through hard times, and instead the couple found themselves mired in financial troubles and difficult circumstances. Al would be the third of five children. His father Gabriele was a well-liked barber in Brooklyn, and his mother Teresina was a devoutly religious homemaker. Life was rough for the Capone family, as they struggled to get by on Gabriele's meager salary. They were poor by most standards, living with no running water and few furnishings in their small apartment situated above Gabriele's barbershop in Brooklyn.

In the early 1900's the streets of downtown Brooklyn were filled with crime, and young Al was exposed to the harsh realties of violence and corruption. He would drop out of school at the young age of fourteen to join a tough youth gang. One of his early mentors during this period was Johnny Torrio, a prominent New York crime mogul who had once been a principal in the gang. Torrio was an important role model for Al as he grew up. The young Capone frequently ran errands for Torrio, who would always compensate him generously. In Lawrence Bergreen's exceptional biography of Capone, the author describes Torrio's influence and mentorship:

> Torrio was above all, a peacemaker; he had no bodyguard, carried no weapon, and always spoke in soft, measured tones. He considered himself a businessman, not a gang leader, and he conducted his rackets in a businesslike way. . . From Torrio he learned the importance of leading an outwardly respectable life, to segregate his career from his home life, as if maintaining a peaceful, conventional domestic setting somehow excused or legitimized the venality of working in the rackets . . . It was a form of hypocrisy that was second nature to Johnny Torrio and that he taught Capone to honor.

But even with his early links to organized crime circles, Capone was extremely popular with almost everyone who knew him. He was considered a respectful man, a capable leader, and a protector of the

A Capone "family" gathering in Chicago Heights in 1926. Pictured top, left to right: Jack "Machine Gun" McGurn, Frank "The Enforcer" Nitti, Charley Fischetti, Ralph "Bottles" Capone, Rocco Fischetti. Bottom left to right: Frank La Porte, Capone's Goddaughter Vera Emery, Al Capone, Sam "Golf Bag" Hunt, and Jim Emery.

families in his neighborhood. He was not a typical ruffian. He helped support his family by taking on legitimate employment, once working in a bookbinding factory, and once as a pinsetter in a bowling alley.

Capone's first invitation to join a formalized crime ring came from gangster Frankie Yale, the owner of a Coney Island bar called the Harvard Inn. Johnny Torrio had recommended Capone to Yale. By design, the Harvard Inn was Brooklyn's preeminent platform for organized crime. Capone was versatile and loyal, and he would quickly develop a strong camaraderie with Yale. Frankie Yale was a resourceful and violent man who flourished thanks to his strong-arm tactics, and he would become another mentor for Capone. Other historians have noted that Yale was involved in a multitude of illegal rackets, which included receiving a sizable flow of illegal "tax money" for protecting local businesses from harassment by other crime networks.

Frankie Yale.

It was also at Yale's club that Capone would receive the famous scar that later became his abhorrent trademark. Frank Gallucio was a smalltime New York crime figure who frequented the Harvard Inn. On one particular evening, Capone reportedly made an advance to Gallucio's younger sister. His suggestive comments instigated a violent fight, during which Gallucio pulled a knife and inflicted a deep laceration on Capone's left cheek. The bloody altercation would leave a permanent scar on Capone, and he was forced to make amends with Yale's associates. Famed gangster Lucky Lucania was brought in to help settle the matter, and to keep peaceful relations between the "families." Lucania scheduled an after-hours truce meeting, and Gallucio and Capone were forced to sit at a table and calmly reconcile their differences.

It was during this period, in early 1918, that young Al met and fell in love with Mae Coughlin, a beautiful middle-class Irish girl. She was two years older than Al, and while it is unknown exactly how and where they met, their courtship was brief. On December 4, 1918, Albert "Sonny" Francis Capone was born, and his birth was followed only three and a half weeks later by Al and Mae's formal wedding. Sonny's Godfather would be none other than Al's old friend and mentor, Johnny Torrio.

After the birth of his son, Capone took legitimate employment with a construction firm as a bookkeeper. It is unclear why he took this job, and left the world of crime. Many historians speculate that he used this time to learn the mechanics of running a viable business. Whatever the case, he continued to maintain strong ties to Yale and Torrio. Then in November of 1920, the Capone family suffered a terrible blow when Al's father Gabriele had a fatal heart attack at only fifty-five years of age. His death would mark the turning point for Al Capone, as he would suddenly become the family's main support, in terms of both income and moral guidance.

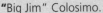
"Big Jim" Colosimo.

Johnny Torrio had relocated to Chicago nearly ten years earlier to manage saloon-brothel rackets under "Big Jim" Colosimo. Colosimo was a tall, heavyset entrepreneur who owned and operated Colosimo's Cafe, one of the most popular and profitable nightclubs in the area, just south of downtown Chicago. Colosimo's wife Victoria Moresco was also a principle player, and she ran a highly lucrative brothel behind the backdoors of the nightclub. Friction arose between Torrio and Colosimo when the Prohibition Law was passed in January of 1920. With smalltime bootleggers springing up throughout Chicago, Torrio saw an opportunity to expand his operations. Prostitution remained as the central business of organized crime in Chicago, and Big Jim Colosimo simply rejected the idea of expanding into other lines. As Torrio cultivated his business, Colosimo became more resistant and more of a hindrance to his activities.

In early 1920, Torrio recruited young Capone to come to Chicago and help him build his empire. He offered Capone a $25,000 annual salary, with percentage profits from the bootlegging business. Capone would start to prepare for his new job even before relocating. "Big Al" sought out the assistance of his Brooklyn mentor Frankie Yale, to permanently end the resistance of "Big Jim." On May 11, 1920, Colosimo was shot to death inside his nightclub presumably by Yale. His funeral would draw over 5,000 mourners, and Torrio publicly grieved his death to counter suspicion.

Capone arrived in Chicago in 1921, bringing his entire family with him. Torrio and Capone progressively built a powerful crime syndicate that would monopolize the entire bootlegging trade in Chicago. The two men found themselves presiding over an immense empire of gangsters, which kept illegal liquor flowing in and around Chicago by paying off the local politicians and police. By 1927 it was estimated that the two men were averaging $240 million a year from their gangland rackets.

Jim Colosimo's nightclub, where Al Capone learned to navigate the treacherous politics of the underground.

Capone had mastered the art of politics, and although he was already a wealthy, powerful gangland figure, he also attempted to balance his activities. Despite his illegitimate occupation, he had become a highly visible public personality. He made daily trips to City Hall, opened soup kitchens to feed the poor, and even lobbied for milk bottle dating to ensure the safety of the city's children. City officials often were embarrassed by Capone's political strength, so they began leveraging his illegal activities through police raids, and by setting intentional fires at his places of business.

In the beginning, the public glamorized Capone's activities and identified with him as a modern day Robin Hood. It wasn't long, however, before public opinion started turning against him, when it was believed that he had ordered the death of a famed local Public Prosecutor named Billy McSwiggin. The young prosecutor had earlier tried to pin the violent murder of a rival gang member on Capone, and he carried a reputation for going after bootleggers. Although many argued against Al's involvement in McSwiggin's death, there was a great outcry over gangland violence at the time, and public sentiment went against Capone.

Capone quickly went into hiding, fearing he would be tried for McSwiggin's murder. He remained out of sight for nearly three months, and then after realizing he couldn't live the remainder of his life underground, he negotiated his own surrender to the Chicago Police. The authorities eventually recognized that they lacked sufficient evidence to bring Capone to trial, and though the decision proved very unpopular with the public, he was eventually set free. The community was outraged, and law officials were left publicly embarrassed by the incident. "Big Al" had become one of the most powerful crime czars in Chicago. It was said that Capone was now larger than life, and more powerful than the Mayor himself.

By 1929 Capone's empire was worth over $62 million, and he was ready to wage war on his most prominent bootlegging rival, George "Bugs" Moran. Bugs was another of Chicago's principal gangsters. He was known to talk openly against Capone, and he maintained an attitude of spiteful arrogance that was said to anger Capone so much that Moran became one of Al's regular topics of discussion. It was rumored that Capone gave orders to take Bugs down by assassinating his gang members from the bottom up, not stopping until they reached Bugs himself.

Capone was now living lavishly in Palm Beach, and he drafted one of his top associates, Jack "Machine Gun" McGurn, to mastermind the hit. McGurn had one of his bootleggers lure members of the Moran gang into a garage to buy liquor at an unreasonably cheap price. The deal was made, and the delivery was scheduled to

A waterfront view of Al Capone's Palm Beach Mansion.

A mug shot of Capone taken in Miami, Florida.

(Below left) The scene of the brutal St. Valentine's Massacre.

(Below right) Seven members of George "Bugs" Moran's gang were lined up against a wall and mowed down by two machine gunners impersonating police officers.

take place on Valentine's Day, 1929. McGurn and his men awaited their victims in stolen police uniforms. When the rival mobsters arrived, McGurn's gang pretended to be policemen making a bust, and ordered all of Moran's men to stand facing the wall. Thinking that they had just been caught by the police, seven members of the Moran gang turned to the wall awaiting arrest. McGurn and his men then opened fire with machine guns, killing all of the gangsters. Bugs himself had seen the police car before stopping his vehicle, and thinking that it was a raid, he fled the scene. Capone was credited with what would be one of the most famous mass murders in American history, the "St. Valentine's Day Massacre."

The Massacre received national attention, and Capone was glamorized in books and newspapers across the country. Capone was now a high-class, family-oriented and self-made gangster-millionaire, who had everyone's full attention. Many local politicians began complaining about Capone and his self-proclaimed political stature. However the publicity surrounding Capone ultimately backfired, by attracting the attention of President Herbert Hoover. Hoover had just started his presidential term, and as one of his first moves, he demanded that Capone be brought to justice. Hoover pressured Secretary of the Treasury Andrew Mellon to spearhead the government's battle against Capone. Mellon collected damning evidence against "Big Al" which exposed his gang affiliations, bootlegging, prostitution rings, and flagrant evasion of taxes.

It would take nearly five years of an intensive undercover operation before Capone was finally convicted. Then on October 17, 1931, Alphonse Capone was sentenced to eleven years in prison and $50,000 in fines, and was forced to pay court fees totaling over $30,000. The judge refused to allow Capone to be released on bail, and the gangster remained confined at the Cook County Jail until arrangements were made for his transfer to Atlanta. On May 4, 1932 Capone began serving out his Federal prison sentence at the Atlanta Federal Penitentiary. Capone flaunted his power even in prison, and quickly secured the ability

A diagram showing how the massacre unfolded at the S.M.C. Cartage Company, at 2122 North Clark Street in Chicago. Chicago Gangster Frank Gusenberg (left) suffered twenty-two bullet wounds, and later died at the hospital. Jack "Machine Gun" McGurn (right) was one of Capone's hit men, and the mastermind of the massacre.

(Left) Capone's criminal history from his inmate file.

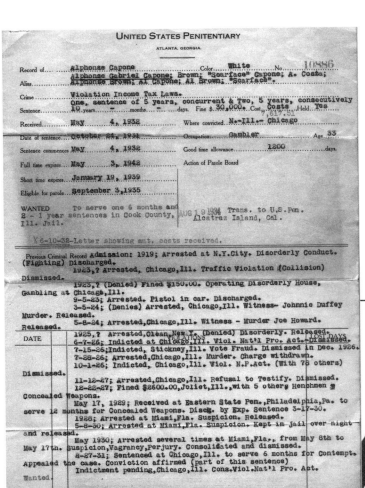

(Right) A recent photograph of Capone's uniquely furnished cell at Eastern State Penitentiary. Before his arrival at Alcatraz, Capone had managed to set the terms of his own privileges while incarcerated at other prisons.

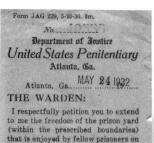

(Above) A request by Capone to use the prison recreation yard at Atlanta State Penitentiary.

DEPARTMENT OF JUSTICE, BUREAU OF INVESTIGATION

IDENTIFICATION DIVISION, WASHINGTON, D. C.

CRIMINAL HISTORY

to dictate his own privileges. He was given unlimited access to the Warden, and was said to maintain large reserves of cash hidden in his cell, often generously "tipping" guards who would assist him by yielding to special requests. His time spent at Atlanta would not be as plush as his confinement at Cook, but he still found means to manipulate the system.

Before arriving at Alcatraz, Capone had already become a master at controlling his environment at the Federal Penitentiary in Atlanta. Despite strict rulings from the courts, Capone was always able to persuade his guards to fulfill his every whim, and he often set the terms of his own privileges. It was said that he had convinced many guards to work for him, and his cell boasted expensive furnishings including personal bedding, and many other amenities that were not extended to other inmates serving lesser sentences. His cell was carpeted, and he had a radio around which many of the guards would sit with him, conversing and listening to their favorite serials. His friends and family maintained residence in a nearby hotel, and each day he was flooded with visitors.

In 1934 Attorney General Homer Cummings and Sanford Bates, the Director of Federal Prisons, made arrangements to send Capone to a facility where he would be unable to leverage the system. Alcatraz was the perfect answer to a problem that no one seemed able to control. On August 19, 1934, without any formal notice, Capone was placed in a secure prison railroad car, and was taken on a journey along with fifty-two other inmates to America's Devil Island. In keeping with the heightened level of security, Capone would remain handcuffed and shackled, and would be personally accompanied to California by Atlanta's Warden, A. C. Aderhold.

To Mrs Theresa Capone   Atlanta, Ga. May 13 19_3

Address 7244 Prairie Av

Chicago Ill

Dear Mother

Its just a simple little word
But it seems the world to me
For it means the best and noblest word
   that anyone can be.
I know that God made that little word to
   stand for all thats true,
I know he called mother because he named
   # after you,
All that I am, all that I hope to be, I owe it all
to you.
Dear Mother with the passing of years the
realization of my debt of gratitude grows more
profound and my love ever deeper and stronger
May God Bless you and love to all
   Your Dear Son
   Al

Name Alphonse Capone

Number 40886

To Mrs Theresa Capone   Atlanta, Ga. Dec. 24 1932

Address 7244 Prairie Ave

Chicago Ill

Dear Mother

Well Ma how are you and
the family, Am wishing all of you at home
a Merry Christmas also give Ralphie and Delores
and Mafalda a real nice big Christmas kiss
for me. Am in hope of seeing you real soon
and will give you yours. Don't worry try
and be merry and may God Bless all of
you. Love and kisses to you the sweetest little
mother in the world.
   Al

Name Alphonse Capone

Number 40886

(Above) These letters were located in Al Capone's inmate file, probably having been censored and retyped before mailing by prison officials. The numerous letters in his file illustrate very affectionate and close bonds within the Capone family.

Al Capone arrived at Alcatraz on August 22, 1934, as inmate AZ-85. From the first moment of his arrival, Capone worked to manipulate the system. Warden Johnston had a custom of meeting the new "fish" when they first arrived at Alcatraz, and he usually participated in their brief orientation. Johnston wrote in a later memoir that he had little trouble recognizing Capone as he stood in the lineup. Capone was grinning and making quiet, smug comments from the side of his mouth to other inmates. When his turn came to approach Warden Johnston, it appeared that he wanted to show off to the other inmates by asking questions on their behalf, as if he were already their leader. Johnston quickly assigned him his prison number, and made him get back in line with the other convicts. During Capone's time on Alcatraz, the famous prisoner would make several attempts to con Johnston into allowing him special privileges, but all were denied. Johnston maintained that Capone would not be given any special rights, and would have to follow the rules, as would any other inmate.

Like every other inmate at Alcatraz in the early 1930's, Capone was to do hard time. He was among the first group that arrived from the Federal Penitentiary in Atlanta, when the rule of silence was being strictly enforced by the correctional staff. Capone would occupy cell B-181 (later renumbered to B-206) located on the west end of B Block. Almost overnight, Capone had been completely stripped of his persona

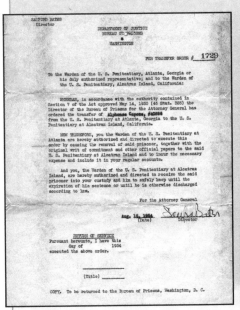

Capone's transfer order to Alcatraz.

as a crime czar. The great Capone was now little more than a common inmate. He received favorable reports at his work assignments, which included a detail in the prison laundry and a stint as a cellhouse orderly delivering books and magazines to other inmates, as well as performing menial tasks such as sweeping and mopping. It is documented that Capone's favorite pastimes at Alcatraz were reading celebrity magazines and playing the tenor banjo.

During his years on The Rock, Capone did receive discipline for misconduct on occasion. On February 20, 1935, Capone was placed in solitary confinement for starting a fight with inmate William Colyer, and it was noted by other inmates that he had been trying to "bully" several of them. Warden Johnston wrote about the event, stating in part:

Alphonse Capone, #85-AZ, and William Colyer, #185-AZ, were working in the laundry on opposite sides of a mangle. Capone was feeding towels in the mangle; Colyer was taking them out the other side.

Colyer became angered because, according to his claims, Capone was not feeding the mangle properly, with the result the towels were coming through partially wet, but Capone's claim was that he was feeding them correctly but faster than Colyer could handle them. At any rate, Colyer,

(Right) A page from Al Capone's conduct report at Alcatraz

SHEET NUMBER ONE

UNITED STATES PENITENTIARY
ALCATRAZ, CALIFORNIA

CONDUCT REPORT

NAME CAPONE, Alphonse   No. 85-AZ

DATE REPORTED	OFFENSE AND ACTION
10-10-34	TALKING IN LINE OF MARCH. This prisoner was talking in line this PM with Collins-#208. This prisoner knows better and has been warned. GUARD NELSON. Action:To lose two weeks yard privileges. C.J.Shuttleworth, Deputy
12-19-34	UNNECESSARY NOISE AT THE TABLE. Caused confusion in the mess hall after meal was finished. GUARD W.B.COTTERAL. Action: To forfeit one weeks yard privileges. C.J.Shuttleworth, Deputy Warden
2-20-35	FIGHTING IN THE LAUNDRY. This prisoner had a fight with Colyer-185 while working in the laundry. He did not resist when I separated them. Some of the prisoners claim he had been doing a lot of bullying lately over the other prisoners who work with him. GUARD- I.B. FAULK. Action: Placed in solitary confinement restricted diet and forfeit all privileges until further orders. C.J. Shuttleworth, Deputy Warden
2-28-35	Removed from solitary to segregation
3-2-35	Removed to regular cell & work assignment, privileges restored. C.J. Shuttleworth, Deputy Warden
5-24-35	SPITTING ON THE FLOOR. While waiting on the range, out side of cell, to be let into his cell, Capone expectorated on the floor, flats, and cell house wall; he left the library about three minutes before and there is no cause for such filthy action. GUARD P.A. HABOUSH. Action:To lose two weeks yard privileges. C.J. Shuttleworth, Deputy Warden.
6-3-35	CONVERSING WITH #43-WALSH. Thsi inmate was talking at cell door with Walsh in adjoining cell. Both men ducked inside when I appeared. GUARD P.A. HABOUSH. Action: Reprimanded and Warned. C.J.Shuttleworth, Deputy.
9-5-35	ENTERING CELL BEFORE SIGNAL. While marching to the cells from evening meal, this man entered his cell instead of stopping at the door and wait-for the signal to enter. GUARD NEELEY. Action: Reprimanded & Warned. C.J. Shuttleworth, Deputy Warden.
9-18-35	WASTING FOOD. Eating the center of piece of cake and leaving the balance on his plate. GUARD J.B. STEERE. Action: To lose breakfast, 9/19/35, C. J. Shuttleworth, Deputy Warden.
4-21-36	FIGHTING WITH #257-HENSLEY. I answered the buzzer for hospital and found #85 and #257 fighting. Mr. Preshaw and I parted them. Mr. Ping witnessed start of agument upstairs. M.A. AMENDE, Jr. Officer
11-11-36	CREATING DISTURBANCE, DESTROYING CLOTHING. Upon being told that he could not go to the yard, this prisoner flew into a rage, kicking the door and cursing evryone. He destroyed his blue uniform and bath robe and threw them over the transom into hall. He kept this up for about one hour. Report #2231, R. L. King, Junior Officer. Action: To forfeit show privileges this date. E. J. Miller, Associate Warden.

receiving some towels on his side that did not suit him, threw them back at Capone, whereupon Capone went around the mangle to Colyer's side and punched him in the eye.

Colyer sought to get a tool to resist Capone but Capone picked up a wooden bench and either struck Colyer in the wrist or Colyer, endeavoring to strike him, hit his wrist against the bench, at any rate the result was a sprained wrist. It all happened very quickly and the guard on-duty separated them and brought them both immediately to the Deputy, who heard their stories and locked them both in solitary.

Capone's various offenses at Alcatraz would range from fighting with other inmates, to spitting, to destroying and throwing his clothing from his cell tier onto the aisle floor. It is documented that Capone attempted to manage the affairs of several other inmates, with little success. He was unable to establish any underground networks at Alcatraz, and his communications to the outside world were strictly censored. Gifts sent to Capone were never accepted, and visits from family members were limited to the same number as for other inmates.

There were also rumors that Al's life was threatened by his fellow prisoners. It is suggested in several documents that other inmates schemed to take advantage of Capone's financial status, in order to secure outside assistance and collaboration in potential escapes. In a letter written to Al's brother Ralph by fellow Alcatraz inmate and music teacher Charles Mangiere on May 18, 1936, it is alleged that some inmates plotted to kill Al if he refused to front the money to hire a gun boat for one such escape attempt. Mangiere stated that inmates Charles Berta and Bert McDonald had told him that unless Al provided them with $5,000, they would never let him leave Alcatraz alive. He further alleged that several others were plotting to frame Capone under a similar pretense.

Jimmy C. Lucas.

Capone himself was aware of these threats, at least one of which would have near fatal consequences. On June 23, 1936, Capone was assaulted by a violent Texan inmate, Jimmy C. Lucas. Lucas was serving time for bank robbery, and he also boasted a previous murder conviction, as well as several reported escape attempts from other institutions. The following reports chronicle the attack:

Re: ATTACK UPON CAPONE #85-AZ 6-23-36

About 9:30 A.M. this date I received a call from Mr. Hansen at the west end of the cell house stating there was a cutting scrape that just happened in the basement. I rushed back there to find out from Mr. Hansen that Lucas #224 stabbed Capone #85 and that both of them were up in the hospital.

I immediately went to the hospital. Waiting outside in the hallway of the hospital was Lucas with Junior Custodial Officer Lapsley. I asked Lucas what happened. He said that he had struck Capone with a pair of scissors. Asked him why he had done it and he said because Capone "snitched to you and had me removed from the barbershop." I told him that Capone had nothing to do with his removal from the barbershop and went on into the Hospital to see the condition of Capone.

Alcatraz California
June 26, 1936

Pursuant to orders of Warden James A. Johnston issued this date, the Board comprising Deputy Warden C. J. Shuttleworth, Chairman, Chief Medical Officer Dr. George Hess and Lieutenant E. J. Miller is now convened for the purpose of providing a hearing for inmate James C. Lucas, Number 224-Az, having been charged that on the twenty-third day of June, 1936, he did attack inmate Number 85-Az, Capone, with a dangerous weapon, inflicting several wounds on the body of this inmate.

  The board is now in session and the prisoner will be brought before the board for hearing. (Prisoner summoned).

  (By Deputy Warden C. J. Shuttleworth, Chairman)
  Lucas, you are called before this Board on instructions of the Warden to try you for an assault on Tuesday morning of this week, June 23, 1936, about 9:30 A.M. on the body of #85-Az, Capone, with a dangerous weapon inflicting several injuries on his body with a part of a pair of scissors, is that correct?

  A. (no audible response)
  Q. What excuse have you got to offer for this attack?
  A. Well, when I was working there, I was minding my own business, getting along and he got a bunch of crazy ideas in his head and messed around—
  Q. What do you mean crazy ideas?
  A. He went to you and told you that I was going to bump him off and some other stuff and I had no such idea in my head, nothing like that, it was not in my mind.
  Q. You state that he went to me about it. Did you see him go to me?
  A. No, but I—
  Q. Did anyone see him go to me with any such stories or hear him?
  A. Well, I couldn't prove that. I don't want to try to prove that, but I know it is so.
  Q. How did you come in possession of these scissors?
  A. Just lay there and I went and got them.
  Q. Just lay where?
  A. In the Barber Shop.
  Q. Where about in the Barber Shop?
  A. On the stand where they always stay.
  Q. Did you break them apart or take the screws out of them?
  A. Unscrewed them.
  Q. Why did you unscrew them instead of using the entire scissors?
  A. One half is better than all of it.
  Q. One half is better—
  A. Sharper.
  Q. Then what did you do after you unscrewed them?
  A. What did I do?
  Q. Yes, how did you know that Capone was in the Clothing Room?
  A. Well, I just knew he was in there, looked and seen him.
  Q. Looked and saw what?
  A. Went on in, knew that he was in there.
  Q. Knew that he was in the Clothing Room. Did you warn him at all before you made the attack on him or just come in without any warning?
  A. What do you mean by that?
  Q. Speak to him?

A. No.

Q. You didn't warn him. What was your intention to do to him?

A. How? What do you mean?

Q. Well, did you just intend to go in there as a threat or what did you go in there for with them?

A. Well, I don't know.

Q. What was you first idea when you got the scissors?

A. Well—

Q. Was it to go in there and kill him if you could, was that what your intention was or just to go in there and have a fight?

A. Well, to just show him not to stool on me and let me well enough alone.

Q. Did you know that when you did this, Lucas, that you might have killed him, that you could have killed him with this?

A. No, I did not think…. not with them.

Q. Did you hold the scissors in your hands, these bare scissors, or did you wrap a handkerchief around them to act as a holder?

A. Well, I wrapped a handkerchief around them.

Q. Wrapped a handkerchief— your handkerchief?

A. Mine.

Q. Have you anything to say in your defense?

A. Well he threatened to kill me.

Q. When?

A. Lots of people around knew—

Q. When?

A. Several occasions. He tried to get guys to kill me. He tried to offer—

Q. Name one.

A.   I would rather not name them now.

Q. That type of evidence is immaterial if you cannot name—

A. I can name him all right. Well, I am not—

Q. What?

A. I don't wantto name him . . . He offered money to get me.

Q. He offered money to get you?

A. But I refuse to name who at the present time for several reasons, and he threatened my life up there. You might have heard that (turning to Junior Custodial Officer Sanders) when I was going up there to the hospital—

Q. That was after the facts.

A. That was Tuesday, but before this—

Q. Afterwards many things might be said after you had executed this unprovoked attack upon him.

A. He offered money to get me done for or he would do it and the other fellow would take the rap.

Q. Who did he offer that?

A. I would rather not say now, at the present time.

Q. That is insufficient evidence. Mr. Sanders what do you know about this case, what did you see on your end of it?

A. (By Junior Custodial Officer Thomas J. Sanders)
    Why, the first I knew is that I saw this man attacking Capone and they were tangled up and fighting and I jumped over and told this man to surrender the weapon, which he did without any resistance to me. I turned the weapon over to you.

Q. What was it?

A. (J.C.O. Sanders) One piece of scissors.

Q. One half of a scissors?

A. (J.C.O. Sanders) One half of scissors.

Q. Did you find the other half of the scissors?

A. (J.C.O. Sanders) No… Oh, yes, the other half, I found it.

Q. Where did you find it?

A. (J.C.O. Sanders) In the Barber Shop on the stand.

Q. Did you find the screw?

A. (J.C.O. Sanders) Yes, sir.

Q. Where was it?

A. (J.C.O. Sanders) It was laying with the other part of the scissors.

Q. Where was it?

A. (J.C.O. Sanders) In the Barber Shop.

Q. This inmate has 3600 days good time, earned or to be earned under a sentence of thirty years. I recommend that he forfeit the entire 3600 days. What is your recommendation (to Doctor Hess)?

Q. (By Dr. Hess) If you don't mind, I would like to ask him some questions. Where are you working, Lucas?

A. In the Laundry.

Q. (Dr. Hess) What were you doing down there?

A. Supposed to get a hair cut.

Q. Down to get a haircut?

A. Yes, to get a hair cut.

Q. (Dr. Hess) Are you sure that you did this because of some threat that Capone made to you or in conjunction with some grievances of others?

A Well, he knows (indicating Deputy) what Capone said about me to him and not only to . . .

Q. Where there any words passed before you struck him?

A. No.

Q. None whatsoever? How long after you went down stairs to get a hair cut before you struck him?

A. Oh, I would say twenty minutes, I don't know just the exact time.

Q. What did you use to loosen the scissors with?

A. They were loose, just a set screw.

Q. I see. Suppose there is any chance of anyone unloosening those scissors purposely.

A. Nobody knew anything about it.

Q. What barber's scissors did you take, do you know?

A. I looked them both over. I don't know what one.

Q. Why did you look them both over?

A. Just looking them over to see which one was the best.

Q. (By Deputy Shuttleworth to Lieutenant Miller). Anything to ask him?

A. (Lieutenant Miller). No.

Q. (By Deputy Shuttleworth to Dr. Hess). What is your recommendation?

A. (By Dr. Hess) I would rather defer my opinion until I can talk to Capone.

Q. (By Deputy Shuttleworth to Lieutenant Miller). Your recommendation?

A. I recommend he lose all his good time.

Q. (By Deputy Shuttleworth to J.C.O. Sanders). That is all, put him away.

A. Dr. Hess requested that #85 be brought before the Board for the purpose of asking him some questions which might aid in finding the cause of the attack. Capone was brought before the board and asked a few questions, which satisfied the Doctor and he "recommended the loss of all his good time."

He was on the table in the Out Patient Office, lying on his side stomach, upper of his body stripped. The Doctor with Guard Attendant Ping was attending to stopping the heavy flow of blood from a small wound on the left side of his back and about half way down his back, near the side.

At this time he was conscious, smiling, and I asked him what had happened and he said that Lucas had come up from behind him, stuck him in the back while he was standing looking at a mandolin which was laying on the counter in the Clothing Room. Upon being attacked he grabbed the mandolin and swung it around, hitting Lucas in the head. Lucas continued to attempt to attack him and in the attempt to disarm Lucas, he got a few minor cut on his hands.

Asked him what the cause of the attack was and he said it was the same old story, because he would not furnish money requested by Lucas.

Guard Sanders who was on duty in the Clothing Room at the time reports that a few minutes before he had gone in the clothing room and went over to a small desk with #107-Best. They were drawing a design for some additional pigeonholes for inmates clothing. Mr. Sander's back was towards the door. He noticed Capone enter the Clothing Room and saw him looking at the mandolin but did not notice Lucas come in. The first he noticed was when he heard a scuffle and yelling.

At that time Capone was trying to protect himself against the attack of Lucas. Mr. Sanders was only about ten feet away, pulled out his club and jumped over to them, pushed Capone behind him and with Lucas in front of him ordered Lucas to surrender the half of scissors he was holding in his hand, which Lucas did without any resistance. Mr. Sanders took Lucas then up the stairs to the cellhouse and turned him over to Mr. Lapsley. At the same time he blew a whistle to attract attention of the cellhouse guard.

#107-Best went with Capone up the stairs through the kitchen to the mess hall gate. Through this gate Best took Capone on up to the Hospital while Mr. Sanders cleared the basement of all inmates. Mr. Lapsley took Lucas to the Hospital and stayed with him.

This is all the information I have been able to obtain up to the present time (3:00 P.M.), excepting that as soon as Lucas had a slight cut on his head dressed I order him placed in Solitary Confinement "D" Cell Block, about 10 A.M.

The second memorandum included with this text was written to Warden Johnston by the Chief Medical Officer, George Hess. The memo provides a detailed summary of Capone's injuries;

On June 23, 1936 the above inmate was brought to the hospital with multiple stab wounds and with a history as follows;

About 9:30 A.M. while engaged at work in the clothing room he was attacked by another inmate with a pair of clothing scissors. He gave the name Lucas, number 224, as the man who stabbed him. His condition at the time he was brought to the hospital was that of semi-shock. He was given the usual circulatory stimulants and then first aid measures and an examination.

The primary examination and treatment was given by Doctor Greenberg. He found several wounds as follows; a small punctured wound in the left chest posteriorly about 2 cm Deep which did not penetrate the chest cavity, a puncture wound on the medial aspect of the left thumb about 1½ cm in length and extending to the bone, several superficial wounds — two on the right arm and one on the right hand. Under the fluoroscope there was seen a foreign body embedded in the first phalanx of the left thumb. This was removed by operation in the operating room under local anesthesia, it was the point of the scissors blade and was about ½ inch in length. The piece of blade was strongly embedded in the bone and much difficulty was experienced in removing the object. He was given 1500 units of tetanus antitoxin.

The patient is recovering from the injuries in a satisfactory manner. The prognosis is considered good at this time. He will probably be confined to the hospital for at least three more days.

In late 1937, Capone started to withdraw further and further from prison society, and spent the majority of his time secluded in his cell. He was witnessed on occasion talking to himself and acting bizarre, and on February 5, 1938 it became apparent that Al was seriously ill. Associate Warden E. J. Miller described the episode:

When we opened the cells this morning at breakfast time, Capone #85-Az came out of his cell with his blue clothes on. On being sent back to his cell to put on his coveralls, he returned, put them on and got in line and came in and drank some coffee.

After the meal was over and men went back to cells, Capone started up on the upper gallery instead of going to his own cell. Officers sent him back to his own cell and being locked in, he proceeded to get sick and threw up what he had eaten for breakfast and then appeared to be all right.

After we let the men go out to work, I went up to Capone's cell and talked to him to see what was the matter with him and what explanation he had for his actions. He was sitting on the toilet and in response to my questions all I could get were indistinct, incoherent mumblings.

At about 8:15, Mr. Amende, Cell House Officer, called me and said that Capone had thrown a fit in his cell. I went to Capone's cell

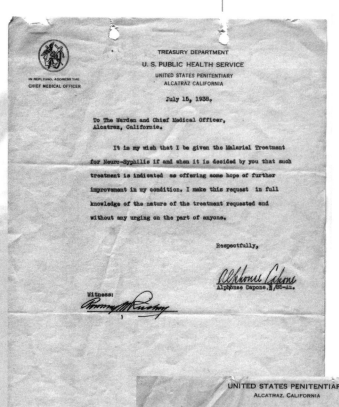

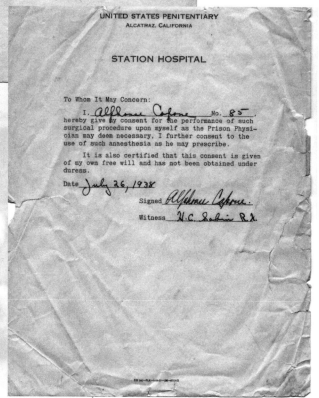

Documents relating to Capone's treatment for syphilis while he was an inmate at Alcatraz.

and found he was laying on the floor and appeared to be in a hysterical fit of some sort. I immediately sent for the doctor and when Dr. Hess came and put him on the bunk and examined him, he said we had better take him to the hospital.

Capone was checked into the Hospital.

Capone had developed symptoms of syphilis, a disease that he had evidently been carrying for years. He was committed to the prison hospital, and would remain there for the duration of his imprisonment at Alcatraz. The prison doctors attempted a variety of treatments with no success. Capone was locked in what was termed a "bug cage" for mentally unstable patients. It was a stiff wired cage that sectioned off a large hospital wardroom, typically housing multiple patients. Inmate Alvin Karpis later recounted a fierce fight that ensued between Capone and an inmate named Carl Janaway.

Janaway shared one of the adjacent wire enclosures, and it is claimed that the two men constantly argued like small children. Their fighting climaxed in an event that would have them both separated, and would finally convince the administration of the need to transfer Capone to a facility that could better care for his medical condition. The altercation stemmed from Janaway's insults, which were reciprocated by Capone using names such as *"Bug House Janaway."* At the peak of their exchange, both inmates started hurling the contents of their bedpans at each other through the wire caging. They would end up so saturated with urine and feces, that

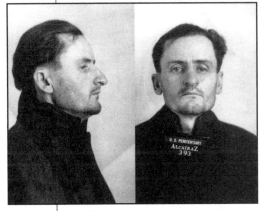

Carl Janaway.

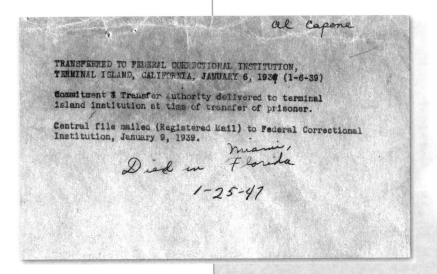

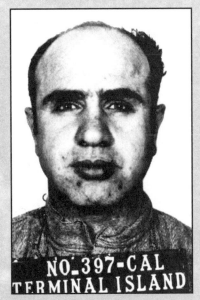

Al Capone's Terminal Island mug shot, taken on January 6, 1938, the day of his release from Alcatraz.

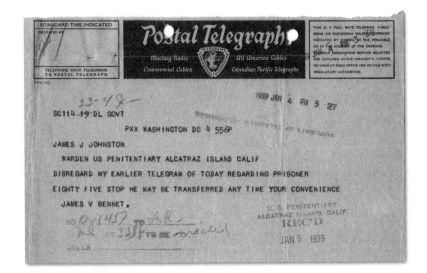

Capone and his brothers Albert and Ralph (wearing their ranger style hats) in Mercer Wisconsin. This never before published photo was taken during a hunting trip in 1944.

they had to be hosed down before being removed from their enclosures to shower. Early on the morning of January 6, 1938, Associate Warden E. J. Miller escorted Capone to the mainland, where Federal Marshals awaited to take custody of the famous prisoner. He was transferred to Terminal Island Prison in Southern California, where he would serve out the remainder of his sentence. He was released in November of 1939, and died on January 25, 1947 in his Palm Beach Mansion from complications of syphilis. His older brother Raffaele would also later serve time for tax evasion at McNeil Island Federal Penitentiary.

The Birdman of Alcatraz
The Life and Imprisonment of Robert Franklin Stroud

Robert Stroud was perhaps the most uniquely memorable of all the prisoners in the annals of American penology. He forever remains as a historical icon, and his legend is woven into the fabric of Alcatraz and its colorful past. However, despite his worldwide fame and notoriety, the public has never gotten to know the real Bob Stroud. His soft image as a humanitarian and gentle bird doctor was the romanticized product of a Hollywood Motion Picture, which largely fictionalized his life story.

The true face of Stroud was violent, intricate, mysterious, and multi-layered. He was far more complex than the handsome and humbled character that actor Burt Lancaster portrayed in the film chronicling Stroud's life. The movie blended gentle images, such as small frail canaries tangling their feet in Lancaster's hair, into a caring portrait of a man of extreme tenderness. His real-life guard-

Burt Lancaster portrayed Robert Stroud in the 1962 classic motion picture *"Birdman of Alcatraz."*

ians failed to see or understand the Hollywood parallels. They characterized him as a *"vengeful manipulator with homicidal traits and impulsively dangerous tendencies."* By the time Stroud had arrived on Alcatraz in 1942, he was fifty-two years old, and had already served thirty-three years in prison.

Robert Franklin Stroud was born on January 28, 1890 in Seattle, Washington, to Elizabeth McCartney Schaefer Stroud and Benjamin Franklin Stroud. Elizabeth was much older than her husband, and was

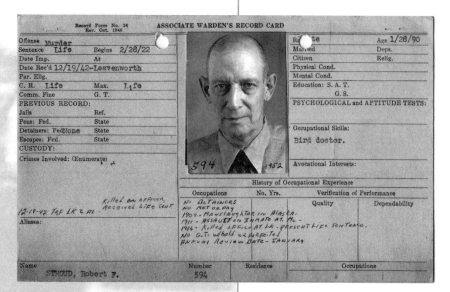

a widow with two daughters from a previous turbulent marriage. Robert was the third of four children, and he was born into an extremely quarrelsome household. His father Ben had apparently despised the very idea of Elizabeth's pregnancy, and some sources indicate that he beat his son frequently from a very young age. Stroud came to feel a deep-rooted hatred for his father, which grew progressively as he moved into adulthood. His mother, however, had a special protective bond with her young son, and was said to favor him over her other children. The scenario was further complicated in 1898 with the birth of Marcus McCartney Stroud, Robert's new baby brother. It is said that Robert's father was pleased with the birth of Marcus. Benjamin Stroud had been steadily employed for some time, and the family's financial future was much brighter at the time of Marcus's birth.

At age eleven Robert contracted a serious case of typhoid fever, which resulted in several months of confinement to his bed. Throughout his repeated bouts of retching illness, his mother always stayed by his bedside. Her loyalty further cemented the bond between them, and this sealed their already close relationship.

By the age of thirteen, Stroud had become a desperately troubled youth, and he left home on foot without a penny to his name. Young Bob set out for the small fishing town of Anacortes, Washington, begging for food and money. He would later claim it was here that he first started having sexual relations with prostitutes, and venturing into the red light districts. Bob also learned to ride the romanticized train rails, and lived by evening campfires with hobos and other runaways. At sixteen Bob finally returned home, and offered fabulous stories of his adventurous escapades to his worshiping younger brother Marcus. At this time, Bob attempted to put his life back on track by working at a series of menial jobs. But despite his best intentions, this would prove to be a barren attempt.

In 1908, at eighteen years of age, Stroud drifted up to Juneau, Alaska, where he fell in love with a saloon prostitute named Kitty O'Brien. Kitty was thirty-six, and she acted as a somewhat motherly figure to Stroud. When Robert developed a severe case of pneumonia, Kitty took care of him and helped nurse him back to health. However, here too there were clouds on the horizon. Charlie F. Dahmer was a bartender at the "Montana Saloon", where Kitty hustled, and he is said to have been an ex-boyfriend who was still in love with her. Whatever their relationship may have been, it was to play a decisive role in the events that followed. Notes from Stroud's Alcatraz admission file would later state that "*Kitty was addicted to the use of dope*," and it was presumed that young Robert might also have been addicted.

The first crucial turning point in Stroud's life came on January 18, 1909, when he murdered Dahmer. There are several narratives of the events surrounding the murder, but the official account given in the Alcatraz Warden's Notebook stated the facts as follows:

> There are two stories connected with the killing, one of which is that this woman (Kitty O'Brien) did not come home one night; that when she returned to her crib in the morning she told Stroud that she had spent the night with one Charles F. Dahmer, a local bartender in a local saloon; that Dahmer abused her and only paid $2.00 whereas the usual and customary fee was ten dollars; that Stroud thereupon proceeded to a local hardware store, now extinct, and asked to buy a few shells for his pistol; that the proprietor of the store refused to sell him anything but a full box of shells; that he thereupon left and returned some time later in the afternoon, purchased a box of shells, went into the residence of Dahmer, fired five shots at him, three of which took effect in his body, proceeded to rob him of whatever money he had on his person and returned to this woman's crib and gave her the money he had taken from Dahmer. The other story is to the effect that he waited several days before committing the murder, but that the reason was the same in both stories. For this crime, Stroud was sentenced to 12 years in the USP, McNeil Island, Washington (rec'd at McNeil about 8-23-09).

Stroud later claimed that Dahmer had beaten Kitty savagely, almost killing her. Furthermore, he alleged that Dahmer had stolen a gold locket that Stroud had given her as a special gift. He later described that when he had walked into her room she was almost dead, and that when he had taken her into his arms, she begged: "*kill him, Robert, please kill him*." Stroud maintained that he went to Dahmer's small cottage demanding an answer as to why he had assaulted Kitty. Dahmer was resistant, and Stroud asserted that Dahmer charged him, and that "*it was either him or me*." Dahmer suffered a fatal gunshot wound to the head and died instantly. After the killing, Stroud turned himself in to the U.S. Marshal's Office. He was subsequently tried and convicted of manslaughter. Since the crime had been committed on Federal territory, Stroud was sent to McNeil Island, the U.S. Penitentiary located in Puget Sound, Washington. Kitty had also been indicted, but charges were dropped due to lack of evidence.

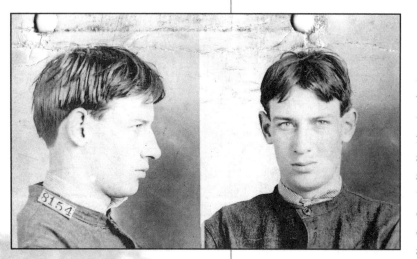

Robert Stroud in 1909, at eighteen years of age.

Stroud arrived at McNeil on August 23, 1909 as inmate #1854-M, and had to learn to live under the rigid prison regulations. The silent system was strictly enforced, and the prison rule resembled that of a tough military establishment. Prisoners moved about the penitentiary in drill formation, and those who violated the rules were thrown into a dark and unsanitary solitary confinement cell, and were fed only rations of stale bread and water. The prison was old and poorly ventilated, and lacked any type of modern plumbing. At McNeil, Stroud worked in the prison laundry and quickly became known as a problematic inmate. His records indicate that he was violent and difficult to manage. There were ceaseless complaints of threats made against other inmates.

After serving nearly twenty-eight months at McNeil, Stroud violently stabbed a fellow inmate who allegedly "snitched" on him for sneaking food back to his cell. He was sent to serve time in solitary confinement, and received an additional six-month sentence for his hostile act. On September 5, 1912, Stroud was transferred by train to the U.S. Penitentiary in Leavenworth, Kansas. Robert Stroud had now become inmate L-17431, in one of the toughest prisons in the United States. Leavenworth was known simply as the "Big Top" among Federal inmates. The move to Leavenworth also further complicated Stroud's personal life. His family was still in Alaska, which isolated him even more from close personal contact. It is recorded that his mother would not make the trip to Kansas for nearly five years.

Leavenworth Federal Penitentiary in Kansas.

Despite his growing reputation as an inmate with a violent disposition, it was at Leavenworth that Stroud started to attend school. His initial foundation studies were primarily in Math and English, but later he undertook more intensive subjects such as astronomy and engineering. Self-study became a newfound outlet for Stroud's energy. But along with his legitimate studies, Stroud also pursued courses in the art of survival, and he crafted weapons under the cover of night from items he obtained covertly. Over the next few years, Stroud would land himself in solitary confinement several times, when guards discovered his crudely fashioned weapons and escape tools.

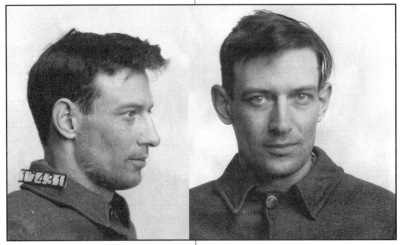

Stroud's first mug shot at Leavenworth, taken in 1912.

The next turning point in Stroud's prison career began on Saturday, March 25, 1916, where Stroud has recounted that he attended a motion picture show in the prison auditorium. Following the film, he was escorted to the mess hall for supper. Stroud would later contend that he didn't feel well that night, and had lost his appetite. To maintain order, correctional officers strolled up and down the aisles, carefully monitoring the activities in the mess hall. A prison guard named Andrew F. Turner made repeated passes by Stroud's table, allegedly delivering hard stares with every pass. Stroud apparently voiced his observation of the guard's behavior to a fellow inmate, thus violating the strict rule of silence. Turner quickly walked over to Stroud, and sharply demanded his prisoner number. Stroud had been put on notice.

The following day, March 26th, Stroud returned to his cell after supper to find a basket of fruit and candy on his cot. The armory guard had left a note for Stroud indicating that his eighteen-year-old brother Marcus had come to visit him from Alaska. Stroud learned that his brother had been turned away simply because he had been in the auditorium at the time, watching a movie. He was infuriated that Marcus had traveled all the way from Alaska, only to be told to come back the following Monday.

Stroud's second murder victim: Leavenworth Correctional Officer Andrew F. Turner. The victim's wedding photo was used during the murder trial.

Stroud would later claim he became worried that Turner would report him for breaching the silence rule during the previous meal, and that the warden would then take away his visitation privilege with Marcus. He asserted that his only option was to speak with

The dining hall at Leavenworth, where Turner was murdered.

Dining Hall, Federal Prison, Leavenworth, Kansas.

Turner again during the next meal period, to ask whether he had reported him. He said that he planned to plead with Turner for leniency.

Stroud recounted to fellow inmate Joseph Duhamel that during the next dinner meal, in sight of nearly two thousand fellow inmates, he raised his hand to talk with Turner. The true sequence of events that unfolded from this point onward is somewhat sketchy. The two started to exchange words, and Turner apparently drew his club from under his left arm. Witnesses state that Stroud went to grab Turner's club, and in a manic rage, pulled a homemade knife and thrusted it violently into Turner's upper chest. Turner fell hard to the cement floor, and gasped a final breath before succumbing to the fatal knife wound. All of the men in the mess hall rose to their feet in shocked silence.

Stroud had just murdered a guard, and everyone immediately knew the ramifications. Stroud would surely die by execution. The Captain of the Guard calmly approached the prisoner and asked him in a soft voice to drop his knife. As Stroud started to explain why he had stabbed Turner, he followed the Captain's order and dropped the bloodied knife onto the floor.

In the timeless classic *Birdman of Alcatraz* by Thomas E. Gaddis, Turner is described as a "*club happy screw*" who was in constant conflict with inmates, and he and Stroud are said to have had a long history of problematic encounters. However, it should be noted that there is no documented proof that Stroud and Turner had any prior conflicts beyond those stated here. At age twenty-six, Stroud had committed his second murder. This time Robert Stroud was destined to face the death penalty.

Stroud's trial began in May of 1916, with Federal Judge John C. Pollack presiding. Stroud entered a plea of self-defense, in front of what would ultimately prove to be an unsympathetic jury. The trial lasted for only a few weeks. On May 22, 1916, Stroud was sentenced to death by hanging, to be carried out on July 21st, 1916. However, the judgment was successfully appealed. That appeal began what would be a series of trials and petitions to have his death sentence reduced to life imprisonment. Stroud's mother Elizabeth hired two prominent attorneys and a skilled psychiatrist—but her attempts ultimately proved futile in the courtroom. On March 5, 1920, by order of Federal Judge James Lewis, Robert F. Stroud was sentenced to be executed on April 23, 1920. The hanging was to be performed at Leavenworth, and the prison began construction of his gallows.

Nevertheless, Elizabeth Stroud did not lose hope, and continued to launch large-scale campaigns to save her son's life. She enlisted the help of women's groups in letter-writing campaigns addressed to President Woodrow Wilson and the First Lady, hoping to secure an executive order commuting his sentence to penalty without death. Stroud's mother was unrelenting, and passionately lobbied the White House to review her son's case. She would base her line of reasoning on the argument that her son suffered from mental illness, and that this was a genetic trait that ran in her family. Stroud's older sister had been institutionalized, and his mother cited case histories in which other convicts had been granted leniency for mental disorders.

Her valiant efforts proved successful; only five days before he was scheduled to hang, Stroud was issued a commutation by the President of the United States. It read:

NOW, THEREFORE, BE IT KNOWN, THAT I, WOODROW WILSON, President of the United States of America, in consideration of the premises, drivers other good and sufficient reasons me thereunto moving, do hereby commute the sentence of Robert F. Stroud to imprisonment for life in a penitentiary to be designated by the Attorney General of the United States. Signed April 15, 1920, by President Wilson.

The commutation was a tough blow for prison officials. The official notebook of the Alcatraz Warden noted:

Rumors were that Stroud was to serve his life sentence in Solitary Confinement. There is no wording, phrases, or riders attached to indicate just how the subject is to serve while confined for the remainder of his life. Such detail was apparently left to the Attorney General or Warden of the Penitentiary.

With no specific direction from the courts or the President, Stroud would have to serve his time under the terms of his original sentence, which stated that he should remain in solitary confinement until his execution. The Warden issued a single statement to reporters that read: "*Stroud is to be kept in the segregated ward during his sentence, which is for life. He will never be permitted to associate with other prisoners, and will be allowed the customary half hour each day for exercise . . .*" It was a perfectly clear and concise message to the public—Stroud would pay his debt. But some recall that Bob Stroud actually embraced the idea of being kept out of the general prison population.

Stroud's fragile family unit began to dissolve after the trial was over. His parents divorced, and his father moved to California to look for work. Marcus Stroud was now leading an eccentric lifestyle in vaudevillian shows as *Marcus the Great*, performing a successful Houdini-like escape act, in which he made use of skills learned from his brother. He formally changed his name to Lawrence Gene Marcus, and traveled throughout the country with his act.

Now confined to a small and dimly-lit solitary cell, Stroud worked to better himself through correspondence courses, and also took to painting and sketching. There is little documentation regarding his activities prior to beginning his bird research. Stroud's biographer Tom Gaddis wrote that Elizabeth had taken a twelve-dollar-a-week job sewing satin casket linings, and that Bob started to craft holiday cards to help supplement his mother's income. It was also Gaddis who best captured the beginning of Stroud's interest in birds. He claimed that Stroud found a baby sparrow in the isolation yard during a storm,

Before Stroud began studying birds, he hand painted holiday cards to help support his mother.

(Opposite page) Stroud's cell with birdcages strewn about, as it was depicted in the biographical film, looked quite similar to his actual solitary cell at Leavenworth.

Hollywood Actress Betty Field's original contract to play the role of Stella in *"Birdman of Alcatraz."* The character was based on Della Mae Jones, and Field was required to furnish her own wardrobe for the film.

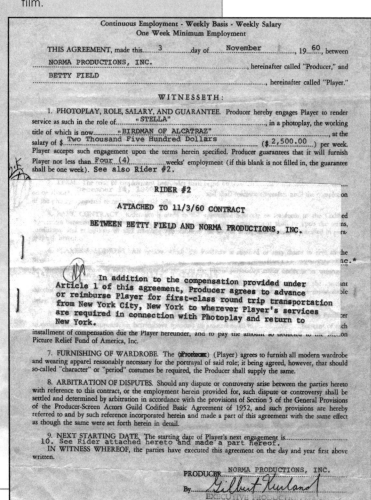

Continuous Employment - Weekly Basis - Weekly Salary
One Week Minimum Employment

THIS AGREEMENT, made this........3........day of........November........, 19..60.., between

NORMA PRODUCTIONS, INC. ...., hereinafter called "Producer," and

BETTY FIELD ...., hereinafter called "Player."

WITNESSETH:

1. PHOTOPLAY, ROLE, SALARY, AND GUARANTEE. Producer hereby engages Player to render service as such in the role of............ "STELLA".., in a photoplay, the working title of which is now............"BIRDMAN OF ALCATRAZ".., at the salary of $..Two Thousand Five Hundred Dollars.............. ($ 2,500.00) per week. Player accepts such engagement upon the terms herein specified. Producer guarantees that it will furnish Player not less than..Four (4)........weeks' employment (if this blank is not filled in, the guarantee shall be one week). See also Rider #2.

RIDER #2

ATTACHED TO 11/3/60 CONTRACT

BETWEEN BETTY FIELD AND NORMA PRODUCTIONS, INC.

In addition to the compensation provided under Article 1 of this agreement, Producer agrees to advance or reimburse Player for first-class round trip transportation from New York City, New York to wherever Player's services are required in connection with Photoplay and return to New York.

installment of compensation due the Player hereunder, and to pay the amount so deducted to the Motion Picture Relief Fund of America, Inc.

7. FURNISHING OF WARDROBE. The (Producer) (Player) agrees to furnish all modern wardrobe and wearing apparel reasonably necessary for the portrayal of said role; it being agreed, however, that should so-called "character" or "period" costumes be required, the Producer shall supply the same.

8. ARBITRATION OF DISPUTES. Should any dispute or controversy arise between the parties hereto with reference to this contract, or the employment herein provided for, such dispute or controversy shall be settled and determined by arbitration in accordance with the provisions of Section 5 of the General Provisions of the Producer-Screen Actors Guild Codified Basic Agreement of 1952, and such provisions are hereby referred to and by such reference incorporated herein and made a part of this agreement with the same effect as though the same were set forth herein in detail.

9. NEXT STARTING DATE. The starting date of Player's next engagement is..
10. See Rider attached hereto and made a part hereof.
IN WITNESS WHEREOF, the parties have executed this agreement on the day and year first above written.

PRODUCER NORMA PRODUCTIONS, INC.

By........Gilbert Kurland........
EXECUTIVE PRODUCTION MANAGER

PLAYER Betty Field

and brought the bird back to his cell to nurture it. Gaddis wrote that Bob would place a sock over the warm light bulb in his cell to create a warm bed, and would feed crushed cockroaches to the sparrow with a toothpick.

Stroud was persistent with his new hobby, and persuaded the warden to allow him to keep and breed birds in his solitary cell. He slowly grew obsessed with this newfound interest, and began collecting materials to make cages, and rearranging his cell in efforts to accommodate his birds. Visitors to Leavenworth were often paraded past Stroud's cell, and were shown the circus-style tricks performed by his small canaries. The guards however were not impressed by his antics. Former Alcatraz Captain of the Guard Phil Bergen stated that the majority of the custodial staff at Leavenworth felt some level of resentment toward the prison administration for allowing Stroud the freedom to breed canaries.

Stroud launched into a new project of assembling a small laboratory in his cell, soon after some of his birds fell ill and died. He had become completely consumed with his birds and their needs. He maintained an observation journal to help understand how the various diseases affected his ever-growing canary population. As well as documenting his observations in detail, he began experimenting with birdseed blends and other pharmaceutically based mixtures. Stroud was allowed to subscribe to a variety of bird magazines, and wrote remarkably detailed theories based on his observations.

Stroud's position as an observer of birds was unique. He lived with the birds in a single room twenty-four hours a day, and was unable to leave his study. Gradually the bird-fancying community began to take notice of this interesting new enthusiast named Bob Stroud. By late 1929 he was breeding his birds in a lucrative business, and he was able to fully support his mother. In addition to his bird sales, Bob also began marketing *"Stroud Effervescent Bird Salts" and "Stroud's Prescription and Salts No.1,"* which rapidly became popular remedies for bird ailments. He claimed that the "Stroud Specific" remedies were the first treatments ever marketed to treat avian diphtheria. Stroud performed detailed autopsies to study the causes of death for his stricken birds, and composed amazingly detailed illustrations of their organs and anatomy. What the public did not know was that the name and address in Leavenworth, Kansas, belonged to a twice-convicted murderer working from a solitary confinement cell in Federal prison.

STROUD'S DIGEST ON THE
DISEASES OF BIRDS

by robert stroud   "The Birdman of Alcatraz"

Della Mae Jones was a widowed middle-aged bird lover who exchanged letters with Stroud, after he won a bird that she had offered in a magazine contest. She became intrigued when she learned that the seemingly gentle bird enthusiast who had written so many articles on bird ailments was actually a Federal prisoner. Bob and Della began a steady stream of correspondence, and quickly developed a closely bonded friendship. After a few years of exchanging letters, Della traveled to Kansas to meet Stroud in April of 1931. After one visit, she immediately began making plans to move to Kansas City and help with the bird business. She moved into the same building as Elizabeth, and soon found herself in conflict with Stroud's dominant mother.

In late August of 1931, Leavenworth Warden Thomas White was directed by the newly formed Bureau of Prisons (BOP) to disband Stroud's mail order business, and to revoke all privileges that allowed him to keep birds in his cell. It was a serious blow to Stroud to have all of his avian studies brought to a halt by prison bureaucracy. He pleaded directly to the BOP with little success. Della and Elizabeth flooded newspaper and magazine offices with plaintive appeals and sorrowful press releases that Bob had written from his cell. Bob's plight drew national attention, and public empathy forced the BOP to change its position. The Bureau's newly appointed Director, James V. Bennett, who was only thirty-seven years of age, was sent to Leavenworth to negotiate new terms with Stroud. After Bennett's visit, the Bureau modified its ruling to state that Stroud would no longer be able to conduct private business ventures from his prison cell. His profitable business of bird remedies and breeding would now fall under the umbrella of prison industries. As a result, Stroud would go from making nearly ten dollars per bird to earning only ten dollars a month as a noncommissioned salary.

Though this was widely considered to be a harsh ruling, the Bureau did make several concessions. They classified Stroud as a special prisoner of the Bureau, and provided him with an additional cell adjacent to his own, with additional electrical outlets to help accommodate his research. The prison even went so far as to hire a construction crew to jackhammer a doorway between the two cells. Stroud once again became engrossed in his research and his self-taught explorations into avian behavior and scientific theory.

In 1933 Stroud's first book, entitled *Diseases of Canaries*, was published by Canary Publishers. It was based on his magazine articles and his independent research techniques, and was intended to be marketed as a comprehensive and authoritative text on canary care for owners and breeders. His well-written reference was as meticulously researched and structured as an avian encyclopedia. The book was, however, not without its critics. Some of the remedies were later found to be harmful to birds. It also drew skeptical responses from some circles in the veterinarian community. Stroud and his publisher E. J. Powell soon clashed over the book's lack of success. Stroud argued that it was Powell who had been responsible for the book's failure, and later attempted to file a lawsuit against him.

Meanwhile Stroud and Della grew closer, and they sought to marry, even though Stroud was incarcerated for life. After reading an out-of-date law book from the prison library, Stroud interpreted the Treaty of Paris, struck in 1803, as granting inhabitants of the Louisiana Purchase (which also included the Kansas territory) the right to marry by signing an officiated contract. Stroud typed the contract on the old Remington typewriter he had in his cell, and the following day their unofficial marriage was published in the *Kansas City Star*, in October of 1933. Della Mae then started penning her name as Della Mae Stroud. Prison officials were furious that Stroud was publicly maneuvering around prison regulations, and it was around this time that rumors started to surface regarding his eventual transfer to Alcatraz.

During the next few years, Stroud would lose many of his closest contacts, and would leave the cell that had been his home and laboratory for so long. In 1934 Elizabeth Stroud ceased her efforts to support the cause of her son, and relocated back to Metropolis, Illinois, along with her daughter Mamie. Elizabeth would have no further contact with her son, and she died only four years later in August of 1938. Meanwhile, prison officials began to complicate the visiting procedures for Stroud and Della, and by 1936 their relationship had also dissolved. To make matters worse, Ida Turner, the widow of the slain guard, had publicly criticized the Prison Bureau for giving Stroud special liberties, and had established a small group of followers.

In spite of these setbacks, the intrepid prisoner continued to conduct and expand his avian research. Stroud had been given professional tools to perform his autopsies, including scalpels and other sharp instruments. He had educated himself in the use of an old microscope that had been donated to the prison by Wesleyan University, and claimed that he had logged more than 3,000 hours at the eyepiece. It was also reported that Stroud had made a microtone from scraps of metal and a discarded razor blade, which could slice tissue to 1/12,000 of an inch—and that he had studied literally thousands of homemade slides. He had spent countless hours sketching his observations in detailed pen-and-ink illustrations.

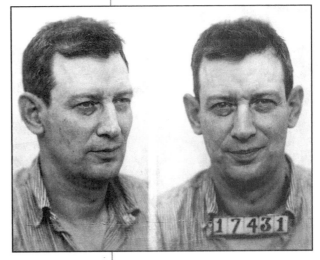

Stroud at Leavenworth in the early 1930's.

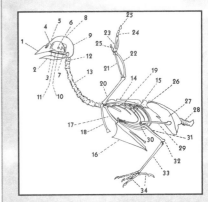

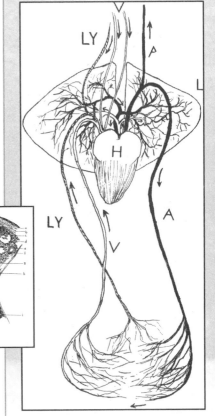

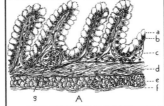

Stroud spent hundreds of hours studying and sketching his avian observations in detailed pen-and-ink illustrations. These sketches were assembled for his book *"Digest on the Diseases of Birds,"* published in 1943.

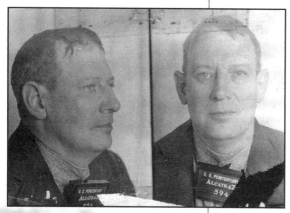
Stroud's mug shot, taken in December of 1942 at Alcatraz.

Then in the early morning of December 16, 1942, Stroud was awakened without any warning by two guards, who advised him to get dressed and prepare for reassignment to Alcatraz. Now fifty-two years old, and having spent over twenty years in his solitary confinement cell at Leavenworth, he would be traveling by train to California. Stroud had been restricted from taking any of his birds. His journey to Alcatraz would be one of wonderment, as he watched through the barred windows of the train. He was viewing a world that he hadn't seen in nearly twenty years.

Stroud arrived on Alcatraz on December 19, 1942, and would now be known as AZ-594. He bypassed quarantine and was immediately taken to the Treatment Unit with all of his accustomed privileges revoked. There would be no birds on Alcatraz, and no special visitors, and the press would be left with only rumors about the famous prisoner. Stroud was assigned to Cell #41 in D Block, located at the far end of the uppermost tier. His cell on Alcatraz was considerably smaller than the one at Leavenworth had been, and his privileges were the same as those permitted to his fellow inmates, with the one exception that he was allowed to finish his manuscript on bird diseases. This change would mean a tough adjustment for Stroud, and he spent the majority of his time proofing the manuscript for his next book. Staff members at Leavenworth reported that they had found numerous contraband articles, including a still to make alcohol and various crudely fashioned knives—all carefully hidden within hollowed sections of his worktables.

In late 1943 with the approval of the Bureau, and with his brother Marcus acting as his agent, he self-published the 500-page reference entitled *Stroud's Digest on the Diseases of Birds*. Marcus had run advertisements in various bird hobby magazines, lobbying for advance orders. His efforts had proved successful, and he had thus acquired enough funds to publish the treatise, to favorable reviews. Though this book was written using scientific terms and was carefully indexed as an informational reference, it also served indirectly as a platform to communicate Stroud's personal opinions, which were sometimes overtly arrogant. In the introduction he attacked E. J. Powell, the publisher of his first book, by stating in part, "... *my former work, DISEASES OF CANARIES, was hastily executed and badly garbled in the hands of the publisher* ..." In this book he also contributed to his own image as a gentle bird doctor. In an interesting chapter discussing post-mortem examinations, Stroud wrote:

Years of work, of study, of careful observation; the lives of literally thousands of birds, the disappointments and heartbreaks of hundreds of blasted hopes have gone through these pages; almost every line, every word, is spattered with sweat and blood. For every truth I have outlined to you, I have blundered my way through a hundred errors. I have killed birds when it was almost as hard as killing one's own children. I have had birds die in my hand when their death brought me greater sadness than that I have ever felt over the passing of a member of my own species. And I have dedicated all this to the proposition that fewer birds shall suffer and die because their diseases are not understood.

The book itself created significant controversy within avian circles. Although it is widely debated whether his remedies were actually effective, he was still able to make scientific observations that would later advance research for the avian species. It is likely that his exhaustive observations were of more benefit to other practitioners with formal training in avian medicine than his remedy theories would ever be. Nevertheless, he was very much a pioneer in his own right.

Not long after the release of this book, the public lost interest in Stroud and his homespun campaigns. He would now spend the majority of his time on Alcatraz studying and learning several languages, including Italian and French. He was also honing his pointed interest in criminal law. He began work on another manuscript, which would be a 200,000 word analytic history of the Federal prison system. This manuscript became a new obsession for Stroud. He would spend years carefully printing his opus onto legal writing pads. The work was a lengthy manifesto that was highly critical of the prison system of the time, and it presented his own biased theories on penology.

Stroud also spent time playing chess with neighboring inmates, and boasting extensively about his endeavors while imprisoned at Leavenworth. Prison reports at Alcatraz continued to describe him as a troublemaker. In one report that required multiple-choice responses, the following items were noted regarding Stroud:

Interest and application: .... Very lazy and avoids work
Ability as worker: .... Poor
Attitude: .... Resistant / Obstructive
Disposition: .... Defiant / Agitator

In May of 1946, the bloodiest and most significant escape attempt ever to occur on Alcatraz left five men dead and several others severely injured. In the course of this explosive event, Stroud would further etch his name in the history of the island prison, as he negotiated with Lieutenant Philip Bergen to help bring an end to the cellhouse barrage of grenades and gunfire. Stroud also would donate several hundred dollars to the defense of the inmates who stood trial for the murder of a correctional officer during the escape attempt. Many believed that this was yet another way in which Stroud communicated his rebellious attitude toward the administration.

Robert Stroud is seen here in a rare photo reading in his wardroom cell in the Alcatraz Hospital Wing. Initially Stroud was forced to use a bedpan to relieve himself, until his attorneys successfully lobbied the Bureau of Prisons to install a toilet. Stroud spent eleven years locked down in this cell with only one visit to the recreation yard per week, usually by himself.

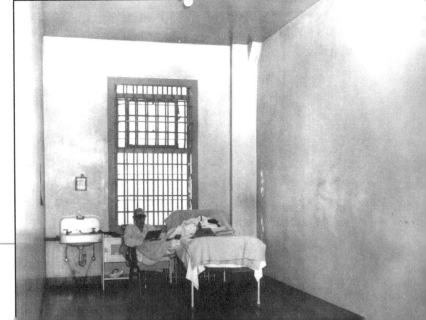

Stroud's cell as it appears today. Little has changed from the days when he occupied this cell. This area of the prison remains isolated, as tourists are not permitted to visit it.

In August of 1948 Stroud helped to instigate a hunger strike, which didn't sit well with prison officials. As a result, Warden Swope, who had the reputation of being a tough disciplinarian, ordered Stroud to be moved into a permanent deep lockdown status inside the prison hospital. Once again, without receiving any notice or explanation, Stroud was walked through the cellblock and up the stairs leading from the mess hall to a new cell.

His new cell was spacious, as it had originally been designed as a hospital wardroom to accommodate up to four patients. The room was painted a hospital style green, typical of the 30's and 40's. It contained little more than a sink, two beds, a steel utility cabinet for storage, and a hard metal-framed chair. For the first eight years there was no toilet, and Stroud was forced to use a bedpan designed for non-ambulatory patients, except on the occasions when he was permitted to leave his cell under escort to use neighboring facilities. The only benefit in these new accommodations was that the room had a window facing the Golden Gate Bridge, and it was also the only single-inmate cell with running hot water.

Stroud would spend his years there in strict isolation, with only an occasional opportunity to speak with an inmate, when his outer door was left open during sick call. His primary link to the outside world was from a sometimes-yielding officer who would consent to a game of chess or checkers, and would endure his longwinded stories and perverse opinions. Former correctional officer George DeVincenzi, who served at Alcatraz from 1950 until 1959, was assigned to the hospital ward for several years. George recalled that playing board games and interacting with inmates on a recreational level was firmly prohibited by the administration.

"I could only play a game of chess with Stroud if the West Gun Gallery Officer was a friend of mine. The gallery officer frequently peered through the port window located at the end of the hallway in the Hospital Ward to ensure I was okay. If the officer was a friend, I could sit at the front of Stroud's cell and play through the bars. It helped pass the time for both of us . . ."

Stroud spent his time in isolation absorbed in his manuscript, and in later years he began exhibiting signs of unusual behavior. During his weekly bathing periods, Stroud would shave all of his body hair, including his face, hands, and fingers. He was still considered dangerous by the correctional staff, and no one let down their guard with him. Lieutenant Bergen would later comment during an interview, *"I can't say I wasn't afraid of Stroud…We all used caution; knowing his capabilities."* Fellow prisoner Jim Quillen stated that he frequently conversed with Stroud when passing by his cell during the course of his duties as an X-Ray technician, a prestigious job assignment for an inmate. *"His outer door was usually open, and he would be standing there like an excited dog, anxious to talk with anyone who walked by.*" A memo addressed to correctional officers on December 20, 1948 sought to end Stroud's freedom to communicate with other inmates. It also implied that on various occasions he was found outside his cell wandering the corridor, and talking with other inmates:

> From time to time it has been noticed that Stroud is permitted to be out of his assigned quarters when other inmates are in the hospital for outpatient treatment. It has also been noticed that he has been able to carry on a conversation with other inmates. It is of course necessary to administer to him as prescribed by the Medical Department, out treatments, baths, taking care of toilet needs or for any other reason it may be necessary to take him from his quarters is to be done when there is no traffic in the Hospital. Under no circumstances is he to be taken from his quarters when an inmate from "D" Block is in the Hospital for outpatient treatment. He is not to be permitted to carry on conversations with other inmates, and when he is out of his quarters he is to be under constant surveillance by a custodial officer.
>
> Signed,
> R.H. Tahash
> *Captain*

Stroud was also allowed fewer yard privileges than were allotted to the general population at Alcatraz, and his walks to the recreation yard were usually carried out when no other inmates were in the area.

Prison Officers' reports typically portrayed Stroud as a difficult inmate to manage, even while in segregation. One example was a disciplinary report written on June 19, 1951. The report submitted by Officer Robert Griffiths to Warden Swope and Associate Warden Madigan reads as follows:

> Violation: INSOLENCE-DISBURBANCE, Under instructions from the Eve. Watch Lieutenant E.F. Stucker, I told the above inmate that I was putting out his light after his treatment was completed. I put out his bright light and he leaped out of bed and switched it on again. I told him not to do it again and switched off the light. He again turned it on, saying, "He didn't give a fuck what Stucker said, the light stays on until midnight."

In 1955, when Robert Stroud had been in prison for over forty years, and had been all but forgotten by the outside world, Thomas E. Gaddis created one of the most intriguing human tales of the 20th Century — the grim story of the Birdman of Alcatraz. Gaddis had left his job as a teacher and probation officer in Los Angeles to chronicle Stroud's amazing life. He had become intrigued by Stroud's story, and had located Marcus in 1950. Marcus ultimately agreed to the idea of a book about his brother's life story. Gaddis acquired hundreds of letters from Stroud's correspondence, and conducted hours-upon-hours of interviews with

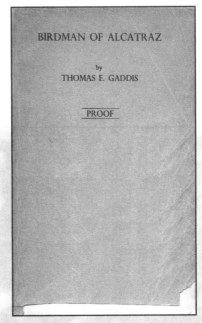

Working from an improvised office inside his small garage, Thomas E. Gaddis penned a book that would become an American Classic— *Birdman of Alcatraz*. Stroud was never permitted to read his own biography or to see the motion picture, for which lead actor Burt Lancaster was nominated for an Academy Award.

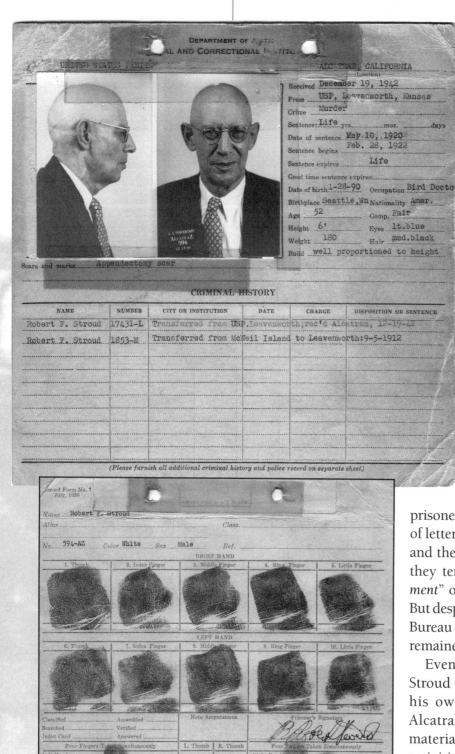

Marcus, extracting every possible detail. While the book relied heavily on second and third-hand information to reconstruct Stroud's side of the story, it appeared to be tangled with a plethora of accurate and fact based material, at least from Stroud's perspective.

In 1951, still early on in his research for the book, Gaddis wrote an article about Stroud for *Cosmopolitan Magazine*. The article helped to finance his project, and once again, public interest started to drift toward Stroud. Working from a manual typewriter in an improvised office in his garage, Gaddis knitted together a classic American tale that would capture the attention of a nation. Gaddis' book, *Birdman of Alcatraz*, was published in 1955 and became an instant success. It also launched a national crusade for the prisoner's release. The public wrote thousands of letters to the President of the United States and the Attorney General, denouncing what they termed "*the government's cruel punishment*" of Stroud, and demanding his release. But despite this exhaustive public crusade, the Bureau of Prisons was unyielding, and Stroud remained in isolation.

Even more interesting was the fact that Stroud himself was restricted from reading his own biography. The strict policy of Alcatraz prohibited inmates from reading materials that referenced any crime-related activities. Morton Sobell, known as the famous "atom spy" and co-defendant of Julius and Ethel Rosenberg, resided on Alcatraz for five years. He later recounted that he was the only inmate on Alcatraz who received the magazine *Scientific American*, and that an article featuring Stroud slipped through the censors in September of 1957. Sobell managed to have the article smuggled to Stroud up in the hospital ward, and this would be one of the first printed biographies he would read on the subject of his own life. Jim Quillen also stated that while he wasn't certain, he had heard that individual pages of the Gaddis book had been slipped to Stroud over a period of several years.

The years of seclusion ultimately took their toll on Stroud, and he attempted suicide twice. His physical health also started to deteriorate visibly. He suffered lengthy bouts of depression, and there were rumors of his failure to thrive. On July 13, 1959, while being escorted to the recreation yard, Stroud was stopped and notified that he was being transferred once again, and was directed back to his cell. After spending seventeen difficult years on Alcatraz, Stroud was to be moved to the Medical Center in Springfield, Missouri. He would arrive there on July 15th.

Stroud was euphoric with his new environment in Springfield. In a brief letter to his attorney Stanley Furman, he wrote in part:

> "I have already been told that I have the run of my ward, have met old friends, one going back to 1913, and have seen my first TV. I have twice as much space to walk as I had in the yard at Alcatraz. I am out in the ward up to 10:00 P.M. and I have a night call button in case of illness."

In addition to being moved to a low security area of the medical prison, he was also given a private room in which he could open and close his own door. He was able to walk the vast grounds of the prison and spend time basking in the sun, which he had not been allowed to do since the beginning of his imprisonment fifty years ago in 1909. In addition to seeing his first television set, he was also able to listen to radio broadcasts freely. Stroud took employment as a bookbinder in the prison library, and then as a tanner in the leather shop. Phyllis Gaddis, the daughter of the famed writer, later wrote that Stroud had made her a hand-tooled purse with his initials stamped on the face when she was a young girl.

Stroud being led to court in Topeka, Kansas in 1959, to appeal his sentence.

A fellow inmate named Joseph Duhamel also took a keen interest in Stroud's tale. He spent two years with Stroud helping to document his story "*in his own words*" for a magazine article that would later appear in *Saga Magazine*. The article was so popular that the issue quickly sold out, and became the magazine's only second print run in its history. To avoid detection by prison officials, Duhamel purchased a World Almanac, and each day he would write notes while Stroud dictated to him in the prison yard at Springfield. Duhamel stated that he used oxalic acid, a chemical employed to treat leather, as a type of invisible ink. The agent would become visible with the application of heat from a clothing iron. Duhamel published the article following his release from prison.

In 1958, 20th Century Fox entertained the idea of making a movie chronicling Stroud's life, but later dropped the project under pressure

List Of Personal Books Of Robert Stroud #594-az Stored In "A" Block

Atlas of Avian Anatomy—Chamberlain.
Stroud's Digest of the Diseases of Birds—Stroud.
Annual Review of Biochemistry—Vol. VIII 1939, Vol. I 1940, Vol. I 1941, Vol. III 1943, Vol. IIII 1944, Vol. XIV 1945, Vol. IV 1946.
Handbook of Hematology, Vols. I, II, III, IV.
Textbook of Biochemistry, 3rd Edition by Harrow.
Yearbook of Agriculture for 1936 and Vol. For 1943.
Annual Review of Physiology: Vol. I, 1939; Vol. II, 1940; Vol. III; 1 941;Vol. IV, 1942; Vol. V, 1943, Vol. IV, 1944; Vol. VII, 1947; Vol. VIII, 1946; Vol. II, 1945.
Fundamental Principles of Bacteriology—Snell
Gould's Medical Dictionary, 4th Edition.
Diseases of Poultry—Giester, 1944
Perspectives of Biochemistry—Cambridge, 1937.
United States Dispensatory, 24th Edition.
Veterinary Medicine (Paperbacks) 19 copies.
Symposia in Quantitive Biology—Gold Springs Bio. Laboratories, 1942
Practical Methods in Biochemistry—Cambridge, 1937.
Biology of Bacteria—Henrici, 1939.
United States Code, Title #8 and Title 9 in one Vol.
United States Code, Title #18 (Paper).
15 Pamphlets University Articles on Birds & Bird Diseases.
Approximately 50 lbs of personal and legal writings in Bores 8½ inches X 14".
1 Box Legal Papers.
1 Bundle Personal Correspondence.
1 Box Business Correspondence.
University Courses in Bacteriology, Part 1 & 2.
1 Box Containing Manuscript to "The Seeds of Destruction"—30 Individually Bound Chapters.
1 Box Containing Manuscript of "The Mulberry Bush", 28 Individually Bound Chapters.
1 Box Containing Manuscript of "The Band Wagon," 22 Bound Chapters.
1 Box of Personal Childhood Biography.
1 Box Containing Manuscript of "The Voice From The Grave"—18 Bound Chapters.
2 Boxes of Original Manuscripts of "The Voice From The Grave" and "The Band Wagon."

This inventory was taken in April of 1959, just four months prior to Stroud's transfer to Springfield.

from the Prison Bureau. Actor Burt Lancaster had reportedly become immersed in Gaddis' book on Stroud, and he lobbied United Artists to join forces with his own production company, Norma Productions (named after his second wife Norma Anderson), to make what he considered a very important film. United Artists finally agreed, and provided a budget of $2,650,000, with shooting to begin in late 1960. Lancaster would soon become obsessed with the project, and he eagerly assembled his film-making team. This team included Cameraman Burnett Guffer (*From Here to Eternity*), who helped to create a cinematographic tone that seemed to capture the essence of Stroud's dark world. The film's producers, Stuart Millar and Guy Trosper, who had also adapted the screenplay, spent nearly $200,000 of their budget building mock sets of Leavenworth and Alcatraz on Columbia Pictures' back-lot in Hollywood, California.

The Bureau of Prisons denounced Lancaster for helping to glorify the actions of a murderer, and pledged to extend no support to the filming. Lancaster had also made attempts to visit Stroud, and Former Correctional Officer Clifford Fish recalled an episode when Lancaster demanded that he be allowed to dock his yacht next to Alcatraz and meet Stroud in person. It was communicated to Lancaster that he would not be permitted to dock at Alcatraz, and that if he approached without permission, his boat would be fired upon by tower guards. Reluctantly, Lancaster conceded.

The original director of the film was Briton Charles Crichton, but after only one month he was fired by Lancaster and replaced with John Frankenheimer. Lancaster had immersed himself in Stroud's very complex character, and the atmosphere on the set had taken on almost a symbolic significance; it was clear that this was the filming of a true epic. Lancaster would be forced to shave half of his head to accurately recreate the appearance of thinning hair, and complicated makeup procedures were used to capture the effect of the aging process over time.

Emotionally the filming was also very exhausting and taxing to the actors and film crew. In January of 1961, during the filming of the 1946 Alcatraz Riot at the Columbia back-lot, Burt Lancaster's brother John died suddenly of heart attack at the early age of fifty-five. It would prove to be an eerie and horrific scene, as the body was taken from the set on an ambulance gurney. Despite this horrible tragedy, the crew continued filming through what would later be described as a surreal event. Guffer would later comment that it had almost felt like he was sitting in the middle of a real riot, as the actors were in a deeply emotional state following the death of Lancaster's brother.

After the film was completed in February, and following initial screenings and an unsuccessful editing, it was decided that the opening segments would need to be rewritten and refilmed. Lancaster had made another commitment to film the movie *Judgment at Nuremberg*, and would need to fulfill this obligation before returning to work on *Birdman* in May of 1961.

Birdman of Alcatraz finally premiered in April of 1962. Lancaster, Gaddis, and Stroud's attorney Stanley Furman held press conferences at the various screenings, attempting to rally support for Stroud's release. Lancaster sent personal letters inviting guests to special screenings of the movie, stating:

". . . I would be delighted to discuss with you the inside details of an incredible epic story. The film, based on the life of the most defiant man I have ever read or heard about. Your understanding will begin when you read the enclosed material on Stroud the killer, convict, scholar, scientist. I am convinced that only by showing you the film personally and talking with you could you comprehend my deep involvement, emotionally and intellectually, with this man and his life."

Critics declared *Birdman of Alcatraz* a masterpiece, and Lancaster won an Academy Award® nomination for his portrayal of Stroud. Meanwhile, Stroud himself continued his legal battle for his own release. Attorney General Robert F. Kennedy had earlier issued a statement based on prior petitions and appeals, stating that he could not "*in good conscience recommend to the President that it would be in the public interest that Mr. Stroud's sentence be commuted.*" But Stroud refused to give up, and by coincidence, his return to court coincided with the film's release in Kansas City. Thomas Gaddis and Burt Lancaster attended the Kansas City hearing, and for the first time, Stroud and Gaddis were able to briefly shake hands without exchanging words. This would be the only time the two would ever meet.

Fellow prisoner Morton Sobell became a close friend of Stroud's at Springfield. Sobell would later write that several of the other inmates hated Stroud because of his eccentric behavior. Stroud himself would never see the classic film that had shaped his character in the public eye. However, it was rumored that he was able to watch Lancaster receive his Academy Award® nomination on TV, as well as a short clip of Lancaster's performance as the Birdman.

On the morning of November 21, 1963, Morton Sobell went to check on Stroud, who had failed to show up for their regular breakfast meeting in the small dining hall. Upon entering his cell, Morton discovered that Stroud had died peacefully in his sleep. Stroud's death was overshadowed in the national consciousness by the assassination of John F. Kennedy,

BURT LANCASTER

April 6, 1962

Honorable James V. Bennett, Director
Bureau of Prisons
H.O.L.C. Building
101 Indiana Avenue, N. W.
Washington 25, D. C.

Dear Mr. Director:

It is my great pleasure to invite you and your guest to join me at a special screening of BIRDMAN OF ALCATRAZ on Wednesday, April 25, at 8:00 p.m. at the Georgetown Theatre, 1351 Wisconsin Avenue, N. W.

A private supper party following the screening, across the street in the Rayburn Room of Billy Martin's Carriage House, 1238 Wisconsin Avenue, N. W., will give us the opportunity to meet once again.

The film, based on the life of one Robert Stroud, is the shocking story of the most defiant man I have ever read or heard about. Your understanding will begin when you read the enclosed material on Stroud, the killer, convict, scholar, scientist. I am convinced that only by showing you the film personally and talking with you could you comprehend my deep involvement, emotionally and intellectually, with this man and his life.

Moreover, you will have the opportunity to meet the two men who have done so much to bring the case of Robert Stroud into world focus, and who are exerting every effort today to free him - Tom Gaddis, a former probation officer whose book, "Birdman of Alcatraz," first revealed the startling story, and Stanley Furman, who has led in vain the legal battle to make Stroud a free man.

Please reply to Miss Whiston, District 7-0728.

I am looking forward to seeing you very soon.

Sincerely yours,

Burt Lancaster
Burt Lancaster

A personal invitation from Actor Burt Lancaster, inviting Bureau of Prisons Director James Bennett to a screening of *"Birdman of Alcatraz"* in 1962.

and the local Metropolis Illinois newspaper contained only a brief editorial, reading in part:

> Stroud, 73, was discovered dead at 5:45 a.m., at the center where Stroud had been confined for the past four years. Stroud was a former resident of Metropolis, and his sister, Mrs. Mamie Schaffer, still lives here. A brother, Lawrence Marcus of Honolulu, is the only other immediate survivor. Several cousins, nieces and nephews also survive him. Arrangements for the funeral are incomplete. The body will be brought to the Aikins Funeral home, and the services will be private. Prison officials said his death was due to natural causes.

At the time of his death Robert Stroud had spent over fifty-four years in prison, until then the longest Federal prison sentence ever served. Throughout his prison term, he never once expressed any remorse for his killings, and was said to have bragged to other inmates about the crimes he would commit if he were ever released back into society. Despite his external associations with affluent celebrities who believed he was no longer a threat, it is clear today that even some of his peers in prison looked upon Stroud as dangerous and unfit to return to society.

When passed a book of Stroud's *Digest on Bird Diseases*, I asked former Alcatraz inmate Jim Quillen if he had any final opinions on the book and on Stroud. Rather than offer any spoken opinion, Quillen pulled out a pen and wrote a small inscription on the inside cover, which read: "Knew Bob Stroud and think he was a smart man but a psycho." Perhaps the famed Public Enemy Number One and fellow inmate, Alvin Karpis stated it best in his 1980 memoir chronicling his twenty-five years on Alcatraz. He simply wrote:

> "...If I had the responsibility of deciding whether or not to release Robert Stroud I would have reached the same conclusion of the parole board."

Stroud's burial site at the Masonic Cemetery in Metropolis, Illinois. He is buried between his mother and his sister.

Alcatraz on Trial
The Life of Henri (Henry) Young

In 1941 the name of Henri Young would saturate newspaper headlines, with stories portraying the prisoner as a casualty of the strict regulations and unrelenting regimen on Alcatraz. Young's trial for the murder of fellow inmate Rufus McCain quickly turned into a debate over the appropriateness of confinement practices on Alcatraz. In the end, Warden Johnston found himself on the witness stand defending his correctional staff against allegations of physical and psychological abuse.

However, the premise that Henri Young was in fact a non-violent and passive inmate driven to murder by his years of confinement, allegedly in moldy and damp underground dungeons, was completely erroneous. In Warden Johnston's personal memoir of his life at Alcatraz, he described Henri Young as an "*alert, shrewd, intelligent, cunning, conspiring criminal with the exhibitionist's desire to dramatize his position and relate his misdeeds.*" Young's inmate file contains an unpublished and unfinished autobiography that he penned after the trial. His memoir reveals a horrendously disturbed and deeply troubled life, with torrid tales of youthful crimes, sexual obscenities, and many painful memories. He claimed to have witnessed the brutal suicide of a relative at only thirteen years of age. Henri Young would become one of the most incorrigible inmates ever to reside on Alcatraz.

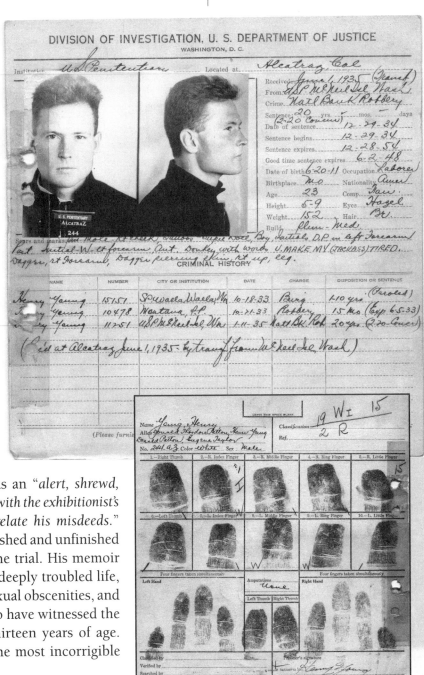

Henri Theodore Young was born in Kansas City, Missouri, on June 20, 1911. He described his own early life in a memoir he began writing during his years in prison:

I was born of Helen E. Young in Kansas City, Mo. Father David E. Young was present. Preceeding [sic] me by 2 years was one girl, Ruth E. Young. Additions were made to our family by one younger girl Naomi and one still younger boy David C. Young. This completes my family.

The true sequence of my earliest memories is hazy to me, but mother told me of fighting with a neighbor woman over some toys her boy and I had some trouble . . . Another time a cousin and I received a spanking for urinating in a garden. Then appears a ghastly white-faced boy who seemed delighted in eating caterpillars. This was repulsive.

We moved from Kansas City to northern Missouri. On a farm there father worked as a laborer. The owners and our family lived in one house. I one day drew a funny picture on the wall of the owners compartment in blue crayon. I would not admit to it. The woman owner was most gracious and I refused to become angry. Here was also a Negro woman cook from whom I would not accept food.

Father bought me a pony. This pony would head for his home each time I got on him. Mother came from a small stream dragging a turtle behind her on a rope, She cooked it. It was delicious. Our family moved from this place to a rickety old farm of our own. Once my uncle Bob whose farm was adjacent beat his horses terribly in full view of our farmhouse. I stood in the window and watched that, but God has been kind enough to obliterate all details of that horror . . . During hog killing time father became angry because his revolver would not shoot. He killed the hog with an axe. On the fence post nearby he placed the bladder of the hog commenting that "dried out it would make a good baby rattle".

I was definitely hurt when my parents one night removed pigeons from the cote, killed them and made me hold their warm bodies. I feel that pain now . . .

Young's memoir also indicates that his family lived in extreme poverty. It reveals that there were many mealtimes without enough food to go around the family table, that Henri only had one pair of trousers, and that he even had to wear his sister's dresses while his mother washed his clothes. In one instance, he recalled spending time at an aunt's impoverished home. He wrote that it was "*filthy*," and that "*hogs and chickens walked about inside the rooms.*" To make matters worse, a war was raging within the walls of his family's home. From his earliest childhood, his mother and father engaged into intense bouts of fighting. Henri recalled one fight so fierce that out of desperate fear he slept all night under the house. His aunt Amelia would later claim that young Henri had learned his future trade of burglary through the encouragement of his father. His parents divorced when Henri was only fourteen, and during this period his school grades steadily declined, until ultimately he failed nearly all of his courses. He later admitted to harboring deep resentment over his family's breakup, and his adult writings show that he was still troubled over the disintegration:

I loved mother, but then I hated her being so stately and elegant away from home to drop into a complacent attitude in our home. She had class, but would use it only on occasions, which threw her into painful blunders. Did she work to save that home? I know, know, know she did. But father, she did not know how to work. Neither did father. The marks of respect they should have observed were lacking. She hurt me often by denouncing my "false pride."

When Henri was seventeen, his mother remarried. Her new husband, Ammie Payne, had six children from a previous marriage, two of whom Henri refers to as *"blunted mentally."* This new marriage was extremely painful for Henri. He clearly adored his mother, and constantly referred to her kindness and immense beauty. But by his own admission, he carried a profound and unwarranted bitterness towards his new stepfather. There were ten children under one roof, and Henri confessed that this caused him a feeling of shame and embarrassment. However, Ammie was in fact quite good to Henri. He taught him how to drive his car, and worked hard at being a good role model—but Henri did not reciprocate. Instead, he began stealing Ammie's tools and selling them cheaply for spending money. He also started spending more and more time away from home. He later would comment: *"I seemed separated from my family."* He left home permanently at age nineteen.

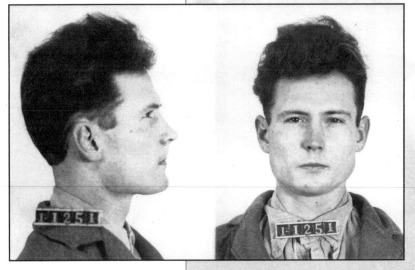

Henri Young in 1934.

After short stints of employment at odd jobs, Henri and his friend Elmer Webb rode freight trains west to California. Henri toured the Pacific Corridor as a drifter, eventually joining a traveling carnival where he worked in an animal sideshow for a middle-aged English couple. He indicated that he liked the work, which consisted of helping with show preparations, setting up the tents, and selling tickets. But after working for half a season, Henri lost interest in the carnival, and started taking on odd jobs while continuing to rove westward. He worked for a brief stint cleaning fruit drying equipment, and even spent time as a respected firefighter in Quincy, California.

Then on October 4, 1932, during an abrupt train stop in Miles City, Montana, Henri and his friend Elmer robbed a fellow drifter, leaving him tied and gagged in a boxcar. Two employees of the Pacific Railroad found the victim in a state of extreme hypothermia due to the near freezing weather. A 1935 police report describes how during his arrest, Young was asked if he had realized that the man could have frozen to death if the two workers hadn't found him in time. He is quoted as stating: *"He was a degenerate and I didn't think it would have been any loss to humanity if he had . . ."* Young was sentenced to serve a term of fifteen months at Dear Lodge Penitentiary in Montana.

Henri Young was released from prison in June of 1933, only to be arrested again on October 9th. This time he was convicted of burglary in the State of Washington, and was sentenced to the Walla Walla Penitentiary for one year. Young served his time, and was paroled on October 12, 1934. A few days after leaving prison, he obtained a gun and held up a man in the parking lot of the Pacific Hotel in Spokane. Young demanded that the man drive him to Cheney, Washington, where police spotted the car careening recklessly, and gave chase. Young would make his first escape from the police in a hail of gunfire.

Young would take part in another kidnapping on October 26, 1934, when he and his accomplice Sherman Baxter, who he had met while incarcerated at the Montana State Penitentiary, abducted a man in Spokane. They drove their victim to a remote location in or near the town of Medical Lake, Washington, and proceeded to rob him. They then wired him to a tree, where he remained undiscovered until the following day. The duo painted their stolen car a different color and drove to Portland, Oregon, where they picked up Jack Baker, a friend of Henri's from his carnival days in California.

On November 2, 1934, the twenty-three-year-old Henri Young and his two accomplices robbed the First National Bank of Lind, Washington. During the hold up, Young forced cashier J. F. Gibson onto the vault floor while they searched for cash. The three men made off with $405, and were captured only 40 minutes later. In the arrest report, Young was described as being arrogant and boastful of his crime. The three young men stood trial, and Henri's accomplices were sentenced to serve 15 years at McNeil Island, while Henri was sentenced to 20 years.

Prison life at McNeil was tough, and Young describes both fistfights and forced sexual encounters. He quickly became known as a difficult inmate, and on January 14, 1935, United States Attorney J. M. Simpson wrote to the Attorney General, pleading for Young's transfer to Alcatraz. Simpson wrote:

> I think Henry Young is the worst and most dangerous criminal with whom I've ever dealt, although I have prosecuted and hung two individuals on the charge of murder. Young's record is bad. He served a term of 15 months in the penitentiary at Dear Lodge, Montana, for the crime of robbery. The circumstances were very brutal.

Four months later E. B. Swope, Warden of McNeil Island and future Warden of Alcatraz, wrote to the Director of the Bureau of Prisons, also advocating Young's transfer to The Rock. Swope wrote that Young was *"fomenting as much trouble as he possibly can."* He went on to describe Henri further:

> I am sure that we are going to have more or less trouble with him. He is vicious, unscrupulous, and is a fomenter of trouble, but still has enough ingenuity to keep undercover. I would very much appreciate that if a transfer is going to be made, that it be done at an early date.

Young Arrives at Alcatraz

Henri Young arrived on Alcatraz on June 1, 1935, and became inmate AZ-244. Just one month later, Young would receive his first write-up for misconduct. Young and inmate Francis L. Keating were reprimanded for talking loudly during mealtime, which was strictly forbidden. His menacing attitude would only intensify under the strict regulations at Alcatraz. Young's first trip to solitary confinement began on July 17, 1935, when he refused to shake out clothes during a work assignment in the laundry. He was also put on a restricted diet, which usually consisted of one full meal a day with two additional servings of bread and water.

Young's arrogant and belligerent attitude only grew worse during his imprisonment on Alcatraz. On January 21, 1936, Young was written up for the following violations:

JOINING IN STRIKE, SUSPECTED OF SABATOGE, Having been reported by Jr. Officer Dixon as having dumped 400 lbs. of vegetables in the vegetable room of the kitchen basement, before walking out on the strike, he was immediately placed in open "D" Block, in a day or two later confessed dumping the vegetables. —C. J. Shuttleworth, Deputy Warden.

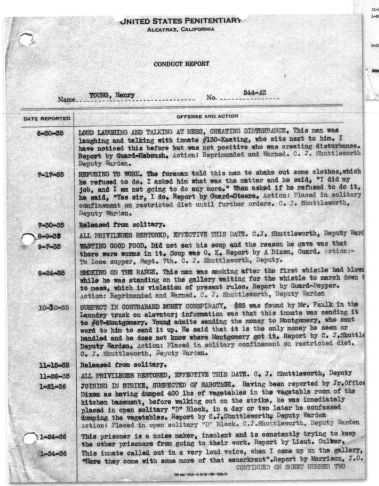

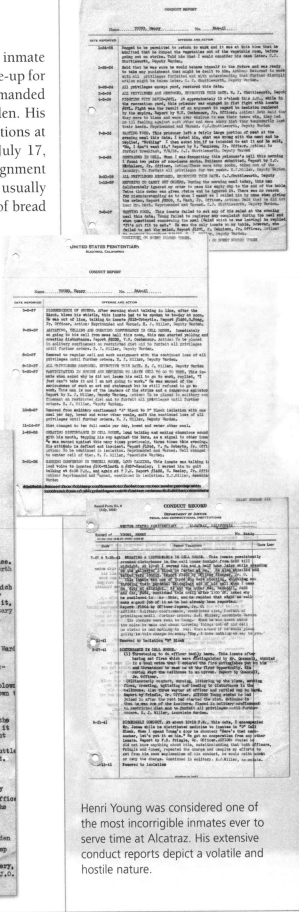

Henri Young was considered one of the most incorrigible inmates ever to serve time at Alcatraz. His extensive conduct reports depict a volatile and hostile nature.

Young would be identified as one of the leaders of the general work strike, and three days later he was written up as "a *noisemaker, insolent, and constantly trying to keep other prisoners from going to work.*" Henri Young had solidified his reputation as a troublemaker, and his antics were infuriating to the correctional staff. He would routinely yell threats, bang his tin cup against the cell bars, and throw items from his cell.

After spending almost four years on Alcatraz, Young joined in a failed escape attempt with fellow inmates Doc Barker, Dale Stamphill, William Martin, and Rufus McCain, on January 13, 1939. Young acted as a lookout while Martin and McCain quickly cut through the bars—the same bars that had been termed tool-proof in D Block. The attempted escape resulted in the shooting death of Barker. Rumors began circulating through the prison that at the last moment, McCain had revealed that he couldn't swim just when they made it to the water's edge, and had begged to turn back as soon as they launched their makeshift raft in the rough bay waters.

Young and the other conspirators were placed in the upper solitary cells in A Block. An entry in Young's conduct report states that he was moved from A Block to D Block isolation cell #587 on January 27, 1939, with continued loss of all his privileges. An official hearing on the escape resulted in Young forfeiting all 2,400 days of his statutory good time. His record does indicate a brief period in which no disciplinary action was taken. This lasted until July 9, 1939, when he again incited a disturbance, which was described as follows: "*Loud yelling, pounding, cursing and attempting to throw water upon an officer. This prisoner was yelling and pounding the front of his cell with the frame of his bed.*"

(Left) Attorney James MacInnis is seen here on the upper tier of A Block, examining the closed-front solitary confinement cells.

(Right) Henri Young's cell in the Solitary Confinement Unit, located on the upper tier of A Block. This photograph was used during Young's murder trial, in an attempt to illustrate the harsh confinement practices at Alcatraz.

Rufus McCain

Rufus Roy McCain was a thirty-seven-year-old offender who seemed to share many traits in common with Henri Young. McCain was the youngest of seven children. His mother died of an unknown illness when he was only five years old, and his father remarried two years later and moved the family to Broken Bow, Oklahoma. McCain's Alcatraz records reflect that he didn't get along with his stepmother, whom he later claimed had mistreated him, and that as a result he was constantly in conflict with his family. He left home at the age of eighteen, and took a job in the oil fields as a driller. McCain claimed to have lived a normal life in a middle class household, working for the same company until he was thirty-two years of age. His file indicates that he drank liquor frequently, and that his only recreational activity was watching motion picture shows.

McCain's first brush with crime occurred in 1931, when he robbed some Indian gravesites, taking valuable relics including jewelry and ceremonial artifacts. For this crime he was sentenced to serve one year at the Oklahoma State Penitentiary. McCain's prison time was served

Rufus McCain, the Alcatraz inmate murdered by Henri Young.

uneventfully, and upon his release, he was unable to find any means of employment. In late 1932 he robbed a bank, hoping to secure enough money to live comfortably until he could find work. He then committed another bank robbery in Oklahoma, and was quickly captured and sentenced to serve twelve years in the Arkansas Penitentiary. Rufus McCain was considered by the prison staff to be very resourceful, and he succeeded in making his escape in April of 1935. On May 14th he stole an automobile with accomplice Samuel Marion Day, and using firearms, they held up the Idabel National Bank in Oklahoma for $2,600 in cash. The two convicts kidnapped two bank cashiers as hostages, and Day was killed in a fierce gun battle following the robbery.

McCain was committed to the Federal Penitentiary at Leavenworth on July 11, 1935. He was subsequently transferred to Alcatraz on October 26, 1935, as a result of his violent outbursts, and because he was considered a high escape risk. McCain had lived a normal life into his thirties, but he had since developed into a violent prisoner. In May of 1938 he attacked inmate Ralph Sullivan with a knife fashioned out of brass. The knife was seven inches long, with edges resembling "*a razor's edge filed to a sharp point*," and the handles were wrapped with electrical tape. McCain was quickly spotted with the knife by correctional officer J. J. Lapsey, and he was stopped before he could inflict any injuries. He continued to build a record of violent acts and rebellion against his guards, and therefore he was no stranger to the solitary confinement cells in A and D Blocks. His conduct report would eventually begin to show similarities to Henri Young's. The two reports show several identical date entries for offenses and misbehavior.

There is no official documentation indicating a reason for the enmity that developed between Young and McCain. Rumors and subsequent trial testimony from other inmates would indicate that McCain had been making death threats toward Young following the failed escape. There were also the tales of McCain panicking during their escape attempt while in the water with Young, and begging to return to shore to reinforce their raft. Many would later state that Young directly blamed McCain for their capture, and for the death of Barker. Whatever the case may be, their animosity would result in a violent confrontation on August 29, 1939.

McCain had earned back work privileges, and had been given a job assignment as an orderly in D Block. On that day, as McCain passed Henri during his noontime lunch break, Young pulled out a dagger and lunged at McCain. Officer Joe Steere witnessed the altercation, and quickly slammed the cell door closed before Young was able to inflict any serious injury on McCain. Young was placed in isolation in D Block, and then transferred to an isolation cell in A Block on September 15, 1939. Less than two months later, Young was written up for violating the silence rule. Associate Warden E. J. Miller revoked his yard privileges for one week after Officer Richard Dennison reported that there had been "*continued talking even when I was known in the vicinity.*" On December 15, 1939, prison officers conducted a search of Henri's cell, and their findings would again place Henri into isolation. Officer M.A. Amende wrote in Young's conduct report:

CONTRABAND IN CELL. While searching this inmate's cell at 2 P.M. this date, I found a brass dagger hidden in the mattress. This weapon was fashioned from a brass plunger used to flush toilet. Report #1898 by M.A. Amende, Jr. Officer. ACTION: Denied any knowledge of the weapon. To be placed in solitary confinement on restricted diet and to forfeit all privileges until further orders. E.J. Miller, Associate Warden.

On September 15, 1939, Young was transferred to A Block with a small group of other inmates, and here he was moved into improvised, but fairly comfortable isolation quarters. Fourteen months later, Henri Young was released back into the general population of prisoners, and was given an immediate work assignment as a janitor in the furniture factory, which was then located on the top floor of the Model Shop Building.

Then on December 3, 1940, the feud that had been smoldering between Henri and Rufus McCain finally turned deadly. Henri, now twenty-nine years of age, fatally stabbed McCain on the second floor of the Model Shop Building. The events of McCain's Murder are best described in several accounts given by correctional officers who filed reports on the incident:

Memorandum

December 3, 1940

To: J. A. Johnston, Warden
From: E. J. Miller, Associate Warden

Re: ATTACK OF YOUNG #244-Az on Mc Cain #267-Az 12-3-1940.

Attached are copies of reports from the following officers relative to the attack by Young #244-Az on McCain #267-Az this date:

Junior Officer R. F. Spencer
Junior Officer Marshall G. Rose
Senior Officer Frank W. Mach
Paul M. Pone, Foreman Clothing Factory
Junior Officer Wesley C. Hicks
Lieutenant H. W. Weinhold

At approximately 10 A.M. this date Officer Ordway in the Captain's Office received a telephone call from Officer Pringle, Model Roof Patrol, that there was trouble in the Tailor Shop. Officer Ordway relayed the message to the Associate Warden and then the Associate Warden sent Officer Ordway to the work area. Lieutenant Weinhold called from the Tailor Shop and stated to the Associated Warden that #267-McCain had been stabbed in the abdomen by another inmate, Young #244, who came down from the Model Shop.

STATION HOSPITAL

UNITED STATES PENITENTIARY
ALCATRAZ, CALIFORNIA

Date ....12-3-40.

Memo: DEPUTY WARDEN.   DISCHARGED.

The prisoners listed below have been ~~admitted~~ to the hospital this date.

Number	Name
267	McCAIN, R.R.

Time 5.10 pm.   Total One.

Romney M. Ritchey, Surgeon (R)
Admitting Officer.
U.S.P.H.S.

Note: Make three copies, send two to DEPUTY WARDEN'S Office, retain one for hospital records.

FPI INC—FLK—1-17-38—500 SETS OF 2—10506

STATION HOSPITAL

UNITED STATES PENITENTIARY
ALCATRAZ, CALIFORNIA

Date 12-3-40.

Memo: DEPUTY WARDEN.

The prisoners listed below have been admitted to the hospital this date.

Number	Name
267	McCAIN, R.R.

Time 10.05 A pp.
A.A.   Total One.

Romney M. Ritchey, Surgeon (R)
Admitting Officer.
U.S.P.H.S.

Note: Make three copies, send two to DEPUTY WARDEN'S Office, retain one for hospital records.

FPI INC—FLK—1-17-38—500 SETS OF 2—10506

DEPARTMENT OF JUSTICE

UNITED STATES PENITENTIARY
ALCATRAZ ISLAND, CALIFORNIA

December 3, 1940

TO WHOM IT MAY CONCERN:

I have this date (DECEMBER 3, 1940) received from James A. Johnston, Warden of the United States Penitentiary, Alcatraz, California, the body of RUFUS ROY McCAIN, #267-AZ.

Signed V. A. Dinsmore
Deputy Coroner

Re. Henry T. Davis J.O.

Lieutenant Weinhold stated that the wound was bad and immediately a truck was sent to the work area to take inmate McCain to the Hospital. In the meantime Dr. Ritchey and Dr. Green were notified that an inmate had been stabbed and McCain was checked into the Hospital about 10:05 A.M.

The associate Warden tried to get a statement from McCain but could secure nothing of value.

E. J. Miller
Associate Warden

• • •

Alcatraz, California
December 3, 1940

Mr. E. J. Miller, Associate Warden

Subject: Inmate Young #244-Az Leaving Model Shop at 10:00 A. M.

From: R. F. Spencer, Junior Officer

At ten A.M. this date I made my count as usual, and every man was at his particular job and accounted for.

Immediately after making check I returned to stockroom where we were taking monthly inventory. Hardly, had I started working when upon hearing a whistle blast I stepped to a window to see what was wrong, I saw at first glance Officer Mach struggling with the above-named inmate on the landing in front of the shoe factory.

I went down and took charge of inmate Young and Mr. Mach returned to his shop.

Within a few moments Officer Rose relieved me of my charge, taking him to the cell house, I returning to my post.

Respectfully submitted,
/S/ R.F. Spencer
Junior Officer

• • •

December 3, 1940

Subject: Statement on inmate #244 (Young).

To: Associate Warden E. J. Miller.

Sir:

This morning, while on duty as a Work Area Officer, I was making my rounds of the Work Area Shops. At 10:00 A.M. I was in the Mat Shop, when I heard a whistle blowing, I ran out of the shop to see what the trouble was. I saw Mr. F. Mach's assistant, he told me that a stretcher was needed, as he thought he had an inmate dying in the Tailor Shop. I obtained the stretcher from the Work Area and I returned with it to the Tailor Shop.

Lt. Weinhold who had arrived on scene, ordered me to take Young #244 to the cell house. This I did without further trouble from Young.

Respectfully,
/S/ Marshall G. Rose, J.O.

• • •

November 3, 1940

To the Associate Warden:

I was on the third table sewing with my back to the Office. I heard a scuffle and a moan, turned around and saw McCain on the floor and Mr. Mach scuffling with Young and had an arm lock on him. At first I thought it was a fistfight, then I saw a knife in Young's hand and Mr. Mach called my attention to it. I took the knife away from him and while Mr. Mach, Mr. Hicks took Young out with the assistance of Mr. Rose and Mr. Spencer. I called up the Hospital to send a Doctor or an ambulance to the Tailor Shop. Lieutenant Weinhold was in the shop, before Mr. Rose came, I turned the knife over to Mr. Mach. This happened approx. ten A.M.

/S/ Paul M. Pone

• • •

MEMORANDUM

Alcatraz, California
December 3, 1940

To: E.J. Miller, Associate Warden
From: W.C. Hicks, Jr. Officer
Re: Stabbing of Rufus McCain #267

At 9:55 A.M. I entered the Tailor Shop and reported to Mr. Mach. He was just about to take a count as he said he took it a little before the hour. After the count, Mr. Mach suggested he show me around the Shop.

We had just started (between 10:00 and 10:05 A.M.) and he was showing me some pattern when I heard someone shout "hey, Ruf." Turning around, I saw Young #244 standing with a knife in his right hand and McCain fall to the floor.

Mr. Mach immediately grabbed him and threw him against the wall and at the same time twisting his right with the knife down to his side. He then called to Mr. Pone and to myself to get his knife. Mr.Pone got the knife in his hand and I found another slipped under his belt in front.
I ran out to the yard for help and while out on the stairs Mr. Mach brought out Young to the top of the stairs and Mr. Spencer (who had come up by this time) and I held him while the other officers were coming. The knife I found on Young I turned over to Mr. Mach.

/S/ Wesley C. Hicks

• • •

Alcatraz, California (corrected report submitted by Officer Hicks)
December 3, 1940

To: E.J. Miller, Associate Warden

From: W.C. Hicks, jr. Officer

Re: Stabbing of Rufus McCain #267

At 9:55 A.M. I entered the Tailor Shop and reported to Mr. Mach. He was just about to take a count as he said he took it a little before the hour. After the count, Mr. Mach suggested he show me around the Shop.

We had just started (between 10:00 and 10:05 A.M.) and he was showing me some pattern when I heard someone shout "Hey, Ruf, Hey, Ruf." Turning around, I saw Young #244 standing with a knife in his right hand and McCain fall to the floor. Mr. Mach immediately grabbed him and threw him against the wall and at the same time twisting his right with the knife down to his side. He then called to Mr. Pone and to myself to get his knife. Mr. Pone got the knife in his hand and I found another slipped under his belt in front.

I ran out to the yard for help and while out on the stairs Mr. Mach brought out Young to the top of the stairs and Mr. Spencer (who had come up by this time) and I held him while the other officers were coming. The knife I found on Young I turned over to Mr. Mach.

/S/ Wesley C. Hicks

• • •

Memorandum to the Warden:

Re: 267-Az, McCain, R.R.

The above captioned Inmate was brought to the Hospital at about 10:00 today, on a stretcher. It was found that he was suffering from an extensive wound of the right side of the abdomen. This wound was about five inches in length and entirely through the abdominal wall. The omentum was exposed and partly protruding. There was considerable oozing of blood from several points on the omentum. He was suffering also from shock. He was given immediate treatment to combat the shock and steps were taken to stop the bleeding. In the meantime Passed Assistant Surgeon George H. Hunt was called from the U. S. Marine Hospital in San Francisco and he came at once to the island and administered an anesthetic and the abdomen explored to determine the extent of the damage. It was found that no viscus was cut through but there were many bleeding points found in the region of the Hepatic flexure of the colon, in which neighborhood there was a hematome. All bleeding points found were ligated and the wound closed with drainage down to the peritoneum. The patient was returned to his room and shock treatment was continued with the administration of fluids and stimulants to support pulse.

As this is written at 2:45 P.M. the patient is still in shock and has a great deal of pain. His pulse is small and slow but his color is fairly good and he complains of great tenderness over the abdomen. Stimulation and fluids will be continued and sufficient narcotic to control the pain. This injury was received at the hands of another inmate. This man is still in a very critical condition and the prognosis is extremely guarded.

Respectfully,

Romney M. Ritchey, Surgeon (R),

Chief Medical Officer

• • •

United States Public Health Service
U. S. Penitentiary, Alcatraz, California
November 4, 1940

Memorandum to the Warden:

Re: 267-Az., Mc Cain, Rufus (Deceased)

The following statement is made to include the several verbal and written reports we made to you yesterday regarding the above captioned Inmate.

At about 10:00 A.M. yesterday the above captioned former Inmate was brought to the Hospital on a stretcher. He was pale and his skin was moist and his shirt was bloody and he was holding with both hands a mass which was protruding from a large opening in the abdomen. He was placed on the table and a hypodermic was given for the pain. The wound was cleansed and inspected and he appeared to be in severe shock from the exposure of the abdominal contents. Bleeding points in the omentum were tied off and active shock treatment instituted. His general condition did not greatly improve but it was imperative that further investigation of the possible injury to the intestines be undertaken. This was done by Passed Assistant Surgeon G. H. Hunt, USPHS, of U. S. Marine Hospital, San Francisco.

No penetrating wound or any viscus was found by considerable oozing of blood from the posterior surface of Omentum. The abdominal wound was then closed with drains into the sheath of the rectus muscle. During this procedure he was given intravenous glucose solution and when returned from the Operating Room his condition was considered fair considering everything, but the pulse was slow and weak. He continued to receive shock treatment and stimulation and some sedative to combat the pain, but by 2:00 P.M. his pulse was only 40 and very thready. He then appeared to rally a little and his pulse returned to 78 but still very small and weak. At about 3:00 P.M. he began to fail again with labored respiration and beginning cyanosis and in spite of continued efforts to relieve him of these symptoms, he died at 3:30 P.M. December 3, 1940, approximately six hours after the injury was received. The cause of death was surgical shock caused by a penetrating wound of the abdomen with internal injuries to the Omentum.

The Associate Warden and myself were both present at the time of death.

Alcatraz on Trial

Word of the murder spread fast, and newspapers quickly latched onto the story of Young's vicious act. In February of 1941, Young was transferred to the Federal Court Building in San Francisco for his arraignment, under heavy guard. Federal Judge Michael Roche was to preside over the case, and the acclaimed Federal Prosecutor, Frank Hennessy, stated from the beginning that he would seek the death penalty for Young. When Judge Roche asked Young if he wished the court to appoint an attorney for him, a soft-spoken Henri approached the bench and requested two young attorneys with no previous record of contributing to unfavorable convictions. Young stated: *"I should like to have the court appoint two youthful attorneys of no established reputation for verdicts or hung juries."* Henri seemed to be contemplating his fate in an inappropriately lighthearted fashion. He joked that although the attorneys probably would not

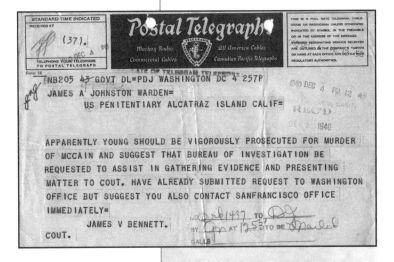

have a positive influence on his trial outcome, the case would at least provide them with some professional experience.

Roche conceded to Young's request, and appointed two youthful attorneys, former Assistant U.S. Attorney Sol A. Abrams, and James M. MacInnis, a recent graduate of Stanford University Law School. Young's trial began in April of 1941, making front-page headlines. The young attorneys would successfully weave a defense strategy which shifted the trial's focus, presenting Henri not as a cold-blooded killer, but as a victim of the extreme conditions at Alcatraz. MacInnis would argue that Young could not be held responsible for his actions after having served three years and two months in the *"most extreme isolation conditions."* He stated that Young had been driven to slay McCain by an *"irresistible impulse,"* and that he had become *"psychologically unconscious"* as a result of his long stretches of inhumane confinement.

The defense team called twenty-two inmates to testify on Young's behalf. These witnesses would further strengthen Young's case by listing allegations of horrible abuse and punishment. Among the many inmates to testify for Young were Harold Brest, who would himself attempt to escape from Alcatraz in 1943; Harmon Waley, a well-known inmate who was a principle architect of the famous Weyerhaeuser kidnapping; Burton Phillips, who in 1937 would viciously attack Warden Johnston in the dining hall on Alcatraz, rendering him unconscious; William Dainard; James Grove; William Dunnock; Carl Hood; and Samuel C. Berlin, who would offer some of the most compelling testimony of all.

Federal Judge Michael Roche.

(Left) Attorney James MacInnis.

(Right) Attorney Sol Abrams.

During Harmon Waley's testimony, the witness claimed that on one occasion he had been severely beaten by guards and thrown into the prison dungeon, simply for asking to be examined by a doctor and given medicine for an illness. Associate Warden Miller testified that Waley had been considered a troublemaker, and had spent frequent periods in isolation for his insolent behavior. Inmate James Grove testified that he was driven insane by conditions at Alcatraz, and that he had to be transferred to the Springfield Medical Facility in a straight jacket. Harold Brest said Young had confided to him that *"he couldn't stop himself from doing what he had done,"* and he also stated that in his opinion, the confining conditions at Alcatraz had contributed to the murder of McCain. Samuel Berlin claimed that many of the deaths that had occurred on Alcatraz had been the direct result of inmate conditions and treatment, specifically referring to inmate Ed Wutke, who had committed suicide.

Young himself also took the stand, articulately emphasizing his time spent in isolation, and the abuse he had suffered. He alleged ghastly beatings by Associate Warden Miller, claiming to have lost

FAMOUS INMATES

several teeth in the assaults. These allegations proved frivolous, since prison records showed no teeth lost during the period in question, and only one tooth extraction performed at Young's request in January of 1941. Young would further testify that he had been left to rot in the dark, damp, and moldy dungeon for weeks, without clothing, light, or running water.

William Wesley Dunnock also claimed to have received beatings from Miller, and stated that he was aware of other inmates being abused—once again mentioning Ed Wutke, whom Defense Attorney Abrams later claimed was "*driven to suicide*" because of his "*unbearable treatment*" on Alcatraz.

Associate Warden Miller testified that he had never assaulted Young, but that he had ordered him to isolation on several occasions due to his unruly conduct. Several witnesses came to testify on Miller's behalf, stating that he always maintained Warden Johnston's policy of proper and fair handling of the inmates. Further testimony was introduced to prove that Johnston had been one of the foremost advocates for inmate rights and rehabilitation. His record as Warden at Folsom and San Quentin supported his record of dedication to helping inmates reform. It was Johnston who had instituted work and educational programs for inmates at San Quentin, and he had brought the same curriculum to Alcatraz. When Johnston was called to the stand, he vehemently defended the Alcatraz regimen. Johnston believed in strict but humane reform, later writing: "*I believed that every human has some good spot, that I always tried to find that spot, and that I never closed the door of hope on any man.*"

Despite favorable evidence supporting Young's just treatment by Alcatraz personnel, the jury proved sympathetic to the defense, and delivered a verdict of "*involuntary manslaughter.*" The ruling enraged Judge Roche, who sternly voiced his displeasure with the jury's decision. On May 3, 1941, Henri Young was given the maximum sentence of an additional three years. Henri attempted to show his gratitude to Judge Roche

Henri Young seen in court, strategizing with attorneys James MacInnis (left) and Sol Abrams (right).

(Below) Henri Young during his famous murder trial.

Senior Correctional Officer Frank Mach is seen holding the murder weapons used by Young to kill Rufus McCain. Young used the thin-bladed knife to inflict the fatal wound.

Inmate Harold Brest during his transfer to the San Francisco courthouse to testify on behalf of Henri Young. Warden Johnston is standing on the left, and Bureau of Prisons Director James Bennett is on the right.

(Right) Inmate Harmon Waley being led to court during the Young trial. Note Alcatraz Correctional Officer Phil Bergen on the right. The inmate on the far left with his head lowered is William Dunnock.

(Left) William Dunnock

by thanking him for appointing the youthful attorneys. Young was sharply cut off by Roche, who hastily remarked to the prisoner and the court: *"I have known Warden Johnston for 30-years. I've watched him work. He is a man most respected in this community. I've visited San Quentin and Folsom unannounced and found everything in order. . . Warden Johnston's work is outstanding. He admits that he made a mistake letting you out of isolation, and letting you go to the prison workshop where you had a chance to murder."* Young listened with a coy smile, and then responded by asking, *"That's a rather perverse attempt to rehabilitate, don't you think Judge?"* Roche nearly rose out of his seat, looking sternly down at Young and stating: *"Some men deserve sympathy, but you're not one of those. You planned a cold and deliberate murder of an unfortunate human being."* Henri Young simply continued to smile.

When the jury requested an investigation of the confinement practices at Alcatraz, Bureau of Prisons Director James V. Bennett released a powerful statement to the press. Many historians consider it as the most revealing commentary on the jury decision in the murder trial of Henri Young:

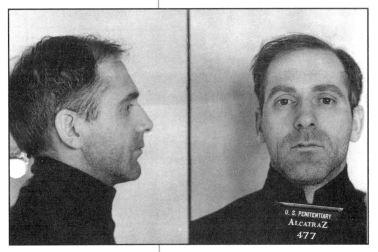

William Dainard

James Grove

Statement of James V. Bennett
Director, Federal Bureau of Prisons
May 4, 1941

I am firmly convinced that the jury which tried Henri Young for murder of another inmate in the Alcatraz Penitentiary has been misled about conditions at the prison. It has been impressed by tactics which sought to free Young through disparaging and attacking a public institution performing humanely and intelligently a most difficult task of protecting the public from hardened and unregenerate criminals. Young has been described by former United States Attorney Simpson and Federal Judge Stanley Webster of Spokane, Washington, as "the worst and most dangerous criminal with whom they ever dealt" and as "one who would not hesitate to kill anybody who crossed his path." He has been permitted to go virtually unpunished on the basis of inferences and innuendoes made by inmates whose criminal records and life histories show them to be wholly unreliable and who were able to commit deliberate perjury with impunity since they could not be reached by any effective legal process. From such information as I have about

(Below) Samuel Berlin

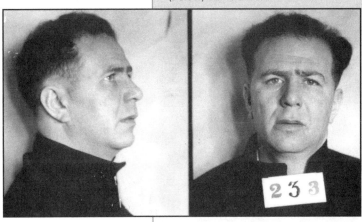

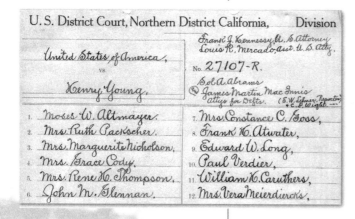

the trial, it is apparent that the Jury had before it no first-hand information or reliable evidence as to the policies or methods followed in the management of the most difficult and desperate group of prisoners ever assembled.

Alcatraz is now and always has been open to inspection and investigation by any qualified or properly commissioned person or groups. It has been inspected by Judges, Congressmen, penologists and qualified private citizens and has been approved as a modern and intelligent method of protecting the public from those desperate criminals who have proved themselves to be wholly intractable.

The institution, for instance, was recently inspected by experts of The Osborne Association of New York, a private philanthropic organization devoted primarily to the investigation of prisons, and was pronounced by them as well managed and operated and as using no improper system of discipline. Members of the Appropriations Committee of Congress in the course of their examination of our estimates also recently inspected the institution and made no criticism of its methods or operations.

I have visited Alcatraz frequently as have various members of our staff and know personally most of the inmates, including Young. As a matter of fact, I have on several occasions personally interviewed Young and done everything possible to obtain his cooperation. I have never found or had called to my attention any authentic case of brutality or inhumanity at Alcatraz.

Corporal punishment is prohibited in all the Federal penal institutions including Alcatraz. We stand on our record as the most modern and humane penal system in the world. I have every confidence in Warden Johnston. He is a just, humane, and intelligent prison warden capably performing the most difficult job any warden was ever asked to assume. The entire institutional staff has consistently displayed their courage, patience, and devotion to the public service. They deserve the support of every fair-minded citizen whose homes and safety they have helped to protect.

The statements made by the prisoners so far called to my attention have already been carefully investigated by the Department [of Justice] and found to be wholly unfounded. When, however, a transcript of the testimony has been received, it will be carefully gone over as in every other case, and if any evidence or facts are found showing brutal or inhuman treatment, vigorous corrective measures will be taken.

Following the trial, Henri Young continued to be a difficult and violent inmate. He would serve several more years in solitary confinement, and he remained insolent toward fellow inmates and staff. One year after the trial, prison staff members started documenting the unusual behavior exhibited by Young. A report filed by Chief Medical Officer Romney M. Ritchey on May 14, 1942 states in part:

> The above captioned inmate who has been in D-Block for some time began showing peculiar conduct last night. The officer on-duty reported that about 5:00 P.M. he started tearing up all of his papers, mostly those he had prepared for Correspondence Courses, etc… He refused to speak to the Officer when addressed. Then he rolled up his mattress and placed it near the back of his cell and sat down on it with his head in his arms and back to the front of his cell . . .

The staff on Alcatraz noted that Young had taken an interest in psychology, but they couldn't be sure whether his new behavior resulted from a legitimate mental disorder, or was simply contrived. There were several documented episodes when Young was found sitting for several days in a near catatonic state, not moving, and refusing to eat meals delivered to his cell. Over the years this condition seemed to worsen, with an increase in the frequency of the sporadic episodes, which usually lasted for a few days. Nevertheless, he continued to be an incorrigibly difficult inmate.

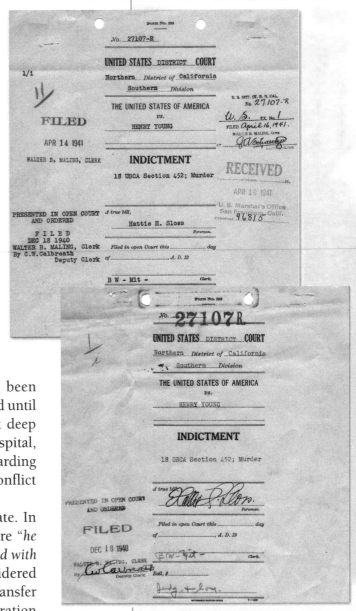

On April 11, 1944, Young instigated a bitter fistfight with inmate Joe Cretzer, who would later murder a correctional officer and injure several others during the escape attempt of 1946. Then on February 27, 1945, inmates Rufus Franklin and Willis Coulter attacked Young in the recreation yard, inflicting a minor stab wound to his back. The inmates had used a kitchen knife that had been sharpened into a dagger. Young remained hospitalized until March 8, 1945, with a puncture wound that went deep into his scapula. Following his release from the hospital, he was returned to D Block. When interviewed regarding the attack, Young would offer no reason for his conflict with Franklin and Coulter.

Young's mental condition continued to deteriorate. In June of 1948 he was admitted to the hospital, where *"he postured, stared, and didn't talk to personnel, but talked with other inmates."* Although his condition was considered suspect, Warden Swope finally received orders to transfer Young to the Springfield Medical Facility for the duration

Institution Alcatraz

DISCIPLINARY REPORT

Name Henry Young _____ No. 244-AZ

Living Quarters Cell 1 ___ Work assignment D Block Iso. __ How Long 7-11-42

Violation Fighting. This inmate stopped Cretzer #548 in the Yard at (9:00 A.M.)
this morning and both began fighting. Kyle #547 came to aid Cretzer. I pulled
Kyle and Young apart.

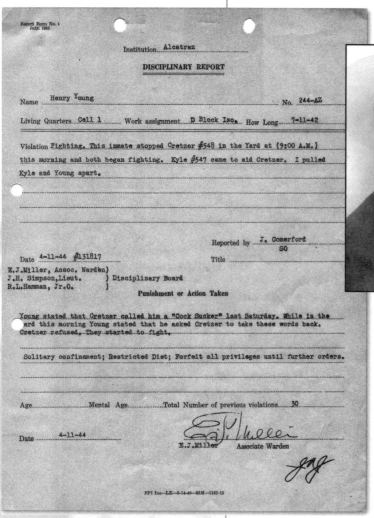

Reported by ___ J. Comerford _____
SO

Date 4-11-44 #131817 ____ Title _____

E.J.Miller, Assoc. Warden)
J.H. Simpson,Lieut.   ) Disciplinary Board
R.L.Harman, Jr.O.   )
        Punishment or Action Taken

Young stated that Cretzer called him a "Cock Sucker" last Saturday. While in the
yard this morning Young stated that he asked Cretzer to take these words back.
Cretzer refused. They started to fight.

Solitary confinement; Restricted Diet; Forfeit all privileges until further orders.

Age ____ Mental Age ____ Total Number of previous violations 30

Date 4-11-44 _____

E.J.Miller Associate Warden

FPI Inc—LK—5-14-40—85M—1163-13

(Above) A disciplinary report describing a fight between Henri Young and Joseph Cretzer. Cretzer, one of the primary conspirators of the 1946 "Battle of Alcatraz," would die during the failed escape attempt.

(Above right) Willis Coulter

of his prison term, and he was sent there on September 13, 1948. The staff at Springfield conducted exhaustive examinations, but they were unable to render an accurate diagnosis or to determine whether he was feigning his illness. Throughout his stay at Springfield Young was considered a model inmate, and he seemed to adjust well to his new environment.

When Young's Federal sentence expired in 1954, he was turned over to the Washington State Penitentiary at Walla Walla to begin a life sentence for an earlier murder conviction. A special progress report dated September 2, 1954 indicates that Young was already planning for his release, and intended to work for a trucking company in Kansas as a shipping clerk. Young was finally paroled in 1972. He subsequently violated his parole by failing to report his status, and despite comprehensive searches, Henri Young disappeared and was never to be seen again. Young's attorney James MacInnis, along with his wife would die tragically in a fatal car accident in 1979.

Coroner F. 1103

STATE OF CALIFORNIA,
City and County of San Francisco

CORONER'S OFFICE
Telephone DOuglas 0461
Telephone DOuglas 0462

THE PEOPLE OF THE STATE OF CALIFORNIA TO *Henri Young # 244 az*
Alcatraz Island

We command you, that all business and excuses being laid aside, you be and appear, before the undersigned, Coroner of the City and County of San Francisco, at Coroner's office, 650 Merchant Street, between Kearny and Montgomery Sts., on

TUESDAY 10th day of DECEMBER ____ 19 40 at 9 45 ____ o'clock A. M.,

to testify upon an inquest then and there to be had on the body of *Rufus Roy McCain* Deceased, and hereof, fail not at your peril.

WITNESS THE HAND OF THE CORONER,
this 4th day of DECEMBER ____ 19 40

JOHN J. KINGSTON, M. D.
Coroner.
By V. A. Dinsmore ____ Deputy.

FILED
APR 24 1941

District Court of the United States

WALTER B. MALING, CLERK

NORTHERN DISTRICT OF CALIFORNIA
SOUTHERN DIVISION

RECEIVED
APR 10 1941
o'clock ____ M.
U.S. Marshal's Office
San Francisco, Calif.

THE UNITED STATES OF AMERICA
                                    }
HENRY YOUNG

vs.

No. 27107 R
Criminal 46813 485
(Criminal)

19

THE PRESIDENT OF THE UNITED STATES OF AMERICA

The Hollywood Version

Fifty years after Young's trial, Warner Brothers Motion Pictures released a powerful drama that claimed to chart the true story of Henri Young, and was entitled *Murder in the First*. The film would succeed in making Young a legend, but it would not present an accurate portrayal of his life and crimes. The film itself was a great dramatic achievement for the filmmakers, but the script written by Dan Gordon was almost wholly fictional. Henri Young's own autobiographical writings, in which he describes his adolescence and his descent into a life of delinquency, fully contradict the movie's portrayal of him as a teenaged orphan sentenced to Alcatraz for stealing $5 from a grocery store in order to feed his starving sister.

The film featured some of the industry's most prominent filmmakers and actors. The executive producer was David L. Wolper, who had previously produced such films as *Willy Wonka and the Chocolate Factory*, and the first documentary ever nominated for an Academy Award, *The Race for Space*. Director Marc Rocco was a young visionary who successfully captured the depth and darkness of the prison. Seasoned actor Kevin Bacon starred as Henri Young in a chilling portrayal, and Christian Slater played his principled and idealistic young attorney. The film also featured actor Gary Oldman in the role of the Warden of Alcatraz.

Shooting for the film began in 1994. During the thirteen-week shooting schedule, the production team for *Murder in the First* spent more than two weeks on Alcatraz to complete the interior and exterior shots. The logistics of filming on location at Alcatraz also proved challenging for Rocco and his crew. The whole company had to be brought over on boats and barges, and the actors' dressing rooms were the actual hospital ward cells once occupied by inmates. Using photographs from the penitentiary era as a reference, crews repainted sections

A letter describing Young's condition after he was found with self inflicted wounds, following an attempt to sever his Achilles tendons.

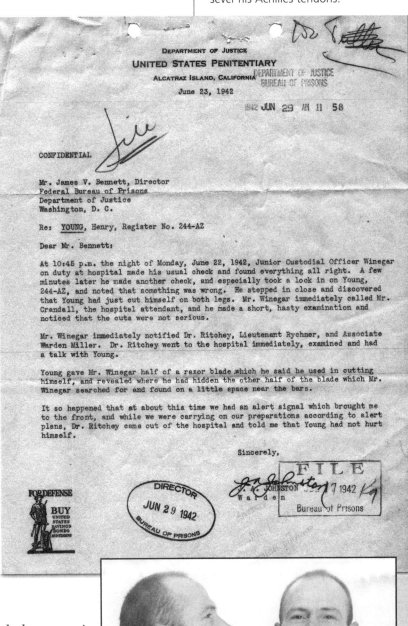

(Right) Young at the Springfield Medical Facility in 1948.

Henri Young in 1954.

of the cellblock to resemble its original state. The cinematographer's visual plan was to create a design in which images would emerge from a stark and desolate landscape. The Alcatraz dungeons were re-constructed for the film on soundstages in Los Angeles, as were the courtroom sets.

Filming around the public tours that were regularly scheduled on the island also proved challenging to the filmmakers. Sometimes they were forced to film scenes with hundreds of onlookers attempting to get a glimpse of the actors, and often interfering in the shots. The film presented the island prison of Alcatraz itself as one of the main characters in the drama. Despite its inaccurate portrayals and its lack of historical verisimilitude, the film still managed to capture some of the imagery and essence of Alcatraz. The film turned Henri Young into both a societal legend and a fictional martyr of the American Justice System.

Hollywood Actors Kevin Bacon (Young) and Christen Slater (Young's attorney), in a fictionalized version of Young's trial portrayed in the Warner Brothers motion picture *"Murder in the First."*

Machine Gun Kelly

Like Al Capone, George "Machine Gun" Kelly has endured as one of the most famous gangsters of the prohibition era. "Machine Gun" was born George Kelly Barnes on July 18, 1895, to a wealthy family living in Memphis, Tennessee. His early years as a child were uneventful, and his family raised him in a traditional household. The first sign of trouble began when he enrolled at Mississippi State University in 1917, to study agriculture and engineering. From the beginning, Kelly was considered a poor student. He was constantly in trouble with the faculty, and spent much of his academic career attempting to work off demerits earned for troublesome behavior.

It was during this time that Kelly met Geneva Ramsey, the daughter of a contractor for whom he worked part-time. Kelly quickly fell in love with Geneva, and made an abrupt decision to quit school and marry. The couple had two children, and in an effort to make ends meet, Kelly worked in various construction camps around the Memphis area. He worked long hours with little compensation for his time.

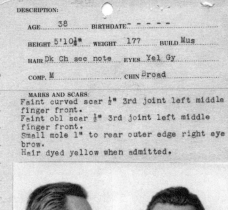

RECEIVED	Oct. 14, 1933	DESCRIPTION:		
FROM	WD-Okla-Okla City	AGE	38	BIRTHDATE _ _ _ _
CRIME	Kidnaping	HEIGHT 5'10½"	WEIGHT 177	BUILD Mus
MILITARY OR CIVIL	Civil	HAIR Dk Ch see note	EYES Yel Gy	
SENTENCE:	Life Yrs. life Mos. Days	COMP. M	CHIN Broad	
DATE OF SENTENCE	Oct. 12, 1933			
BIRTHPLACE	Ill	MARKS AND SCARS: Faint curved scar ½" 3rd joint left middle finger front. Faint obl scar ½" 3rd joint left middle finger front. Small mole 1" to rear outer edge right eye brow. Hair dyed yellow when admitted.		
RELIGION	Cath.			
EDUCATION	College 2			
OCCUPATION	Hosp. Attendant			
MARRIED	Yes CHILDREN 2			
RESIDENCE	Ft Worth, Texas			
HABITS	Smokes, drinks mod.			

, a prisoner in the United States Penitentiary, Leavenworth, Kansas, do he Warden of said Penitentiary, by himself or his authorized representative, to open and examine all letters, papers and and all express packages which may be directed to my address so long as I am a prisoner in said Penitentiary.

Geo R. Kelly.
Signature of Prisoner.

George "Machine Gun" Kelly

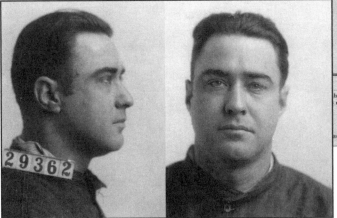

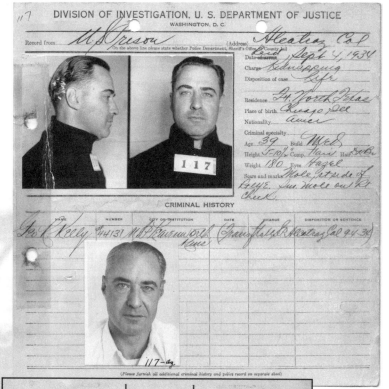

Kelly and Geneva were struggling financially, as the construction work was failing to provide enough money to support their family. Distressed and broke, Kelly left his job to seek other ways to make ends meet. The strain proved to be overwhelming. At nineteen years of age, he found himself without steady work and separated from his wife. Kelly then hooked up with a smalltime gangster, and started a new venture as a bootlegger. He seemed to enjoy the financial rewards of his new trade, as well as the notoriety.

But along with this new success came the difficulties of working in the underworld. After being arrested on several occasions for illegal trafficking, Kelly decided to leave Memphis with a new girlfriend and head west. This was when he adopted the alias of George R. Kelly, to preserve the reputation of his upstanding family back home. Kelly's luck varied, with hugely profitable scores alternating with several unfortunate mishaps. By 1927, Kelly had already started to earn a reputation in the underground world as a seasoned gangster, having weathered several arrests and various jail sentences. In 1928 he was caught smuggling liquor into an Indian Reservation, and was sentenced to three years at Leavenworth Penitentiary.

After serving another long sentence at the State Penitentiary in New Mexico in 1929, Kelly gravitated to Oklahoma City, where he hooked up with a smalltime bootlegger named Steve Anderson. Kelly soon fell for Anderson's attractive mistress Kathryn Thorne, a seasoned criminal in her own right. Thorne came from a family of outlaws, and had been arrested for various charges ranging from robbery to prostitution. She was twice divorced and her second husband had been a bootlegger, who was later found shot to death under suspicious circumstances. The official determination held that his death was a suicide, but many people (including one of the investigators) had long suspected that Kathryn was involved, because of assorted threats she had been known to make against him. Kelly and Kathryn became inseparable, and they married in Minneapolis in September of 1930.

Up until he began his relationship with Thorne, Kelly had been a relatively smalltime criminal. But Kathryn's influence soon became obvious, as Kelly's crime sprees would win him the prestigious status of "Public Enemy Number One." Kathryn purchased a machine gun for

Kelly, and pressured her husband to practice. It was said that her purpose was premeditated — she was a master at marketing her husband to underground circles and to the public. She was known to take the spent gun cartridges and pass them around to acquaintances at many of the underground drinking clubs, introducing them as souvenirs from her husband "Machine Gun Kelly."

Many historians and fellow inmates of Kelly believe that Kathryn was the creator of the "Machine Gun Kelly" image, and she became known as the mastermind behind several of the successful small bank robberies that Kelly pulled off throughout Texas and Mississippi. In August of 1933, the FBI published "wanted" posters describing Kelly as an "*expert machine gunner*," and thus creating a public frenzy that would later place Kelly into the history books.

In July of 1933 Kathryn and George Kelly plotted a scheme to kidnap wealthy oil tycoon and businessman Charles Urschel. A formal report written on January 16, 1934 by FBI agent Paul Hansen described the events in detail:

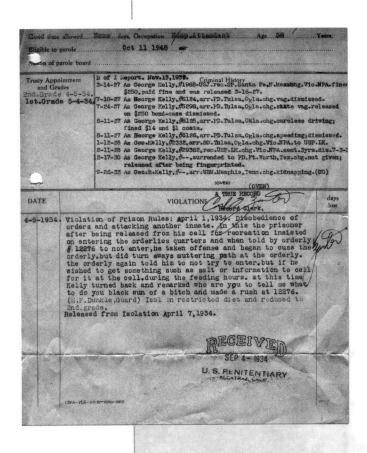

On the night of July 22, 1933, Mr. And Mrs. Charles F. Urschel were engaged in a social bridge game with their friends, Mr. and Mrs. Walter R. Jarrett in the sun-parlor on the ground floor of the Urschel home in Okalahoma City, Oklahoma. At approximately 11:15 P.M., two widely known underworld characters entered this room; one was Albert L. Bates, who is known by that and many other names throughout the United States as a thief, burglar, bank robber, safe blower, extortionist, and kidnapper, and he carried an automatic pistol; and the other was George Kelly Barnes, more familiarly known as George Kelly and "Machine-gun Kelly," who is known throughout North America as a liquor runner, thief, robber, kidnapper, and close associate of organized underworld gangs. And he carried a machine gun. The latter demanded, "Which is Urschel? We want Urschel." As no one present replied, Barnes there upon said, "Well, we will take them both." Then, by force of arms, they marched Urschel and Jarrett out through the backyard to a car, which was parked in the driveway of the Urschel home. Shortly after leaving the Urschel home, the abductors took from the possession of Urschel his wallet containing about $60.00 in cash, and from Mr. Jarrett his wallet with approximately $50.00 in cash. At a point about ten miles northeast of Oklahoma City, the kidnappers had satisfied themselves, from an examination of the identification cards in each wallet and a statement made by Mr. Urschel, which was Urschel, and Jarrett was released.

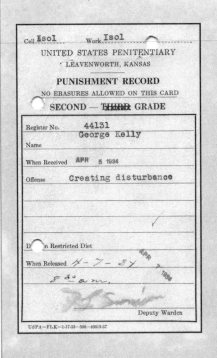

Approximately twenty miles from Oklahoma City, the victim of this kidnapping was blindfolded by the use of adhesive tape. He was driven at a fair rate of speed over what seemed to be country roads until a short time before daybreak Sunday Morning, July 23, when he changed to another car on the farm of R.M. Coleman near Stratford, Oklahoma. After about thirty minutes wait, the abductors proceeded with their victim to the farm home of Robert Green Shannon, father-in-law of Barnes, near Paradise, Texas, in whose home he was held that night. The next morning he was removed to another house located on the Shannon farm about three-quarters of a mile from the R.G. Shannon home, where his son, Armon Crawford Shannon, lives. He was held in this house in a miserable blindfolded condition, being always chained to the chair, and part of the time being forced to sleep on the floor, while a continuous guard watched over him with two .45 caliber automatic pistols. When one of the abductors was not guarding their victim, he was guarded by R.G. Shannon, who is known as Boss Shannon, or his twenty-two year old son, Armon Shannon.

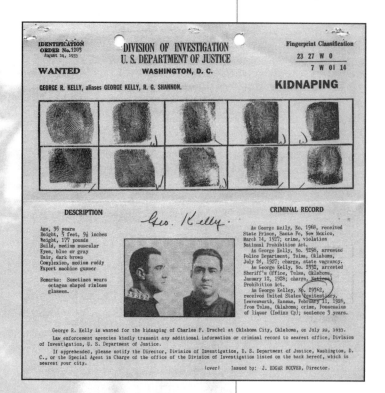

The kidnappers demanded that Urschel designate a friend who would act as a intermediary with his family and John G. Catlett of Tulsa, Oklahoma, was selected to make this contact. Through a well planned arrangement of having the Urschel family place an ad in a daily Oklahoma City Newspaper, negotiations were opened, and E.E. Kirkpatrick, friend and business associate of Urschel, was instructed to take $200,000 in used Federal Reserve Twenty Dollar Notes in a light colored tan handbag and in a certain directed manner and appointed time, should go from Oklahoma City to Kansas City, Missouri where he was to receive further instructions. As directed in Kansas City, about 5:30 P.M., July 30, 1933, Kirkpatrick using the appointed name of E.E. Kincaid, took a yellow cab to the La Salle Hotel and walked west on Linwood Boulevard a short distance where he was met by a man identified as George Kelly Barnes, who took the bag and told him Urschel would be released shortly. A record of the number on each of these ten thousand bills had previously been made.

About 3:30 P.M., July 31, 1933, Mr. Urschel was taken from his temporary imprisonment in the Armon Shannon home by one of the abductors and they were later joined by the other and he was driven to Norman, Oklahoma, and released about 10:00 P.M., being instructed by the kidnappers to hire a car and proceed immediately to his home and not communicate with any officers concerning his experience. This Urschel did. It was not until after a very detailed and extensive investigation, which covered the entire United States, was made that the identity of the kidnappers and those who conspired with and assisted them was established.

After splitting the ransom money with their accomplices, Kathryn and Machine Gun started hopping from state to state, trying to stay ahead of law officials. Aided by the clues that Urschel was able to provide, the FBI raided the ranch and arrested one of the other conspirators. The bills that had been used for payment in the ransom had traceable serial numbers, and the Central Bureau of Investigation (now the FBI) started a nationwide search for the ringleader, who they now suspected was George R. Kelly.

George and Kathryn bounced around in several states, with Chicago as their main hub. Both dyed their hair to conceal their identities, and they enjoyed a lavish lifestyle. After several weeks in hiding, the couple finally made their way back to Memphis to stay with longtime friend John Tichenor. On the morning of September 26, 1933, Memphis police and FBI agents surrounded the Tichenor house, and then made a violent forced entry. It is said that this was the moment when Kelly coined the phrase: "*G-Men, please don't shoot.*" Kelly was found still in his pajamas and badly hung over from the prior evening's drinking binge, while Kathryn was still in bed asleep. The couple was quickly flown to Oklahoma, where they stood trial and both received life sentences. Another accomplice, Albert Bates, was taken into custody in Denver, Colorado, on August 12, 1933, on an unrelated charge. At the time of his arrest, he had in his possession $660.00, later identified by Bureau agents as part of the Urschel ransom money.

Albert Bates

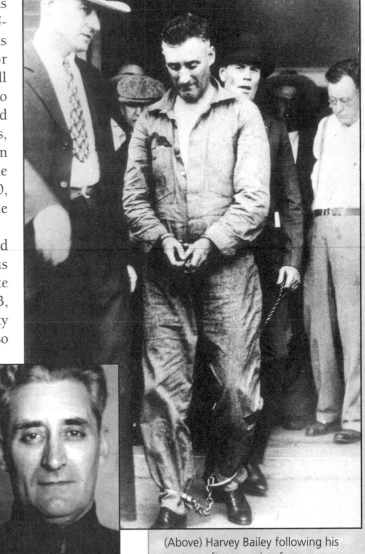

The FBI then raided the Shannon residence and took into custody Harvey J. Bailey, a notorious criminal who had escaped from the Kansas State Penitentiary at Lansing, Kansas, on May 30, 1933, where he had been serving a sentence of ten to fifty years on a charge of bank robbery. Bailey was also wanted in connection with the murder of three police officers, a FBI Special Agent, and their prisoner. Eventually all of the accomplices were apprehended, and of all those involved in the kidnapping, six were given life sentences.

Kelly was transferred to Leavenworth in Kansas, and Kathryn was sent to a Federal prison in Cincinnati. Kelly was arrogant toward prison officials, and he bragged to the press that he would escape, then break his wife out of jail, and they would spend Christmas

(Above) Harvey Bailey following his capture after escaping from a Kansas prison in 1933.

(Left) Harvey Bailey's Alcatraz mug shot.

(Right) Kathryn Kelly and George Kelly being led to court for sentencing in 1933.

(Below) George and Kathryn Kelly during their sentencing.

(Below) Following her conviction, Kathryn Kelly was transferred to the Federal prison in Cincinnati, Ohio.

together. It was decided that these threats should be taken seriously, and in August of 1934, Kelly and fellow inmates Albert L. Bates and Harvey J. Bailey were transferred by train from Leavenworth to Alcatraz. Arriving on September 4, 1934, they would be among the first prisoners received on the island. Kelly was now inmate #AZ-117, Bates was #AZ-137, and Bailey was #AZ-139.

In prison, Kelly constantly boasted about robberies and murders that he had never committed. Although this was said to be an apparent point of frustration for several fellow prisoners, Warden Johnson considered him a model inmate, and his life at Alcatraz was largely uneventful. He took a job as an altar boy in the prison chapel, worked in the laundry, and served out his time quietly. Warden Johnson noted that Kelly would become depressed when receiving mail from family members. He seemed to feel remorse for his crimes, and always felt that his wife Kathryn and their other accomplices were treated too harshly.

Inmate Willie Radkay, who occupied a cell next to Kelly, stated that he had many fond memories of getting to know him, and working together in the prison Industries along with Basil "The Owl" Banghart. Every day they would work side-by-side, enduring all of Kelly's "*big tales*." When asked about his most prominent memory of living next to Machine Gun, Radkay said that nearly every night

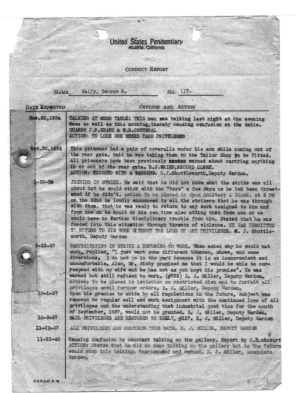

(Top, middle, bottom) George Kelly was transferred to Leavenworth Federal Penitentiary under heavy guard.

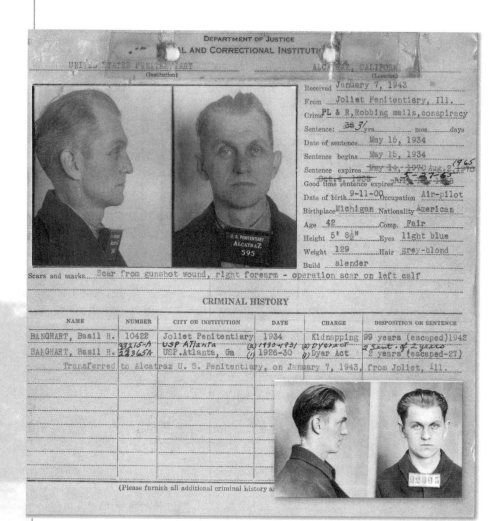

Basil "The Owl" Banghart and Machine Gun Kelly were close friends at Alcatraz.

George Kelly's Leavenworth mug shot, taken in 1951.

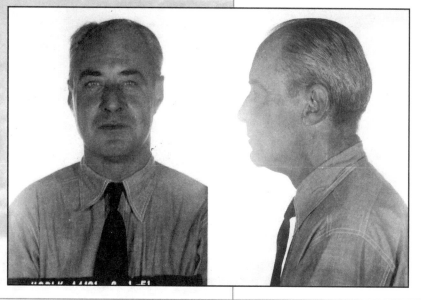

Kelly would accuse Willie of snoring, reach out of his cell, and slap him in the head with a magazine.

Kelly wrote several remorseful letters to Urschel begging his help in pleading his case. His letters provide a genuine sense of the pain and loneliness he suffered during his imprisonment on The Rock. In one letter written to Charles Urschel on April 11, 1940, Kelly penned perhaps some of the most profound observations ever written on the subjects of crime, and time served on America's "Devil's Island." He wrote in part:

I feel at times you wonder how I'm standing up under my penal servitude, and what is my attitude of mind. It is natural that you should be infinitely curious. Incidentally, let me say that you have missed something in not having had the experience for yourself. No letters, no amount of talk, and still more, no literary description in second-

From Geo. R. Kelly #117,   November 20, 1944.
Alcatraz Island, Cal.   To Mr. Francis Biddle, Washington, D.C.

Dear Sir,

About two years ago I talked with Mr. Hope Bennett concerning my being transferred to some other Institution. At the time he implied that, in my particular case, his hands were tied; that it was entirely up to the Attorney General. The inference was that Attorney General Cummings had instituted some ruling to the effect that if the question of my being transferred did arise, the decision was wholly up to him. What I should like to know is, does that ruling still stand, now that Mr. Cummings has been out of office for six years?

I am one of the original homesteaders of Alcatraz, having been here now for over ten years. There are only about eight or ten of us left who came out in the first shipments and I understand that at least five of them do not wish to be transferred either because they have relatives close by who visit them each month, or because they feel that their time is now too short to make a change.

Last week I talked with Warden Johnston and he was non-committal as to whether he would recommend my transfer but did suggest that I see Mr. Bennett when he next came to Alcatraz. In view of the fact that Mr. Bennett told me at my last interview that it was out of his hands, I thought it

Letters from Kelly to the Attorney General, requesting an immediate transfer from Alcatraz.

rate books, and books on crime cannot but be second-rate—could ever give you the faintest idea of the reality.

No one can know what it's like to suffer from the sort of intellectual atrophy, the pernicious mental scurvy, that come of long privation of all the things that make life real; because even the analogy of thirst can't possibly give you an inkling of what it's like to be tortured by the absence of everything that makes life worth living.

Maybe you have asked yourself, "How can a man of even ordinary intelligence put up with this kind of life, day in, day out, week after week, month after month, year after year." To put it more mildly still, what is this life of mine like, you might wonder, and whence do I draw sufficient courage to endure it.

To begin with, these five words seem written in fire on the walls of my cell: "Nothing can be worth this." This—kind of life I'm leading. That is the final word of wisdom so far as crime is concerned. Everything else is mere fine writing . . .

to get your advice . . . that I am trying to commercialize in my boy's name but I have two sons in the armed forces. My #1 boy is a First Lieutenant in the Air Corps and has been overseas for thirty-three months. My other son is a corporal in the medical corps and is now stationed at Camp Howze, Texas. My son-in-law has taught aeronautics and ground flying at the University of Oklahoma for over two years. I mention this merely to show you something of my background.

Regardless of what you have heard of Alcatraz it is far from being a pleasant place to do time. The climate is murderous and I, personally, have suffered from chronic sinus trouble for years. The recreation facilities are practically nil. I realize that is the way the department wants it, but to me it seems like an exceptionally wide discrimination is drawn between the men of Alcatraz and the men in the other Federal Institutions. I should like to be where I could read a newspaper and listen to the radio for a change after ten years here. If I were in Leavenworth or Atlanta my children could also visit me. I incidentally, both my conduct record and my work record are good here.

This letter is intended solely in the vein of one seeking advice, shall I go further into the matter with the Warden and Mr. Bennett or is it entirely in your hands? I should appreciate your advising me as to what steps to take.

Very truly yours,
Geo. R. Kelly - #117.

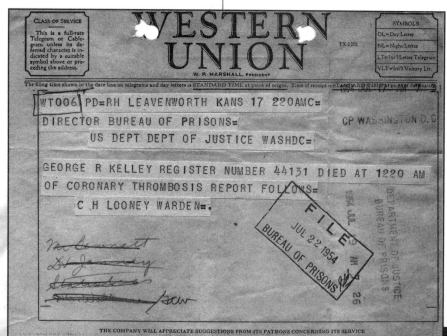

A telegram to the Director of the Bureau of Prisons, announcing George Kelly's death in 1954.

Charles Urschel apparently never responded to any of Kelly's letters. George "Machine Gun" Kelly would spend seventeen years on Alcatraz, and was returned to Leavenworth in 1951. Kelly died of a heart attack on July 18, 1954. Ironically, it was his fifty-ninth birthday. Kathryn was released from prison in 1958, and took a job at an Oklahoma hospital as a bookkeeper. Albert Bates died of a heart attack on July 4, 1948 while still an inmate at Alcatraz.

The last known photo of Machine Gun Kelly, taken just prior his death in 1954.

(Right) Kathryn Kelly playing the piano at the women's correctional facility in Ohio.

Morton Sobell

In March of 1951 Morton Sobell, known internationally as the notorious "*Atom Spy*," was brought to trial for conspiracy to commit espionage against the United States. He was the co-defendant of Julius and Ethel Rosenberg, and their court case remains one the most famous and controversial trials in American history. Their alleged acts were declared the "*Crime of the Century*" by J. Edgar Hoover, and the trial would result in the execution of both of the Rosenbergs. Sobell would escape the death penalty, but would receive a harsh thirty-year Federal prison term. In an attempt to apply one of the most severe punishments that the Federal prison system could impose, J. Edgar Hoover personally requested that Sobell be sent to Alcatraz for his alleged crimes.

In 1950 the Federal Bureau of Investigation arrested Julius Rosenberg, then an electrical engineer employed by the U.S. Army Signal Corps, and his wife Ethel, a political activist. They were indicted for conspiracy to transmit classified military information to a foreign power. During the course of their trial, the prosecution charged that the Rosenbergs had persuaded Ethel's brother David Greenglass, an Army Technical Sergeant at a top-secret governmental laboratory in Los Alamos, to furnish a Soviet agent named Anatoli Yakovlev with classified data on nuclear weapons. Greenglass had allegedly sketched schematics of the atomic bomb design, and provided several other key documents. It was revealed during the trial that he had full military clearance, with access to the most sensitive Defense Department data.

Morton Sobell was born on April 11, 1917, to Russian immigrants who had remained active in the Communist Party after immigrating to the United States. Morton met Julius Rosenberg while attending the City College School of Engineering in New York. Both men belonged to a young communist league, and were active in promoting their political views. After completing their studies, Sobell and another colleague, Max Elitcher,

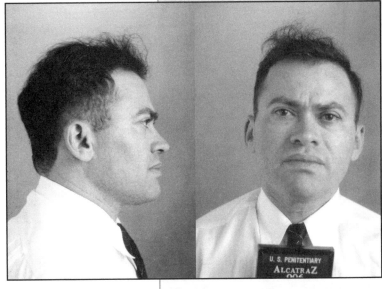

Morton Sobell

moved to Washington D. C., where they shared an apartment while working at the Bureau of Ordnance in the Department of the Navy.

Years later during the famous trial, the sole evidence that would be introduced against Sobell was the testimony of Max Elitcher. Elitcher had admitted to being a communist, attributing this to Sobell's influence. It was also through Sobell that he had become acquainted with the Rosenbergs, who he alleged were known to him as secret Soviet agents. He testified that he had acted as a courier between Sobell and Julius Rosenberg. Despite Elitcher's incriminating testimony, the prosecution failed to present any substantial proof that Sobell had any connection with atomic bomb research, and supplied no evidence of the alleged transmission of information on his part. Nevertheless, the prosecution asserted that an extensive spy ring had been in operation, of which Sobell had been a principle member. They built their case around his previous political and personal affiliations, and his connection with the Rosenbergs.

The case was further based on a decision Sobell had made in 1950, when two days before the Korean War broke out, he left with his family to seek sanctuary in Mexico—perhaps knowing that he would be sought in connection with the Rosenbergs. Initially he made no attempts to conceal his identity in his travels. He used his own name to book the flight, and to rent property during his stay in Mexico. But the fact that Sobell then assumed an alias to seek passage to Europe would prove seriously detrimental to his case. The prosecution was able to link Sobell further with the Rosenbergs' activities, because he departed for Mexico during the same time window in which Greenglass was paid by the Russians for transmitting atomic bomb secrets.

Although the evidence linking Sobell to the case was weak, the prosecution effectively persuaded the jury to convict him, stating in part: "*Sobell's conduct fits the pattern of membership in this conspiracy and flight from an American Jury when the day of reckoning had come.*" On March 29, 1951, the jury pronounced all three defendants guilty of conspiracy to commit espionage, and the Rosenbergs were sentenced to death. The judge asserted that while he was fully confident that Sobell had also engaged in espionage activities, he was bound to recognize the lesser degree of his implication. Soviet agent Anatoli Yakovlev managed to escape back to Russia before the F.B.I. could apprehend him.

Despite many court appeals and pleas for executive clemency, Julius and Ethel Rosenberg were executed by electrocution on June 19, 1953, at Sing Sing Prison in New York. They became the first U.S. civilians to suffer the death penalty in an espionage trial, and the controversial case received worldwide attention. Some supporters claimed that the political climate in the country had made a fair trial impossible, while others questioned the value of the information that had been transmitted to the Soviet Union, arguing that the death penalty was too severe in this case. President Eisenhower was unsympathetic and unyielding, stating: "*I can only say, that by immeasurably increasing the chances of atomic war, the Rosenbergs may have condemned to death tens of millions of innocent people all over the world.*"

"I AM INNOCENT"

Prisoner on Our Conscience

Morton Sobell, imprisoned in Alcatraz on a 30-year sentence, asserts his innocence and is fighting for a new trial. Millions of people believe he is telling the truth — that he is victim of a terrible injustice. Eminent Americans have declared that he was convicted on perjured testimony in an atmosphere of public hysteria. Our committee, made up of people who want to uphold justice in our country, asks YOU to look at the facts.

No Evidence

There was no documentary evidence — not so much as a scrap of paper introduced by the prosecution to prove Morton Sobell had committed a crime. The charge against him was "conspiracy to commit espionage," and he was tried in 1951 with Julius and Ethel Rosenberg. Sobell was convicted on the unsupported testimony of one witness, a man named Max Elitcher. **Elitcher admitted on the witness stand that he had previously lied under oath, and that he feared a prison sentence for perjury.** Would you want your fate to depend on the word of an admitted liar who stood to save himself by accusing you?

Trial Never Reviewed

Despite the illusion that the Rosenberg-Sobell case has been reviewed, it is a fact that the fairness of the trial has never been reviewed by the Supreme Court. As Supreme Court Justice Hugo Black said: "It is not amiss to point out that this Court has never reviewed this record and has never affirmed the fairness of the trial below." Surely a case of this magnitude requires a review.

Justice Demands New Trial

We say let there be a new trial so the full truth can come out. A man's life is at stake. Justice is at stake. Attorneys for Morton Sobell have new evidence that perjured testimony was used against Morton Sobell . . . President Eisenhower has authority to direct the Justice Department to agree to a new trial. Or he can pardon Morton Sobell, or commute his sentence to the six years already served. Will you do as thousands of others are doing? **Write a letter today to President Eisenhower, Washington, D. C., asking him to take favorable action.**

HEAR MORE FACTS at the

MEETING FOR MORTON SOBELL	FRIDAY, JUNE 22 — 8 P. M.
in memory of Julius and Ethel Rosenberg	HOTEL SIR FRANCIS DRAKE EMPIRE ROOM POWELL AND SUTTER STREETS

SPEAKERS: PROF. MALCOLM SHARP
MRS. ROSE SOBELL
WARREN K. BILLINGS

Admission: 50¢

Auspices: Bay Area Council of Sobell Committees

No other case in American history has had such global ramifications. The description of the Rosenbergs' executions reverberated throughout the world, and would forever call into question the cruel process of death by electrocution. The Associated Press printed a disturbing and vivid account of Ethel's death, which ultimately weakened public support for capital punishment.

Morton Sobell arrived at Alcatraz on November 26, 1952, as inmate AZ-996. His background as an engineer was not parallel to the criminal

Morton Sobell

histories shared by his new neighbors, and he seemed an unusual candidate for The Rock. The administration had worried that because of the nature of his crimes, Sobell could be targeted by the other inmates, who by nature were generally extremely patriotic. But Sobell was also Hoover's archenemy, and this would in fact earn him a special status amongst the inmate population. In his personal memoir entitled *On Doing Time*, Sobell recounted his experiences in seemingly unbiased detail. He wrote that the environment at Alcatraz was different from that of any other prison he had seen. The inmates seemed unusually curious, and the guard staff was openly courteous, initially going as far as to address him as "Mr. Sobell." Like most other new "*fish*," he was placed in B Block for a quarantine cycle, and it would be several weeks before he was given a job assignment.

Sobell also commented that the population at Alcatraz seemed unusually subdued when he first arrived, and that the prison was "*like a tomb of living souls.*" Unlike many of the other inmates, he was able to adjust to his environment at Alcatraz, and used his idle cell time productively by reading extensively from the prison library. Sobell was eventually moved to cell #C-156, located at the far corner of C Block. Warden Swope frequently stopped at Sobell's cell when giving tours to special visitors. He would later reside on the top tier in cell #C-342, where it was significantly warmer, and he had a spectacular view of the Golden Gate.

On March 7, 1958, Sobell was received at Federal Penitentiary in Atlanta, and then on May 30, 1963 he was transferred to the Medical Facility for Federal Inmates in Springfield Missouri. At Springfield Sobell developed a close friendship with Robert Stroud, the "*Birdman of Alcatraz*," and would later be the one to find him dead of natural causes in his cell. Sobell was transferred to the Federal Penitentiary in Lewisburg, Pennsylvania on January 30, 1965, and was finally released on January 14, 1969.

Roy Gardner

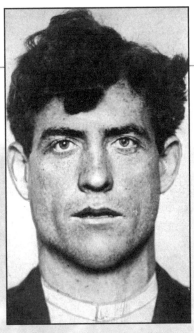

Roy Gardner

I n the late 1930's Roy Gardner was known as one of the last notorious train robbers from the old western era, and in the first years after Alcatraz became a Federal prison, Gardner's name was synonymous with the island institution. He spent two years incarcerated on the island from 1934 until 1936, and after his ultimate release in 1938, he peddled a small informational book and narrated boat tours for San Francisco tourists. Jim Quillen once said that if the walls of Alcatraz could talk, every cell would be novel of tragedy and despair, and he felt that this was especially true in the case of Roy Gardner. When Gardner arrived on one of the first trains from Leavenworth to Alcatraz, he was already considered a "*solid con*," or a seasoned inmate. Gardner was known to the public as a brilliant escape artist, and he was famous for his Houdini-like jailbreaks. Up until his arrival at Alcatraz in 1934, he had seemed nearly impossible to keep caged.

Gardner was born on January 5, 1886 to a poor family in Trenton, Missouri. He entered the U.S. Army, and served in the 22nd Infantry stationed in the Philippine Islands from 1903 to 1905. After returning to the U.S., he deserted the military because of what he described as "*serious gambling debts*." Fearing for his life, he fled to Mexico and took a job working in the mines. In 1909 Gardner was arrested in Mexico for smuggling weaponry, and was sentenced to death by a firing squad for his involvement with the Mexican Revolutionary Army. While awaiting his execution, he was confined in a dungeon under the most horrific conditions. The cells were rat-infested and dimly lit, and he was forced to relieve himself in a bucket that was emptied infrequently. Just three days before his scheduled execution, he amazingly overpowered his sentry and fled to Arizona. From there he eventually traveled northwest to San Francisco.

On December 22, 1910, during the busy Christmas shopping season, Gardner robbed Glindemann's Jewelry Store on Market Street in San Francisco. Posing as a distinguished customer, he waited as the clerk laid a full tray of diamond rings before him. After taking some time to examine the gems, he grabbed the entire tray and fled into the street, but he was quickly spotted and tackled by a San Francisco police officer. Following his trial he was sentenced to serve five years in a California state prison, and he

Dolly Wades-Gardner

entered San Quentin on February 16, 1911. He was by all accounts a model inmate, and worked productively in the Prison Industries. He was released in September of 1913, and secured a job at a copper mine in Kennett, California. He eventually took a welding job at the Mare Island Naval Ship Yard, and sold war bonds during World War I. During his short reprieve from crime, Gardner met and married a pretty waitress named Dolly Wades. But despite this interlude of normalcy, Gardner's link to the world of crime had not yet dissolved.

After a busted gambling spree during a business trip in April of 1920, Gardner was again arrested for robbing a postal mail messenger in San Diego, taking approximately $75,000 in bonds and securities. He was sentenced to a twenty-five-year Federal term at McNeil Island. The thought of enduring another prison term was unbearable to Gardner, and during his transfer by train, cuffed in hand and leg irons, he made a bold escape from the Federal marshals who were accompanying him. He somehow managed to secure their guns, and made them take off his shackles. He fled, and immediately thereafter committed another robbery. This time he had truly struck gold, as his heist would net him over $200,000. But his luck was to prove short-lived. Only days after the robbery, Gardner was recognized while playing poker at a saloon in Roseville, California. The Porter House Saloon was only blocks from where he had committed the robbery. He was captured, and was sent back to McNeil to serve out an additional prison term. Amazingly enough, just like a modern-day Houdini, he again escaped from the Federal marshals. But he was recaptured soon after, and this time extensive precautions would be taken to ensure that he had no means of escape.

In September of 1921 Gardner was transferred to Leavenworth Federal Penitentiary, and he immediately fell into conflict with the prison administration. He was transferred to Atlanta in October of 1925, and in July of 1926, he attempted another daring escape. Gardner and four other inmates secured weapons and attempted to take hostages, but their plan failed, and Gardner was placed in a deep lockdown status where he would remain for several months.

Surprisingly, Gardner volunteered to be transferred to Alcatraz. He claimed that he wanted to go straight, and felt that this would bring him closer to friends and family. Following his unsuccessful escape, Gardner had finally acquiesced under the strict prison rules. He eventually earned the reputation of a model inmate, and was granted his request for transfer to what he would later call "Hellcatraz." Gardner was destined to do hard time during his twenty-five month imprisonment at Alcatraz. Warden Johnston had assigned him to work in the Mat Factory, and he would later comment that Leavenworth and Atlanta were summer resorts compared to The Rock. He wrote:

The hopeless despair on the Rock is reflected in the faces and actions of almost all of the inmates. They seem to march about the island in a sort of hopelessness, helpless daze, and you can watch them progressively sinking down and down . . . On "the Rock" there are upwards of three hundred men. One hundred fifty will die there. Sometime—in ten, fifteen, twenty-five years—the others come out into the world. These, too, are dead; the walking dead. The men confined there, to all intents and purposes, are buried alive. In reality they are little more than animated cadavers—dead men who are still able to walk and talk. Watching those men from day to day slowly giving up hopes is truly a pitiful sight, even if you are one of them.

Gardner was transferred back to Leavenworth in 1936, and was finally released from prison in 1938. He drifted back to San Francisco, and set up an exhibition booth at the Golden Gate Pan Pacific Exposition on Treasure Island. Gardner recounted to patrons his murderous stories of violence and torture, and autographed his personal memoir entitled *Hellcatraz*. Gardner's show, entitled *Crime Doesn't Pay*, failed to draw large crowds, and it eventually closed. He then spent a brief period working as a narrator on a San Francisco tour boat, but was later forced to take employment as a baker in San Francisco.

(left and above left) Following his release from Alcatraz, Gardner worked as a guide on a San Francisco tour boat for a short period.

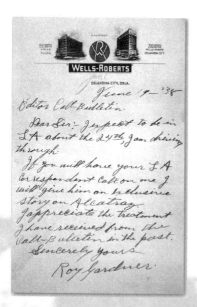

Gardner eventually found himself with no friends, and his wife had left him and remarried. He finally committed suicide in a small San Francisco hotel on January 10, 1940. Using cyanide, sulfuric acid, and a bath towel, he draped the bathroom sink and covered his head, creating a makeshift gas chamber. On the door was a note warning the maid: "*Do Not Open Door - Poison Gas - Call Police.*" Gardner had also left the maid a small cash tip for cleaning out his belongings. His suitcase stood neatly in a corner of his room, and the shower curtain was neatly folded across the floor to prevent any mess. He wrote a note to the *San Francisco Call-Bulletin* that read: "*I'm old and tired and don't care to continue the struggle. Please let me down as light as possible.*"

(Right) Using cyanide, sulfuric acid, and a bath towel, Gardner created his own makeshift gas chamber, and committed suicide by draping the bathroom sink with a towel and covering his head.

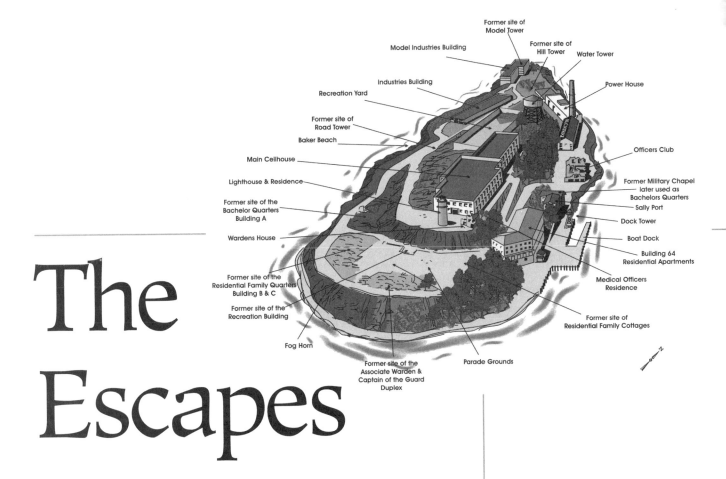

Former site of
Model Tower

Model Industries Building

Former site of
Hill Tower

Water Tower

Industries Building

Power House

Recreation Yard

Former site of
Road Tower

Officers Club

Baker Beach

Main Cellhouse

Former Military Chapel
later used as
Bachelors Quarters

Lighthouse & Residence

Sally Port

Former site of the
Bachelor Quarters
Building A

Dock Tower

Boat Dock

Wardens House

Building 64
Residential Apartments

Former site of the
Residential Family Quarters
Building B & C

Medical Officers
Residence

Former site of the
Recreation Building

Former site of
Residential Family Cottages

Fog Horn

Former site of the
Associate Warden &
Captain of the Guard
Duplex

Parade Grounds

The Escapes

Alcatraz was designed to be an "escape-proof" prison for the nation's most hardened criminals, incorporating multiple layers of redundant safeguards to eliminate all possible routes of escape. The island's size, location and topography were also ideal in this regard, as it lay accessible to the mainland, yet surrounded by icy waters and treacherous currents, with a barren rocky landscape that offered little cover for potential escapees. The prison buildings were constructed to enhance even further the natural inaccessibility of the site, and even the interior Gun Galleries were designed so that they could only be entered from outside of the prison perimeter. But despite the seemingly foolproof design of the prison, inmates were still able to identify weaknesses in the system, and some made it down to the shore and into the ice-cold water—never to be seen again.

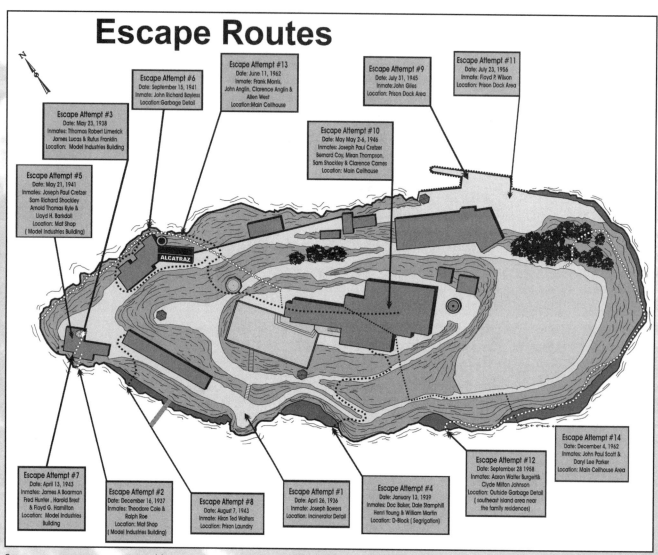

Escape Routes

Escape Attempt #13
Date: June 11, 1962
Inmate: Frank Morris,
John Anglin, Clarence Anglin &
Allen West
Location: Main Cellhouse

Escape Attempt #9
Date: July 31, 1945
Inmate: John Giles
Location: Prison Dock Area

Escape Attempt #11
Date: July 23, 1956
Inmate: Floyd P. Wilson
Location: Prison Dock Area

Escape Attempt #6
Date: September 15, 1941
Inmate: John Richard Bayless
Location: Garbage Detail

Escape Attempt #3
Date: May 23, 1938
Inmates: Tthomas Robert Limerick
James Lucas & Rufus Franklin
Location: Model Industries Building

Escape Attempt #10
Date: May May 2-6, 1946
Inmates: Joseph Paul Cretzer
Bernard Coy, Miran Thompson,
Sam Shockley & Clarence Carnes
Location: Main Cellhouse

Escape Attempt #5
Date: May 21, 1941
Inmates: Joseph Paul Cretzer
Sam Richard Shockley
Arnold Thomas Kyle &
Lloyd H. Barkdoll
Location: Mat Shop
(Model Industries Building)

Escape Attempt #7
Date: April 13, 1943
Inmates: James A Boarman
Fred Hunter , Harold Brest
& Floyd G. Hamilton
Location: Model Industries
Building

Escape Attempt #2
Date: December 16, 1937
Inmates: Theodore Cole &
Ralph Roe
Location: Mat Shop
(Model Industries Building)

Escape Attempt #8
Date: August 7, 1943
Inmate: Hiron Ted Walters
Location: Prison Laundry

Escape Attempt #1
Date: April 26, 1936
Inmate: Joseph Bowers
Location: Incinerator Detail

Escape Attempt #4
Date: January 13, 1939
Inmates: Doc Baker, Dale Stamphill
Henri Young & William Martin
Location: D-Block (Segrigation)

Escape Attempt #12
Date: September 28 1958
Inmates: Aaron Walter Burgett &
Clyde Milton Johnson
Location: Outside Garbage Detail
(southeast island area near
the family residences)

Escape Attempt #14
Date: December 4, 1962
Inmates: John Paul Scott &
Daryl Lee Parker
Location: Main Cellhouse Area

Some escape routes presented here are considered speculative.

Escape Attempt #1

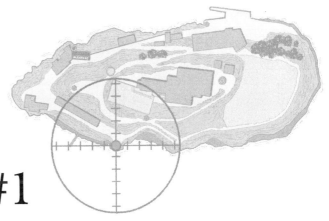

DATE: APRIL 27, 1936

INMATE: JOSEPH BOWERS

LOCATION: INCINERATOR DETAIL

The first recorded escape on Alcatraz during its tenure as a Federal Penitentiary occurred on April 27, 1936. However, several historians consider the escape attempt by Joseph Bowers as a suicide rather than a conventional prison break. Joseph Bowers was among the first group to be transferred to Alcatraz from McNeil in 1934. In a report submitted on September 4, 1936, shortly after Bowers' arrival, Chief Medical Officer George Hess concluded: *"He is a man of extremely low mentality upon which is superimposed an extremely ugly disposition, he is a custodial problem and will probably have to be dealt with by firm measures."*

Joseph Bowers

Joseph Bowers is thought to have been born on February 18, 1897 in El Paso Texas, and he was thirty-eight years old when he arrived at Alcatraz as inmate AZ-210. From his birth onward, his life had been a fragmented model of instability. Bowers was born to circus performers, and was deserted by his parents at birth. He was raised by various people within the circus environment, and although he was never given any formal schooling, he claimed to have learned to read and write from others in the circus. Bowers traveled the world extensively, and he later asserted that he could read and write in six different languages. At age thirteen, Bowers decided to leave the circus and take employment as a seaman on a commercial schooner. In 1919 he was married in Russia, but he separated from his wife later that same year.

A neuro-psychiatric report written by Dr. Romney Ritchey at McNeil states that it was "believed" that Bowers had served in the German Army, but that he would not admit to this. There was significant circumstantial evidence to corroborate this however, as Bowers had suffered what appeared to be combat injuries. These included a lost testicle due to a bullet wound, and a *"bullet scar"* on his chest. Bowers also claimed that at the age of twenty-five he had secured employment in Germany as an interpreter, making $350.00 per month. When it was discovered that he didn't possess a valid passport or proof of citizenship, he was deported back to the U.S. to obtain documentary evidence of his birthplace. It was further recorded that he could not find any traces of his parents.

In 1928 Bowers was arrested for car theft in Oregon, and he served ten months in jail. He was again arrested in Washington in 1930 for drunken driving, fined $75, and released. The Federal crime that would lead him to Alcatraz was committed in 1930, and it would garner him a mere $16.63. Bowers' description of the crime, which he claimed he did not commit, was included in the neuropsychiatry summary by Dr. Ritchey of the McNeil Island Penitentiary in Washington State. It is further worth noting that in 1938, Dr. Ritchey left McNeil Island to replace Dr. George Hess as Chief Medical Officer at Alcatraz. A pertinent section of Dr. Ritchey's report on Bowers reads:

> His present crime he says was committed because he was out of funds and was actually hungry most of the time. He says he met a man sleeping in a Park in Sacramento who persuaded him to go along while they robbed a store and post office near Orville California. He claims that he did not actually go with the man to Orville but that the man himself proceeded with his plan and robbed the store and finally was arrested and confessed and lay the blame on Bowers, he himself going free for his testimony.

Dr. Ritchey's 1933 report at McNeil Island stated Bowers' official mental diagnosis as *"constitutional psychopathic state, inadequate personality, emotionally unstable and without psychosis."* However, fellow inmates of Bowers' at Alcatraz considered him "insane." In a subsequent report by Dr. Hess, there were references to Bowers that indicated some suggestion of mental illness. Bowers believed that other inmates were plotting against him, and he alleged that he could *"hear"* them talking about him at night after lights out. On March 7, 1935, he attempted suicide by trying to cut his own throat with a broken glass lens. The attempt was unsuccessful, as the wound was only superficial. He apparently reported hearing voices, and would continually ask to be admitted to the hospital for protection. But each time he was admitted, he would quickly demand to be released.

The silence rule and strict unrelenting routine at Alcatraz seemed to weigh heavily on Bowers' mental state. In one incident which occurred on June 1st, 1935 and was documented by Deputy Warden C. J. Shuttleworth, Bowers was waiting in line to go to work in the laundry when he started shouting: *"Put me in the dungeon. I do not want to go to work."* While this may have seemed to some like a relatively minor misbehavior, Bowers was punished harshly by being placed in solitary confinement with the *"solid door open,"* and put on a restricted diet. At around the same time, a letter from an inmate was smuggled to a San Francisco newspaper, alleging *"cruelty practices on prisoners"* at Alcatraz, which were causing inmates to go insane. The letter was rumored to have been smuggled out by a correctional officer, and Bowers was one of four inmates named in the case.

Warden Johnston later wrote that he looked at Bowers as *"a weak-minded man with a strong back who would get peace of mind by exercising his body."* This essentially translated to a trivial and tough labor work assignment for Bowers at the island's incinerator, which was located on the lower level on the west side of the island, close to a wire fence that rimmed the shoreline. It appeared that Bowers was coping well with his job until the day of the escape. There have been several versions proposed as to the etiology of Bowers' ascent of the fence.

On the day of the escape attempt, Correctional Officer E. F. Chandler reported his recollection of the events to Warden Johnston in a formal memorandum:

> While on duty in the Road Tower at about 11:00 A.M., I suddenly looked to see inmate Joseph Bowers 210-AZ on the top of wire fence attempting to go over, I then yelled at him several times to get down but he ignored my warning and continued. I fired two shots low and waited a few seconds to see the results. He started down the far side of the fence and I fired one more shot, aiming at his legs. Bowers was hanging on the fence with his hands but his feet were pointing down toward the cement ledge. After my third shot I called the Armory and reported the matter. When I returned from calling the Armory, the body dropped into the bay.

Several other correctional officers witnessed the shooting, and essentially confirmed Chandler's report. Guard Joe B. Steere also described what he had witnessed in his report to Deputy Warden C. J. Shuttleworth:

The island's garbage incinerator, where inmate Joe Bowers attempted to escape by scaling the barbed wire fence. He was shot and killed while climbing down the other side.

> At about 11:00 A.M., I was in the industries area between the Mat Factory and Blacksmith Shop, when I heard a shot fired apparently from the Road Tower. I ran to the corner of the building and looked at the tower and saw Mr. Chandler raise his rifle for another shot. I looked in the direction he was aiming, expecting to see a boat, but saw Number 210 with his back to me going over the fence in back of the incinerator. Mr. Chandler fired and I started to run towards the incinerator. When Mr. Chandler fired a third shot, I was between the Renovating Plant and the Rock Crusher. I looked at Number 210 then and could see only his head due to the fact I was running parallel to the fence at this point and Number 210 was around a bend in the offset where the incinerator is located. He then disappeared from my sight.
>
> When I reached the incinerator and looked down through the bars over the concrete chute, I could see him lying on his back on the rocks just at the edge of the water. The Deputy Warden was in the Road Tower and instructed me to attempt to reach the body by going over the side of the cliff. I then went through the gate and down the lower road and dropped down from the retaining wall to the rocks of the cliff, and tried to go down the face of the cliff, but I was unable to proceed very far. I remained here until the trucks arrived with slings and ropes. Then I assisted Mr. Curry who went down on a rope and secured the body until the Launch "McDowell" arrived.

Correctional Officer E. F. Chandler

Sanford Bates, Federal Director of Prisons, was on Alcatraz at the time conducting an inspection of prison workshops, accompanied by Warden James A. Johnston. Following the inspection, the two were entering the office of the warden when the gunfire broke out. Johnston would then request that the escape siren be sounded for the first time ever on Alcatraz, and several guards were directed to report to the escape location. Dr. George Hess also responded after hearing of the injuries inflicted, and he pronounced Bowers dead before the body was secured with ropes and pulled into the launch.

During the initial examination, Hess reported that in his opinion, Bowers might have broken his neck in the fall. After the body was brought to the mainland and transferred to the coroner's office, Dr. Hess was permitted to attend the autopsy performed by Dr. Sherman Leland. Although Bowers had fallen approximately seventy-five feet, his physical trauma was limited to two gunshot wounds. Hess recorded:

> A bullet wound into the right posterior chest, just lateral to the scapula and penetrating the right lung. Upon opening the chest cavity it was found that the bullet had transversed the chest cavity and had emerged from the left chest just below the clavicle leaving a ragged wound about two inches in length. As the bullet emerged from the chest it fractured the second rib on the left side. There was also found a bullet wound of the right buttock and right thigh. These wounds were made by fragments of a bullet and no whole bullet was found. No other bones of the body were fractured.

Following Bowers' death, tension increased between the correctional staff and the inmates of Alcatraz. During the investigation, Correctional Officer Chandler was reassigned to work in the Armory. There were several rumors going around that Bowers had been shot in cold blood. The *San Francisco Examiner* published former inmate Henry Larry's account of the incident in a feature article entitled "Inside Alcatraz," which described tales of abusive incarceration practices at Alcatraz. Larry alleged that Bowers had simply climbed the fence to feed a seagull, and suggested that Bowers' disturbed mental condition was a result of the treatment he had received at Alcatraz. Other inmates later reported that Bowers had been ordered to clean the area, and he was only attempting to pick up papers that were lodged high up on the fence. These accounts were quickly dismissed, as the correctional staff confirmed that Bowers was "*aggressively*" attempting to "*go over.*" It was determined in the investigation that Chandler's actions were fully justified. One report stated that any lesser response would have been deemed a breach of duty. Bowers was buried at the Mount Olive Cemetery in San Mateo, California.

The San Francisco Examiner published former inmate Henry Larry's account of the Bowers escape attempt in a feature article entitled "*Inside Alcatraz.*" Larry's article was one of the first "inside stories" to surface in the press.

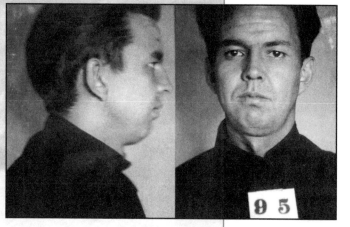

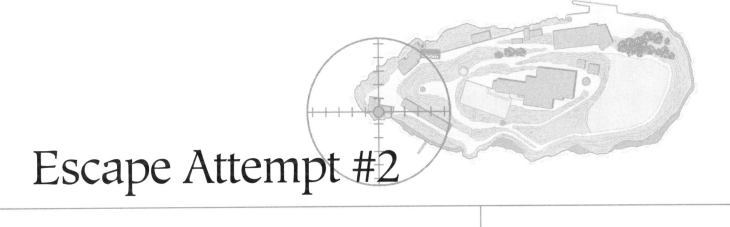

Escape Attempt #2

DATE: DECEMBER 16, 1937

INMATES: THEODORE COLE

RALPH ROE

LOCATION: MAT SHOP (Model Industries Building)

The second fateful escape attempt would end in the suspected death of two inmates in the icy waters of the turbulent bay. The headlines would read: "*ISLAND LEGEND SHATTERED*," as the name "Alcatraz" had until then been synonymous with the word "escape-proof." Fellow inmates Theodore Cole and Ralph Roe had been long-term associates at McAlester and Leavenworth prisons, both had established escape records, and each was known in their own right as a Houdini of escape. Their crafty escape plan would give them the opportunity to sneak beyond the view of a correctional officer, and then slip past the barbwire fences and into the chilly waters of the fog-laden bay, never to be seen again.

Theodore Cole

Theodore Cole was a violent killer who had escaped a death sentence through "*sentimental pressure*." Born April 6, 1912 in Pittsburg, Kansas, Cole began his life of violent crime in his early teens. He was the youngest in a family of one brother and two sisters, and grew up primarily in Tulsa, Oklahoma. His father died when he was only two years of age, and his mother eventually remarried in July of 1925. It is documented that his mother and his new stepfather were both strict disciplinarians. His family moved about frequently as his stepfather, a paving contractor, strived to maintain steady employment.

Theodore Cole

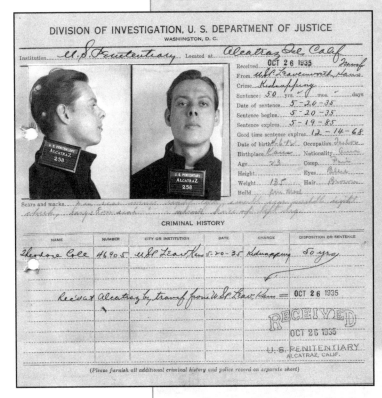

In February of 1927, at only fourteen years of age, Cole robbed a gas station using a handgun. Cole's criminal record would grow over the coming years to include a variety of burglaries, one of which would involve the non-fatal shooting of a police officer in Hot Springs, Arkansas. At seventeen, Cole robbed the Dr. Pepper Bottling Works in Tulsa, and this crime resulted in another conviction for armed robbery. His parents spent everything they had to defend their son, but their efforts ultimately proved unsuccessful. Cole was prone to intensely violent and unpredictable outbursts, and District Judge Saul Yager sentenced him to die in the electric chair stating, "*The boy is a potential killer and deserves such a sentence*." Cole had been sentenced to death without having committed murder, and this initiated nationwide sentimental protests led by various women groups and civil rights organizations. The groups were successful in getting his sentence reduced from life to fifteen years, but it was a barren victory. . .

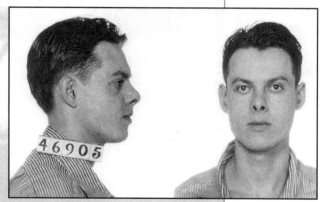

Cole in 1935.

In November of 1933, while imprisoned at McAlester Penitentiary in Oklahoma, Cole attempted to escape, and was critically wounded in the process. Only a few months after his failed attempt, Cole's violent tendencies would resurface when he murdered cellmate William Pritchard, using a homemade knife to stab him twenty-seven times. Amazingly, Cole was able to convince the jury that Pritchard had attempted to kill him, and therefore that he had acted in self-defense. On November 30, 1934 Cole managed to escape the Oklahoma prison by concealing himself in a laundry bag, which was loaded onto a truck and driven into town. On the afternoon of December 5th, Cole secured a pistol and approached a forty-eight year old gentleman named James A. Rutherford, pleading that he was stranded and needed a ride into the next town. Rutherford obliged, and as they drove away, Cole drew his pistol and took him hostage. He forced Rutherford to drive him to Illinois, where he released him. Cole then stole another vehicle and traveled south, committing a few small robberies along the way for quick cash. Finally, on January 6, 1935 in Dallas, Texas, Cole was captured and extradited back to Oklahoma. This time the court showed less leniency, stating "*He is moronic, vicious, and a killer*"—and Cole was sentenced to fifty-years in prison.

Throughout his trial, Cole continued his efforts to escape from the Oklahoma County Jail, where he was incarcerated during the proceedings. He succeeded in sawing through several bars of his cell using a razor, and he continually boasted that he would eventually break out. He was considered such a high escape risk that a sensitive ribbon microphone was installed to monitor any unusual sounds emerging from his cell. On May 20 1935, Cole was transferred to Leavenworth Penitentiary in Kansas, where he renewed a longstanding friendship with Ralph Roe, a fellow inmate he had known at McAlester.

Ralph Roe

Ralph Roe was born on February 5, 1906 in Excelsior Springs, Missouri, and like Theodore Cole, he had endured a troubled childhood. Roe's mother died of tuberculosis when he was only nine, and he later lost his two sisters to the same disease. At fourteen, Roe quit school and ran away to California. It was in Los Angeles that Roe was convicted of his first robbery in April of 1923, and this would be only the beginning of his lengthy criminal record. In July he was sent to the Preston Reformatory in Ione, California, but he escaped and trekked onward to Little Rock, Arkansas. Roe would then go on to commit a string of robberies throughout the west. His robberies became ever more violent, and one resulted in a gun battle which left accomplice Wilbur Underhill wounded and bleeding to death, hiding in the back of a furniture store.

Then on September 10, 1934 Roe and his accomplice Jack Lloyd robbed the Farmers National Bank in Sulphfur, Oklahoma, and took hostages. This Federal crime would earn him a ninety-nine-year sentence, and a recommendation for transfer to Alcatraz. Like Cole, Roe had also previously attempted to escape from McAlester. He had gotten another inmate to nail him into a utility crate, but he quickly started to suffocate inside of it, and thus was forced to abandon his plan. Both Cole and Roe were transferred via the same train from Leavenworth to The Rock.

Ralph Roe

Roe in 1934.

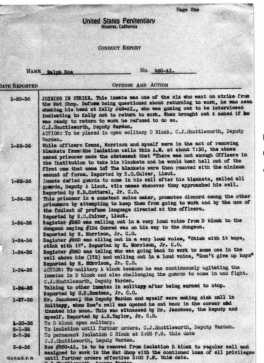

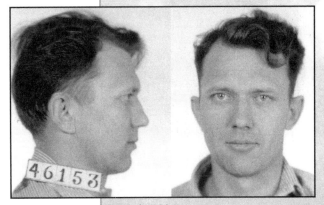

(Left) Ralph Roe's conduct report at Alcatraz.

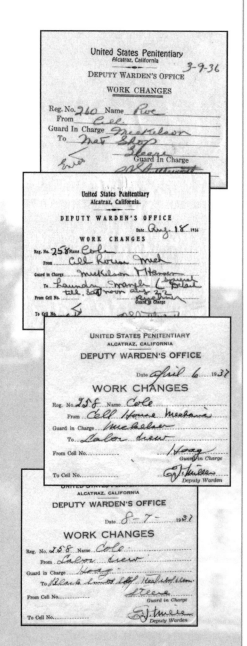

Alcatraz

The two inmates maintained a close friendship at Alcatraz, both taking paying jobs and working side-by-side in the Mat Shop. The Mat Shop was a facility where prison workers transformed used car tires into rubber mats for the Navy, and it was located on the bottom floor of the Model Shop Building at the northernmost tip of the island. The area was recognizable by the piles of discarded tires that were pitched down from the industry building, littering the waterline.

Roe and Cole had spent several weeks in preparation for their escape, studying the habits of the correctional staff, and working to identify potential loopholes in the security system. Using a stolen hacksaw blade, they were able to saw their way through the steel sash window grill, packing the saw gaps with grease and shoe polish to avoid detection. On the morning of Thursday, December 16, 1937, dense fog forced the docking of almost all the small vessels in the area. The forceful currents leading out past the Golden Gate Bridge and toward the Pacific Ocean were fluctuating between seven to nine knots, creating what were considered death-trap conditions for anyone willing to try their fate in the perilous waters. The two inmates were likely not aware of how dangerous the currents and foggy conditions could prove to be. It was speculated that they might have seen the spell of bad weather as an opportunity to escape under the cover of dense fog.

At about 12:50 P.M., the inmates returned to the Industries Building from the mess hall after lunch, and underwent a count by Junior Officer Joe Steere, who found all inmates present and accounted for. Steere was alternating his patrol between the Blacksmith and Mat Shops, and he

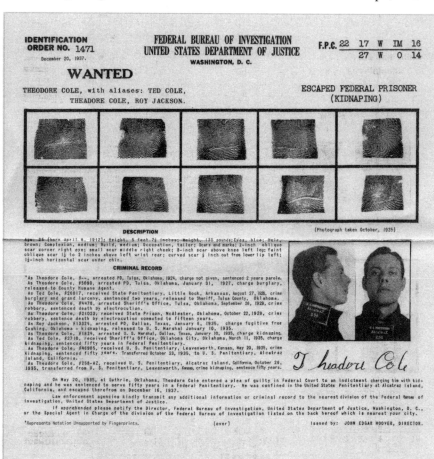

left the Mat area unattended while performing his routine watch. Steere returned to the Mat Shop for the 1:30 P.M. count, but inmates Cole and Roe were not at their assigned work detail. He hurriedly searched the shop and immediately noticed the punched-out panes of glass and bent-out steel grilling. Officer Steere ran to the phone and sounded the escape sirens, in what was known among the custodial staff as a "22-Alarm."

It is speculated that Roe and Cole bent out the sawed bars using a heavy wrench, punched out two panes of glass, and climbed through the window, dropping down to the ground below. They swiftly ran to a locked gate that led down to the waterline. It is also believed that in preparation for the escape, the two inmates had constructed floats from lightweight metal five-gallon fuel canisters with specially made handles, and they carried these makeshift floats with them. Using the wrench, the inmates quickly unfastened the bolts of a chain-link gate, and then laid the gate over the five rows of sharp barbwire, thus making a protected pathway down to the water's edge.

In his book *On the Rock*, former Public Enemy Number One Alvin Karpis stated that the winter of 1937 started off with severe rains and flooding along the Sacramento River. Large pieces of debris floated down the River toward the Pacific Ocean, and the fragmented wreckage ranged from large sections of barns to dead livestock carcasses. The currents were so fierce that the debris could often clearly be seen floating swiftly past the island from the Industries Building windows. Another inmate, "Blackie" Audett, wrote in his 1954 memoir *Rap Sheet* that he was able to watch the two inmates as they made their entry into the bay and began their swim. He noted that he saw Roe come up out of the water

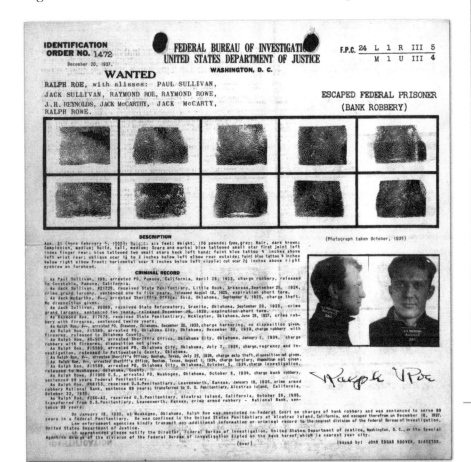

several yards off the island, appearing to be struggling desperately, and attempting to stay afloat in the rough waters. Audett recalled that Roe came up and then drifted into the dense fog, never to be seen again.

Despite the dangerous fog, Warden Johnston dispatched the launch, which started a circular search pattern around the island, but found no signs of any debris from the inmates' improvised floats. The officers in the towers searched with binoculars, but were hardly able to see much of the surrounding waters because of the thick fog. Associate Warden E. J. Miller described his actions following the escape in a December 18, 1937 memo to Warden Johnston. He wrote in part:

> We searched the area in the back of the Model Building and found where the lock on the gate where we throw the old tires through had been broke with a Stillson Wrench and the wrench was laying beside the gate also. Made a complete search of the area without finding any additional clues or signs of the men, no footprints, no clothing. The caves were searched with lights and the big cave was flooded with tear gas and in the evening with sickening gas and had men stationed to see if there was any movement or anyone came out, without result. We combed the Island thoroughly, entered all residences, inspected every nook and cranny, all along the shoreline, in the rocks, the emergency dock, the regular dock, beneath the docks, the sewers, all shrubbery, covering every inch of the island.

The path to the waterline, showing where Roe and Cole entered the freezing Bay waters.

For several weeks after the escape there were reports that people had seen the escapees, and with the FBI leading the investigation, every lead was followed up—but with no success in locating the two men. It was believed that both men had unquestionably met their death on that foggy afternoon, but the FBI kept the investigation open, and continued their vigorous search.

Los Angeles champion open-water swimmer Lisa Johnson stated in a news report that she felt it was impossible for the men to have survived the swim during such a strong ebb tide, even using float devices. She stated that the fog alone would have caused serious disorientation because no fixed landmark references could be seen, and that they would not have been able to swim on any direct route toward land. She further stated: "*They were probably unable to swim back to Alcatraz once they realized that they were in grave danger. Even with my experience and conditioning, I would never have put one toe in that turbulent water.*" Roe also had a debilitating factor that could have contributed to his supposed demise. It is documented in a Leavenworth report that he had a slight deformity of his right tibia, due to a serious fracture that he had sustained from a gunshot wound during his last escape attempt. It was noted that the cold weather sometimes caused "*aching pains*" in his leg, but this was not further substantiated, and no medical records show any complaints of leg pain while at Alcatraz.

For nearly twelve weeks following the escape, Johnston continued a policy that every corpse found floating in the bay would be investigated by the Alcatraz launch *McDowell*, to help identify the body in case it proved to be one of the escapees. It was later officially concluded that the two inmates had drowned in the bay. Johnston wrote in his 1949 memoir:

> I believe when that when they jumped into the bay they jumped to their death. There wasn't any boat there to meet them and the impenetrable curtain of fog that hampered the visibility of the guards, also made it

San Francisco Police Chief William Quinn is seen here handing out photos of Roe and Cole to street officers.

impossible for them to see anything and they just floundered until they were no longer able to keep up and then sank to the bottom of a bay that seldom gives up its victims.

The press continued to cover the escape with great interest. Johnston worked to defend the integrity of the island's security, and was harshly critical in his response to any comments that might lead the public to believe that the prisoners had successfully escaped. On February 18, 1938, the Associated Press ran an article claiming that the Bureau of Prisons was *"chagrined and embarrassed"* over the escape attempt by Roe and Cole. The article suggested further that the security at Alcatraz was not up to "required standards," and Bureau Director Bennett subsequently asked the House Appropriations Subcommittee to increase the institution's budget from $305,600 to $309,535 for the 1939 fiscal year. The additional funding was approved, and it allowed for an additional captain and two junior officers to man additional fixed sentry posts.

The *San Francisco Chronicle* would later run several reports of various sightings of the escapees, and all leads were rigorously investigated, with no fruitful results. Nonetheless, the articles kept alive the idea that such a discovery was possible, since both inmates remained listed as unaccounted for. In an article published following the date of the escape, the closing statement read simply:

With long years of prison ahead of them, Ralph Roe, Muskogee, Okla., robber and Theodore Cole, Cushing, Okla., kidnapper, defied science, the natural hazards and the guns of guards, escaped and shattered a national byword, the legend of "escape proof" Alcatraz.

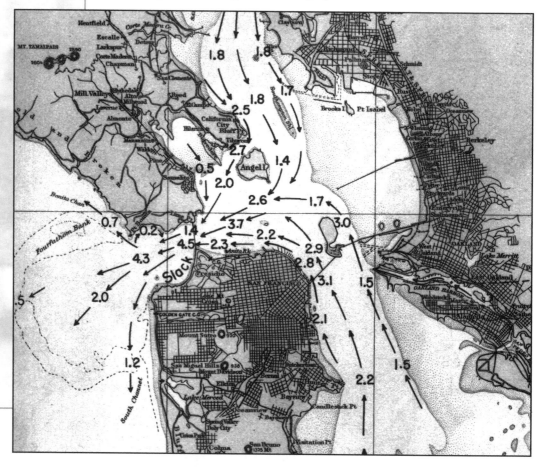

A tide chart showing the forecast ebb tide conditions for December 16, 1937.

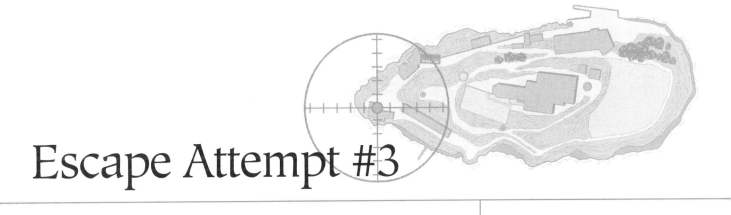

Escape Attempt #3

DATE: MAY 23, 1938

INMATES: THOMAS ROBERT LIMERICK

JAMES LUCAS

RUFUS FRANKLIN

LOCATION: MODEL INDUSTRIES BUILDING

T he third escape attempt at Alcatraz would forever stand as one of the most vicious and violent ever seen on The Rock. It would result in the tragic murder of a well-liked senior correctional officer, and the death of an Alcatraz inmate. The plan was uncomplicated and essentially required no more than a few simple tools. These circumstances, combined with the desperation of the convicts, created a deadly formula for tragedy.

Thomas Robert Limerick

Thomas Robert Limerick was born in Council Bluff, Iowa on January 7, 1902. It was recorded that he lived in a harmonious family environment until his father's death, when Robert was only fifteen years old. His father worked as a farm equipment mechanic, and the family enjoyed a comfortable middle-class lifestyle until his untimely death. Thomas was the oldest of one brother and three sisters, and the family quickly fell into extreme poverty living in a "*tar-paper shack*" in a poverty-stricken farming community. Thomas was forced to leave school, and took a job as a laborer in a self-sacrificing attempt to help support his stricken family. The circumstances of his father's death are sketchy, but Thomas would later assert that his father had been "*murdered*" by the police, and that because "*nothing was done about it*" he had decided that he would "*even the score*" himself.

At the age of nineteen, Limerick found himself convicted of grand larceny and sentenced to serve five years at the Iowa State Reformatory. Records also show that Limerick had diffi-

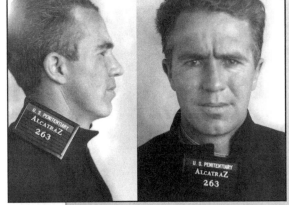

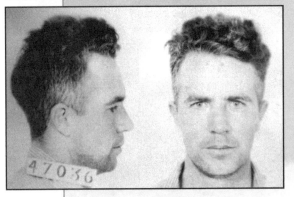

Thomas Limerick

cultly adjusting to the conditions of his confinement. Immediately upon his release he again found his way into more trouble when he traveled to Lincoln, Nebraska, violating his parole and stealing an automobile. He served seven years in the Nebraska State Penitentiary, after which was sent back to Iowa to serve additional time for his parole violation.

Following his release on June 20, 1934, Limerick continued to be implicated in various crimes throughout the state. He was retained for questioning in Sidney, Iowa for the suspected burglary of a railroad boxcar, but no charges were filed. A string of robberies followed, and officials were starting to close in on Limerick as the culprit. Then at thirty-two years of age, Limerick met Catherine Cross and they married in September of 1934. The couple had been married for less than two months when Limerick would permanently seal his fate.

On November 7, 1934, using a sawed-off shotgun and a pistol, Limerick and an accomplice *"forcibly, violently, and feloniously"* robbed the First National Bank in Dell Rapids, South Dakota. They were able to secure $4,812.51 in cash, and $6,900 in stocks and bond certificates. Limerick and his accomplice took three bank employees hostage at gunpoint, and fled. By 1935, Limerick was known as the *"No. 1 bank robber of the Northwest."* He was captured that year and sentenced to life in prison. Limerick arrived at Leavenworth Penitentiary as inmate 47036-L on June 4, 1935, and was transferred to Alcatraz in October of the same year as AZ-263.

James C. Lucas

Another accomplice in the escape would be twenty-six-year-old career criminal James "Tex" C. Lucas, who was serving out a thirty-year sentence for bank robbery, in addition to sentences for attempted murder in Texas and an escape while incarcerated in Huntsville. His prison record featured a series of violent outbreaks. In June of 1936, Lucas attempted to stab Al Capone with a single scissor blade while Capone was working in the clothing room. Without warning, Lucas pulled the concealed shear from a handkerchief and started jabbing at Capone, managing to inflict several minor stab wounds. He would later claim that Capone had threatened to have him *"snuffed."* Capone denied the allegation, stating that Lucas had earlier demanded money, which he had refused to give. As a result of the stabbing, Lucas had all of his *"good time"* earnings revoked and was sent to serve time in solitary confinement.

James "Tex" Lucas

Rufus "Whitey" Franklin

The third accomplice, Rufus "Whitey" Franklin, was born on January 15, 1916 in Kilby Alabama, and began his career in crime when he stole an automobile at only thirteen years of age. He was born into a large family of ten siblings as the middle child. At age sixteen Rufus was arrested for carrying a pistol, and only one year later he was sentenced to life in prison for first-degree murder. When he was allowed a temporary parole to attend the funeral of his mother, he and an accomplice named John Austin Cooper held up a bank in Cedar Bluff, Alabama, taking $558.65 in cash. Because of his long criminal record, the nature of his offenses, and what was documented as "*an assaultive and vicious demeanor,*" he was sent to Alcatraz in August of 1936, and there he was registered as inmate AZ-335.

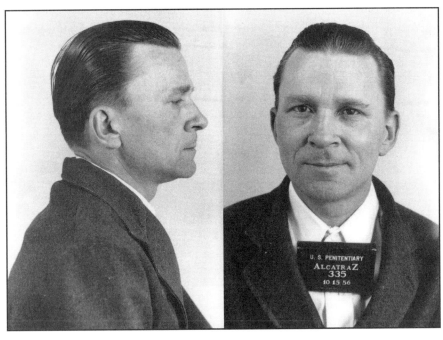

A mug shot series of Rufus Franklin. Rufus spent nearly his entire adult life behind bars.

The Escape

Warden Johnston described the escape in great detail in a formal memorandum to the Director of the Bureau of Prisons, James V. Bennett. The memo, dated June 4, 1938, was written following an intensive investigation of the escape. It chronicled the following events:

Immediately following the attempted escape of prisoners Limerick, Franklin and Lucas, their assault on Senior Officer Royal C. Cline, their assault on the guard tower manned by Junior Officer Harold P. Stites, I reported the matter to you by telephone and followed it by making additional telephonic reports on the following day, informing you of the death of Officer Cline and death of prisoner Limerick.

At noon on that day I went to San Francisco to act as honorary pall-bearer at the funeral of Jesse S. Cook, former Chief of Police of San Francisco. While I was in the Masonic Temple where the services were being held, somebody tapped me on the shoulder and told me I was wanted on the telephone. I went at once to the telephone and called my secretary who told me there had been some shooting on the lower end of the Island in the work area and apparently some prisoners had tried to escape, that Officer Cline had been hurt, but beyond that he could not give detailed particulars. I ordered the launch sent off and I proceeded immediately to the wharf and reached the Island shortly after Mr. Cline and Prisoners Franklin and Limerick had been moved to the Hospital.

As soon as I got on the grounds and questioned the Associate Warden, Lieutenant of the Watch and officers who had participated, I found that this is what had happened:

Junior Officer Harold P. Stites was on duty in the tower on the roof of the Model Shop Building. Junior Officer Clifford B. Stewart was patrolling the roof of the building at the northwest side where he could keep an eye on the ground below the rear and side of the building nearest the Bay where contractors' workmen were boring holes in the concrete building in preparation for the installation of tool-proof steel window guards, the workmen being under supervision of Junior Officer George D. Hoag.

At about 2 P.M. or even before that hour, Officer Stites was inside the tower and heard noises behind him and turning in the direction of the sound saw Prisoners Lucas, Franklin and Limerick on the roof to which they had ascended from the top floor of the shop building. Subsequent examination showed that they had reached the roof by standing on a window shoved out-ward which they held steady with a timber frame and making an aperture in the barbed wire guard around the roof, cutting the wire with pliers.

Almost as soon as Officer Stites saw the prisoners, they rushed the tower from several angles each of them firing iron missiles (note: these consisted of heavy metal objects including hammers and heavy wrenches), their apparent purpose being to try to knock him out and seize his arms.

Officer Stites endeavored to halt them by warning and by firing the first shot into the frame of the window but they kept advancing and then he kept dodging and firing shots through the glass in his tower. Several of the missiles they fired went through the glass in the tower but many others failed to go through, showing that the shatterproof glass is a very valuable protection. Only one of the missiles that went through hitting Officer Stites. He did not leave his tower but fired through the glass.

The Associate Warden happened to be in his work area on the west side near the incinerator. Lieutenant Culver was making his regular afternoon inspection of the work area and at the time was in the laundry. The Associate Warden heard the shots and went toward the Model Shop Building where he saw Prisoner Franklin laying on the barbed wire which goes around the edge of the roof, Model Shop Building. Lieutenant Culver coming from the Laundry also saw Franklin, as did several other Officers.

Associate Warden (Miller) used the emergency telephone to call all the officers from the front of the building and instructed the Armorer to get those that were on the island but off duty to go into the work area, and had the launch go to that part of the Bay back of the building, not knowing just whether or not anybody had succeeded in getting out.

When he learned that Officer Stites and Officer Stewart had the three men under control on the roof, Associate Warden Miller and Senior Officer Nickelson went up to the top floor of building to see if all of the other prisoners were there and had all of the shops in the building checked.

When they got to the fourth floor where Franklin, Lucas and Limerick had been assigned to work, they found the remaining prisoners assigned to that shop up at one corner and looking around for Mr. Cline they found him in a corner of the storeroom with his head battered in and bleeding.

He sent for stretchers and immediately moved Mr. Cline to the hospital, then went to the roof and removed Prisoner Franklin who still had the hammer in his hand with which he had been trying to hit Officer Stites, and from the blood appearing on it, it appears that this hammer was used in assaulting Officer Cline. Limerick was lying on the roof, shot in his head, unconscious. Lucas was held in corner, apparently in attitude of surrender, kept covered but not fired upon by Officer Stewart while Officer Stites was engaged in the battle with Franklin and Limerick.

(Left) The Model Shop Tower, where Officer Harold Stites was attacked by the would-be escapees. Stites opened fire on the inmates, fatally wounding Limerick.

Senior Officer Royal Cline was brutally murdered by Thomas Limerick during the escape attempt. In his final moment of bravery Cline refused to aid the escapees, and subsequently was killed.

Limerick and Franklin were then removed to the Hospital and Lucas was taken to the cell building and locked up. The Associate Warden interviewed both Lucas and Franklin. He secured a statement from Lucas which was reduced to writing and signed by the prisoner and afterwards he turned it over to the F.B.I. Agent.

At the request of Dr. Ritchey arrangements were made to move Officer Cline to the Marine Hospital, San Francisco, and he was moved over there at 5 P.M.

Dr. Creel, in charge of the Marine Hospital, telephoned to me during the evening and said that Mr. Cline's condition was very critical and it was doubtful if he would survive the night.

I telephoned to the United States Attorney and the San Francisco Office of the Federal Bureau of Investigation and arranged for their representatives to be at the Hospital so that in case Mr. Cline recovered consciousness and was able to talk they might secure a dying statement but he did not show any signs or consciousness during the night.

During the night Prisoner Limerick died and I immediately called the Coroner and arranged to transfer the body to him very early the morning of May 24, 1938. The afternoon of May 24, 1938, Mr. Cline died and the Marine Hospital notified the Coroner and arranged to transfer the body to him.

After autopsies, the bodies were released to the undertaking parlor and the body of Limerick was prepared and shipped to the Woodring Funeral Parlors, Des Moines, Iowa, in accordance with the request of his relatives.

The body of Mr. Cline was prepared for shipment to home in Sweetwater, Texas, in accordance with request of Mrs. Cline. Prior to shipment, services were held at undertaking parlors in San Francisco, about which I will write you a separate letter. On the morning of May 24, 1938, Agents T. P. Geraghty and Orval H. Patterson at the San Francisco office of the F.B.I. came over to the Island at my request and I related what had happened, gave them the names of all of the officers who had any knowledge, names of prisoners who worked in the shop, gave them sketches which one of our officers, George D. Hoag had made of the roof and fourth door of shop building and helped then in the taking of photographs of the roof of the shop building, the window, the barbed wire, and the tower.

They interviewed all persons having knowledge and they tagged with identifying marks all of the missiles that had been found on the roof as well as the hammer and the pliers and the shattered portions of the glass from the tower.

This detailed report has been held awaiting action of the Coroner who held inquest on both cases Thursday, June 2, 1938. In the meantime I had consulted with United States Attorney Frank J. Hennessy and after reciting all that happened to him, decided upon the witnesses who could give the essential testimony necessary for the inquest—E. J. Miller, Associate Warden; Clitton C. Nickelson, Senior Officer; Harold P. Stites, Junior Officer and Clifford B. Stewart, Junior Officer. These officers appeared at the inquest and testified in response to the questions of the Coroner. United States Attorney Hennessy was present, as was T. P. Geraghty, F.B.I. Agent.

Mr. Hennessy observed the proceedings and asked some questions. The Coroner's Jury returned a verdict that Royal C. Cline, officer of the prison had met his death at the hands of the convicts named who assaulted him in their attempt to escape, and that Prisoner Thomas H. Limerick met his death from wounds inflicted by Officer Stites who shot him in the performance of duty in order to frustrate his attempt to escape.

The verdict of the Coroners Jury is what I have received orally but I am awaiting the copy of the verdict as well as the death certificate so that I may enclose copies with this report. United States Attorney Hennessy in bringing the matter to the attention of the Federal Grand Jury and states that he will present it on Tuesday, the Seventh of June, at which time he intends to ask the jury for indictments for Franklin and Lucas. Subsequent developments will be reported as they occur so that you will be kept fully advised.

J.A. Johnston, Warden

Chief Medical Officer Doctor Romney Ritchey wrote the following memorandum to the Warden, describing the condition and injuries of Limerick when he was received at the prison hospital:

United States Public Health Service
U.S. Penitentiary
Alcatraz, California
May 24, 1938

Memorandum to the Warden: Re. Reg. No. 263-A Limerick, Thomas R.

The above captioned inmate was brought to the Hospital at 3:00 P.M. on a stretcher yesterday afternoon, May 23, 1938. He was entirely unconscious and found to be suffering from a gunshot wound of the head. There was a large bleeding hole in the forehead just to the right of the midline. The right eye was badly swollen and prominent. His breathing was heavy and the pulse was small and rapid. There was no wound in the back of the head, but there was some slight prominence at one point about opposite the point of entrance, which might indicate that the bullet had reached the skull posteriorly but had not entirely penetrated it. He was in a very critical condition and medication and treatment was administered to combat the shock. His condition appeared to be absolutely hopeless from the first and he gradually grew worse until about 08:00 P.M. when stertorous breathing set in and the pulse became weaker and he died at 11:18 P.M. May 23,1938, without ever regaining consciousness. Several verbal reports were made regarding this case both to the associate warden and yourself, and the associate warden was notified when he died.

Respectfully,
Romney M. Ritchey, Surgeon.
Chief Medical Officer

The trial of Franklin and Lucas lasted three weeks. It was an emotional process, due to the brutal circumstances of Cline's murder. The jury was forced to examine the grisly weapons used in the crime. They were shown graphic photos of the blood trail left behind when the body was dragged, the hammer which delivered the fatal blows, and the vivid death mask showing the viciousness of the attack. These factors contributed to the jury's quick decision. Franklin and Lucas were convicted of first-degree murder, and both received life sentences for Cline's death.

Franklin, who had been found with the bloodied hammer used in Cline's killing, would be sentenced to serve nearly fourteen years in a closed-front solitary confinement cell. He would spend the longest term in solitary of any inmate in the history of Alcatraz. Nevertheless, Franklin was eventually extended a few special privileges. After a long period, he was allowed to keep the door front open and to enjoy a non-restricted diet. His long-term isolation status made him an underground hero among his fellow inmates. Even while being held in the most controlled cell row, he was able to communicate with others in the general population via orderlies, and thus to obtain contraband.

On February 27, 1945, Franklin was allowed time in the recreation yard along with famed inmate Henri Young. In an interrogation of Young while he was under the influence of the drug Sodium Amatol, the prisoner asserted that Whitey Franklin was the "*coolest*" inmate at Alcatraz. However, Franklin apparently didn't reciprocate Young's feelings. During their brief meeting in the yard, the two quickly engaged in conflict, and Franklin produced a kitchen knife and inflicted a minor stab wound to Young's right shoulder. In a telegram written to Bureau of Prisons Director James Bennett, Warden Johnston suggested that an inmate assigned to the kitchen detail had planted the knife in the yard.

Jimmy Lucas and Rufus Franklin being transferred to court via the prison launch on November 18, 1938.

(Above left) Lucas (left) and Franklin (right) during their highly publicized court appearances. Both inmates were convicted of first-degree murder for their role in Officer Cline's death.

Franklin was released back into the general population in 1952. Because he refused to participate in a culinary strike that lasted from March 18th until April 4th, Franklin was forced back into the Treatment Unit for protection from the hostility of other inmates. He was allowed to continue work, and was permanently returned to the general population on February 12, 1954. Records show that Franklin readjusted easily to the normal prison routine. He increased his reading habits and was noted to take special interest in spiritual and philosophical subjects. Franklin gradually became more trusted by the custodial staff, and was later awarded a privileged position in the prison's hospital. He was trained as an X-Ray technician and later qualified as a surgical assistant, and was even allowed to prepare and handle the surgical instruments during operations.

After spending twenty years at Alcatraz, Franklin was allowed to transfer back to Leavenworth Penitentiary for a brief ten-month stay, and then to Atlanta Federal Prison to be closer to his family. In a letter written in August of 1958, Franklin boasted about the train ride through New Mexico and Arizona in a Pullman car, and the emotion of seeing life outside of prison for the first time since the murder trial of Royal Cline. He wrote frequently to Warden Madigan and other "*friends*" at Alcatraz, keeping them up-to-date on his progress. Madigan seemed to reflect pleasantly on Franklin's progress, and in a letter dated October 15, 1959, he wrote in part:

Rufus Franklin in court, awaiting the jury's verdict.

> It has been a long time since you first came to Alcatraz and you have been through many difficult years and trials. You were a young man when you first came to us and as many young men you possessed the fire that got you into difficulty. You grew out of those years and by application improved your education and work habits. It was not easy for you since there were many pressures brought to bear that made it most difficult for you to conduct yourself as you wished to do. At any rate, you accomplished what you set your mind to do and are now in a position to accomplish still more.

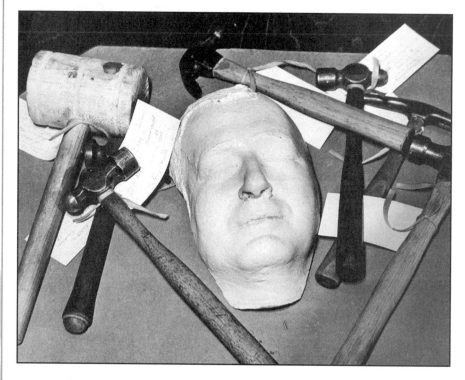

(Above left) Coroner's Technician Paul Green testifying in the Franklin and Lucas trial. Mr. Green is seen pointing to indentations in the skull, which the prosecution claimed were caused by hammer blows inflicted when Cline resisted the escapees.

(Above right) Death mask of slain guard R. C. Cline; the hammers used in his murder; and other tools found in the Model Shop that were used in the escape attempt.

Franklin would spend nearly his entire life behind bars. He was finally paroled on October 29, 1974, and died only a short time later on May 27, 1975 in Dayton, Ohio. He was living with his sister Ruby Farrow at the time of his death, and was said to have enjoyed cooking every morning, and rode the bus into the city everyday to savor his freedom.

Correctional Officer Royal Cline tragically had been only thirty-six years of age at the time of his death in 1938. His wife Etta remained faithfully at his side in the hospital until he succumbed to his injuries. Fellow correctional officers were profoundly affected by Cline's death, which was especially sobering to the island's families since Cline left behind four young children. His death would emphasize the reality that convicts would commit murder in trade for potential freedom. Warden Johnston would be quoted in the *San Francisco Chronicle* as stating: *"I greatly regret that one who was so attached to his duty should meet such an end."*

Harold P. Stites is sworn in to testify at a coroner's inquest on November 4, 1938. On the table is Limerick's death mask, showing the bullet wound from Stites' fatal gunshot. Stites himself would later die in the brutally violent "Battle of Alcatraz" of 1946.

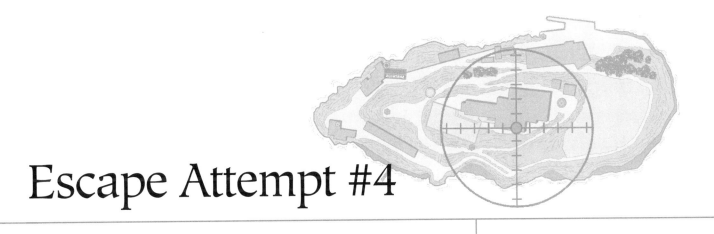

Escape Attempt #4

The Barker-Karpis Gang
and the Escape Attempt of 1939

DATE: JANUARY 13, 1939
INMATES: ARTHUR "DOC" BARKER
          DALE STAMPHILL
          HENRI YOUNG
          WILLIAM "TY" MARTIN
          RUFUS MCCAIN
LOCATION: D BLOCK (SEGREGATION UNIT)

It seemed almost predestined that "Doc" Barker would ultimately meet his death as the primary conspirator in the first escape that would demonstrate a weakness in the security of the main cellhouse. Doc's life as a desperado is the fascinating and bleak story of an American tragedy. A memo from FBI Director J. Edgar Hoover to Attorney General Homer Cummings dated August 15, 1935 states in part: "*Arthur 'Doc' Barker is beyond doubt among the most dangerous criminals with which this Bureau has had to deal.*"

Arthur "Doc" Barker

Doc was a member of the notorious "Ma Barker Gang" that terrorized the Midwest during the early 1930's. He was born in 1899, into an impoverished family in the remote Ozark Mountains of Missouri. Short in stature, he was the third of four sons who had all been reared into a life of crime by their mother, the legendary Kate Barker, known affectionately by associates simply as "Ma."

The FBI chronicled the family's history extensively, and a confidential report dated November 18, 1936 includes the following description:

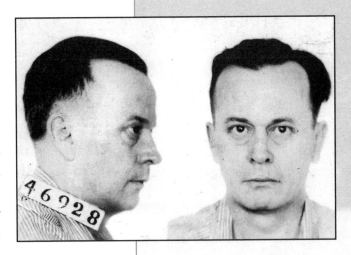

DIVISION OF INVESTIGATION, U. S. DEPARTMENT OF JUSTICE
WASHINGTON, D. C.

Institution _U. S. Penitentiary_ Located at _Alcatraz De Calif._

Received _OCT 26 1935_

From _U.S.P. Leavenworth Kans_

Crime _Conspir. to transport kidnapped persons_

Sentence: _Life_ yrs. ____ mos. ____ days

Date of sentence _5-17-35_

Sentence begins _5-17-35_

Sentence expires _Life_

Good time sentence expires _Life_

Date of birth _6-4-99_ Occupation _Painter_

Birthplace _Mo_ Nationality _Amer._

Age _36_ Comp. _Ruddy_

Height _5-5_ Eyes _Brown_

Weight _150_ Hair _Dk Brn_

Build _Low Med_

Scars and marks _9½ pears, ✗ long under left ear_
½ pear, under left ear.

CRIMINAL HISTORY

NAME	NUMBER	CITY OR INSTITUTION	DATE	CHARGE	DISPOSITION OR SENTENCE
Arthur R. Barker	46978	U.S.P. Leav., Kans	5-17-35	Consp. to kidnap	Life
		Recd from Leavenworth Kans (Transfer)	OCT 26 1935		

RECEIVED OCT 26 1935 U.S. PENITENTIARY ALCATRAZ, CALIF.

(Please furnish all additional criminal history and police record on separate sheet)

Arthur "Doc" Barker

Arthur Dunlop and Kate "Ma" Barker.

Ma Barker in the formative period of her sons' lives was probably just an average mother of a family which had no aspirations or evidenced no desire to maintain any high plane socially. They were poor and existed through no prolific support from Ma's husband, George Barker, who was more or less a shiftless individual . . . The early religious training of the Barkers . . . was influenced by evangelistic and sporadic revivals. The parents of the Barkers and the other boys with whom they were associated did not reflect any special interest in educational training and as a result their sons were more or less illiterate . . . Ma was more intelligent than any of her sons, she ruled them with an iron will and found this expression of dominance easily exerted because of the submission of her sons Fred and Arthur.

Hoover further characterized Ma Barker as "*a monument to the evils of parental indulgence,*" and according to legend, she instructed her boys from an early age in the finer points of robbery, kidnapping, larceny and murder, romanticizing the life and the wealth of the outlaw.

The family eventually moved to Tulsa Oklahoma, where the Barker boys quickly became community nuisances, engaging in petty thefts and forming a youth crime group dubbed the "Central Park Gang." During his adolescence Doc would form strongly bonded relationships with these town hoodlums, including Volney Davis and Harry Campbell, who years later would also find their way to Alcatraz. Another gang associate, William Green, would conspire in a 1931 mass escape from Leavenworth Prison, and would ultimately commit suicide to avoid recapture.

The eldest Barker son, Herman, was arrested on March 5, 1915 for highway robbery in Joplin, Missouri, and this would mark the beginning of the family's private crime wave. It is documented that Ma Barker liked to live well, and purchased expensive clothing, furniture, and other necessities from the spoils of her sons' depredations. FBI records disclosed that Ma was exceptionally jealous of her sons' girlfriends, and would purposely attempt to sever their relationships. Her personality would be sharply described as that of a "*gutty old girl with a fantastic loyalty to her sons, who wouldn't tell cops or G-Men the time of day and backed her boys to the hilt, right or wrong.*"

Herman left the Barker household and continued his criminal antics while traveling through the Midwestern States. He was arrested several times and ultimately landed himself in prison, serving moderate terms for grand larceny and robbery. Fred Barker would also leave the family homestead, and venture out to pursue his own career in crime. He would eventually join forces with Herbert Farmer, who owned a renowned chicken ranch with his wife near Joplin, Missouri, and over the years they would harbor several fugitives, including Bonnie and Clyde. Farmer would later find himself sentenced to serve time on Alcatraz after being convicted as a conspirator in the famous 1933 Kansas City Union Station Massacre, an event which had a profound impact on the image of the American gangster. As Hoover described it, the Massacre was a "*turning point in the nation's fight against crime.*" The savageness of the attack had stripped away the glamour and romantic mystique of the early gangster era, and U.S. Attorney General Homer Cummings had used the Massacre as a pretext for proclaiming the Federal government's "*war against crime.*"

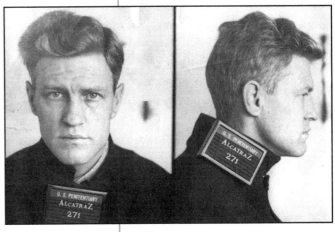

Volney Davis

The Fourth of July would seem an ironic date for Doc Barker to establish his role as a public enemy of the nation, but as fate would have it, on July 4, 1918 he stole a government vehicle in Tulsa, Oklahoma, and was quickly apprehended. Doc somehow managed to escape from the county jail, and then for nearly two years he maintained a low profile, working as a glass blower and later on a labor detail. On February 19, 1920 Doc was captured and charged in connection with the escape. He pleaded guilty, and was released less than a year later. On January 21, 1921 Doc and his longtime friend Ray Terrill were arrested for the attempted armed robbery of a bank firm in Muskogee—Doc under the alias Claud Dale, and Ray under the alias G.R. Patton. Surprisingly, Doc was released in June of 1921 without any formal charges being brought against him. Only two months later, on August 26th, Doc and his old companion Volney Davis allegedly murdered James J. Sherrill, a security watchman at Tulsa's St. John's Hospital, during a break-in. On February 10, 1922 Doc and Volney were given life sentences for this crime, and were sent to serve their time at the State Penitentiary in McAlester, Oklahoma. Volney would escape in 1925, and he quickly started building his resume for Alcatraz. It was rumored that Doc was innocent of the murder, and another criminal would claim responsibility several years later.

Despite the raging criminal activity of her young sons, Ma Barker continued to defend them vehemently, with unrelenting requests for their release. However, Ma did not extend the same loyalty to her husband George, whom she had married when she was only fifteen. In 1927 Ma Barker left her husband for a man known as Arthur Dunlop. He carried a low reputation in the community as a drunkard, and an arrogant and illiterate nomad. It was further rumored that the Barker Boys were resentful of Dunlop, who apparently did little more than freeload and boast about the criminal escapades of his youth.

Herman Barker had also found himself deep in the criminal life, roaming the Southwest with the Kimes-Terril Gang, robbing banks, stores, and other establishments. In late January of 1928, Herman and several accomplices broke into an Oklahoma bank, and under the cover of night, made off with a cash safe containing nearly $45,000. On a tip from a witness, police quickly raided their hideout in Carterville, Missouri. A fierce gun battle ensued, and Herman and the others were forced to surrender. Herman was sent to Arkansas to stand trial for another robbery, and he later managed to escape by sawing through the bars of his jail cell.

In early August, Herman and his wife were pulled over by Deputy Sheriff Arthur Osborne, and before the officer was able to draw his gun, Herman fatally shot him. Less than a month later Herman engaged in another gun battle with police while attempting to escape a roadblock, and he was severely wounded. Bleeding profusely from his bullet wounds and with no hope of escape, Herman turned the gun on himself and committed suicide. Herman likely had pondered the certain fate of death by electrocution that would await him if he surrendered to police. His wife would later be convicted as an accomplice to Osborne's murder, and would be released a few years later. She subsequently became a prostitute and the mistress of Alvin Karpis, another notorious Alcatraz inmate.

Alvin "Creepy" Karpis

Alvin Karpowicz was born in Montreal, Canada in 1908, and his father moved the family to Topeka, Kansas when Alvin was still a young boy. It was an elementary school teacher who decided to shorten his name to simply Alvin Karpis, and he would later be given the nicknames "*Creepy Karpis*" and "*Old Creepy*." Alvin would have the unique distinction of enduring a twenty-five year residence at Alcatraz, and he was designated as "Public Enemy Number One" by J. Edgar Hoover himself. He would live a quarter of a century in a place where he would never be allowed to walk astray, and would never see many areas that were only a few yards from his cell. In his memoir published in Canada in 1980, Karpis claimed that his first encounter with crime had occurred when he stole a gun at only ten years of age. Like many other criminals of his day, Karpis' first arrest was for illegally hopping trains. He was sentenced to a Florida chain gang, and after his release he was again arrested for robbery. He subsequently escaped from prison, and became a fugitive.

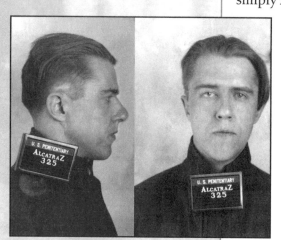

Karpis joined the Barker gang after meeting Fred Barker in 1930 at the Kansas State Penitentiary in Lansing. Karpis and Fred had formed a close relationship in prison while working together in the coalmines. Karpis had made arrangements to "*buy*" himself an early release. Prisoners who worked in the mines were required to dig a specified amount of coal, and each day that they dug over their quota, they were given special "*good time*" credits that they could apply toward their release. Karpis paid other inmates to turn over their coal to him, which helped him to secure an early release in May of 1931. Only a month later, Karpis and Fred Barker were arrested for robbing a jewelry store. Both managed to pay restitution, and they were paroled.

Then on December 18, 1931 Karpis and Fred Barker robbed another store using a new 1931 DeSoto as their getaway car, and several witnesses were able to identify the vehicle. The following day an officer named C. R. Kelly was sent to investigate a sighting of the car at the Division Motor Company in West Plains, Missouri. Alvin and Fred had stopped there to have a flat tire repaired. When the officer approached the car to question the two occupants, Karpis opened fire on him, inflicting fatal

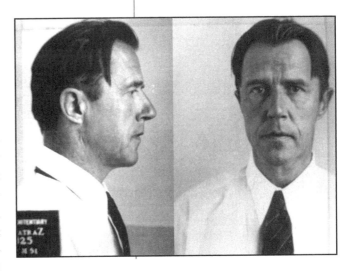

gunshot wounds to the chest. Not long after the murder the two were identified, and on a tip from a witness, Dunlop's cottage in Thayer, Missouri was raided by the police. The fugitives had already fled, but the police discovered stolen merchandise from other robberies, and thus were able to identify the players.

Karpis was quickly accepted as one of the Barker family, and he almost seemed to replace Herman. Doc was released from prison in 1932, and as a condition of his parole, he was directed by authorities never again to return to Oklahoma. Once more the Barker gang went into full swing, pulling various bank and business heists. The family rented a house with Karpis and Dunlop at 1301 South Roberts Street in West St. Paul, Minnesota, but the landlady soon became suspicious on seeing them frequently entering and leaving the house carrying violin cases. Her son also recognized Fred Barker and Alvin Karpis from a detective magazine which featured a story about the killing of Officer Kelly. On April 25, 1932 the police raided the house, only to find that it had just been abandoned. The following morning, the body of Arthur "Old Man" Dunlop was found on the shores of Lake Frendsted near Webster, Missouri. Dunlop had been stripped of his cloth-

Alvin "Creepy" Karpis became known in the 1930's as America's "Public Enemy Number One." Karpis would spend twenty-five hard years at Alcatraz.

ing and shot three times at close range. Not too far away, the police found a bloodstained woman's glove that was believed to belong to Ma Barker. The FBI later contended that Alvin and Fred had shot Dunlop to death, believing that he had been the one who tipped off the police.

The FBI had now started to close in on the Barker gang, which forced the outlaws to flee to Kansas City. Karpis posed as one of Ma's sons, and the family bought a luxury home in an exclusive residential district known as Country Club Plaza. They attempted to masquerade as an upstanding family that worked in a successful insurance firm. The men ultimately teamed up with convicts Francis Keating, Thomas Holden, and Harvey Bailey (later an accom-

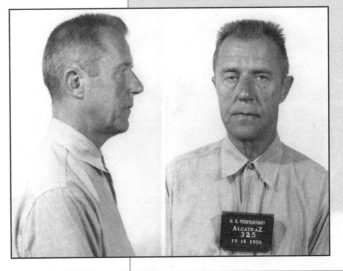

plice of "Machine Gun" Kelly), who had all escaped from Leavenworth Penitentiary. Another accomplice was Bernard Phillips, a corrupt police officer who had become a professional bank robber. The family started to move from one location to another, attempting to evade the FBI. On July 7th the FBI apprehended Bailey, Holden and Keating while they were playing golf at the Old Mission Golf Course in Kansas City. Phillips was also with the men, but he happened to be inside the country club, and watched from afar as the others were handcuffed and shoved into law enforcement vehicles. Phillips carried the news back to the gang, and Alvin and Fred quickly packed their belongings and fled. When the FBI raided the apartment they found cooked meals on the table, indicating an unplanned and rapid departure.

In July of 1932 Karpis, Phillips, Fred and Ma Barker, and another accomplice named Jess Doyle fled together from Kansas City to White Bear Lake in Minnesota, where they rented a summer cottage in a small resort. The gang maintained a low profile with the exception of frequenting a small nightclub called the Hollyhocks, which was owned by an associate named Jack Peifer. Their crime spree continued with a daring daylight robbery of the Cloud County Bank in Concordia, Kansas, where they secured over $240,000 in bonds and thousands of dollars in cash.

The family paid for the services of a private detective named Jack Glynn to help negotiate the release of Doc, who was imprisoned at Leavenworth at the time. Glenn conducted independent investigations, and managed to win Doc's release on September 10, 1932. Glynn had also attempted to achieve the release of Lloyd Barker, who was likewise imprisoned at Leavenworth. But the authorities were unmoved by Glynn's attempts, and denied Lloyd's appeal. Doc spent a short time visiting with his father and a small stint attempting to make an honest living as a glass blower, and then reunited with Ma and the others back in Minnesota. Volney Davis was also successful in getting paroled, and he soon joined up with Doc.

On December 16, 1932 the Barker-Karpis Gang robbed the Third Northwestern Bank of Minnesota, and the violent aftermath left one bystander and two police officers dead in a hail of machine gun bullets. The gang had thought that the bystander was attempting to get their license plate number, and had therefore shot him to death. Gang member Larry DeVol was captured, and he was found to have $17,000 in his possession from the Third Northwestern Bank robbery. The others took flight once again, this time making their way to Reno, Nevada, where they stayed for only a short period.

The reign of terror would continue as the Barker-Karpis Gang raged through the Midwestern States, eventually ending up in Chicago, where they murdered another police officer. The gang split up and kept separate residences, Ma living on the exclusive South Shore Drive, and Alvin cohabiting with Dolores Delaney, the sister-in-law of Pat Riley, a mobster from the Dillinger Gang. In 1933 the Barker-Karpis Gang had returned to St. Paul and was keep a low profile while they began to meet and plan the kidnapping of William A. Hamm, Jr., the President of Hamm's Brewing Company. On June 17, 1933 the gang abducted Hamm, demanding a $100,000 ransom from his family and threatening his certain death if they tried to involve police. The ransom money was paid two days later, and Hamm was released unharmed.

The gang's next victim was Edward G. Bremer, a prominent community leader and President of the Commercial State Bank in Minnesota. Edward Bremer was the son of Adolph Bremer, one of the most well known figures in Minnesota, who owned his own brewing company. On the morning of January 17, 1934 Bremer drove his nine-year-old daughter to school, as part of his normal daily routine. After dropping her off, he proceeded to a crossroad and stopped to check for oncoming traffic. Volney Davis approached the Lincoln Sedan and held a pistol to Bremer's head, directing him to "*move over*." Another man then entered on the passenger side and struck Bremer over the head several times with a blunt object, then covered his eyes with a pair of goggles that had black electrical tape over the lenses.

At 10:40 A.M. Walter Magee, a very close friend of the Bremer family, received a call at his St. Paul office from a man who called himself Charles McGee. The caller explained that Bremer had been kidnapped, and that a note could be found on the side of the building providing further instructions. Under a side door, Magee found a note which read:

You are hereby declared in on a very desperate undertaking. Don't try to cross us. Your future and B's are the important issue. Follow these instructions to the letter. Police have never helped in such a spot and won't this time either. You better take care of the payoff first and let them do the detecting later. Because the police usually butt in, your friend isn't none too comfortable now so don't delay the payment. We demand $200,000. Payment must be made in 5 and 10-dollar bills—no new money —no consecutive numbers—large variety of issues. Place the money in two large suit box cartons big enough to hold the full amount and tie with heavy cord. No contact will be made until you notify us that you are ready to pay as we direct. You place an ad in the Minneapolis Tribune as soon as you have the money ready. Under the personal column you must write: We are ready Alice. You will then receive your final instructions. Be prepared to leave at a minutes notice to make the payoff. Don't attempt to stall or outsmart us. Don't try to bargain. Don't plead poverty; we know how much they have in their banks. Don't try to communicate with us; we'll do the directing. Threats aren't necessary—you just do your part—we guarantee to do ours.

Magee promptly notified the FBI, and they began a full-fledged investigation. Bremer's abandoned car was discovered with bloodstains on the steering wheel, the gearshift, and all of the car seats. It was clear that a struggle had taken place, and the Bremer family feared that Edward was already dead. The gang quickly learned that the police had been summoned, and sent several more letters warning of the outcome if the family didn't pull the police off the case. The gang also devised a new signal, which would be to place a special sticker on the office window when the money was ready, and they warned again that they would kill Bremer if the family failed to come through with the ransom. On January 25, 1934 another note and a key were found inside a can of Hills Brothers coffee. The note instructed Magee to open a locker at the Jefferson Lines Bus Station, located in downtown St. Paul, and stated that additional instructions would be found inside this locker. Magee complied fully with their demands, assuming the name of John B. Brakesham and boarding a bus that departed at 8:40 P.M. for Des Moines, Iowa. But despite Magee's efforts, the payoff failed to transpire as planned, and officials later found another note canceling the whole thing.

The kidnapping finally came to an end on February 6, 1934, when Magee received new instructions to locate a vehicle that had a note hidden in the glove box. Magee followed the additional instructions, which eventually led him down a dark dirt road at night, where he was to drop off the money. The FBI allowed the transaction to take place according to the wishes of the family, but they carefully recorded the serial numbers of the five and ten dollar bills. The following day, Bremer was released in the middle of an intersection near Rochester, Minnesota, and was told to stand with his back to the car and to count to fifteen before removing the large bandage covering his eyes.

After the kidnapping was safely resolved, U.S. special agents immediately embarked on an intensive investigation. Bremer had not been kept blindfolded all of the time, and he told agents that he could hear children playing outside of the hideout and two dogs barking frequently close to the house. Bremer had also studied his surroundings with great care. He had memorized the wallpaper and furnishings in the house, and the FBI searched for matching samples using old store receipts and other investigative means. Bremer had also heard traffic, and he told agents that when buses approached he could hear the drivers apply their brakes. Magee took agents to where he had dropped off the ransom money, and they found four flashlights that had been left behind. A young girl at a local store later identified photographs of Alvin Karpis and Doc Barker as the ones who had purchased the flashlights in downtown St. Paul. Bremer also remembered that his captors had thrown away a gas can that had been used to refuel the car during his kidnapping. The FBI recovered the gas can and it was found to have Doc's full hand and fingerprints all over it.

The bills that had been used to pay in the ransom soon started surfacing in various banks around the Chicago area. Officials also later confirmed that Karpis and Fred Barker had met with Dr. J. O. Moran, a physician with close ties to Capone and the Chicago Crime Syndicate. Both of the criminals had received surgery to alter their facial features, and had also attempted the removal of their fingerprints. The operations were apparently severely painful, and the FBI later documented that Fred became a "*raving maniac*" from the acute distress. Volney Davis and Doc later underwent similar surgery, also attempting to conceal their identity. The Barker-Karpis Gang then started to split up to avoid apprehension, since word was growing stronger that the FBI was closing in on them.

Karpis moved to Cleveland, Ohio with Dolores Delaney, taking enough funds to live happily for several years. Soon thereafter Fred Barker followed them, and rented a home in a nearby housing development. Doc and several of the others also moved to Cleveland and led a fairly quiet existence. According to FBI reports, the gang still had about $100,000 of the original ransom money in their possession. The idyll was soon disrupted however, when a few of the female members were arrested for being drunk and disorderly in a hotel, and were quickly linked to the Barker-Karpis Gang. Karpis moved around the states, ending up in Miami, Florida, and then he and Dolores made their way to Havana, Cuba, where Alvin felt confident that agents would not find them. But Alvin Karpis would not be granted any rest, as his picture was already being circulated in the newspapers of Havana. He fled back to Miami, where once again several of the other gang members were starting to reassemble.

The FBI noted that during this period, Doc Barker spent time hiding in Toledo, Ohio, where he became infatuated with a woman named Mildred Kuhlman. Until then, many of Doc's associates had termed him as a woman hater, who spurned female companionship with the exception of his frequent visits to houses of prostitution. He persuaded Mildred to accompany him back to Chicago, where he promised a life of luxury and riches. When she agreed to go with him, the FBI had already put her under surveillance. On January 8, 1935 special agents surrounded the Barker house on Pine Grove Avenue in Chicago, and took them both into custody. Agents also found a Thompson submachine gun, and the crime lab determined that it had been used in a robbery on August 30, 1933, in which a policeman had been killed with that very weapon. Also found in the house was a map with a street in Ocala, Florida circled in pencil. Doc received a life sentence for his role in the Bremer kidnapping, and was sentenced to serve his time at Alcatraz. He was shipped to The Rock in 1934.

Special agents quickly descended on the town of Ocala and began an extensive investigation, believing that the map found in Chicago indicated the whereabouts of other Barker-Karpis gang members. Their hunch was right, and they soon learned that Fred and Ma were living in a remote cottage located on Lake Weir at Ocklawaha, Florida. At 5:30 A.M. on the morning of January 16, 1935, special agents surrounded the cottage and told Fred and Ma to surrender. No answer or movement was detected for nearly fifteen minutes, and then finally the voice of Ma Barker was heard shouting: "*all right, go ahead.*" This was interpreted as indicating that they were going to surrender, but still no one emerged from the cottage. Seconds later the true meaning of the message was clear—the agents were forced to take cover under an intense bombardment of machine gun fire. The agents returned fire with a heavy barrage of machine gun rounds, rifle shots and tear gas grenades, and finally everything became quiet.

FBI agents waited for nearly an hour before entering the bullet-riddled gang hideout. When they went in, they found Ma Barker dead with a machine gun lying by her left hand, and Fred spread out on the floor next to the window, dead from multiple bullet wounds. He was still clutching a .45 caliber pistol. In the aftermath of the shootout, agents discovered a small arsenal of weapons and nearly $14,000 in large bills. The bodies of Fred and Kate (Ma) Barker would remain unburied from January 16, 1935 until October 1st, when George Barker finally received assistance for their burial. The two would be laid to rest in a small unknown and unmarked countryside cemetery in Welch, Oklahoma, next to the eldest Barker son Herman.

Agents had also learned that the hideout where Bremer had been held during his kidnapping was in Bensenville, Illinois. Bremer returned to the house and made a positive identification, which would ultimately led to more arrests. Special agents from the FBI continued their search to locate the other fugitives from the Barker-Karpis Gang. Their efforts were successful and they continued to make arrests, including the capture of Volney Davis and Dolores Delaney. Delaney gave birth to a baby boy while in prison, and the child was named Raymond Alvin Karpowicz after his father. The boy was ultimately turned over to Alvin's mother and father to care for until Dolores was released a few years later.

Following the deaths of Fred and Ma Barker, Alvin Karpis would continue his criminal activities with other gangsters. After he and an accomplice returned to Toledo, Ohio, Karpis recruited another underworld figure and future resident of Alcatraz, Freddie Hunter. Karpis, Hunter and some other gang members pulled off a few more successful robberies, including a railroad station heist in which they made off with $34,000 in cash and nearly $12,000 in U.S. Treasury Bonds. It was reported that Freddie Hunter held the station's mail clerk at gunpoint with a Thompson machine gun, while Karpis and the others gathered up the money. Hunter was later identified as the driver of the gang's getaway car.

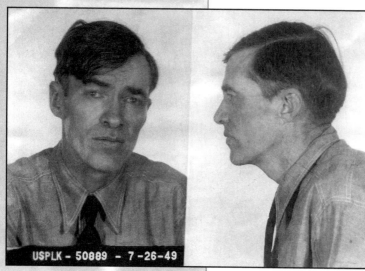

USPLK - 50889 - 7-26-49

Fred Hunter

Meanwhile J. Edgar Hoover had initiated an intense pursuit to capture Karpis and his associate gang members. On May 1, 1936, under Hoover's personal direction, the FBI descended on Karpis and Hunter in New Orleans. Hoover was on hand to command the squad of FBI agents who performed the arrest. Karpis would later laugh at Hoover's claim that he had been present for the arrest, stating that Hoover was actually nowhere to be seen until Karpis and his accomplice had already been cuffed, when he quickly emerged for the photo opportunities.

Karpis would not formally participate in the 1939 escape attempt, and would remain at Alcatraz for twenty-five years, the longest term

(Above) Alvin Karpis is pictured here being apprehended by FBI agents in May of 1936. FBI Director J. Edgar Hoover is seen in the foreground, and he would later claim to have planned the capture and the arrest himself. Karpis would comment that Hoover was *"nowhere to be seen"* during the arrest, and that he came out only after the suspects were handcuffed.

ever served on The Rock. He was sent to McNeil Island in 1962, and finally released in 1969 under condition of deportment to his country of birth, Canada. Karpis would later write two books about his life at Alcatraz, including one bestseller, and he would thus acquire enough funds to fulfill his longtime dream of moving to Spain. His life in Spain is largely undocumented, but on August 26, 1979, Karpis was found dead from what appeared to be an intentional overdose of sleeping pills. It was speculated that Karpis had likely run out of money, and had no other means to support himself.

A photograph of Alvin Karpis taken during his release from prison in 1969.

Henri Young

Rufus McCain

A mug shot series of William "Ty" Martin.

Henri Young and Rufus McCain

Two other accomplices in the escape of 1939 were Rufus Roy McCain and Henri Young. Both of their biographies are covered extensively in a separate chapter. Rufus McCain maintained a reputation as a difficult and violence-prone inmate at Alcatraz. He had built a record of violent acts and rebellion against his guards, and therefore he was no stranger to the solitary confinement cells in A and D Blocks.

Henri Young would later become one of the most famous inmates ever to reside on Alcatraz. He would also be the subject of several books and of the Hollywood motion picture *Murder in the First*, which chronicled the psychological effects of the harsh punishment he allegedly received while imprisoned on The Rock. Like McCain, Young had a long record of outbursts and unusual behavior. He was a problem inmate whose ill-mannered acts would frequently land him in solitary confinement.

William "Ty" Martin

William "Ty" Martin was another accomplice in the escape who had a close association with inmate Bernard Coy, the gang leader of the 1946 "*Battle of Alcatraz*," which was debatably the most significant escape attempt ever to take place on the island. Ty was an African-American from Chicago, serving a twenty-five year sentence for armed robbery. He was well liked among the Caucasian inmates, which was unusual at the time, as there was heavy racial segregation among prisoners during this period.

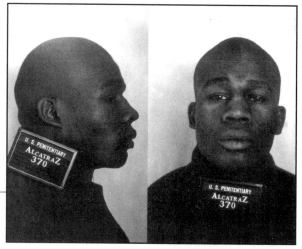

Dale Stamphill

The last of the inmates who participated in the escape of 1939 was Dale Stamphill, born March 12, 1912. Stamphill was a habitual criminal serving a life sentence for kidnapping and robbery. On February 17, 1935, while serving time at the State Reformatory in Granite, Oklahoma, Dale and twenty-one other prisoners escaped after killing a tower guard. Then on February 27, 1935, Stamphill and two accomplices, W. L. Baker and Malloy Kuykendall, robbed the 1st National Bank in Seiling, Oklahoma, and kidnapped Dr. Fred Myers from his residence at gunpoint. Dr. Myers was forced to treat a hip injury that Kuykendall had received during the bank robbery, and then to drive the men to Grazier, Texas, with a shotgun trained upon him. The outlaws were captured by the police, and Stamphill was sentenced to life imprisonment on October 26, 1937. He was initially sent to Leavenworth, but then was transferred to Alcatraz on January 21, 1938, because of his escape history.

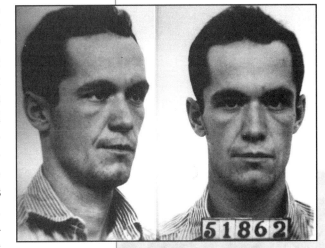

Dale Stamphill

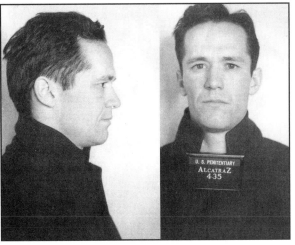

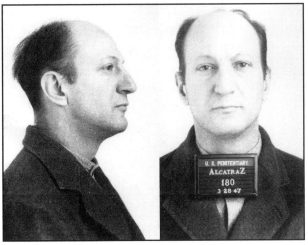

Malloy Kuykendall

The Escape

In the autumn of 1938, several months before the escape, Barker started recruiting his accomplices and plotting a breakout from D Block. After striking deals with other inmates to have a hacksaw blade and makeshift bar spreader delivered to him in D Block, Barker worked on getting himself thrown into segregation. On October 30, 1938 Barker assaulted fellow inmate Ira Earl Blackwood, while standing in line in the recreation yard waiting to file down to their work detail. Karpis later wrote that Ira had a reputation with most cons as a stool pigeon. Associate Warden E. J. Miller, nicknamed "Meathead" by the inmates, was on a month-long vacation, and Acting Deputy Warden C. J. Shuttleworth had Barker thrown into isolation for the full nineteen-day duration. After completing his time in isolation, Barker was moved to a standard segregation cell where he would remain until the escape.

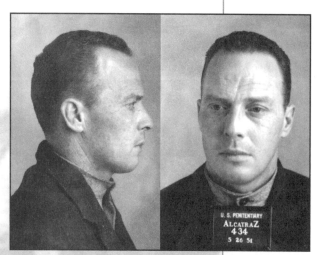

Ira Earl Blackwood

D Block was one of the few areas besides A Block that had remained in its original state, just as it was when it was utilized during the military years. The cell bars were still of the flat soft iron type, with outward swinging door hinges similar to those found in A Block. The inmates would exploit this weakness to their advantage by using their hacksaw blade to saw methodically through the soft iron bars in sequence, filling the gaps with debris and paint to avoid detection. The bars that encased the windows of D Block were made of tool-proof alloys, and this would make gaining access an even greater challenge.

The D Block area had not yet been walled off from the rest of the prison, which allowed for the easy transfer of contraband from inmates performing clean-up details and other assignments inside the main cellhouse. It was further rumored that inmate William "Slim" Bartlett, who apparently had worked as a machinist before being incarcerated, had requested permission to build a lap steel guitar. It was said that once it was completed, he smuggled the makeshift bar spreader into the main cellblock inside the guitar, so that another collaborator could pass it to Barker in D Block. The bar-spreader was in some respects similar to the device that would later be used by

A typical cell in D Block, prior to the 1940 remodeling. Note the flat soft iron bars.

Bernard Coy in the 1946 escape attempt. It was small, consisting of two bolts with a cross thread, and if used in combination with a crescent style wrench, it could exert enough force to reposition and force apart the bar section.

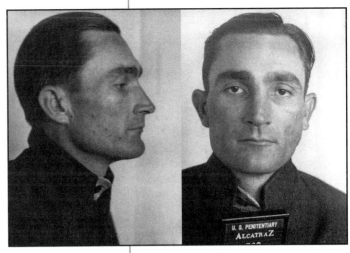

William "Slim" Bartlett was rumored to have a smuggled a bar-spreader device to Doc Barker.

Before the escape could be attempted, a few of the inmates would have to leave their cells and try to displace one of the window bars, during a period when the guards would be performing duties in the main cell house. This was a risky undertaking, since they would have to leave their cells when noise levels allowed some degree of cover, also taking care not to be spotted by any of the custodial officers. During the early evening hours when the cellhouse inmates were herded into the dinning room hall for dinner, two of the inmates left their cells to work on the window bars, while another went to act as a lookout, keeping an eye on the guard inside the gun gallery. The inmates manipulated a wrench to exert enough force against the bar, which snapped free from its foundation. Using putty and cement, they set the bar back in its place to avoid raising suspicion. As the inmates worked, other prisoners around the cellhouse banded together to flush toilets and make various other subtle noises, in order to keep the guards from hearing the inmates working outside their cells in D Block. Once they were able to sneak back into their cells undetected, with the window bar prepared for easy removal, the inmates were ready to make their escape.

On the fog-laden morning of Friday the thirteenth at 3:00 A.M., the guard in D Block performed his customary counts of the inmates, thinking all of them to be asleep. At this hour there was only one guard on the cellhouse floor, and one in each gun-gallery. After the guard finished the count in D Block, he walked over to B Block and started his next round of counts. As soon as the path was clear, the escape accomplices bent out the lower bars of their cells, which they had been preparing for weeks, and made their way to the window. Karpis later wrote that Ty Martin was the first to climb through the window, and when his large shoulders became stuck, he hung helplessly attempting to squeeze through without making any noise. With Stamphill's help he managed to painfully cram himself through the small opening and drop to the path eight feet below. After the five inmates had all made their way out from the cellhouse, they stealthily hiked down to a small clearing at the water's edge, and then started to gather wood, attempting to build a makeshift raft. The harsh waves pounded against the jagged rock forms as the men stripped down to their underwear, using clothing to tie the pieces of wood together.

By 3:30 A.M. the guard had started making another round, and he reached the disciplinary section at about 3:45. In a shocking discovery, he found one of the D-Block cells empty with the sheet stripped from the bed. He quickly ran to the administration phone and called the Armory, anxiously communicating the news of the escape. Minutes later, sirens and searchlights saturated the fog-shrouded island, and a quick phone call was placed to the Warden. Johnston quickly dressed himself and was met at the front door by Associate Warden Miller. Little information was available other than that the inmates had all been present during the 3:00 A.M. count. Captain Weinhold had been awoken, and he quickly reported to D Block. It was found that the five inmates, all of whom shared adjacent cells, had sawed through the bottom bars of each cell and were now missing. Meanwhile down by the water's edge, as the sirens wailed in the distance, the inmates became separated and hurried to complete their improvised wooden rafts.

The off-duty correctional staff poured into the Armory to get weapons, and then started to search the island in groups. The launch *McDowell* was sent out to begin searching the shorelines through the dense fog. It was well known among the staff that the inmates would try to take hostages in their desperation to attain freedom, and officers were sent to search every conceivable hiding spot around the living quarters, including the Warden's basement. As the officers walked quietly along the roadway, one of them heard voices coming from a remote cove below, but was unable to see anything because of the fog. Finally, the road tower guard shined the powerful searchlight into the cove, and followed two figures running for the water. One officer observing from the roadway yelled at the inmates to halt, and fired several warning shots ahead of them. The two men hit the water, and the officers, now able to target the inmates, opened fire with a shower of machine gun and rifle bullets raining into the cove.

The fronts of Rufus McCain's cell (Above) and Dale Stamphill's cell following their escape (Below).

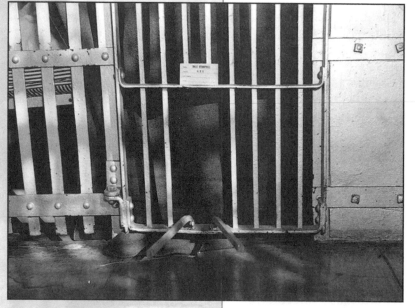

The first men to be captured were Young and McCain, who were stripped of their clothing, and stood chattering and cold from exposure. The two inmates were brought up to the visitor's area of the administration building and given blankets until they could be escorted to the prison hospital. The cove proved to be too dangerous for the *McDowell*, so two officers took a small rowing boat into the shallow water, and pulled the wounded inmates Stamphill and Barker into the craft. Stamphill was lethargic and had suffered serious gunshot wounds to each leg, both of which had sustained serious bone fractures, with one bleeding profusely from a

D Block as it appeared following the 1939 escape. Note the spread bars on one of the cell fronts. Also note the extended cell front toward the rear of the cellblock. This was one of the early closed-front solitary confinement cells.

severed artery. Barker was pulled into the boat and was also found to be critically injured. He had suffered gunshot wounds to the head and thigh, and he had an obvious fracture in his left leg that most likely resulted from a stray bullet. Ty Martin was found standing almost completely naked, wearing only a pair of water soaked socks, bleeding from several cuts and bruises, and nearly frozen from exposure. Warden Johnston later wrote that when Miller shined the light onto him, Ty started yelling, "*I give up, I give up.*" Martin was also taken to the hospital for an examination.

McCain and Young were found to be uninjured, and both were immediately sent to solitary confinement in A Block. Martin was also treated and released back into solitary confinement. Barker was semi-conscious when he arrived at the hospital, and complained that he was in severe pain. Warden Johnston stated that they tried to get a formal statement from Barker, but his last words would be simply, "*I was a fool to try it. I'm all shot to hell.*"

In a memorandum to the Warden dated January 14, 1939, Dr. Romney Ritchey described Barker's condition:

Re: Barker, Arthur, 268-AZ

This will inform you that the above captioned Inmate, who came to the Hospital yesterday morning with injuries mentioned in a previous memorandum, showed a gradual loss of strength during the day and died at 5:40 P.M. last night.

When first brought in he was greatly confused but partly conscious and complained of pain in the left leg which was broken, and of being cold. Later on during the morning he was restless in bed and would rally to look around him but made no statement or gave any indication that he understood the situation more than to realize at times his own precarious physical condition. Everything possible was done to improve his condition and Dr. E. M. Townsend of the U.S. Marine Hospital was called in consultation. During the afternoon he became more restless and confused and was constantly rolling about in bed. His circulation became weaker more rapidly during the afternoon and his breathing more labored and it was realized that he probably would not survive the night. A Spinal Puncture revealed a large amount of blood in the cranial cavity

The area where the escapees entered the water, known today as Barker's Beach.

weaker more rapidly during the afternoon and his breathing more labored and it was realized that he probably would not survive the night. A Spinal Puncture revealed a large amount of blood in the cranial cavity resulting from a skull fracture. His condition showed little change after 3:00 P.M. until 5:30 P.M. when he became rapidly worse and in spite of stimulants died at 5:40 P.M.

Cause of Death: Fracture of Skull

Doc Barker's father could not afford to have his son brought back to Oklahoma. Warden Johnston arranged for a small formal service and burial in Colma, California, where ironically several other celebrity crime figures have been laid to rest, including the famous old-west lawman Wyatt Earp. Services for Barker were held on January 17th at the Lasswell Funeral Parlor, and he was laid to rest in a pauper's grave in the Mount Olivet Cemetery late that afternoon. Protestant Chaplain Wayne Hunter wrote a memo to Johnston stating that the only people in attendance were a prison clerk, two men from the funeral parlor, the manager of the cemetery, and four other cemetery employees.

The only unusual occurrence reported was that when Barker's casket was being prepared to be driven to the cemetery, a drunk staggered into the funeral parlor and yelled out only one word, "Barker." When asked what he wanted, he turned around and walked out.

Doc's grave was marked only with his Alcatraz inmate number, #268.

Stamphill's wounds proved serious but not fatal, and he would remain in the hospital until April 8, 1939. He was subsequently transferred to isolation, and was kept there until August 3, 1940, when he was released back into the general prison population. The experience of the escape attempt seemed to have changed Stamphill; from then on he would maintain a fairly clear conduct record, and he held several jobs in various departments at Alcatraz. Stamphill was approved for transfer to Leavenworth in 1950, and he remained there until his parole in 1956. Once paroled, Stamphill started a small tax preparation and business accounting firm, which kept him out of trouble for nearly ten years. He married, but soon after started having personal and business problems that ultimately led to severe debt, and he eventually would violate his parole following another burglary. He was returned to Leavenworth and released several years later. He died in September of 1998 in Kansas City.

A coroner's inquest conducted by Coroner T. B. W. Leland following the death of Doc Barker resulted in a deluge of negative press about the security practices at Alcatraz. Associate Warden Edward J. Miller ap-

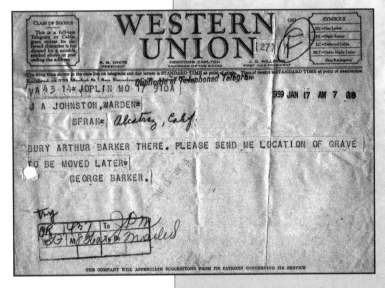

A telegram from Barker's father asking that his son be buried in San Francisco. Barker would regret his escape attempt, and his final words were recorded in the Alcatraz hospital as: "*I was a fool to try it. I'm all shot to hell.*"

peared as the sole witness in the inquest. Miller admitted that the officers on duty could have been asleep during the escape, and that they were *"definitely not alert."* However he did make it clear that the officers were required to call the Armory every half hour, which made it seem very unlikely that they were taking a nap during the time period when the inmates had escaped from D Block. Miller testified that no saws had been found, and no trace of filings or any material which might have been used to conceal the progress of work on the iron bars. The instrument that had been used to force the *"tool-proof"* outside bars was likewise never found. The jury findings of the inquest stated the following:

> We, the jury, find that the said Arthur R. Barker met his death attempting to escape from Alcatraz Prison from gunshot wounds inflicted by guards unknown.

On December 30, 1940, Henri Young fatally stabbed Rufus McCain. He would later claim that this act resulted from conflicts that arose during the failed escape attempt of 1939. In news reports describing the murder trial, it was reported that Young stated to the jurors: *"McCain held a great deal of animosity toward me. He wanted to use the wives of the guards as shields in the break, but I wouldn't do it. I obstructed the plan. I told McCain freedom wasn't everything, but he wouldn't listen."* Young's life would later be fictionalized in the book and motion picture *Murder in the First.*

The escape of 1939 had been the first ever on The Rock to demonstrate a weakness in the main security system. This would be last escape to initiate from within D Block.

Escape Attempt #5

DATE: MAY 21, 1941

INMATES: JOSEPH PAUL CRETZER

SAM RICHARD SHOCKLEY

ARNOLD THOMAS KYLE

LLOYD H. BARKDOLL

LOCATION: MAT SHOP (Model Industries Building)

The 1941 escape attempt by inmates Joseph Cretzer, Sam Shockley, Arnold Kyle, and Lloyd Barkdoll would unexpectedly serve as a prelude to the bloodiest chapter in the prison's history, known today as the *Battle of Alcatraz* of 1946. The biographies of Joe Cretzer, Sam Shockley, and Arnold Kyle are covered extensively in a later section chronicling the events of 1946. Prior to their capture in 1939, Cretzer and Kyle had been considered the number-one bank robbing team in the nation. They had previously made spectacular breaks from other penitentiaries, and they would seize upon the slightest opportunity to break from The Rock. All four men were serving life sentences, and were assigned to work details in the Rubber Mat Shop.

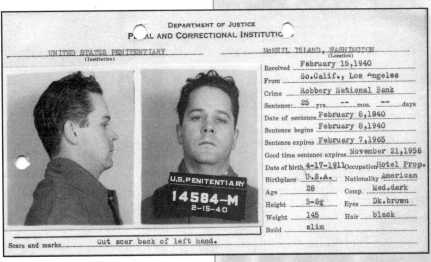

Joseph P. Cretzer

Lloyd Barkdoll was later said to have been the principle instigator of this escape attempt. He had previously been serving a life sentence for a series of bank robberies in Oregon, and he was transferred to Alcatraz on October 13, 1937 from the Federal Penitentiary at McNeil Island, where prison officials believed that he was planning a mass escape. Barkdoll had also been a key witness during the famous Henri Young trial, and Warden Johnston had subsequently stated in a newspaper interview that Barkdoll's sole purpose for testifying had been to seek an opportunity for an escape.

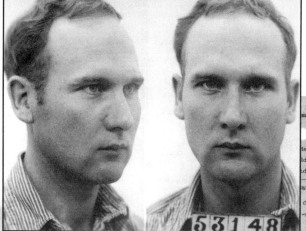

Sam Richard Shockley

(Below) A report written while Shockley was incarcerated at Leavenworth, describing a knife that was found hidden in his cell mattress.

REPORT OF CUSTODIAL OFFICER
U. S. PRISON SERVICE
DEPARTMENT OF JUSTICE
N? 15281
June 26th 1938

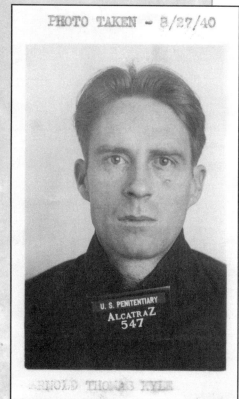

Arnold Thomas Kyle

The Alcatraz escape attempt took place on May 21, 1941. Just after the inmates had returned from lunch, Clyne E. Stoops, a correctional officer assigned to the Industries, was lured into the mat shop under the pretense that a piece of equipment had stopped working. As the officer started to examine the piece of machinery, the four inmates overpowered him, bound his hands and feet with heavy gauge twine, and gagged him. The prisoners then took control of the workshop and moved eight other inmates who chose not to participate into an adjacent room.

Taking turns and using a heavy piece of pipe, they struggled to pry open the inside casement, which was made of heavy wire. After nearly thirty minutes of intense prying, they were caught off guard when another officer entered the workshop. In a newspaper interview with the *San Francisco Chronicle*, Warden Johnston later recounted the following events:

They had worked at it about half an hour when Manning, who wasn't expected, entered the shop on a routine inspection tour. They had a lookout posted. When Manning entered one grabbed him on each side and one from behind, and they hustled him into the room with Stoops, binding him but not gagging him.

Then they went back to the window. By this time they had pried off part of the casement. They dragged over a small motor driven emery stone and began grinding away at one of the toolproof bars.

One of the convicts remained posted at the door as a guard, and when Officer Johnson entered he was hustled in with the other officers. So far as I can gather they at no time used any weapons on the officers, just overpowering them by surprise and strength of numbers. Barkdoll is a big, husky man and took the lead.

Finally Captain Madigan entered the shop. They overpowered him too. But Captain Manning pointed out to them that it was time for the officers to ring in to the administration building, and that an alarm would be sounded if the officers failed to ring in. They were about ready to give up anyway. They had to cut through at least and probably three of the bars before they could drop down to the outside and they hadn't even cut through one.

So they freed Madigan. He phoned the administration building, and by the time we got there he was leading them away.

In a later report, Barkdoll was commended for protecting the officers from being assaulted. It read: "*It was reported that during the escape attempt, when Cretzer, Kyle, and subject tied up the officers and threatened them with hammers and other weapons, Barkdoll kept the others from injuring the officers and protecting them from assault.*" All four men were immediately sent to solitary confinement. Shockley would serve the remainder of his time at Alcatraz in the segregation unit, until the 1946 escape attempt.

After he had been integrated back into the general prison population, Barkdoll would earn the designation of a model inmate. His progress reports reflect unanimous praise for his leadership abilities promoting positive conduct. The correctional

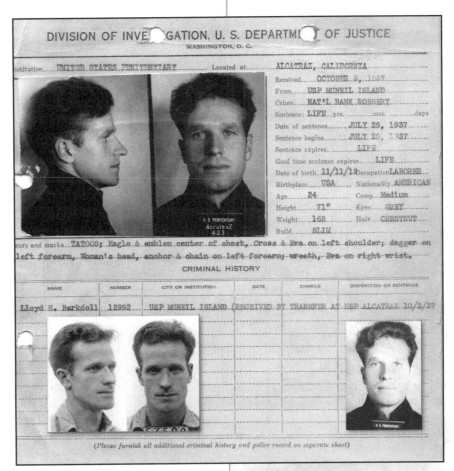

Lloyd H. Barkdoll

DEPARTMENT OF JUSTICE
UNITED STATES PENITENTIARY
ALCATRAZ ISLAND, CALIFORNIA

March 8, 1950

MEMORANDUM TO THE WARDEN

Re: Barkdoll, L. #423-Az., Death of,

This is to inform you that the above captioned inmate subject was taken ill in his cell at about 3:30 p.m. Mar. 7, 1950 complaining of severe pain in his upper chest. Medication was administered to patient while he was still in his cell but he did not respond satisfactorily and he was then admitted to the hospital for further treatment and observation. Patient expired about 5:15 p.m. Mar. 7, 1950. Apparently the cause of death was Coronary Occlusion.

Respectfully,
R.S. Yocum
R.S. Yocum
Sr. Surgeon, USPHS.
Chief Medical Officer.

by direction.

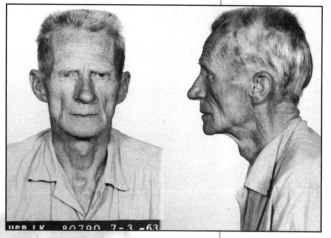

A photograph of Arnold Kyle, taken in 1963. The effects of decades spent in prison are plainly evident.

staff characterized him as cheerful, friendly, and cooperative, with a pleasing personality and all the qualities of a natural leader. On March 12, 1945 he was assigned to the kitchen detail, and was later promoted to work in the Officer's Dining Room. He would also be credited with starting an inmate orchestra. When other inmates participated in a culinary strike in October of 1948, Barkdoll stayed on the job, helping wherever he could. He was clearly liked and respected by prison officials, who provided him with monetary rewards even though he worked in a non-compensated industry assignment. On March 7, 1950, Barkdoll developed severe chest pains while walking in the recreation yard. He was taken to the hospital, and shortly thereafter suffered a fatal heart attack. Under the direction of his wife, Barkdoll's body was sent to Schroeder Mortuary in Coquille Oregon for burial.

Although the escape attempt of 1941 had proved unsuccessful, it was destined to become a prelude to a later prison tragedy...

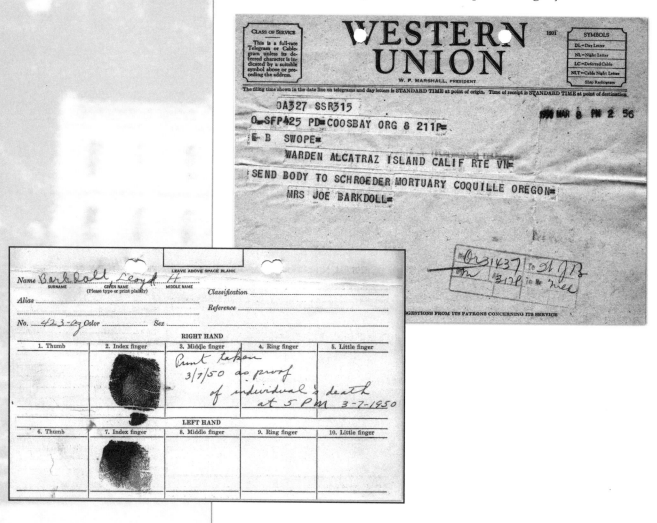

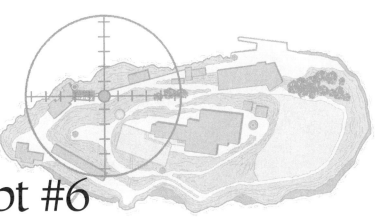

Escape Attempt #6

DATE: SEPTEMBER 15, 1941
INMATE: JOHN RICHARD BAYLESS
LOCATION: POWERHOUSE

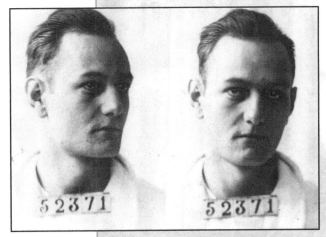

John Bayless was one of a small select group of inmates who were sent to Alcatraz twice, under two completely separate convictions. He was born on May 16, 1915 into a middle-class family in Wichita, Kansas. His father was steadily employed as a railroad worker, and his mother was an affectionate and devoted homemaker. Like many boys of the age, he became a Boy Scout, developed an avid interest in science, and attended church every Sunday. It wasn't until he turned sixteen that his life started to change for the worse. While he was still in high school, his parents decided to divorce, and this was apparently a very traumatic experience for Bayless. He was sent to live with his grandmother in Willow Springs, Missouri, and after graduating high school in 1933, he decided to enlist in the U.S. Navy.

In the Navy Bayless was trained as an aircraft mechanic on the Aircraft Carrier USS Saratoga, based out of Long Beach, California. But despite his naval training and a promising future in aviation, he detested military life. On July 28, 1935, Bayless wrote a bad check for a payment on a 1931 Ford Roadster, deserted the Navy, and drove back home to Missouri. The car was immediately reported stolen, and Bayless was soon arrested after being caught trying to forge his grandmother's signature on another check. He was convicted of forgery and a dyer act on December 16, 1935, and was sentenced to serve two years at the U.S. Southwestern Reformatory, in El Reno, Okalahoma.

Within only a few months of his release, Bayless met and married an attractive young girl named Gwendolyn, and the two quickly moved into a furnished apartment. However, his wife soon grew suspicious that her

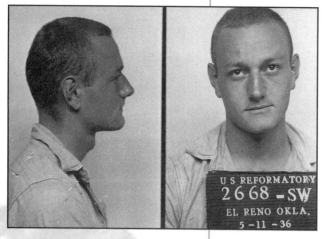

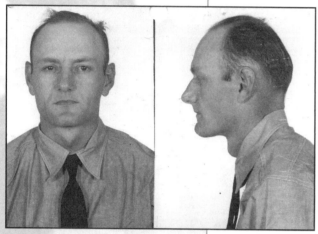

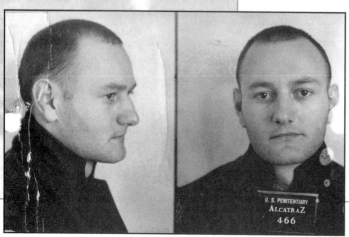

new husband didn't work, yet somehow always seemed to have money. He would leave with friends for long periods during the day, and return without volunteering any information about his activities. He finally told his young bride excitedly that he had inherited money, and that they would receive the entire sum the following month. She too was excited, and was now starting to adjust into her new life.

On October 29, 1937 the couple decided to drive to Wichita, Kansas with John's seventeen-year-old friend Orville Sims and his wife Orletta, so that Gwendolyn could visit her mother. When John tired during the drive, Orville took over the wheel, and began driving erratically. Orville lost control, and the car rolled over numerous times before plunging violently into a ditch. John and Gwendolyn, who were riding in the backseat, found themselves pinned underneath the wreckage. They were finally able to free themselves, and hurried to the nearest hospital. Gwendolyn had suffered serious injuries including a fractured vertebra in her neck, and a broken femur in her right leg. John walked away with only a minor back injury and a few stitches in his left hand. Gwendolyn would need to remain in the hospital for several weeks, so Bayless decided to rent a car and head back home to get some money.

A local newspaper, *The Wichita Eagle*, ran a story on the accident, and this helped to alert law enforcement officials to the location of Bayless and his partner in crime. After meeting with Gwendolyn, police decided to raid the Bayless apartment, where they found bank diagrams and other items that linked John to a series of crimes. At the same time that agents were raiding the apartment, Sims and Bayless were in Mansfield, Missouri, casing a bank. Dressed in dark blue overalls, each with a watch chain dangling from his pocket, the men drew guns on two female employees at the downtown Merchants Bank. They locked the two women in the bank vault, and made off with all of the cash from their tills.

When news of the bank robbery was broadcast over police radios, the agents headed to Sim's residence, where they found both men asleep. On awaking, Bayless made a comment that would be entered into his arrest report: "*Lucky you caught me asleep copper, or I'd have blasted you.*" In early 1938, several FBI agents and Deputy United States Marshals, all armed, escorted the young men to the courtroom. The prisoners wore handcuffs, which were slipped from their wrists as they entered. Bayless and Sims stood before Judge Albert L. Reeves in the Federal Court of Kansas City, pleading guilty to two Federal Grand Jury indictments for robbery of an FDIC bank using force, violence and deadly weapons. They were sentenced to serve twenty years for the first count, and twenty-five years for the second. Bayless would arrive at Leavenworth on February 1, 1938, and he was transferred to Alcatraz on November 29, 1938, as inmate #AZ-466.

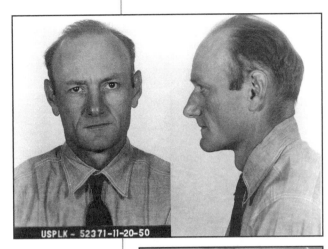

At Alcatraz, Bayless was considered a low-maintenance inmate who rarely sought trouble. He was a loner, and spent most of his time during recreation periods by himself. On September 15, 1941, Bayless was assigned to the garbage detail, which was generally considered a choice assignment by the inmates. This work detail permitted Bayless to collect garbage and debris from all over the island, under limited supervision. On this day at the end of his shift, Bayless made a spontaneous decision to escape under a dense layer of fog. Just before the inmates were rounded up for the final count and rallied back to the main cellhouse, Bayless slipped away and dropped to the rocky shore near the powerhouse. But by the time he had made it to the water's edge, the guard staff noticed him missing from his work detail and immediately notified the Control Center. The piercing sound of the klaxon siren rang out over the island.

Bayless removed his shirt, shoes, and socks, then immersed himself in the water until he was chest-deep. He would later state that once he was in the ice-cold water, he had trouble staying afloat, and quickly realized that he would be unable to make the swim across the Bay. Wilkinson, one of the officers assigned to the same detail, quickly spotted Bayless in the water. The prisoner didn't resist capture, and after being shackled, he was marched

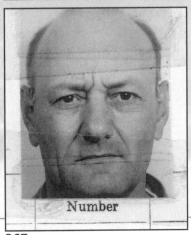

Number

directly into D Block. When Bayless was brought to trial in San Francisco on January 28, 1943, he again demonstrated his desperation by breaking free and making a dash from the U.S. Marshals while they were inside the courthouse. He was immediately tackled, and was sent back to isolation on Alcatraz. In April of 1943 he was convicted of attempted escape, and was sentenced to serve an additional thirty years.

Bayless would serve his time quietly in segregation, and would eventually earn a transfer back to Leavenworth in November of 1950. He

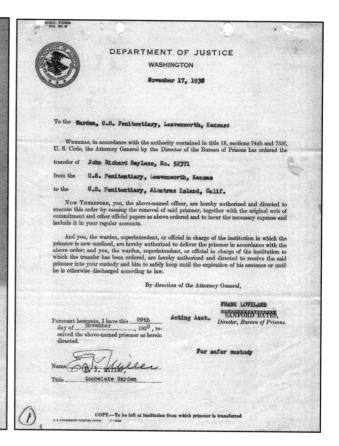

DEPARTMENT OF JUSTICE
BUREAU OF PRISONS
WASHINGTON

September 15, 1941

MEMORANDUM FOR THE FILES:

Warden Johnston called me on the phone today and told me that John R. Bayless had made an abortive attempt to escape. He was workong on the "garbage crew" near the dock. At the time the inmates were brought in for count Bayless was missing.

Officer Wilkinson immediately noticed that Bayless was gone, rang the alarm and went to the wharf and found Bayless in the water and called to him to return. Bayless evidently feeling that he could not safely make his getaway and returned to the institution. He seemed so cold and nervous at the time he was taken into the institution that he was committed to the hospital where he was at the time Warden Johnston phoned me.

The Warden could not inform me of the ressons for Bayless' apparently foolhardy attempt to escape other than that he was discouraged.

There was no violence connected with the affair and not more than four of five minutes elapse in all probability between the time Bayless left the detail and when he was found in the water.

James V. Bennett
Director.

DEPARTMENT OF JUSTICE
WASHINGTON

November 17, 1938

To the Warden, U.S. Penitentiary, Leavenworth, Kansas:

WHEREAS, in accordance with the authority contained in title 18, sections 744b and 753f, U. S. Code, the Attorney General by the Director of the Bureau of Prisons has ordered the

transfer of   John Richard Bayless, No. 52371

from the   U.S. Penitentiary, Leavenworth, Kansas

to the   U.S. Penitentiary, Alcatraz Island, Calif.

NOW THEREFORE, you, the above-named officer, are hereby authorized and directed to execute this order by causing the removal of said prisoner, together with the original writ of commitment and other official papers as above ordered and to incur the necessary expense and include it in your regular accounts.

And you, the warden, superintendent, or official in charge of the institution in which the prisoner is now confined, are hereby authorized to deliver the prisoner in accordance with the above order; and you, the warden, superintendent, or official in charge of the institution to which the transfer has been ordered, are hereby authorized and directed to receive the said prisoner into your custody and him to safely keep until the expiration of his sentence or until he is otherwise discharged according to law.

By direction of the Attorney General,

FRANK LOVELAND
SANFORD BATES,
Acting Asst.   Director, Bureau of Prisons.

Pursuant hereunto, I have this   29th
day of   November   , 1938 , received the above-named prisoner as herein directed.

For safer custody

Name   E. J. Miller
Title   Associate Warden

COPY.—To be left at institution from which prisoner is transferred

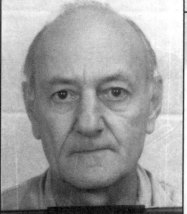

was awarded a conditional parole release on August 19, 1951, and landed himself back in jail on February 26, 1952, after committing another bank robbery. This time he was convicted and sentenced to serve thirty-five years. One year to the day after his release, he arrived for his second term at Alcatraz on August 19, 1952, as inmate #AZ-966.

Bayless would be among the last inmates to depart Alcatraz when it finally closed on March 21, 1963. He was sent back to McNeil Island, and would not serve his time there idly; once more he would find himself involved in a violent and desperate prison break. On November 8, 1965, Bayless and fellow inmate Dennis Hubbard concealed themselves behind another prisoner as he passed through an electric sentry gate into a minimum-security dormitory. Using a hand-fashioned knife, they overpowered a guard, and bound and tied him using duct tape. They escaped through a non-barred window and under the cover of heavy rain, scaled the perimeter fences and disappeared into the landscape.

The duo found a vacant house that belonged to the prison's physician, who was away on a hunting expedition. They remained inside the house undetected for five days, until the physician returned home. When prison officials came for them, they offered no resistance, and Bayless again stood trial for escape. He was sentenced to another forty-five years, and would again be paroled for good time served on August 20, 1973. But just one month later he was back in prison at Leavenworth for attempted bank robbery. Bayless was re-paroled to a community treatment center in Long Beach California, and died on July 30, 1981. He had finally returned to the city in which he had committed his first crime.

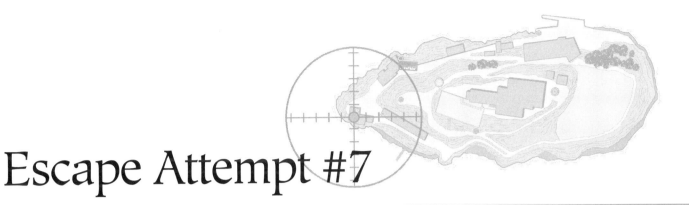

Escape Attempt #7

DATE: APRIL 13, 1943

INMATES: JAMES A. BOARMAN
FRED HUNTER
HAROLD BREST
FLOYD G. HAMILTON

LOCATION: OLD MAT SHOP

On the cold morning of April 13, 1943, a densely strewn layer of fog lay over the prison fortress. The escape attempt that was about to unfold would involve four inmates who were assigned to the old Mat Shop, employed in manufacturing cement blocks that were used to weigh down heavy submarine nets during the war. The inmates had each acquired smuggled military uniforms from the prison laundry, and had stuffed them in specially made float canisters, which were smaller but nearly identical to those used during the escape of Theodore Cole and Ralph Roe in December of 1937. The four hollow one-gallon fuel containers offered perfect concealment and water protection for their clothing, and a seemingly perfect float device with which to swim quietly across the bay. Their plan would also incorporate some of the more successful aspects of the 1941 escape attempt by Cretzer, Barkdoll, Shockley, and Kyle, which ultimately ended in failure.

James A. Boarman

James A. Boarman

James Arnold Boarman, a small time bank robber from Indianapolis, was only twenty-four years old at the time of this ill-fated escape attempt. Born on November 3, 1919 in Whalen, Kentucky, he was the sixth in a family of eight children. His father, who had supported the

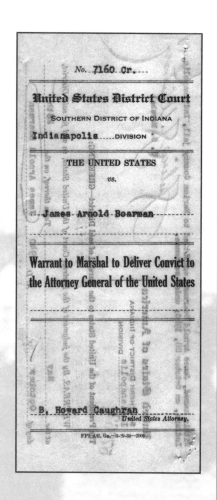

family as a carpenter, died of an accidental drowning when James was only seven years old. His mother, who was a homemaker, relocated the family to Indiana where they would all share residence in a small apartment. Boarman attended St. Patrick's Catholic School in Indianapolis, and dropped out to work as a gardener at age fourteen. His mother would later state that James always had brought his earnings home, and never complained about the family's financial troubles. Despite their hardships and their dependence welfare support, reports state that his family was close, and all worked together to help and support each other.

Boarman's bouts with crime first began when he was still very young. In May of 1936 he stole his first automobile, and after being arrested and placed on probation, he stole two other cars and headed for California with two accomplices. His mother pleaded his case in court, stating that she had been hospitalized due to illness, and that he had lacked proper supervision when he needed it most. The court proved unsympathetic to her pleas, and on January 30, 1937, Boarman was sentenced to three years in the Federal Reformatory at El Reno, Oklahoma.

Boarman and four other inmates plotted an escape from El Reno, and carried out their plan on September 9, 1937. A special progress report chronicled the events:

> After arrest, he was taken to jail in Golden, Colorado, and while there involved in several fights. Also, in a scheme to effect his escape hid under a table in the jail and tried to jump a turn-key. While an inmate at El Reno, connived with four other inmates to escape from the institution. This was frustrated, but subject admitted his participation in the scheme, which was to climb a fence, seize the physician upon his arrival at the parking area, drive away in his car and hold him as hostage.

Boarman was recommended for transfer to a more secure prison facility, and was sent to Lewisburg Federal Penitentiary on September 28, 1937. At Lewisburg he continued to assemble a record of conduct violations. The most significant of these was being found with an eight-inch dagger hidden in a magazine inside his cell. He apparently disclaimed ownership, stating that he was *"just putting a handle on it."* His reports were all unfavorable, with one stating: *"This inmate is a reckless, very unstable psychopath who is not material for rehabilitation. He has been making a very poor institutional adjustment and has had several disciplinary infractions of a serious nature."*

He was finally released from Lewisburg on December 15, 1939, and was immediately provided with employment by the R.C.A. Radio Company in the labor compound department. After a series of layoffs and rehires by R.C.A., he again emerged into the crime scene. He was later quoted in a progress report as saying: *"When I come out of Lewisburg, I intended to go straight. I got me a job and did go straight. I lost that job, and couldn't find another one for hell. I tried to join the Army, the Navy, and the Marine Corps and didn't get in, so I went and got me a gun and started robbin'."* His probation officer also documented his own attempts to help

Boarman enlist in the Army, but apparently the recruiters felt that his criminal conduct made him unacceptable for the armed forces.

The following report describes Boarman's character in the eyes of the correctional system, and the reasons for his transfer to Alcatraz:

On August 12, 1940, at about 9:30 P.M., this defendant stole an automobile in Indianapolis after flourishing a gun on a salesman, which he drove to Lexington, Ky. He traded said gun for another and on the morning of August 15, returned to Indianapolis, and entered a branch of the Fletcher Trust Co., again flourishing a gun in the presence of bank employees and patrons, escaping with $12,812.00. He drove said stolen car to a point near Loogootee, Indiana, abandoned that car and stole another and hence drove it to Owensboro, Ky. After abandoning this car, he appeared at a motor sales agency and purchased a Buick car for which he paid $600 in cash, using a part of the funds stolen from the forgoing bank. In addition he purchased a rifle and an assortment of clothing and was subsequently arrested in a hotel room at Frankfort, Ky. $11,710 of the stolen funds were recovered. Defendant admitted numerous hold-ups, including filling stations, grocery stores and two ladies in a parking lot. He has previously been convicted as shown by the attached F.B.I. report.

Subject is apparently a confirmed offender and a vicious menace to society as indicated by the instant offense and the series of armed robberies which he committed prior to the instant bank robbery. He is a highly unstable and impulsive youth who is apparently quite proud of the fact that he committed the instant offense without the aid or advice of other persons. He is convinced, outwardly at least, that he is entirely capable of whipping the whole world and providing himself with funds even if it is necessary to resort to physical force and the aid of firearms.

Note, in the Central File a report from the United States Marshal which may be more indicative of his attitude toward the sentence and confinement than his own personal statements:

Deputy Taff states that while crossing a bridge or large culvert on Highway #71, two miles north of Plat City, this prisoner suddenly tried to wreck the car by raising both feet and kicking against the back of the driver's seat throwing the guard, who was driving at the time, against the steering wheel. The guard happened to be a man of large stature, and while thrown against the steering wheel he did not lose absolute control of the car although the incident did cause the car to leave the highway. Boarman likewise made an attempt to get the deputy's revolver but was unsuccessful.

In view of this subjects traits in the instant offense of vicious nature, his previous institutional adjustments during confinement in the Federal Reformatory at El Reno, and the Federal Prison at Lewisburg, his present indifferent attitude and the indication that his future adjustment in confinement here or elsewhere is very definitely problematical. It is believed advisable that he be CONSIDERED FOR TRANSFER TO THE FEDERAL PRISON AT ALCATRAZ ISLAND, CALIFORNIA.

Harold M. Brest

Harold Martin Brest would be another one of the few select inmates to be committed to Alcatraz twice during their lifetime. Born on January 2, 1913, Harold was the third in a family of six children, and he was reared in what was considered a good home environment in Sharon, Pennsylvania. Brest and his family suffered the loss of his mother when he was only seven years of age. His father was a skilled laborer, and struggled to raise his children in a "*congenial atmosphere.*" Early prison reports reflect an angry tempered individual with little restraint in his dealings with fellow inmates and correctional staff. Brest was originally sentenced in June of 1939 to serve two twenty-five-year sentences, one five-year sentence, and a life sentence for kidnapping and bank robbery.

Brest's criminal history is fully described in his Alcatraz inmate file:

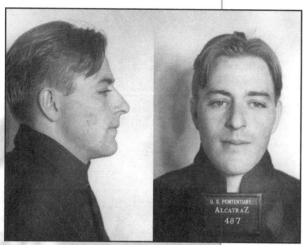

Harold M. Brest was another inmate who would serve two separate terms at Alcatraz, under two separate register numbers.

At the age of 15, the subject first became a delinquent serving a 5-day jail term for trespassing. The following year he served a 10-day jail sentence, and in 1932 he received a one-year probation term in his hometown for larceny of auto. Again in 1933 he went to the State Prison, at Pittsburgh, PA., to serve a three to six year term for blackmail. The Parole Director of this institution advises this man while incarcerated there received a disciplinary report for being implicated with another inmate in an attack on an officer and suspected of degeneracy, and was held six months over the minimum sentence. He was paroled in 1936, and in January of 1937, less than a year later, he was sentenced to a term of life and 55 years concurrently for Kidnapping, Bank Robbery, and Dyer Act, and committed to Leavenworth Penitentiary, later being transferred to Alcatraz in March of 1937.

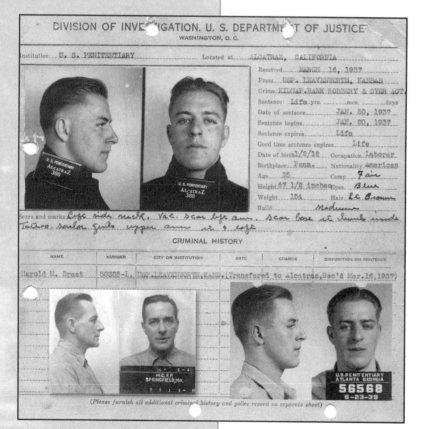

The circumstances of this crime are revolting and are outlined in detail in the Deputy Warden's abstract of admission summary prepared at Leavenworth, copy of which is in the record.

Harold Martin Brest was indicted, in one count, with Harry James Logan, by the Federal Grand Jury at Erie, Pennsylvania, on September 24, 1936 for seizing, kidnapping, and carrying away one Deloria Lester Santee, for the purpose of robbing him of his money and his automobile, and by causing him to be transported by means of his automobile, by threats, by force and arms, against his will, from Sharon, Pennsylvania, to Youngstown, Ohio, on or about July 2, 1936.

On January 14, 1937, Brest and Logan were indicted by the United States Grand Jury, at Pittsburgh, Pennsylvania, charged in four counts, first, with taking from the person and presence of P. M. Cox, Cashier, and Mrs. Mabel Simpson Brown, Assistant Cashier, L.P. Hauschild and L.W. Morgan, National Bank Examiners, on September 15, 1936, lawful money of the United States, in the sum of $5,846.50, which money belonged to and was in the care and custody of the First National Bank of Volant, Pennsylvania; second, with perpetrating the said offense by the use of dangerous weapons and devices, two revolvers or pistols; third, with the robbery of the same bank on December 18, 1936, in the sum of $3,910.36, and fourth, with the use of dangerous weapons and devices in the perpetration of this robbery, to wit, two automatic pistols.

Brest further admitted that he, with Logan, on September 10, 1936, robbed the Farmer's State Bank of Spring Green, Plain Station, Plain, Wisconsin, where by the use of arms and threats to kill the Cashier, he obtained, a little over $300.00. Brest stated that the banker was "scared to death, white as a sheet and almost dropped dead;" and that he, Brest, cocked his gun, ready to shoot the banker if he asserted himself, or resisted in any way; that but for the fact that Logan became uneasy, Brest stated he would more than likely have killed this banker.

In addition, thereto Brest admitted that he and Logan participated in so many robberies of drug stores, filling stations, and the like in the states of Pennsylvania, Ohio, Illinois, Michigan, Wisconsin, and Minnesota, that it would be impossible for him to recall all of them. On being informed by an F.B.I. Agent that he, Brest, entered the Volant National Bank but fifteen minutes prior to Pennsylvania State Policeman and that he probably would have been killed had they met there, Brest boldly said: "That all depends on who would have got the first shots in".

On or about July 25, 1936, Logan and Brest while seated in an auto at a point near Zeeland, Michigan, they were observed by an officer, who gave chase, and caught up with them in Holland Michigan. While the officer drove up beside the car, Brest drew fourth his gun and shot the officer in the mouth. This officer, for a time, was not expected to live. However, the bullet was removed from the base of the officer's skull and he is on the way to recovery. In conversing with the F.B.I. Agent, Brest readily stated that he would shoot it out with any officer who attempted

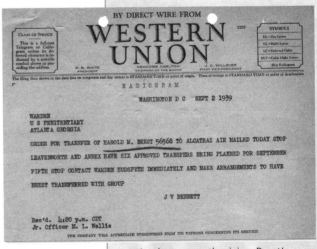

A telegram authorizing Brest's transfer to Alcatraz.

to apprehend him, and that had it not been for the fact that he was unarmed at the time of his arrest, which, incidentally, was the only time he went unarmed, in Boise, Idaho, he would have probably have shot and killed both policeman who apprehended him. During the conversation Brest at one time expressed regret that the shooting of the Police Officer did not result fatally.

Following transfer to Alcatraz, where he was sent for safer custody, he received three disciplinary reports; one on May 23, 1937 for creating confusion at the mess table; and two on September 20, 1937, for participating in a strike and refusing to go to work, and for agitating, creating a disturbance, and insolence to an officer and also for threatening an officer, agitating and causing a disturbance. On this date, after being placed in solitary, inmate told the Deputy Warden: "If I am ever turned out of solitary, I am going to kill you the first time you turn your back. I have killed men before and I would enjoy killing you." It is clear from subject's past criminal record and adjustment that notwithstanding his age, he is a confirmed criminal type with vicious and dangerous traits, impulsive and apparently devoid of any moral or social restraints.

Floyd Garland Hamilton

The third accomplice in the 1943 escape attempt was one of the most famous inmates ever to inhabit a small five-by-nine-foot cell at Alcatraz. He had reached the top of the FBI's most wanted list, and had chauffeured one of the most well known crime couples of the 1930's, Bonnie and Clyde. His brother Raymond had been a member of the Barrow-Parker Gang, and later met his death by electrocution for his role in a prison escape from a Huntsville prison, which had resulted in an officer's death. Floyd and his brother Ray had grown up with Bonnie and Clyde in a small town near Dallas, Texas. Newspapers of the era characterized Floyd Hamilton as a suspect in almost every act of violence that occurred in the Dallas area during the 1930's.

Floyd Hamilton was born on June 30, 1908 in Henrietta, Okalahoma. He was the second in a family of six children, and his parents were divorced. Records indicate that he was raised in a normal family setting, attended Sunday school,

Floyd Garland Hamilton

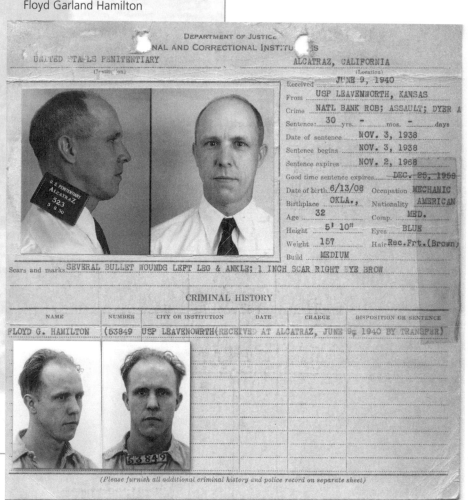

and left home at the age of nineteen to marry a young woman named Mildred Stract. During the early years of his marriage, Floyd worked as a pipe fitter in an oil refinery, but he later lost his employment when the plant closed down.

Floyd then began a crime spree that would eventually place him at the top of the FBI's Ten Most Wanted List. He worked as a getaway driver for Bonnie and Clyde, and later teamed up with Alcatraz alumnus Huron Ted Walters, who would himself attempt to escape from The Rock in another incident. Both men would engage in several other robberies, with targets including a Coca-Cola Bottling Company. This was the heist that would ultimately lead to Hamilton's arrest in Dallas on August 21, 1938.

Hamilton was incarcerated at Leavenworth, and would be recommended for transfer to Alcatraz in January of 1940, after attempting to enlist a released inmate to smuggle weapons and hacksaw blades into the institution. His Leavenworth report also stated that he and a few other inmates had attempted to have a shotgun and shells fabricated in the machine shop for use in an escape. He arrived at Alcatraz several months later on June 9, 1940, as inmate #AZ-523.

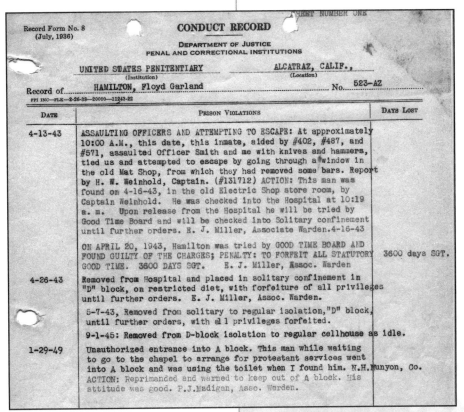

Floyd Hamilton's conduct reports from Alcatraz.

Fred Hunter

Fred Hunter

Fred Hunter, another "public enemy" and former member of the Karpis-Barker Gang, was also an accomplice to the planned escape. Hunter was serving twenty-five years for his involvement in the kidnapping of William A. Hamm Jr., the president of Hamm's Brewing Company, and Edward G. Bremer, a prominent community leader and the President of the Commercial State Bank in Minnesota. His criminal history is covered in the chapter describing the Barker Escape of January 1939. There were rumors from Hunter that the group of inmates had been prepared for an escape attempt nearly two weeks earlier, but Boarman had allegedly insisted that they wait for the right fog conditions so that they could enter the bay without being seen.

The Escape

At approximately 10:00 A.M. on April 13, 1943, conditions seemed ideal for the escape, with densely layered fog enveloping the island. It was later speculated that the inmates had cut through one of the steel-mesh window guards in the old Mat Shop during the previous weeks, hiding their work by using grease mixed with other agents to fill in the tiny sawed gaps. Custodial Officer George Smith was busy supervising the inmates who were mixing concrete. He was called to the yard gate to escort four other inmates who were reporting to their work assignments. When Smith returned only a short time later, he noticed that Hunter was the only prisoner at his position near the entrance to the Mat Shop. Officer Smith was quickly intercepted by Hamilton, who forcefully grabbed him by the arm, while Boarman stepped into his path gesturing deadly threats with a knife and hammer. When Smith resisted, he was beaten into submission by all four of the inmates, and then bound and gagged.

Captain of the Guards Henry Weinhold, known to many of the inmates as "*Bullethead*," was a tough former Marine making his routine rounds. Not suspecting any trouble, he entered the Mat Shop and was quickly captured by the inmates, who by were now stripped down to their underwear. Weinhold resisted and nearly managed to grasp one of Boarman's weapons, when the other inmates tackled him, dealing several painful blows of a carpenter's hammer to his extremities. He too was incapacitated, then tightly bound and gagged and laid beside Officer Smith.

Hamilton was the first to climb through the window, and he managed to maintain a grip on the remaining security bars while the other inmates passed out a wooden filling guide to be used as a ramp from the window to the barbed wired security fencing. After maneuvering the makeshift plank properly into place, Hamilton was passed a large rolled section of canvas to drape over the barbed-wired fencing. Boarman and

Brest now stripped to their underwear and belts (which they planned to secure to the canisters to keep them afloat), and smeared their bodies with engine grease as insulation.

Boarman and Brest attempted to maneuver the float canisters through the window without success, so they were forced to leave them behind, along with the clothing they contained. One by one, the men climbed through the window, negotiated the wire fencing, and then hurried down to the rocky shore. Hunter had injured himself when dropping from the fence, and he took refuge in a small island cave that was recessed under the industry buildings. The cave was dark and littered with discarded tires, and was flooded with varying levels of seawater depending on the tide levels. Boarman, Brest, and Hamilton each started their swim to freedom, partially obscured by the breaking fog.

Meanwhile Officer Weinhold had succeeded in loosening his gag, and started yelling for help, but due to the noise of the loud machinery in the Industries, his cries went unheard. At about the same time, Officer Frank L. Johnson, who was assigned to the tower atop the Model Shop, was attempting to reach Smith, and had already contacted Cliff Fish in the Armory. Fish, who was just being relieved from duty, responded to the Industries to investigate the problem, accompanied by Phil Bergen and Earl Long. Officer Johnson stepped outside of the tower booth, and immediately spotted several figures in the water, swimming away from the island. Smith, while unable to undo his gag, was able to move his body against Weinhold, who then managed to maneuver Smith's

The old Model Industries Building

A letter to the Warden from Harold Brest, asking that he be transferred from Alcatraz.

whistle into his mouth. Weinhold started frantically blowing the shrill whistle, which was clearly audible from Johnson's post.

Lifting his rifle, Johnson strained to peer into the target site as several faint figures continued to advance away from the island in the foggy seascape. Watching the figures move in rhythm with the sea, he drew his grip tight, and squeezed the trigger until the pressure of the spring gave way to a ragging shot. He repeated the process, sighting each moving figure, then firing his Springfield .30-06. Each round released a caustic smell of burnt gunpowder mixed with the misty salt air. Brest and Boarman saw the geyser-like splash patterns in the water around them, accompanied by the distant sharp cracking sound of a high-powered rifle. After each round was fired, silence would drape the water until the next blast racked the air. As Brest and Boarman swam almost side-by-side a few hundred yards from shore, the sounds of Boarman's thrashing suddenly stopped. As Brest reached out to examine the now silent form of his fellow inmate, the water surrounding them started to turn an eerie red.

Boarman's eyes were open, but glazed over by the seawater as Brest tried to maintain his grip on his accomplice's limp body. Boarman was bleeding profusely from what appeared to be a bullet wound behind his left ear. The prison launch *McDowell* pulled alongside the two inmates, with Officer Sutter aiming his muzzle at Brest's head. Brest struggled to hang on to Boarman's belt, but as the officers attempted to latch it with a boat hook, the belt broke, and Boarman slowly disappeared into the green murky depths. Brest was pulled into the launch and wrapped in blankets, then returned to the island. He was immediately taken to the prison hospital and examined. He had sustained only a minor bullet wound to his elbow.

Hamilton had been able to swim to "*Little Alcatraz*" using the large wood plank as a float, but when he heard the bullets whizzing past his head he tried to keep himself submerged for as long as he could hold his breath. He apparently clung to the small rocks of "*Little Alcatraz*," and then swam back towards the island, lifting his head out of the water only long enough to take a deep breath. Hamilton made his way back into the island cave where Hunter was hiding. Warden Johnston had already assembled a team of three officers to explore the rocky shoreline in an attempt to locate the stranded inmates. Associate Warden Ed Miller walked the island perimeter, while a boat with a powerful spotlight covered the officers from the water. Standing near the mouth of the cave, Miller noticed a blood smear on one of the rocks. He yelled into the small cavern, demanding that any hiding inmates surrender or be fired upon. When he received no response, he decided to fire a round from his colt .45 pistol into the dark void. Fred Hunter, who was hiding behind some tires and nearly neck deep in water, immediately raised his arms to surrender. Unknown to Miller, Hamilton was still in hiding under several tires.

Officer Johnson had reported back to the Warden that he had fired upon at least three inmates, and that Hamilton had probably met his death, as Boarman had. The prison launch patrolled the waters around the island for hours, but when there was no sign of Hamilton, Johnston started to feel confident that the inmate had perished in the downpour of gunfire alongside his accomplice. He was so convinced of this that he

"Little Alcatraz" is seen just beyond the buoy.

released a statement to the press reading in part: "*Hamilton is dead. He was shot, and we saw him go under.*"

Hamilton would remain in hiding until April 16th, when cold and hungry, he decided to seek shelter in the old Electric Shop. Captain Weinhold, who had returned to reexamine the scene of the escape, found Hamilton curled in a fetal position, weak from hunger and exposure. He was admitted to the prison hospital and treated for a multitude of inju-

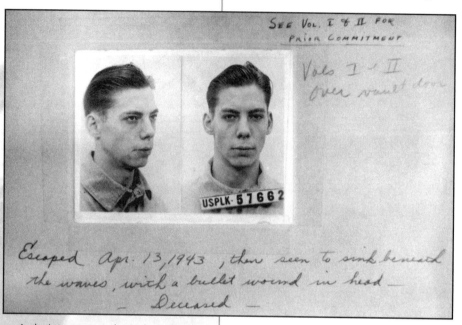

ries. Hamilton was then moved into the D Block segregation unit, and would remain there until September 1, 1945. Hunter would be released back into general prison population on January 22, 1945. Brest remained in D Block segregation until May 21, 1944.

Hamilton was released from Alcatraz in August of 1952, and was sent back to Leavenworth. He was eventually set free, and returned to Dallas on July 2, 1958. While at Leavenworth, he had enrolled in Otto Lang's religious training program, designed to help participants become men-

A closing note on the jacket of Boarman's inmate file.

tors for other inmates. Following his release he started an organization named ConAid, which was eventually credited with assisting over 1,200 inmates. On December 23, 1966, Hamilton received a full Presidential Pardon from Texas native President Lyndon B. Johnson. Hamilton died of natural causes in 1984, at his home in Dallas, Texas. During a lecture he gave on the anniversary of his Alcatraz escape in 1961, when asked what he had learned from his escapades in crime, he stated simply: "*Happiness comes from within; not from without. Crime always leads to prison, and prison is a void of living bodies in a state of death. Lucky for me, Alcatraz became my birthplace and not my grave.*"

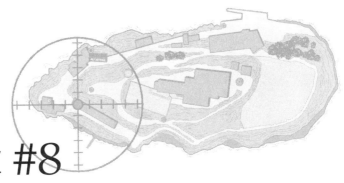

Escape Attempt #8

DATE: AUGUST 7, 1943
INMATE: HURON TED WALTERS
LOCATION: PRISON LAUNDRY

In August of 1943, Alcatraz was suffering from personnel shortages as a result of the War efforts. The prison industries were overwhelmed with the sheer volume of military clothing being delivered for laundering, and there were barely enough officers to cover the critical posts. Many of the officers assigned to the industries were required to alternate their rounds, sometimes leaving certain posts unattended for brief periods. These circumstances would figure in a Saturday morning escape attempt by Huron Ted Walters.

Huron Ted Walters (known to many as "Terrible Ted") was a habitual criminal and former crime partner of Floyd Hamilton, another Alcatraz inmate. Born on October 25, 1913 in Wylie, Texas, Walters was the youngest of three children. His father died when he was only two years old, and his mother remarried two years later with a gentleman employed as a machinist. Ted's home life was considered fairly normal, and at seventeen years of age he left his parents' forty-acre ranch to pursue a career as a truck driver. He immediately began getting involved in criminal activities, and was soon arrested for stealing automobiles. In 1936, after being sentenced to serve time for auto theft, he successfully escaped from a Texas jail, and continued his criminal escapades.

Walters, Floyd Hamilton, and another accomplice named Jack Winn were involved in a series of robberies, with targets ranging from banks, to stores, to beer taverns, to a Coca-Cola Bottling Company plant. Their crimes spanned several states, and involved several police chases, as well

Huron Ted Walters

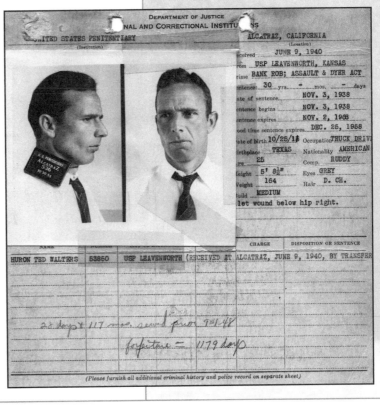

Huron Ted Walters

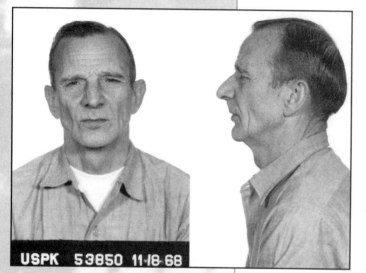
USPK 53850 11-18-68

as other dire scenarios. On August 13, 1938, the day following the Coca-Cola Bottling Company robbery, the trio held up a salesman near Weldon, Arkansas, and stole his 1938 green Plymouth Sedan. They were spotted near DeQueen, Arkansas, and after an intense gun battle with Arkansas State Highway Patrolmen, they disappeared into the remote woods on foot. Both men were captured eight days later in Dallas, Texas when Winn, who had been arrested several days earlier, identified his accomplices to the police. Walters had suffered a minor gunshot wound to his right thigh, and Hamilton was also found to have sustained injuries.

On November 3, 1938, both men were sentenced to thirty years in prison for their crimes. When Walters was later questioned by FBI Agents, he would be quoted as saying that his only regret was that he had not killed a few of the officers before being apprehended. Walters and Hamilton were both sent to the Federal Penitentiary in Leavenworth, Kansas on November 5, 1938. Ever true to their chosen lifestyle, they would remain outlaws within the prison walls. Associate Warden C. J. Shuttleworth, who had formerly held the same position at Alcatraz, documented an escape plot that would earn the two inmates a cross-country train ride to Alcatraz. He wrote in Walters' conduct record:

Information has come to my attention that this inmate, together with Floyd Hamilton, and inmate Reed were planning and plotting an escape from the institution by concealing themselves in an institutional sawdust truck driven by Lee Barker, No. 53385-L, a confessed conspirator with Steffler and Miles in a similar plot. While definite information is meager, regarding this particular conspiracy, it was upon this same information that the plot was of Steffler and Miles were finally discovered. The plot had also included the fabrication of homemade shotguns, shells, and sixteen bombs that were to be made in the prison factories. An inmate not connected with the plot furnished the information. In talking with Hamilton relative to this plot, Hamilton admits that Reed and Walters were his only trusted associates in the institution. Further, early in December, Walters was observed at about 3:30 PM sitting outside the Shoe Factory, "casing" the East Gate and the general truck shakedown. This at a time when he was supposed to have been at his work in the Clothing Factory. This inmate has a long dangerous record, and is one of the most vicious criminals in the Southwest, and co-partner of Hamilton's. In view of his long sentence and the actually known conspiracies of his co-partner Hamilton, it is recommended that he be transferred to Alcatraz for safer custody.

Walter and Hamilton arrived at Alcatraz on June 9, 1940. Here too, both men continued to receive negative conduct reports for numerous infringements of prison regulations. On April 14, 1943, as described in the preceding chapter, Hamilton and fellow inmates James Boarman, Harold Brest, and Fred Hunter participated in a failed escape that would cost Boarman his life.

On August 7, 1943, only months after Hamilton's luckless escape attempt, Walters decided to try his fate against The Rock. He had been assigned to the laundry for nearly two years, and in the spirit of Hamilton's escape, he had been collecting military clothing stuffed in one-gallon containers, which he would attempt to use as floats. Even though the concept had been tried unsuccessfully on three previous attempts, it still seemed to be the most promising scheme. Walters had also been able to acquire $42, which he stuffed into one of the pant pockets for use once he made it to shore.

It was a Saturday, sometime between 2:15 P.M. and 3:45 P.M., when Walters slipped from sight. Because of staffing shortages, the number of officers posted in the Industries Building had been reduced. Clutching his two one-gallon containers, and with no officer in direct view, Walters

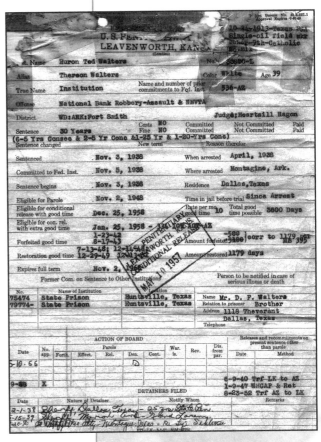

carefully made his way to the fence line. He had also acquired a pair of electrician's wire cutters, which he intended to use to cut through the heavy security fencing. But no matter how hard he squeezed the small handles against the stiff galvanized wire, the cutters proved completely ineffective. Keeping a close eye on the towers, he carefully stacked some packing crates next to the perimeter fence, and then risked scaling it in view of the tower guards, who failed to spot the escapee. As he maneuvered over the skin-piercing barbed wire at the top, he lost his grip and fell. The fall proved to be treacherous, and resulted in a serious back injury. In acute pain, Walters descended the steps that led to the water's edge, and then contemplated his swim to the mainland.

In the laundry, a supervisor making his rounds noticed Walters was absent from his workstation, and immediately contacted the Armory. The alarm was quickly sounded, as Walters stood by the water's edge, now stripped to his underwear, and facing the reality that his plan had failed. A Coast Guard cutter was quickly dispatched and found Walters standing stripped down on the bank. Captain of the Guards Henry Weinhold and Associate Warden E. J. Miller captured Walters without any resistance, and brought him to the hospital to be examined. Walters spent nearly ten days in the hospital before being taken to D Block.

In a letter from Bureau of Prisons Director James V. Bennett to Warden Johnston dated August 12, 1943, it is clear that Bennett was unsatisfied with the performance of the officers. He also alleged in two memorandums that Walters should have been spotted by the tower officers when he was climbing the fences. A telegram to Warden Johnston read:

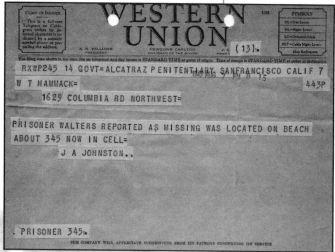

Have asked Captain Conner to check on the Ted Walters escape and confer with you as to what action if any should be taken with respect to the officers since I cannot understand how Walters could have climbed the fence in plain daylight without being noticed by tower officers unless they were inattentive to their duties in which case disciplinary action should be taken. Captain Conner will arrive August sixteenth.

After being released from the hospital, Walters was tried by a specially assembled disciplinary board. The following is a transcript from his hearing:

In accordance with the regulations of the Bureau of Prisons governing the forfeiture of GOOD TIME, a special court was appointed by the Warden for the purpose of trying Huron Ted Walters, Reg. No. 536-AZ, and for his misconduct, specifically:

Leaving place to which he was assigned in laundry, dropping from walk-way to get out of sight of road tower guard, carrying wire cutters and soldier clothing stolen from laundry, climbing over two wire fences, then hiding out at water's edge in attempt to escape: All of the above occurred at about 2:15 P.M. to 3:45 P.M., on Saturday, August 7, 1943.

The board met at approximately 10:40 A.M., Tuesday, August 17, 1943, and consisted of the following members:

E.J. Miller, Associate Warden, Chairman
Isaac B. Faulk, Lieutenant, Member
Neal W. Mcrisson, Lieutenant, Member
Dr. Romney M. Ritchey, Chief Medical Officer, Consultant

The following transcript of the testimony, questions by E.J. Miller, Associate Warden and Chairman, except, where noted:

Huron Ted Walters, Register No. 536-Az, you are called before the GOOD TIME BOARD to try you for the credits for the things done by you on August 7, 1943. (Mr. Miller then read the charges above.)

Q: You heard the charges. How do you plead?
A: Guilty.
Q: Have you anything to say?
A: No, sir.
Q: Did you get the soldier's clothing out of the laundry?
A: Yes, sir.
Q: Where did you get the wire cutters?
A: I picked them up down there.
Q: Did you try to cut the wire with them?
A: Yes, sir.
Q: Wouldn't they work?
A: No, sir.
Q: You then climbed over both fences?
A: Yes, sir.

Q: Where did you get the one-gallon buckets?
A: Out of the laundry.
Q: Did you have any money on you?
A: No, sir.
Q: Did anyone give you money?
A: No, sir.
Q: Did you use any boxes?
A: There was a couple of packing cases that I used to climb over the first fence.
Q: What did you use on the second fence?
A: I climbed up the wire by the gate.
Q: When you got over the fences where did you go?
A: Down the steps to the bank.
Q: Did you try the water?
A: Yes, sir.
Q: What was the reason you didn't go in?
A: I hurt my back and figured I couldn't make it.
Q: How did you hurt your back?
A: I fell off the fence.
Q: How long did you plan the escape?
A: Two or three days previous.
Q: Do you wish to say anything for yourself?
A: No, sir.
Mr. Miller: After questioning you, Walters, I recommend that you forfeit 3100 days Statutory Good Time.

Walter was immediately brought to D Block and placed into the strip-cell, where he remained until August 28, 1943, when he was placed in segregation. He would again be placed in an isolation cell in May of 1944, after officers found a six-inch hacksaw blade hidden beneath the linoleum flooring of his D-Block cell (#23). He would ultimately remain in segregation until May 10, 1945, and then as surprising as it may seem, he was released back into the general population and given a work assignment back in the prison laundry.

Despite his years in segregation, little had changed in Walters' attitude toward the administration. He continued to receive write-ups, which described him as making threats against officers, claiming that they made too much noise when opening the cells of the kitchen workers in the early morning. He also was reported for being intoxicated on homemade brew. In what could probably be considered one of the more unusual write-ups for possession of contraband on Alcatraz, Walters was also sent to isolation for having a toy rubber duck hidden in his cell in April of 1949.

Walter was released from Alcatraz and returned to Leavenworth on August 23, 1952. His admission record at Leavenworth certainly offered a profile of an inmate who had failed to make a positive adjustment on The Rock. It read:

At Alcatraz, he was reported for fighting, refusing to work, insolence, possession of a contraband knife, assaulting another inmate with a knife, attempting to smuggle food from the dining room, wasting food, attempting to escape, creating a disturbance and using profanity, fighting and having part of a band saw in his cell, refusing to do work directed, inciting a riot, interfering with the count and intoxication.

At Leavenworth Walters would be assigned to the Shoe Factory, and he was said to make an excellent adjustment following his transfer. He was paroled and returned to Dallas in 1958, and then he married only a year after his release. He found a job working in a small bakery, and for a short period his life seemed normal. It wasn't anything remotely like what he had experienced sitting in a solitary cell at Alcatraz. But in spite of his recently won freedom and his new wife, he continued to struggle with his past. He would eventually revert back to his old familiar life as an outlaw.

Walters' final brush with the law would occur on October 13, 1971. At about 10:00 A.M., he and an unidentified female passenger were pulled over on a routine traffic stop in Euless, Texas. As Texas Ranger Bill Harvell approached the passenger side of the vehicle, Walters drew a pistol. Harvell was able to retreat to the rear of the vehicle, when Walters punched the accelerator to flee the scene. Harvell opened fire on the 1962 Plymouth Valiant with his service revolver, emptying the entire chamber. Harvell then returned to his patrol car and gave chase, while summoning other law enforcement officers on the radio.

Walters sped through a residential district, stopping only briefly to release his female passenger. Carrying his pistol and a sawed-off shotgun, he then took off on foot into a remote pasture. An intensive manhunt ensued, and Walters stayed ahead of the police for a short time. At daybreak, Hoyt Houston of Bedford, Texas entered his garage to find Walters sleeping there in a small fishing boat. Walters ordered the man into his house at gunpoint, and took his family hostage. Hoyt had two young daughters, and one had been able to escape through her bedroom window to run and get help.

When the police arrived at the Houstons' home, Walters aimed his shotgun at the family and demanded that the police drop their weapons, which they did. He then forced his hostages into the family's 1969 Mercury, and directed Mrs. Houston to drive while he kept his loaded shotgun aimed at the head of her husband, who was sitting in the passenger seat. After a slow and careful pursuit, the police were able to force the vehicle to stop on a bridge just outside of Grapevine, Texas. A police car had been positioned at the end of the small overpass, creating a roadblock. While police attempted to negotiate the safe release of the Houston family, a Texas Ranger named Tom Arnold took aim at Walters through the target scope of his .30-06 rifle. During a brief moment when approaching officers distracted Walters, Tom Arnold fired a fatal shot at Walters' head. As the window shattered, Arnold dropped his rifle and aimed his pistol steadily at the slumped figure, then fired several more rounds into Walters' body. None of the Houston family members were injured in the hail of gunfire. Ironically, Walters died only 300 feet from where Bonnie and Clyde had slain two police officers on April 1, 1934.

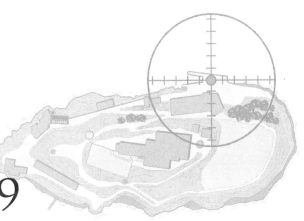

Escape Attempt #9

DATE: JULY 31, 1945
INMATE: JOHN GILES
LOCATION: DOCK AREA

John Giles was described by Warden Johnston as a deep and quiet gentleman with a lone wolf personality, who was somewhat difficult to figure out. While his attempted escape is not remembered as the most famous, it certainly was known in the circles of Alcatraz as one of the most ingenious escapes ever attempted at The Rock. John Knight Giles was born in Elgin, Tennessee on February 16, 1895 to a local engineer, as the youngest of three boys. His father had migrated south from New York and his mother was from Georgia, and the couple apparently separated frequently throughout their marriage. It is documented that John's mother suffered from mental illness, and was admitted to mental institutions several times during his childhood. John attended high school in Everett, Washington, and for unknown reasons, he decided to quit school at age fifteen. He took a job as a Surveyor's Assistant in the U.S. Reclamation Service near British Columbia, where he worked for almost four years.

Giles' first brush with the world of crime came in 1915, when he was given a five to ten year sentence for robbery, and was incarcerated at the Washington State Penitentiary in Walla Walla. It would appear that officials were lenient with Giles, and he was issued a pardon in 1918, probably

John Knight Giles

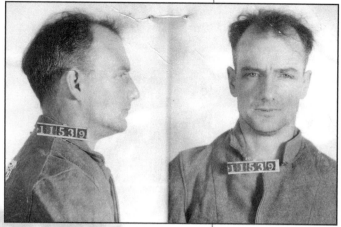

John Knight Giles

John Knight Giles

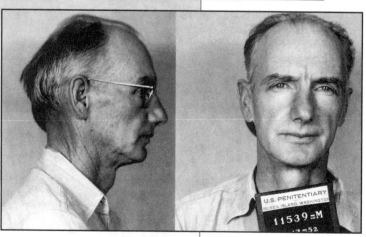

to allow him to enter the U.S. Army for the First World War. He failed to enlist, and only months after his release he committed another robbery. In November of 1918 Giles planned what he thought would be an easy burglary, targeting an interstate bridge tender in the state of Oregon. He robbed the tender at gunpoint, and then attempted a getaway. He was swiftly apprehended by Deputy Sheriff Frank W. Twombley, and during the arrest, the officer was killed. An all-points bulletin was issued on Giles, and he was quickly taken into custody.

Giles was convicted of murder, and sentenced to life in prison at the State Penitentiary in Salem, Oregon. He was considered a quiet inmate, and he took to writing short fictional stories. Records show that he was somewhat successful in selling his work, and wrote for a variety of pulp magazines. After serving several years, Giles would boast to officials that he had helped to prevent riots and other uprisings by acting as a leader among the inmates. In November of 1934, after sixteen un-eventful years, Giles managed to escape from the State Penitentiary. He was later identified in connection with a theft in Redding California, but managed to elude officials for over a year, always keeping one step ahead of them. However Giles would soon participate in a crime that would finally seal his fate.

In May of 1935, Giles and six accomplices made the ill-fated decision to rob the Denver and Rio Grande Mail Train in Salt Lake City. Reports show that the gang jumped onto the train, forcing the engineer to halt the locomotive, and a few of the men then climbed into the cabin and held the engineer at gunpoint. They made their way back to the locked mail car and attempted to break a window to gain access, without success. The gang fired randomly into the car through its windows, then threw in a large bottle of ammonia, attempting to force out the mail clerks with the pungent fumes. Their plan failed, as one of the mail clerks who was armed with a gun returned fire and forced the gang to retreat to an awaiting truck. Law officers quickly apprehended four of the men, along with Giles. Giles was sentenced to an additional twenty-eight years for the Federal crime of attempted mail robbery.

Giles arrived at McNeil Island Federal Penitentiary on June 17, 1935. Because of his escape record and the length of his sentence, he was transferred to Alcatraz on August 28, 1935. Giles seemed to adapt well to the routines at Alcatraz, though he was described in a 1943 progress report as follows: *"he mixes little with other inmates and pretty well keeps to himself, being considered by some as odd."* Nevertheless, he was highly regarded by the correctional staff, and was generally considered to be friendly. Giles' mother, who was now in her late 70's, had moved to Los Angeles where one of his brothers was now residing, so that she could be closer to her two sons. But Giles refused all visits from his mother, stating to the Warden that he didn't want her to see him in prison. He seldom wrote to his family, and appeared to be leading a very quiet existence. His 1943 progress report states that Giles had been working as janitor at the dock,

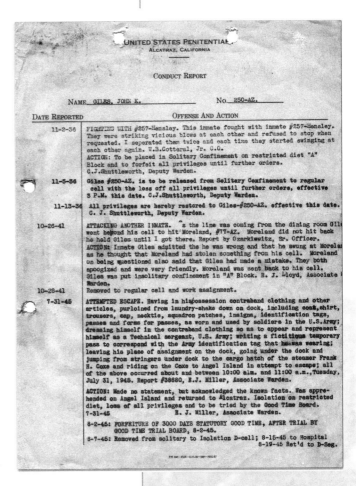

and he was noted as an obedient and good worker, performing his job quietly and *"without friction to others."* What officials failed to realize was that despite his calm disposition, Giles had been plotting a very elaborate escape plan for nearly a full decade.

Over the years, Giles had devised a system of monitoring the laundry deliveries made by an Army vessel dispatched from Fort McDowell, which was located across the bay on Angel Island. When the laundry arrived, the bales would be dumped onto a panning table and searched for contraband before being sent down to the Industries. Giles would carefully wait for a safe opportunity, and then, out of sight of both correctional officers and other inmates, he would conceal a garment or other potentially useful item in his jacket, and later hide it in a canvas bag under the dock. The dock security procedures were extremely tight, but there were frequent counts and searches of the inmates before they were allowed to return to the cellhouse. When the Army launch departed, Giles was always permitted to walk to the ramp area and sweep up, which provided the perfect opportunity to pull out his hidden bag and secrete his newly acquired items. Opportunities to lift items were scarce, and the process was tedious. It would take nearly ten years before he acquired all of the materials needed for his attempt.

On the morning of July 31, 1945, Giles was prepared for his escape, now having pieced together a complete Technical Sergeant's uniform. At 10:10 A.M. the Army vessel *General Frank M. Coxe* pulled up next to

Warden James A. Johnston
United States Penitentiary
Alcatraz Island
San Francisco, California

Re: John Knight Giles

Dear Warden:

Pursuant to your request the following personal effects which were found in the possession of the above captioned subject at the time of his apprehension at Angel Island on July 31, 1945 are being listed below:

One set of prison underwear.
One pair of prison socks.
One pair of brown prison shoes.
One regulation Army tie.
One pair of regulation U.S. Army pants labeled Kane Manufacturing Company, 1/19/43.
One Khaki Army overseas cap, red bordered #K-9699.
One regulation Army shirt bearing laundry mark #P2587.
One U.S. Army field jacket, size 38 L, bearing no identification marks, with Technical Sergeant's chevrons on sleeve.
One white pouch containing small comb.
One navy blue pouch containing two flashlight bulbs, one Texaco touring map of San Francisco and the Bay Area, one State Auto Association map of Marin County, one small taped ball containing odd change.
One navy blue pouch containing shoulder patch U.S. Army, Pacific Coast Frontier Defense Sector.
One navy blue pouch containing two glass cases, one case containing subject's silver rimmed glasses, the other containing a white powder believed to be stomach powder.
One handkerchief, brown striped border.
One small memo book approximately three by five inches, contents blank.
One small piece of white cloth.
One U.S. Army official dog tag in the name GEORGE F. TODD, #38409746 T43.
One enlisted man's temporary pass issued in the name of TODD dated 0730 July 31 to 0730 August 2, '45 "to visit Bay Area". The above described tag and pass were used by subject in an ineffectual attempt to elude detection at Fort McDowell.
One white cloth pouch containing U.S. Army dog tag in the name of ARTHUR L. WADE #34506347 T43, Army dog tag in the name of ERNEST D. BENNETT, #33573388, one broken tube Barbasol shaving cream containing $1.38 in change.

One Pall Mall cigarette package containing seven assorted shoulder patches, U.S. Army, two chevrons U.S. Army Staff Sergeant, one new U.S. Army Air Corps shoulder patch wrapped in tissue paper.
Four undated enlisted men's temporary passes in the name of A.L. WADE, Staff Sergeant, #34506347, Hq. Btry. A 256 AAA, granting permission to visit Bay Area.
Six blank enlisted men's passes.
Three blank temporary passes bearing the stamped signature of WILLIAM B. BURCH.
One fountain pen, gold colored.
One gray flashlight marked "USM" containing two Every-Ready batteries marked for use before June, 1944.
One small cardboard box containing blank furlough paper form #31, War Department, A.G.O.
One metal Bayer Aspirin box containing sixty cents in assorted change and several strands of what appears to be human hair.
One small Colgate toothpaste tube painted green containing a brown substance believed to be glue.
One seed envelope containing unidentified white powder.
One Army tie.
One pair regulation Army socks.
One traced insignia of Pacific Coast Frontier Defense Sector.
One small cardboard box containing two wooden objects both carved in the shape of a "U" approximately one inch in length, covered with waxlike substance.
One small tin box containing piece of broken mirror.
One small medicine bottle containing ink.
One small cardboard box containing razor, fourteen cents in change, one pen point and three taped balls containing change.
One Dennison label box containing unidentified white powder, and five safety pins.
One small wooden cylinder (pencil lead holder) containing three wooden matches each tightly wrapped with small needle and tan thread.
One small bar green soap.

I should like, at this time, to express my appreciation to you for the assistance rendered Special Agents HARTLEY and CROW during the investigation of this matter.

Very truly yours,

N. J. L. PIEPER
Special Agent in Charge

the Alcatraz dock, parallel to a descending ramp. The soldiers exited onto the wharf and they were quickly counted, and then permitted to begin off-loading the laundry. Giles moved down the ramp and swiftly slipped on his improvised uniform. The uniform looked as though it fit Giles well, but it had a tousled and wrinkled appearance. Armed with only a flashlight, Giles boarded the vessel through a freight hatchway located just below deck. It is believed that Giles found his way to the boat's lavatory and waited until the *Coxe* departed before venturing back out into a secluded area of the boat. Sergeant-at-Arms Corporal Paul Lorinz later stated that he was tipped off by deckhand Jerry Van Soest that a soldier was wandering below deck. Lorinz investigated and found Giles standing alone in a secluded area, and he asked him *"Where are you going Sergeant?"* Lorinz noted that Giles failed to look at him di-

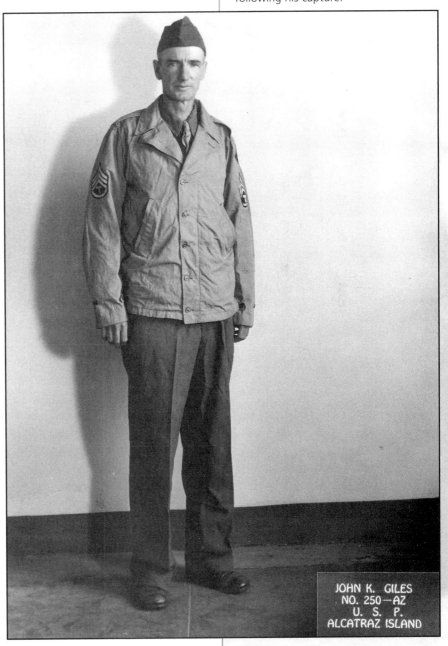

John Giles would devise one of the most clever escape plans ever conceived at Alcatraz. Over the course of several years, he worked to collect and assemble a full Army uniform out of the Army laundry that was delivered to the dock area. This photo was taken immediately following his capture.

JOHN K. GILES
NO. 250—AZ
U. S. P.
ALCATRAZ ISLAND

rectly, and responded by stating he was heading to *"Fort McDowell."* When questioned further by Lorinz, Giles stated that he was a line repairman who was checking cables. He then pulled out a notebook and acted as though his was making notes. Lorinz made his way back up to the deck and reported that a soldier was onboard who had failed to present a pass.

Back at Alcatraz, Giles' absence had already been detected after he missed the routine departure count. Associate Warden E. J. Miller was contacted, and he and Phil Bergen quickly summoned the prison launch to rendezvous with the Army vessel, which was heading toward Angel Island. Warden Johnston was already on the phone making arrangements to have Giles apprehended once the *Coxe* arrived at Fort McDowell. Giles was completely unaware that his short taste of freedom had ended before it even began. As the *Coxe* arrived at Angel Island, Lieutenant Gordon L. Kilgore approached him asking to see his passes. As Giles disembarked from the launch, Miller and Bergen approached him and without any struggle, they handcuffed him and took him aboard the *Warden Johnston* to head back to the island. *"You*

really felt kind of sorry for him once you saw the look on his face" Captain of the Guards Phil Bergen would later recall. "*He really should have won some sort of an award with that uniform.*"

Giles was immediately returned to the island, and was placed directly into the solitary strip cell. The FBI investigated the escape and put together an inventory of the items that had been found in Giles' possession. Over the course of nearly ten years, Giles had acquired more than forty smuggled articles ranging from clothing to dog tags. Giles was punished harshly, and he would remain in segregation for nearly three years. In 1948 he was integrated back into the general population, and was given the incinerator detail, considered one of the island's toughest work assignments. He was eventually transferred to Leavenworth and paroled several years later. Upon his release, Giles moved to Los Angeles to live with his brother and never returned to prison. John Giles died in February of 1979 at age eighty-four.

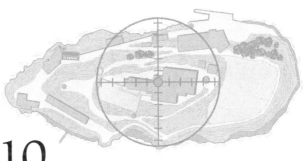

Escape Attempt #10

DATE: MAY 2–4, 1946
INMATES: BERNARD COY
JOSEPH CRETZER
MARVIN HUBBARD
MIRAN THOMPSON
CLARENCE CARNES
SAM SHOCKLEY
LOCATION: MAIN CELLHOUSE

The Battle Of Alcatraz

On May 2, 1946, six convicts embarked on one of the most violent escape attempts ever made on The Rock. Many historians rank this as the most significant event in the island's twenty-nine-year history as a Federal penitentiary, and it was appropriately labeled by the contemporary press as the *"Battle of Alcatraz."* Of the thirty-nine convicts who attempted to escape over

FINAL MORNING EXTRA

San Francisco Chronicle
THE CITY'S ONLY HOME-OWNED NEWSPAPER

FOUNDED 1865—VOL. CLXII, NO. 108   CCCCAAAB   SAN FRANCISCO, FRIDAY, MAY 3, 1946   ◀DAILY 5 CENTS, SUNDAY 15 CENTS

ALCATRAZ SIEGE!
Photos of Prisoners' Rebellion!
One Guard Killed, 16 Injured

A message scratched onto one of the flat bars of cell #23 in A Block, where several inmates were temporarily housed during the Battle of Alcatraz.

Bernard Paul Coy was the primary architect of one of the most ingenious escape plots ever implemented at Alcatraz. He would be the only inmate in the prison's history to successfully secure prison firearms.

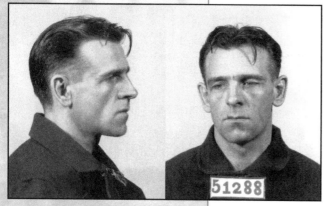

the years, only one successfully plotted and executed a plan to secure weapons—and they were used with deadly consequences. In the wake of the conflict, two correctional officers and three inmates lay dead from bullet wounds, and several others were left seriously injured. This legendary escape attempt would remain a topic of discussion by inmates and guards alike until the prison's closure in 1963.

The Conspirators

BERNARD PAUL COY

Forty-six-year-old Bernard Paul Coy was a hillbilly bank robber serving out the remainder of a twenty-five-year sentence on The Rock. Bernie was born to a hauntingly poor Kentucky hill family of one brother and four sisters, all of whom suffered the consequences of their extreme poverty. By the time Bernie reached his late teens, his teeth were horribly decayed, and he was afflicted with excruciatingly painful gums, a condition that was often exacerbated by his shoddily fashioned false teeth. It was rumored that Coy had been neglected as a child, and had received frequent beatings from his father. Even in his earliest years, Coy had allegedly exhibited violent tendencies.

At sixteen years of age, Bernie decided to leave home and enlist in the U.S. Army. It was in this context that he would enter into his first battle: World War I. Coy served in the Army with great distinction until the war ended in 1918. After finishing his tour of duty, he fell in love with a woman from Wisconsin, and the couple soon married. In order to maintain a steady income, Bernie reenlisted in the Army in 1920. As the war effort wound down, Coy frequently found himself in trouble, and it was during this period that he changed the direction of his life, and began moving toward his eventual destiny. In 1921, Bernie was arraigned in Chicago for abandoning his post assignment and going AWOL. He was found guilty of desertion and was sent back to Camp Taylor in Kentucky, where he served fifteen days in the military detention center. Soon afterward, he received a dishonorable discharge, and therefore had to make the transition back to civilian life with few job opportunities and limited prospects.

Coy feverishly attempted to find work, in hopes of making a decent life for himself and his wife. He was a gifted artist, and had made use of his talents before as a decorator and painter. However, despite his earnest attempts, the Great Depression had left him unemployed and desperate to support himself. Bernie found himself backed into a corner, with few options left by which to survive. In 1923 Coy was arrested in Draper, Wisconsin for violating liquor laws, and he was also charged with assault and battery. He was released with time served and fined $250, which he clearly could not afford to pay in his state of unemployment. He was convicted of larceny charges in 1928 and 1930, and eventually served nearly five years in the Wisconsin State Penitentiary.

Reading Coy's letters from the years prior to his Alcatraz escape attempt, it would be nearly impossible to predict his violent and premeditated break for freedom. His letters articulated what appeared to be a true desire to reform, as is illustrated in these excerpts written to the superintendent of the prison where he was incarcerated on August 30, 1936:

> I regret that this request [for release consideration] must be made under the present unfavorable conditions, rather than under circumstances relevant to the continued progress of some noble social service. Please believe me sincere in my regret, and if there is a loyalty of promise incapable of future betrayal, you may be assured, Sir, that your confidence in me, however great or small, shall never be abused. Since my incarceration, I have made a record which is the envy of everyone. Not one time have I been disobedient, or sullen, nor have I set an example which would not be commendable in the best society. I am a firm believer in discipline, and regulate my actions according to my belief. I believe I have proved myself trustworthy. I am president of the Holy Names Society here inside the prison, a Catholic society, and I know that I have acquitted my office satisfactorily every moment. I do know right from wrong, and certainly try to be well thought of by everyone I meet. The Army and the World War, at age seventeen, gave me a background upon which to build a life equally as remarkable as your own; and I may yet put the right foot first. I am not too proud to ask for help, nor too weak to win if refused. I am not guilty of any crime and have nothing of which to be ashamed. Your will is my determination, Sir, in prison or, at home. More than this no man can promise.

Only six months after composing this letter Coy was released from prison, but he was soon involved in another crime. On April 18, 1937, armed with a sawed-off shotgun, Coy robbed the National Bank of New Haven Kentucky with a friend named Delbert Lee Stiles, and a relative named Richard Coy. The three fugitives made off with just over two thousand dollars, and retreated into a small cave by the Rolling Fork River. Three days after the heist, local farmers noticed smoke from their campfire and alerted officials. During the trial that followed, Coy was identified by cashier A. E. Kirkpatrick as the man who had walked up to the cage, drawn a sawed-off shotgun, and held him at bay while an accomplice scooped up the

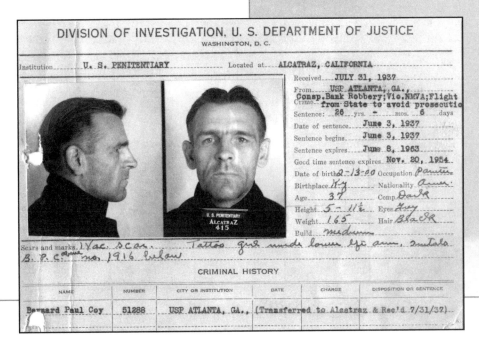

money. On June 3, 1937, Bernard Paul Coy was sentenced to twenty-five years and five days in a Federal penitentiary. The trio would all be sent to serve out their respective sentences at the Federal Penitentiary in Atlanta.

Bernie did not adjust well to prison life, and frequently found himself in isolation as punishment for engaging in altercations with other inmates. It is recorded that Coy physically attacked another inmate with a brutal implement consisting of a razor blade mounted onto a toothbrush handle, and this incident would earn him his one-way ticket to Alcatraz. Bernie arrived at Alcatraz on July 31, 1937, and he got off to a rough start during his first years on The Rock. On September 21, 1937 he participated in a work strike, stating: *"I'm not a big shot or looking for glory, I just want to be locked up in my cell and not be bothered by anyone."* He thus received his first introduction to D Block, and was placed into segregation for one week.

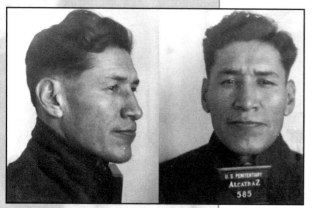

Joe Varsalona

On April 4, 1939 a heated dispute broke out between Bernie and fellow inmate Joe Varsalona while they were working in the prison kitchen. In a violent fury, Bernie hit Varsalona, knocking him to the floor. One of the guards came up from the basement, and after trying unsuccessfully to break up the fight, he summoned other correctional officers. But before the other guards could intervene, Varsalona grabbed a butcher knife and inflicted several minor stab wounds on Coy. Bernie was admitted to the prison hospital for seven days, and then released back into the general prison population. His first aborted escape attempt came in December of the same year, when it was suspected that Bernie was trying to cut through a steel window-guard in the bakeshop. His actions were quickly halted, and as a punitive measure he was thrown into the strip cell and placed on a restricted diet.

It wasn't long before Bernie found himself back in the general prison population, quietly serving out his time. He soon became what could be considered a model inmate. Despite his limited education, Bernie was a passionate reader, and was thought to be very intelligent. He also found the opportunity to reengage his passion for art. In October of 1944, Warden Johnston wrote Coy a lengthy congratulatory letter regarding a few paintings of landscapes and wartime subjects that Coy had contributed for an exhibit in Washington D.C., at the Congress for the American Prison Association. Johnston remarked that Coy's paintings were very popular, and mentioned how pleased he was to have them representing Alcatraz.

JOSEPH PAUL CRETZER

Joseph Paul Cretzer had vowed that he would not concede victory to Alcatraz, and despite formidable odds, he declared that he would find a way to escape the island. Cretzer was born on April 17, 1911 to deaf-mute parents in Anaconda, Montana. He was the youngest of three boys and two girls, and constantly lived under the scrutiny of his older broth-

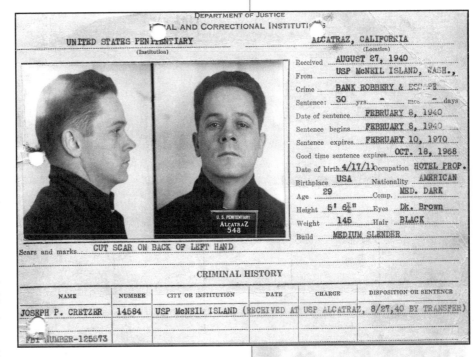

		DEPARTMENT OF JUSTICE			
		PENAL AND CORRECTIONAL INSTITUTIONS			

UNITED STATES PENITENTIARY (Institution) ALCATRAZ, CALIFORNIA (Location)

Received: AUGUST 27, 1940
From: USP McNEIL ISLAND, WASH.,
Crime: BANK ROBBERY & ESCAPE
Sentence: 30 yrs. — mos. — days
Date of sentence: FEBRUARY 8, 1940
Sentence begins: FEBRUARY 8, 1940
Sentence expires: FEBRUARY 10, 1970
Good time sentence expires: OCT. 18, 1968
Date of birth: 4/17/11 Occupation: HOTEL PROP.
Birthplace: USA Nationality: AMERICAN
Age: 29 Comp.: MED. DARK
Height: 5' 6½" Eyes: Dk. Brown
Weight: 145 Hair: BLACK
Build: MEDIUM SLENDER

U. S. PENITENTIARY ALCATRAZ 548

Scars and marks: CUT SCAR ON BACK OF LEFT HAND

CRIMINAL HISTORY

NAME	NUMBER	CITY OR INSTITUTION	DATE	CHARGE	DISPOSITION OR SENTENCE
JOSEPH P. CRETZER	14584	USP McNEIL ISLAND		(RECEIVED AT USP ALCATRAZ, 8/27,40 BY TRANSFER)	
FBI NUMBER-125673					

Joseph Paul Cretzer

ers. One prison report stated that all of the siblings had been in conflict with the law, and all held poor reputations within the communities in which they resided. His brothers George and Donald, with whom he had the closest ties, had also served long sentences in the Colorado State Penitentiary. In prison interviews, Cretzer described that he had enjoyed a friendly relationship with his father, but other reports alleged that his father led him into crime by encouraging him to perform "*sneak thefts*" and burglaries at a very young age. News clippings in his inmate file showed that his father, who was sixty years old at the time of the reports, was institutionalized at the Colorado State Hospital in Pueblo.

His parents separated when Joe was very young, and the mother and children took up residence with his grandmother. His mother soon remarried, which caused family friction, as Joseph had difficulty getting along with his new stepfather. His first bout with crime occurred when he was only fourteen years of age. His sister would later recount that Joe was first sent to a reformatory after stealing his grandfather's pocket watch. His grandfather referred Joe to juvenile court, and he was later also tried for stealing an automobile in Pueblo. It would be a tough time for Joe and his family, as his mother Lillie would die the same year from acute asthma. Joe continued engaging in petty crimes until he was sixteen, at which time the courts committed him to the Colorado State Reformatory at Golden, Colorado, from which he would escape three times. When he was formally released, Cretzer made his way via freight train to San Francisco, where he would take up residence with his older sister.

Reports reveal that Joe attempted to hold honest employment during this period, making license plates at the Norton Manufacturing Company in Oakland for about five months, and later working at the American Can Company for about nine months. But he soon returned to the life of crime. On January 28, 1929 Cretzer, who was now seventeen, and his accomplice Floyd Willoughby, aged twenty-two, broke into a home on Park Boulevard in Oakland. The robbery attempt ended in a hail of revolver shots when Police Officer L.S. Trowbridge fired at the suspects as they attempted to flee the scene.

Despite his youth and his contrition before the court, Cretzer was deemed incorrigible and sentenced to serve one year at the Preston Reformatory Industrial School in Ione, California. He was later released, having earned "*good time*" credits, and he moved to Portland Oregon. There he soon committed another robbery, and was caught and sent to

FBI
LAW ENFORCEMENT
BULLETIN

SAN FRANCISCO
48597

A complaint was filed before the United States Commissioner at Portland, Oregon, April 7, 1937, charging Joseph Paul Cretzer, and others, with the robbery of the Rose City Branch of the First National Bank of Portland, Portland, Oregon, on March 29, 1937, in violation of the National Bank Robbery Act.

Federal Bureau of Investigation
United States Department of Justice

John Edgar Hoover, Director

Washington, D. C.

VOL. 6 NO. 9
VOL. 7 NO. 9
SEPTEMBER 1, 1937

serve ninety days in the Multnomah County Jail. It was here that he first met fellow inmates and future accomplices Arnold Thomas Kyle, Jack Croft, Dick Kane, and Mickey Lynch. After all of the inmates had been released, they met again in Seattle, Washington, and committed a series of robberies together. Then during the early part of 1930, all of the fugitives made their way to San Francisco. Cretzer returned to Oakland, where he was soon arrested on several counts of burglary and larceny, and was again sentenced to serve out his time back at Preston, along with his future brother-in-law Arnold Kyle. Their time at Preston only seemed to bond the two even more closely.

Kyle had also served time for committing several robberies in various communities throughout California before he met Joe Cretzer. Remarkably, Kyle and Cretzer had endured similar childhoods. Kyle too was born in Montana, his parents had separated when he was only three, and as a result he and his siblings had been raised by their grandparents. He moved in briefly with his father and stepmother, but because of family friction, he soon found himself boarded in a home for orphans at only eleven years of age. At fifteen he was convicted of petty larceny, and placed in the Montana State Industrial School. Kyle would later marry Joe's sister Thelma.

Cretzer was unexpectedly paroled almost at the same time as Kyle, and immediately upon their release, the two young men quickly returned to their criminal habits. On the run once again, the fugitives found shelter with Arnold's younger sister Edna Kyle, who was now living in Pittsburg, California. Edna was no stranger to organized crime circles, and under her alias of Kay Stone Wallace she had made her own mark in the flesh trade. Edna and Joseph soon fell in love, and they became inseparable. The two were ultimately married in Flagstaff, Arizona on April 17, 1930.

The trio then continued their illegal escapades, helping to operate Edna's house of prostitution. For several years the business continued to thrive with little interference from the police. Then on June 23, 1936, the four outlaws violently robbed the American Trust Company in Oakland, making off with over five thousand dollars in cash. However, the robbery did not go off smoothly, and during their exit they engaged in a fierce gun battle with a police officer. They then moved their base of operations to Los Angeles, and ran a prostitution racket at the Garden View Hotel. During the years 1936-1937 they ran the Fern Hotel in San Pedro, which proved to be another lucrative prostitution venture. When their accomplice Jack Croft accidentally shot himself during a robbery, they left him behind and headed back home to Northern California.

U. S. PENITENTIARY
ALCATRAZ
547
10 29 51

Arnold Kyle

In January of 1938, things began to go wrong when a nineteen-year-old Montana farm girl named Jeanne Walters was arrested in a Berkeley hotel, and relayed a compellingly torrid tale of being abused in a white slave ring. Walters told police that she had been unwillingly sold as a prostitute, and she named Kay Wallace as one of the gang leaders and as the owner of the Bruno Hotel where the illicit activities usually took place. The police subsequently exposed a statewide prostitution ring, and it was discovered that Kay was one of the key players. Another woman also accused Kay, stating that she was only seventeen years old when Wallace had forced her into prostitution. The investigation further revealed that Cretzer had beaten the woman severely after she withheld some of her earnings. In an FBI Report dated February 24, 1940, it is stated that Cretzer beat her so severely that he knocked out several of her teeth, and left her with numerous cuts and bruises. Law enforcement officials quickly intervened, shutting down the brothel and seizing the hotel assets. Kay jumped her ten-thousand-dollar bail, and the trio then began a bank-robbing spree that would take them from Southern California up into Seattle.

Edna Kyle (a.k.a. Kay Stone Wallace)

It was at about this time that Cretzer and Kyle teamed up with two other professional bank robbers, John Hetzer and Jim Courey, who were well known for their *"quick style"* robberies. Their method was to rush in, clear out a few cash drawers, and then rush out, usually spending no more than one or two minutes inside the bank. Although the individual returns from each bank were smaller, the volume of robberies and their successful evasion of law enforcement made for a very lucrative cash flow. It was estimated that the gang robbed nearly eighty banks, taking in almost $72,000 in only a few months. The FBI began a comprehensive investigation of the heists, and suspicion soon fell on Joe Cretzer.

The FBI intensified their search, and began a national campaign to bring Cretzer and Kyle to justice. Joe was said to enjoy his notorious high-ranking status as a public enemy. Joseph Cretzer was now ranked number four on the FBI's Most Wanted List. He and Arnold decided to leave the Bay Area, since the FBI would likely be concentrating their search efforts throughout the Northwest. Jim Courey, unable to face the prospect of spending his life in prison, committed suicide in a Los Angeles hotel room when agents sought to arrest him.

In an effort to maintain a low profile, Cretzer and Kyle made a quick journey to Chicago, hoping that they could thus escape the watchful eye of the Bureau. Kyle stayed only a short while, then continued his travels back through Denver, Colorado, and on to Wichita, Kansas. He was finally apprehended on May 19, 1939 in Minneapolis, following another robbery. Kyle would not reveal the whereabouts of his other accomplices. While in Chicago, Joe and Edna had bought and operated another hotel, this time attempting to run a legitimate business. However, they had underestimated the magnitude of the FBI's search effort, and were apprehended in late August of 1939 and extradited back to Southern California to be tried for one of their earlier bank robberies in Pasadena. The FBI reported that Edna would stand charges for harboring a fugitive, and also that she was a suspect in the shooting of a police officer in Michigan City, Indiana, which had occurred on June 10, 1939. She would eventually be sent to Terminal Island in Southern California, where Al Capone had briefly been incarcerated after leaving Alcatraz.

During the preparations for the trial the Federal government intervened, claiming that they held ultimate jurisdiction and would elect to try both Kyle and Cretzer in Washington State before addressing the charges in Southern California. The defendants' cases also attracted a high level of media attention, with pertinent events regularly reported to the fascinated national public. Arnold Kyle and Joseph Cretzer were put on trial for the robbery of three Seattle banks, and both were convicted on February 8, 1940. Both were given twenty-five-year sentences at McNeil Island, a Northwestern Federal penitentiary located in Puget Sound, Washington. The official conviction report would declare them guilty in the case of "*National Bank Robbery.*" Cretzer had already started to build his résumé for Alcatraz, when officials caught him with a handcuff key in his mouth, which he had fashioned from a belt buckle. It was noted that the key was almost an "*exact duplicate.*"

Both Kyle and Cretzer arrived at McNeil on February 15, 1940, and they maintained a close relationship, just as when they had served time together at Preston. On April 11, 1940 the two were assigned to a labor detail, from which they attempted an escape. Armed with the axes they used for cutting roadside trees, they stole a prison truck, slammed through the yard gate (nearly running down a prison guard), and drove to a remote area. They then fled far into the woods of the four-thousand-acre island (Alcatraz in comparison is only twelve-acres). The duo hid for three days without food or water, attempting to keep cover under heavy brush, until they were finally captured and immediately placed into isolation.

Following the attempted escape, it would almost seem as if Cretzer didn't feel that he would be convicted of any serious crime. In a letter written to his wife, who had just been released from Terminal Island in Los Angeles on May 27th, Cretzer wrote: "*The charge is not serious & nothing to become alarmed over. We are being treated exceptionally well & feeling in fine spirit. I am certain everything here isn't as serious as it appears.*" On July 20, 1940, the two friends were tried for unlawful escape at the U.S. District Court of Tacoma, Washing-

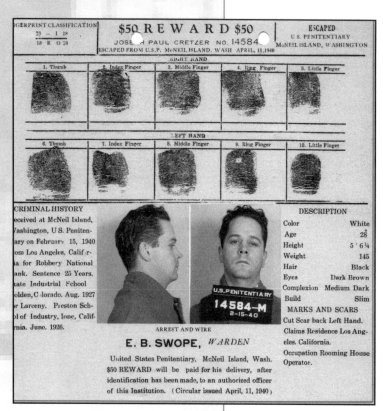

GERPRINT CLASSIFICATION
23 - 1 18
18 R O 20

$50 REWARD $50

JOSEPH PAUL CRETZER NO. 14584
ESCAPED FROM U.S.P. McNEIL ISLAND, WASH. APRIL, 11,1940

ESCAPED
U.S. PENITENTIARY
McNEIL ISLAND, WASHINGTON

RIGHT HAND
1. Thumb | 2. Index Finger | 3. Middle Finger | 4. Ring Finger | 5. Little Finger

LEFT HAND
6. Thumb | 7. Index Finger | 8. Middle Finger | 9. Ring Finger | 10. Little Finger

CRIMINAL HISTORY
eceived at McNeil Island, Washington, U.S. Penitentiary on February 15, 1940 om Los Angeles, California for Robbery National ank. Sentence 25 Years. tate Industrial School olden, Colorado, Aug. 1927 r Larceny. Preston School of Industry, Ione, California. June 1926.

ARREST AND WIRE

E. B. SWOPE, *WARDEN*

United States Penitentiary, McNeil Island, Wash. $50 REWARD will be paid for his delivery, after identification has been made, to an authorized officer of this Institution. (Circular issued April, 11, 1940)

DESCRIPTION
Color — White
Age — 28
Height — 5' 6¼
Weight — 145
Hair — Black
Eyes — Dark Brown
Complexion — Medium Dark
Build — Slim
MARKS AND SCARS
Cut Scar back Left Hand.
Claims Residence Los Angeles. California.
Occupation Rooming House Operator.

U.S. PENITENTIARY
14584-M
2-15-40

ton, and both entered pleas of not guilty. As a result, they were given a full trial. But on August 22, 1940, during the noon recess from the proceedings, they viciously attacked U.S. Marshal Artis J. Chitty, causing his death. The following is a report sent to the McNeil Island Warden by Lieutenant C. Zukowsky, who had supervised the inmates while they were in the custody of the court. His report describes in detail the events surrounding the Marshal's death:

August 23, 1940

To: P.J. Squire, Acting Warden
Via: L. Delmore, Acting Associate Warden
W.F. Swift, Acting Captain

From: C. Zukowsky. Lieutenant

Subject: DESPERATE ATTEMPT BY INMATES KYLE AND CRETZER, AND DEATH OF MARSHAL CHITTY.

Sirs:

Thursday, August 22, 1940, Lieut. Bass and myself were detailed to go dress out inmates Kyle and Cretzer for court. Upon the arrival of the Marshals at the institution, Inmates Kyle and Cretzer were turned over to the custody of Marshal Chitty, Lieut. Bass and myself accompanying the Marshal to the Federal Building, Tacoma.

We left the Island at approximately 08:40 A.M. arriving in the Marshal's Office at approximately 09:40 A.M. The Marshal immediately locked inmates Kyle and Cretzer in the Detention Cell at the Marshal's Office.

At 10:00 A.M. inmates Kyle and Cretzer were taken into court. The trial of inmates Kyle and Cretzer inmates immediately began, and at 12:00 noon was recessed for lunch, court to begin again at 2:00 P.M.

Inmates Kyle and Cretzer were handcuffed together (Cretzer's right arm to the left arm of Kyle). Then they were led back to the Detention Cell and locked up. Lieut. Bass and myself relieved each other for lunch, I returned from lunch at approximately 1:40 P.M. and seated myself on the corner of a table in the Marshal's office, directly in line of Detention Cell front, approximately twenty feet away.

At approximately 2:30 P.M. word came in that court was ready for inmates Kyle and Cretzer. Marshal Chitty unlocked the cell door and called the inmate's attorney to come out of the cell, as soon as the attorney had passed out of the cell Marshal Chitty called for inmates Cretzer and Kyle to come out.

At the time the Marshal called he was standing in front of the open cell. Inmates Kyle and Cretzer were seated against the wall.

As inmates Kyle and Cretzer were arising from the bench, inmate Cretzer called to Chitty, and beckoned with an upward motion of his head; at this point Marshal Chitty stepped forward into the cell, and at the same time Inmates Kyle and Cretzer moved toward Marshal Chitty.

As I saw Chitty step inside the cell, I automatically moved toward Marshal Chitty. Marshal Chitty made two steps forward into the cell, Inmates Kyle and Cretzer made the same move toward Marshal Chitty.

I was about at the open cell door when inmate Cretzer applied the "Inside Waist Hold" from the front, on Marshal Chitty.

Inmate Kyle's left hand was handcuffed to Cretzer's right hand, Kyle attempted to swing around to Marshal Chitty's back and was reaching with his free right hand for Marshal Chitty's right hand rear pocket.

At this point I knocked Kyle's right arm downward, the memento of the same swung Kyle around backward. I then stepped between Marshal Chitty and Inmate Cretzer, Cretzer releasing the hold, just as I was forcing Chitty away from the pair. Inmate Kyle with his free right hand started a long right swing, striking Marshal Chitty a blow on the face.

Marshal Chitty fell face forward, I immediately forced inmate Kyle to the floor. As inmate Kyle struck the floor he thrust his free right hand toward Chitty's right hand hip pocket.

At this point, Marshal Chitty was laying face downward on the floor; I noticed the gun in his right hand rear pocket.

As Inmate Kyle's hand reached the Marshal's holster, enclosing the gun, I dropped to my knees, pinning his right wrist with my left hand, and pinning his arm down with my left knee. Inmate Kyle attempted to rise up more on his right side but I forced him down, to lie on his back. Freeing Kyle's right hand from the holster and gun, which was still in Marshal Chitty's right hand hip pocket, I bent his arm upward and toward his head.

At this point I saw Marshal Chitty's body raise upward, and Deputy Marshal Vargo stepping in front of me and grapping Kyle's arm and twisting same into an arm-lock. I looked to the right and back of me and saw Cretzer lying down face forward, with Captain Delmore and Lieut. Bass standing over him.

Inmates Kyle and Cretzer were raised and seated back on the bench. Captain Delmore was wiping the blood dripping from a cut below Inmates Kyle's left eye.

Marshal Chitty stepped into the cell and ordered the inmates taken to the washbasin in the corner of the Marshal's office so they could be washed.

The inmates were led to the washbasin; upon reaching the washbasin inmates Kyle and Cretzer had just started to wash their faces when I heard something fall to the rear of us. I looked back and saw Marshal Chitty's body lying on the floor, and Captain Delmore standing just in back of me. I nodded to Captain Delmore, I staying with the inmates and Captain Delmore going toward the Marshal's body.

Captain Delmore returned immediately and ordered the inmates locked in the detention cell, which was immediately done.

In the meantime Marshal Chitty's body had been removed to the Marshal's private room and laid on a cot.

Captain Delmore came out of the private room and asked me to assist him in moving Chitty's body from the cot onto the floor, so artificial respiration could be easier administered.

This being done, I was about to start administering artificial respiration. I noticed the gun in Marshal Chitty's pocket. I removed same from his pocket and handed it to Deputy Marshal DeLine and told him to take care of the Marshal's gun.

Captain Delmore and myself relieved each other at administering artificial respiration until the doctor pronounced Marshal Chitty dead.

Captain Delmore took charge of the inmates and they were again taken to the courtroom, surrounded by Deputy Marshal's and Custodial Officers.

The inmates upon receiving their sentence were immediately rushed to the Steilacoom Dock, placed on a waiting boat, and arrived back on the island at approximately 5:45 P.M.

Respectfully Submitted,
C. Zukowsky, Lieutenant

The struggle ultimately contributed to Chitty suffering a fatal heart attack, and both Cretzer and Kyle subsequently changed their pleas to guilty. Each was given an additional five-year sentence, to be served concurrently with their previous twenty-five-year sentences.

Only a few days after Cretzer and Kyle were sentenced for their attempted escape, a Federal Grand Jury returned an indictment charging the convicts with murder in the first degree. Both entered pleas conceding to the charge of second-degree murder, and on October 21, 1940, they were sentenced to serve out the remaining course of their natural lives in prison. In some respects, they could consider themselves lucky. The prosecutors had fought vehemently to uphold a charge of capital murder, and had demanded death by the electric chair. But the defendants' council successfully argued that Chitty's death was accidental and not a case of premeditated murder, and therefore that the accused were not eligible for the death penalty. Both escaped the electric chair, but they received harsh life sentences that would ensure they would never walk free again.

In the midst of the trial both Cretzer and Kyle were transported to Alcatraz, arriving on August 27, 1940. The two men would now become residents of America's most notorious prison. Cretzer, had practically grown up just across the Bay, and would find serving time on the island even more difficult, as he was able to see familiar landmarks on the mainland. Now only twenty-nine years of age, he would have to adapt to the rigid structure of Alcatraz and its relentless routine, coupled with the realization that he was facing a dark and dismal future.

By any standard, Cretzer did not adjust well to life on The Rock, and he frequently found himself at odds with the administration. Less than one year after their arrival, Cretzer and Kyle participated in a failed escape attempt while working in the Mat Shop. Cretzer was sentenced to "*permanent segregation,*" and the few privileges he had been allotted were completely revoked. On September 19, 1943, now thirty-two years old and still residing in D Block, Cretzer incited a disturbance after an air vent fan failed. He was again stripped of all privileges, and was forced to serve additional time in segregation.

Then on April 11, 1944 Cretzer was allowed to spend some time in the recreation yard, when he was assaulted by the now famous inmate Henri Young, whose tale would later be portrayed in the Hollywood motion picture *Murder in the First*. The two convicts engaged in a bitter fistfight, which was broken up before anyone could be proclaimed the victor. Cretzer would again find himself isolated in cell #D-19, in a com-

Letters from Cretzer pleading with the Warden to be moved out of isolation and back into the general prison population. His commitment to staying out of mischief would prove to be short-lived.

plete lockdown status with all of his privileges rescinded. It was under these circumstances that Cretzer came to know Bernie Coy, who visited his cell in his role as the library orderly. Through this interaction they would build a close relationship, and the two friends would later conspire in the 1946 escape attempt.

On May 26, 1945, at thirty-three years of age, Cretzer wrote a letter to Warden Johnston pleading that he be allowed to start work again. This indicated to the administration that after spending three years in segregation, Cretzer was ready to be integrated back into the general prison population. The letter stated in part, *"You may rest assured that, considering the time spent in lock-up, I will not become involved in any future mischief. Wherever Mr. Miller wishes to work me will be okay. I will feel very much obligated to you, and will show my appreciation by conducting myself in a favorable manner."* The Warden took this letter to be sincere, and recommended Cretzer for release from segregation and assignment to a work detail. Cretzer would be transferred to cell #152 in B Block.

While Cretzer was imprisoned at Alcatraz, his wife Edna made frequent visits to the island, and she often wrote kind letters to Warden Johnston, sometimes offering her help in persuading "Dutch" to behave through her *"letters and visits."* Johnston was usually accommodating in this regard, and in July of 1945 he allowed Edna to see both her brother Arnold and her husband Joseph in back-to-back visits. His trust, however, was obviously misplaced. Cretzer had no intention of living up to the promises made in his letter.

MARVIN FRANKLIN HUBBARD

Another accomplice in the 1946 escape attempt was Marvin Franklin Hubbard. Marv (as he was called by fellow inmates) carried the reputation of a ruthless gunman, and he had earned his transfer to Alcatraz through a series of brutal escape attempts at other prisons. He was given a work assignment in the kitchen, and he became a good friend of Arnold Kyle. Like Kyle, Hubbard had also fallen prey to the Great Depression. Born August 13, 1912 to a farming family in Boaz, Alabama, he was the third of five siblings. His father died when he was only three years old, and he would be forced to drop out of school in 1918 after completing only the first grade. Hubbard worked on the family farm throughout his childhood, and assumed the tough responsibility of helping to provide income to support his family. At ten years of age, Hubbard ran away to live with Willie Wiggins, a relative of his stepfather, who taught the young Marvin the skill of masonry.

A letter written by Hubbard's wife to the Warden at the Atlanta Penitentiary on October 17, 1942 provides more insight into his personal history and upbringing. Herein are some excepts from the letter:

Dear Warden,

In answer to your letter received this week, I hardly know where to begin, I did not know where my husband was at, at this present time until I received your letter, it came as a quite a surprise, or rather a shock, as we had not been corresponding lately, I'm afraid I don't know very much of anything that would be of help to you, but will give you my best.

We were married at my mother's home in Dekalb County, on January 8, 1928. Neither of us were previously married, this being the only marriage for either of us. We only have one child. . . . My husband's attitude towards me and the child, were very fine at times, he didn't ever mistreat us in no-way except staying away from us for so much of his time, that he could have been with us, the harm he done was more of his own self than any-one else, only heartbreaks and sorrows, I had a fair share of that at an early age, my life has been filled with disappointments and heartaches. My husband has taken the responsibility of his family serious at times, and other times, he would leave us for a long time, as much as five or six months at a time, during this time he would never give us any support.

Marvin Franklin Hubbard

He was born and raised in Alabama, in Boaz, Route #3, we have lived out there part of our time together as well as here in Georgia. As far as where we have lived for the past five years is rather hard to explain, he spent a large portion of it in Kilby Prison as you no doubt already know, and the other part just here and yonder. His occupation has mostly been a bricklayer since I have known him, he does beautiful brickwork. Although he had farmed some during times when that trade was dull. His greatest handicap during these years, have been having no education, he was raised by a dear old mother who was left a widow with five children to raise, she did the best she could but could not educate the children. My husband's difficulties he has faced in recent years, I think depends on him getting started with the wrong kind of characters at a early age, which gives him the wrong opinion of life, before life was hardly started for him. Before he got started with the bad characters he was very kind and generous hearted, made good friends with all of whom he met, was well thought of in the community which he lived.

I just wish to say here, that anything you can do for him to make his stay in your institution, profitable to him, and as comfortable as possible, will highly be appreciated by me, although we have been separated a large portion of our time, it didn't take away the love and care I have for him. He was once good and kind and made home a place worth living for. I shall like very much to visit him as soon as possible, as I have not seen him since one year ago, last July 18th, 1941. Trusting this will be of some help to you in preparing my husband for his stay there.

Yours Very Truly,
Mrs. Lola Belle Hubbard

Hubbard's involvement with crime had started in his teenage years, with a series of forceful, violent robberies that usually ended in his arrest, and for which he ultimately served several short-term sentences. In late 1942, Hubbard and his accomplices were arrested after robbing a liquor store at gunpoint. His prison record includes a summation of his criminal history:

On August 7, 1942, Marvin Franklin Hubbard, George Kelly Matthews, and Kenneth Jackson escaped from the Walker County Jail, Jasper, Alabama, by assaulting the jailer and stealing a submachine gun, a .38 caliber revolver, property of the Walker County SO. They then stole a taxi at the point of a gun from Robert Pow and Roy Seals and forced them to accompany subjects to Double Springs, Alabama, to Moulton, Alabama, and to Madison, Alabama, where they had a blowout. They then obtained a 1939 Dodge truck from R.U. Dublin to accompany them in the truck to Huntsville, Alabama, and to Grassy Mountain, Alabama, where they tied the three victims to trees and abandoned them about nine P.M. on the same date. Subjects then proceeded in a truck to a secluded spot in the mountains near Cedartown, Georgia, where they stayed in hiding, except for short visits to a country store to purchase food, until three P.M. August 13, 1942. Subjects then hijacked W.A. Cason near Cedartown, Georgia, and stole his 1940 Ford sedan, releasing Cason at a nearby lake. They proceeded in the Ford to Tallapoosa, Georgia, to Anniston to Alabama, to Gadsden, Alabama, and to Collinsville, Alabama, where they parked in a secluded spot and slept from eight A.M. August 14, 1942, to the afternoon of the same date. They then proceeded on a country road to Trenton, Georgia and to Chattanooga, Tennessee.

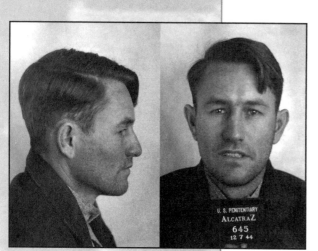

Marvin Franklin Hubbard

About 7:30 P.M. on August 14, 1942, subjects kidnapped Logan Stroud, traffic officer, Chattanooga P.D., when he attempted to arrest them for not having a safety sticker on their car and by threats of death at the point of a gun they forced him to accompany them from Hamilton County, Tennessee, to Catoosa County, Georgia. Subjects took refuge at the home of Henry Christian, tied Stroud, and locked him in a milk shed at the rear of the house. Stroud escaped about 4:30 A.M. August 15, 1942. Hubbard and Matthews were apprehended at 5:30 A.M. August 15, 1942, by FBI agents, and Georgia and Tennessee police officers after a gun battle in which Kenneth Jackson was killed. Hubbard and Matthews waived removal to Chattanooga. Authorized complaint was filed August 15, 1942, at Chattanooga, Tennessee, charging Hubbard and Matthews with violation of the kidnapping statute. Both subjects entered a plea of guilty before Commissioner Morgan on August 17, 1942, and in default of $25,000 bond each was remanded to the Knox County jail, Knoxville Tennessee.

On September 11, 1942, while being held at the Knox County Jail Marvin Franklin Hubbard, together with others, escaped from said jail by overpowering the turn key and the elevator operator who were locking up the prisoners in their cells for the night. Hubbard was apprehended by the Sheriff's Office, Knoxville, Tennessee, at Concord, Tennessee, on the night of September 14, 1942. When arraigned before the Commissioner on September 15, 1942, he entered a plea of guilty, and in default of $3000 bond was remanded to the custody of the US Marshal and incarcerated in the Knox County Jail, Knoxville, Tennessee.

On September 15, 1942, Marvin Franklin Hubbard addressed a letter to the United States Attorney at Chattanooga, Tennessee, requesting that he be indicted and arraigned at the next term of court at Greenville, Tennessee, on September 21, 1942, and expressed the desire to plead guilty to a charge of escaping from Federal custody.

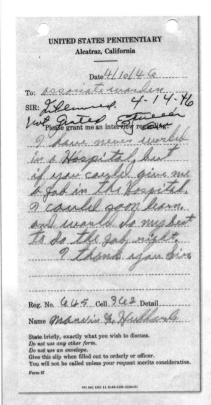

A request from Hubbard for a work assignment in the Prison Hospital. This request, dated April 10, 1946, suggests that Hubbard was probably recruited as an accomplice weeks or even days before the mass escape attempt.

In October of 1942, having been convicted of kidnapping and illegal transportation of firearms across state lines, Hubbard was sent to the Federal Penitentiary in Atlanta, where he reportedly participated in riot activities. Hubbard was deemed incorrigible, and in 1944 he received his ticket to The Rock.

MIRAN EDGAR THOMPSON

Miran Edgar "Buddy" Thompson had been on Alcatraz only since October, a little over six months, but his criminal record seemed endless. At only twenty-nine years of age, Buddy was already a seasoned felon. Before even disembarking from the prison launch, he had accumulated no less than eight successful escapes on his inmate profile record.

Thompson left home at an early age, and soon found himself in a reform school after being convicted of armed robbery before his eighteenth birthday. Reform school failed to reform him, and when he set out to support himself, he immediately began a chain of violent burglaries, targeting almost any establishment that had a cash register. Thompson was arrested frequently, but he had an exceptional ability to escape from his captors. His early crimes included everything from forgery, to drunk and disorderly conduct, to assault, and he ultimately graduated to armed robbery. Thompson

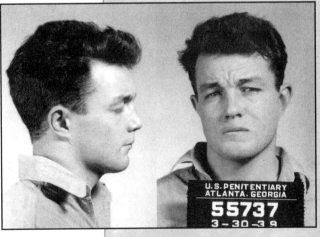

Miran Edgar Thompson

traveled through various states committing robberies, up until March 12, 1945. Although historians often dispute the details of the events of that day, it is certain that Miran and a twenty-seven-year-old accom-

Miran Edgar Thompson

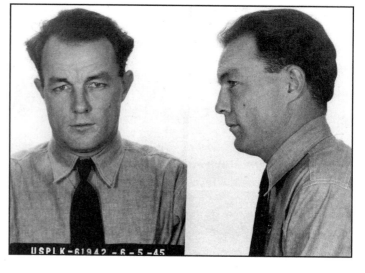

plice named Elmer Day were arrested by a Police Detective Lem Savage. During the course of the arrest, Thompson for some reason was not handcuffed, and he pulled a revolver and fatally shot the officer. Officer Savage's body was then kicked out of the car, and the pair fled west, later kidnapping a young New Mexico woman and commandeering her vehicle. They were captured a short time later at the New Mexico-Texas state line, but not before they had crossed the state border. This meant that Federal kidnapping charges would be filed against them.

Miran was tried in Federal court for the kidnappings, but somehow managed to escape the death penalty, receiving a ninety-nine-year sentence with no possibility of parole for the kidnapping, and a life sentence for the murder. With his long history of successful escapes and his conviction for the violent murder of a police official, Miran was quickly selected by the Bureau of Prisons to serve out his time on Alcatraz. Thompson arrived on the island on October 15, 1945, as inmate #AZ-729. His reputation as a vicious cop killer had followed him to Alcatraz, and this gave him special status among the inmate population.

SAM RICHARD SHOCKLEY

Sam Shockley was another resident of The Rock who had truly earned his place there. It was revealed during the trial of the escapees that Shockley had an IQ ranging in the low to mid-sixties, the mental equivalent of a child of eight to ten years. He was considered by all of the correctional staff as "*impulsively dangerous,*" and many thought that his imprisonment on Alcatraz was inappropriate, since he suffered from mental illness, and therefore was unable to blend into the general population. He often suffered hallucinations, which resulted in violent fits directed toward the correctional staff. He had a reputation for throwing articles from his cell, breaking plumbing fixtures, starting fires, and viciously attacking officers when they attempted to restrain him. Shockley had become one of the most frequent residents of the strip cell. One of the least disputed facts surrounding the 1946 escape was that inmate Sam Shockley was considered by nearly all to be dangerous and psychotic.

Shockley had been transferred to Alcatraz from Leavenworth in September of 1938, and he spent the majority of his imprisonment in segregation. He had suffered emotionally throughout his childhood growing up in rural Oklahoma, and eking an existence under conditions of severe poverty. He was forced to leave school and work on the family farm before completing the elementary grades, which limited his education to basic reading and writing. He developed no trade skills, and was often involved in petty crimes. It was also documented that while serving out a sentence in a state reformatory, Sam was badly beaten by a fellow inmate and suffered a severe head injury. One year later he would receive another head injury, this time inflicted by a correctional officer. His family remained very supportive, securing an attorney named E.W. Schenk, who endeavored to attain clemency for Sam, but the effort was ultimately unsuccessful.

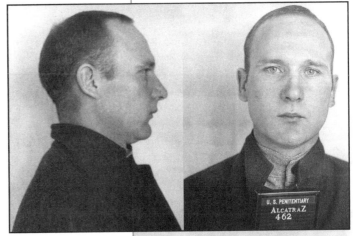

Sam Richard Shockley

On March 14, 1938, Shockley and an accomplice named Edward Leroy Johnston burglarized a farmhouse near Pauls Valley, Oklahoma, stole a shotgun, and devised a plan to rob the Bank of Paoli, located in Paoli, Oklahoma. The following day at 4:45 A.M., Shockley and Johnston stole a car from a gentleman who ironically was named Jesse James. They bound and gagged him with bailing wire, and then beat him severely. After shoving a handkerchief in James' mouth and securing it by wrapping utility tape around his head, they made off with his Chevrolet Coupe. At approximately 1:00 P.M., the two criminals entered the Paoli Bank with Shockley posing as a customer who needed to cash a labor check. Once Shockley had arrived at the teller's window, he pulled a revolver on bank president D.F. Pendley, his wife, and the assistant cashier, demanding that they turn over all of the cash. While Shockley stood over the couple, Johnston collected $947.38 in silver and currency. The official report also stated that Shockley abused the couple verbally with vulgar profanities and death threats.

After they had bagged the cash, the couple were taken as hostages and transferred to the vehicle that had been stolen from James. The car eventually broke down, and the four were forced to head into the mountains on foot. Police reports state that a young teenage farmer interceded and initiated a gun battle, thus allowing the two hostages a chance to escape. Shockley and Johnston were able to flee into the mountains, and were not captured until ten days later when they were apprehended at a farm belonging to Shockley's brother near Tom, Oklahoma. Shockley made a mad attempt to escape out the back door, but was quickly hunted down by the police. He later denied having any role in the robbery, but his accomplice Johnston readily admitted that both of them had been involved.

Shockley was committed to Leavenworth on May 16, 1938, where he was frequently reported as behaving violently toward the correctional staff. After his transfer to Alcatraz this pattern apparently continued, and he was often placed in segregation. Shockley would always be released back into the general prison population, but then he would quickly find himself in some type of mischief again, and be returned to isolation. Despite his low IQ, he occasionally devised some witty schemes. For example, in June of 1943 when Shockley was assigned to work in the kitchen detail, he stole six pounds of tenderloin steak from the freezer, and managed to sneak it into the bakeshop and roast it. He wasn't caught until after he had eaten a healthy portion. He was then sent back to solitary, placed on a restricted diet, and permanently removed from his work assignment in the kitchen. The correctional officers on Alcatraz dreaded Shockley's outbreaks, and only one week prior to the 1946 escape attempt, he participated in a large-scale disturbance that reverberated through D Block.

On the evening of April 26th, Robert Stroud, better known as the *Birdman of Alcatraz*, started yelling at the top of his lungs that he was suffering from severe abdominal cramps and needed immediate medical attention. The D Block Correctional Officer made an attempt to see if Dr. Roucek, the official prison physician, was still on the island. After calling around and not being able to locate the doctor, the officer informed Stroud that he would have one of the MTAs (Medical Technical Assistant) from the prison hospital come down and examine him. Stroud protested profusely, insisting that he wanted to see a *"real"* doctor, and bragging that he was smarter than any of the MTAs. The correctional officer apparently had a difficult time getting the MTA to come down to D Block. After some time had passed, with Stroud becoming progressively more vocal, the rest of the inmates started to join in, insisting that a doctor be brought in to examine him immediately. After a wait of nearly two hours, the MTA finally made his way into Stroud's cell, which was located on the top tier in the far corner. The MTA performed a quick and superficial exam, offered Stroud a few aspirin, and prescribed rest.

Stroud continued to complain into the evening that he had been misdiagnosed, and repeatedly demanded to see a doctor. By this time Dr. Roucek had returned, and he came up to examine Stroud. After performing a thorough examination, he explained to Stroud that there were no pertinent findings, and that the trouble would probably pass by morning. Soon afterward Stroud again began yelling, stating that he would die unless someone got him medical help. By this time the other inmates had started rallying on his behalf. Their rebellion implied that the prison administration was cruelly leaving an inmate to suffer, and this led the inmates to start vandalizing their cells. Shockley and several of the others began to destroy everything in sight. The frenzy raged throughout the cellblock as the majority of inmates threw their belongings out onto main floor from their respective tiers.

Jim Quillen was a fellow inmate who had been sentenced to serve time in D Block after a failed escape in the kitchen basement area. With the assistance of a few other inmates, Quillen had attempted to escape through a narrow tunnel housing steam pipes which were thought to lead down to the prison powerhouse. The temperatures in the tunnel were unbearably hot, and when the inmates reached the end of the cellhouse, they would unfortunately find that the tunnel was sealed with a five-foot block of cement. A fellow prisoner had meanwhile betrayed their plan to the administration, and they were sent to serve time first in isolation and then in segregation.

Quillen would later describe some of the events that Stroud incited, such as inmates draining the water from their toilet, and using bedding and other flammable items to start a fire in the bowl. Once the fire had reached a sufficient temperature, the inmate would flush the toilet and the cold water would shatter the porcelain. The sharp, heavy pieces would then be thrown out of the cells and over the tier railings, presenting a hazard to the correctional staff, and sometimes even shattering the outside windows. By the early morning hours on April 27th, water was flooding over the upper levels, and massive pools had saturated the lower cellblock floors. The block was fogged with smoke from smoldering fires as the chilling bay breeze ripped through the cellhouse, intensifying the cold, and the inmates were left alone in their wet cells with no warm place to rest.

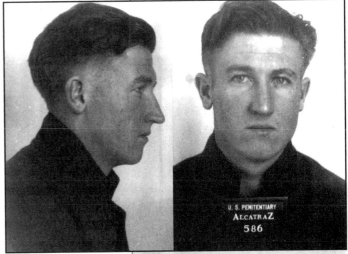

Jim Quillen

By daybreak the correctional staff had started to assess the damages, and they set up a desk at the end of the block to hold hearings with Warden Johnston. On the morning of April 28th the hearing board convened, and met with each and every inmate who had caused destruction to his cell. The board was comprised of Associate Warden E. J. Miller, Captain H.W. Weinhold, Lieutenant N.W. Morrison, Dr. Roucek, and the Warden himself. Quillen later recalled that Stroud's cell was found completely intact with his bed nicely made, and that he was angered that Stroud had used the other inmates to get back at the administration.

Warden Johnston punished the inmates harshly, ensuring that each one was penalized for their collective rebellion against the administration. It was decided that the inmates would remain in their own cells until proper repairs could be made. Since many of them had destroyed their sink and toilet, they were forced to use a tin bucket to relieve themselves. It was left to the correctional staff to determine how frequently the buckets would be emptied—usually only once a day—and the inmates were completely at their mercy in this regard. In addition, the inmates who had been involved received nineteen days in isolation, and were forced to pay for all damages before they were allowed to transfer out of Alcatraz. This would require each inmate to remain on good behavior, integrate back into the general population, and secure a paying job in the industries. It was a severe punishment delivered directly by Warden Johnston himself. Quillen later commented that the inmates long resented Stroud for using them as pawns in his own futile cause.

CLARENCE VICTOR CARNES

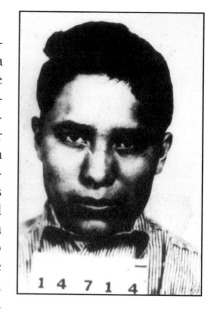

Clarence Victor Carnes, born on January 14, 1927 in rural Oklahoma, was a full-blooded Choctaw Indian, and like many of the other inmates he was exposed to a troubled and poverty-stricken childhood. His father struggled to support his family through the Depression years, and tried to create a stable life for his children, but was largely unsuccessful. Carnes would become what was later described as a *"natural fighter,"* and he developed into a gang leader during his early teens. He was constantly in and out of trouble, and at only fifteen years of age he would participate in an armed robbery that would cost him his freedom.

Carnes' fate was sealed when he and a school friend attempted to hold up a small gas station in Atoka, Oklahoma. Carnes threatened station attendant Walter Weyland with a stolen revolver, but Weyland refused to take the youths seriously. He apparently attempted to disarm Carnes, and the struggle ended with a fatal gunshot wound to the attendant's chest. Carnes and his accomplice were quickly apprehended and placed in the county jail, where they were to await trial on charges of first-degree murder. But only hours after their capture they somehow managed to overpower the jailer and escape, taking with them his stolen pistol. Within hours they were recaptured, and in October of 1943, Carnes was found guilty of first-degree murder and sentenced to life in prison.

Then on February 3, 1945, while incarcerated at the Oklahoma State Reformatory in the city of Granite, Carnes and two accomplices escaped from a hard labor chain gang at work in a rock quarry. Carnes and his accomplices made it to town without being detected, stole a vehicle, and kidnapped the owner. The trio then crossed the state line into Shamrock, Texas, wrecked the stolen vehicle, and made their way back into Oklahoma in another stolen car, leaving their kidnap victim behind. They were quickly apprehended, and on March 19, 1945 Carnes would receive an additional ninety-nine years for kidnapping under the Federal Lindberg Act. Carnes was sent to the State Reformatory in McAlester, Oklahoma, and later to Leavenworth Federal Peniten-

(This page and opposite top) Clarence Victor Carnes—A life in pictures. He would spend almost his entire adult life in maximum security prisons.

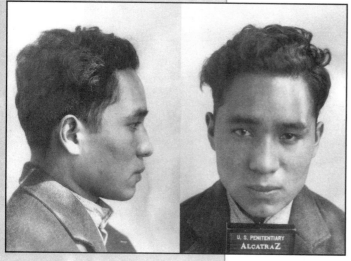

tiary in Kansas. He soon became a serious disciplinary problem at Leavenworth, and was recommended for transfer to Alcatraz by the Warden. Carnes arrived on Alcatraz on July 6, 1945 at only eighteen years of age. Many who knew him described him as being somewhat out of place on Alcatraz. He was quiet and very easy going, and rarely got involved in altercations. Carnes was also very fit, and did not back down when trouble arose. It is likely that these traits appealed to Coy when he recruited him for the prison break.

Preparations for the Escape

The famous escape of 1946 did not happen spontaneously; on the contrary, it was the fruit of careful planning by the group of inmate conspirators, and particularly by Bernie Coy. He was the architect of the scheme, who studiously watched the habits of the guards, meticulously selected his accomplices from among the pool of prisoners, and arranged for all of the necessary tools and supplies to be constructed and secreted around the prison.

EARLY PLANNING STAGES

In late 1945, Bernie Coy had earned his way to a job as the library orderly, which gave him special privileges to move about the cellhouse freely. This job assignment also allowed him to provide his own special "*reading privileges*" to other inmates in return for "*special favors*," whenever the need would arise. Another advantage was his new ability to venture into D Block, in order to deliver reading materials. D Block was strictly off-limits unless an inmate had a specific reason to enter. Former inmate James Quillen later stated that Coy was thus able to study activities within the cellhouse discreetly, and to identify potential systemic weaknesses that could offer a future prospect for escape. Coy's assignment as a library orderly proved to be a choice position, as it also provided additional opportunities to interact with the correctional officers, and to study their individual work habits. In addition to his primary assignment, he was also allowed to take an additional job as a cellhouse orderly, fulfilling these duties in the afternoon. Coy was well liked by the correctional officials, and was said to have an easygoing attitude. He was respectful toward inmates and guards alike, and as one correctional officer recalled, he was a "*mature con*" that "*got on well with most everyone.*"

However, behind this mask of innocence, Bernard Paul Coy actually had no intention of finishing out his time at Alcatraz. During his sentencing in 1937, he had stated that "*murder meant nothing,*" and that no prison could hold him. True to his vow, Bernie embarked on an intense study of procedural operations at the prison, exploring the systemic frailties that he believed would ultimately grant him freedom. Coy recognized that the West End Gun Gallery had one weak point that could possibly be penetrated if he acquired the necessary tools. He noticed that at the top of the Gallery, the bars encasing the upper tier ran from the back wall, curving downward until they reached a horizontal cross-member several feet from where the bar-base was anchored. The bars were parallel and spaced approximately five inches apart, and he decided that if he could force the bars and separate them far enough to accommodate his body, he could gain access to the Gallery, secure weapons, and take hostages. It was a brazen plan, and it seemed to have great potential.

As Coy carefully studied the individual routines of the guard staff, he also began to select his co-conspirators. He understood that in order for the escape to be successful, his plan would require exquisite orchestration, as well as the total commitment and cooperation of his accomplices. It is clear that his choice would fall on individuals who were capable of following a prescribed plan, and doing whatever became necessary to carry it out, even if this meant murder.

During Coy's rounds of delivering books and magazines to inmates, he routinely stopped at cell #152 to visit Joseph Paul Cretzer, also known to many of the inmates as "Dutch." Cretzer was an ideal choice as an accomplice, and he had already proven his capabilities during an aborted escape attempt in May of 1941. That attempt had involved taking guards hostage, which was also an element of Coy's plan. Although the previous attempt had failed, inmate Clarence Carnes stated afterward that Cretzer had kept calm when it became clear that the plan was doomed, and this had won him a solid reputation with the other convicts. It is likely that Coy took this into consideration in deciding that Cretzer would make a perfect accomplice.

Inmate Clarence Carnes would later comment that Coy had consistently reminded his accomplices of the virtue of patience and thorough planning. Coy had prepared himself for the day of the escape both physically and mentally, continually refining the procedures and chronology of the plan. He lost twenty pounds by adhering to a strict diet regimen over a period of several months, and improved his muscle tone and physical strength by performing exercises in his cell. He also arranged for pre-placement of the crudely fabricated tools that would be needed to spread the bars in the West End Gun Gallery. It is believed that inmate and cellhouse plumber Ed Mrozik smuggled pliers to Coy, and also assembled the makeshift bar spreader with the help of a fellow inmate in the Machine Shop.

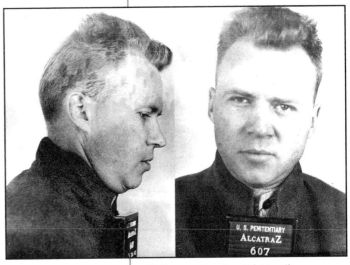

Cellhouse Plumber Ed Mrozik

The inmates of Alcatraz had developed a complex system for smuggling items past the elaborate security mechanisms within the prison. Inmates who risked smuggling contraband for others generally were given special payoffs or rewards. Despite the watchfulness of the correctional officers, inmates often successfully used covert networks to pass and smuggle items to one another. For example, if an inmate working in the machine shop wanted to "*mail*" a contraband item, he could wrap it in a soiled rag and send off to the laundry, making sure that the laundry bag carried a special secret marking. The contraband could then be folded in with clean kitchen linens and delivered to an appropriate recipient in the kitchen. Since problems such as clogged drains were common occurrences in the kitchen, the inmate plumber could intercept the smuggled item, which could be disguised as a common plumbing tool or fixture, and he could introduce it into his tool kit, thus ensuring final delivery. The security focus was generally on the inmates themselves, so these covert activities went largely unnoticed.

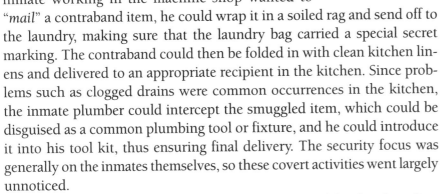

It is likely that Coy and Hubbard extended special food and reading privileges to inmates who helped smuggle materials for the escape. It is also possible that Coy granted favors to some correctional officers, who would eventually contribute to the success of the plan. Coy had earned a great deal of trust amongst the custodial staff through his frequent interactions with the guards. He was thus allowed to make his rounds within the cellhouse with minimal supervision. Several books written on the escape have further speculated that Coy actually helped to determine the officers' routines, by distributing popular reading materials at specific time intervals to the guards posted in the gun galleries.

THE SCENE OF THE BATTLE

Correctional Officer Bert Burch was assigned to the West End Gun Gallery for the afternoon watch on the day of the escape attempt, May 2, 1946, and it is clear that Coy had been able to study his work habits in advance. It was at first believed that during his preparations for the escape, Coy had observed that Burch usually spent the after-lunch hours in the D Block end of the Gallery, where he would read for most of the afternoon. But a second theory, extracted from notes handwritten by Carl Sundstrom a few days after the escape attempt, held that Burch did not always maintain a strict routine. Instead it is suggested that he would be lured into that section of the cellblock for an extended period of time by the acting-out of an inmate in D Block.

Correctional Officer Bert Burch

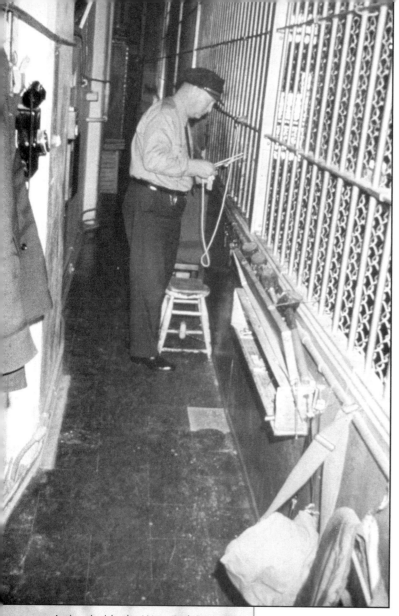

A view inside the West End Gun Gallery. An officer is seen here lowering a key to a colleague. The Gallery posting was one of the assignments most favored by the prison officers. Up until the events of 1946, it was also considered the safest.

Access to the West End Gallery was from an exterior catwalk located on the southwest end of D Block, with entry and exit monitored by the Road Tower officer. Changing shifts in inclement weather was no easy task, since the correctional officer would have to climb the metal staircase on the side of the cellhouse, battling the rain and wind that was intensified by the oceanfront exposure. It was, however, one of the most secure areas of the cellhouse, and several officers considered it a good assignment. Officers who worked in the Gallery brought their own meals, since they would be locked inside for their entire shift, which usually lasted eight hours.

The Gallery was a dual-level, narrowly enclosed area with a passage width of only about four and a half feet. The west end of the Gallery was situated over the area known to inmates as *Times Square*, and ran from each end of the cellhouse through the southwest end of D Block. This arrangement allowed the officer on duty to patrol all three main cellblock aisles (and to pass through a door into D Block), simply by walking the length of the Gallery, which generally provided an excellent and protected view of all cellhouse activity. Most importantly, the officers assigned to the East and West Galleries each carried a .30-06 Springfield rifle, and a semi-automatic Colt .45 handgun. Should any of the unarmed officers walking the cellhouse floor find themselves in a compromising situation, the Gallery officer could regain control with this powerful and accurate weaponry. This impression was projected to the inmates on a daily basis, as the heavily armed Gallery officers paced the length of the shielded passage.

Directly across from the Mess Hall at the opposite end of the cellhouse, and located off the main entrance corridor, was the prison Armory. The Armory was considered the most secure part of the prison, and it was the center of communications as well. Situated across from the control room, it had a secure switchboard, and also contained the prison's weapons reserves. The Armory could only be unlocked from the inside, and it was considered almost impossible to infiltrate. Encased in steel and bulletproof glass, the Armory was the operational nucleus of Alcatraz, and the vital hub for island activities and correctional officers' posting status. It housed the prison's arsenal, and its control center monitored the movements of anyone leaving or entering the cellblock. The Armory switchboard linked the telephones throughout the entire prison network for internal communications. There was also a special marine radio for prison launch communications, in addition to a short-wave

transceiver, standard telephones, and a Teletype machine that could be used to wire messages to the mainland. In the event of a large-scale riot or takeover of the cellhouse, the integrity of the Armory could always be maintained.

The scene was set and the plans were laid, and all that remained was for the final signals to be given. The conspirators believed that they had thought of everything, and had prepared for every eventuality—but through a sequence of unforeseen circumstances, their careful plans were destined to go terribly wrong.

The Armory served as the weapons arsenal for the prison, and it was also the stronghold for all of the prison keys, as well as the communications center. The Armory Officer had the ability to lock himself inside the weapons vault, to which there was no possible outside access. The Armory was the impenetrable nerve center of Alcatraz.

The Battle of Alcatraz

The explosive sequence of events that would eventually come to be known as the *Battle of Alcatraz* began early on the morning of May 2, 1946, and would gradually build in a tragic crescendo over the next two days. During this period, numerous prisoners and guards we be wounded or lose their lives, and the reputation of the island prison would change forever. For the first time, inmates would secure weapons from the prison armory, and turn them against their guards with deadly force. When the smoke had settled and the dust had cleared, a new legend would have arisen from the rocky soil of Alcatraz.

On the morning of May 2, 1946, Marvin Hubbard was tending to his duties in the prison kitchen, which was his official work assignment. Although Arnold Kyle did not play an active role during the escape attempt, it is speculated that he was responsible for involving Hubbard in the plan, as he had been on the same work detail before being reassigned to a paid position in the laundry. At 6:30 A.M. Lieutenant Joe Simpson rang the first bell, waking the prisoners and allowing them time to enjoy a cigarette, make their beds, and prepare for their work assignments. The inmates assigned to the kitchen detail were always released from their cells a few hours earlier to prepare the food carts. At 6:50 A.M., Simpson sounded the second bell, and the cell doors racked open with the powerful resonance of heavy steel. The inmates began to line up outside their respective cells, in preparation for their customary count and organized march to the Mess Hall.

At 7:00 A.M., Simpson rang the bell a third time. The inmates from the lower tiers of B and C Blocks then started to march into the Mess Hall, followed in an orderly fashion by the prisoners from the second and third tiers. The steam tables were placed buffet style to accommodate the flow of inmates in two parallel lines. The inmates from C Block would walk in order to the steam tables on the left, and those from B Block would file in on the right. After obtaining their food tray and meal, the prisoners would sit on their respective sides of the Mess Hall, reflecting the cellhouse arrangement. The process was refined for efficiency and allowed for no variances, since the breakfast period would last only twenty minutes.

The steam tables were manned by Hubbard and fellow inmates Floyd Harrell, Lavelle Bush, and Harold Brest. Brest had participated in a failed escape at Alcatraz in April of 1943, in which his accomplice James Boarman had been killed by a bullet to the head. In May of 1946, Brest had been out of segregation and on work assignment for less than one month, and probably had no interest in getting involved in another escape, with the memory of Boarman's violent death still fresh in his mind.

As the inmates were assembling for breakfast on the morning of May 2nd, the next shift of correctional officers started to come on duty, relieving those coming off the graveyard shift. Officer Bert Burch made his way up the narrow stairway running up the side of the cellhouse, to begin his shift in the West Gun Gallery.

Main Cellhouse
1946 Riot Events

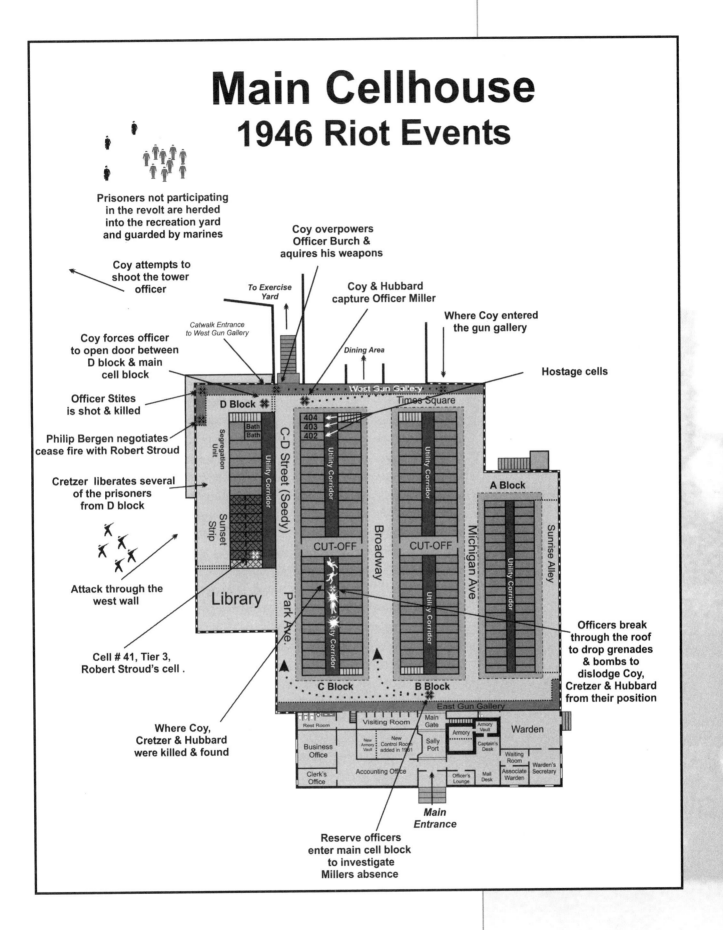

Prisoners not participating in the revolt are herded into the recreation yard and guarded by marines

Coy attempts to shoot the tower officer

Coy overpowers Officer Burch & aquires his weapons

Coy & Hubbard capture Officer Miller

Where Coy entered the gun gallery

To Exercise Yard

Catwalk Entrance to West Gun Gallery

Coy forces officer to open door between D block & main cell block

Dining Area

Hostage cells

Officer Stites is shot & killed

West Gun Gallery

D Block

Times Square

Philip Bergen negotiates cease fire with Robert Stroud

Bath
Bath

Segregation Unit

Utility Corridor

404
403
402

Utility Corridor

Utility Corridor

A Block

Cretzer liberates several of the prisoners from D block

C-D Street (Seedy)

Sunset Strip

Suntise Alley

Utility Corridor

Attack through the west wall

Library

CUT-OFF

Broadway

CUT-OFF

Michigan Ave

Cell # 41, Tier 3, Robert Stroud's cell .

Park Ave.

Utility Corridor

Utility Corridor

Officers break through the roof to drop grenades & bombs to dislodge Coy, Cretzer & Hubbard from their position

Where Coy, Cretzer & Hubbard were killed & found

C Block

B Block

East Gun Gallery

Rest Room

Visiting Room

Main Gate

Armory

Armory Vault

Warden

Business Office

New Armory Vault

New Control Room added in 1961

Sally Port

Captain's Desk

Waiting Room

Clerk's Office

Accounting Office

Officer's Lounge

Mail Desk

Associate Warden

Warden's Secretary

Main Entrance

Reserve officers enter main cell block to investigate Millers absence

Armory Officer Clifford Fish

Correctional Officer Ernest Lageson

Cliff Fish was the day watch officer assigned to the Armory in May of 1946. As the officers reported to their assigned locations, they would individually call in to Fish so that he could record the post changes in the official activity register. As part of standard procedure, the officers were required to call in to the Armory every thirty minutes to report on their welfare. The status of each inmate was likewise recorded every thirty minutes. As the inmates congregated in the Mess Hall for breakfast, the correctional staff reported and prepared their posts for the transfer of inmates to the work industries.

Following breakfast the inmates were marched back to their cells, and those with work assignments were allowed time to smoke and get ready for work. After all of the inmates had been locked back in their cells, Joe Simpson sounded the bell signaling inmates to stand in silence at their cell door until the count activities were concluded. Ernest Lageson, who was the officer in charge of the cellhouse, sat at the desk situated just outside of the Mess Hall at the west end of the cellblock. He compiled the numbers from the six officers performing the counts, and phoned the final tallies to Fish in the Armory.

After the counts were complete, the inmates who were assigned to work details usually changed into their work clothing, and ensured that their cells were clean in case of a surprise inspection. Being assigned to a work detail was a great privilege, and inmates rarely disobeyed rules regarding cleanliness and hygiene. After the count bell sounded indicating that no discrepancies had been found, the officers in charge of the industry work details gathered near the recreation yard, preparing to release the inmates from their cells to start work.

Joe Simpson would then give the signal to release those on work details from their cells. The cells were unlocked, just as at meal periods, with all of the cells on each tier racking open to allow the men to step outside of their cells. They would then await the okay signal to march down into the recreation yard and line up for their work assignment. Bert Burch in the West Gun Gallery lowered key #107 to Officer William Miller, who opened the heavy steel access door to the recreation yard, and then started signaling the inmates to file down into the lineup. As the convicts passed through the cellhouse door, Miller counted each one. The inmates then walked into the yard area, lining up on a painted stripe in accordance with their specific assignment. Once again they would participate in yet another count, for purposes of identification, and to ensure that they reported to the proper work detail.

The inmates inside the cellhouse likewise were subjected to an additional count, and once it was complete, Captain Miller signaled Officer John Barker, who was posted on the recreation yard perimeter catwalk (considered the least favored assignment by the correctional staff). He then lowered the key to Officer Al Shield, who would open the yard door leading to the Industries. When the signal was given, the inmates would march line-by-line down the narrow steep stairwell and pass through the "*snitch box*," a name affectionately given to the metal detector by the inmates. When each inmate had arrived at his assignment, before they were all allowed to start work, the officers performed a final count. Once this process was complete, the numbers were called in to the Armory, where Cliff Fish tallied the latest figures. Then the yard was again secured, and the key was passed back up to Barker on the catwalk.

After the inmates assigned to the Industries were situated and the recreation door was secured, those who were assigned to "*inside details*" were released from their cells. Then when all of the count data had been submitted to Fish in the Armory, Ernest Lageson started assembling and issuing equipment to the twelve men assigned as cellhouse orderlies. He also assisted Bernie Coy, who was assigned to the library detail, and briefly supervised the orderlies' activities as they began reviewing the request and distribution lists. Cretzer was forced to remain in his cell, since he still had not been assigned to a work detail, while the other inside-detail inmates lined up, waiting to start work.

The breakfast detail was supervised by Chief Steward Bob Bristow and Steward Charles Scanland, assisted by Officer Larry O'Brien. There were twenty-three inmates assigned to the Culinary Department, and their work schedules were among the most demanding in the prison, though these assignments were also the most highly coveted by the inmates. The culinary workers often labored seven days a week, and their cells were located close together at the west end of the cellhouse. They generally worked long hours, starting their day around 5:45 A.M., and ending sometime after 6:00 P.M. The culinary employees were not paid, unlike those working in the industries. However, there were many benefits that made this assignment worthwhile. The workers could sample fresh foods, and could even make special dishes, provided they managed to squelch the suspicions of the correctional officers. It was also said that many of the culinary inmates were able to concoct their own "*special brews*." For convicts serving long sentences and life terms, there was little use for the money that they could earn in the industries. Additionally, all of the inmates assigned to the "*inside work details*" were often allotted special daily recreation yard privileges, away from the normal inmate population. If their work in the cellhouse was completed satisfactorily, they were allowed a short respite in the yard every afternoon.

By 11:10 A.M. most of the inside detail activities were complete, and the inmates would then returned to their cells for a count and to prepare for lunch. On this particular day, Henry Langston was the only inmate assigned to the yard for clean up and maintenance duty. Convicts assigned to this detail were nicknamed "*yard birds.*" Langston too was eventually called into the cellhouse, since inmates would soon be lining up in the yard in preparation to return to the Mess Hall. At 11:30 A.M. the powerhouse steam whistle blew, signaling the inmates to com-

Officer Al Shield

Chief Steward Bob Bristow

plete their tasks and prepare for the march back up into the main block. If the winds were blowing to the east, the industries whistle could often be heard at Fisherman's Wharf in San Francisco. As an inmate recalled in an interview years later, several of the prisoners referred to their walk down the steep narrow path from the Recreation Yard as the "*The Lonely Walk Down*." It was the only time when the inmates could see the city of San Francisco with minimal obstruction from fences and barbwire.

When Captain Weinhold gave the okay, the inmates began their controlled march through the metal detector, up the steep and narrow stairwell and into the yard for another count. All the while, they were watched intensely by the watchtower guards, who were ready to aim and fire their rifles should this become necessary. As the inmates lined up in their rows, Officer Shield completed his counts. Once the counts from all of the industry assignments were tallied and verified, the inmates were quietly marched back through the second metal detector and in to their cells. Once again as they carried out their tasks according to the strict protocol, Officer Miller hooked Key #107 to the lanyard clip, and Burch hoisted the key back up into the Gun Gallery. The inmates then took the time to rest and have a cigarette before the lunch whistle sounded.

At 11:55 A.M. the sound of a whistle resonated throughout the cellhouse, signaling for the inmates to line up outside their cells, and then at Captain Weinhold's direction, they filed into the dining hall as usual. It has been suggested that this meal period was the meeting hub where the final signals were given that the prison break was on. The lunch period progressed according to its usual strict customs, and at 12:20 P.M., when all of the inmates had finished their meals and the eating utensil counts were completed, the inmates were marched out of the Mess Hall and back to their cells for another count. After this process had been completed, all those assigned to the industries would line up for their march into the recreation yard, and return to their specific work assignment. There was also a second sick-call for inmates wishing to be examined by the island's physician. The inmates would notify their correctional officer, who in turn would provide them an approval slip to leave their assignment and fall into the designated line. Miran Thompson would be one of the first inmates to line up for sick call, while several others would form special lines for interviews with the Associate Warden, and the most favored would cue for visits that had been pre-approved by the Warden.

The cellhouse activities then started to shift focus to D Block, where the inmates were to be fed, and those with limited privileges were to be prepared for a brief excursion to the recreation yard. Marvin Orr, one of the officers assigned to the kitchen detail, helped wheel the food carts over to D Block, then started serving lunch to the inmates inside their cells, assisted by Correctional Officer Cecil Corwin. Officer Bill Miller had just returned from lunch, and he initiated the 1:00 P.M. inmate count. At that time, Bernie Coy gathered his broom and electric floor polisher and started preparing to clean the smooth-surfaced cement floors. With the majority of inmates back at work in the Industries, the cellhouse had grown fairly quiet, almost like a library.

By 1:30 P.M., the correctional staff was at its minimum level. Burch remained stationed in the West End Gun Gallery, where he usually spent his time after lunch on the D Block side, because the majority of the inmates would be found there during standard work hours. Of the prison's operational staff on duty at the time, Correctional Officer Ernest Lageson was leaving the main cellhouse to take a short lunch break; Corwin would be on duty solo on the D Block floor; Bill Miller would be alone in the main cellhouse overseeing routine maintenance and cleaning activities; and lastly Joseph Burdett, a correctional officer from Joplin, Missouri, would be supervising the clean-up in the kitchen and dining areas.

Before Lageson departed, he met with Bernie Coy to give final instructions about the areas that would likely require the most attention. Feeling confident that Coy understood his work directive, Lageson made one last round to ensure that the workers had started in on their assigned tasks, and then made his way to the main entrance of the cellhouse, where he would leave the building for lunch. Lageson's exit would mark the onset of an event that would forever be ingrained into the history of The Rock. As Coy pushed his broom, sweeping the aisle down "Broadway" toward "Times Square," he carefully made his way to the edge of the cellblock, watching Lageson gesture to gate Officer Al Phillips at the main entrance to let him through. In D Block, the period following lunch was usually very quiet, since most of the inmates would take naps around this time. Coy hurriedly made his way to the library, and then made a tapping sound on the access door to D Block, to signal that the escape was commencing.

The sound of the taps would be the signal for Sam Shockley, who had been confined to D Block for his role in the bold May 1941 escape attempt with Joe Cretzer. He was residing in cell #D-5. Sam's role was to start a disturbance in D Block, in order to shift attention away from the main cellblock. As Shockley screamed and shouted violent threats, Officer Corwin called for assistance to help calm the inmate, who was nicknamed "Crazy Sam" by inmates and guards alike. Officer Burch made his way to the D Block end of the Gallery, attempting to size up the situation before calling down to Miller.

Meanwhile, Bernie Coy was making his way toward the kitchen to signal Marvin Hubbard. Marv was stalling as he completed his clean-up tasks, pacing himself so he could stop work as soon as he received the signal from Coy. Hubbard had made careful efforts to ensure that everything was in perfect order, so that Officer Burdett would not become suspicious. In accordance with their meticulous plan, Hubbard made a final stop at the wooden knife rack, and carefully slipped a large butcher knife into the underside of his shirtsleeve with the handle resting in his palm. Hubbard then approached Burdette, stating that he had finished his work and was ready to get some fresh air out in the yard. Not suspecting anything unusual, Burdette granted Hubbard permission to leave. Hubbard then went to the dining room entrance and waited for Officer

Cells #404 and #403, located at the end of C Block, were used by the escapees to lock up their hostages. This would also be the site of a vicious murder.

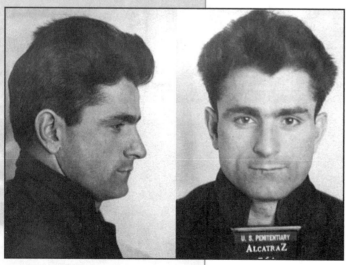

Joseph Moyle

Miller to open the gate and let him pass. Miller, who was unaware of the recent problems in D Block, opened the gate and let Hubbard pass through. As procedure dictated, Marv then stood at the base of the West End Gun Gallery waiting for Miller to search him. Miller locked the gate after Hubbard and approached the inmate. Meanwhile Coy, who was closely watching the two while walking toward them from C Block, carefully started pushing his broom closer and closer, trying not to spark suspicion.

Hubbard stood at attention, slightly lifting his arms so that Miller could start his head-to-toe search. Suddenly Coy grabbed Miller from behind with the quiet skill of a silent assassin, pinning his arms around his back. Hubbard started delivering violent blows to Miller's head using his clenched fists, and Miller slumped over into unconsciousness. The East Gallery had been left unmanned as a result of budgetary cuts from the previous year, and no one was at this post to monitor activity at the east end of the cellhouse. Bert Burch had rushed into the D Block side of the Gallery to assess the disturbance that Shockley was causing. Officer Miller was thus left helpless, with no other prison guard aware of his plight. Hubbard and Coy each grabbed an arm, and starting dragging him around to cell #404 at the end of "*Seedy Street*," which was used by guard staff and cellhouse workers as a common bathroom. Coy pulled the large key ring from Miller's belt clip, and opened the control box that housed the cell access levers. Having carefully watched the correctional staff open and close the various inmate cells, Coy was able to rack open #404 without a hitch. The inmates pulled Miller into the cell and Hubbard removed his pants and jacket. Miller was then gagged and tied to the cell bunk.

Joseph Moyle, an inmate who had just happened to pass through the main gate less than a minute before, was shocked to witness Coy and Hubbard pulling Miller into cell #404. Joseph Moyle and Bill Montgomery were both assigned as Warden Johnston's "*passmen*." This was the most coveted work assignment on Alcatraz, as these men were allotted the most freedom of all the inmates, in order to serve as the Warden's personal stewards. The passmen worked directly in the Warden's house, and often spent several hours each day outside of the normal confines of the prison. The inmates who worked as the Warden's stewards were hand picked and were generally nearing their release date. Though it may seem hard to believe, the passmen did most of the Warden's cooking and cleaning, and some reported that the Warden's wife would put on the radio (allowing them to listen to baseball games), leave out newspapers (which were prohibited inside the prison), and give them special treats like homemade cookies. Though the assignment came with many great perks, these men were generally not trusted by the general inmate population, as they spent so much time with "Old Saltwater" himself. Therefore as Moyle approached the escape accomplices, Hubbard motioned him to enter the cell with Miller to ensure that he didn't "*rat them out*" to an unsuspecting guard.

Bill Montgomery

At about the same time two other inmates who were assigned to painting details, Earl Egan and George Pichette, were walking up "Park Avenue" when they witnessed the activities that were transpiring just ahead. As Coy motioned them forward, Egan apparently indicated that he didn't want any part of the escape. But the men weren't taking any chances, and Egan was also directed into the cell. Pichette had turned at the end of the cellblock and disappeared. The door of cell #404 was quickly racked closed, and Coy started running to the block control boxes and opening the cells of his other accomplices. Thompson, Cretzer, and younger inmate named Clarence Carnes all emerged from their cells in a state of near disbelief that Coy's plan had actually succeeded, even to this point. Carnes seemed an unlikely type to participate in the escape, as he was the youngest inmate ever to be sentenced to The Rock, at only eighteen years of age.

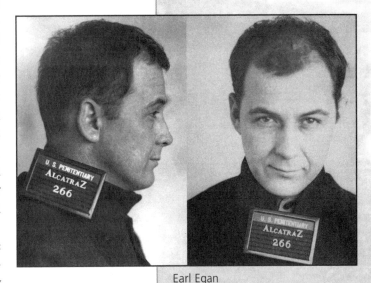

Earl Egan

When Coy had released his accomplices, he made a swift dash down the C Block utility corridor to where his toolset was hidden. Coy emerged from the passageway with a cotton pouch of the type that inmates generally used to carry their dominos into the recreation yard. While the other inmates stood watch for Burch in the West Gallery, and for any other correctional officers who might enter the cellhouse, Coy quickly stripped down to his underwear and with Cretzer's help, smeared axle grease over his chest, head, and extremities. He then briefly inventoried the tools in his sack and started climbing up the West End Gun Gallery from the juncture at Times Square and Michigan Avenue. Hand over hand, he scaled the barred cage until he reached the top.

Clenched in Coy's teeth was the small bag containing his crudely fashioned bar-spreader device, which had been made from toilet fixtures in one of the prison workshops. He set the tool firmly between the two bars (which were approximately five inches apart), and using pliers, he was able to exert enough force to create an opening nearly ten inches wide. With Cretzer eagerly watching his progress from below, Coy painfully squeezed his body through the opening and slipped into the West Gun Gallery.

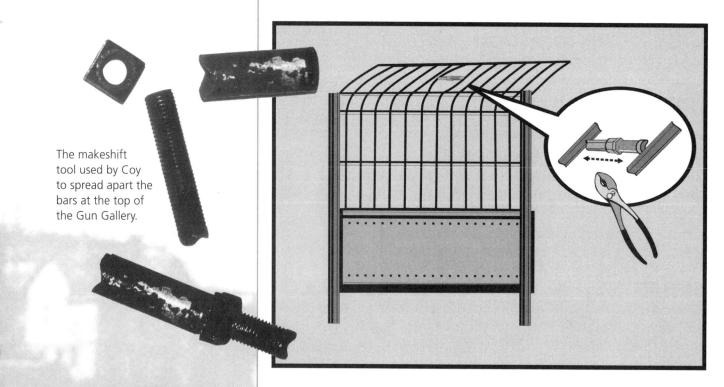

The makeshift tool used by Coy to spread apart the bars at the top of the Gun Gallery.

An officer looks up toward the area where Bernard Coy scaled the Gun Gallery. Using plumbing fixtures that had been fashioned into a makeshift bar spreader, Coy quietly entered the Gallery and secured weapons.

Without delay, Coy secured a riot club and positioned himself in a low crouch so that Officer Burch couldn't see him when looking through the window in the door. On Coy's signal, Cretzer sharply tapped the recreation yard access door with Miller's key ring, a standard indication to the Gallery officer that the cellhouse guard needed a key for access. Burch was unknowingly being lured straight into an ambush. By now, Shockley had ceased his staged screaming fit, and Corwin was sitting at his desk talking casually with D Block orderly Louis Fleish, the famed onetime leader of Detroit's "Purple Gang" of the early 1930's.

When Burch passed through the doorway, Coy forcefully hurled the heavily framed door forward, throwing the unsuspecting guard off balance. With brutal force, Coy clubbed the officer and forced him to the floor, then strangled him till he lost consciousness. Inmate Jim Quillen later recalled that all of the residents of D Block could hear the struggle in the Gallery, and the first rumor to travel down the row of cells was that the "hacks" were fighting among themselves. But the prisoners quickly realized that an inmate had amazingly managed to infiltrate the Gun Gallery.

Coy quickly lowered a Colt .45 pistol with twenty-one rounds of ammunition and several riot clubs to Cretzer, who was standing on the officers' work desk. Coy then pitched down a large key ring that he was confident would hold the yard door access key, #107. After dropping these items down to Cretzer, and now armed with a Springfield rifle and fifty rounds of ammunition, Coy entered the D Block Gallery, taking aim at the unarmed Officer Corwin. Coy directed Corwin to follow his orders carefully, and to stay away from the phone. He instructed him to walk slowly over and open the steel door that divided the segregation unit from the main prison. As soon as Corwin had rotated the key and the door swung open, he was met by Cretzer, who aimed the .45 directly at his forehead. As the barrel of the .45 was pressed against Corwin's forehead, the cold metal felt as though it was biting into his flesh. Louis Fleish had opted not to get involved, but he encouraged Corwin to follow Cretzer's demands so that he wouldn't get hurt.

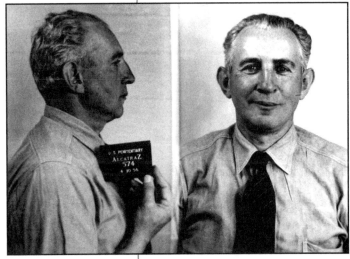

D-Block Orderly Louis Fleish

Coy headed back to Officer Burch and stripped him of all his clothing, then tied him to electrical piping that ran near the floor. After ensuring that Burch would be unable to trip an alarm if he regained consciousness, Coy retraced his steps to the top of the Gallery, carefully squeezed through the bars, and climbed back down to the cellhouse floor. Meanwhile Cretzer demanded that Corwin rack open #D-14, the cell of Rufus "Whitey" Franklin, an inmate who was notorious as a guard killer and a master escape artist. Franklin was serving time in isolation for the vicious murder of Alcatraz Officer Royal C. Cline in 1938. Corwin pleaded that he couldn't open the cell because the locking mechanism for all of the isolation cells was controlled from the Gallery. Since Coy had already made his way back down, and would thus be able to open the cell doors himself, Corwin was stripped of his jacket, hat, and keys, and placed into cell #404 along with Captain Bill Miller, who was still unconscious. Coy then racked open the cells in the top two tiers of D Block, and Shockley and the other inmates started to emerge, attempting to size up the situation.

Though Franklin was left behind because they had been unable to access the lock mechanism to release him from his cell, Cretzer ordered an inmate to open the outer steel doors to all of the isolation cells on the bottom row. It is suspected that Floyd Hamilton, former outlaw and driver for Bonnie & Clyde, had also been in on the plot, though he did not take part in the attempt. In Hamilton's inmate file there is a notation that reads:

> Although Hamilton received but one misconduct report, the testimony of Mr. E. Lageson, cellhouse officer, who was one of the hostages in the prison escape plot of May 2nd to 4th, 1946, was to the effect that Coy, #415-AZ, ringleader to the rioters, was trying to get Hamilton unlocked from his cell so that he could join in the plot. This, with the fact that Hamilton had secured a lay-in for that day indicates he knew something about the plot and may have been involved to a certain extent.

The desperate inmates searched feverishly for key #107, but a brave correctional officer had concealed the key inside the hostage cell.

As Cretzer passed through the steel D Block access door, he observed Burch straining against his restraints, and looking over the steel shield of the Gun Gallery. Cretzer yelled to Burch in the Gallery while pointing the .45: *"I'll kill you if you try to reach that phone!"* Coy and Cretzer then started shuffling through the keys on the Gallery ring, trying to find Key #107, which would grant them access to the recreation yard. After several minutes of fruitless attempts, both became frustrated and tried to force the lock with any key that would fit, as their plan was starting to fall behind schedule. They had hoped to get into the recreation yard, snipe off the tower guards, and then escape through the yard access door. They planned to get down to the dock area by using hostages, so the next item on the agenda was to secure captives, probably family members of the correctional staff. They would then hijack the prison launch to take them over to the mainland, where they would make their final escape. Everything had run smoothly, up until now…

Standing at the recreation yard door, Coy and Cretzer methodically debated where the right key could be found. Cretzer seemed certain that it had to be one of the keys in their possession. Carnes called over to Cretzer and Coy from his lookout post, warning them that he had heard a gate inside the sallyport open and then close. About a minute later the main cell door swung open and Chief Steward Bristow emerged, walking briskly down Broadway towards the Dining Hall. Bristow was in charge of the prison's culinary division, and he was completely unaware that armed convicts were roaming the cellhouse. He approached the Dining Hall door realizing that something was amiss, as the gate was not secure and Bill Miller wasn't anywhere to be seen. Attempting not to make any suspicious gestures, he turned quickly as if he had forgotten something, and headed back to the main gate, hoping Officer Phillips would be there to greet him. Carnes positioned himself in the cutoff corridor after quietly running up from Park Avenue, and he watched Bristow to see if he would enter the kitchen. Carnes was now armed with what an officer would later describe as a pair of sharp *"artist's dividers,"* and he intercepted Bristow at the cutoff and led him to Cell #404 without any struggle.

Coy and Cretzer were now becoming very frustrated, as they had not anticipated being unable to locate the yard key. The two inmates walked up to cell #404 where Bill Miller was now fully conscious, and sternly demanded to know where key #107 was hidden. Miller denied having any knowledge of the key's location, since it was strict protocol to return it to the Gun Gallery officer after using it. He insisted that the key must be in the Gallery, adding that the inmates had witnessed the procedure numerous times themselves, and therefore must know that this regulation was stringently followed by all correctional officers. Coy and Cretzer walked a short distance to the officer's desk in D Block, and laid out all of the keys, searching for #107. What they didn't know was that Miller had failed to follow protocol, and for convenience's sake, had slipped key #107 into his shirt pocket. It was a stroke of luck, but Miller's act of mild nonconformity was in fact upsetting the entire escape effort.

Suddenly, one of the inmates signaled that someone was coming through the main gate. At about 1:45 P.M., the gate opened and an unsuspecting Ernie Lageson strolled into the main cellhouse. While making his way down Broadway, he quickly noticed that something was wrong. Turning to look back, he recognized Bernie Coy wearing a pair of officer's pants and no shirt. But before he could act, Coy aimed a rifle at him, leaving him no chance of escape. Coy forced Lageson to walk through the cutoff and onto Seedy Street, where he was searched and stripped of his keys and other valuables. With few words exchanged, he was shoved into the now crowded cell #404.

Sam Shockley then turned up at the cell front, yelling that Lageson had assaulted him previously when shoving him into the strip cell. Shockley insisted that his comrades let him at the officer, but Hubbard and Cretzer only pointed their weapons, discouraging this foolish behavior. Still Sam was fixated on injuring Lageson, and he stood at the cell front making threatening slurs. Finally Cretzer aimed the pistol at Shockley's head, warning him to back off and calm himself.

As Lageson entered and moved to the middle of the crowded cell, Corwin quickly briefed him as to what had happened. It baffled them as to how Coy had managed to penetrate the Gun Gallery and access the weapons. Their initial assumption was that Coy had perched himself on something, then grabbed Burch by his clothing from outside, repeatedly smashing him against the tool-proof steel bars. Another hypothesis was that a guard had been held hostage until Burch surrendered the weapons. The Gun Gallery had once been thought to be one of the most secure positions in the prison, and it was hard to imagine how its security had been breached.

Officer Joseph Burdette had been busy tending to his duties down in the kitchen basement, and had finally come up to inspect the dining area. Like Officer Bristow, Burdette was puzzled to find the Dining Hall gate open, with no sign of any floor officers in the vicinity. As he carefully looked around the area he noticed Coy walking by, and thinking that the prisoner was about to get into a fight with another inmate, Burdette made the ill-fated decision to venture out into the cellhouse and investigate. In a matter of only seconds, Burdette was captured, escorted through the cutoff, and thoroughly searched before being placed in #404 with the five other occupants.

By this point, Coy was in a frenzy to locate key #107. He probably realized that his time was running out, and that someone would soon notice that the guards were missing from their post assignments. Once the island's siren was activated, it would be all over. The prison would go into lock-down mode, and every guard, including all of the reserves, would be issued firearms and stationed at all points on the island. Coy started to verbally trace the chain of custody of Key #107. The guards being held captive could hear Coy's desperation as he struggled to locate the key. Then Lageson and Bristow asked Cretzer if they could untie Miller, who was still bound to the bunk, and surprisingly, Cretzer agreed. While Lageson and Bristow were untying him, Miller covertly passed the key to Burdette, who stealthily slid to the back of the cell. As the other guards stood at the front of the cell, blocking the view and distracting everyone's attention by asking questions, it is alleged by some historians that Burdette quietly dropped the key into the toilet bowl, and then submerging his hand, pushed it back until it was out of view (*It should be noted that in at least one of the official FBI statements, it was indicated that the key was simply hid behind the toilet and not submerged. The above is simply the most common written theory, and it is likely inaccurate*).

A few minutes later Coy returned to the cell front, and demanded that Miller tell him where he had put the key. Quite heroically, Miller maintained that the key must still be in the Gallery, since he remembered passing it to Burch. But Bernie Coy was furious, and opened the cell demanding that Miller's person and every inch of the cell be thoroughly searched. Miller was forcefully removed from the cell, and was searched in an aggressive manner by Cretzer while standing in the aisle of "Seedy Street." Still in acute pain from the attack, Miller held his ground, telling Coy that he would have to go back into the Gun Gallery if he wanted to find the key. Coy was incensed.

The conspirators then transferred the officers from cell #404 into cell #403. The two inmate hostages, Egan and Moyle, begged Cretzer to let them go, pleading that they didn't deserve to be locked up with the guards. In what may have been his only act of kindness, Cretzer nodded and told them to go back to their cells. Both scurried out, looking for any open cell in which to take cover. Hubbard and Cretzer thoroughly searched the other officers, sometimes jabbing them with the barrel of the pistol. Thompson and Coy took a box of keys from the cellhouse officer's desk, and tried every key in hope of finding a duplicate disguised with a dummy number. Both inmates went key by key, forcefully inserting them into the yard door lock tumbler, hoping to find a match.

Correctional Officers Ed Stucker and Emil Rychner.

Officer Ed Stucker was assigned to the cellhouse basement, to supervise inmate barbers Joe Fisher and William Bartlett, as well as the activities in the clothing room and the shower area. Stucker carried the reputation of a by-the-book guard who generally engaged in very little small talk with the inmates. There were eighteen other inmates under his supervision, and some of them were getting haircuts, while others were on work detail sorting clothing. Two inmates asked if they could be released back to the main floor after getting their haircuts, as they had been promised some time in the recreation yard if they finished early. Stucker agreed, and the two ascended the stairs that led up to the base of the West End Gun Gallery, at the juncture of Times

Square and Michigan Avenue. When the inmates reached the top of the stairs, they looked around through the large-link steel caging that enclosed the stairwell, but couldn't locate Miller or any other officer. After calling out and brashly tapping the steel mesh access door, the two inmates descended and asked Stucker if he could get someone to come and let them out, as no one had responded to their calls.

Stucker was puzzled that the inmates couldn't get the attention of any officer. If Miller was busy, then Burch would usually hear the tapping from the Gallery and summon an officer. Stucker instructed the inmates to remain in the basement, and went up to see if he could catch Miller's attention. Once he reached the top, he looked through the steel grating and was shocked to see a few inmates standing around unsupervised. Stucker swiftly secured the padlock, which was generally used as an added security measure, and headed back downstairs. At the bottom of the stairwell he pulled the receiver from the only phone that he could access in the basement, and dialed the Armory (*Note: Stucker in an FBI interview, indicated that he had seen Cretzer with a pistol and reported this information to the Armory. Although not verifiable, for the sake of accuracy, his testimony should be considered as an equal account*). As soon as Fish picked up, Stucker explained that he thought there was something seriously wrong in the cellhouse. Fish immediately hung up and started ringing the West Gallery and dining area. After dialing several phones in the west cellhouse with no response, Fish immediately contacted Lieutenant of the Watch Joseph Simpson, who was in the Administration Office doing paperwork. Fish explained that there seemed to be a problem in the cellhouse, and that he could not reach any of the officers at their posts.

Simpson quickly summoned Records Officer Carl W. Sundstrom and Bob Baker, the mail officer who spent most of his time reading and censoring inmate mail. The three men quickly entered the Armory and inquired whether Fish had received any updates from the floor or Gallery officers, but still no one had picked up the cellhouse phones. Fish now suspected the worst, and started communicating to the others that he felt it was not safe to enter the cellhouse. All three officers ignored his advice, and prepared to make entry. Simpson and the three others navigated their way through the sallyport gates, and carrying only wooden billy clubs, they entered the cellhouse heading straight down Broadway toward the Dining Hall.

Unfortunately, they would meet the same fate as the other officers. The armed inmates all stood waiting at the west end of the cellblock, and they ambushed the three officers. The captive guards had been moved out of #404 and into #403 to allow for the cell search, and Bristow and Simpson were led to cell #402.

Back at the Armory, Officer Fish had finally been able to get through to the hospital, where the staff members on duty were going about their business, unaware of the events that were transpiring just downstairs. Fish instructed them to secure themselves, because something was happening on the cellhouse floor. Fish then called back to Stucker, explain-

Joe Fisher

Officer Bob Baker

ing that no one was answering the phones, not even Officer Burch. It was becoming evident that something serious was afoot. The two officials quickly got off the phone, and Stucker explained to the twenty inmates that there was a "*problem*" in the cellhouse. He said that they would need to remain in the basement for a little longer than usual today, since he didn't want any of them to get involved. He tried to downplay the prospect of any serious trouble, realizing that if the inmates caught on to what was happening in the cellhouse, his life could potentially be placed in jeopardy. Stucker quickly and calmly moved the inmates into the band practice area, explaining that they would be allowed to head back upstairs shortly. He walked to the base of the stairs, looked up, and noticed someone attempting to pry open the basement door. Not wanting to tip anyone off, he casually walked back into the band practice room and secured the door.

Meanwhile Coy went back into cell #404, and he and Cretzer started methodically going through the cell inch by inch in case the guards had been bold enough to try and hide the key there. Suddenly Coy had the idea that they might have attempted to flush the key. This seemed like a long shot, but there was a slim chance that it was lying hidden inside the toilet, just out of view. Coy took off the guard's coat, positioned himself on his hands and knees, and reached into the saltwater-filled

The heavy steel door leading to the recreation yard from the main cellhouse.

toilet bowl. As he groped along the bottom, he suddenly felt a piece of metal with the shape and texture of a brass key. He maneuvered the key out with his fingers, and strained to read the number. Sure enough, it was #107. Coy handed the key to Thompson, who carefully guided it into the slot, and attempted to turn the mechanism . . . But the key still would not work. The dead bolt had been specially designed to jam if it was sufficiently tampered with. The security design had worked, and despite the inmates' frenzied efforts, the key would not budge the heavy steel dead bolt.

By now Cliff Fish was incredibly nervous, and he rang all of the phones located at the main internal posts. The ringing phones could be heard throughout the cellhouse, and this seemed to contribute to the stress of the inmates involved in the plot. Still there was no answer, and at about 2:00 P.M. Officer Fish called the Warden at his residence. Mrs. Johnston answered the phone, and explained that the Warden was taking a nap and had asked not to be disturbed. Fish explained that there was a crisis in the cellhouse, and stressed that he needed to speak with the Warden urgently. Fish then briefed Johnston about the situation. Johnston instructed him to contact all of the tower posts, as well as the Associate Warden, and added that he would wash up and meet Fish in the Armory within a few minutes. Fish then found himself in a rare predicament—the Warden had left him to decide whether or not to sound the siren. At this point, he had been unable to confirm any serious problem. But once the siren was engaged, it would sound for three minutes with no way to deactivate it—and the siren's wail would signal to the world that there was a major situation at Alcatraz. At 2:07 P.M., Fish reached over and unlocked the siren cover and pressed the activation key.

When the siren began to sound, it could be heard across the Bay as far as the town of Marin. The conspirators were keen to the obvious. This was it—they now knew that the chances of escape were almost nonexistent. The island would soon be swarming with armed officers, and measures were probably already in place to prevent them from gaining access to the launch. Jim Quillen would recall in a later interview that he left D Block around this time and walked out onto Seedy Street, asking Cretzer if he and fellow inmate Jack Pepper could come along. Cretzer was apparently conscious that their chances of escape where dashed, and he shook hands with Quillen and told him to go back to his cell, because he didn't think that they were going to make it to the mainland. He asked Quillen to try to get Sam Shockley to return to his cell too, but Shockley motioned them to wait a minute, and then walked away. This was the last he would ever see of them.

Coy had entered the bakery carrying the Springfield rifle, and he lined up a shot to take out the Hill Tower guard, Elmus Besk. Upon hearing the siren, Besk walked out onto the catwalk to check for any unusual activity. Coy carefully punched out one of the windows and then opened fire. Elmus was struck in the legs, and dropped to the deck in severe pain from several fragments of a bullet that had struck the railing and broken apart. Fish would later recount that Besk crawled back into the tower and phoned him, reporting that he had been shot with what had seemed almost like a shotgun. Besk communicated that he would hold out until they could get him help, and dressed his own wounds using rags.

Coy then ran up into the kitchen and punched out a pane from another window, this time targeting the Road Tower guard, Irving Levinson. The first bullet ripped through the window, and Levinson quickly dropped to the floor for cover. He scanned the prison windows to see if he could make out where the shot had come from. He noticed the yard wall officer who was lying on the catwalk, looking over at him and motioning toward the kitchen. Levinson pulled his rifle over and remained ready to fire, while attempting to determine where the shot had come from. Coy then punched out another pane, this time taking aim at the Dock Tower guard, Jim Comerford. Coy squeezed off another round, and the bullet sliced through the Dock Tower window. Comerford dropped onto the narrow perimeter catwalk, taking aim at the cellhouse with his rifle as he heard the bullet whiz past his shoulder. Comerford's wife heard the shot and ran toward the tower, attempting to see if her husband was injured. Comerford waved that he was not hurt, and directed her to go back home and take cover. The powerful rifle shots reverberated all over the island, and it was later reported that they had been heard as far away as the shores of Marin and San Francisco.

One interesting detail is that the Armory Officer was usually responsible for calibrating and adjusting the target sights on every Springfield that was returned, on a routine schedule. Fish would later note that his

Dock Tower Guard Jim Comerford.

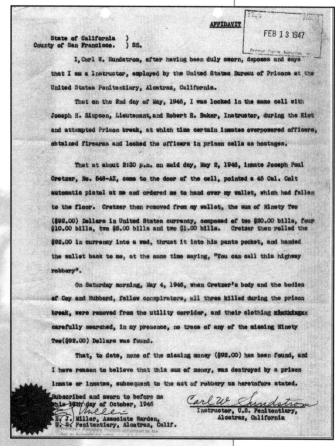

An official affidavit written by Officer Carl Sundstrom, describing the theft of his wallet by Joe Cretzer.

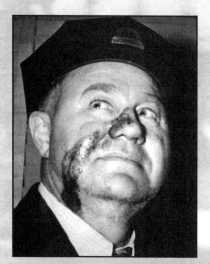

Associate Warden E.J. Miller suffered moderate burns to his face after his gas billy exploded during an altercation with one of the conspirators.

adjustments had been off by nearly six inches, and this probably had affected Coy's aim, thus saving the lives of a few officers. Several of the island's residents heard the rifle fire and retreated into their homes. They knew that the chance of an inmate acquiring weapons was remote, but that nothing was impossible.

Captain of the Guards Henry Weinhold was an ex-marine, and he had the reputation among his peers as very capable but rigid officer. After talking with Fish, Weinhold took a gas billy and demanded that he be admitted to the cellhouse. Fish had been vehemently protesting against anyone entering the embattled building, but his pleas fell upon deaf ears. Weinhold went into the cellhouse by himself. He too was quickly captured by the armed convicts, and was led off to join the other hostages. But before Weinhold could be put into the cell, Shockley viciously attacked him. Jim Quillen later stated that he saw Shockley throw a punch at Weinhold, who was able to duck and avoid the blow. Shockley apparently fell into a deep rage, charging Weinhold and attempting to kick him in the groin. Weinhold blocked the force of the kick by lifting his leg, then clenched his fist and struck Shockley straight in the mouth. Shockley then went crazy, just as Carnes appeared with Officer Sundstrom, jamming the billy club sharply into his back and pushing him forward into the cell. Sam struck Sundstrom in the head, knocking him off balance. The other inmates then calmed Sam down, while Cretzer made Sundstrom strip, and confiscated his pants and wallet.

Associate Warden Edward J. Miller, known to his peers as "Ed" but nicknamed "Meathead" by the inmates, was at home when he received the call from Fish. Without wasting any time, Miller hiked up the steep path to the main building, and hurriedly reported to the Armory. After receiving a full briefing from Fish he decided to enter the cellhouse on his own, to help ensure the safety of his fellow officers, and to straighten out what he believed was a simple cellhouse fight. Once again Fish protested, knowing that something had gone seriously awry. But without further consideration, Miller grabbed a gas billy and entered the east end of the cellhouse. As he cautiously starting walking up Broadway, he observed someone who he thought to be an officer walking towards him. But within seconds he had caught a closer glimpse, and he recognized that it was actually Bernie Coy, carrying a rifle. Miller quickly attempted to retreat, and armed the gas billy. Coy started to run at Miller, and managed to fire off two rounds. One of them struck the gas billy, causing it to explode in Miller's face, and Miller withdrew into the sallyport, half-blinded and with moderate burns. Gate Officer Al Phillips quickly secured the main door while Miller walked back toward the administrative offices, where the Warden had just arrived.

By now, word was coming in that a sniper taking aim from the cellhouse kitchen might have injured a couple of the tower guards. Ed Miller, still in pain from his facial injuries, started to brief Johnston on what had taken place. Then as the sirens wailed, resonating off nearly every structure of the island, Johnston gave the directive to assemble all of the off-duty officers immediately, as it was now obvious that the inmates intended to blast out of the prison. Johnston and Miller started to plan their strategy, and using a procedural matrix, they initiated calls to the neighboring police departments in San Francisco, Marin, and Oakland, as well as to the FBI, the Coast Guard, the U.S. Marshal, the Justice Department, and the Bureau of Prisons.

(Above and below) Reinforcements were brought in from a variety of agencies and organizations. They included personnel from the Bureau of Prisons, law enforcement agencies, and the US Military.

Johnston pulled out the cellblock diagrams, and charted the areas that appeared to be secure and those that were now controlled by the inmates. Then he and Miller began to post officers at critical observation points, and to follow the prescribed protocol for securing the island. All of the resident off-duty officers were speedily armed and assigned to established posts on an anti-escape perimeter around the prison building. The prison launch was searched and then sent out to patrol on a 200-yard-wide security area around the island, with an armed officer onboard. The Control Room officer had been instructed to try to contact all of the off-duty guards who resided on the mainland. The inmates who were working at the dock and outside the normal security area were quickly marched to the prison industries work area at the northwest end of the island, under armed supervision. Specific measures had been taken to secure the inmates at work in the industries within their respective buildings, until more officers were available to facilitate their safe transfer to the recreation yard.

Meanwhile inmates Coy, Hubbard, Cretzer, Thompson, Shockley and Carnes, desperate and without any alternative plans, found themselves in a stalemate. None of them knew exactly what their next step should be, but Coy, Cretzer, and Hubbard made it clear that they didn't intend to be taken alive. Carnes would later comment that he was surprised at how casually they had talked about

A correctional officer firmly warns an approaching vessel to maintain its distance.

the possibility of dying. The trio made a pact that they would not surrender, and would try to stay alive for as long as possible, hoping to the end that some opportunity would arise for them to complete their escape. Coy headed off to cover the main entrance, as he knew that Miller would return with reinforcements to try to infiltrate the cellhouse.

Hubbard remained at the entrance of D Block, talking with some of the inmates who were still wandering around. It was becoming more evident that the prison escapees would most likely be attacked with heavy gunfire, and so he started instructing the other inmates to return to their cells and take cover. With the sirens blaring and the distantly ringing phones echoing from various points in the cellhouse, Cretzer was starting to get panicky. He conveyed to the others that all of them would get "*the chair*" if Coy had killed any of the tower guards. He explained that if the guard staff was able to regain control, which would most likely be achieved by sheer brutal force, the hostages would certainly testify against them. Cretzer started pacing indecisively in front of the cells, and Shockley stood loyally by, awaiting Cretzer's next directive. It was now becoming painfully clear that their escape had failed, and that the full wrath of the prison administration would soon fall upon them.

It was later reported that Captain Weinhold tried to reason with Cretzer at this point, but this only seemed to agitate him even more. Weinhold tried to explain to Cretzer that every point of the island would soon be swarming with armed guards, and that the conspirators didn't stand even a remote chance of escaping. There was also a well-known rule that the Prison Bureau would not trade the life of a hostage for the freedom of an inmate. This was a hard and fast policy in the prison system, which still exists today. Thompson had completely given up on opening the yard door, and Cretzer hesitantly floated the idea that they should rid themselves of their hostages. If they killed the captives, then no one could ever identify the ringleaders. Thompson stood in agreement— they simply could not afford to leave any witnesses. At this point Shockley became manic, and started yelling in front of the cells, "*shoot'em all dead, go ahead and kill'em!*" Shockley couldn't control his rage, and he repeatedly urged Cretzer to pull the trigger. Weinhold calmly appealed to Cretzer to be sensible, and to stop before anyone was hurt. But Cretzer, with little sign of emotion, walked to the front of cell #404, cocked the hammer on the .45, and pulled the trigger, shooting Captain Weinhold in the chest. Shockley's cheers resonated throughout the cellhouse, as he wildly screamed: "*shoot the fuckers dead.*"

Weinhold fell to the floor of the crowded cell as Cretzer, in a manic rage, again took aim and opened fire. A bullet struck Miller, ripping through his chest and exiting through his arm. Corwin was hit in the face and crumpled to the ground, bleeding profusely. As Cretzer coldly aimed and pulled the trigger in a series of staccato shots, the other officers fell to the floor in a mass of human carnage. Cretzer then pulled out the ammunition clip and slowly assessed the fallen officers. The captives in the next cell listened in horror as he methodically loaded bullets into the clip and then snapped it back into place. He walked to cell #403 and calmly raised the pistol between the bars, taking aim at the terrified officers and firing off several more rounds. The piercing sounds of gunfire rang through the cellhouse as Simpson took a bullet in the abdomen, and Baker fell to the floor as another shot hit his left leg, shattering his femur. Sundstrom lay cringing on the floor, expecting pain to riddle his body, but surprisingly the bullets had missed him. The officers lay on the floor of the cramped cells, waiting helplessly for the next flurry of bullets.

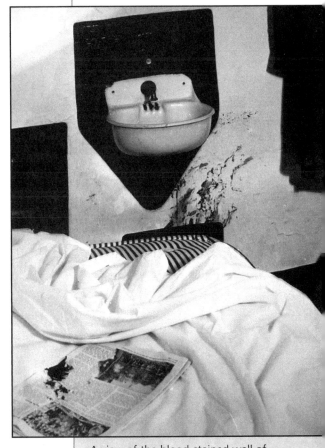

A view of the blood-stained wall of cell #403, where four officers were shot in cold blood by Joseph Cretzer.

Thompson and Shockley paced in front of the cells, watching for any signs of movement within. Finally Shockley yelled that he saw a "*screw*" moving, and begged Cretzer for the gun to finish him off. Cretzer walked to the front of cell #404 where Ernie Lageson bravely emerged from among the wounded officers, trying to calm the irrational inmates. Cretzer made some surprisingly positive comments to the others about how well he got along with Lageson, adding that perhaps he should be spared. But Shockley and Thompson demanded that no witnesses should remain. If Lageson survived, he would make sure that each one of them received the death penalty, so Lageson could not be spared. Cretzer raised the pistol to Lageson's head, stating simply, "*I'm really sorry, Mr. Lageson,*" as he firmly pulled the trigger. Stillness spread over the cells, and pools of blood started to saturate the cement floors.

As Cretzer peered into the cells he could still see some movement, and he heard a few muffled moans from what appeared to be Baker and Simpson, still alive and in terrible pain. Again he raised the pistol and clipped in a few more rounds, then fired. The cell was still once more, with patches of dense smoke slowly dissipating into a fogged haze. Coy had heard the barrage of gunfire, and he appeared at the front of the cells, observing the aftermath of Cretzer's mass execution. Weinhold was completely unconscious and unresponsive, due to a large bore bullet wound that had torn straight through his body and left him bleeding profusely on the cell floor. But Lageson had only been slightly grazed with a minor burn to his left ear, and he covertly lifted his head to assess his surroundings. Corwin's condition appeared critical; he had clearly been struck in the facial area, as his jaw was grimly deformed. Burdett and Bristow had both escaped injury. Miller was unconscious, and his condition was also extremely critical. He lay bleeding from a gaping wound, and his breathing was labored and shallow. In the other cell, Sundstrom was completely uninjured, and was attempting to lie as still as possible on the floor of the cell. Simpson and Baker had both been hit again during Cretzer's frightening attack. Simpson was unconscious and immobile, and Baker was lying immobile, praying that Cretzer would not fire again.

Carnes was now armed with the butcher knife that Hubbard had taken from the kitchen, and he was directed by Cretzer to stand watch at the cell fronts. Cretzer sharply ordered him to go in and *cut their throats* if he noticed any movement. Carnes peered into the cells, carefully watching over the officers, who were lying amid the murky pools of blood. As he looked intently at each officer, he soon noticed slight breathing movements. But when Coy and Cretzer returned and asked him if the captives were all dead, Carnes risked his safety by assuring his accomplices that Cretzer's bullets had killed them all. The inmates then walked off, discussing the strategy of their next move. Carnes and Thompson realized that their cause was hopeless, and jointly pleaded with the others that they didn't stand a chance without weapons, and that they wanted to return to their cells for shelter. Carnes and Thompson then wished the trio luck, and headed back to find open cells in which to take cover. They would both carefully attempt to wash the officers' blood from their clothes, hopeful that no one would identify them as having played a role in the escape attempt.

Back in the bloody cell, Ernie Lageson carefully looked up, and seeing that no one was watching over them, he slowly reached into his shirt pocket and pulled out a pencil. On the cell wall he inscribed the names of Cretzer, Coy, Carnes, Hubbard, Thompson and Shockley. He then circled the names of Cretzer, Coy, and Hubbard, and placed a check next to Cretzer's. The list was written indistinctly but legibly on the cell wall, and was clear enough to serve as evidence if the guards were all killed. The circled names indicated the ringleaders, and the check mark would leave no question as to who had committed the murders.

(Author's note: It has also been argued that it was Officer Carl Sundstrom who inscribed the names on the cell wall. Armory Officer Clifford Fish vehemently insisted that Sundstrom had told him immediately after being rescued from the cellhouse that he had performed this act. I have been unable to find any other references that provided proof of this argument, but Fish's account should also be considered, as he seemed adamant about this fact, and his recollections of events were usually exceptionally precise. For the sake of accuracy, it should also be noted that a feature article in the San Francisco Chronicle [May 5, 1946, p. 8] reported that Sundstrom had first made notations on a blank piece of white paper, and had then inscribed on the cell floor: "Cretzer killed or shot Joe Simpson in the stom-

Officer Lageson had the foresight to scrawl the names of the conspiring inmates on the cell wall, circling the names of the ringleaders. This would prove to be a key piece of evidence in the trial of the surviving inmates.

ach and chest twice and shot Baker also. He missed me so far." It is possible that these two details have been confused, and that Lageson was actually responsible for the wall inscription.)

Cretzer, Hubbard, and Coy then started toward C Block, entering the utility corridor and cautiously ascending the array of plumbing pipes and electrical conduits. After making the climb and reaching the top, each inmate carefully perched himself so as to have a clear view of the entryway, with the intention of eliminating as many officers as possible. The inmates probably considered this as the most strategic platform from which to monitor all the activities of the assault teams that were sure to come. The cellhouse had descended into an eerie quiet. The sirens had stopped wailing, and the ringing phones had finally gone still. Most of the inmates had returned to their cells, and the noise level had flattened into a dead silence, broken occasionally by the screech of a passing seagull.

It was approximately 2:45 P.M., and Lieutenant Phil Bergen was enjoying a quiet day off with his wife on the mainland, while his two daughters were still in school. By now, news of the Alcatraz "blast out" was spreading around San Francisco, with most of the facts terribly exaggerated by the newscasters. When Bergen heard the news, he immediately found a phone and contacted Cliff Fish in the Armory. Fish stated that there was little information that had been confirmed, but that they could identify one of the attempted escapees as Bernie Coy. They also knew that Bernie was armed with a .30-06 Springfield, which he had somehow managed to seize from Bert Burch in the Gun Gallery. Fish further explained that he and his colleagues had been unable to contact any of the officers within the cellhouse, with the exception of Stucker in the basement and the hospital officer, who hadn't been aware that there were problems downstairs. Bergen immediately reported to Pier #4 at Fort Mason, where Coast Guard cutters were standing by to carry off-duty officers who were reporting back to the island.

As the reserve officers reported for duty, they were immediately readied and posted at various points around the prison. Prior to Bergen's arrival, two officers had been sent to take up positions in the East Gun Gallery, and Officers Harold P. Stites and Joe Maxell had been posted to the west side. But as soon as the two officers attempted to enter the west end of the Gallery, they were immediately faced with a barrage of gunfire and were forced back out. They did however manage to fire off a few rounds, and to throw two teargas grenades through the Gallery bars and onto the cellhouse floor. It was evident that they would be unable to enter without sending in an assault team to do battle with the inmates, and to take the Gallery by force.

By the time the 3:45 P.M. launch arrived at the island, the boat had transported enough officers to begin the slow process of moving the inmates who were still secured in the Industries up to the recreation yard. Prison officers organized supply details that helped to bring up several bales of blankets from the prison laundry. The recreation yard was set up to give as much shelter to the inmates as was possible under

Correctional Officer Harold P. Stites

The American Red Cross was enlisted to assist the families as they were slowly evacuated from the island.

(left) Lieutenant Isaak Faulk; (right) Lieutenant George Boatman

Warden Johnston's Secretary, Walter Bertrand

the circumstances. The San Francisco Chapter of the Red Cross, headed by Robert S. Elliot, was contacted for support. They started to put together supplies of sandwiches, coffee, water and cigarettes to serve to the inmates and the riot support personnel alike, since it was unclear when the guards would be able to regain control of the cellhouse and restore order. There were even some delicacies provided to the inmates, such as potato chips and filtered cigarettes. Federal agents were now beginning to arrive, and several men were assigned to positions on the yard wall catwalk. They were instructed to keep a close eye on the recreation yard inmate population, and sharpshooters stood ready to suppress any gunfire that might originate from the kitchen areas.

Johnston quickly put together a planning conference with Associate Warden Miller and a few of the lieutenants. The group started a painstaking review of all the available officer counts, and all of the status updates from Officers Virgil Cochenour and John Mullen, who had been monitoring the activities in the cellhouse from their positions in the East End Gallery. Isaac Faulk, who was normally in charge of the tower officers, had set up headquarters with Officer Fish in the Armory. Lieutenant George Boatman offered his assistance in rescuing the captive officers, and started designating support assignments to those just arriving. Ike Faulk was already aware that at least one of his tower officers had been injured, and with Boatman's assistance, he devised a plan for the Federal agents to provide cover while the prison officers climbed the towers to rescue their comrades. Hill Tower Officer Besk was found lying on the floor, and was quickly given first aid, having lost a large amount of blood.

With several vessels from the Navy, the Coast Guard, and the San Francisco Police now patrolling the waters, word was spreading that something very bad was unfolding on Alcatraz, so Johnston broke the twelve-year silence and decided to make a formal public announcement about the current events. Johnston and his Secretary, Walter Bertrand, stood in the Armory and started delivering the solemn news to the world. The first Teletype messages were sent to B.O.P. Director James Bennett, the F.B.I., and finally to Western Union, which would communicate the grave news to all of the press associations in the following telegram:

Serious Trouble . . . Convict has machine gun in cellhouse . . . Have issued riot call . . . Placed armed guards at strategic locations . . . Many of our officers are imprisoned in the cellhouse . . . Cannot tell extent of injuries suffered by our officers or amount of damage done . . . Will give you more information later in the day when we can control . . . J.A. Johnston, Warden, Alcatraz.

Formal planning was then initiated to discuss the rescue of the captive officers. Warden Johnston assigned Lieutenants Phil Bergen and Frank Johnson to organize and lead the assault team. There were few updates coming from the officers now posted in the East Gallery, who reported only that there was virtually no activity on the cellhouse floor. The island's residents had started to take cover, and most had barricaded themselves inside their apartments. There were several others who secured themselves in the air-raid shelter, which had been established during World War II following the Japanese bombing raid on Pearl Harbor. Mutual aid plans had been initiated, and eleven correctional officers from McNeil and five from Leavenworth were boarding planes to San Francisco. Johnston had arranged to have them flown to Hamilton Field, and from there they were quickly driven to Sausalito and then transferred to Alcatraz by what the Warden termed as "*crash boats.*" Many of those who volunteered to come to San Francisco had worked on the island, and were familiar with the landscape and the posts.

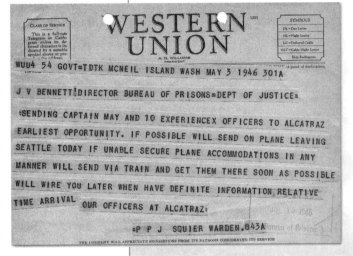

As the Warden and the other men carefully worked through the formal anti-escape procedure manual, Bergen and Johnson chose their men, and started plotting their entry into the West Gun Gallery. The situation quickly grew tense, as the East Gallery officers started firing shots at the silhouette of an inmate who was running across the floor with a rifle. As the sun started to set on the prison, Bergen and fellow officer Harry Cochrane met with Associate Warden Miller, pleading to be allowed to enter the cellhouse and begin the rescue of their fellow officers. Miller had been instructed by Johnston to refrain from entering the cellhouse until more reinforcements arrived. But Bergen was ready, and he firmly stated that if the hostages were still alive; they would be waiting for them to make a move. Bergen and Cochrane were assigned the dangerous task of securing a ladder to the side of the cellhouse, so that they could report on any activity that was not visible to the officers in the East End Gallery. As Bergen ascended the ladder he carefully peered into the building, but could see only a dense haze of teargas. No inmates were visible, and the cellhouse seemed abandoned. Bergen and Cochrane reported to Associate Warden Miller with this update.

At approximately 3:30 P.M. the first detachment of marines arrived from Treasure

Officers are seen here peering through the main cellblock portholes, attempting to observe the activities of the rioters.

Island. They were equipped with a full arsenal of weaponry, and they started manning the yard wall and assisting Alcatraz officers at various other posts. Bergen and Cochrane were summoned to the Associate Warden's office and informed that once all of the marines had received assignments and reported to their posts, they would enter the cellhouse to rescue their fellow officers. There was, however, one change in plan. Johnston felt that it would be a better strategy to gain control of the West End Gallery first, and to have armed officers cover the team that entered the main floor of the prison. It was agreed that once Bergen and his armed assault team had taken control of the West Gallery they would be relieved by reserves, and then they would immediately enter the main cellhouse to perform the rescue.

Bergen, however, strongly voiced his opposition to this plan. He reasoned that his team could easily enter the main cellhouse using armed force, and quickly bring out the hostages. Bergen was adamant about not wasting time, and following Johnston's orders, he decided to assemble his team and have them briefed on the West Gallery entry plan. Bergen and his men made a quick stopover at the Armory, and then made their way to the catwalk outside of D Block. The men advanced along the catwalk in strict formation, crouching down as they quickly moved into position at the Gallery entrance. There were eight officers lined up along the catwalk. Phil Bergen, Harry Cochrane, and Harold P. Stites would be the first to enter the Gallery. Stites carried a solid reputation among his peers, and he had bravely put an end to the 1938 escape attempt by inmates Thomas E. Limerick, Rufus "Whitey" Franklin, and James Lucas.

The other men in the assault team were assigned to their stations, and it was planned that they would hold the West Gallery once Bergen, Stites, and Cochrane had completed the rescue of Officer Bert Burch. It was still unclear whether they would be recovering his corpse or rescuing him alive, since no one knew his true fate. The reserves were mostly seasoned officers. The remaining group was comprised of Lieutenant Frank Johnson, and Officers Alvin Bloomquest, Fred Mahan, Herschel R. Oldham, Fred J. Richberger, and Joe Maxell, who had made the first attempt at entering the Gallery with Stites, but had been forced to retreat.

While the guards crouched at the entrance, Bergen made a final review of the plan, and then on cue he carefully swung open the door just enough to allow them passage. As they entered the building they remained cautiously silent, while searching for any visible movement on the cellhouse floor. The interior was mysteriously quiet, and masked with an eerie haze of smoke that clouded the air. The acrid smell of teargas slightly irritated their eyes as they tried to adjust to the dim lighting. As they searched the cellhouse for any sign of the hostages and the escapees, they could see little except broken glass littering the floors, and several of the cells standing open with no movement inside. Bergen and Cochrane advanced steadily to the middle of the Gallery, stopping at the stairwell that led up to the middle level. Stites covered the entrance area, and scanned for any sign of movement.

Coy armed with his rifle and Cretzer with his .45 watched the officers make their entry into the Gallery. They carefully took aim at the shadows moving down the caged corridor, and then once they had a sure shot, they fired almost in unison. As soon as the shots were discharged, Stites, Bergen and Cochrane instantaneously dropped for cover under a volley of return fire. The officers on the catwalk squeezed into the entrance, and they too started shooting into the cellhouse. A brief gun battle ensued while Bergen and Cochrane made a concerted effort to locate the origin of the gunfire, without success. Meanwhile, the deafening barrage was heard all the way to the city's shores. Bergen yelled out to Stites to head for the stairs, where they could take cover and secure better positions from which to return fire. As Cochrane attempted to climb the stairs, he was violently struck by a bullet in his right arm. Bergen yelled emphatically to cease fire, and led the reluctant Cochrane back to the entrance. Richberger had also suffered a major gunshot wound to the leg, and in a painful low stance, he limped along the catwalk back to safety. Bert Burch, still tied and unable to move, tried to remain as still as possible to avoid being hit or targeted.

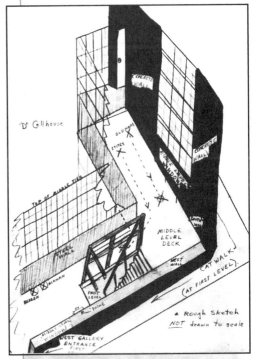

A diagram drawn by Lieutenant Phil Bergen, showing the positions of the officers when Stites was struck by friendly fire.

The team quickly regrouped outside the Gallery entrance, and Bergen, full of strong determination, prepared to reenter and take control of the Gallery. Bergen and Stites, now followed by the reserve officers, quickly rushed back into the building. Bergen had just begun a feverous search for Burch when the gunfire intensified, causing him to stop and take cover. Bergen and Mahan rushed to the stairwell while Stites and Oldham maintained their positions in the D Block section of the Gallery. The Gun Gallery in the D Block section had an "L" shaped curve that paralleled the south cellblock wall. This section provided an excellent frontal view of the cells and the activity of the inmates. Bergen and Mahan carefully positioned themselves in a low stance, and prepared to return fire into the ghostly haze of smoke. As the reserves fired off piston-like bursts of gunfire into the cellblock, the assault team quickly navigated the stairwell, hoping to locate and extricate Officer Burch. Suddenly and without warning, while Stites was slowly advancing along the south wall of the Gun Gallery, he was struck by a bullet and fatally wounded.

The interior of the Gun Gallery section inside of D Block. Visible at floor level is the window from which the fatal shot struck Stites.

Unconscious and completely unresponsive to his surroundings, Stites was lying supine and motionless at the southwest corner of D Block, bleeding profusely from a flank wound. Bergen and Mahan heard Oldham yelling out that Stites was badly hit, and quickly came to his aid. They immediately recognized the severity of his wounds, and each officer grabbed a leg to drag him along the Gallery to the stairwell. Oldham joined in to help them carry the wounded officer, and he was struck in the arm as he passed one of the Gallery windows. Stites was dragged out to the catwalk, where he lay bleeding in full view of the other officers positioned on the hillside. He was quickly carried into the administration area, where he was immediately pronounced dead. It was a sobering indicator of the gravity of the situation, and a final confirmation that this would not end peacefully. Bergen was now more determined than ever to free his fellow officers.

Bergen and Fred Mahan were now all alone in the West Gallery, studying every sound and every shadow. The cellhouse remained still, and free of any movement. They could only hear an occasional cough or a muffled voice from an anonymous cell. Mahan maintained his position in the D Block end of the Galley, while Bergen advanced alone into the main area of the cellhouse. Bergen was especially cautious, and he studied every discernible figure and shadow that he could make out through the Gallery bars. As he progressed cautiously through the darkened Gallery, he finally came across Burch, who was cold and shivering, and relieved to hear Bergen's voice. Burch briefed Bergen on what little he could remember. He didn't recall being struck, but had some recollection of the fight that had ensued with an inmate who he believed to be Bernie Coy. Burch was sore and had several scrapes and bruises, but amazingly he didn't appear to have suffered any other injuries. He was unclothed, except for his undergarments and socks.

Bergen and Burch slowly crawled their way back into D Block. As soon as they met up with Mahan, they called the Armory and notified the staff there that they had located Burch, and that he appeared to be unhurt. Burch was assisted out of the Gallery and walked back into administration, where he was examined and provided with clothing. Against the advice of the physician, he immediately returned to the Gallery to provide support. Bergen had decided to make another excursion into the West Gallery, where he would attempt to locate his fellow officers. Holding his pistol at the ready, he skillfully advanced into the narrow corridor. He again studied every tier of cells, looking for even the slightest indication of where the captives could be located. He ascended the staircase at the north end of the Gallery, careful and alert, and ready to react should the convicts attempt to ambush him. As he made it to the top level, the mystery of how Coy had infiltrated the Galley became clear. From a crouched position he could see the bars and how they had been bent. It was clear that Coy had somehow acquired tools that were capable of bending the steel that had been termed "*tool-proof.*" Bergen inspected the Gallery, and was finally confident that no inmates were waiting in ambush. He descended back into the D Block section, where he was met by Mahan, and he reported his findings back to the Armory via the Gallery telephone. Bergen and Mahan maintained their positions and continued a close surveillance of the cellhouse, awaiting further orders from the Warden's office.

The Warden was behind closed doors, plotting with his aides about how to perform a stealthy rescue and free his men. With Lieutenants Isaac Faulk and Frank Johnson and Associate Warden Ed Miller, he debated the pros and cons of making entry into the cellhouse without firm knowledge of the whereabouts of the captive officers. It was later reported that Warden Johnston had also felt uneasy about sending in a team carrying weapons, which could potentially be seized by the already armed inmates. It was known that the inmates had only a small

Correctional Officer Fred Mahan

arsenal of weapons and ammunition, and the prison staff realized that the battle could intensify if the convicts secured more firearms and drew more inmates into their scheme. This had been one of the most critical elements of the security system at Alcatraz. Weapons were never to be allowed into the cellhouse under any circumstances. But clearly this type of situation had never been anticipated, and some invasive action would have to be implemented, beyond what was dictated by protocol.

The injured guards, Richberger, Cochrane, and Oldham, were driven down to the dock area. Johnston made a solemn trip over to meet with Bessie Stites and deliver the news of her husband's tragic death. Her friends and children would assist her, as they gathered their belongings and met at the dock where her husband's body lay tightly covered with a dark green army blanket. Harold P. Stites had become the first known fatality, and his body was lifted onto the bow of the launch for the brief trip over to the Van Ness Pier. As they arrived, they were met with a barrage of reporters snapping photos, desperate to get any information that was available. The news of Stites' death was starting to spread, and the tension rose among the families, who feared the worst for their loved ones on the island. Ambulances lined the dock access path with their flashing red lights radiating against the buildings and water. When the launch arrived at the dock, four prison officers, Fred Richberger, Harry Cochrane, Herschel Oldham, and Elmus Besk, were rushed by ambulance to the Marine Hospital in the Presidio. The body of Harold Stites was solemnly loaded into the back of an ambulance and driven to the Medical Examiners Office, where it would immediately undergo an autopsy.

Warden Johnston had made a final decision that it was still too risky to send in an armed assault team. The plan would therefore be to attempt to communicate with the cornered inmates, to see if they could strike some limited bargain for the hostages' return. Ed Miller was assigned the task of attempting to negotiate with the inmates. Breaking out a pane from a window over the D Block catwalk, Miller yelled blindly into the cellhouse, trying to reason with the escapees, and pleading for them to surrender. At first there was no response, but then after a brief moment, Cretzer yelled from an indiscernible location that they would not be taken alive, and challenged Miller to "*come'n and get us.*" From his position in the Gun Gallery Bergen listened carefully to the sound of the voice, and cautiously looking over the Gallery's steel barrier, he attempted to locate where the voice was coming from. As Cretzer and Miller briefly exchanged words, Coy fired off several rounds toward the window where Miller was standing. This action incited a response, and soon there was an intense barrage of gunfire into D Block.

Former "Public Enemy Number One" Alvin Karpis later recounted that the first bombardment of gunfire took the inmates completely by surprise. They had not expected the barrage of bullets to be so severe. The inmates in D Block were nearly deafened as the artillery attack reverberated throughout the cellhouse, and to the many spectators who lined the shores of San Francisco, it was reminiscent of a Fourth of July fireworks display. Former inmate Jim Quillen later reported that when

(Above and below right) Scenes of Alcatraz at war. Armed with mortars and bazookas, United States Marines used heavy artillery to bomb the cellhouse in an effort to regain control.

the rifle grenades fired by marines penetrated into the cellhouse, the steel casings of the segregation cells could be seen expanding and contracting from the massive impact of the explosions. The inmates took cover behind piled mattresses, bedding, and books. As grenades traveled through the barred windows of D Block and clumsily landed, they would detonate hot shrapnel fragments across the cells. The individual blasts sent violent shockwaves across the tiers, and in one case inmate Burton Phillips was knocked completely unconscious, and all of the plumbing fixtures within his cell were destroyed. Each time a grenade hit, it would rupture the water lines, creating what Quillen later described as a "*free-flowing river*" that flooded each tier. There was a collective mood of terror as the inmates were forced to take cover behind the icy-cold water-soaked mattresses, which slowly increased in density, acting as large porous sponges. The chilly Bay winds started to creep into the cellblock, but this also dispersed some of the harsh and acrid haze of teargas. It was later recounted that each time the clouds of teargas started to dissipate, another canister would be thrown onto the cellhouse floor.

By 9:00 P.M. the cellhouse was completely dark, with only ambient lighting glowing though the exterior windows. Bergen was now positioned in the "L" section of the Gun Gallery, observing the attack of the administration forces. As the barrage of fire lessened, voices from the catwalk again pleaded with the inmates to surrender their weapons and release the hostages. Coy was now taking cover behind the cement wall next to the D-Block entrance, and he yelled more obscenities at the guards, then fired several rounds toward the window from which the voice had emerged. The attack would again rage on, as the cellhouse was shelled with powerful artillery. Bergen and Mahan, who were now rejoined by Burch, fiercely opened fire on Coy, but they were unable to

see him well enough to aim precisely. After nearly forty-five minutes of fierce battle, the rapid pulse of gunfire slowed to an irregular pattern, with only occasional deafening bursts aimed at briskly moving shadows. Coy retreated back into the utility corridor, where he climbed the labyrinth of piping, hoping to find a point on top of the cellhouse from which he would have a clear, unobstructed shooting radius.

Tension was now also rising for the inmates in the recreation yard. Each time shots were fired into the cellhouse, the inmates would yell obscenities at the marines and guards along the wall. These slurs would generally be met with aimed rifles and machine guns, challenging the prisoners' unruliness. The sharp winds had also added to the inmates' misery, and the blankets seemed to offer little protection against the salty ocean mist. The guards in the East Gallery were aware that Coy and his accomplices were pinned down in the C Block Corridor. The inmates decided that they would need to position themselves more advantageously, and they decided to make a run for the Dining Hall, where they could stock up on food supplies, and perhaps attempt another attack on the yard wall guards. As they slowly opened the access door they were immediately met with intense fire, and were forced to retreat into the corridor. On the outside, Bergen, Burch, and Mahan spread out to see if they could detect any movement. There was virtually none, and all they heard was the loud whispering of the inmates amongst themselves. Bergen got back on the phone with Miller, and he conveyed his confidence that his team now controlled both Galleries, and that they were in a good position to attempt the rescue.

Warden Clinton Duffy of San Quentin had shared a long and close friendship with Warden Johnston. Duffy's father had also served as Warden of San Quentin, and he himself had actually been born inside the prison grounds. A mentor to both Johnson and Duffy was the former Warden of "Q," James B. Holohan. Holohan and Johnston had been among the driving forces behind recent progress in the area of inmate reform and education. Duffy and Holohan interfaced extensively with Johnston, and both men continued many of the programs that were introduced by Johnston during his days at San Quentin. When word came of the current debacle, Duffy committed a large group of his full-time correctional staff to help support their peers on Alcatraz, including the San Quentin physician, Dr. Leo Stanley. A Coast Guard cutter made a special trip across the Bay, bringing the San Quentin guards straight over to the island. Captain Bernard McDonald of the San Francisco

Spectators lined the shores of San Francisco, watching the embattled prison. The sounds of gunfire and bombing resonated throughout the city.

Police Department also brought over several heavily armed officers, who were prepared to engage in battle with the inmates.

At approximately 10:30 P.M. Johnston finally agreed to put together a large armed assault team that could enter the main cellhouse and carry out the rescue. The Associate Warden and Lieutenant Isaac Faulk assembled their group of ten additional men, and planned their entry. The rescue would be aggressive, and they were prepared to do battle with the inmates should they attempt to ambush the team. The inmates affectionately referred to the special troops that carried out this type of task as "The Goon Squad." By approximately 11:00 P.M. the assault team had lined up outside the main entrance, awaiting the signal to enter. Miller slowly opened the main steel door, and carefully assessed the main floor of the prison. With no suspicious movement visible, the team advanced inward and started an articulate search, with their flashlights glaring into the squinting eyes of timid inmates as the officers closely examined each cell they passed along the flats. As they slowly progressed towards Seedy Street with their weapons poised and ready to fire, they heard whispers from one of the captive officers in one of the end cells on the C-D aisle. Officer Mowery was able to advance forward and locate the hostages. He also managed to open the cells and begin preparing the men for evacuation.

But as the officers moved toward the cells, they were suddenly fired upon by Coy, who was perched on top of C Block. Officer McKean and Lieutenant Faulk were able to secure and lock the door to D Block as well as the C Block utility corridor access door, and then they took cover. Coy fired off several shots, thus giving away his position. Officer Fred Roberts took a bullet in the arm, and plummeted to the floor. The team then retreated under one of the walkway balconies below a cell row, and pulled Roberts under for cover. The officers had seen the muzzle flashes, and they emerged from their hiding place with a rapid barrage of gunfire aimed at the top of C Block, forcing Coy to retreat. Then without delay, the officers started pulling the injured men from the cells.

Sundstrom, Burdette, and Bristow were found unharmed, and Lageson had only minor wounds; all were able to walk on their own. Weinhold, Simpson, Corwin and Miller were all in extremely critical condition, and had to be carried out to safety by the other officers. The freed hostages were brought in through the sallyport and laid on the floor outside of the Warden's office. Alcatraz physicians Roucek and Bowden, assisted by Dr. Jones of the Public Health Department, all started feverously treating and bandaging the injured officers' wounds. At about midnight, the wounded officers were taken aboard the prison launch and quickly ferried to the Van Ness Pier. When the launch pulled up to the dock, there were abundant crowds of onlookers and reporters watching attentively as the critically injured officers were loaded into waiting ambulances. As each ambulance departed, the wailing and fading sirens could be heard by everyone on the island.

With the hostages rescued and large numbers of reinforcements swarming the island, the officers would now aggressively attempt to flush out the armed convicts. Warden Johnston and his staff sat with Officers Lageson, Sundstrom, Burdette, and Bristow, and exhaustively interviewed the men, attempting to extract every minute detail of how the escape had transpired. They were able to ascertain conclusively that Coy, Cretzer, Hubbard, Thompson, Shockley, and Carnes were the active armed conspirators. Other convicts were also named, mostly by individual officers, but their level of participation could not be precisely determined. It seemed possible that they might not even have been involved, and might have been present purely by coincidence. Johnston was also unable to pinpoint the conspirators' exact location in the cellhouse. The group discussed the various possible origins of the gunfire, but the evidence was not conclusive, since the guards had heard gunshots from a variety of locations. Ed Miller was confident that Roberts had been shot with a rifle from on top of C Block, because he had seen the muzzle flashes as they were fired upon during the rescue.

Lieutenant Bergen had watched Miller's team during the rescue, and had helped to return Coy's fire. He had already moved more men up to the top of the West Galley, and had situated them so they would have a sound vantage point from which to suppress gunfire. Officers O'Brian and Green used heavy sledgehammers to knock out the bullet-proof panes from the Visitors' Gallery, and prepared to take aim on any of the armed convicts who might appear. Three other armed officers named Mowery, Jones, and Runnels entered the cellhouse, and climbed to the top of B Block. They carefully watched for any movement on top of C Block, and fired whenever they saw a moving shadow. Bergen had left the Gallery phone off the hook to maintain an open line, and he continued to convey updates on activities to the Armory. When the Armory officer needed to speak to Bergen, he would blow a whistle into the receiver, which would generate just enough sound to capture his attention. Warden Johnston had contacted Bergen personally as soon as he had confirmed the identities of the conspirators. He had asked Bergen and his men to maintain a careful lookout for these convicts.

By 2:10 A.M. Simpson and Weinhold were in surgery having the fragmented Colt slugs removed from their bodies. Miller and Corwin were scheduled next, and they initially appeared to be doing well. Miller had provided a sworn statement to FBI agents, positively identifying Joseph Cretzer as the gunman who had shot them one by one in cold blood. Reporters flooded the hospital waiting rooms, attempting to grab photos and any statements that they could get from the doctors and from the ambulance attendants who had transported the men. The city morgue had also sprung to life, with journalists lining the entryway, hoping to glean information on how Stites had met his fate. One of the morgue attendants who had transported Stites from the dock acknowledged that he had stayed to watch Stites' uniform cut away, and had seen some of his wounds. However, he misinformed the hungry reporters, stating that it looked like Stites had taken "*several machine-gun bullets*" in his back. Meanwhile the battle continued through the night, with the officers and marines launching attacks on both D and C Blocks. Lieutenant Faulk managed to secure the entrance door to D Block, and it was believed that one of the armed men was trapped there. The battle raged on as

Officer Bill Miller is shown being transferred to the Marine Hospital just hours before he succumbed to a fatal gunshot wound.

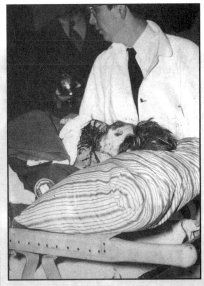

(Above) Officer Cecil Corwin was critically injured by a gunshot wound to the head. Luckily, Corwin would survive his injuries.

(Below) One of the injured officers is seen being wheeled into the Emergency Room following the historic rescue.

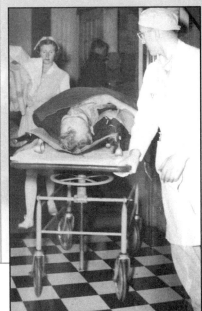

Charlie L. Buckner lowered demolition grenades into the cellhouse from the roof using string. He strategically detonated the grenades inside the utility corridors, in an attempt to flush out the rioters.

The cement scar patterns are still visible today where Buckner detonated the explosives.

thousands lined the shores throughout the night, watching the tracers of artillery fire bludgeoning the cellhouse.

As the sun started to rise on San Francisco, Ed Miller assisted Warrant Officer Charlie Buckner to the roof, and started shooting gas grenades into the C-Block corridor through the ventilators. They continued to call to the inmates, urging a peaceful surrender, but there was never any reply. Charlie L. Buckner was a decorated World War II veteran, who had been stationed on Treasure Island after the war. He was a demolition expert, and had prevailed in some of the bloodiest battles of the war. The Alcatraz guards had been able to achieve virtually no precision with the gas grenades, because they would bounce off of objects and land far from their target. Buckner's experience would be invaluable, because during the war he had become an expert at rigging devices designed to expel Japanese soldiers from the burrowed tunnels in which they concealed themselves during battles. He was a master at lowering the grenade into the tunnel on a thin string, armed with a detonation system that was extremely effective and precise.

Buckner told Warden Johnston that if he could obtain demolition grenades, he could lower these explosives into confined areas with great accuracy, and without risking the lives of his officers. Johnston quickly made arrangements to have the ammunition boated over from a military arsenal in Benicia. When the supplies arrived, the rescue team started drilling holes through the ceilings directly above the corridors. The holes were drilled large enough to allow fist-sized grenades to pass through the openings. In a systematic process, Buckner rigged a wire around the casing cap to hold the grenade, and then delicately lowered it through the opening. The string was generally measured to a specific length, and thus the explosive device was lowered to a precise height. Once the string was spooled out and the grenade had reached the desired position, Buckner would sharply jerk a second string that was affixed to the discharge mechanism, and this would expel the pin. He was later described by one of the correctional officers as having the skill of a "*masterful puppeteer*."

Warden Johnston was also pleased to welcome two other visitors, General Joseph W. "*Vinegar Joe*" Stilwell, and General Frank Merrill, who had come over to the island on an Army vessel. Johnston and the two Generals evaluated the situation in meticulous detail, and reviewed every officer's post assignment, as well as the strategy for regaining control of the cellhouse. The Generals seemed impressed with the containment procedures already in place, and they reviewed some of the artillery configurations that they had recommended to help reestablish control. The light fragmentation explosives they had been using was replaced with anti-tank shells, which were dropped through the drilled ceiling portals.

The guards and Marines also fired rifle grenades from the lawn on the side of the building that faced the Golden Gate Bridge. Army-style cots were set up in the administration building so the officers could remain close by while they rested. Many of the officers had been up for over twenty-four hours, including Burch, who had been tied up for nine hours following the brutal attack, and had then stayed up all night on watch in the Gallery with Bergen. Bergen and the others had also begun to tire after having been up all night, but before turning in, both men met with the Warden and described in detail all of the events that they had witnessed from their perspective in the Gun Gallery. At 7:00 A.M., the Alcatraz staff received the dreadful news that Bill Miller had gone into cardiac arrest, and that the surgeons had been unable to resuscitate him. One of the doctors explained to Johnston over the phone that Miller had fallen into a deep state of shock as a result of severe blood loss, and had subsequently died. Cecil Corwin was still deemed to be in critical condition, but he was expected to survive his injuries. Weinhold and Simpson had done well in surgery, and had been moved into the intensive care ward where they were now listed in critical but stable condition. They had both been placed in oxygen tents, and allowed to rest. The other guards were also in a stable condition, and were expected to recovery fully from their injuries.

After interviewing Burch and Bergen, the Warden walked the short distance to his house and retired for a short nap. Sleep would be difficult however, as more marines were landing on the island, and the artillery attack had intensified. Dr. Roucek pulled out a small flask and provided Burch and Bergen with a shot of whisky to help soothe their nerves. By 11:00 A.M. the situation was still considered to be out of control, and heavier artillery was brought to the island, including anti-tank mortars and bazookas. The firing grew more and more intensive, and a staccato rhythm of bombing began against the exterior walls of D Block, launched from the grassy slopes below the south wall. Small brush fires started below the cellhouse, and a heavy blanket of dense pungent smoke could be seen from all points of San Francisco. Large groups of journalists keenly watched the events from boats that were idling in the waters only a few hundred yards away. Jack Eoisie was one of the reporters who had been assigned to cover the escape attempt by the *San Francisco Chronicle*. He described the events in sharp detail on page four of the May 4th edition:

Five stout men, protected by a ledge about 100 yards directly beneath and out from the "hot" cell block window are doing the job of keeping the convicts from reaching the window ledge–and a possible dash for freedom through the shattered bars. They are doing the job by firing, about every five minutes, four fragmentation grenades launched from either an Army rifle or carbine. During the hours we watched, no other weapon was used–no bazookas and nor mortars. Earlier in the day a few smoke grenades churned up outside the beleaguered cell. It is understood that of the five men who can be seen operating the grenade launcher with methodical precision, one is a Marine. He is Warrant Officer C.L. Beckner [sic], who commands the Marine detachment on the island.

They are preparing to fire now. The grenade is inserted carefully into the launcher device attached to the muzzle of the gun. There is a slight report as the grenade leaves the gun, but it is drowned out by the sharp concussion as the projectile strikes the wall. A flash of yellow flame lights up, and then curling black smoke. This one, then, missed the cell, but immediately another is fired, and all that can be heard is a smothered concussion. Black smoke drifts out the window. The one went in. Each grenade sprays the cell area with sharp metal for a radius of 50 feet, forcing the convicts inside to keep down on the floor or behind sheltering objects in corners. Two more grenades are fired and then, the stronghold relaxes. The men can be seen lighting cigarettes and stretching out on the beds of bright purple flowers.

Bergen returned to his post in the West Gallery after a short rest. As he drew near, the bombing increased, causing the men to take cover under the low sheath of thin metal plating across the front of the Gallery. The grenades were deafening even to the officers, and the fury of the bombing was unrelenting. In a later memoir co-written by Bergen entitled *Alcatraz '46*, the officer recalled giving a wry look to Mahan and joking: *"That's one hell of a breakfast they're serving."* Buckner continued his carefully calculated barrage of explosives, drilling along the corridor path and dropping the grenades into the cellblock. The men imprisoned in the isolation cells were trapped and unable to take cover behind any fixed objects, which would have offered some protection. As the shrapnel from the explosives grew more intense, the inmates began to scream and plead for someone to close the heavy steel cell doors.

Bergen would later recount one of the most intriguing events that occurred during the escape attempt. Robert Stroud, known as the "Birdman of Alcatraz," had remained in cell #41 on the topmost tier, until the bombardment grew so intense that he was forced out. Stroud soon noted that the majority of the bullets were actually striking closest in proximity to *his* cell. He finally fled down the tier, and took refuge in another cell. Bergen recalled that he could hear the sheer panic of the inmates confined in the cells along the flats, until finally Stroud emerged and walked to the end of the tier against the wall closest to his cell. Remarkably, he climbed over the railing and lowered himself onto the second tier rail, at great risk of being struck by gunfire or shrapnel. This was an amazing feat for a man of fifty-six years. He then balanced himself, crossed over the second rail, and dropped to the cellblock floor where he quickly closed each of the cell fronts. He then went to the cells beyond, and hoisted himself up, climbing tier by tier back to the top. Bergen and Mahan watched in complete amazement. Stroud, who had once been a savior of sick birds, had now attempted to help his fellow inmates when they were in danger's way.

At about 1:10 P.M., Bergen was still in the Gallery when he was hailed by Stroud. Bob Stroud yelled across the smoke-filled cellblock to Bergen, who was pitched low for cover. Stroud pleaded with him to stop the bombing before someone was needlessly killed. He swore to Bergen that there were no guns in D Block, and insisted that the bombardment was senseless. As he made his plea, he offered to strip his clothes off and stand in the middle of the cellblock floor, where he could be used as a hostage for barter. Bergen had always seen Stroud as a "*homicidal maniac*," but nevertheless, he believed that the prisoner was telling the truth. Bergen got this message to the Warden, and the shooting finally ceased. Bergen yelled to the inmates that the shooting would not resume, but warned them to stay in their cells and not to wander along tiers. Quillen would later recount in an interview, "*Most respected Bergen; he treated inmates fair, but several of the men didn't dare move from behind their barricades since they thought it was a trap. Bergen had yelled all night to surrender the rifle so a lot of the men didn't move since they thought no one was going to believe what Stroud told them.*" Walter Bertrand, the Warden's secretary, had been working non-stop, attempting to answer all of the phone calls and Teletype inquires that flooded the office. Amid the smoke in the aftermath of the battle, the United States flag was brought down to half-mast, and reports were now delivered to the mainland that various areas of the prison had been secured.

Amid the smoke in the aftermath of the battle, the United States flag was brought down to half-mast in honor of the officers who lost their lives during the siege.

Marine Major Albert Arsenault is shown describing the events of the battle into a microphone.

Then at 6:55 P.M. Officer Joe Steere was fired on while passing the C Block utility corridor, and quickly took cover. The bombardment of gunfire started up again, and Buckner made his way back up to the roof with more small explosives. Ed Miller and an armed team of officers approached the access door and swung it open, and each fired several rounds into the darkness. There was no detectable movement, and no voices responded to Miller's demands for surrender. It seemed evident that the inmates were now trapped within the corridor, so Miller rapidly closed the door and locked it. The correctional staff started implementing plans to move the inmates from the recreation yard back into the cellhouse, housing them all in A Block. Extra mattresses were moved into A Block so that inmates could be assigned two per cell, and guard staff from San Quentin, Atlanta, McNeil Island, Folsom, and Leavenworth helped to ready the cells as quickly as possible. The prison's locksmith, Earl Waller, was summoned to fix the jammed lock in the door to the recreation yard.

The inmates who had now been trapped in the recreation yard for more than twenty-four hours were ushered down to A and B Blocks. The East and West Gun Galleries were both heavily fortified with officers ready to fire at anything that posed a potential threat. Once all of the inmates had been secured, the guard staff started delivering boxed meals

Officer Joe Steere

to those who had been locked up for over twenty-four hours. Buckner resumed dropping explosives with increasing accuracy into the dark passage of the narrow utility corridor. Heavy utility lights were aimed at the top of the corridor of C Block from the Galleries, blinding any inmates who might be there. The corridor had become more difficult for the inmates to navigate and climb, as the barrage of explosives had severed most of the piping. Each time Buckner prepared to drop an explosive device, an officer would pass the muzzle of the Springfield .30-06 through the drilled cement hole and fire blindly into the corridor. The movements of the inmates in these final hours are unknown. Perhaps the last sight their eyes were to register before death was a small grenade slowly being lowered on a black spun string, or the muzzle flash of a rifle the split second before the concussion echoed into silence. As the sun began to rise on the east face of the prison, the shadowy silence was broken only by the occasional cries of airborne seagulls.

At 8:40 A.M., the Associate Warden and several other officers including Bergen and Mowery stood on ready to enter in the C Block utility corridor. Officer Mowery opened the door, shining his powerful searchlight and yelling a warning, but his call was met only with silence, and a harsh stench from the raw sewage still dripping from the severed piping. The guards entered into the dark and eerie silence, and slowly advanced through the flooded passageway, shining their bright flashlights. The first inmate they came across was Coy, who lay nearest the door with his eyes open and glazed over. His body was stiffened with rigor mortis, and the rifle was at his side, loaded and ready to fire. He was wearing Weinhold's jacket, and still had rounds of ammunition in his pocket. Cretzer was found next to Coy, also stiffened by hours of death, wearing a guard's uniform and ammunition belt. Hubbard was found at the end of the corridor, still flexible and warm. The bodies were pulled out of the dark passage and examined by Dr. Roucek. He carefully assessed the wounds on each, articulating every detail to his assistant Jesse Riser.

In Dr. Roucek's official report to Warden Johnston, he dictated the following after examining Coy's corpse:

The C-Block utility corridor where inmates Coy, Hubbard, and Cretzer made their final stand. All three inmates where eventually found dead inside this area.

May 4, 1946
To: The Warden
Subject: Report of Death of Bernard Paul Coy, No. AZ-415.

Examination of the body of this inmate revealed the following: Body was cold and rigor mortis had set in. Pupils were fixed. Left arm was extended in a 15-degree angle; right arm was flexed at the elbow at approximately a 45-degree angle. He was wearing an Officers uniform coat marked Captain and underwear marked No. 415 with blue trousers marked No. 415.

Further examination revealed a small laceration of cheek over left maxilla and a large penetrating wound through left border of Sternal Mastoid muscle and apparently through upper border of Trapezius. Laceration of scalp approximately 2 cm to left and down from natural whorl of hair. There were no apparent wounds on the posterior side of body. There was bleeding from the nose. In the examination all clothing was cut from his body. This inmate was pronounced dead at 10:12 A.M. this date.

Examination was witnessed by the following Officers:

Medical Technical Assistant, Jesse A. Riser, USPHS
Lieutenant P.R. Bergen, Custodial Force
Senior Officer, John Delling, Custodial Force
Jr. Officer, D.H. Mowery, Custodial Force

Signed,

Louis G. Roucek, Surgeon
Chief Medical Officer

Bureau Director James V. Bennett arrived at the prison from Washington D.C. just in time to see the three deceased inmates sprawled on the cold cement prison floor. The bodies were covered, and had been prepared for transport back to the mainland. Ed Miller now switched his focus to the living ringleaders. A team of guards converged on the cells of Thompson, Carnes, and Shockley, and the inmates were marched one by one into separate isolation cells in A Block. The Alcatraz staff then assessed the aftermath of the battle. The wind whistled through the mortar holes in D Block. Correctional staff from the other prisons assisted in searching the cell of each inmate, and then placing them into lockdown. Jim Quillen would later write in his personal memoir, *Alcatraz from the Inside*:

> The entire flat was covered with armed, nervous and tired guards. Each guard had been assigned an inmate to cover as he stepped from his cell. The guard assigned to cover me was a stranger, possibly from another institution. He was armed with a shotgun and was so nervous that I could see the gun trembling in his hands.

As the bodies of the three convicts were placed on the bow of the *Warden Johnston*, the press stood shoulder to shoulder at the gate of Van Ness Street Pier, snapping hundreds of photos as the boat approached. The bodies of the dead convicts were lifted and carried to the waiting ambulances. FBI officials then flocked to the island, and began an in-

Bureau Director James V. Bennett arrived from Washington just in time to witness the three deceased inmates being pulled from the utility corridor.

(Below left and right) The *Warden Johnston* pulling up to the Van Ness Street Pier, with the bodies of the three dead inmates clearly visible on the deck.

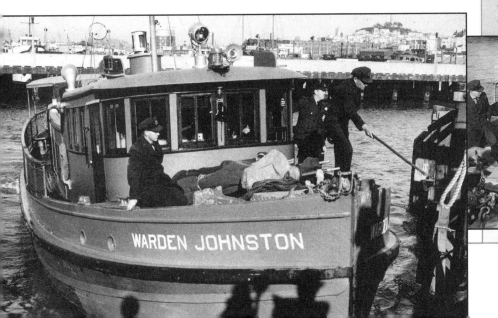

355

(Below) The lifeless bodies of the inmates were loaded into waiting ambulances at the pier.

tensive investigation. A press conference was quickly held by U.S. Attorney Frank Hennessy in the San Francisco Federal Building, and he explained that the three survivors of the break would be charged with the murder of the two slain officers, as well as conspiracy to commit murder, and conspiracy to escape. Later that evening Johnston and Bennett would hold the first ever press conference on Alcatraz, and would walk reporters through the prison explaining how the escape took place. Johnston escorted the all-male group of reporters and photographers through the prison as inmates chanted and shouted at them. He walked the group of visitors to the foot of the Gun Gallery and then over to the cells where Cretzer had fired upon the helpless guards, and where the blood stains were still fresh on the walls. The inmates yelled slurs, and several of the reporters wrote them into their features. In one case an inmate yelled *"Oh Saltwater Johnston, tell them how you starve us in the dungeons."*

The Aftermath

On May 5, 1946 at 7:40 A.M., Medical Examiner Dr. Gus T. Kerhulas began his autopsy examinations of the three inmates, to determine their exact cause of death. He removed several bullet fragments from Coy's brain, and ruled that his death had been instantaneous at the moment of projectile entry. Cretzer's autopsy followed at 8:30 A.M. The doctor carefully examined his injuries, and described Cretzer's post mortem condition in his autopsy report:

APPEARANCE: The body is that of a well-developed, well-nourished, adult, young white male revealing evidence of head injury. In the center of the scalp in the mid-cranial vault there is a laceration of linear type with crusted margins, apparently of twenty-four hours duration. There is no evidence of fracture at this point. The wound is gaping. There is a wound of entrance at the left temporal region with a smooth margin, measuring approximately 1cm., and a wound of exit at the right temporal region with ragged wound margins, measuring approximately 1.5 cm in diameter and revealing evidence of fragmentation of bone with evidence of compound fracture at this point. The right temporal, frontal, and parietal bone in this area is likewise apparently shattered as on palpitation it reveals crepitation and abnormal mobility of the cranium on this side. In addition, there are abrasions on the anterior upper chest, hands, and left knee. There are no other abnormalities. Rigor mortis and post-mortis lividity are present.

HEAD: On reflecting the scalp back in the region of these wounds, there are hematomas present and the bony cranial vault is fractured at the wound entrances and exits with fractures of the left temporal and the right temporal, frontal, and parietal bones. On opening the cranial vault, the brain is found to be severely lacerated and penetrated through and through from the left temporal lobe to the right temporal lobe running across the base and also destroying the brain stem. On removing the brain, the pituitary fossa and sphenoid body is also seen to be involved in this fracture. There is no evidence of metallic objects present in the cranial vault.

(Above left) Warden James Johnston and Bureau Director James Bennett examine the tools utilized by Bernard Coy to gain access to the Gun Gallery.

(Above right) During the first press conference ever held inside Alcatraz, Warden Johnston shows members of the press where Coy made his entry into the Gallery.

(Below) Cell #403, where Cretzer coldly shot the helpless correctional officers.

DIAGNOSIS: Gunshot wound with fracture of skull and laceration of brain.

Hubbard's injuries were also found to have afforded him a quick death. It was confirmed that Hubbard had died hours after Coy and Cretzer, but it was somewhat puzzling that there were no firearms within his reach when he was found, and he was armed with only the butcher knife that he had carried with him from the kitchen. Investigators were bewildered to find that he appeared to have waited out his death. Like the others, Hubbard had taken two fatal bullet wounds to the head. Medical Examiner Kerhulas allowed reporters to view the deceased convicts and to photograph them. The sound of camera shutters flickering and blinding flashes of light saturated the room, which smelled of formaldehyde. The Coroner documented in his report:

External Appearance: The body is that of a well developed, well nourished adult young white male revealing evidence of gunshot wounds of the head with a wound of entrance in the left temporal region having smooth margins and measuring approximately 1 cm in diameter, and a wound of exit at the right temporal parietal region with evidence of extensive compound fracture of the right temporal, frontal and parietal region bones at this point. In addition there is a wound of entrance at the inner corner the left eye with exit in the right occipital region of the skull. There are abrasions of the right temporal posterior auricular region.

Officer William A. Miller was mourned in a small service at St. Brigid's Catholic Church

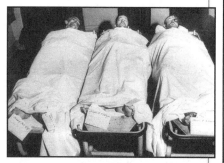

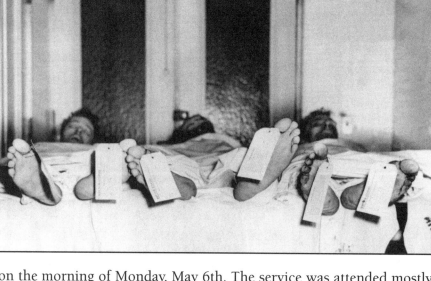

(Above and right) Medical Examiner Dr. Gus T. Kerhulas invited the press to photograph the deceased inmates, and openly discussed his autopsy findings.

Attorney General Thomas Clark (seen with his arm around Stites' son) and Warden Johnston gave a brief testimonial for Harold Stites during a ceremony held at Alcatraz.

on the morning of Monday, May 6th. The service was attended mostly by the wives and children of his fellow officers. Miller's widow Josephine would hold a larger family service when his body arrived in Pennsylvania. His body was prepared at the Halstead Funeral Parlor in San Francisco, and then following a small open casket service, his remains were placed in a hearse and driven to the train depot for the final ride home. His wife and two young children accompanied him on the train.

Officer Harold Stites' services were held on Tuesday, May 7th at the Maneely Chapel in San Francisco. The services were heavily attended by the press, and James Bennett and Warden Johnston both sat in the front pews, giving support to his widow Bessie and his four children. Following the ceremony, there was a large funeral procession led by the San Francisco Police to the Golden Gate National Cemetery, where a graveside service was held before Stites' final burial. Chaplain Lieutenant Rodney Shaw presided, while the family sat in solemn silence on a bench placed next to his grave.

Bernie Coy's body was released from the San Francisco Morgue after eleven days, as no family member had claimed his remains. He was buried in a plain pinewood coffin in an unmarked gravesite at the Woodlawn Cemetery in Daly City, just south of San Francisco. Officials had attempted to contact Coy's ex-wife, but all their telegrams were returned undelivered. On May 16, 1946 Coy's sister Anna Long wrote a short letter to Warden Johnston, asking him to send all of Bernie's belongings back to her in Kentucky. Johnston replied that Coy had only $6.16 in his account, and a small cloth container filled with what appeared to be family photos. Anna's letter simply stated, "*I was told by his [Coy's] attorney that it was best not to bring him back here.*"

Marvin Hubbard's body had been taken to the Godeau Funeral Home, as his wife had made arrangements for his remains to be transferred back to Oklahoma. Hubbard's family came to San Francisco and quietly accompanied Marvin back home for a proper burial. Joseph Cretzer's body was cremated, and his ashes were placed in a burial vault at the Cypress Lawn Cemetery in Daly City. There were only two people who attended his service, his attorney and his ex-wife Edna.

In the weeks that followed, a sensational trial ensued in which Carnes, Shockley, and Thompson faced charges for their roles in the escape and in the murder of Officer Miller. The trial commenced on November 20, 1946, with Judge Louis E. Goodman presiding. The inmates were transferred to and from the courthouse chained together and under heavy guard on each day of their trial. The inmates were not charged with Stites' murder, since it was deemed probable that he had been struck by friendly fire. The court appointed defense attorneys William Sullivan and Archer Zamlock to represent Carnes and Shockley, and Ernest Spagnoli and Aaron Vinkler to defend Thompson. The four attorneys would argue that the men had been held under heavy duress, similar to the mitigating factors that had been presented during the Henri Young murder trial. Robert Stroud donated $200 to the inmates' defense, and several other inmates came to testify on their behalf. Quillen also testified, and argued that Shockley was not fit to stand trial due to his mental state, adding that he felt Sam was more of a victim than a conspirator. Quillen further contested the chronology of the events as they have been described here. He stated that Shockley never incited any disturbance prior to the break, and that he most likely had limited knowledge, if any, of the planned escape plot.

Prior to the trial, Dr. Roucek had conducted extensive evaluations of Shockley. In one interview performed on November 5, 1946 in the prison hospital, Shockley complained of hearing voices. This transcript was taken directly from Roucek's handwritten notes:

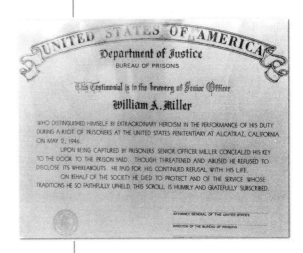

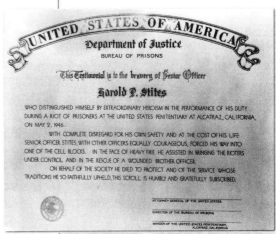

ROUCEK:	Do you hear voices?
SHOCKLEY:	Yes, I hear voices.
ROUCEK:	What do they say?
SHOCKLEY:	I've heard so many that it'd be a long story. On May 4th when the officers came into "D" Block with guns, three officers had guns pointed at me. One had his thumb on the trigger and the voice said, "Let it go off."
ROUCEK NOTE:	When asked more questions the patient stated, "I'm not in a thinking mood this morning because the ra-

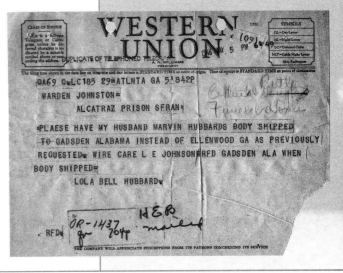

May 15, 1946

Dear Bob & Naomi,

This is the first time I have had an opportunity to write you since the awful escape attempt of May second. I am now cold. All of the windows were bombed and shot out, and all of the radiators were broken up by shells. Workmen are laboring to get the place warm again. And I am writing this on a Life news magazine held on my knee.

When that terrible escape started I was writing a letter to Aunt Amelia. A while later I tore it up because if I didn't come through all the shooting I didn't want anyone else to read it. At first the shooting was light. Another fellow and I sat on the floor until he caught a deflected shell in his shoulder. He wasn't hurt badly. We however grabbed some mattresses and built a barricade at the front of the cell door. Then we stacked all my books up behind that. Things got hotter. The noise of the gun firing was terrific. We crawled under my steel bunk and stayed there nearly all of the time. Those anti-aircraft and anti-tank bombs the Navy and Marines threw into isolation lifted my cell up and crashed into my eardrums with an awful din. I'd lay there and wait to feel the pain from a fragment or a shell. But I never even got touched.

The real close calls scared me. One came at the very first and one at the last. But after I got used to the firing I slept awhile over different periods. I raised up to take a look around the cell block during some of the heaviest firing. The place was truly beautiful. There was a steady stream of brilliant white and red flares casting their lights over everything. Tracer bullets were lancing through the smoke. Actually the worst of the whole thing physically was that pungent smoke from smoldering mattresses. I could hardly breath and my eyes ran a steady stream.

When I wasn't sleeping or talking I was praying for all of us fellows, the officers I knew were in danger of getting killed, and that the officials and guards would have the courage to come in and capture those who had caused such horror. It was a sheer miracle that so few innocent inmates were slightly wounded. Even the guards couldn't hardly believe their own eyes when they saw us all walking.

There was a big colored fellow among us who was through the Italian Campaigns during the recent war. He laughed aloud and said that even Italy was never so bad as what we went through.

Yours, with love,

Henri Young 244-AZ

dio irritated me before coming up this morning."

ROUCEK:	What type of words does the radio use?
SHOCKLEY:	Evil words; murder and hung.
ROUCEK:	Has there ever been any change since the break?
SHOCKLEY::	Not so many evil words used and the minerals in the food has been cut down.
ROUCEK:	Are any of the inmates insane?
SHOCKLEY:	We are all insane at times.
ROUCEK: :	Are the voices men or women?
SHOCKLEY:	Always men voices.
ROUCEK:	What is your trouble?
SHOCKLEY:	It's the minerals in the food here that gives me pains all over my body, and the rays of light shot at me.

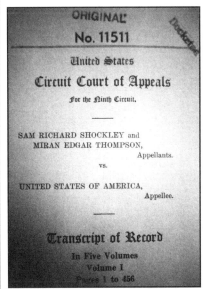

(Above left) Inmates Miran Thompson, Sam Shockley, and Clarence Carnes being transferred to court under heavy guard. All three were arraigned on murder charges for the death of Officer Bill Miller.

ROUCEK:	Who puts them in the food?
SHOCKLEY:	Put there by the prison hospital for treatment when we come into the institution.
ROUCEK:	What rays shoot at you?
SHOCKLEY:	The rays from the lights in the cellblock have shot at me ever since I've been here. It is arranged automatically. In bed at night the lights flash . . . flash . . . flash.
ROUCEK:	Where do you feel these rays?
SHOCKLEY:	On my head. When I came up here today I felt them on my head. Sometimes I can feel them on my shoulders.
ROUCEK:	Do you have any sickness?
SHOCKLEY:	Yes . . . I have cancer in the lower part of my stomach.
ROUCEK:	Do you eat all your meals?
SHOCKLEY:	No, can't eat breakfast. Milk is too cold and acid and doped up to make you crazy.
ROUCEK:	Do you plan to eat dinner?
SHOCKLEY:	Yes . . . I'll eat dinner. The food around here is better since the break. The more you eat the more you want.
ROUCEK:	What do the minerals do to you?
SHOCKLEY:	They give me marks on my body all over.
ROUCEK NOTE:	Showed doctor a reddish area in his groin area which he claims to scratch.

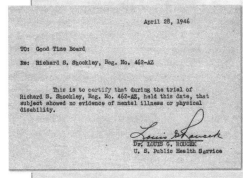

An affidavit from Alcatraz Physician Louis Roucek, stating that Shockley was mentally competent.

(Below) Sam Shockley during his trial for his role in the death of Officer Miller.

The trial continued for over a month, and people across the nation followed its progress in the newspapers. Despite the efforts of several inmates who provided favorable testimony, Shockley, Carnes, and Thompson were convicted of the first-degree murder of William A. Miller on December 21, 1946. On the same day, Shockley and Thompson were given the death penalty for their role in the crime, and sentenced to die in the gas chamber at San Quentin on September 24, 1948. Carnes was spared the death penalty, and was instead given an additional life sentence due to mitigating factors, as he had shown leniency toward the officers held hostage, which ultimately saved their lives. Shockley and Thompson were transferred from Alcatraz to San Quentin State Penitentiary across the Bay.

The prisoners' time on San Quentin's "Condemned Row" was not spent idly. In October of 1947, Thompson and another inmate were discovered to be making a contraband key, as part of what was thought to be a plot to escape. San Quentin Warden Clinton Duffy had warned Warden Johnston that Shockley and Thompson were apparently plotting a "*spectacular dash out of the Condemned Row.*" Thompson wrote several letters to Duffy claiming that officers were trying to exploit him. In one specific letter he wrote that pictures from his cell had been confiscated following the May '46 events, and had been published in a detective magazine. He wrote frequently to his brother Horace in Alabama, and in nearly all of his letters he commented that he was the victim of a "*frame-up.*" The two inmates were afforded minimal interaction with each other while on Condemned Row. Most of their time together would transpire during the appeals of their death sentences.

The sentences of both Shockley and Thompson were appealed to higher courts. On March 10, 1948 the Ninth Court of Appeals confirmed the convictions, and on June 17, 1948, the Supreme Court denied their petition and ordered their execution. Nevertheless, Thompson continued to vehemently deny any role in the death of Miller. In a letter written to President Harry Truman on August 11, 1948, he pleaded that he had not had proper resources to defend himself, stating that he had only been educated to the third grade level, and thus that he was ill-prepared to deal with legal matters. Thompson added that even though it had been proven that Joseph Paul Cretzer had murdered the guard, he himself "*was somehow found guilty*" of the same crime.

On December 2, 1948 the Death Watch Squad moved inmates Shockley and Thompson into two adjacent holding cells on Death Row. It is documented that Shockley did not appear to fully comprehend his fate, and that Thompson was nervous and spent much of his time with the San Quentin Chaplain. He had little appetite in his final hours, and reportedly chain-smoked throughout the night. Shockley refused any religious support, and spent his time meeting with a few relatives, including his niece Anna, who had supported him during the trial and lived close by in the town of Richmond.

On the morning of December 3, 1948 at 7:00 A.M., two years after the violent escape attempt, the two prisoners were seated in adjacent cells for their final meal. At 9:35 A.M., the cyanide pellets were fastened into place inside

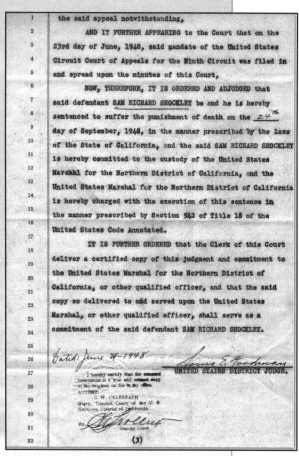

A court order for Shockley's execution.

the gas chamber. At 9:50 A.M., visitors started to line the Witness Room facing the airtight octagonal steel chamber. There were three officers from Alcatraz in attendance to witness the execution. The two inmates were walked side by side into the chamber, with Shockley seated first, followed by Thompson. Ironically the next person to enter the chamber was Dr. Leo Stanley, who had helped to treat the injured officers during the events of '46. He affixed a remote tube stethoscope to each of the prisoners' chests, and then exited to monitor the proceedings from outside the chamber. The two prisoners were seated in adjacent steel chairs, with leather straps pulled tightly around their wrists, ankles, and chests. Judge Goodman had ordered U.S. Marshal George Vice to carry out the execution of both men, and he stood in the doorway with Warden Duffy, who asked the men if they had any final words. Shockley uttered angry slurs, and Thompson sat quietly. The steel door was swung closed, and a guard turned a mechanism that resembled the hatch of a submarine, pneumatically sealing the chamber.

At 10:04 A.M., Warden Duffy nodded the signal to allow the small fluid wells under each man's chair to begin filling with sulfuric acid. As the curtains were opened, the men peered at the witnesses sitting outside the chamber. One minute later, the cyanide pellets were dropped into the sulfuric acid pans. It was later stated that both men strained violently against the straps as they breathed in the deadly gas. At 10:12 A.M., the two men were pronounced dead. At 10:15 A.M. the eyewitnesses left the Witness Room, and the five-man execution team started to clear the gas from the chamber in order to remove the corpses. The sulfuric acid was neutralized by flushing the seat wells with distilled water. A powerful blower fan connected to a large duct on top of the chamber was used to dissipate the residual gases. The bodies of the prisoners were carefully pulled from the seats, and their clothing was removed and incinerated.

Thompson was shipped to Harry M. William's Mortuary in San Rafael, and when his brother Horace was unable to claim his body, he was buried in grave plot #235 at the Marin County Farm Cemetery on December 9, 1948. Shockley's remains were taken to Kenton's Mortuary for embalming, and then shipped back to his sister Myrtle in Oklahoma. As an interesting endnote, Warden Duffy, who had overseen the execution of the two inmates, had long opposed the death penalty. But while he opposed the practice of execution, he did believe that the inmates executed were unquestionably guilty of the crimes for which they were convicted. He later wrote: *"I have never presided over the execution of an innocent person, although several of the ninety whose deaths I ordered . . . claimed innocence right up to the last minute. The evidence against these people was so convincing that I seriously doubt miscarriages of justice."*

Thompson and Shockley were both sentenced to die in the gas chamber at San Quentin. They were executed seated side by side on December 3, 1948

Following the trial of the inmates, Clarence Carnes was returned to Alcatraz, and he remained in segregation until 1952. Carnes was celled next to Robert Stroud, and he would develop a lasting relationship with the "Birdman of Alcatraz." Stroud took fondly to his new pupil, and taught him to play chess. By the time Carnes had integrated back into

(Right) Miran Thompson was buried in this peaceful unmarked graveyard, located in the foothills of Marin County. His grave is just a few feet from the tree seen in the foreground.

the normal prison population, he had been the titleholder of the institution's chess championships for over ten years. After years of imprisonment, Carnes became a model inmate, and began to thrive in the prison environment. He would remain at Alcatraz up until a few months before its closure in 1963, when he was transferred to the Federal Prison Medical Adjustment Center in Springfield Illinois to undergo gallbladder surgery. Following his recovery he would be transferred to Leavenworth, and then paroled on Christmas Eve of 1973. Carnes moved in with his sister in Kansas City, but he found life outside of prison confusing and difficult. After having spent the majority of his life incarcerated, he found freedom overwhelming, and he took to heavy drinking and habitual drug use. He eventually violated parole, and was sent back to Leavenworth for a short period.

In late 1978 Carnes' life story was dramatized in a screenplay, which was later produced as a made-for-television movie entitled *Alcatraz— The Whole Shocking Story*. Carnes worked as a consultant on the production, and a fellow inmate reported that he was paid $20,000 for the story. Carnes lived a short interlude of luxury and fame, which in the end would lead him only to a harder fall. He spent a brief period back at Alcatraz after it was opened as a national park, meeting with the public and talking about his experiences. The movie aired on the NBC Television Network on November 5–6 in 1980, featuring some of Hollywood's most accomplished actors, including Academy Award winner Art Carney in the role of Robert Stroud. But when the money from the film finally ran out, Carnes found himself homeless on the streets of Missouri. He suffered from ill health, and eventually found his way back to prison after purposely violating parole in order to get off the streets. He died in 1988 at the Springfield Facility at the age of sixty-one. His story would again be told in another made-for-television special, based on the book *Six Against the Rock* by Clark Howard. The feature presentation was aired on NBC-TV, on May 18, 1987.

Ed Miller retired less than a year after the incident, and moved back to Leavenworth, where he had begun his career with the Bureau of Prisons. He died in March of 1967 at age seventy-seven. Robert Baker finished out his career at Alcatraz and later retired to Napa, California, in the heart of the wine country; he died in March of 1978 at age sixty-seven. Robert Bristow took a custodian job for a school district in Sacramento, where he lived throughout his retirement. Ernest Lageson became a schoolteacher in nearby Pittsburg, California, and died tragically of cancer at the young age of forty-two. Lieutenant Joe Simpson died on January 31, 1960, and was buried at Fort Leavenworth.

Cecil D. Corwin recovered from his wounds, and returned to work in the prison system. He continued to have medical problems as a result of his injuries, including blindness in his left eye, and was declared permanently disabled in May of 1948. Cecil and his wife Catheryn moved to Stockton, California, where he undertook studies in psychiatry. He later moved to Pomona, California, and worked as a psychiatric technician for the remainder of his career. He retired to Long Beach, California, and suffered a fatal heart attack in July of 1967. Joe Burdett retired to Woodland, California, and died in October of 1983 at age eighty-seven. Carl W. Sundstrom retired to Alameda, California, directly across the Bay from Alcatraz, and died in March of 1973 at age sixty-seven. Irving Levinson retired to Lake Ellsinore in Southern California, and died in 2002. Officer Elmus Besk remained in San Francisco following his career at Alcatraz, and passed away at the age of sixty-one, before reaching his retirement, in March of 1972. Ed Stucker remained in the Bay Area and retired to Palo Alto, California; he died on March 11, 1990, at age eighty-six. Isaac Faulk also remained in the Bay Area following his departure from Alcatraz, and sought other employment opportunities. He retired to Novato, California, and died in December of 1986 at age eighty-seven.

Henry W. Weinhold was classified as permanently disabled due to his injuries, and lived out his retirement across the Bay from Alcatraz in Marin; he died in April of 1967 at age seventy-six. Bert A. Burch moved to Arizona and retired in Coconino; he died in November of 1974 at seventy-three. Emil Rychner remained in San Francisco following his long career on The Rock and passed away in January of 1980 at age eighty-six. San Quentin Warden Clinton Duffy retired and successfully authored two books about his life as the Warden of San Quentin. Duffy and his wife Gladys retired to Walnut Creek, California, where he died in October of 1982 at eighty-four. Cretzer's brother-in-law Arnold Kyle was paroled in his senior years, and died in November of 1980 in Lynnwood, Washington at age seventy-one.

Clifford Fish had one of the most prominent careers on Alcatraz, serving from August of 1938 until March of 1962. In total he worked for twenty-four years on the island, serving the majority of his time in the Control Center. Fish retired to Grass Valley, California, and passed away in November of 2002. He remained an extraordinary historian of 1946 events.

CONDUCT RECORD

DEPARTMENT OF JUSTICE
Penal and Correctional Institutions

U. S. PENITENTIARY   ALCATRAZ, CALIFORNIA
(Institution)   (Location)

Record of.. THOMPSON, Miran Edgar   No... 729-AZ
FPI—LK—4-7-48—4M—688-8

Date	Prison Violations	Days Lost
5-4-46	Joining in desperate escape attempt, and riot with other inmates attacking officers, with use of firearms & other weapons, causing death to officers & wounding others, May 2, 1946. TO SOLITARY A-BLOCK, 5-4-46.	
5-10-46	OUT OF SOLITARY INTO SEGREGATION D BLOCK	
12-21-46	FOUND GUILTY OF MURDER IN FIRST DEGREE BY JURY AT SAN FRANCISCO, CALIFORNIA AND SENTENCED TO DEATH, SAME DAY. 12-27-46 TRANSFERRED TO SAN QUENTIN, CALIF. ST. PRISON.	
	Date of Execution set for Sept. 24, 1948, by Judge Louis Goodman, on June 29, 1948. Executed 12-3-48 S.Q. gas chamber	

Phil Bergen led a remarkable career navigating his way up the promotional ladder of the Federal Bureau of Prisons, and enjoyed a sixteen-year term of service at Alcatraz. Following the escape events of '46, he received a promotion to Captain of the Guards. In 1955, he accepted the position of Associate Warden in La Tuna, Texas, and then was promoted to Correctional Inspector for the Bureau in Washington D.C. In this capacity, he would help to investigate the 1963 Morris-Anglin Escape at Alcatraz. Bergen remained as one of the great Alcatraz historians until his death on June 16, 2002.

The Battle of Alcatraz endures as one the most significant events in the entire history of criminal imprisonment. Of all the inmates who participated in escapes over the years at Alcatraz, Bernie Coy was the only one who successfully devised a workable plan to secure weapons, and then managed to use them in his break for freedom. After the escape attempt, the correctional staff would look differently upon some of the more trusted convicts. Even the men who held the roles of "passmen" were restricted from work until stricter measures were implemented. The question of why the three inmates chose death over life in their final hours will forever remain as one of the true mysteries of Alcatraz.

Fifty years after the Battle of Alcatraz, former inmate Jim Quillen (right), who was barricaded inside D Block during the incident, and officer Phil Bergen (left), who led the assault teams into the West Gun Gallery, met with the author in 1997 to recount the 1946 events from the inside perspective. They are seen here looking up at the West Gallery where Phil Bergen was positioned during the events. At the time, it would have been unthinkable that fifty years later they would become friends, and reflect on the events together. Both men have since passed away.

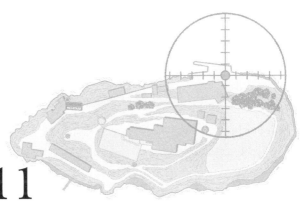

Escape Attempt #11

DATE: JULY 23, 1956
INMATE: FLOYD P. WILSON
LOCATION: PRISON DOCK

Floyd P. Wilson

Born in Chilhowie, Virginia on March 22, 1915, Floyd P. Wilson's life would begin with a hard luck story that eventually led to murder. In the cold winter of 1947, Wilson was a jobless carpenter when he set out to steal seventeen dollars for a ton of coal to heat his near-freezing home in Maryland. He was desperately trying to support his wife and five young children, and as he would later testify, he was *"trying to keep them from freezing to death."* Distraught and cold, he decided to prey upon a young food market messenger who was driving to a local bank with a cash deposit of $10,162 from the store where he worked. The messenger apparently resisted, and Wilson would later testify that everything seemed to move in slow motion as he opened fire on the innocent man. Floyd watched in horror as his victim dropped to the ground in a pool of blood. Floyd was quickly identified as the perpetrator of the crime, and he soon found himself in a Washington, D.C. jail cell awaiting trial.

Wilson ultimately received a conviction for first-degree murder, and he was sentenced to death by electrocution on June 27, 1947. His attorneys appealed the verdict, stating that Wilson was only a desperate man trying to support his ailing family. He was presented to the court as an honorable family man who had been reduced to crime because of his inability to find work. On August 3, 1948 President Harry Truman proved sympathetic to Wilson's case, and in consideration of the mitigating circumstances, he commuted the death sentence to life in prison. Wilson was transferred to the Federal Penitentiary at Atlanta in April of 1949. Shortly thereafter, he was found in possession of a rope and some pipe segments, which officials speculated

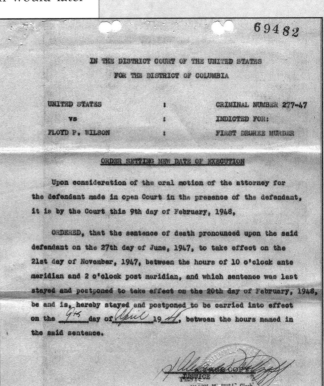

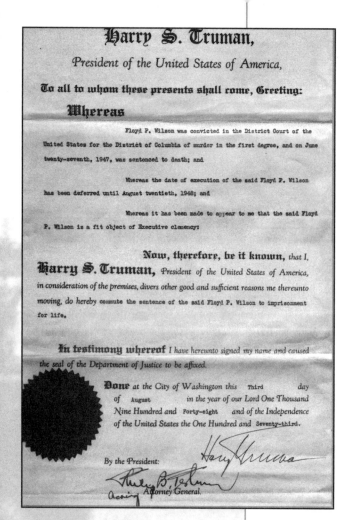

Floyd P. Wilson was convicted in the District Court of the United States for the District of Columbia of murder in the first degree, and on June twenty-seventh, 1947, was sentenced to death; and

Whereas the date of execution of the said Floyd P. Wilson has been deferred until August twentieth, 1948; and

Whereas it has been made to appear to me that the said Floyd P. Wilson is a fit object of Executive clemency:

Now, therefore, be it known, that I, Harry S. Truman, President of the United States of America, in consideration of the premises, divers other good and sufficient reasons me thereunto moving, do hereby commute the sentence of the said Floyd P. Wilson to imprisonment for life.

In testimony whereof I have hereunto signed my name and caused the seal of the Department of Justice to be affixed.

Done at the City of Washington this Third day of August in the year of our Lord One Thousand Nine Hundred and Forty-eight and of the Independence of the United States the One Hundred and Seventy-third.

By the President:
Acting Attorney General.

President Harry Truman was sympathetic to Wilson's case, and commuted his sentence to life imprisonment in 1948.

were likely intended for use in an escape attempt. Based on the length of his sentence and his high risk of escape, he was recommended for transfer to Alcatraz.

Floyd P. Wilson arrived at Alcatraz on January 6, 1952, and was registered as inmate AZ-956. His conduct report reflects a man completely in conflict with his environment. While it was common knowledge that a significant percentage of inmates never fully adjusted to the rigid regimen of the penitentiary, this was especially evident with Floyd. Within his first year at Alcatraz, he received multiple disciplinary reports for insubordination and poor job performance. These reports reveal that Wilson rarely interacted with fellow inmates, and generally limited his conversation to correctional staff and older inmates.

Even in later years, Wilson minimized his interactions with prisoners as much as possible and insisted that he be fed separately, claiming that other inmates had threatened to kill him. It was also documented that over the course of his imprisonment at Alcatraz, Floyd rarely visited the recreation yard. When he did, he kept to himself. He preferred to spend his leisure time reading in his cell.

On July 23, 1956 Wilson was assigned to the dock crew, and after a routine count in the late afternoon, he disappeared without a trace. His only hope for an escape to the mainland lay in a length of rope that he planned to use to tie logs together. Once he reached the water's edge, he would try to collect wood and construct a makeshift raft. Warden Madigan best described the details of Wilson's escape in a memo written to the Bureau of Prisons Director on July 27, 1956:

July 27, 1956
DIRECTOR, Bureau of Prisons
Warden Madigan—Alcatraz
Attempted Escape—Floyd P. Wilson, Reg. No 956-AZ

The following is an account of the events occurring on the afternoon of July 23rd when inmate Floyd P. Wilson, Reg. No. 956-AZ ran from the dock crew and was able to hide out on the island for a period of several hours.

Four inmates were assigned to the dock crew that day, plus one inmate assigned to the garbage pick up detail. At 3:25 P.M. when the launch was due to leave on a scheduled trip, the water barge was also about to leave, and the inmates were called on the line for counting purposes which is customary procedure. The four dock inmates were on the line and the garbage truck, with Officer Jones and one inmate, had arrived at a position under #1 Dock Tower at that exact time. Mr. Jones stopped his truck until the boat and barge had cleared the docks. He then drove to the dock proper, let the inmate out of his truck and went about his duties, but told us later that he saw inmate Wilson take a rubber automobile tire and throw it on the bonfire that was burning at the end of the dock. This created some black smoke that belched up, but not too much thought was given to this fact because Wilson had spent most of the day in burning excess refuse that had been around the dock.

At 3:40 a routine count was made by Mr. Black, Dock Officer in Charge, and all inmates were present. At 3:50 P.M. just as the launch "McDowell" was returning from the mainland, the inmates were called to the line where they could be easily counted, and Wilson was missing. A hasty search was made but he was not found so a call was put into the control center advising that Wilson

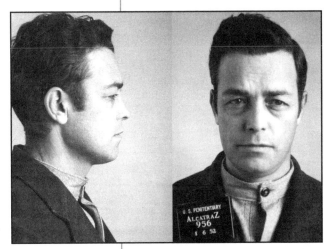

(Above and below) Floyd P. Wilson

was not present. The alarm was sounded on the island and in the matter of a few minutes the Evening Watch Officers and several officers on their day off arrived on the launch. These men were all pressed into service and started searching around the East end of the Island since it was felt that Wilson had gotten thorough the fence surrounding the end of the dock. Searchers immediately found an area near the bonfire Wilson had been attending where the fence was pried up which would permit him to crawl through and follow the sea-wall around until he was out of eyesight of #1 Tower Officer.

The FBI, plus the San Francisco Police Department, Coast Guard, Fort Mason and Presidio Military Police were immediately notified and our escape plan put into operation. All posts were covered and ten searching parties from two to three men each were sent out to several predetermined areas. The Coast Guard immediately sent two patrol boats which surrounded the island regularly, and the FBI sent a large number of officers to Fort Mason and the Fort Mason Dock, as well

as Dock #4 where our launch lands. San Francisco Police covered the waterfront and the piers opposite Alcatraz, and they in turn notified the various Sheriffs and Highway Patrol. By all estimates Wilson had about a ten-minute start before searchers were out on his trail. He certainly did not have much time to secrete himself in that period, but was able to avoid detection until 2:55 A.M. the next morning.

My wife and I arrived at Dock #4 at 5:15 P.M. and quickly saw the activity around the dock and the patrolling by the Coast Guard Boats at Alcatraz. One of our officers notified me immediately that Wilson was missing, and it was the first thought of everyone that he had probably been able to secrete himself on the water barge and might have reached the mainland. Until

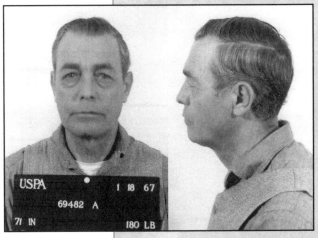

I had talked to Mr. Jones after arriving on the island, I was convinced he was probably on the barge, however, Mr. Jones was so positive that he had seen him throwing the rubber tire on the fire at approximately 3:40 P.M. that I was convinced then he was hidden somewhere in the island.

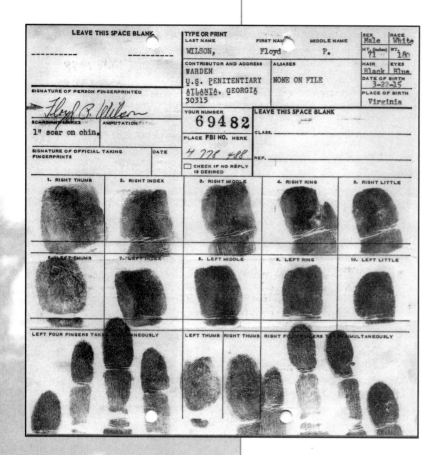

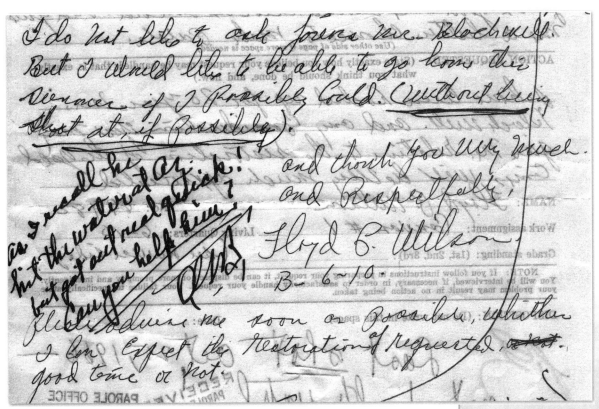

An excerpt from a letter written to Warden Blackwell by Floyd Wilson while he was serving time at the Federal Penitentiary in Atlanta. Both Wilson and Blackwell were Alcatraz alumni. Wilson requested that his "good time" be restored, in consideration of his upcoming parole hearing. Floyd displayed a sense of humor in his letter, stating: *"I would like to go home this summer if I possibly could—without being shot at, if possible."* Wilson was paroled in 1971.

In going over what transpired that evening with Mr. Willingham, it does not seem that our officers were derelict in their duty, however this hideout points out clearly that we must take further precautions in order to have a officer watching these men at all times. During the course of the day when freight is coming and going, and the dock is a very busy place, it seems easier to watch the men than in a situation such as confronted us at this time. Two of the inmates were in the process of changing clothes and getting ready to go into the institution; the inmate mechanic was doing some work around a truck in the garage, while Wilson who usually is a lone wolf type and stays off by himself, apparently was able to scamper under the hole in the fence under cover of the smoke produced by the burning tire.

We have one satisfaction of knowing that our procedure was tight enough to prevent any of these men from getting on the water barge, but we are red-faced in the fact that Wilson was able to elude us for the number of hours that he did.

P. J. MADIGAN
Warden

Wilson remained at Alcatraz until its closure in 1963. He was then transferred to the Federal Penitentiary in Atlanta, and only a few months later to Lorton Reformatory in Virginia. In August of 1966 it was documented that he had once more assembled contraband materials for use in another escape attempt. He remained a problematic inmate until his parole on April 5, 1971. Upon his release Wilson went back to the trade

of carpentry, and returned to Maryland where he had been living prior to his arrest. His parole report states that once he returned to normal civilian life, he seemed to adjust well despite his years of incarceration. A 1972 report read: *"Floyd Wilson has led a rather quiet and orderly life since his release on parole. He visits with relatives, enjoys sports, and engages in other reputable pursuits when not working."* Wilson died of natural causes in January of 1974.

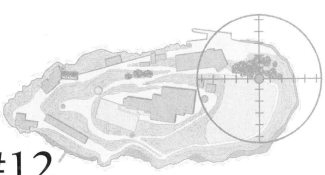

Escape Attempt #12

DATE: SEPTEMBER 29, 1958

INMATES: AARON WALTER BURGETT

CLYDE MILTON JOHNSON

LOCATION: OUTSIDE GARBAGE DETAIL (southeast island area near the family residences)

O n a murky September afternoon in 1958, Clyde Johnson and Aaron Burgett were to engage in what would be the last forceful escape attempt ever made on Alcatraz. Both inmates had been assigned to an outside garbage detail, and they were accompanied by a solo officer tasked to supervise their activities as they walked freely outside the normally authorized perimeter. Using a smuggled paring knife, a rope and some tape, they overpowered the unsuspecting guard, and bound and tied him to a eucalyptus tree. They then slipped away under the cover of heavy fog . . .

Clyde Milton Johnson

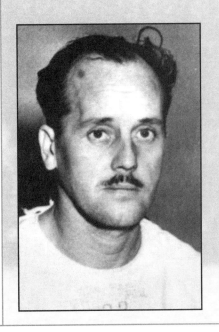

Clyde Milton Johnson was born in Minneapolis, Minnesota on August 16, 1918, the second of two siblings. Johnson's father, whose profession was officially listed as a "truck driver," died when Clyde was only two years of age. With no other means of financial support, his mother relocated the family to Glendale, California, where she secured exhausting employment as a laundress. Johnson's file shows no record of delinquency as a juvenile, but after joining the Army in 1941 he deserted on several occasions, and during the same period he was linked to twelve Safeway grocery store robberies. He was sentenced to serve one year to life at San Quentin State Penitentiary, and was dishonorably discharged from the Army in 1943.

After his release in 1949, Johnson and an accomplice committed an armed robbery in a Memphis bank, making off with $43,662 in cash. They made their getaway in a stolen car, and were later apprehended in Florida, in February of the same year. While awaiting extradition at the Dade County Jail, the two convicts were able to escape with the help of

ESCAPE ATTEMPT #12   373

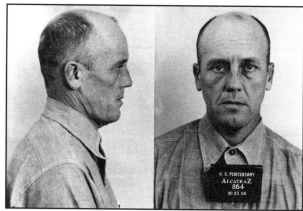

(Above and below) A mug shot series of inmate Clyde Milton Johnson. Taken during the period from 1949 until 1993, these photographs illustrate the effects of a lifetime of incarceration. Johnson and fellow inmate Aaron Burgett bound and gagged a guard at knifepoint during their attempt to escape from The Rock.

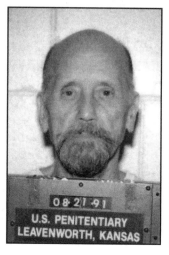
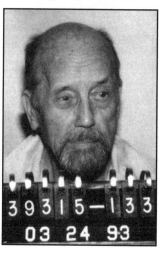

Johnson's girlfriend, Billie Hayes, would commit four other robberies before being apprehended again in April. FBI documents show that Johnson resisted arrest and fired upon FBI agents during his capture. Johnson had been listed by the FBI as Public Enemy Number Two, and was believed to have committed numerous armed robberies across the United States. On July 13, 1949 he was sentenced to serve forty years in a Federal Penitentiary.

Johnson arrived at the Federal Penitentiary in Atlanta on August 10, 1949, and then was transferred to Leavenworth on November 19, 1949. In view of his long sentence and his high escape risk, he was recommended for transfer to Alcatraz. His transfer recommendation reads: *"He has escaped on several occasions and is considered a serious escape risk at this time. He has committed a number of armed robberies, is considered a vicious gunman who thinks nothing of the lives of others and will stop at nothing less than murder to meet his goal."* He would arrive at Alcatraz on March 22, 1950, as inmate AZ-864.

Aaron Walter Burgett

Aaron Burgett was born on October 24, 1929, in Potts Camp, Missouri. His mother had died of an illness when he was only three years old, and his father worked to support the family as a Railway Section Hand, and later as a cotton picker. Burgett's inmate record would indicate that his father had had trouble caring for the young Aaron during his childhood. Burgett's nickname "Wig" was given to him by his father, because of his long blond curls. The death of Aaron's mother weighed heavily on the family, and his father was only a minimal presence in the home, as he attempted to maintain employment in order to support his ten children. At only sixteen years of age Aaron dropped out of school to work on the family's small farm, but this would prove to be only a brief interlude. On April 20, 1945, the young Burgett was arrested for breaking into a candy truck, and sentenced to serve two years at the State Training School in Booneville, Missouri. After serving out nearly a full year, Burgett and another accomplice successfully escaped from the minimum-security institution. In close succession, he would be captured, released, and then arrested again for other burglary-related crimes.

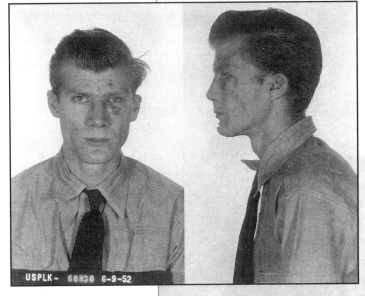

Aaron Walter Burgett

On April 4, 1948, Burgett was committed to the State Penitentiary in Jefferson City, Missouri, after being charged with *stealing chickens in the night time and breaking escape from the county jail.* But despite his early problems, he did experience some good luck as well. In February of 1951, after his release from prison, Burgett met a young girl named Mary Frances Cauley at a party. The couple courted for several months, and then married in Piggott, Arkansas, on August 25, 1951. By Burgett's account, this would be the best year of his life—but trouble was not far away. Burgett was unable to hold a steady job, and this began to create friction between him and his wife, who was now pregnant. He fell back into a life of crime, and by 1952, Burgett had established himself as a career felon.

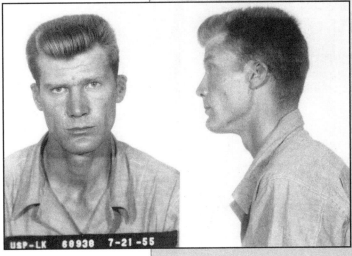

Burgett and his accomplices Earl Wilhelm and John Oliver would go on a spree of over thirty armed robberies in the St. Louis area, some of which turned seriously violent. Generally they robbed their victims by having them lie on the floor while they emptied cash registers and removed personal jewelry. On some occasions, the victims would be struck with the guns. Burgett's robbery targets ranged from post offices to beer taverns, and during one episode, a gunfight ensued in which Wilhelm and a patron were injured by gunfire. On May 16, 1952, Missouri State Trooper David Walker apprehended the trio, who were packing eight loaded guns. All three men would

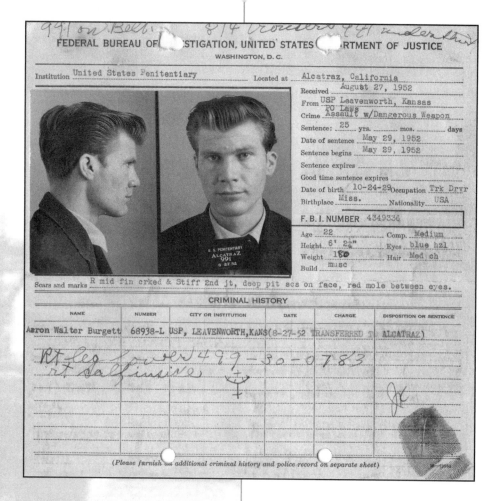

FEDERAL BUREAU OF INVESTIGATION, UNITED STATES DEPARTMENT OF JUSTICE
WASHINGTON, D.C.

Institution **United States Penitentiary** Located at **Alcatraz, California**

Received **August 27, 1952**
From **USP Leavenworth, Kansas**
Crime **PO Laws / Assault w/Dangerous Weapon**
Sentence: **25** yrs. _____ mos. _____ days
Date of sentence **May 29, 1952**
Sentence begins **May 29, 1952**
Sentence expires _____
Good time sentence expires _____
Date of birth **10-24-29** Occupation **Trk Drvr**
Birthplace **Miss.** Nationality **USA**

F.B.I. NUMBER **4349336**

Age **22** Comp. **Medium**
Height **6' 2½"** Eyes **blue hzl**
Weight **150** Hair **Med ch**
Build **musc**

Scars and marks **R mid fin crkd & stiff 2nd jt, deep pit scs on face, red mole between eyes.**

CRIMINAL HISTORY

NAME	NUMBER	CITY OR INSTITUTION	DATE	CHARGE	DISPOSITION OR SENTENCE
Aaron Walter Burgett	68938-L	USP, LEAVENWORTH, KANS	8-27-52	TRANSFERRED TO ALCATRAZ)	

(Please furnish an additional criminal history and police record on separate sheet)

stand trial and plead guilty, and each defendant was sentenced to serve twenty-five years in a Federal institution.

Then on June 9, 1952, while Burgett and his two co-defendants were being transported to the Federal Penitentiary at Leavenworth, Kansas by a Deputy Marshal and a prison guard, Burgett made a desperate attempt to escape. The inmates had been shackled to one another with chains and handcuffs, with Burgett seated in the middle of the back seat, and at around 2:50 A.M. prison guard LeRoy Tozer dropped a lighted cigarette onto the seat beside him. Burgett pleaded to the Marshal to pull over, as the cigarette was burning the seat and his clothing. Tozer ordered Burgett to raise himself so he could reach under him and grab the cigarette. Tozer found the cigarette, and started rolling down the window to throw it out. As he turned toward the window, Burgett threw his legs over Tozer to pin him down on the seat. Using great force, he then kicked the back of Deputy Marshal Davidson's head several times, knocking his glasses off and throwing his head forward into the steering wheel, which forced the car to veer off the road.

As the car came to a halt at the side of the roadway, Davidson drew his pistol and Tozer forcefully restrained Burgett, leaving multiple cuts and bruises about his face. On arrival at Leavenworth, Burgett still refused to cooperate, and stated that he would rather die than be forced to serve his time there. This event would buy him his ticket to Alcatraz, in consideration of the length of his sentence. He would arrive on Alcatraz as inmate AZ-991, on August 27, 1952.

At Alcatraz, Burgett briefly enjoyed a reputation as a good inmate. His progress report states that he enjoyed playing cards and table games in the recreation yard. He also played the Hawaiian guitar and subscribed to the magazine *Flying*, and he purchased books on system navigation and other related subjects. It is speculated that Burgett planned his escape from The Rock for several months in advance, collecting sections of raincoats, plywood, and electrician's tape over a long period of time.

Alcatraz Guard Harold Miller had worked as a casket maker before entering the prison service. He was only twenty-seven years of age, and had been working at Alcatraz for about ten months. The garbage assignment was a tough and potentially dangerous detail for the correctional staff. Inmates on this detail would sometimes trim trees and shrubbery, and had access to sharpened gardening tools, even including axes. Inmates had to possess good conduct records to be chosen for this detail, as it was considered a privileged assignment. Both Burgett and Johnson had been on this detail for nearly six months at the time of their escape attempt. Miller had just started supervising the detail, and this would only be his fourth shift on this assignment.

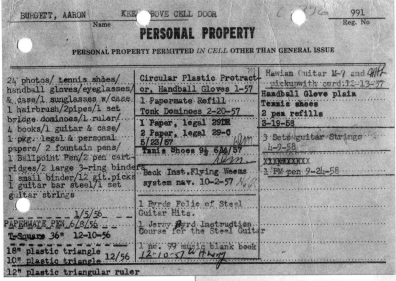

At 2:30 P.M., Miller checked in at the control room, and logged his assignment and report time. Shortly thereafter, the inmates working at the southeast tip of the island made their way down a path to throw some refuse into a bed of century plants. Without warning, Johnson pulled a paring knife on Miller, and Burgett grabbed the unsuspecting guard, taking him to the ground. The inmates warned Miller that if he cooperated, he would not be harmed. Burgett stuffed a piece of clothing into the guard's mouth, and then the two quickly tied his hands with tape, and wrapped more black tape around his head and eyes. The events that followed are described in an interview with Johnson following the inmates' eventual capture:

Subsequent to the capture of inmate Johnson #864, he was interviewed by the Warden and Associate Warden. This interview took place at least an hour after Johnson had been brought to the Administration Building from the Beach. Part of the interview was conducted with both the Warden and Associate Warden, and part of it while the Warden was out of the room.

Johnson states that the officer Mr. Miller made his check call at 2:30 P.M. (Sept. 29, 1958) from the vicinity of the foghorn station. He says that he, Mr. Miller, and inmate Burgett proceeded directly from this station to the gate by the Associate Warden's house and Mr. Kaeppel's cottage. He said that he and Burgett had convinced Mr. Miller that they should go into this area to clean the roadway and drainage outlets. He claims that they had swept up and picked up considerable trash and they suggested to Mr. Miller that they carry the trash over the stone wall and dump the trash down the face of the cliff. He says that they also told Mr. Miller that it was part of their duty to keep the cactus trimmed alongside the pathway leading from the gate to the Beach facing Fisherman's Wharf and that they suggested looking this over to see if it needed trimming.

As they were returning along the path toward the gate, Burgett was in the lead followed by Mr. Miller, with Johnson coming up the rear. Johnson says that a point some 20 feet from the gate they pulled a knife on Mr. Miller and taped his eyes and mouth. They tied his hands behind him and then the two of them guided Mr. Miller directly down the hillside towards the vicinity of the large wooden warning sign. They then went a short distance northward where Mr. Miller was tied to a tree. Johnson states that the two of them then went westward toward the cement steps at the foot of the pathway leaving from the Associate Warden's house. At this point they observed a boat approaching near to the island. They became alarmed and headed back toward the place where they had left Officer Miller. Johnson states that they then examined Mr. Miller's bindings to make sure that he was suffering no ill effects and to be sure that he had not loosened the bindings.

Johnson claims that when they left Mr. Miller the second time that he and Burgett parted company. He repeatedly stated that he had not seen Burgett after parting with him after this point. He says that he continued on westward and finally removed a plastic bag from underneath his sweatshirt where he had been carrying it folded. He says he then inflated this bag to the best of his ability and fastened the opening securely. He says the bag was some 2 x 3 feet in size. Johnson claims that up to this point he had intended to hide out until dark but after inflating the bag he decided to try it immediately. When he stepped in to the water he states that, "the bag was torn from my hands and I lost not only the bag but just about everything I had including my dental plate." He claims that at this time he gave up all hope of escaping, as he did not think it possible to escape by swimming or even floating in the cold water. Johnson also claims that inmate Burgett changed his mind several times; and one time he would argue that they should try to escape into the water as quickly as possible, at another time he would feel that they should wait until dark before getting off the island.

Johnson again and again emphasized the fact that they had picked this particular time for attempting to escape because of the change from daylight savings to standard time. He says that they had waited for this change in order that darkness would come sooner than under daylight savings time. He further admits that the timing at the change of job rotations were definitely to their advantage, inasmuch as the officers were not yet familiar with their new assignments. He steadily maintains that they had not waited for a dense fog but that the fog on the date of the escape was purely accidental so far as their planning was concerned.

When Miller failed to report in at the routine roll call, the other guards immediately launched a search. Within minutes, the piercing sound of the klaxon alarm resonated throughout the island, and radio bulletins went out to the patrol officers on mainland San Francisco. All of the guards were called to duty, and they began the extensive search. Walking in groups of two with one unarmed lead-man and the other carrying a .45 pistol, they were finally able to locate Miller after nearly an hour of searching. Miller was found tied to a tree, unharmed.

A Coast Guard cutter was dispatched to aid in the search, which was hampered by the dense fog. At approximately 5:00 P.M. the Coast Guard managed to locate Johnson, who was standing waist-deep in the fifty-degree water, shivering. They drew their rifles on him, and waited until guards on shore were able to apprehend him. Johnson didn't resist.

In a letter to Burgett's father on October 9, 1958, Warden Madigan wrote that at approximately 3:15 P.M., a member of the staff had heard cries for help, but could not locate where the sound was coming from. A massive search effort was initiated to locate Burgett. It was speculated that he had drowned, as there was a three-knot ebb tide that day, which would have made it impossible for him to swim. Several days later, divers were brought in to search the kelp beds in hopes that they would locate Burgett's body.

On October 12th Alcatraz Guard Lyndon Cropper reported to his assigned post in the road tower, and noticed a body floating a few hundred feet from the eastern end of the island. A Coast Guard patrol boat was dispatched to retrieve the body. In his official report on the incident, Warden Madigan described how the body of Aaron Burgett was identified:

On Sunday, October 12, 1958, at approximately 09:30 A.M., J.B. Latimer, Associate Warden, and I reached Pier No. 45½ in the Fisherman's Wharf area, San Francisco, California. There were two Police Officers, Harbor Patrol Officers, and about five members of the Coast Guard present.

I saw a wire net litter-basket stretcher covered with a blanket and a right and left toe protruding. The stretcher was in the rear section of a small boat. I climbed down a ladder into the boat and partially uncovered a body, which was resting on the stretcher with the front side up. The face was beyond recognition because of the missing flesh and the damaged condition probably due to decomposition and sea life. The putrid odor of decaying flesh was evident. All of the hair was missing from the top of the head, but there was sandy colored hair around the sides and back of the head. Most of the fingers appeared to be in good condition; however, the skin was hanging from some of the fingers and it is probable that the end joints of two fingers were missing. The skin on the inner sides of both thumbs were in good condition. I placed the fingerprint card from Burgett's institutional file beside the right thumb and determined that the two were identical. The ridge counts to the core were identical. Several ending ridges below a line extending from the left to right deltas were identical. All bifurcations, islands, and other characteristics were identical.

A khaki cotton belt commonly worn by prisoners at Alcatraz was around the abdomen, but not passed through the belt loops of the trousers, with the number "991" in large numbers on a white cloth which was sewn on the belt. The body was clothed in a heavy "T" under shirt, white cotton shorts, two pairs prison trousers, a heavy khaki undershirt with the legs through the sleeves and the bottom pinned around the waist, three pairs of socks, and brown low-cut work shoes. A broken piece of plywood was secured to the bottom of the left shoe by means of electricians tape and a copper wire. A cotton bag similar to those carried by inmates to carry dominoes to the

The actual fingerprint card that was used to identify Burgett's body.

exercise yard was fastened to the belt which was buckled in the rear of the body. The bag contained two smooth stones, the larger of which was about two inches in diameter, a roll of black electricians tape about 2½ inches in diameter, about ½ cup sand, approximately 10 feet of cord and shoe laces, and a piece of wire about 10 inches long. The large stenciled numbers, "991" appeared on the belt, undershirt, underwear, and one pair of trousers. The stenciled number, "814" was on the outer pair of trousers. A stainless steel knife was removed by one of the morgue officers and retained by me. This knife was enclosed in plastic, initialed, and submitted to the Warden. The teeth appeared to be in good condition. The body was then covered with a blanket and removed to by uniformed City Morgue Officers to the City Morgue, 650 Merchant Street, San Francisco, California.

Mr. Latimer and I then went to the City Morgue where I watched the clothing being removed form the body. The body measured 6 feet and 2 inches in length and weighed 228 pounds. The inside surface of the right calf of the leg had the tattoo, "499-30-0783", in large blue-black numbers. (This is the number on Burgett's Social Security card now in his personal belongings.) There was also a "pachuco" tattoo in the form of an "X", arc with rays, and a cross, below the series of numbers and upside down when viewed from the feet.

The officers at the Morgue assured me that their technicians would obtain pictures of the corpse and fingerprints for the institution. A copy of the dental chart furnished by Agent Keith, F.B.I., was placed with the body and the remains were wheeled into the refrigeration room.

It is my opinion, based upon my acquaintance with inmate Burgett, clothing commonly worn by inmates at Alcatraz, the stiff right middle finger, tattoo marks, identical ridges on the fingers with the fingerprint cards on file, weight and measurements of the corpse, and other features, that the body was that of Aaron Walter Burgett, Reg. No. 991-AZ, beyond any reasonable doubt.

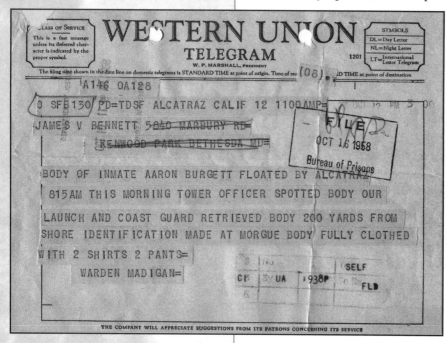

Burgett's body was released to Godeau Funeral Directors on Van Ness Avenue in San Francisco.

Clyde Johnson was paroled from prison in 1971. While on parole, he was again convicted of armed bank robbery, assault with a deadly weapon, assaulting a Federal officer, and attempted escape. He was sentenced to serve thirty-six years for his crimes. In August of 1994, Johnson was diagnosed with lymphoma of the stomach and colon. He died at the Men's Federal Correctional Institution in Lexington, Kentucky on October 29, 1995.

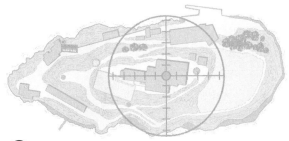

Escape Attempt #13

DATE: JUNE 11, 1962
INMATES: FRANK LEE MORRIS
JOHN AND CLARENCE ANGLIN
ALLEN CLAYTON WEST
LOCATION: MAIN CELLHOUSE (B-BLOCK)

The "Escape from Alcatraz"

If there was ever an inmate who was destined to escape from Alcatraz, it was Frank Lee Morris. In the 1979 movie *Escape from Alcatraz*, Clint Eastwood accurately portrayed Morris as the brilliant mastermind of one of the most famous prison escapes in history. The escape plan took nearly seven months to design, and required the fabrication of clever decoys and water survival gear. Today it is considered one of the most ingenious escape plans ever attempted.

The classic motion picture *"Escape from Alcatraz"* featured Academy Award-winning actor Clint Eastwood in an amazingly accurate portrayal of Frank Morris.

(Right and below) Frank Lee Morris—a chronology of mug shot photographs, representing a hardening lifetime spent in prison. On Morris' Alcatraz admission card, officials listed one of his formal occupations as *"escape artist,"* and noted his superior intelligence. He would escape from nearly every prison to which he was ever committed.

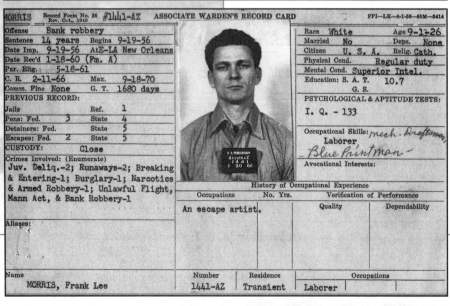

Frank Lee Morris

Frank Lee Morris had spent a lifetime navigating the prison system before his arrival on Alcatraz. From his infant years until his teens, Morris was shuffled from one foster home to another. Frank's years as a toddler are poorly documented, but it is known that he was convicted of his first crime at the youthful age of thirteen. Whether by fate or misfortune, Frank's rudderless course had been dictated by his mother long before his birth. Some sources indicate that his Morris' mother was the daughter of an upper-middle-class family, and that she began her misadventures as a runaway at a very young age.

It is alleged that Frank's mother was in her teens when she found herself pregnant. Frank was born on September 1, 1926, in Ednor Maryland. In his responses to a questionnaire that he completed at sixteen years of age, Frank documented that his mother was born in Ireland, his father was born in Spain, and both were dead (he claimed that his father had died when he was two or three). He went on to reflect that their passing had affected him very deeply. He was raised in foster homes with extremely strict foster parents who delivered harsh discipline, and on occasion he resided with his aunt and her children. His responses to the questionnaire also indicated low self-esteem. In one question asking his opinion of his own appearance, he stated "not so good."

Frank was convicted of his first crime at only thirteen years of age, when he burglarized several homes. He was arrested by the Sheriff's Office in Clarksburg, West Virginia, and was listed as a runaway from Washington. On November 13, 1940, at age fourteen, the young freckled-faced Morris was again arrested for burglary, and was sentenced to six years and nine months. His sentence was to be served at the National Training School for Boys in Washington D.C., not far from the reformatory where his mother had once allegedly been interned. His teachers considered him highly intelligent but difficult to manage and uninterested in his studies. In one incident during his first few weeks of imprisonment at the boys' school, he drew a sexually explicit sketch of his female teacher, including sexual comments and signing it "*from guess who?*"

Morris was prone to violent outbursts, as was illustrated on the morning of July 31, 1941. He had been caught stealing oranges from the kitchen icebox, and was told by the senior officer to put them back. When he refused to obey the order, the officer stated that he would have him benched for three days. But as soon as the officer turned his back, Morris threw a large kitchen knife, which struck him on the blunt side, luckily causing no injury. After receiving harsh discipline for this act, he began planning his escape. Thus began Frank's career in what would later be listed on his Alcatraz record card as his official occupation, that of an "*escape artist.*"

By the time Morris reached his late teens, his criminal record included a multitude of crimes ranging from narcotics possession to armed robbery, and he had become a professional inhabitant of the correctional system. His repeated escapes and quite brazen acts of non-conformity earned him his way to ever-larger penitentiaries. His life was a merry-go-round of short bouts of freedom interspersed with long terms of imprisonment. Meanwhile, he graduated from small burglaries to large bank heists. Then one day in late April 1955, while serving a ten-year sentence in the Louisiana State Penitentiary for armed robbery and possession of narcotics, Morris and fellow inmate Bill Martin were on a work detail cutting sugar cane when both slipped away—and their escape went undetected for several hours.

The fugitives made their way to New Orleans, and after several months of lying low, devised a plan to rob a bank in Kansas City. Because they knew in advance that alarm mechanisms were wired to the bank doors, Morris, Martin, and a third accomplice named Earl Branci decided to cut a hole through the rear wall to minimize the risk of detection. After gaining access, Morris torched through the rear of two vaults, and removed $6,165 in coins, weighing a total of 1,200 pounds. The three men retreated to the home of a woman living in Baton Rouge, where they were harbored for several weeks. Soon after, all of them were apprehended by the FBI. Morris earned a Federal prison term of fourteen years, and he would eventually find his way to Alcatraz.

While serving his Federal term in Atlanta, Morris once more attempted to escape. On September 20, 1959 at 8:30 P.M., prison officer Paul Legg heard a loud crash and ran to see what had happened. He later would report that Morris had run toward him, attempting to conceal his identity, and had subsequently tried to sneak back into his cell without being noticed. Morris was reported, and was sentenced to punitive segregation in addition to forfeiting privileges. In 1960, Federal officials decided that Morris' pattern of escape attempts, termed as "*shotgun freedom*" (although his escapes had never involved the use of a shotgun), would end at The Rock. On January 20, 1960, Morris disembarked from the prison launch, and became inmate #AZ-1441. However, Frank's long history of escape attempts would not end at Alcatraz—on the contrary, he was to go down in the annals of the island prison as one of its most daring escape artists ever.

John and Clarence Anglin

Frank's future accomplices were equally well acquainted with life amid the dark world of organized crime. Brothers John and Clarence Anglin were also serving sentences at Alcatraz for bank robbery. They came from a large Florida family of fourteen children, and had been convicted along with their brother Alfred. On January 17, 1958, the brothers had cased the Bank of Columbia in Alabama, and had made off with nearly $20,000 in cash. Five days later they were apprehended by FBI agents while hiding out in a small two-bedroom apartment in Hamilton, Ohio.

All three brothers served sentences at the Federal Penitentiary in Atlanta, where they first became acquainted with Morris. On April 11, 1958, Clarence Anglin was sent to Leavenworth Penitentiary to be separated from his brothers, though John was soon transferred there as well. Then on October 8, 1960, John was caught assisting Clarence in an escape attempt at Leavenworth. John Anglin was working in the prison bakery at the time, and the escape would involve cutting the top out of one

(Below) John W. Anglin. These mug shot photos illustrate the passage of approximately only two years, but Anglin's physical characteristics show significant changes. Note the handwritten entry on the Associate Warden's Record from Leavenworth (opposite page, top), stating that Anglin was not to be celled with his brother Clarence. At Alcatraz they inhabited neighboring cells in B Block.

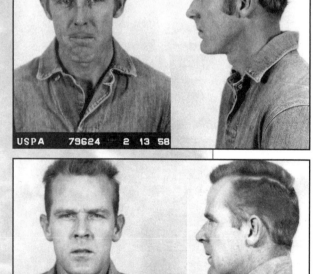

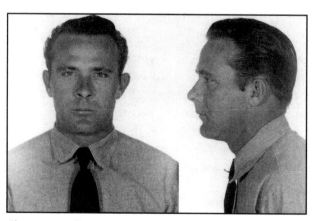

Clarence Anglin

breadbox and the bottom out of another, which provided ample room for Clarence to stand inside when they were stacked one on top of the other. After the breadboxes were stacked and Clarence was safely hidden within, John pushed them into the kitchen elevator—but a prison officer noticed that something was amiss, and halted the escape. Both brothers were subsequently transferred to Alcatraz. John was relocated on October 22, 1960, and Clarence followed on January 16, 1961,

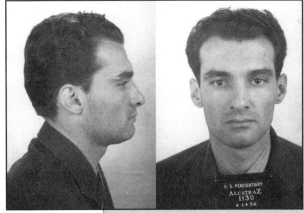

DNA	Record Form No. 86 Rev. Oct. 1940	ASSOCIATE WARDEN'S RECORD CARD		FPI—LK-4-24-59—66M—6640

Offense	Bank Robbery		Race White	Age 29 1931
Sentence	10 yrs Begins 2-10-58		Married Single	Deps. None
Date Imp.	2-10-58 At MD:ALA		Citizen U.S.	Relig. Prot.
Date Rec'd	1-22-60-NE		Physical Cond. Reg. Duty	
P. lig.	6-9-61		Mental Cond. No Report	
C.	12-28-64 Max. 2-9-68		Education: S. A. T. 3/	
Comm. Fine	G. T. 1200		G. S. 18	
PREVIOUS RECORD:	38 EOT		PSYCHOLOGICAL & APTITUDE TESTS:	
Jails	Ref. 1-SIS			
Pens. Fed.	State I		Occupational Skills:	
Detainers: Fed.	State I		Labor	
Escapes: Fed.	State			
CUSTODY: CLOSE			Avocational Interests:	
Crimes Involved: (Enumerate) 1-Inv B & E; 1-PL; 1-Vag; 1-GL				

USP LK 77350 1-25-60

Occupational Experience			
Occupations	No. Yrs.	Verification of Performance	
		Quality	Dependability
5-9½ 160 lbs			

Escape Risk not to cell with his Brother 75456 -

Aliases: None		Name ANGLIN, John William 1476	Number 77350-L	Residence Ruskin, Flor.	Occupations Labor

their transfer records stating the reason for the move as: *"to ensure safer custody."*

John Anglin, now inmate #AZ-1476, was assigned to cell #158 while Clarence, as inmate #AZ-1485, moved into #152. Warden Olin Blackwell had shown some leniency in allowing the brothers to reside in adjacent cells. This privilege also entitled them to sit together during meal periods. Meanwhile Frank Morris, who had been assigned to cell #138 on the same ground-level tier, was already considering the odds of making an escape from the island, and had begun his formative planning.

Allen Clayton West

Convict Allen Clayton West, a native of New York, was also brought into the scheme—though he later claimed that *he* had been the one to design the plan that resulted in the successful escape. Some have strongly disputed his claim, since Morris had previously masterminded similar types of escapes, and pertinent reading materials on fabricating the apparatus used in the escape had been found in his cell. The style of this escape was also reminiscent of Morris' earlier bank heists.

Allen Clayton West would later claim that he had masterminded the escape.

West resided in cell #140 on the same tier as Morris and the Anglins, and regardless of who had actually masterminded the scheme, he proved to be the perfect accomplice. West carried a reputation as an arrogant criminal. He was serving out his second term at Alcatraz for a relatively unglamorous crime, interstate transportation of stolen vehicles. West also had a history of failed and aggressive escape attempts. In one such attempt at a Florida prison, West had held a gun to the Associate Warden's head, demanded his car keys, and then escaped in his car. West had become acquainted with John Anglin while serving time with him at the State Penitentiary in Florida.

Thomas Kent was one of several inmates who helped to smuggle materials that were used in the escape.

The plan for the Alcatraz escape started to take shape in December of 1961. It was a complex strategy that involved the design and fabrication of ingenious lifelike dummies, water rafts, and life preservers, all made from over fifty rain coats acquired from other inmates (some donated and others stolen), and a variety of crudely fashioned tools. In later interviews with the FBI and Alcatraz Prison Officials, West indicated that he had masterminded the escape, and had brought Morris in last of all, after the Anglins. Although it is still unclear who actually conceived the scheme, West's interview provides significant insight into the planning and details of the escape. It establishes that he was at least a key participant, and likely the most reliable source of a specific chronology for the planning sequence and the escape itself.

In the FBI interview, West stated that he began pondering the idea of escaping from Alcatraz in May of 1961. It was apparently common knowledge among inmates that there were eight ventilator holes in the ceiling of C Block that had not been used for several years. The vent covers had allegedly been cemented closed, according to many of the inmates in the general prison population. West stated that during a routine painting assignment he noticed that one of the ventilators had not been cemented shut. He said that after covertly examining the vent opening, he determined that that it would be possible, with minimal labor, to make a successful escape onto the cellhouse roof. West also claimed that during one of his painting assignments he had noticed that there was a vent duct which ran down the side of the cellhouse. He stated that given these two factors, he felt that a well-planned escape could conceivably succeed.

At around this time plumbers were working in the utility corridor, and after they had completed their work, West was ordered to clean out the refuse from inside the narrow space. While cleaning smaller particles from the floor on his hands and knees, he noticed something wrapped in soiled paper and hidden beneath a cement support. When he opened the package, he found that it contained several old rusty saw blades and some makeshift metal files. He guessed that they had been hidden for ten to twenty years, based on their severely rusted condition.

During a routine painting detail, inmate Allen West noticed that one of the roof ventilators had not been cemented shut. This marked the beginning of his collaboration with Morris and the Anglins on one of the greatest prison escapes ever recorded.

West said that sometime after making this discovery he reported his finding to John Anglin, who was apparently already aware of the possibility of escaping through one of the ventilation openings in the roof. The two engaged in a lengthy conversation about the odds of success, and various methods of breaking out of the prison and swimming to the mainland. After considering several other options, one of which involved cutting the cell bars, they determined that the best escape route would be through the six-by-nine-inch iron ventilation grills at the rear of their cells. West explained to Anglin that he had already studied civil engineering references that he had obtained through the prison library, which contained a formula to break down the composite structure of cement by heating it to a temperature of 500 to 900 degrees. He also confided to Anglin that at one point he had obtained element wires similar to those of a bread toaster, and had plugged the wires into the electrical outlet in his cell, but could not generate enough heat to affect the cement.

West alleges that he brought Clarence Anglin and Frank Morris into the scheme in December of 1961. John Anglin had apparently gotten hold of a sharpened spoon, and had started digging around the ventilator grill inside his cell. He had already made significant progress in penetrating the cement. After several weeks' time, the three inmates were all able to procure spoons, and they initiated a concerted digging schedule that began after the 5:30 P.M. count and continued until 9:30 P.M.

Because the Anglins shared adjacent cells and Morris and West were also neighbors, they alternated daily digging schedules while the cellmates opposite stayed on lookout. After nearly a full month of work the inmates had made considerable headway, digging over fifty

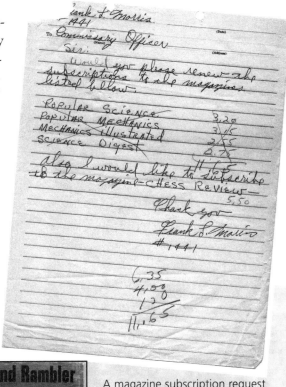

A magazine subscription request by Frank Morris. The list included several technical magazines, including Popular Mechanics, from which Morris would extract useful information on crafting materials to aid in his escape plot.

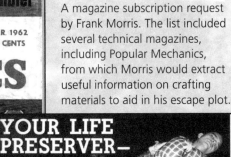

This March 1962 issue of Popular Mechanics was found in Morris' cell, and it was believed to have helped provide him with examples and ideas for fabricating the life vests that were used in the escape.

June H. Stephens

small holes around the perimeter of the vent. The excess debris was flushed down the toilet or brushed back into the corridor. Once each hole was completed, they used a mixture of soap and toilet paper to fill it in, and touch-up paint to conceal the tiny cavities. They also fabricated fake grills out of cardboard, painstakingly matching the paint finish. The fake grills were amazingly convincing and difficult to detect.

Morris and John Anglin finished digging their holes

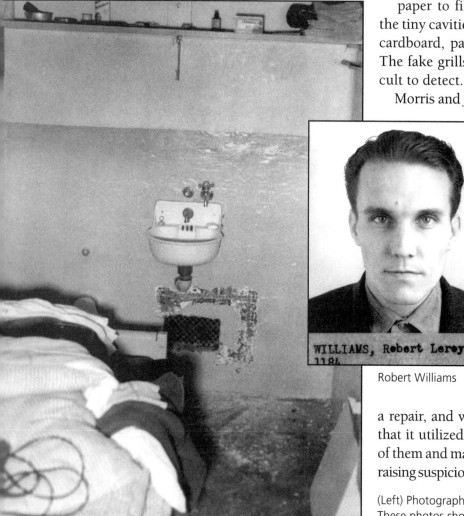

WILLIAMS, Robert Leroy
1184

Robert Williams

first, and John assisted Clarence by digging from the back wall of his cell. West later told officials that he had decided to leave his grill intact, to avoid arousing the suspicion of anyone doing maintenance work in the corridor. In May of 1962, Clarence Anglin was the first to climb the maze of plumbing and make it to the cellblock ceiling. Using a screwdriver, he attempted to loosen the 18½-inch-diameter metal coupling that secured the ventilator, without success. West then learned that the prison's vacuum cleaner was broken. He was permitted to attempt a repair, and while inspecting the machine, he found that it utilized two motors. He carefully removed one of them and managed to get the other working, to avoid raising suspicion. Morris was able to modify the smuggled

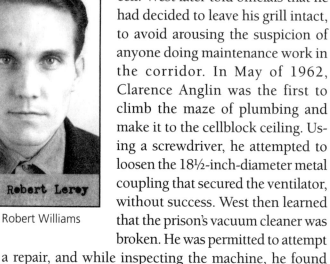

(Left) Photographs showing drill holes around the cell vent grill. These photos show cells B-346 and B-134, the homes of Robert Williams and June Stephens. Both cells were found to have drill holes around the ventilation grills.

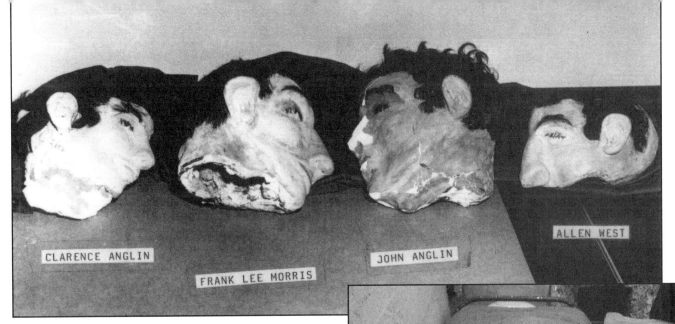

CLARENCE ANGLIN

FRANK LEE MORRIS

JOHN ANGLIN

ALLEN WEST

motor into a motorized drill. They attempted to use it in drilling out the roof ventilator, but achieved only limited success. The motor proved too noisy and not very effective.

After some lobbying, Morris was able to secure a work detail that required him to paint the uppermost areas of the cellblock. He fashioned a clamp out of clasps he had taken from his bed and bolted together, and this tool provided ample leverage to loosen the sticking bolts. He left the ventilator in place to avoid detection. Meanwhile with John's help, Clarence had created their first dummy head. It was crudely fashioned from soap packed over a bundle of white cotton rags, painted with flesh tones from an artist's paint kit, and topped with human hair acquired from the barbershop. In his official statement West remarks that Clarence, in jest, had named the dummy head "Oink."

Using glue stolen from the glove shop, the inmates then started to cut and bond the raincoats into a makeshift raft and life preservers. Each evening following the completion of their self-imposed work details, they would hide the materials on top of the cellblock to minimize any chance of being caught with the contraband goods. The inmates also acquired an elaborate array of forged tools. West was able to lift an electric hair clipper while working on a paint detail in the barbershop. He used the clipper, along with drill bits stolen from the Industries Building by another inmate, to fashion a makeshift motorized drill. The motor later proved too small, and the drill would require something more effective.

After months of preparation, the inmates had fashioned all of the gear they needed to aid them in their escape, and they had

The inmates used clever decoys to fool the guards during the late night counts. The amazingly detailed and lifelike dummy heads that were tucked under the blankets were fashioned primarily from scrap bits and pieces. The materials used included soap chips, concrete, wire, plaster, glue, paint, and hair that had been smuggled from the prison barbershop.

Concealed contraband materials that were used in the escape, and were later found in one of the inmates' cells.

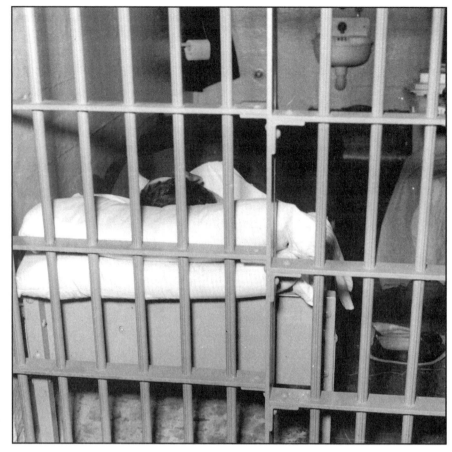

A Photograph of Frank Morris' cell taken on June 12, 1962. This view shows how the cell appeared as the officers conducted their counts on the night of the escape. After lights out at 9:30 P.M., the cellhouse was considerably darker, and the heavy blanketing likely made it difficult to discern the mannequin figures.

meanwhile continued loosening the ventilator grill on top of the cellhouse. John Anglin carefully completed the valve assembly on a six-by-fourteen-foot raft constructed from raincoats. Morris modified an accordion-type musical instrument called a concertina, which would be used to inflate the raft. While the others progressed well in their activities, West fell behind in digging out the ventilator grill at the rear of his cell. His primary role had been to construct the life preservers and special wooden paddles for the raft, which didn't require him to leave his cell.

On the night of June 11, 1962, Morris indicated that the top ventilator was loose enough, and he felt that they were ready to make their attempt. At 9:30 P.M., immediately after lights-out, Morris brought down the dummies from the top of the cellblock and announced that the escape would take place that night. Clarence Anglin attempted to assist West with his grill from the utility corridor, but was unsuccessful. Applying great force and dealing hard kicks to the grill proved futile. In the end, Morris and the Anglins had no choice but to leave West behind. The inmates made their final thirty-foot climb up the plumbing to the cellhouse roof, traveled one hundred feet across the rooftop, and then carefully scaled down the fifty feet of piping to the ground. This would be the last anyone ever saw of Morris and the Anglin Brothers.

By 1:45 A.M. West was finally able to complete the removal of his grill and climb to the rooftop, but by then all of his accomplices had disappeared. With no raft or other means to escape, he was forced to return to his cell. Some of the inmates would later report that they had heard an unusual disturbance among the seagulls during the late evening hours.

On the morning of June 12, 1962 at 7:18 A.M., Correctional Officer Lawrence Bartlett discovered that Frank Morris was missing from his cell. After some verbal prodding, Bartlett had nudged what he thought was Morris' head. When it shockingly rolled off the bed and onto the floor, he then realized that it was only a decoy. Alcatraz immediately went into complete lock-down status with scores of officers deployed in search of the missing inmates. The FBI quickly arrived on Alcatraz, and using bloodhounds they successfully tracked the inmates' path to the water's edge.

In one of the interviews he gave after the escape, Allen West described how their plan had been to use the raft to make their way to Angel Island. After resting, they would reenter the bay on the opposite side of the island and then swim through a waterway called Raccoon Straights and on into Marin. They would steal a car, burglarize a clothing store, and then venture off each in their own direction. West told a correctional officer that he had in fact been the mastermind of the escape. He was immediately taken to A Block under strict isolation precautions. FBI Agents and military personnel combed the bay waters in search of potential leads. The FBI would find several significant pieces of evidence in the bay waters of San Francisco.

On June 14, 1962 one of the search boats found a small eight-by-ten-inch rubber packet floating in an active whirlpool about two or three feet below the water's surface. The location of the find was approximately 2,700 yards off Angel Island, which is a little more than a mile north of Alcatraz. The container was made from the same olive drab material as the inmates' raincoats, and held several personal items believed to have belonged to Clarence Anglin. Inside were seventy-nine photographs of family and friends, many with personal inscriptions to Clarence, and several other miscellaneous slips of paper with addresses and phone numbers.

Also found floating was a makeshift oar, which was later confirmed to have been constructed by the inmates. The Coast Guard of Angel Island located the oar floating just off the Stuart Point Lighthouse on the northwest side of the island. One of the rafts that had apparently been used by the inmates was found just offshore in the same vicinity. It had deflated, apparently due to a breached seal along one of the seams. Another raft was also found in the same condition near the Standard Oil Wharf at Point Richmond on the other side of the bay.

A life jacket was found about fifty yards east of Alcatraz by the prison launch during its routine trip to Fort Mason. The Mae West style life preserver was identified as being fabricated from the same materials as the one found on top the cellblock, and it also contained other interesting clues. It had brown stains, which later were confirmed to be blood. The air valve bore teeth marks, likely indicating that the convict had held it with his teeth to prevent air leakage. This tended to support the theory that the clip may have come off in the icy waters, thus contributing to the inmate's exhaustion and eventual drowning.

The cellhouse utility corridor where inmates Frank Morris and brothers John and Clarence Anglin emerged from the tunneled openings in the back of their cells, and ascended through the maze of plumbing to the top of the cellblock.

The rooftop ventilator through which the inmates made their final exit from the cellhouse.

The inmates quietly trekked across the rooftops of the cellhouse and the hospital before making their descent down a pipe along the west wall of the prison.

Another lifejacket was found by a couple walking along a section of Cronkite Beach in Marin County, almost four miles from the Golden Gate Bridge. The couple saw an object floating fifty feet from the shore, and waited a few minutes for it to wash up. It was a life jacket identical to the one made for West, which had been found on top of the cellhouse. This one also revealed additional interesting clues. The jacket was deflated, and the paper clip that held the air tube closed was missing. There was also a small tear at the seam, which had allowed air to escape. West stated that their plan had been to cut up the floats once they came ashore, and throw them back into the water.

For decades people speculated as to whether this famous escape attempt had been successful. The FBI launched an intensive investigation, following every possible lead, and after spending nearly two decades painstakingly exploring physical and circumstantial evidence, the Bureau finally resolved that the inmates had not succeeded. There were several key points of the investigation that would ultimately cast doubt on the success of the escape attempt by Frank Morris, and John and Clarence Anglin. Through careful examination of the available evidence, one can form one's own opinion as to whether or not the inmates made it to freedom. Consider the following evidence assembled by the FBI:

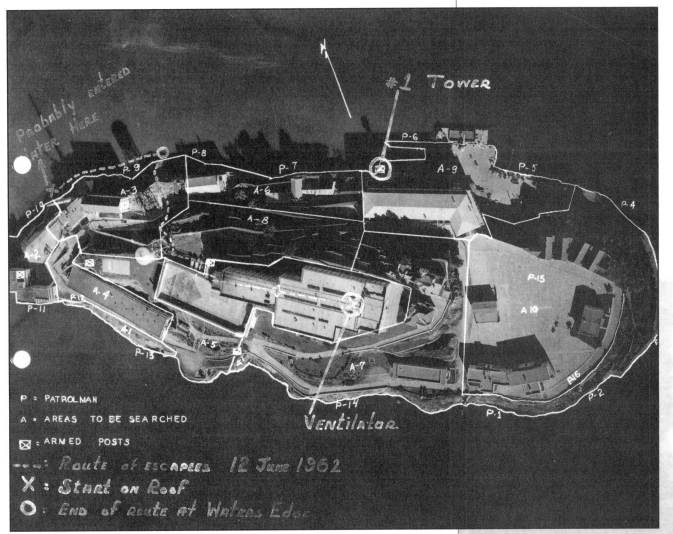

Within the map image:
- #1 TOWER
- Probably entered water here
- P-6
- P-8
- P-9
- P-7
- A-9
- P-5
- A-3
- A-6
- P-19
- A-8
- P-4
- A-2
- A-4
- P-15
- A-10
- P-12
- P-11
- A-5
- P-13
- A-7
- P-16
- P-2
- P-14
- P-1
- Ventilator
- P = PATROLMAN
- A = AREAS TO BE SEARCHED
- ☒ = ARMED POSTS
- --- = Route of Escapees 12 June 1962
- X = Start on Roof
- O = End of route at Waters Edge

(Above) The perimeter search map utilized by the prison officials and the FBI. Investigators plotted the presumed path of the escapees to the water's edge.

(Below) An officer examining the false grill sections behind Allen West's cell.

- The formal plan was to steal a car and then perpetrate a burglary at a clothing store. No reports of any such crime were filed in Marin County within a twelve-day period following the escape. None of the other surrounding counties, including San Francisco, Alameda, Contra Costa, Santa Clara, Monterey, and several others, reported any related or suspicious crimes within a similar time period. It was also rumored that Morris, who had a passion for reading about aviation-related subjects, had talked about stealing a helicopter to make a rapid departure from the Bay Area. The FBI and the FAA came up with no potential leads on this angle, and in any case, it is very unlikely that Morris could actually fly a helicopter, as he had claimed to a fellow inmate.

- Sources reported that these three men had neither friends nor relatives with the resources to come to San Francisco and assist in the escape. The cost of putting a boat in the Bay night after night to assist in the escape would have been thousands of dollars. The families and friends of the trio were investigated regarding their financial resources, and their hypothetical role as accomplices was eventually ruled out. There would have been no possible way for

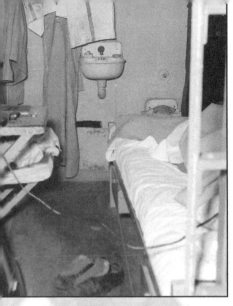

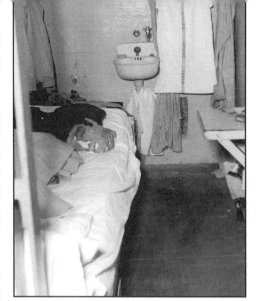

(Above left) A frontal view of Clarence Anglin's cell following the escape.

(Above middle) John Anglin's cell (B-158). The towels and clothing were used effectively to hide the ventilation grill.

(Above right) Allen West's cell, with a section of the fake ventilation grill visible on the bed. The inmates used cardboard tobacco boxes to create the false grills, and carefully measured and cut the grill patterns using contraband razorblades.

(Below right) Frank Morris succeeded in covering the ventilation grill inside his cell with the case of his concertina, thus diverting any suspicion from the planned escape.

(Below left) An officer seen examining the opening where the ventilation grill was originally located.

the inmates to communicate with outside contacts in order to confirm the date and progress of their break.

- Critics on the other side of the debate claimed that the fact that no bodies were found amounted to "proof" that the inmates had made it successfully to the mainland. The reality was that it was common for people who perished in the Bay waters never to be found. On the very night of the escape, a thirty-three-year old African-American gentleman named Seymour Webb, reportedly despondent over a failed relationship, abandoned his car mid-span on the Golden Gate Bridge and tragically jumped to his death in front of sixty-two horrified eyewitnesses. Despite a quick response from the Coast Guard, his body was never recovered. The significance of this event is that the suicide entered the water about the same time as the escapees, and his body was never found.

- On June 19, 1962, Robert Panis, an eighteen-year-old Filipino male, also drowned in the waters of Half Moon Bay, approximately twenty-five miles south of the Golden Gate Bridge. On the day of the drowning, a Coast Guard Helicopter noticed a floating body wearing attire that matched that of the missing man. A surface vessel was dispatched to the location, but the authorities were never successful in recovering the body. The FBI cited this as another example of the extreme difficulty in recovering drowned bodies from the Bay. The Bureau also referenced the case of Theodore Cole and Ralph Roe, who escaped from Alcatraz in 1937. Despite intensive searches these men were likewise never located, and it was concluded that they had drowned.

- The Bay water temperatures ranged from fifty to fifty-four degrees. It was determined that exposure to the elements would have affected body func-

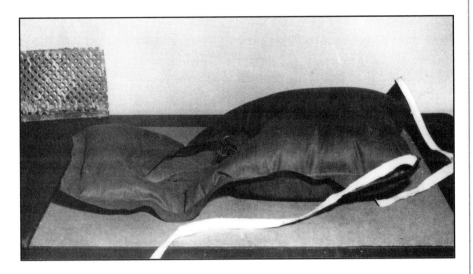

(Left) Allen West's life vest, shown here fully inflated.

(Below) A life jacket that was found just fifty yards east of the Alcatraz Dock. The vest was saturated with stains, and there were teeth marks around the air tube. Based on this evidence, it was concluded that the inmate who wore it was desperately attempting to maintain enough air pressure to keep afloat. The prisoners had used binder clamps to seal the air inside the vests, and these were probably unable to sustain adequate air pressure.

tions after approximately twenty minutes. The showers at Alcatraz were always supplied with moderately hot water, in order to hinder inmates from becoming acclimated to the freezing Bay waters.

- On July 17, 1962 the Ship S.S. Norefjell, a Norwegian Freighter departing from Pier 38, reported seeing a body floating twenty miles northwest of the Golden Gate Bridge. The ship was en route to Canada, and the crew noted the sighting in the ship's log, but did not make a formal report until returning to the United States on August 8, 1962. The S.S. Norefjell was not equipped with a transceiver that could broadcast on the marine radio bands used in the United States. The crewmembers logged the notation that sometime between 5:45 P.M. and 6:00 P.M. they noticed something bobbing in the water, and used binoculars to confirm that it was a body floating face down. The hands and feet were dangling down in the water, but the buttocks were clearly visible. Although bleached from the ocean and sun, the body was clothed in full-length denim trousers that appeared identical to

---

U. S. PENITENTIARY
Alcatraz, California

REPORT OF MISCONDUCT

Inmate's Name *ANGLIN JOHN WILLIAM* No. *1476 AZ* Work Assignment *Clothing Room* Quarters *B150*

Nature of charge *ESCAPE*   Date *6-12-62*

Inmate John William Anglin #1476 AZ is charged with breaking out of the rear of his cell (B150) and escape from Alcatraz Island.

He was discovered missing at about 7:18 AM (above date) by this officer while making a count. A plaster head was found in his bed.

Reported by *[signature]* C.O.

U. S. PENITENTIARY
Alcatraz, California

REPORT OF MISCONDUCT

Inmate's Name *Frank Lee Morris* No. *1441 AZ* Work Assignment *Brush Shop* Quarters *B138*

Nature of charge *ESCAPE*   Date *6-12-62*

Inmate Frank Lee Morris is charged with breaking out of the rear of his cell (B138) and escape from Alcatraz Island.

He was discovered missing at about 7:18 AM (above date) by this officer while making a count. A plaster head was found in his bed.

Reported by *[signature]* C.O.

Record Form No. 8
(July, 1960)

UNITED STATES DEPARTMENT OF JUSTICE
BUREAU OF PRISONS

CONDUCT RECORD

U. S. Penitentiary   Alcatraz, Calif.
_____(Institution)_____   _____(Location)_____

Record of   MORRIS, Frank Lee   No. 1441- AZ
FPI-LK-5-15-59-24M-3896

DATE	PRISON VIOLATIONS	DAYS LOST
5-10-60	DRINKING CONTRABAND COFFEE IN CELL: About 7:30 P. M. this date while making a routine check of the cellhouse I observed the above named inmate with what appeared to be a cup of coffee. I said to Morris, that looks like coffee to me, he replied that's what it is. The aroma to me was that of instant coffee. R. Jimerson INMATE'S VERSION: Admitted he had been drinking coffee. Claimed he had carried it from the dining room in a small varnish bottle. ACTION: 5-11-60 Two (2) weeks restriction. O. G. Blackwell, Assoc. Warden	
6-12-62	ESCAPE. Inmate Frank Lee Morris is charged with breaking out of the rear of his cell (B-138) and escape from Alcatraz Island. He was discovered missing at about 7:18 A. M. (above date) by this officer while making a count. A plaster head was found in his bed. Lawrence Bartlett, D. O. ACTION: It was unanimously recommended that inmate forfeit all SGT and EGT up to date of the offense. A. M. Dollison, Chairman	483 SGT 69 EGT

(Above top) The inmates concealed their discarded tools and equipment inside a five-gallon container, and then filled it with plaster. Investigators found wire, spoon handles, steel bars, the vacuum cleaner motor, staples, a homemade flashlight, ladle handles, and other bits of contraband embedded in the hardened plaster.

(Above bottom) In the aftermath of the escape, correctional officers swarmed through the cellhouse, conducting meticulous inspections of every cell in B Block.

prison issue. Coroners from San Francisco, San Mateo, Alameda, and Marin Counties all confirmed that a body could float for five weeks after drowning. The FBI determined this to be one of the most significant leads in the case. Their official report established that there was no other individual missing or drowned at that time who had been wearing similar trousers, and concluded that it was reasonable to state that this was likely to be one of the escapees.

• The families of the Anglin brothers stated that the escape had been a topic of family discussions for several years. None of them have ever been contacted by the brothers, and they felt that had the inmates survived, they would have made contact in some form. The Anglin family would soon suffer yet another tragedy. The third brother, Alfred, was electrocuted on a high-voltage security wire when attempting to escape from Kilby Prison in Montgomery, Alabama in 1964.

Allen West remained at Alcatraz until February of 1963, leaving only one month before the prison's final closing. He then continued his journey through the Federal penal system until he was eventually released in 1967, in the state of Florida. His taste of freedom was brief, and he quickly landed himself back in prison less than a year later. In 1972 West fatally stabbed another inmate, and thus permanently sealed his fate, condemning himself to a life in prison. Allen West died of peritonitis in the Florida State Prison hospital in December of 1978, at only forty-nine years of age.

The mystery is still being explored decades after the Great Escape, and it is unlikely that anyone will ever be able to prove with absolute certainty whether Morris and the Anglins found death or freedom. Frank Morris wrote in an institutional questionnaire in 1943 that if he were granted three wishes, he would wish for the following:

1. To get out of prison.
2. A nice home with everything to go with it.
3. Plenty of money.

He was granted only one.

WANTED BY THE FBI

ESCAPED FEDERAL PRISONER – BANK ROBBER
CLARENCE ANGLIN

FBI No. 4,731,702

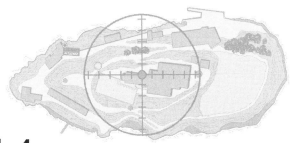

Escape Attempt #14

DATE: DECEMBER 4, 1962
INMATES: JOHN PAUL SCOTT
DARYL LEE PARKER
LOCATION: KITCHEN BASEMENT

By December of 1962, plans had already been set in motion to close the prison due to crippling costs and structural deterioration of the main cellhouse. Decades of exposure to the harsh environment of the damp salt ocean air had taken its toll on the prison. The last attempted escape at Alcatraz may have been facilitated by the dilapidated state of the prison facilities. In any case, it finally demonstrated that with properly constructed floats and a favorable current, it was technically possible for an inmate to enter the icy Bay waters and paddle to the mainland. John Paul Scott and Daryl Parker were two of the tough incorrigibles that Alcatraz was designed to cage, but they proved that even The Rock was not invulnerable to a well-planned prison break.

John Paul Scott was a university educated bank robber of the modern era. His inmate file details a multitude of bank heists, dramatic prison breaks, and spectacular shootouts with police. Like Scott, Daryl Lee Parker's attempted escape at Alcatraz would be merely a brief episode in a lifelong diary of crime. In this chapter, the stories of John Paul Scott and Daryl Lee Parker will be illustrated through firsthand reports and inmate records that chronicle their lives in prison as well as their various escape attempts.

Daryl Lee Parker

Daryl Lee Parker

An entry in a 1967 classification study report recounts the early life of Daryl Parker, and it includes a letter from his mother describing his childhood:

Daryl's childhood was normal. He was number five of a family of eight children. No bad habits like drinking or smoking early in life. At the age of twelve to fourteen he began taking bottles and

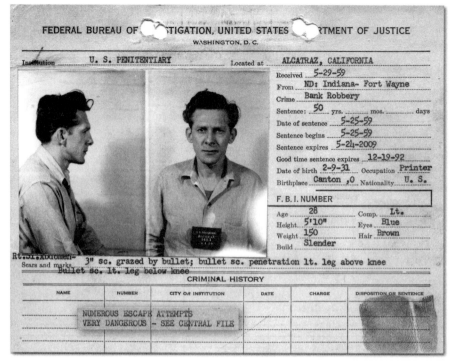

Institution	U. S. PENITENTIARY	Located at	ALCATRAZ, CALIFORNIA

Received 5-29-59
From .... ND: Indiana- Fort Wayne
Crime .... Bank Robbery
Sentence: .... 50 .... yrs. .... mos. .... days
Date of sentence 5-25-59
Sentence begins 5-25-59
Sentence expires 5-24-2009
Good time sentence expires 12-19-92
Date of birth .... 2-9-31 .... Occupation .... Printer
Birthplace .... Canton ,O .... Nationality .... U. S.

F. B. I. NUMBER

Age .... 28 .... Comp. .... Lt.
Height .... 5'10" .... Eyes .... Blue
Weight .... 150 .... Hair .... Brown
Build .... Slender

Rt.51.Abdomen—
Scars and marks .... 3" sc. grazed by bullet; bullet sc. penetration lt. leg above knee
.... Bullet sc. lt. leg below knee

CRIMINAL HISTORY

NAME	NUMBER	CITY OR INSTITUTION	DATE	CHARGE	DISPOSITION OR SENTENCE
	NUMEROUS ESCAPE ATTEMPTS VERY DANGEROUS – SEE CENTRAL FILE				

cashing them in for spending money. The habit of thievery grew rapidly with it ending in your institution. Daryl was a beautiful baby and much loved by his brothers and sisters. Therefore, might have been spoiled somewhat. He was sent to the Boys Industrial School at the end of eighth grade. He also entered Timkin Vocational and finished all but two credits in high school. He lost out in Industrial School with there being a war on and a shortage of math teachers. He took printing in Timkin Vocational School. After this he worked at Isaly's Dairy store and he married Margaret Davis, also of Tinkin Vocational School, in a church here in Canton. There were no children. His father, Howard, is a foreman at the Timkin Roller Bearing Company. He also fixes TVs in his spare time as a hobby. He was born in Morgan County, Ohio. Georgia (Walker) Parker, his grandmother, was also born in Morgan County, Ohio, and was a schoolteacher prior to her marriage.

All I can say in conclusion was Daryl was high-strung, quick-tempered, and very nervous. At age 6 he developed a stammer. It was not bad, but irritated him a lot. He changed schools three times by our moving, and he resented the last school bringing home all F's in every department. He has been in the Boys Industrial School, Mansfield Reformatory, Lorton and the prison in Maryland. He came nearer adjusting himself after leaving Mansfield, staying out of trouble three years. He returned from Lorton Prison in very bad shape having made friends with an elder criminal, which he ended where he is now, with you. Each time Daryl has been in trouble we hope and pray it will be his last. That hasn't happened yet and we hope that he will come out of your prison a better boy for our faith in prisons is very low at the moment.

The inmate is married but has no children. He married Margaret Davis January 19, 1952, at Canton, Ohio, and stated there had been no discord with his wife, who is self supporting as a secretary, and he stated that in view of his long sentence, he had advised her to obtain a divorce.

(Top, left, and opposite page) Daryl Lee Parker

By 1957 Daryl's criminal record was already full of entries, ranging from juvenile stints as a runaway beginning in 1944, to armed robbery charges in 1957. A bank robbery that he committed in that year with his friend John Bartholomew is detailed in his criminal summary:

Attached to the form 792, U.S. Attorney's Report, accounting for the sentence of 20 years on count 1 and 25 years concurrently on count 2 for Bank Robbery and assault with a deadly weapon was the statement, Defendant, Daryl Lee Parker, which John T. Bartholomew, robbed the Clinton and Rudisill Branch of the Lincoln National Bank and Trust Company, Fort Wayne, Indiana of the sum of $50,104.00 on Friday, October 18, 1957.

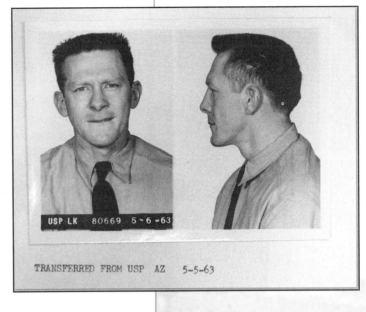

The men became acquainted while both were doing time in the Federal Reformatory at Lorton, Virginia. Daryl Lee Parker, though the younger of the two men, carefully laid all of the plans and made all of the arrangements for the bank robbery. He furnished the weapons used and stole two automobiles used as getaway cars. Both Parker and Bartholomew wore grotesque Halloween masks during the actual robbery. The defendant Daryl Lee Parker disguised his appearance by the use of black hair dye and of suntan theatrical grease paint. Both men entered the bank together. Bartholomew carried a .45 automatic pistol, while Daryl Lee Parker carried a .357 caliber magnum revolver, which, we are informed, is the most powerful handgun made, so powerful that it will drive a shell through the motor block of an automobile engine.

Bartholomew took up a position near the front of the of the bank, menacing the branch manager and the assistant branch manager with his gun, and directing them to fill a laundry bag with the bank's money from the teller's cages. Daryl Lee Parker proceeded to the rear of the bank menacing tellers behind the teller's cages with his magnum revolver, and compelling a youthful vault casher to take money from the drive-in windows of the bank and put it in one of the bank's money bags. During the time of

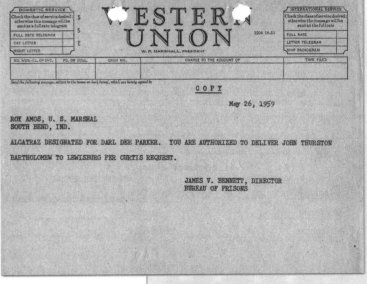

Parker's transfer order to Alcatraz.

the robbery there were 15 to 20 customers in the bank. Daryl Lee Parker vaulted over the gate in the area behind the teller's cages, held the magnum revolver to a young girl cashier and on the youthful vault cashier whom he ordered not to take another step or he would "blow your head off." Daryl Lee Parker ordered all of the clerks away from their teller's cages and said that if the police should come during the robbery he and his fellow robber would take 3 hostages and that they would kill the hostages without hesitation.

Defendant Daryl Lee Parker planned this bank robbery with such meticulous attention to detail that it required months of intensive investigation to assemble the evidence required before his arrest on March 19, 1958. Daryl Lee Parker said to a fellow prisoner at the Allen County Jail at Fort Wayne, Indiana, that he was sure to be convicted of the Fort Wayne bank robbery charge on which he was held and that escape was the only way out.

Daryl Lee Parker on June 11, 1958, stated to Donald Byington, Warden, United States Penitentiary, Terre Haute, Indiana, that he would try to escape at the first opportunity he had and stated: "I am in too much trouble, having robbed four banks and I couldn't do all that time"; the defendant's brother, Robert Parker, who probably has more than just simple guilty knowledge of Daryl's activities, has admitted that they have a total of $226,000.00 hidden away. *Both Daryl Lee Parker and his brother Robert Parker are known to have made flights to Cuba soon after the Fort Wayne bank robbery.*

Parker was charged with two counts of robbery, and was committed to the Allen County Jail in Fort Wayne. The following report describes his escape, which would prefigure his eventual break from Alcatraz:

Parker was at first confined in Cell Block "A" on the first floor of the County Jail. There he approached a fellow prisoner, who was a trustee, showed him a hundred dollar bill concealed in a package of cigarettes, and solicited his aid for escape. Parker told the trusty that a large negro man would place some hacksaw blades near a flag pole in the front yard of the jail. Parker suggested that this trusty, who had freedom to go in and out of the jail, might pick these hack saw blades up, conceal them in a magazine and deliver the magazine to Parker. Parker offered $1,000.00 to this trusty if he would smuggle these hacksaw blades into the jail. The trusty immediately reported Parker's offer to the jail officials.

Parker was thereupon moved upstairs to the maximum-security cellblock of the County Jail, adjacent to the section where mental patients were held. Jail officials and F.B.I. agents searched Parker's cell for the $1,000.00, which he offered to pay to the trusty. Parker was even required to strip his clothing and to be examined by a physician as part of the search. Parker's shoes were taken to a local shoemaker for examination. The shoemaker tore the heels off the shoes and discovered two packets made of black electrician's tape, each of which packets contained five one-hundred-dollar bills. Each packet was secreted in special indentations, which had been cut out of the heel of each shoe. The shoemaker who made the examination expressed the opinion that the work had been done by a skilled shoemaker. Further investigation showed that the shoes had been taken to a shoemaker in Canton, Ohio, to have the work done. The packets of money were already made up for insertion under the heel in each of the shoes.

Parker managed to smuggle out of the jail, plans of the jail to certain persons to enable those persons to deliver to him the tools necessary for escape. At this time, Parker was confined in a cell to the left of which was a cell occupied by a person named [deleted entry]. Immediately to the left of this person's cell was a cell in which there was located a bathtub for the use of prisoners. [Deleted entry] had been the trusty detailed to empty the garbage from the basement kitchen of the jail. At the time the practice of the jail had been to entrust the cook in the kitchen with the key that unlocked the barred door from the kitchen that led directly to the outside. [Deleted entry] had secured the key, had unlocked the barred rear door of the kitchen and had gone out to empty the garbage. He did not return and was later apprehended and returned to the jail cell next to the cell occupied by Parker. Parker inquired and learned from this prisoner how he had secured the key.

On a stormy night prior to Tuesday, June 10, 1958, two men scaled the wall of the County Jail with an extension ladder. One of these men carried a dark oilcloth bag tied around his neck. He was able to get onto a roof below the barred window of the jail cell used by the prisoners for bathing. He tied the bag to the end of a rope, the other end of which had been previously tied to one of the cell bars of this cell. The rope had been painted black and was long enough to allow the bag to lie on the jail roof in such a way as be unnoticed from the window. The bag contained a .45 automatic pistol, ammunition, hacksaw blades, and money. Perhaps $75 to $80 dollars.

Parker himself admitted that he took a bath and concealed this black bag under his clothing when he returned to his own jail cell. Parker spent three nights trying to saw through the bars on the window of his jail cell. The bars were of such hard steel, that he was unable to make any headway. Then he commenced working on the bolt which locked his jail cell door, discovering in the process that it was of a softer steel and that he was able to cut through it.

On Tuesday morning, June 10, 1958, a jail guard and a trusty came into the cellblock to feed the prisoners. Parker did not eat that morning, and the trusty and the jail guard continued on past Parker's cell to feed the patients held in the mental section. Thereupon, Parker opened the steel barred door of his jail cell, menaced the jail guard and the trusty with a .45 caliber pistol, and compelled them to get into one of the jail cells. He compelled the jail guard to take off his Deputy Sheriff's uniform. Parker then put the Deputy Sheriff's uniform on himself over his own clothing and fled downstairs into the jail kitchen. There he was unable to obtain the key to unlock the door that led immediately outside, because after the other prisoner's escape from the kitchen, the practice had been changed. The cook was no longer entrusted with the key.

Parker then went back upstairs into the jail office. With his .45 caliber pistol, he shot the lock off the door of the jail guard's office. The office was completely bullet proofed except for one little spot just behind the door's lock. Parker compelled the guard on-duty to press the button, which electrically unlocked the iron barred door to the front of the jail.

Parker then fled out of the jail, through an alley behind the jail to an intersection at which traffic was regulated by stop-and-go lights. There he commandeered the private automobile of a Fort Wayne mail carrier, who had been stopped by the red light. At gunpoint Parker compelled the mail carrier to drive him out of Fort Wayne, Indiana, in the direction of the Ohio state line. Parker became lost on the back roads, which they followed and ran into a roadblock. The roadblock was manned by the

Chief of Police and by an Ohio State Policeman. A gun battle followed in which the life of the mail carrier was gravely endangered. Parker was shot in the hip by the Ohio State Policeman and thereby recaptured. He had been free from the Allen County Jail a total of approximately five hours. Subject was then confined to the Terra Haute Penitentiary in the hospital, and also in the Federal Medical Center at Springfield until he was well enough to appear before the court. He was sentenced to fifty years in a Federal Penitentiary for his crimes.

Daryl Lee Parker arrived at Alcatraz May 29, 1959, as inmate #AZ-1413. Even prior to his attempted escape from the island, Parker's incarceration was problematic. For example, on March 15, 1960 he was placed in the closed-front solitary confinement cell for exploding a homemade bomb, and only one month later he was caught behaving intoxicated after having ingested a specially concocted homebrew.

John Paul Scott

J. Paul Scott was born on January 3, 1927 in Willisburg, Kentucky, the second of six children in the family of Buelah and William A. Scott. His father, who served as the postmaster of Springfield, Kentucky from 1950 until his death in 1966, was an affectionate parent. He provided a good living for his family, and offered all of his children a college education. His mother was also a college graduate, and she never worked outside the home. From all indications, the home situation was most amicable.

In 1944 Scott graduated from Springfield High School in Springfield, Kentucky. He entered the University of Kentucky in 1950, and subsequently attended Western State Teachers College, the University of Georgia, and Georgia State University. During his attendance at these universities, he maintained an above-average academic standing and amassed a total of 170 hours of credit toward his Bachelors degree. The last school he attended was Georgia State University, during the winter quarter of 1970.

(Above and below right) A mug shot series of John Paul Scott.

Scott enlisted in the U.S. Army Reserve on July 13, 1944, and entered active duty in June of 1945. He left the U.S. Air Force with an honorable discharge on December 28, 1946. He also enlisted in the Aviation Cadet Program on September 24, 1949, and was honorably discharged on November 2, 1949. He experienced only minor disciplinary problems while in the Air Force, but was discharged because it was discovered that he had a prison record. The highest rank he attained was that of private.

Scott's first arrest occurred in February of 1949, and he was charged with possession of stolen merchandise. During the years following, he would be arrested on various other charges including burglary and armed robbery. On the weekend of December 15, 1956, J. Paul Scott and his brother Don R. Scott forcibly entered the National Guard Armory at Danville, Kentucky with accomplice Earl Morris, and stole two .45 caliber submachine guns and three .30 caliber rifles, with a sizeable quantity of ammunition. On January 6, 1957, J. Paul Scott and the same two accomplices entered the Farmers and Traders Bank of Campton, Kentucky, armed and carrying acetylene cutting equipment. While in the bank, Scott was struck in the mouth and the arm by two bullets fired by a bank guard. Meanwhile, Morris was perched outside of a window and Don Scott was on the roof of the bank, standing guard. As the robbers fled from the bank they engaged local officers in a gun battle, which resulted in the wounding of a Wolfe County Sheriff.

Scott began serving his sentence at the Federal Penitentiary in Atlanta, where he received two disciplinary reports, one for attempted escape and one for a homosexual act. In March of 1959 he was transferred to Alcatraz, and there his disciplinary reports would include an escape from the island.

The Alcatraz Escape Files of Parker and Scott

The following report was written by Warden Blackwell to the Director of the Bureau of Prisons on December 20, 1962, describing the events from his perspective:

December 20, 1962

To: Director, Bureau of Prisons
From: O.G. Blackwell, Warden
Re: Escape Attempt, December 16, 1002 - John Paul Scott
           1403-AZ and Daryl Parker 1413-AZ

On Sunday, December 16, 1902, the two above inmates were missed from their detail in the Culinary unit, at 5:47 P.M. We have definitely established that both of those individuals were accounted for on the official 5:20 P.M. count and again counted by the lieutenant on duty, Mr. Harold Robbins, at 5:30 P.M.

The alarm was sounded, immediate search of the area was instituted, and the entire escape procedure was placed into effect. At 6:10 P.M. our boat officer spotted Parker clinging to a rock some 100 yards off the northwest end of the island, known as "Little Alcatraz." At approximately 7:20 P.M. inmate SCOTT was spotted clinging to a rock off Fort Point, which is located almost directly under the south end of the Golden Gate Bridge. SCOTT was spotted by two teenagers who reported to the Presidio MPs. They reported to the scene and called for a fire department rescue team, rescued SCOTT from this rock and took him immediately to the Letterman Hospital for emergency treatment. For the first thirty minutes several doctors worked with SCOTT and stated that they were very much uncertain as to whether he would live or die. He was suffering from numerous cuts and bruises and from severe shock as a result of extreme lowering of body temperature, caused by the cold water of the Bay, which normally runs from 52 to 54 degrees, the year around. PARKER, of course, was returned to the institution, examined by the medical staff and locked up immediately after he was found. SCOTT was returned to the institution following release from the emergency unit of the hospital by the doctors.

Of course both you and Mr. Aldredge came to the institution and are very familiar with the incident and all of the findings. However, I might review some of the more outstanding points for the benefit of others who might read this report.

During the investigation it became obvious that the two sets of bars that were removed had been worked on over a long period of time and obviously by more people than just SCOTT. A check of the records indicates that ex-inmate BURBANK, No. 1369, now in custody by the Missouri State Penitentiary, was assigned to the kitchen basement for a long period of time and could have well have started the removal of the bars. Following his assignment, inmate Leonard WILLIAMS, No. 1045, was assigned to the basement area and he too could have contributed to these cuts. It is noted by the record that WILLIAMS was involved in several escape attempts, including an attempt to escape while being transported to Alcatraz.

We are not quite sure of all instruments used to sever these bars; however, we are rather positive that a spatula, with serrated edges; a grease scraper, used by fry-cooks in scraping down grills, that had serrated edges, and string, which had been impregnated with floor wax; and institution scouring powder were at least three items that were used to sever these bars. One set of these bars, incidentally, is commonly referred to as "tool-proof-steel."

As we see the picture, and as admitted now by SCOTT and PARKER, SCOTT almost completed severing the bars, alerted PARKER that he expected to try to escape, and invited him then to go along. On the evening of the sixteenth, immediately after the 5:30 count, under the guise of taking the garbage to the basement, SCOTT got on the elevator, took the elevator half-way down, jumped off and completed severing the bars, which he states took approximately five minutes. He then dashed to the elevator shaft and signaled for PARKER, who jumped down the shaft, landing on the elevator halfway down, then jumped off to the floor and they both went out through the window.

Investigative reports suggest that inmates Charles Burbank (above) and Leonard Williams (below) may have begun cutting through the steel window bars several months before the escape, when they were assigned to the kitchen detail.

This window is the last window on the south side of the kitchen basement and is partially hidden by two butane tanks that service burner units in the hospital. They eluded the officer who was patrolling back of the Kitchen by seeing that he had checked that side of the building and started in the other direction. They then hurriedly climbed two pipes at the corner of the building, gaining access to the roof. They crossed the roof and lowered themselves to the ground directly behind the Library on a length of extension cord that they had tied knots in, approximately three feet apart. This cord was removed from the buffing machine that is used to polish the basement floor. They then slid and fell down the steep hill directly behind Apartment Building "A." During this fall PARKER apparently broke his foot and received several cuts and bruises. They then went down the rather high bluff to the water's edge by sliding down a sewer pipe. At this point they inflated rubber gloves that they had inserted in shirtsleeves, and pieces of shirt that had been crudely stitched together, making a set of so called "water-wings" to be used as flotation equipment.

It was dark and rainy. Visibility was extremely poor. PARKER stated that SCOTT moved out first and he followed after checking his flotation equipment and immediately lost SCOTT, but thought he saw him. As it turned out, it was a bucket floating in the bay. He fought the tides as hard as he could but could make no headway and it washed him back in to the rock known as "Little Alcatraz," and he hung on to this rock until found by our boat. He received further cuts and bruises attempting to stay on the rock. SCOTT claims that he almost drowned when he hit the rock at Fort Point because the waves were coming over his head, and he could not find any protection on this rock at all.

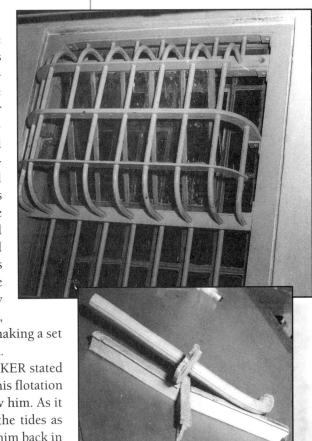

(Above) The cutaway bar section of the south-end window at the east end of the kitchen basement, through which inmates Parker and Scott made their escape.

In searching the basement area several times, we found items which included the impregnated string, and a twelve-inch crescent wrench that had been missed over two years ago from the old Furniture Factory and apparently had been secreted in the Kitchen basement behind one or the huge refrigerators. The rubber gloves obviously had been stolen from the hospital unit and SCOTT claims they had been there for a long time. The crescent wrench was used to twist out the last section of the outside detention sash, which was extremely eroded from the elements and of course, was never designed to be first-rate security material.

As attached reports will indicate, searches of the basement area had been ordered and apparently completed. The bars had been tapped by officers on both Saturday and Sunday, the day of the escape. At first glance it seemed strongly indicated that disciplinary action should be instituted against

An exterior view of the window that was used by inmates in their attempted escape.

7930 - 205 - 2868

SCOURING POWDER

FED. SPEC. P - S - 311a

TYPE I – with bleaching agent

CLASS 2 – coarse abrasive

16 OUNCES NET WT.

NEWPORT PRODUCTS CO.

SAN FRANCISCO, CALIF.

Supplement # 6   Aldredge, Capt

(Above) This is the actual label from the scouring power that was combined with floor wax and soaked into string, then used as an abrasive to cut through a steel bar over a long period of time.

(Below) Surgical rubber gloves were inflated and sewn into shirtsleeves that were successfully used as a flotation device.

those who were ordered to knock the bars in this unit. However, after careful examination of all of the facts it became highly conceivable, from a technical or mechanical standpoint, that the officers hammering these bars with rubber hammers could very well have struck them a heavy blow (and they insist they did) without noticing any particular difference from any other bar. It is obvious, of course, that their visual inspection was not effective. However, since the cuts were on the back side of the main bar, and the duty of hammering bars is rather monotonous, it is highly possible that they could have overlooked the carefully concealed cut, thinking that they were doing a good job. With all of this in mind, and after careful consideration of all of the facts by the Captain, Associate Warden, Mr. Aldredge, and myself, at this point we do not feel that disciplinary action against the officers is indicated.

To further explain the reasoning, the top of the upright bar was not cut, but was eventually removed by SCOTT through the use of a three by two foot piece of oak, and it required considerable leverage to break loose the welds at that end. SCOTT claims that enough of the lower section of the bar was left solid that it took him five minutes to remove it, which would have fastened that end, making both ends rather solid and quite capable of receiving a heavy blow with a rubber hammer without showing any appreciable movement.

In reviewing our obvious weaknesses and in endeavoring to correct as many weaknesses as possible, we have instituted the following:

(1) We welded in bar material to replace that which had been removed. We then fabricated an additional set of stainless steel bars and

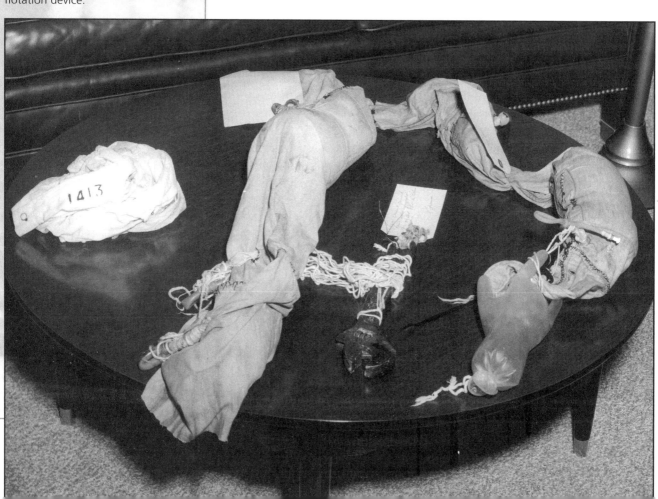

secured them on the outside window, which now makes three sets of detention material that must be gone through to escape from this unit.

(2) We have completely secured with expanded metal the entrance to the elevator at the Kitchen level. This will be kept locked at all times unless actually in use, and then under direct supervision.

(3) Under existing operations the officer furnishing coverage for the back of the Kitchen was patrolling from side to side on the cat-walk around the yard wall in order to check both sides and the end of the Kitchen area. We have now stationed one man on the northeast corner of the cat-walk, which will permit him to constantly observe the east side of the Kitchen and the north end at any time inmates are out of the cellhouse, and in any part of the Kitchen area. We have stationed another officer on the yard wall that can observe the west side of the kitchen and dining roof unit as well as assist in viewing the north end.

(4) We have issued a specific order that no inmate, or inmates, will be permitted in the basement of the Culinary unit unless under direct and constant supervision, and any time an employee takes inmates to that unit he must advise the Control Center first, indicating who he is taking. He must call the Control Center each fifteen minutes and must advise the Control Center as soon as he departs and secures the Kitchen basement area. This is, of course, to prevent an employee from being overpowered or otherwise incapacitated without someone being aware of it.

(5) We have issued an order that in order to protect all employees' families, in the event of escape, the gates on the Parade Ground near "B" Building will be secured during the hours of darkness and more specifically, from 5:40 P.M. until 8:10 A.M.

(6) All lieutenants have been instructed to issue specific and detailed instructions to any officer or group of officers that are designated to make searches or to check bar facilities, and then to make periodic checks to insure that they are being carried out as intended.

(7) Since we are in the process of phasing-out and have some thirteen custodial vacancies, at present we are not following our normal annual leave schedule, and are urging that those employees who do not need annual leave on an emergency basis cancel out any leave that may have been scheduled. We are not, of course, refusing leave to people who have already made specific plans or have sound reasoning for taking leave. With this arrangement we feel that additional coverage can be satisfactorily carried out without an enormous amount of overtime being paid.

Copies of reports of all employees concerned with this incident are attached, and a complete set of pictures of all specific items of interest are also attached. Copies are furnished for the inmate Bureau files and the institution inmate files. The FBI investigated this incident and reported their findings to the U. S. Attorney, who in turn presented the cases to the Grand Jury, who in turn indicted both inmates. It is expected they will be prosecuted for the escape in the early part of next year. Any further items that may develop in connection with this case will be reported promptly.

O.G. BLACKWELL
Warden

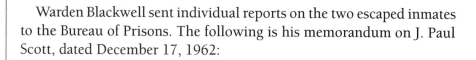

Warden Blackwell sent individual reports on the two escaped inmates to the Bureau of Prisons. The following is his memorandum on J. Paul Scott, dated December 17, 1962:

UNITED STATES DEPARTMENT of JUSTICE
BUREAU OF PRISONS
UNITED STATES PENITENTIARY

ALCATRAZ CALIFORNIA

December 17, 1962

MEMORANDUM FOR FILE

Re: Statement of Inmate JOHN PAUL SCOTT #1403-AZ

At approximately 11:00 p.m. Sunday, December 16, 1962 inmate SCOTT was returned from the emergency section of Letterman General Hospital by Associate Warden Williard and Business Manager Bones, and brought to the Warden's office for questioning.

During the questioning SCOTT talked fairly freely and made several pertinent statements. In sequence he claims that over a period of time, which he refused to define, he impregnated string with floor wax and scouring powder and used this to cut the bars in the south-end window on the east side of the kitchen basement. He further claims that he had the bars partially cut and filled in with soap and painted over so officers would not detect it, and on both Saturday, December 15th and Sunday, December 16th, the officers were tapping bars and broke the spreader bar cut loose to the extent that he attempted to glue it back to prevent further detection. He claims that on the spur of the moment he decided he had better "go" before the cutting of the bars was detected, and asked PARKER if he would like to go with him. PARKER agreed and he (Scott) finished making the small cuts necessary on the bars, signaled to PARKER, and PARKER came down the elevator shaft and they went out the opening in the window.

He then claims they climbed some drain pipes in the corner to prevent an officer in the tower from seeing them; gained access to the roof; and lowered themselves to the ground on the opposite side of the building and behind the library by use of a knotted electric cord he had removed from the kitchen basement waxing machine. This particular descent was made, again, to prevent the tower officer from seeing them.

He then claims that he and PARKER went down the steep hill where PARKER fell and bruised himself considerable; they emerged near the north end of "A" Building, then slid down a steep cliff by holding on to a sewer pipe where they reached the water. At this point they inflated their floatation equipment, which consisted of two or three rubber gloves blown up and tied inside a piece of inmate shirt material that was crudely stitched together, this then being tied around their body. They then entered the water and for only a short time did he observe PARKER, and did not know what happened to him after that.

He claims that he spotted lights on the mainland; attempted to swim towards them and the tide carried him by; he then selected another light and repeated the performance, and this continued until he was washed on to a rock out near the Golden Gate Bridge. The tide was so swift and waves so high at this point that he claims to have almost drowned and could not maneuver around on the rock to keep the waves from covering him closing off his breath. It was at this point that he was rescued by members of the Fire Department at the Presidio of San Francisco and taken into custody by the Military Police at the Presidio. He was taken to the emergency hospital for treatment, but claims he does not recall the Associate Warden entering the room, and fails to remember several other things for a short period of time.

Over and above this, he stated he had heard in the yard for some months that there was a hole in the kitchen basement. He inferred but would not flatly state that some other inmate had partially cut through this window a long time ago. He indicated that the outside section of the window was partially cut by the use of a spatula that had notched edges. He added that the spatula and scraper used for this had been disposed of by putting them down the old butcher shop drain, and it should be noted that several days ago a spatula and scraper fitting that description was actually removed from that drain, and it was deteriorated to the extent to indicate that it had been there for several months.

He further claimed that the rubber gloves used for floatation purposes had been in the kitchen basement hidden behind one of the refrigerators for a long long time. He would not establish a definite or approximate date. He claimed that he had made up five or six strings immersed in floor wax and thoroughly coated with scouring powder, and left them in his trousers that were hanging in the kitchen basement. These trousers were found but no such string could be located.

The two sections of bars had been removed and concealed underneath the large refrigerator to prevent early detection. He continually insisted that the so-called tool-proof stool bars were severed by this homemade abrasive string, and inferred that it had not taken very long to complete the job. The actual cuts on the bars had circular grooves and were highly polished and fresh, indicating that his described method was highly plausible. He offered as an excuse for his escaping that he had a long sentence and had no desire whatsoever to return to his detainer.

O.G. BLACKWELL
Warden

(Above top) The inmates slid down this sewage drain pipe to make their escape into the icy Bay waters.

(Above bottom) Under the cover of night, rain, and heavy fog, John Paul Scott washed up at Fort Point near the base of the Golden Gate Bridge, exhausted and lethargic from the freezing water.

The following is Warden Blackwell's report to the Bureau of Prisons on Daryl Parker, also dated December 17, 1962:

UNITED STATES DEPARTMENT of JUSTICE
BUREAU OF PRISONS
UNITED STATES PENITENTARY
ALCATRAZ CALIFORNIA

December 17, 1962

MEMORANDUM FOR FILE

Re: Statement of Inmate Daryl Lee Parker, #1314-AZ

At approximately 6:30 P.M. Sunday, December 16, 1962, inmate PARKER was returned from escape status and brought to the Associate Warden's office. During questioning he was very reluctant to make any statements, however, eventually he did say that he and inmate J. PAUL SCOTT, #1403-AZ, left the main dining hall shortly after the 5:20 P.M. count, gained access to the basement by way of the elevator, and escaped through the end window on the east side of the kitchen basement after having removed two sections of the bars. From this point, he claims that he climbed up the drainpipe and gained access to the roof, crossed over and went down the other side by means of an electric extension cord, then proceeded to the water and entered. From this point on he does not know what happened to SCOTT, or how he reached "Little Alcatraz."

Following this, he refused to make any further statements.

O.G. BLACKWELL
Warden

An inventory list submitted by Officer Irving Levinson, representing contraband items that were found in the kitchen basement following the escape of Parker and Scott.

By all accounts, Scott very nearly died in his quest to reach the shore. Open-water swimmer Lisa Johnson would later state that Scott really couldn't take credit for "*swimming to shore,*" but that actually he "*was carried*" by the three-knot-per-hour tide. Even Scott himself admitted that he hadn't anticipated how violent the ocean currents could be. In fact, they were so powerful that Scott was washed onto the rock at Fort Point and lay naked except for his socks, after his clothing had been ripped from his body by repeated banging against the rocks. When Scott was revived at Letterman, he was shaking so convulsively that he could not speak. His body temperature had dropped to 94 degrees, or 4.6 degrees below normal. He was lucky to have been spotted in his near-death state. John Paul Scott's spectacular but futile swim from Alcatraz Island to Fort Point destroyed once and for all the official position that escape from this Federal prison was impossible. As the press snapped photos of Scott wrapped warmly in knit army blankets when he was being taken from Letterman at 10:45 P.M. for his cruise back to Alcatraz, he gave them a coy smile. He had come the closest of any escape artist yet to breaking The Rock.

Both inmates would be transferred from Alcatraz following its closure in 1963, and Parker would make another unsuccessful escape attempt in March of 1967, while imprisoned at Atlanta. He built a makeshift ladder nearly thirty feet in length, but his attempt ended when a tower officer opened fire on him, forcing him back down. Parker was later paroled on August 20, 1974.

Scott would also continue to build his resume of crime. In May of 1963 he was transferred back to Atlanta, where he was again found with contraband materials for an escape. His record states that he worked in the hospital as an X-Ray Technician, and was finally paroled on July 10, 1968.

Scott got married for a second time on January 20, 1970 in East Point Georgia, to Margie Morgan, a middle-aged widow. A later arrest report would indicate that Scott resided with his wife "*in a very comfortable, spacious, ranch-style home.*" The report went on to say, "*he himself built this home and has resided there since 1970. Estimated value is over $50,000 dollars.*" It was also documented that he owned four other homes, but had placed them in his wife's name. Scott also re-enrolled at Georgia State University for a short period. He later took a job as a lab technician at Clayton General Hospital in Riverdale, Georgia, and was described as a model employee. He then started his own business, and built and sold several homes. But despite his successful integration back into society, his skeletons haunted him.

The following is a case report filed by the U.S. Attorney following another bank robbery in which Scott participated:

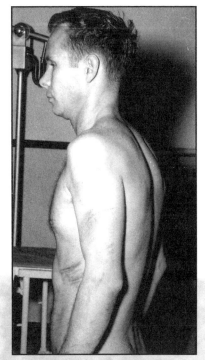

Scott sustained several cuts and bruises from the sharp rocks when he washed up at Fort Point.

Details of the offense reveal that at approximately 3:18 P.M. on September 5, 1975, Ronald Coleman Anderson, J. Paul Scott and Leon Johnson entered the Hearon Circle Branch of the Spartanburg Bank & Trust Company located on the Asheville Highway, Spartanburg, S.C. All three were dressed in coveralls, dark ski masks and brown jersey gloves. All were carrying pillowcases. Anderson was armed with an AR-l6 rifle, Scott was armed with a Model 10 shotgun, and Johnson was armed with a .22 handgun. During the course of the robbery, two deputies of the Spartanburg County Sheriff's Office appeared at the drive-in window in a marked car, and were observed by the bank robbers. The robbers fled the bank, and shooting

Scott's driver's license, issued during a short stint of freedom in 1974.

ensued outside the bank between the robbers and one of the deputies, with no injuries being sustained to either of the deputies, the robbers, or either of their vehicles. A chase ensued which culminated in the parking lot of a construction company located approximately one mile from the bank. As the car containing the deputies rounded the corner into the parking lot, the bank robbers fired on them, rendering the sheriff's car inoperable and slightly wounding one of the deputies in the rear of the neck. The getaway vehicle utilized by the robbers was determined stolen the previous night from a motel parking lot in Greenville, S.C. Witnesses at the switch site believe the bank robbers drove from the construction company parking lot in a two-tone blue Ford Granada, Mercury Monarch, or late model Monte Carlo.

Scott was again arrested in June of 1976 with Morris Lynn Johnson, one of the FBI's ten most wanted fugitives, in eastern New Orleans. In the following report, Scott described his plight in his own words, and recounted the story of yet another attempted escape:

In February of 1977, I received a 25-year sentence for Bank Robbery in Columbia, South Carolina. I was first confined at the USP Atlanta, Georgia, however, on March 15, 1977, I was notified that I was being transferred to the USP, Leavenworth, Kansas. I was to be transported on a Federal Bureau of Prison bus.

I was confined in a Jackson, Miss. County Jail during the night of Friday, March 18, 1977. Another inmate gave me a full-length hacksaw blade. On Saturday, March 19, 1977, I smuggled the hacksaw blade on the prison bus. There were about 25 other inmates on the prison bus. I was handcuffed and had leg irons on. I sat by myself on the right hand side near the middle of the bus. I had made up my mind that I would try and escape, since on Friday I had also obtained a paperclip and a ballpoint pen cartridge.

During the morning ride thru Louisiana I was able to pick the lock on first my handcuffs and then my leg irons. It took me about one hour to cut through the bar on the bus window. I had ripped a piece of my shirt and used it to get a good grip on the hacksaw blade. No one knew what I was doing until I had finished cutting the bar and had kicked out the window. No other inmates helped me in any way.

I was able to kick out the window and escape thru the hole I had cut in the window bar. The bus came to a stop but I still fell when I escaped thru the window. I ran approximately 100 feet from the bus, but stopped when the bus guards started shooting at me. They must have fired about five or six times, however, I was not hit. I was placed back in the bus, and they radioed ahead to FCI about my escape and capture.

Scott remained a violent and incorrigible inmate until his death at the Federal Correctional Institution in Tallahassee, Florida on February 22, 1987. His bold escape from Alcatraz with Daryl Parker remains as one of the most notable incidents ever to occur in the history of the island prison.

An excerpt from Parker's inmate record in 1982, showing that he still maintained his passionate desire to escape from prison.

The Closing
of Alcatraz

An aerial view of Alcatraz before its closure in 1963.

The Fall of an Icon

Perhaps one of the greatest ironies of Alcatraz was that the frigid and treacherous waters of the San Francisco Bay, which had proved to be the ultimate deterrent to escape for nearly three decades, finally contributed to the downfall of America's super-prison. Immediately following the escape of Morris and the Anglins, the prison fell under intense scrutiny due to its deteriorating structural condition and the diminishing security measures that resulted from governmental budget cuts. These developments should not be credited to the escape, as many of the decisions were already in process before the attempt was made. In a January 1963 structural report, the following conditions were described:

> The cellblocks which are located over the basement areas are considered unsafe for occupancy during a severe earthquake. For minor earthquakes and normal loadings the supporting structures are considered safe at this time, although further deterioration will result in an unsafe condition. The present structural condition of the basement does not conform to the 1961 Uniform Building Code . . . The present structural damage in the basement area is of continuing nature, which structural members deteriorated to a point where they will soon be inadequate to support the cellblock structures under normal loading conditions.

Attorney General Robert F. Kennedy would give the final order to close Alcatraz due to the exorbitant operational expense required to maintain the prison.

(Below) In August of 1961, a state-of-the-art Control Center was built in the Armory to enhance prison security.

Several photographs from 1962, showing the severe deterioration of the concrete structure.

Criminologists were also starting to publicly cast doubt on the effectiveness of Alcatraz as a deterrent for organized crime. The corrosive effects of the saltwater and the exorbitant cost of running the prison (Cost per inmate had risen to over $13.00 per day, as compared with $3.88 at USP Atlanta, not including an estimated five million dollars in expenses for restoration) provided U.S. Attorney General Robert Kennedy with grounds for closure. In the autumn months of 1962, the Federal Bureau of Prisons started to transfer inmates to other institutions, and prepared to shut down the facility. Bureau Director James Bennett wrote:

During the 1960's, financial considerations determined the issue and freed me from my dilemma. Alcatraz's buildings and steel towers were gradually being eroded by the salt spray, and would cost several million dollars to restore. The cost of supplying the island prison was exorbitant since food and water had to be brought across the bay. Alcatraz was also expensive to run, because it was located far from the continental center of population, far from most of the other prisons, and men had to be transported long distances from and back to the East and Middle West.

The daily per-prisoner operating costs at Alcatraz were far higher than at any other federal institution. So we drew up plans for a new maximum security prison to be built in the heart of the continent at Marion, Illinois, which could be built and operated at a lower cost. When the federal funds were made available for the new prison, we could close Alcatraz down.

On March 21, 1963, the final day of operation for Alcatraz, Warden Blackwell invited a press pool to witness the last small group of inmates

The base of the north wall of the utility corridor inside the main cellhouse. Senior Officer James Lewis is seen indicating the gaps that had appeared in the crumbling cement, due to years of environmental corrosion.

leaving The Rock. On that day, twenty-seven inmates filed into the Mess Hall for the last time, and lined up at the steam tables for one final breakfast. Even on the last day of the prison's operation, the meal period would last only twenty minutes, as the Warden was determined to adhere to the rigid regulations right up to the final hour. While the inmates sat in the Mess Hall, Deputy Director of the Bureau of Prisons Fred T. Wilkinson answered questions for the press, and took reporters on a brief tour of the cellhouse. After the inmates had filed back to their cells, each one was met by an officer and then handcuffed and shackled, and prepared for final departure.

The inmates stood quietly until the cellhouse officer gave the final signal to march quietly down Broadway in a single-file procession. There were only the eerie sounds of the inmates' shackles, and the snapping shutters from the press-pool cameras. Several men covered their faces as the flash bulbs burst off in quick succession, trying to capture the final march of prisoners at Alcatraz. Interestingly enough, the last inmate to be incarcerated at Alcatraz would also be the last to leave. Frank C. Weatherman, inmate #AZ-1576, was the last inmate to board the prison launch. When the press asked him how he felt about the closure, he uttered what would become the prison's eulogy: *"Alcatraz was never good for anybody."* The members of the press were then invited back into the cellhouse for coffee and donuts in the Mess Hall. Meanwhile the remaining officers left their posts and secured their weapons for the last time. USP Alcatraz then closed its doors after twenty-nine years of operation.

During the history of Alcatraz as a Federal prison, there were 1576 register numbers issued, with twenty-eight inmates receiving two numbers under separate prison terms. Theodore "Blackie" Audett would be alone in the distinction of having been issued three numbers, for three separate terms at Alcatraz. In the final assessment, 1546 inmates served time at Alcatraz Federal Penitentiary.

In July of 1964, the abandoned prison was turned over to the General Services Agency, which offered use of the property to other governmental agencies. John Hart, a former correctional officer at Alcatraz, remained on the island with his family as a lighthouse keeper and caretaker for the island. They continued to receive the *San Francisco Chronicle*, which was regularly dropped by a news helicopter, but otherwise lived in relative isolation.

The island remained essentially abandoned while several parties presented proposals for its use, ranging from erecting a West Coast version of the Statue of Liberty, to building a monument in honor of America's Space Program, complete with a memorial

(Above) Correctional Officer Keith Dennison standing guard inside the main cellhouse corridor on the day of the prison's closure.

(Below) The final march down Broadway by the last group of inmates, on March 21, 1963. The prisoners were subjected to the strict Alcatraz regimen even in the final hours of the prison's operation.

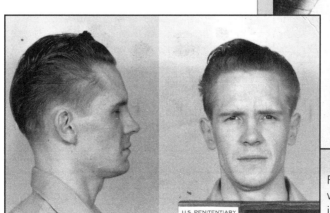

Frank C. Weatherman was the last inmate to be incarcerated at Alcatraz.

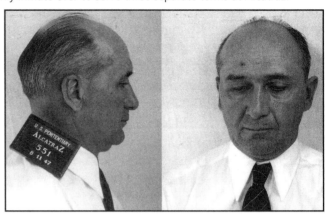

Correctional officers watching a plane carrying the last group of prisoners from Alcatraz, as it took off from San Francisco International Airport after the closing of the prison on March 21, 1963.

(Below) On November 20, 1969, a large group of American Indians landed on Alcatraz and claimed it for the Indian Nation. They offered to purchase the island for twenty-four dollars, payable in beads and red cloth—the same amount paid by the government to natives for "a similar island 300 years ago."

modeled on an Apollo space capsule. In June of 1968, San Francisco Mayor Joseph Alioto issued an appeal for public propositions. After a series of long battles and debates, which included an acceptance by the board of a proposal by Texas millionaire Lamar Hunt to develop the island as commercial property, the Secretary for the Department of the Interior ordered a draft plan for public recreational use of the abandoned prison site. But the battles over Alcatraz were not yet over. A group of Native American activists would also choose the island as the ideal place to make a political stand.

The Indian Occupation

On November 20, 1969, a large group of American Indians landed on Alcatraz and claimed the island as Indian property. The group articulated great plans, and hoped to establish an educational Native American Cultural Center. Overwhelming public support had developed for the movement, with advocates ranging from celebrities to members of the Hell's Angels. The Indians had the attention of both the media and the government. Federal officials met with the group, often sitting crossed-legged on blankets inside the old prison Dining Hall, discussing the social needs of the Indians. The volume of visitors became overwhelming, and the island started to become a haven for the homeless and the less fortunate. The Indians soon were faced with the same problems that had assailed the prison administration: there were no natural resources on the island, and all food and water had to be ferried over by boat. This was an expensive and exhausting process.

Despite special prohibitions that had been declared by the Native Americans, drugs and alcohol were prominently smuggled onto Alcatraz, and the situation quickly became unmanageable. The social organization of the group soon fell apart, and the Indians were forced to resort to drastic measures in order to survive. In an attempt to raise money to buy food, they allegedly began stripping copper wiring and tubing from the island buildings for sale as scrap metal. The worst tragedy occurred when Yvonne Oakes, the daughter of one of the key activists, fell to her death from the third story balcony of an apartment building. The Oakes family left the island in grave despair, and never returned. Then late on the evening of June 1, 1970, fires started by the occupants raged through several of the prison buildings, as well as the Warden's home, the lighthouse keeper's residence, and the Officers' Club, and badly damaged the historic lighthouse that had been built in 1909.

A Native American tee-pee is clearly visible next to one of the island pathways in 1970. This was a symbol of their quest for *"peace and freedom"*.

By now tensions had developed between Federal officials and the Indians, as the Federal agents blamed the activists for the destruction, and the activists blamed government saboteurs. The press, which until this point had been largely sympathetic toward the Indians, now turned against their cause, and began to publish stories of alleged beatings and assaults among the island's new residents. Public support for the Indians fell drastically. The original organizers had all deserted the island, and those who remained fought amongst themselves, thus providing clear evidence of a loss of solidarity in their society. On June 11, 1971, twenty Federal marshals and Coast Guard officers descended on the island and removed the remaining residents. All were taken to Treasure Island under protective custody, and this marked the official end of the Indian occupation of Alcatraz.

The massive fires that were started on June 1, 1970 during the Indian Occupation ultimately destroyed several key structures, including the Warden's mansion and the lighthouse.

Despite the fact that Alcatraz has been closed for several decades, its reputation still lives on, and continues to inspire both fictional and non-fictional books and films. The fictional movie *"The Rock,"* starring Sean Connery, Nicholas Cage, and Ed Harris, is one of many films set against the backdrop of Alcatraz.

Alcatraz will forever remain woven into the fabric of life in San Francisco, and it will stand as an iconic symbol in the annals of American history and folklore.

From Penitentiary to National Park

In 1972, Congress created the Golden Gate National Recreation Area, and Alcatraz Island was included as part of the new National Park Service unit. The island was opened to the public on October 25, 1973, and it has since become one of the most popular Park Service sites, with more than one million visitors from around the world each year. Today Alcatraz is considered an ecological preserve, and it is home to one of the largest western gull colonies on the northern California coast. The thrill of touring Alcatraz derives both from the awareness of its historical significance, and from the various portrayals of prison life that have been popularized through Hollywood motion pictures. People come from all over the world to meet eye-to-eye with the ghosts of America's toughest criminals. Meanwhile, many of the former inmates are still trying to come to terms with their imprisonment on Alcatraz, and they seek to understand why people would visit a place that represented for them only a monument of pure anguish and deep despair.

"There will always be the need for specialized facilities for the desperados, the irredeemable, and the ruthless, but Alcatraz and all that it had come to mean now belong, we may hope, to history."

—James V. Bennett, Director of the Bureau of Prisons

Each year, former Alcatraz inmates reunite with officers and family members at an annual reunion. Seen here are former inmates Nathan Glenn Williams (left) and Jim Quillen (right). Both men have written compelling books about their time served at the infamous prison.

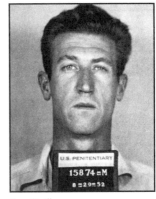

Jim Quillen

Nathan Glenn Williams

(Left and below) Willie Radkay, a veteran of Alcatraz. He is seen here during one of the reunions in 2002, at age ninety-one. He celled next to Machine Gun Kelly, and was also close friends with Dale Stamphill and Basil "Owl" Banghart.

(Below) Armory Officer Clifford Fish returned to Alcatraz in 2002, which was the first time since his retirement from the prison in 1962. He is seen with a Discovery Channel film crew filming in the Alcatraz "Dungeon".

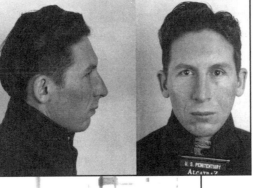

(Above) Former inmate Tom Kent and Father Bernie Bush meet with visitors inside the cellhouse chapel to discuss their memories of Alcatraz during a reunion event.

Inmate Regulations, 1956

Note: These "Institution Rules & Regulations" were in effect at the United States Penitentiary, Alcatraz, during Warden Paul J. Madigan's administration (1955–1961). They were issued to all inmates in the form of a typewritten booklet to be kept in the cell.

REGULATIONS FOR INMATES U.S.P., ALCATRAZ, REVISED 1956

INMATE Reg. NUMBER, _____

This set of Institution Regulations is issued to you as Institutional Equipment. You are required to keep it in your cell at all times.

INDEX

REGULATIONS FOR INMATES U.S.P., ALCATRAZ

This booklet is issued for the information and guidance of inmates of the U.S. Penitentiary, Alcatraz, California. It outlines the Institution's routines and explains what is expected of you in the matter of conduct and work. You are expected to learn and obey the rules and to perform your assigned work to the best of your ability.

1. **GOOD CONDUCT** means conducting yourself in a quiet and orderly manner and keeping your cell neat, clean and free from contraband. It means obeying the rules of the Institution and displaying a co-operative attitude. It also means obeying orders of Officials, Officers and other employees without delay or argument.
2. **GOOD WORK RECORD** means the reputation you establish as a willing, capable workman, doing your best at whatever work you are told to do.
3. **YOUR GOOD CONDUCT RECORD AND YOUR GOOD WORK RECORD** will be reviewed every time you are considered for work assignments, cell changes, and disciplinary action.

4. **STATUTORY GOOD TIME, MERITORIOUS GOOD TIME AND IN-DUSTRIAL GOOD TIME** are types of reduction in sentence which can be earned only by inmates who establish and keep a good conduct record and a good work record.

5. **PRIVILEGES.** You are entitled to food, clothing, shelter and medical attention. Anything else that you get is a privilege. You earn your privileges by conducting yourself properly. "Good Standing" is a term applied to inmates who have a good conduct record and a good work record and who are not undergoing disciplinary restrictions.

6. **DISCIPLINARY ACTION** may result in loss of some or all of your privileges and/or confinement in the Treatment Unit.

7. **TREATMENT UNIT** is the segregation section of the Institution where privileges may be restricted to a minimum.

8. **PROSECUTION IN THE U.S. DISTRICT COURT** in addition to Institutional disciplinary action may result if you commit any serious offense such as assault, escape, attempt to escape, rioting, destruction of government property, etc.

9. **FORFEITURE OR WITHHOLDING OF EARNED GOOD TIME, STATUTORY OR INDUSTRIAL,** in addition to disciplinary action and/or prosecution in the District Court, may result if you become involved in any serious misconduct.

10. **RESTORATION OF FORFEITED OR WITHHELD GOOD TIME** will not be recommended unless you can show at least one year of better than average good conduct and good work when you are called for your annual Classification Hearing.

11. **TRANSFER TO OTHER FEDERAL INSTITUTIONS** will not be recommended unless you can show a better than average good conduct record for several years at this Institution.

12. **RECOMMENDATION FOR CLEMENCY FOR MILITARY PRISONERS** will not be made unless they can show better than average good conduct and good work records for several years at this Institution.

13. **YOUR COMMITTED NAME AND REGISTER NUMBER** are used as a means of identification. You will be addressed by your surname (last name) only. Your register. number is also used as the laundry mark on your Institutional clothing.

14. **COMMENDATORY REPORTS** may be submitted by Officers who observe your behavior and find it better than average. Such reports are filed and help you to establish a good record.

15. **DISCIPLINARY REPORTS** may be submitted by Officers who observe your behavior and detect violations of the Institutional regulations. If you are interested in keeping a good record, you should conduct yourself according to the rules.

16. **CONTRABAND.** Anything found on your person, or in your cell, or at your work place, which was not Officially issued to you, or Officially approved and purchased by you, and Officially listed on your property card, will be classed as contraband. Possession of contraband of any sort is a serious offense and will result in disciplinary action. If you steal anything from other inmates or from employees, or from the Institution, you will be punished.

17. **ATTEMPTING TO BRIBE EMPLOYEES** by giving, or promising to give them anything, is a serious offense. You must not give or sell or receive or buy anything except through the Official channels.

18. **THREATENING, RIDICULING, OR ATTEMPTING TO INTIMIDATE OR ASSAULT OFFICERS, OFFICIALS, EMPLOYEES OR VISITORS** is a very serious offense.

19. **TRADING, GAMBLING, SELLING, GIVING, OR LOANING** your personal property or your government issue items or services, or contraband of any kind is a serious offense. You are expected to keep the things that are legitimately in your possession. If they are found in another inmate's possession, disciplinary action will result for both parties. If anything is stolen from you, report the loss to the Officials as soon as possible.

20. **RECREATION.** As a general rule, you will work eight hours a day, five days a week, with Saturdays, Sundays and Holidays devoted to recreation. Movies are shown twice each month. Exercise Yard activities include baseball, handball and various table games. Newly arrived inmates are kept in Quarantine Status for 30 days and are not allowed recreation during that period.

21. **WORK.** You are required to work at whatever you are told to do. Usually your first assignment will be to temporary maintenance jobs around the cellhouse. Other maintenance jobs include the Culinary Unit, the Clothing and Bath Room, the Library, and the Yard Detail. By doing good work on your maintenance assignment you earn Statutory Good Time. You may also qualify for additional Meritorious Good Time and/or pay, if your work and behavior are outstandingly good and are of outstanding value to the Institution. If you make a better than average work and conduct record while on your maintenance job, you may be considered for an assignment to a Federal Prison Industry Shop where you may earn Industrial Good Time and pay in addition to your Statutory Good Time.

22. **LOAFING, LOITERING, VISITING, OR UNAUTHORIZED ABSENCE FROM WORK** will result in disciplinary action, and may result in loss of your job, and withholding of, or forfeiture of, good time.

23. **YOUR CONSTRUCTIVE SUGGESTIONS OR LEGITIMATE COMPLAINTS** if made by you to the proper Officials, will receive careful consideration. However, if you make groundless complaints for the purpose of creating dis-satisfaction and/or stirring up trouble; or if you agitate' or rib' yourself or others into trouble, you will be subject to disciplinary action.

24. **INTERVIEW REQUEST SLIPS** may be obtained from the Cellhouse Officer. When you wish to ask an Official for information, for an interview to request some service or when you want to make a constructive suggestion or a legitimate complaint — use an interview slip. Instructions are printed on the slips.

25. **MONEY.** You are not allowed to have money of any kind in your possession while in this institution. Use of cigarettes or other items as jail money' is forbidden. Your earnings and whatever funds you brought with you, or which may be sent to you by approved correspondents, will be kept on deposit for you in the Prisoner's Trust Fund.

26. **PRISONER'S TRUST FUND** is operated like a savings account in a bank, except that it does not draw interest. With the approval of the Associate Warden, you may authorize the withdrawal of funds from your account for legitimate purposes such as the payment of attorney's fees and/or purchase of text books and educational materials. You are required to save a part of what you earn, and may contribute part of your earnings to dependents.

27. **THE PRISONER'S MAIL BOX** in each Institution is designed to provide any inmate an opportunity to write directly, without inspection by institutional authorities, to the Director of the Bureau of Prisons, the Attorney General, the Parole Board, the Surgeon General, Federal Judges, Department of Justice Officials, and in the case of military prisoners to the Secretary of War or Navy, or the Judge Advocate General, or the Adjutant General, regarding any matter of importance to the individual, to the inmate group as a whole, or any matter of importance affecting the institution and its personnel or Officials. The Prisoner's Mail Box is open to all inmates regardless of their status. See Section #41.

28. **DAILY ROUTINE:**
   7:00 A.M. Weekdays . . . 7:15 A.M. Saturdays, Sundays & Holidays: Morning wake-up bell. See Section 30 for instructions in making bed, policing cell, etc.

7:20 A.M. Weekdays . . . 7:50 A.M. Saturdays, Sundays & Holidays: Count Bell. Stand up by your cell door, facing out, remain there until the bell signal sounds again, indicating the count is correct. Absolute silence must prevail during all counts.

7:30 A.M. Weekdays . . . 7:50 A.M. Saturdays, Sundays & Holidays: Breakfast. When your door opens come out promptly and proceed in single file to the Dining Room in a quiet orderly manner. Do not change places in line by moving forward or backward. You may carry books and magazines to the library exchange table but do not carry books or anything else to exchange with other inmates nor put anything in other inmates' cells.

The Officer at the tray-dispenser cart will direct you to file past the steam table to the right or left, as he sees fit, to balance the lines. You must follow his instructions without question. See Section #33 for other Dining Room Rules.

Upon returning to your cell after breakfast, tidy up your cell, placing all trash in your wastebasket. Place this basket outside the cell door at the first opportunity so that orderlies may empty it. If you leave the building for work or recreational activity, put on appropriate clothing. Caps are not worn inside the cellhouse at any time.

8:00 A.M. Weekdays: Outside Work Call.

Industries and other outside details will proceed in single file through the rear cellhouse door to the yard.

In rainy weather, all outside workers are called out by details. Remain in your cell until your detail is called, then proceed promptly to the West End of the cellhouse. Your detail officer will escort you as quickly as possible to your place of work.

In fair weather, or when it is not raining too hard, details will remain on the Yard until the Lieutenant gives the signal to line up. You will have a few minutes to smoke and converse. When the line-up bell rings, move promptly to your proper place in your detail and face the South wall. Smoking is not permitted between the Yard and your place of work. Your detail officer will give the signal to proceed through the rear gate to the Work Area. Move in single file.

Laundry workers will turn right at the ramp and enter the Laundry. Gardeners and incinerator operator will wait at the Garden Area Gate. If you work in a lower-level shop or outside, proceed to the lower level and stop at the designated lines. Form a column of Twos and await the signal from your detail Officer to proceed.

When you reach your place of work, change in to your work clothes and go about your work as directed by your detail Officer or Foreman.

Smoking is permitted in the shops except where there is some hazardous condition. Smoking is a privilege. Be very careful about putting matches and butts in the butt-cans.

8:25 A.M. Count Bell on Saturdays, Sundays & Holidays.

8:30 A.M. Saturdays—Main Line Bath. (See Section #29)

9:25 A.M. Saturdays—Count Bell.

9:30 A.M. Saturdays—Yard. (See Sections #37 & #42)

8:30 A.M. Sundays—Religious Services. (See Sections #40 & #48)

8:40 A.M. Sundays—Yard.

8:30 A.M. Holidays—Yard.

8:40 A.M. Weekdays: Inside details will proceed directly and quietly to their places of work. They will confine their activities strictly to their assigned duties and upon satisfactory completion of these duties will return directly and quietly to their cells.

Culinary Detail inmates have a special schedule of work and recreation hours.

11:35 A.M. Weekdays: Outside details will stop work, check in tools, wash, change clothing and prepare for return to the cellhouse.

11:45 A.M. Weekdays: Outside details leave shops on signal and proceed in column of twos to the cellhouse. Do not carry on loud and boisterous conversations. Do not jostle or indulge in horseplay with others.

YOU MAY BE STOPPED AND SEARCHED AT ANY TIME. DO NOT ATTEMPT TO CARRY CONTRABAND.

11:50 A.M. Weekdays: COUNT BELL.

12:00 Noon. Saturdays, Sundays & Holidays—Return to cellhouse from recreation Yard. Line up in Yard according to cell block and gallery area and proceed to the cellhouse on signal.

12:00 Noon. Weekdays: Dinner.

12:10 P.M. Saturdays, Sundays & Holidays: COUNT BELL.

12:15 P.M. Saturdays, Sundays & Holidays: Dinner.

12:30 P.M. COUNT BELL.

12:35 P.M. SICK CALL. See Section #36.

INTERVIEWS: You will be notified if you are scheduled for an interview with any Official. See Section #24.

1:00 P.M. Weekdays: Outside Work Call. Same as A.M. Routine.

1:00 P.M. Saturdays, Sundays & Holidays: COUNT BELL.

3:10 P.M. (TUESDAYS ONLY): Return to cellhouse for Tuesday bathline.

3:25 P.M. COUNT BELL. (Tuesday only).

3:30 P.M. Bath lines — Tuesday Only.

3:30 P.M. Weekdays. (Other than Tuesday) Yard recreation period ends. Return from recreation area.

4:10 P.M. Stop work on outside details.

4:20 P.M. Outside details leave shops to cellhouse.

4:35 P.M. COUNT BELL.

4:40 P.M. Supper.

5:30 P.M. COUNT BELL. Final Lock-up Count.

SATURDAYS, SUNDAYS & HOLIDAYS:

3:45 P.M. Return from Yard.

3:55 P.M. COUNT BELL.

4:00 P.M. Supper.

4:40 P.M. COUNT BELL. Final Lock-up Count.

RECREATION PERIODS: Saturdays: 9:30 A.M. to 12:00 Noon: 1:15 P.M. to 3:40 P.M.

Sundays: 8:40 A.M. to 12:00 Noon: 1:15 P.M. to 3:40 P.M.

Holidays : 8:30 A.M. to 12:00 Noon: l:15 P.M. to 3:40 P.M. Movies are shown twice monthly on Sundays and Holidays in the afternoon.

29. BATH ROOM RULES: Bathing and laundry exchange are scheduled for mainline bath inmates every Tuesday afternoon and Saturday morning. Items of clothing will be exchanged as follows:

TUESDAY:

    1 handkerchief
    3 pairs of socks
    1 face towel
    1 sheet
    1 pillow case
    1 lt. undershirt
    1 shorts or drawers

SATURDAY:

    1 handkerchief
    3 pairs of socks
    1 face towel
    1 B & W pants
    1 blue shirt

1 lt. undershirt

1 shorts or drawers

When you go to the bathroom you will display all items of soiled clothing before the inspecting Officer. You will then deposit this clothing in the proper hampers and take your bath. You are expected to bathe in a reasonable length of time. Go to the issue window and draw your clean clothing. Check each item. Minor repairs and replacements will be made immediately, if possible. If this cannot be done, the Clothing Room Officer will take your name and number and place you "on call."

Special issues of' clothing and equipment will not be handled during bathline. Give your name and number to the Clothing Room Officer and he will place you "on call" for these special items.

Do not carry blankets, coats, shoes or other articles to the bath room. Special arrangements are made for collection and laundering of woolen articles and for the repair of shoes.

CULINARY DETAIL BATH LINES: The culinary details will bathe on Mondays, Wednesdays & Fridays, in two groups as designated by the Steward. Each group will go to and from the bathroom in a body. When the first group has finished bathing and returned to the Culinary department or to their cells, the second group will proceed to the bathroom. Exchange items and days will be as follows:

MONDAYS:

1 Face towel

1 pr shorts

2 pairs of socks

1 lt undershirt

1 white pants

1 white pants

1 handkerchief

WEDNESDAYS :

1 face towel

1 pr shorts

2 pair socks

1 lt. undershirt

1 white pants

1 white shirt

1 handkerchief

1 sheet

1 pillowcase

FRIDAYS:

1 face towel

1 pr shorts

2 pair socks

1 B & W pants

1 blue shirt

1 heavy undershirt

1 lt. undershirt

1 white pants

1 white shirt

1 handkerchief

On Wednesdays and Fridays, Culinary inmates will draw those other supplies which are issued to the Mainline on Tuesdays & Saturdays.

30. **CELLHOUSE RULES.** Caps are never worn in the cellhouse. You may smoke in your cell, in the Library or in A-Block, but not elsewhere in the cellhouse. DO NOT SMOKE OR CARRY LIGHTED CIGARETTES OR PIPES ON THE GALLERIES OR FLATS IN THE CELLHOUSE AT ANY TIME. WALK—DO NOT RUN when moving from one place to another.

Upon entering the cellhouse, remove your cap and walk directly and quietly to your cell. Loud talking, loitering or visiting on the galleries, stairs or aisles is not permitted. Don't enter any other inmate's cell at any time.

When you talk in the cellhouse, talk quietly. Don't create a disturbance. Keep your cell neat and clean and free from trash and contraband. Keep your property neatly arranged on your shelves, as shown in the cell diagram on Page #8 [**not included here**]. Don't leave things stacked on the bars or on your folding table and seat. Don't paste or tack anything on the walls or shelves in your cell. Keep the floor and the bars of the cell-front free from dust and dirt. The only articles permitted on the cell floor are shoes, slippers, trashbaskets, drawing boards and musical instruments.

Your cell is subject to search at any time. Contraband items found in your cell will be confiscated and a disciplinary report will be placed against you for possession of same.

Any dangerous articles such as money, narcotics, intoxicants, weapons, or tools, found in your cell or on your person, that could be used to inflict injury, destroy property, or aid in escape attempts will result in disciplinary action and possibly U.S. District Court action. The presence of articles of this nature on your person or in your cell will be considered evidence of intent to use them for unlawful purposes. "Extra" razor blades are classed as dangerous weapons.

At the wake-up bell in the morning you must get out of bed and put on your clothes. Make up your bed properly (as shown in the diagram on Page #8) with your pillow at the end near the bars, blankets tucked neatly under the mattress, and extra blankets folded neatly at the foot of the bed. Sweep your cell and place the trash in the trash basket. Don't attempt to flush trash down the toilet. Don't sweep trash or dirt out onto the gallery or off the gallery.

At 9:30 P.M. lights out, retire promptly. All conversations and other noises must cease immediately.

Keep your person, clothing, bedding, cell equipment, toilet articles, personal property, library books, etc., clean and in good order at all times. You must not mark or deface your cell, library books, furniture, equipment or fittings of the institution. Do not throw anything from your cell at any time.

Advise the cellhouse Officer when you need hot water and a mop to clean your cell. You will be required to remain in your cell and clean it whenever it is reported for being dirty.

Loud talking, shouting, whistling, singing or other unnecessary noises are not permitted. You are permitted to hold QUIET conversations and to play games QUIETLY with your adjoining neighbors ONLY.

Do not tamper with the electric outlets or radio fixtures in your cell. If they do not operate properly, notify the Cellhouse Officer.

Your cell light must be turned out when you leave your cell except when you go to meals. LEAVE YOUR CELL LIGHT BURNING WHEN YOU GO TO MEALS.

A - 12 Books (Maximum)

B - Personal Papers

C - Paint Box etc.

D - Radio Headphones

E - Ash Tray & Tobacco

F - Extra Soap

G - Mirror

H - Toothpowder
I - Razor & Blades
J - Shaving Brush
K - Shaving Mug
L - Drinking Cup
M - Face Towel
N - Bathrobe
O - Raincoat
P - Calendar
Q - Coat & Cap
R - Soap
S - Sink Stopper
T - Cleaning Powder
U - Toilet Tissue
V - Extra Shoes & Slippers
W- Musical Instrument/Case
X - Broom
Y - Trash Basket
Z - Extra Blankets

N.B. Extra Blanket is to be folded neatly at foot of bed. Pillow at the head of the bed toward the bars. Blankets are to be tucked in under the mattress. Shoes, slippers and musical instruments & cases are to be under the bed with the shoes or slippers under the leading edge of the bed.

No fires are permitted in the cell for any purpose whatsoever. Do not attempt to heat water in your cell.

Cell changes are made only on the approval of the Associate Warden. Submit a written request to the Cellhouse Officer who will forward it to the Associate Warden for consideration.

Each inmate is given a property card on which the cellhouse Officer has listed all his personal property. UNLISTED articles which are found in your cell will be confiscated and considered as contraband. At no time will you change or alter your property card. The cellhouse Officer will list any authorized additions to your card. In addition to the personal property listed on your property card, you are allowed the following articles in your cell:

CELL ISSUE EQUIPMENT
2 shelves
2 sheets stationary
2 envelopes
1 can cleanser
3 pencils
1 Radio Headset
1 sink stopper
1 75-watt light bulb
4 wall pegs
1 whisk broom
1 lamp shade
1 set INSTITUTION REGULATIONS
1 roll toilet tissue
1 drinking cup
1 ash tray
2 cleaning rags
1 wastebasket

NO SPECIAL SHELVES, BOXES, DESKS OR PICTURE FRAMES WILL BE ALLOWED

BEDDING
2 Mattresses (Maximum)
2 sheets
2 pillows
1 to 4 blankets
2 pillow cases (if 2 pillows]

TOILET ARTICLES
1 shaving cup
2 razor blades
1 safety razor
1 cake soap
1 comb
1 shaving brush
1 pair nail clippers
1 mirror
1 can toothpowder
1 face towel
1 toothbrush
1 cake shaving soap

You will keep your property card listing your personal property, above your cell door behind the locking mechanism.

31. **CLASSIFICATION, PAROLE, EDUCATION AND SOCIAL MAT-TERS**: At this institution, these functions center in the Parole Office and you are free to request an interview with the Parole Officer when problems arise concerning these matters.

CLASSIFICATION: You will be reclassified each year shortly before or during the month of your parole eligibility date (except military prisoners who are reclassified just prior to their military annual review dates) and you will be given an opportunity to appear at the Classification Committee meeting to present any problems you may wish to discuss with the Committee.

PAROLE: A few months before your Parole Eligibility Date, you may file an application for a parole hearing. If you do not choose to file at that time, you may sign a waiver. This waiver will not interfere with your right to file for a hearing at a later date.

EDUCATION: Although there are no school classes at this institution, limited facilities are provided for cell study of books available from the library or from correspondence schools. Library rules are listed in Section #45.

SOCIAL MATTERS: If you have social problems outside the institution, such as correspondence problems, you are free to request an interview with the Parole Officer. The Parole Officer will also help you with the development of your release plans.

32. **CLOTHING**: The standard inmate uniform for all normal activities inside the cellhouse consists of: blue chambray shirt, Blue & White (B&W) trousers, web waist belt and issue shoes. This uniform is worn at visits, interviews, meals, movies, etc. Your shirt will be buttoned except for the top collar button. The sleeves will be rolled down and buttoned. Your belt will be worn with your register number in plain view, at the center of your back.

You are required to wear this standard uniform to and from outside work or the Recreation Yard, but you may add to it your cap, jacket, coat or raincoat. You may wear tennis shoes to the Recreation Yard only.

You will wear your robe and slippers or shoes when going to and from bath.

You are not allowed to change or alter any of your issue clothing. Keep your clothing neat, clean and in good repair at all times.

Special work clothing is issued for work details. This special clothing will be kept at the place of work and will not be brought to the Yard or cellhouse.

Culinary inmates wear a special work uniform consisting of white cap, white shirt and white pants. This uniform is issued for work only but is worn between the cell and Culinary Unit. Culinary workers are cautioned to be wearing their complete uniform with all buttons except the top collar button fastened before leaving their cells to go to work.

INMATES WILL BE ISSUED ON ARRIVAL:

- 1 B & W Pants
- 1 Cap
- 1 wool coat
- 1 Blue shirt
- 1 belt
- 1 pr shorts
- 1 bathrobe
- 3 pairs socks
- 2 handkerchief
- 1 Rain coat
- 2 pairs shoes
- 1 wool undershirt (on request)
- 1 pair slippers
- 1 lt undershirt

AUTHORIZED EXTRA CLOTHING ISSUE:

Culinary workers: 1 white shirt: 1 white cap: 1 white pants.
Barbers: 1 white shirt.
Office Orderlies: 1 white shirt.
Passmen: 1 white shirt: 1 white pants.
Hosp. Orderlies: 1 white shirt: 1 white pants.

When they are available, heavy undershirts may be issued upon request to the Clothing Room Officer. They are issued on the call-out list after the Saturday bath. Heavy undershirts are worn for a full week and are not exchanged on Tuesday bath line.

Clothing issue, replacement and repair are scheduled during Saturday bathline. Inspect your issue clothing when you receive it. Make certain that you have your own clothing and that all of it is in the lot. Report immediately any discrepancies to the Clothing Room Officer and tell him of your needs for replacement or repairs. If the service cannot be provided immediately, you will be recalled after the bathline for attention.

If you damage your clothing accidentally during the week, notify the Cellhouse Officer and you may be permitted to go to the Clothing Room for repairs or an emergency issue.

33. **DINING ROOM RULES:** Meals are served three times a day in the dining room. Do not exceed the ration. Do not waste food. Do not carry food from the dining room.

Wear standard uniform. (See Section #32).

Conduct yourself in a quiet, orderly manner. You may converse in normal tones with persons near you. Boisterous conduct will not be tolerated in the dining room.

Observe the ration posted on the menu board and take all that you wish to eat within the allotted amounts, but you must eat all that you take.

You may go to the coffee urn on your side of the dining room only when no other inmate is there. Do not go to the urn for the purpose of visiting with others.

Do not pass or exchange food, cigarettes, notes or any other items anywhere in the dining room.

You will be given ample time to eat but no loitering will be permitted.

Shortages of silverware at the table must be reported to the Officer immediately before beginning to eat.

After you have finished eating, place your silverware in the right hand compartment of your tray. Empty bread, cake or pie trays and pitchers will be passed to the end of the table toward the center of the Dining Room. Inmates seated at that end of the table will arrange them for inspection by the officer assigned to the table.

When all inmates on a table have finished eating, the inspecting Officer will give the signal to rise and leave the dining room. Proceed in single file directly to your cell. Enter your cell without delay. Do not loiter or visit on the galleries. Do not enter another inmate's cell at any time. Cell door will be locked as soon as you enter your cell.

34. **HAIRCUTS AND SHAVES:** Haircuts will be of regulation type. You are not permitted to wear your hair in an unusual manner or have any special haircut except as authorized by the Associate Warden.

You will be placed on call for a haircut approximately every three weeks. You will be told when you are scheduled for it.

You may be allowed to go to the Recreation Yard after your haircut if you are in good standing. You will shave in your cell. Razor blades are exchanged each Saturday by the Evening Watch Officer. Two new blades are issued in exchange for your two old blades. Failure to account for both of your blades at any time will result in a disciplinary report. Loss of a razor blade must be reported to the Cellhouse Officer immediately. Do not wait until issue night to report the loss. You must be clean shaven at all times. No special beards, mustaches or goatees are allowed.

35. **INTERVIEWS:** If you wish an interview with the Warden, Associate Warden, Captain, or other Official, submit a written request slip stating briefly what you wish to discuss and give the request slip to the Cellhouse Officer. You will be notified when to remain in your cell for the interview.

36. **MEDICAL ATTENTION:** Medical attention is available to all inmates. A member of the Hospital Staff conducts a daily Sick-Call line in the Cellhouse at about 12:30 P.M. To attend sick-call, proceed directly to the West End of the Cellhouse and stand quietly in line until called. After consultation, return directly to your cell. Do not loiter or visit on the gallery. If you become ill at any time, notify an Officer and you will receive medical attention. Do not make unnecessary disturbances. When you receive a medical lay-in, you will remain in your cell except for religious services, meals and movies. If you are notified by the Medical Officer at sick-call to remain in your cell for Hospital call-out, you must do so. You are allowed to keep in your cell only those medications issued to you by the Hospital Staff. Empty and unused bottles are to be returned to the West End desk. No medications will be kept in your cell longer than 30 days.

37. **MOVEMENT OF INMATES:** All inmate movements will be by block and galleries, to yard, work, meals, sick-line, band room and bathline. Movements will be from cells to West End of the Cellhouse and then to destination. Movements to picture shows and Religious Services will be from cells to East End of cellhouse and then to Auditorium. All movements from yard will be by galleries. Inmates will line up by cellblocks and galleries in the designated areas on the yard and proceed to the cellhouse as called by the Yard Officer. While awaiting the signal for your gallery to come in, do not wander around in other gallery lines, or indulge in scuffling or jostling with others. Industries and other "outside" details will return tn the cellhouse without lining-up in the yard.

38. **SUPPLIES:** Toilet tissue, matches, soap, cleanser, etc., will be issued on Tuesdays and Saturdays during bathlines. Writing paper and envelopes are issued only on Tuesdays. Toothpowder will be issued on either of the bathdays in exchange for your empty container. Toothbrushes, combs and fingernail clippers will be issued by the Clothing Room Officer,

after a proper request slip has been submitted. Your old item must be exchanged for the new item.

39. **WORK REGULATIONS:** If you are assigned to an Industries shop, go to your place of work as stated in Section #28. Do not leave your assigned station in the shop without permission from your Foreman or Officer.

Work assignments are made by the Associate Warden. If you wish a work assignment or re-assignment, send a request slip to the Associate Warden and state your experience in the type of work you are requesting. Send a separate slip with this information for each job application. Work changes will not be made for trivial reasons. Your request will be considered only on the basis of merit, and then only when a vacancy exists.

When in need of advice regarding your work or work assignment, consult the Associate Warden by interview slip.

The regular work-reports submitted by your superiors, supervisors, foremen, shop Officer or other Official are taken into consideration at all hearings for other matters. Special attention is paid to work reports at your hearings before Board meetings for consideration of restoration of forfeited good-time, transfer, parole reports, clemency and/or work changes.

Do not take issue with an Officer, foreman, supervisor or civilian employee on account of any order he may issue to you. If it should seem to you that such person is exceeding his authority or abusing his office, do not argue. Follow his instructions and report the matter to the Associate Warden after the duty is performed.

Smoking is permitted in designated areas. If in doubt, ask your foreman or Officer.

Do not carry any unauthorized articles to or from your place of work.

Do not carry work clothing from the work area to the cellhouse.

Removing tools or other articles from your work area is forbidden. Do not loan any tools or other work material to any inmate without the express approval of your superiors.

Immediately report any injury received while at work. If you become ill, report to your foreman.

Do not manufacture any unauthorized or contraband article, nor perform any unauthorized service for yourself or for any other inmate. Do not assist or interfere with another inmate's work except as directed by an Officer or foreman.

40. **AUDITORIUM RULES:** When preparing to attend religious services or movies, in the Auditorium, you must remove everything from your pockets except your handkerchief and eyeglasses and eyeglass case. All other items will be classed as contraband. There is no smoking permitted in the Auditorium and you are not allowed to wear or carry, caps, coats, jackets, cushions, blankets or pillows. Use the East-End cellhouse stairs when going to and from the Auditorium. Walk quietly and be co-operative if and when you are searched for contraband. Upon arrival at the Auditorium, take the seat assigned. If you have poor vision, and wish to sit in the front seats tell the Officer who is directing the seating. After being seated, remain in your seat until the Officer directs you to leave. Loud talking, pushing or boisterous conduct is forbidden. In general, you are expected to conduct yourself in an orderly manner, with proper consideration for the rights of others.

Leaving the Auditorium before the end of the program is permitted only in emergencies. Quietly notify the Officer in charge and he will permit you to leave. You will not be able to return to the Auditorium. The privilege of attending Religious Services and movies is important to you. This privilege may be withdrawn for violation of the rules.

41. **CORRESPONDENCE:** Upon entrance to the institution, each inmate will be given a form to fill out, listing the persons with whom he wishes permission to correspond. After approval of the list, inmates may correspond only with the approved correspondents. You will refrain from discussing other inmates or institutional affairs. Violent or abusive letters will not be mailed. Correspondence is limited to two (2) outgoing and seven (7) incoming letters a week. All regular inmate mail will be collected by the evening watch Officer in the cellhouse. Writing materials are issued during the Tuesday P.M. bathline, at the supply table in the clothing room.

SEALED CORRESPONDENCE: As stated in Section 27, sealed correspondence may be addressed to certain Officials. Such letters may be sealed and placed in the special mail box which is located at the West End of the Cellhouse. You are not required to place any identifying information on the envelope and it will be forwarded to the Bureau without inspection.

SPECIAL HOLIDAY MAIL: In addition to your regular mail privileges you will be allowed to send your Mother an extra letter on Mother's Day. At Christmas time you will be allowed to mail (4) Christmas Cards. You may receive greeting cards only on the following occasions: Christmas, Easter, Father's Day and your birthday.

Inmates will not ask Officers, Officials or civilians to write or post letters for them or receive mail through Officers, Civilians or Officials except when acting in their official capacity.

42. **YARD PRIVILEGES:** Exercise yard rules:

All inmates in good standing are allowed the yard privilege on Saturdays, Sundays, and Holidays, if the weather permits. In addition, inmates who have completed their assigned tasks, or who have been "laid in" by detail foremen, or who have been "held in" for haircut, medical attention, interview or other Official business, may be allowed the yard privilege on weekday afternoons if they are otherwise eligible.

Inmates who are "restricted" or who are in "idle" status because they have quit a job, or refused a job, or were removed from a job for disciplinary reasons, are not eligible for weekday afternoon yard.

Inmates held in for dental or hospital call may have yard after their appointments, subject to the Doctor's approval.

Inmates using cushions, tables or other institutional athletic equipment must return the same to the metal detector when recreation period is over.

No gambling is allowed. You may play chess, checkers or backgammon. Authorized card games are Hearts, Cribbage, and dominoes. No card game will be allowed if it is a "draw" type of game or does not use the full deck on the deal.

All card tables will be set up behind the screens at the West-End of the yard. All games will cease immediately when the bell rings for the termination of the yard period. No loitering will be permitted to finish uncompleted hands or games.

43. **USE OF TYPEWRITERS:** You are permitted to work on your own case or to hire a lawyer to represent you. A typewriter is available if you are able to type. Apply to the Associate Warden for permission. You are not permitted to work on another inmate's case or to give another inmate legal advice or instructions. After you obtain permission to use the typewriter, you will be notified when a machine is available. You will bring all materials to "A" Block where they will be inspected. All typing material, books, papers, etc., will remain in "A" Block until the typing has been completed. All papers will be signed and labeled. One copy of all papers typed shall be made for the Insti-

tution records. After the Associate Warden has inspected the papers, your copy will be returned to you.

44. **LIBRARY RULES**: Each cell contains a catalog which lists all of the books contained in the library. If you do not have a library catalog or library card, address a request to the Librarian to obtain one. Fill out this card with your name, register number and cell location.

(1) To request delivery of library books to your cell, refer to the catalog for the "Call" or identification number of the book you want and place that number on your library card. Place the card on the table at the entrance to the dining room on your way to breakfast. Return books in the same manner.

(2) The library books you request are checked out to you and must be returned within the time limit shown on the DATE-DUE slip inside the back cover of the book. Failure to return the book to the library prior to or on the date due, may result in forfeiture of library privileges.

(3) You are permitted to have not more than three CIRCULAT-ING library books in your cell at one time. Keep your books and magazines neatly arranged on the shelf in the cell when they are not being read.

(4) In addition to the circulating books, you are permitted to have a Bible, Dictionary and study books up to a maximum of twelve (12) in your cell at one time. This includes all books, personal, library and study course books. Books beyond the maximum of 12 will be confiscated.

A maximum of 24 pamphlets may be kept in your cell at one time. Pamphlets beyond this maximum will be confiscated.

(5) Handle library books carefully. Many of the worn out books, especially fiction books, can not be replaced since they are out of print. You are cautioned not to loan or exchange books with other inmates or to toss books to other tiers or the flag. Defacement, mutilation or destruction of books will be cause for disciplinary action even to the extent of forfeiture of good time.

MAGAZINES: The library subscribes to a few magazines such as the National Geographic and these magazines can be obtained from the library, not by using the library card, but by submitting a request form. Library magazines must be handled with care and promptly returned to the library for redistribution. Do not remove articles or pictures.

You are permitted to purchase (by subscription) not more than eight (8) magazines from the approved list. Requests for the purchase of magazines are submitted to the Mail Censor using the regular request slip. When magazines arrive at the institution, the mail Censor marks your number on them and forwards them to the Library for distribution. Magazines are withdrawn from circulation 30 days after delivery.

MOVIES: Movies are shown twice monthly for inmates in good standing. See the AUDITORIUM RULES in Section #40.

46. **MUSIC RULES**: Musical instruments may be purchased if approved by the Associate Warden.

Guitars and other stringed instruments may be played in the cellhouse in a QUIET manner only between the hours of 5:30 P.M. and 7:00 P.M. No singing or whistling accompanyments will be tolerated. Any instrument which is played in an unauthorized place, manner, or time will be confiscated and the inmate placed on a disciplinary report.

Wind instruments, drums and pianos will be played in the band or Orchestra Rooms on Saturdays, Sundays and Holidays. At no time will you play any wind instrument in the cellhouse.

Permission to play instruments in the Band, Orchestra or bathrooms may be granted by the Associate Warden to inmates in good standing. The Band room is a privilege and permission to play there must be requested from the Associate Warden.

A limited number of inmates may be allowed to take musical instruments to and from the recreation yard. Permission must first be obtained from the Associate Warden.

No inmate on "idle" status or on "report" or restricted will be allowed to use the Band Room, Orchestra Room or to take instruments to the yard.

An inmate whose musical privileges have been restricted or revoked shall be removed from all musical lists, and his instrument stored in "A" Block until otherwise authorized by the Associate Warden.

No inmate is allowed to give, sell, trade, exchange, gamble, loan or otherwise dispose of his personal or institutional instrument or to receive such from another inmate.

Institutional instruments may be loaned to inmates in good standing upon the approval of the Associate Warden.

All instruments will be listed on personal property cards. Institutional instruments shall be listed as "On Loan" from the institution, together with the date of the loan and the identification number of the instrument. Surplus parts for musical instruments together with and including extra sets of guitar strings shall be kept in "A" Block. Guitar strings shall be purchased in the regular manner and stored in "A" Block until needed. An old set of strings must be turned in to the cellhouse Officer to draw a new set.

47. **RADIO**: Radio programs are carefully selected for the enjoyment of all concerned. Protect your radio privileges by conducting yourself properly with consideration for the rights of other inmates during broadcasts.

You are issued a radio headset on the signing of a receipt for the same. Do not tamper with your radio outlets, phones, or other equipment. If they do not work properly, notify the cellhouse Officer quietly. Your headsets are of a "tamper-proof" type. Evidence of tampering with any part of your radio equipment will result in a disciplinary report.

The operator of the radio is not in the cellhouse. Do not shout any instructions, advice or abuse.

Programs are scheduled for the following hours:
Weekdays: 6:00 PM to 9:30 PM
SATURDAYS, SUNDAYS & HOLIDAYS: 1:00 PM to 9:30 PM

Loud laughter, yelling, cheering or clapping will not be tolerated. Your headset must be kept at the rear of the cell when you are out. Do not leave your headset plugged-in when you leave the cell. Headsets found plugged-in or hanging on the outlet box will be picked up.

48. **RELIGIOUS SERVICES**: Catholic and Protestant Services are held regularly on Sundays in the Chapel. Jewish Services are held on appropriate occasions. Religious advice and counsel are available by sending a request slip to the Chaplain. The menu board in the dining room will indicate the schedule of the Religious Services.

Regular Auditorium Rules will be observed during all Services. See Section #40 for Auditorium Rules.

49. **SPECIAL PURCHASES**: There is no commissary at Alcatraz. The institution supplies all your needs. You are not allowed to have anything sent to you from home, friends or relatives. You may be allowed to purchase certain items such as text books, correspondence courses, musical instruments, or magazine subscriptions. All such purchases must be listed on your property card by the cellhouse Officer.

After your purchase request is approved, you must sign a withdrawal slip and return it to the cellhouse Officer. If you receive only a part of what was signed for on this withdrawal slip, the balance of the money will be returned to your account. Only those items actually received are charged to you.

All purchases will be entered on your property card. No bartering, trading or giving as a gift of any purchase is allowed. You are not permitted to loan any items to any other inmate nor to borrow from another inmate.

50. **TOBACCO AND SMOKING REGULATIONS**: Pipe and cigarette tobacco is available from the dispensers at the West-End of the cellhouse. Take what you need for immediate use, not to exceed six packs altogether. Don't hoard tobacco. Don't waste tobacco.

Cigarettes: One pack of cigarettes may be issued to each inmate in good standing, each Monday, Wednesday and Friday evening. Inmates who are restricted or on report will not receive cigarettes. You are not permitted to have more than 3 packs (60 cigarettes) at any one time. If you are found to have in excess of 60 cigarettes at any one time, all will be confiscated and you will be placed on a disciplinary report.

Matches: Matches and cigarette papers are distributed during bathlines. Do not accumulate more than 10 books of matches nor more than two of the 150-paper size books of cigarette papers.

Smoking: Smoking regulations vary for different areas. If in doubt, ask your foreman or Officer. No smoking is permitted in the Cellhouse at any time except within the cells, library or "A" Block. Smoking is not permitted in the dining room or kitchen except for certain areas assigned for kitchen workers. Smoking is permitted in the yard but not between the yard and your place of work.

51. **VISITS**: You are allowed to receive one visit each month from members of your immediate family or other persons approved by the Warden. Visiting hours are approximately 1:30 PM to 3:10 PM weekdays.

In all personal visits you will confine your talk to personal matters and refrain from discussing other inmates, Institutional matters, etc.

Visits with your Attorney of record may be arranged through the office of the Associate Warden.

52. **THE GOOD TIME LAW**: Revised Title 18 of the United States Code, effective September 1, 1948, provides in Section 4161 as follows:

"Each prisoner convicted of an offense against the United States and confined in a penal or correctional institution for a definite term other than for life, whose record of conduct shows that he has faithfully observed all the rules and has not been subjected to punishment, shall be entitled to a deduction from the term of his sentence beginning with the day on which the sentence commences to run, to be credited as earned and computed monthly as follows:

Five days for each month, if the sentence is not less than six months and not more than one year.

Six days for each month, if the sentence is more than one year and less than three years.

Seven days for each month, if the sentence is not less than three years and less than five years.

Eight days for each month, if the sentence is not less than five years and less than ten years.

Ten days for each month, if the sentence is ten years or more.

When two or more consecutive sentences are to be served, the aggregate of the several sentences shall be the basis upon which the deduction shall be computed."

Section 4165 provides as follows:

"If during the term of imprisonment a prisoner commits any offense or violates the rules of the institution, all or any part of his earned good time may be forfeited."

Section 4166 provides as follows:

"The Attorney General may restore any forfeited or lost good time or such portion thereof as he deems proper upon recommendation of the Director of the Bureau of Prisons."

53. **GENERAL RULE**: Though not mentioned in these rules, any disorder, act or neglect to the prejudice of good order and discipline, and any conduct which disturbs the orderly routine of the institution shall be taken cognizance of by the Warden or his representative, according to the nature and degree of the offense, and punished at the discretion of the Warden or other lawful authority.

Inmate Roster

LISTED IN ORDER OF REGISTER (AZ) NUMBER

1 Bolt, Frank Lucas
2 Copp, Charles R.
3 Gregory, Leon Harold
4 Harrison, Joseph Constantine
5 Henry, Forrest B.
6 Hicks, Clyde F.
7 Hills, Ralph L.
8 Hoke, Albert D.
9 Hood, Alan Whitney
10 Hulme, Frederick Lasalle
11 Janda, Edward Joseph
12 Johnson, Charles E.
13 Johnson, Luby L.
14 Landers, William D.
15 Limas, Manuel
16 Marud, John
17 Miller, John Leroy
18 Mumma, William J. F.
19 Nelson, Jack
20 Paris, Angelo George
21 Payne, William G.
22 Petarson, John H.
23 Prokopf, Leo
24 Riley, Joseph F.
25 Sodoma, Frank
26 Soliwode, Joseph
27 Vinson, Harold Ray
28 Walters, Ervie R.
29 Weber, George Watson
30 Wilde, George Earle
31 Wolfe, Gilbert D.
32 Woody, Harold Orville
33 White, Frederick Grant
34 Moxon, Robert Bradford
35 Cole, Elmer Hutchinson
36 Raap, Verrill Hersey
37 Souza, Frank
38 Reynolds, Perry
39 Fernandez, Hal Joseph
40 Burke, Joseph Francis
41 Dean, Harry E.
42 Boyd, William Edward, Jr.
43 Walsh, James John
44 Smith, Mack
45 Kerr, George William "Red"
46 Stadig, John Millage
47 Wutke, Edward
48 Lewis, Edgar Robert
49 Kelly, Walter
50 Kennedy, Willie
51 Brown, Thurman Alexander
52 Weston, Herbert Sheely
53 Fontaine, Harold
54 Goleboski, John
55 Moten, Frank Edward
56 Brown, Benjamin A.
57 Simmons, William Joseph
58 Kronz, George Safford
59 Fondren, Pearl Turner
60 Colson, James
61 Eaton, Ruey
62 Bearden, Walter Edward
63 Coleman, Robert
64 Waters, Francis Leo
65 Marsh, James C.

66 Messamore, John Richard
67 Montgomery, Harold Leroy
68 Watts, James W.
69 Marques, Armand
70 Fulbright, Floyd
71 Schmidt, Ludwig "Dutch"
72 Krug, Charles Richard
73 Gogich, Lazar
74 Mcintosh, Leo Dale
75 Mcnealy, James Lester
76 Zuckerman, Louis
77 Morland, Thomas Leroy
78 Cleaver, Charles
79 Wareagle, Thomas W.
80 Bender, John Francis
81 Denny, Theodore
82 Hooker, Stanley Richard
83 Walton, James H.
84 Thomas, John Virgil
85 Capone, Alphonse "Scarface"
86 Carter, William Jackson
87 Van Gorder, Hayes Overn
88 Matchok, Joseph John
89 Buckner, Walker Beverly
90 O'brien, Edward William
91 Patterson, Lester William
92 Bicks [Bajczyk], Frank Joseph
93 Costner, Isaac Allen
94 Gempp, William Phillip
95 Larry, Henry Kenneth
96 Lepinski, Frank Alexander
97 Mangiere, Charles Patrick
98 Reiss, Charles
99 Ritchey, William Malcolm
100 Wilmoth, Virgil Edward
101 Murdock, Theodore (Nmi)
102 Walden, Spencer
103 Dickerson, Howard C.
104 Donohue, John
105 Kendrick, John Allen
106 Sweeney, Elmer "Bull Dog"
107 Best [Besmanoff], Albert
108 Reisner, John Joseph
109 Mcdonald, Arthur T.
110 Gardner, Roy G.
111 Grindle, Hubert Alexander
112 Brownie, Frank B.
113 Morris, Daniel Joseph
114 Alcorn, Gordon Francis
115 Mcdonald, Bert
116 Dixon, Riley
117 Kelly, George R. "Machine Gun"
118 Varsalona, Joe
119 Westbrook, Charles E.
120 Alexander, Joseph
121 Talarico, Mike
122 Badgett, Lewis
123 Lagomarsino, Ray Louis
124 Perry, James Francis
125 Chapman, Frank
126 May, William David
127 Stevens, Olin Dewitt
128 Pettijohn, Milton T.
129 Sargeart, James Louis

130 Keating, Francis Lawrence
131 Brown, Stanley
132 Berta, Charles
133 Boyd, John
134 Ryan, Phil Francis
135 Sherwood, Erwin Ralph
136 Barnett, Howard E.
137 Bates, Albert Lawrence
138 Holden, Thomas James
139 Bailey, Harvey John
140 Underwood, Tom
141 Nolan, George
142 Grauer, Harry
143 Rogers, George
144 Miller, Edward A.
145 Warren, Byron W.
146 Sobalesky, John
147 Ballew, Andrew
148 Beane, Clement Wallace
149 Thomas, Lafayette David
150 Delbono, Frank
151 Belcastro, Rocco
152 Chiesa, Frank
153 Johnson, Harry "Limey"
154 Rowland, Edward
155 Tesciona, Frank
156 Gouker, Frank
157 Gill, Willie
158 Grove, James
159 Dotson, Louis
160 Jones, Robert (Nmi)
161 Wallace, Abraham
162 Taylor, Acie
163 Fitzmaurice, William Alfred
164 Martini, Louis
165 Stroud, Mack
166 Harden, Alfred
167 Anderson, Frank
168 Lawrence, Louie
169 Serfess, Walter B.
170 Sullivan, Daniel
171 Owen, William Aloysius
172 Poulos, James "Jimmy The Greek"
173 Bowen, Hugh Allen
174 Davis, Robert
175 Wolf, Ralph Edward
176 Fisher, Gerald Perry
177 Sieman, Jack
178 Bouman, Joe
179 Ballin, George (Nmn)
180 Blackwood, Ira Earl
181 Reed, Pet
182 Young, Cal
183 Wiggins, Walker Harris
184 Hanna, William J.
185 Colyer, William E.
186 Levin, William Hyman
187 Loomis, Alfred Merritt
188 Mckee, Frank (Nmi) "Blackie"
189 Ryan, James
190 Kelly, Harry C.
191 Tatum, Ralph William
192 Thompson, Orville Ulesse
193 Warden, Walter Lee
194 Green, Charles
195 Youngberg, Arthur Henry
196 Smith, Clint
197 Satterfield, Joseph Hiram

198 Sullivan, Harry
199 Cherrington, Arthur S.
200 Spark, Walton
201 Fallon, Daniel Joseph
202 Moore, Ross W.
203 Norton, James
204 Telfian, Charles
205 Collins, Floyd L.
206 Minnema, Howard
207 Macklin, Elmer
208 Audett, Theodore James
209 Carroll, John Patrick
210 Bowers, Joseph "Dutch"
211 Allen, Jack
212 Kilpatrick, Steward M.
213 Urbaytis, Joseph
214 Mahoney, Frank William
215 Baker, Jack
216 O'brien, Michael
217 Armes, Monroe Harry "Blackie"
218 Raymond, Robert
219 Conroy, Earl Francis
220 Hardin, Jack
221 Spain, Loren
222 Snow, Cecil
223 Kyne, Harry Paul
224 Lucas, James C.
225 Skoog, Albert Winfield
226 Doll, Edward
227 Kulick, John
228 Hall, Harlan Karl
229 Watkins, Jesse R.
230 Whitaker, Norman T.
231 Cochran, Cecil Elmo
232 Dunn, John
233 Berlin, Samuel Charles
234 Carroll, John H.
235 Vessila, James
236 Terry, Milton Edward
237 Davis, George W.
238 Chase, John Paul
239 Bartlett, William Edward
240 Deshelley, Luis Eduardo
241 Delmar, Frank
242 Clark, James
243 Smiddy, Ennis Fay
244 Young, Henry J.
245 Wiley, Edward E.
246 Kalinoski, Joseph Frank
247 Berman, Jacob
248 Waley, Harmon Metz
249 Thompson, George
250 Giles, John Knight
251 Gayden, Walter
252 Mcglone, John Patrick "Sonny"
253 Fisher, Joseph
254 Rettich, Carl
255 Harrigan, Charles Joseph
256 Dugan, Thomas John
257 Hensley, Rudolph "Jack" (Nmi)
258 Cole, Theodore
259 Phillips, Burton Earnest
260 Roe, Ralph
261 Goode, John Elmer
262 Rector, Rollie "Hardrock Roy"
263 Limerick, Thomas Robert

264 Lloyd, Jack
265 Unsell, Aubrey Curtis
266 Egan, Earl John
267 Mccain, Rufus Roy
268 Barker, Arthur R. "Doc"
269 Binkley, Homer Eldridge
270 Cert, Warren
271 Davis, Volney Everett
272 Kralj, John Thomas
273 Verheul, Ernest
274 Leaman, William Frank
275 Rhodes, Jack Robert
276 Pivaroff, James
277 Clay, Clarence Clyde
278 Brammer, Webb
279 Carter, James Alex
280 Clayton, Hicks
281 Kales, Louis M.
282 Huffsttler, John William
283 Harper, Francis Virgil
284 Persful, Rufe
285 Sadler, (Sidney) Herman
286 Neumer, Richard Adam
287 Butcher, Hugh
288 Dupont, John
289 Johnson, Roy
290 Brown, Charles Edward
291 Minor, Andrew Davis
292 Sullivan, Ralph C.
293 Conway, [James] Bryan
294 Harpin, Harold
295 Donald, Phoenix
296 Streng, Arend John
297 Sawyer, Harry
298 King, William Patrick
299 Farmer, Elmer Charles
300 Miller, Robert V.
301 Gilmore, Dewey Earnest
302 Brown, Floyd Emmett
303 Gulick, Virgil
304 Cooper, Russell Land
305 Porter, Frank Howard
306 Lambert, Robert Everett
307 Bentz, Edward Wilhelm
308 Williams, Frank
309 Epplesheimer, Frank Francis
310 Nichols, Robert Elmer
311 Davis, Andrew Webb
312 Pierce, Amin
313 Cossack, Loeb L.
314 Garrett, Donnie
315 Fitzgerald, Charles Joseph
316 Nelson, Neils
317 Yanowsky, Charles
318 Medley, Philip Henry
319 Stein, Joe
320 Fleisher, Harry
321 Reese, Fred
322 Campbell, Harry
323 Mckinney, Marshall
324 Dimenza, Philip
325 Karpavicz, Alvin Francis
    "Creepy Karpis"
326 Selbin, Jack
327 Fleisher, Sam
328 Sparger, Clarence
329 Walker, Jack Charles
330 Mulloy, Frank B.
331 Galatas, Richard Tallman
332 Farmer, Herbert Allen

333 Hawk, Henry
334 Parker, Homer Zeamon
335 Franklin, Rufus William
    "Whitey"
336 Bequette, Charles
337 Von Glahn, George
338 Murrietta, Lorenzo
339 Mcdonald, John
340 Anderson, Allie Theodore
341 Wylie, Arlin Price
342 Roubideaux, Jefferson
343 Hesly, Daniel Ferdinand
344 Ripley, James
345 Murphy, Patrick Edward
346 Koonen, Ernest "Red"
347 Deane, Claude Rowlett
348 Snyder, Lee
349 Edwards, Edison Jackson
350 Backner, Joseph Paul
351 Seals, Taylor
352 Harvey, Leland Legrea
353 Phillips, Bob
354 Wells, Ernest Marion
355 Howder, Elzear John
356 Palmersino, Carmine
357 Holmes, Kellory Weston
358 Hewitt, George Ormand
359 Harris, James
360 Spinks, Donald
361 Brown, Fred (Nmi)
362 Lynch, William
363 Kendrick, William
364 Dixon, Major
365 June, Harold C.
366 Sladowski, Henry
367 Lovvorn, James A.
368 Conley, John Carl
369 Brandt, Rudolph
370 Martin, William
371 Lucas, William
372 Myers, Henry Lloyd
373 Minntole, Alfred
374 Brunette, Harry Walter
375 Schatz, Morris
376 Giacalone, Vito
377 Gebhart, Marvin
378 Phipps, Earl
379 Robinson, Thomas Henry, Jr.
380 Brest, Harold Martin
381 Melton, Virgil "Red"
382 Moore, Jesse Ernest
383 Cannon, Jerry
384 Logan, Harry James
385 Pickens, Elmer Bentley
386 Saccotello, James Samuel
387 Franzeen, Richard C.
388 House, Evans Earl
389 Sullivan, John Lawrence
390 Hansen, Frederick T.
391 Fusco, Charles Robert
392 Kress, Robert
393 Janaway, Carl
394 Cumby, Ernest Emerson
395 Remine, Ramon
396 Stewart, Jackson Luther
397 Fisher, George M.
398 Martinez, Jesus
399 Moffitt, Thomas C.
400 Lewis, Charles
401 O'keith, Charles

402 Hunter, Fred John
403 Voss, John Wilbur
404 Ward, George Henry
405 Pringle, Robert Lee
406 Stanley, Herbert Alvin
407 Brown, Royce Rockwood
408 Hathaway, Robert M.
409 Wade, George Claire
410 Cline, Charlie William
411 Lewis, Edward
412 Vance, Robert (Nmi)
413 Bell, Robert Vivion
414 Sink, George
415 Coy, Bernard Paul
416 Mcneill, Thomas Michael
417 Mancuso, Salvatore
418 De Stefano, Pier
419 Boyd, Marl
420 Northcutt, Guy Burruss
421 Morgan, David Crockett
422 Holiday, Forrest
423 Barkdoll, Lloyd H.
424 Bailey, Reese Lloyd
425 Crockett, William Cecil
426 Brown, Glen P. (Bill)
427 Hood, Carl Owen
428 Mercer, Martin Ralph
429 Norman, Paul Kenneth
430 Hitesman, George Lorenzo
431 Cavanaugh, James Buchanan
432 Collins, Arthur Elmer
433 Osborne, George Guy
434 Kuykendall, Malloy
435 Stamphill, Dale Evert
436 Widmer, James H.
437 Shauver, Ray
438 Bird, Frank
439 Garrison, Orville Chester
440 Harris, James W.
441 Palmer, William Wallace
442 Baker, Vincent T.
443 Ross, William Henry
444 Gant, Hugh Archer
445 Levy, Hymie Herbert
446 Leigh, Arthur William Oliver
447 White, Samuel Williams
448 Bundy, Richard Clay
449 Yoakum, Mack
450 Barker, Clarence Russell
451 Hill, Floyd Allen
452 Mcdaniel, Dennis Barkley
453 Stevenson, Ray Chilton
454 Coulter, Ira L.
455 Oley, John Joseph
456 Geary, Percy
457 Mccollum, Fremont
458 Wells, Selvie Windfield
459 Price, Homer Carl
460 Nelson, Thomas
461 Edwards, Harry Herbert
462 Shockley, Samuel Richard
463 Mcgrew, Sam
464 Murry, Harry (Peck)
465 Pyle, Raymond Howard
466 Bayless, John Richard
467 Barker, Raymond Loyd
468 Couch, John
469 Washington, John James
470 Lewis, Morson Johnson
471 Price, Richard

472 Burns, Robert
473 Vacca, Herman (Nmi)
474 Long, [Jeremiah] Samuel
475 Burman, Willard
476 Parnell, Terry Wesley
477 Dainard, William
478 Darlino, Jimmie
479 Griesemer, Charles Wayne
480 Burall, Louis
481 Embry, George
482 Bruce, Floyd
483 Bruce, Ray
484 Miller, Raymond
485 Habermann, Leonard
486 Paris, Peter Joseph, Jr.
487 Brest, Harold Martin
488 Miller, George
489 Turner, William
490 Long, Willard
491 Herring, Maurice Merle
492 Evans, Everett
493 Jazwiak, George
494 Cox, Earl
495 Johnson, Raymond Stanley
496 Wofford, Thomas Merryl
497 Wilson, Herbert "Hub"
498 Pendergast, Donald Ward
499 Mcdowell, John Robert
500 Baker, W. L., Jr.
501 Wright, William
502 Smith, Allen Treat
503 Houghtalin, Victor
504 White, Ernest Newton
505 Ramos, Raul San Miguel
506 Jones, Kenneth Hural
507 Vigouroux, Joseph Clarence
508 Mahoney, Harry Alfred
509 Montgomery, William
    Edward
510 Aeby, Aubrey
511 Keeney, Winfred
512 Duke, Curtis
513 Pifer, Louis Andrew
514 Murray, James (Nmi)
515 Lockhart, William Henry
516 Chandler, Elmer
517 Dobbs, Robert Eugene
518 Johnson, Wallace
519 Perrine, Edward Marshal
520 Smith, William Lee
521 Howell, Frederick Richard
522 Breshears, Eldridge Owin
523 Hamilton, Floyd Garland
524 Pyles, Clifford
525 Warner, Edward John
526 Ritter, Paul
527 Reed, Chester Herman
528 Rogers, David
529 Walker, Robert Raymond
530 Reynolds, George
531 Kelley, Eichler Odell
532 Mahoney, Truman Richard
533 Hughes, L. D.
534 Steffler, Fred William
535 Cole, Charles Franklin
536 Walters, Huron Ted
537 Parrish, Hardin
538 Booth, Eugene Edward
    [Thomas]
539 Gilreath, Leonard

540 Williams, Virgil Leroy
541 Byrd, [John] Bowling
542 Thompson, Sidney James Owen
543 Dunnock, William Wesley
544 Butler, Howard
545 Sweetney, Clarence Mackle
546 Orloff, John
547 Kyle, Arnold Thomas
548 Cretzer, Joseph Paul
549 Lynch, Joseph Pershing
550 Willis, Thomas Arthur
551 Audett, Theodore James
552 Barber, William
553 Abernathy, Forest
554 Bartholemew, John Thurston
555 Deloura, Anthony
556 Dressler, Oliver Lawrence
557 Davis, John Boyce
558 Smith, Bruce Richard
559 Taylor, Lee William
560 Wilfong, George Marion
561 Moyle, Joseph Anthony
562 Willmont, Robert
563 Steinmetz, Charles Merle
564 Aurechio, Carmine
565 Souza, Frank
566 Brooks, George
567 Macomber, Ora Bernard
568 Mcmillan, William
569 Langston, Talmadge Henry
570 Bledsoe, Billy Bernard
571 Boarman, James Arnold
572 Stalling, Raymond
573 Sanford, Norman Harding, Jr.
574 Fleish [Fleisher], Louis
575 Tippett, Ellis Matthew
576 Lynch, Jay William
577 Davis, Paul
578 Michener, Elliott Wood
579 Wright, Cecil Lester
580 Freeman, John
581 Jackson, Isaac
582 Bartlett, William Edward
583 Austin, Thomas Ostend
584 Chappell, Robert C.
585 Pichette, George
586 Quillen, James John
587 Russ, Lonnie Lee
588 Wilson, Raymond John
589 Pepper, [Joseph] "Jack" William, Jr.
590 Swihart, Ralph Thomas
591 Glivinski, Leo
592 Nard, Jettie (J. T.)
593 Daniel, Lathan
594 Stroud, Robert F. "Birdman Of Alcatraz"
595 Banghart, Basil Hugh
596 Ludwig, Kurt Frederick
597 Hart, John Marion
598 Clendenon, Russell Raymond
599 Moses, Joseph Ernest
600 Newagon, Arthur
601 Dunbar, Floyd
602 Mcdonald, Walter (Nmi)
603 Young, Ike
604 Morneau, Walter Joseph
605 Rutkowski, Frank C.
606 Gould, John Murray

607 Mrozik, Edward Richard
608 Crapo, Alton F.
609 Murphy, Edward
610 Carrollo, Charles Vincent
611 Decloux, Lawrence
612 Mccready, Loyal Dean
613 Hoskins, Edward Garrett
614 Vasilick, William
615 Scott, James Moore
616 Lovett, Charles Joseph
617 Richards, Larry
618 Beland, Charlie L.
619 Heck, George Franklin
620 Waldon, John Frank
621 Coulter, Willis Tipton
622 Rausch, Gerald
623 Buckles, Luther Nave
624 Branch, Claude Clyde Colbert
625 Owens, Clifford Houston
626 Cunningham, Ross
627 Erskine, Harry Albert
628 Reyes, Edward Guerrero
629 Brown, Russell Berlin
630 Cory, William Frank
631 Johnson, John Elgin
632 Kammer, Warren Joseph
633 Atkeson, Marvin Hazel
634 Lampaces, George Thomas
635 Acton, Frank Harry
636 Trammell, Berlis
637 Hilliard, Hughes Robert
638 Kimbrough, Vernon Paul
639 Spear, Ben
640 Greene, Ralph Waldo
641 Orick, Guy
642 Mugavero, John (Nmi)
643 Burton, George King
644 Aldrich, Wayne Charles
645 Hubbard, Marvin Franklin
646 Kern, Edward John
647 Haskins, Frank Jones
648 Nimerick, Clyde H.
649 Zidack, Joseph Edward
650 Robbins, William Vester
651 Roedel, Heinrich Herman
652 Mcmiller, Benjamin Harrison
653 North, James
654 Hope, Edgar (Nmi)
655 Schank, James William
656 Smith, Henry
657 Luckett, Willis
658 Colonna, Anthony James
659 Gent, Charles William
660 Merrill, Frank
661 Chinn, Sehon Stephenson
662 Bell, Edward Howard
663 Greco, Raphael
664 Dohrman, Leroy
665 Pugowski, Anthony Joseph
666 Radkay, William Isaac
667 Bracey, Jack Harold Wilber
668 Sanders, Hilliard Alton
669 Smith, Albert E.
670 Turner, James Carlo
671 Fagan, Henry Carroll
672 Moore, Perry William
673 Bishop, William Jennings
674 Oddo, Joseph Peter
675 Bush, Lavelle Homer

676 Livers, Charles Thomas
677 Cloud, Donald Lee
678 Morris, Luther Eugene
679 Strignano, Michael Benny
680 Jensen, Howard T.
681 Roper, Delton Eugene
682 Massey, William Jesse
683 Graham, Frank Ernest
684 Phelps, Robert
685 Palmer, Kenneth George
686 Ison, Burgin
687 Thompson, Walter
688 Whitehead, Thomas Jefferson
689 Sharpe, Edwin Wade
690 Tyree, Ernest
691 Hollingsworth, George Cecil
692 Myles, Richard Arthur
693 Adams, Jack Floyd
694 Cantrell, Paul Ellis
695 Temple, David
696 Westley, Willie James
697 Lopez, Ernest Barragan
698 Benjamin, Arthur
699 Dillon, George Donald
700 Lucas, Cecil Stanley
701 Peabody, Gerard Rushton
702 Miller, Robert Daniel
703 Burke, Lee Bonnie
704 Mcmahan, Dorsey Willard
705 Kitchens, Joseph Archie
706 Fleming, Frank Douglas
707 Blankenship, Julius
708 Newell, Fred Augustus
709 Robinson, Thomas Henry, Jr.
710 Cook, Edgar William
711 Stubblefield, George William
712 Mcgary, Leroy (Nmi)
713 Walton, Calvin
714 Carnes, Clarence Victor
715 Newell, William Wood
716 Testerman, James Edward
717 Harrell, Floyd Henderson
718 Altmayer, Michael Robert
719 Whitehurst, Samuel Phillip
720 Duboice, Ray L.
721 Brussart, Leroy
722 Bradford, James Roy
723 Estes, Albert Bennett
724 Spencer, William Ellsworth
725 Gilbert, Flavis Godfrey
726 Connelly, Patrick Raymond
727 Gooch, Lonnie Clyde
728 Mcdowell, John Leonard
729 Thompson, Miran Edgar
730 Stallings, Roy Carlton, Jr.
731 Cartwright, Thomas M.
732 Cumming, Robert Alexander
733 Dunn, William Howard
734 Phillips, Ellis Franklin
735 Roberson, Samuel
736 Mcknight, Marvin William
737 Powell, John Richard
738 Mayberry, Edward R.
739 Buchan, Woodrow Wilson
740 Tippett, Ellsworth John
741 Smith, John Eddington
742 Skinner, Orval Lloyd
743 Mitchell, Eugene Richard
744 Anderson, Irvin

745 Brewster, Herrie
746 Varnado, Joseph (Nmi)
747 Evens, William James
748 Jefferson, Curtis Purken
749 Hart, John Marion
750 Wilson, Sherman Leon
751 Cheser, Joseph Lee
752 Price, L. Z.
753 Tiverny, Theophil
754 Forbush, Walter Haywood
755 Washington, James
756 Payne, Harry Joseph
757 Haughton, Charles Frank
758 Davis, William Roscoe
759 Watson, Walter Ellsworth
760 Isenberg, Joseph Gordon
761 Mcnealy, James Lester
762 Pierce, Joel Thomas
763 Porter, Robert Lee
764 Norris, Thomas Nathan
765 Mansour, John
766 Mignogna, Louis Thomas
767 Austin, Eugene Rex
768 Townsend, Charles Edward
769 Sweat, John Calvin
770 Graham, Ben I.
771 Carter, Frank F.
772 Winhoven, Willard Arthur
773 Davis, Dando Tennyson
774 Penska, Gazie Alexander
775 Eklund, John Eugene
776 Fleck, Frank Earl
777 Melton, Ollie Oliver
778 Larson, George Fabian
779 Thomas, Richard (Aka Williams, Richard)
780 Mayes, Henry Leslie
781 Wilson, Robert Thomas
782 Stidham, James William
783 Webb, Henry C.
784 Ellis, William Willard
785 Horase, Willie
786 Spradley, Douglas
787 Watson, Arthur Vernon
788 Herbert, Raymond
789 White, Henry William
790 Neason, Paul
791 Knight, Leander
792 Oden, Guy Edward
793 Hopkins, Willie Lee
794 Karabelas, Spiro Peter
795 Bruinsma, Ray Nelson
796 Stephenson, Floyd R.
797 O'leary, William Patrick
798 Irvin, Theodore Andrew
799 Mcgee, Mickey
800 Watson, John Theodore
801 Taylor, Carl Mendel
802 York, Kilburn Jack
803 Sorrentino, Stephen
804 Nunes, Gilbert Walter
805 Bedient, Robert Burr
806 Cookston, Clarence Leonard
807 Crump, William Max
808 Byrd, Clarence W.
809 Ludwick, Roger Paul
810 Edwards, Leon William
811 Pearson, West
812 Mann, Floyd George
813 Beck, Harold Willie

814 Williams, Alvin
815 Dewitt, Joseph Charles
816 Schillo, Duke
817 Merritt, Billy Eugene
818 Williams, Jewell James
819 Bullock, James A.
820 Nettles, James Edward
821 Frazier, Bivens
822 Brunson, William M.
823 Cooper, Henry Lee
824 Osborne, Floyd J.
825 Wyatt, Charles Sumner, Jr.
826 Macintyre, David Merrill
827 Barker, Houston Hubert
828 Barker, Paul Dean
829 Birchfield, D. L.
830 Williams, George Benjamin
831 Mainhurst, Richard Lewis
832 Kovalik, George Michael
833 Smith, Clayton Roby
834 Hawkins, William Murray
835 Scott, Nick Julius, Jr.
836 Castone, Lonnie Alfonso
837 Mason, Joseph Stone
838 Manuel, Ono
839 Womack, Edison Russell
840 Stevens, Wilborn K.
841 Lawhon, Walter Lee
842 Thomas, Morris
843 Kenney, Paul Lester
844 Davis, Lawrence Alvin
845 Robinson, Andrew
846 Strickland, Harry
847 Lindsey, Roland Junior
848 Walker, Ross, Jr.
849 Humphrey, Hezkiah
850 Stevens, Williams Charles
851 Guzman, Josefino Pacapac
852 Wilson, David C.
853 Russell, Moses
854 Smith, George Edward
855 Jackson, Edward, Jr.
856 Fuller, Leroy E. Alex
857 Martin, Edward Dennis
858 Smith, Johnny Ray
859 Philpott, James Floyd
860 Evans, Theodore Roosevelt
861 Alred, William Edward
862 Rivers, Joseph Bernard
863 Close, Carl
864 Johnson, Clyde Milton
865 Denormand, Kingdon William
866 Gimple, Erich
867 Bistram, Carl Harvey
868 Messamore, William Dessie
869 Scribner, Sam
870 Landreth, Walter Joseph
871 Mitchell, Edward E.
872 Abbott, Charles Melvin
873 Runnels, George Williamson
874 Medina, Robert Victor
875 Webber, Raymond Seymoure
876 Kuehl, Roger Walter
877 Wayne, Patrick
878 Grover, James Mason
879 Wagner, Richard Peter
880 Carter, Charles Joseph
881 Baker, Joseph
882 Blakeney, John Jaymond

883 Hayman, Herman Robert
884 Barsock, Joseph
885 Duverney, Lawrence
886 Wells, Charles L.
887 Morris, Isaac
888 Buswell, Lyle Howard
889 Bynum, Jesse (Atlas)
890 Collins, Ernest
891 Anderson, Paul L.
892 Green, John Leroy
893 Thomas, Freddie Lee
894 White, George Alvin
895 Moore, Sidney (Nmi)
896 Jordan, William Thomas
897 Hawkins, Benjamin Franklin
898 Baker, Oliver, Jr.
899 William, Eddie
900 Allen, Robert Neal
901 Nite, Robert Allen
902 Ross, Jack
903 Rowley, Eugene Gilford (Clifford)
904 Bois, Joseph Roland
905 Demos, John
906 Burnaugh, Poney Max
907 Romano, Michael Anthony
908 Robertson, Robert Lee
909 Shelton, Henry Harland
910 Henley, William John
911 Wagner, Ivan Laughlin
912 Byers, Vernon Howard
913 Davenport, Franklin Thomas
914 Hammond, John Larry
915 O'carter, Patrick
916 Meeks, George Harrison
917 Mckinney, Joseph Cecil
918 Cook, William Edward, Jr.
919 Layman, Talbert Jackson
920 Sanetsky, John
921 Willis, Donald Walter
922 Hill, Floyd Allen
923 Forrester, J. D.
924 Cooper, Gaith
925 Kennon, Paul Clifford
926 Gilford, Robert Lee
927 Holloman, Earl Ulysses
928 Rhodes, William L.
929 Steen, Leroy (Nmi)
930 Anderson, Nathaniel Boss
931 Mckinney, Willard Derondo
932 Gilliam, James Samuel
933 Tollett, Henry Clay
934 Brown, Darrell James
935 Carignan, Harvey Louis
936 Garcia, Victor Margreto
937 Dunn, Joe Kenneth
938 Hall, Edwin
939 Henry, Winston Churchill
940 Jakalski, Joseph
941 Mann, Floyd George
942 Kahl, John Raymond
943 Dauer, John Henry
944 Davidson, Richard Wayne
945 Harrington, Hoyt K.
946 Tassos, Christopher
947 Cole, Alexander
948 Collins, Walter Woodrow
949 Anderson, James Averster
950 Kirby, John Edward
951 Shope, William Mckinley

952 Allen, Hank
953 Hardaway, Willard
954 Johnson, Robert Ebon
955 Saxton, Gaylord Miles
956 Wilson, Floyd Page
957 Harrington, James
958 Walton, Johnnie Lee
959 Sanders, Timothy
960 Vasquez, Emerito Rivas
961 Miller, Robert (Nmi)
962 Ward, Charles Earl
963 Forrest, Frank, Jr.
964 Hodges, H. L.
965 Custer, Lloyd Lester
966 Bayless, John Richard
967 Higgins, Wilbert
968 Merrill, Elmer Anthony
969 Wright, Luster
970 Parker, John Nelson
971 Stevenson, William Asbury
972 Galmon, Ben
973 Mitchell, John Paul
974 Bell, Robert Alonzo
975 Obery, Leonard Reginald
976 Thomas, Joseph
977 Washington, Willie
978 Rich, Lester Griffin, Jr.
979 Havicon, Albert Charles
980 Bell, James Lee
981 House, Albert Ross
982 Brown, Henry Floyd
983 Nipp, Gale Kenneth
984 Ward, Arley Irvin
985 Estep, Ted Lee
986 Lopez, Serapio Delasara
987 Kitts, Kenneth Allen
988 Consolo, Frank
989 Jackson, Orba Elmer
990 Colbert, Wesley Leon
991 Burgett, Aaron Walter
992 Wilkins, Joseph R.
993 French, John Burke, Jr.
994 Fry, David Richard
995 Smith, Joseph Orby, Jr.
996 Sobell, Morton
997 Fontenot, Pershing Lee
998 Grills, Thomas Francis
999 Ray, Ervin
1000 Smith, Calvin
1001 Taylor, Earl William
1002 Chebetnoy, John Max
1003 Addison, Irving
1004 Oughton, Chester Leroy
1005 Butler, Oscar Larry
1006 Copley, Jay Paul
1007 Satterwhite, Clarence Andrew
1008 Butterfield, Wilbert William
1009 Dounias, Peter Nicholas
1010 Johnson, Raymond Vincent
1011 Gregory, Cleo
1012 Cole, Donald William
1013 Glascoe, Clinton Lemuel
1014 Lee, John
1015 Kay, Richard Willard
1016 Wilfong, Robert
1017 Rainey, Hiram Russell
1018 Pogolick, Henry Ford
1019 Pruett, Charles Edward
1020 Duncan, Lawrence Robert
1021 Gaynor, Frank

1022 Holtshouser, Edward Joseph, Jr.
1023 Holland, Raymond Evan
1024 Bent, Joseph Franklin
1025 Kimes, Roy
1026 Coons, Clarence Earl, Jr.
1027 Fuller, Arthur Eugene
1028 Rayborn, Benjamin Franklin
1029 Thomas, Artus Floyd
1030 Hoyland, James Alva
1031 French, Charles, Jr.
1032 Borecky, Joseph
1033 Edgerly, David Whalen
1034 Newman, Eli Olen
1035 Kimmy, Hiram Walter
1036 Kimbaugh, Charles
1037 Neuman, James Edward Howard
1038 Taylor, Courtney Townsend
1039 Beaird, William A.
1040 Campbell, Warren Arealous
1041 Hayes, Hiller Arthur
1042 Knight, Willie Lee
1043 Chalupowitz (Or Chapman), Abraham
1044 Thompson, Robert George
1045 Williams, Leonard James
1046 Bellew, Richard Bernard
1047 Tucker, Forrest Silva
1048 Charles, James D.
1049 Angell, Henry Carl
1050 Atwater, Chester
1051 Butterfield, Dwight Richard
1052 Chesney, Vincent Nichols
1053 Gallagher, Hammond Nesterfield
1054 Morden, Edward Neil
1055 Osborne, Kethel
1056 Smith, Earl E.
1057 Watson, John Edward
1058 Butler, Rex Melrose
1059 Kawakita, Tomoya "Meatball"
1060 Bielizna, Joseph
1061 Bradham, John Wesley
1062 Brooks, Louis Rafe
1063 Catalano, Daniel, Jr.
1064 Dougherty, Wilbur Webb
1065 Hill, Charles Ray
1066 Hoffler, Sylvester
1067 Mockford, Stanley Edward
1068 Revense, John Harold
1069 Robinson, Oscar O'brant
1070 Sumpter, Joseph Obbie
1071 Vasquez, Emerito Rivas
1072 Wagstaff, Joseph Alfred
1073 Rodriquez, Henry
1074 Zavada, George (Nmn)
1075 Catalonotte, Guisseppe
1076 Dekker, John F.
1077 Frazier, Kenneth Douglas
1078 Hale, Calvin Gene
1079 Hixon, James A.
1080 Manzulla, Victor
1081 Powers, Carl William
1082 Sommerville, Robert A.
1083 Tomblinson, James J.
1084 Jacobanis, David Stanley
1085 Current, Fleet Robert
1086 Bremmeyer, Jerie
1087 Hawkins, Benjamin Franklin

1088 Thompson, William Elwood
1089 Deloach, William Lawrence
1090 Hendrikson, Harold Emil
1091 Riehl, Wallace Conrad
1092 Turpin, Dave
1093 Quilop, Eufemio Jacob
1094 Nelson, Robert John
1095 Tryanowski, Stanley (Nmi)
1096 Mccauley, Neil Ade
1097 Jupiter, Earl
1098 Mabane, Willie D.
1099 Raskin, David
1100 Robinson, Thomas Junior
1101 Truman, John Arthur
1102 Williams, Marion John
1103 Williams, Nathan Glenn
1104 Toliver, Charles Edward
1105 Barry, Lee William
1106 Bonner, Ferrell Cannard
1107 Cox, Meredith Leroy
1108 Crawford, Glen Cleveland
1109 Chittenden, Robert Eugene
1110 Davis, Jimmie Lee
1111 Dyer, Johnny Crosswaite
1112 Eidson, James Billy Thomas
1113 Freeman, Victor Dwight
1114 Guthrie, James Albert
1115 Harbison, Henry Lee
1116 Herrera, (Jose) Arsenio
1117 Johnson, Ellsworth Raymond "Bumpy"
1118 Luke, Robert Victor
1119 Morgan, Emmanuel Nunez
1120 Pavlovich, Alexander Vasljie
1121 Smith, Thomas Francis
1122 Winchell, Milton Emerson
1123 Dancy, Oscar, Jr.
1124 Edwards, Edward Charles
1125 Larson, Lewis Woodard
1126 Michael, Joseph Charles
1127 Piatt, Edson
1128 Sawyers, Walter Hamilton
1129 Trumblay, Lawrence Alfred
1130 West, Allen Clayton
1131 Simcox, Ronald Eugene
1132 Bridges, Fred Douglas
1133 Banner, John Richard
1134 Gauvin, Edward Horace
1135 Banks, William
1136 Barber, Isaac Orbin
1137 Craddock, Clarence Julian
1138 Hamlin, Wade Darnell
1139 Hayes, Harold Raymond
1140 Hayes, William Sheridan
1141 Lipscomb, Robert Edward
1142 Mcclelland, Hubert
1143 Phillips, Raymond Harold Holmes
1144 Tarbett, Birdson Francis
1145 Ukena, Tracey William
1146 Ward, William Andrew
1147 Hildebrandt, Howard
1148 Huckeby, Harold Montdean
1149 Irving, Marshall
1150 Neal, Joseph
1151 Roberts, Jesse James, Jr.
1152 Robinson, Clarence Eugene Joseph
1153 Thomas, Raymond Andrew
1154 Schultz, Charles John, Jr.

1155 Banks, Chester
1156 Cooper, Charles
1157 Mcmahan, Dorsey Willard
1158 Merrill, Elmer Anthony
1159 Ragan, Jack V. K.
1160 Roberts, Lawrence John
1161 Whitacre, George Thomas Alden
1162 Young, Thomas Edward
1163 Miranda, Rafael Cancel
1164 Page, Enoch Benford
1165 Sanchez, Carmel
1166 Armitage, Joseph Taylor
1167 Ho, Herbert Kim Leong
1168 Beck, Harold Willie
1169 Campbell, George Joseph
1170 Hattaway, Ray Orlen
1171 Stone, Ronald Lee
1172 Kast, Donald Dean
1173 Thomas, Walter Howard
1174 Duncan, Charles Wesley
1175 Lathman, David Lee Roy
1176 Nichols, Oscar Alvin, Jr.
1177 Quatsling, George (Juraj)
1178 Barton, Clifford Gerald
1179 Dunn, William Howard
1180 Green, Theodore
1181 Reed, William Andrew
1182 Bird, Donald Walter
1183 Brown, James Boyd
1184 Williams, Robert Leroy
1185 Ellis, George John
1186 Hopkins, Charles Edward
1187 Stegall, Charles Edward
1188 Carpenter, Kenneth Darrell
1189 Heflin, Lorton Lewis, Jr.
1190 Juelich, Herbert Eugene
1191 Inman, Defoye
1192 Gillette, Thomas James
1193 Drake, John Franklin
1194 Murdock, Raymond Leo
1195 Bishop, Jack Allen
1196 Sizemore, Delbert Herschel
1197 Iozzi, John Guido
1198 Brennan, John James
1199 Austin, Robert Roe
1200 Gross, Sidney Louis
1201 Smith, Leaman Russell
1202 Morris, Farris Egbert
1203 Dewey, Donald Francis
1204 Carriker, Charles Boyce
1205 Mccoy, George Junior
1206 Bailey, Donald Everett
1207 Devine, Charles Everett
1208 Nolen, Earl Loftin
1209 Radcliff, Robert James
1210 Austin, Roe Robert
1211 Bostick, Ezzie
1212 Spinosa, Joseph Elmo
1213 Trevino, Ruben Dominguez
1214 Hall, Jack Walter
1215 King, Robert Douglas
1216 Pahmahmie, Dale Rome
1217 Audett, James Henry (Theodore)
1218 Brown, Gene Carrol
1219 Callaway, Sherman Thomas
1220 Laclair, Bernard Edmond
1221 Langford, Charles Emery
1222 Lewis, Richard Ray

1223 Pamplin, Billy Ray
1224 Smith, Earl Kill
1225 Stephens, June Heyward, Jr.
1226 Weaver, Robert Theodore
1227 Wilburn, Haywood Floyd
1228 Armstrong, Charles Harper
1229 Bell, Roland
1230 Clark, David
1231 Francis, William French
1232 Lowe, John Paul
1233 Mckinney, James Franklin
1234 Nolan, James Wilson
1235 Payne, Harry Joseph
1236 Rimanich, Robert Michael
1237 Skinner, Ralph Newton
1238 Smith, Carl George, Jr.
1239 Teller, Louis Emery
1240 Waites, Jack Dempsey
1241 Williams, John Henry
1242 Allen, Solomon King
1243 Cooper, Vernon
1244 Floyd, Louis Ellis
1245 Hawkins, William Murray
1246 Kendrick, John Allen
1247 Mccord, John Wesley
1248 Small, Samuel Richard, Jr.
1249 Thomas, James Bernard
1250 Thompson, Joseph Haywood
1251 Barchard, Richard Robert
1252 Drake, Roy Rudolph
1253 Albert, Morris
1254 Breaton, Marvin Ferris
1255 Harris, Eddie
1256 Taylor, Earl Curtis
1257 Miles, Lawrence Melvin
1258 Allmond, Bruce Edward
1259 Baker, William Garnett
1260 Ballin, George (Nmn)
1261 Boyes, Trent
1262 Bennett, James Jefferson
1263 Clermont, Raymond William Joseph
1264 Peabody, Gerard Rushton
1265 Tiblow, Samuel
1266 Henderson, Woodard Peyton
1267 Thomas, Herschell Carl, Jr.
1268 Dalton, William Henry
1269 Bright, Joseph Dayton
1270 Jones, Robert Lloyd
1271 Post, Raymond Louis
1272 Cooper, Delmar Eugene
1273 Kimbrough, Vernon Paul
1274 Davis, William D.
1275 Williams, Robert
1276 Duncan, William Howard
1277 Mcdole, Francis Laverne
1278 Conklin, Lawrence Doyle
1279 Lebolo, Andrew Arby
1280 Seiber, Byrel Franklin
1281 Guy, Frank
1282 Gomez, Isaac Gomez
1283 Mendoza, Armando Javier
1284 Gussman, Harry
1285 O'rourke, Domingo Edward
1286 Russell, Charles Benton
1287 Evans, William (Nmi)
1288 Nirenberg, Abraham
1289 Swann, Harold (Nmi), Jr.
1290 Wilson, Eugene Kenneth

1291 Leyvas, Rudolph Reyes
1292 Farley, Charles Leo
1293 Reyes, Severo C.
1294 Clinton, Homer Richard
1295 Curl, Roosevelt
1296 Hatfield, Frank
1297 Lawrence, William Jr.
1298 Jenkins, William Ernest
1299 Montos, Nick George
1300 Nicholson, Joseph Cevac
1301 Drew, James Frederick
1302 Hahn, Edward Phillip
1303 Lee, Morris Wilbur
1304 Shannon, Andrew Jackson
1305 Baker, Joseph
1306 Cantrell, Johnny
1307 Flynn, Derotha Lee
1308 Martin, William Paul
1309 Blassingame, Samuel
1310 Rhodes, Clifford Edward
1311 Sloan, Richard William
1312 Woods, Vernie Samuel, Jr.
1313 Tillman, Levi
1314 Banks, Henry
1315 Brent, Percy Russell
1316 Burdette, Jesse
1317 Carter, Robert
1318 Deford, Frank Raymond
1319 Fitch, James Hodge
1320 Jones, Carl Redginald
1321 Lyles, Archibald
1322 Mcelroy, Elah Cisero
1323 Quarles, William Jerome
1324 Riston, George
1325 Roy, Herbert Lee
1326 Sawyers, Walter Hamilton
1327 Spaulding, Lindsey
1328 Burton, Carl Edward
1329 Davis, Harold Wayne
1330 Mcchan, George H.
1331 Hart, George Washington
1332 Jefferson, Garland Lloyd
1333 Mollett, Walter David
1334 Pyles, Jonathan Plato
1335 West, Allen Clayton
1336 Alvarez, George Nunez
1337 Bassett, Eugene Thorpe
1338 Boyles, Joe Albert
1339 Clymore, Jerry Wayne
1340 Crespo-crespo, Hiram
1341 Garnett, Russell George
1342 Griggs, James Trammell
1343 Heffington, Landon Flournoy
1344 Hess, Louis Clifton
1345 Hughes, Felton Lee
1346 Hinsley, Billy James
1347 Johnson, Eugene Clifford
1348 Leather, James Joseph
1349 Long, James Edward
1350 Lowe, Glen Franklin
1351 Mantell, Lloyd Emerson
1352 Mcewen, Malcolm Lewis
1353 Riley, John Calvin
1354 Rouwenhorst, John Bruce
1355 Schibline, Robert James
1356 Scusselle, Gino
1357 Skinner, Donald Blaine
1358 Spasoff, Richard
1359 Duncan, John Douglas

1360 Eves, Samuel	1416 Dillon, Edward Joseph	1469 Stewart, Charles Willis	1524 Macey, Peter William
1361 Gilliam, James Samuel	1417 Chamberlain, Kenneth Wayman	1470 Weber, Isaac	1525 Jenkins, James Francis
1362 Twining, Jack Wright	1418 Chamberlain, Gary Lee	1471 Fernandez, Manuel Cordiera	1526 O'brien, James Joseph
1363 Watson, Lewis Frank	1419 Smith, Lee Harold	1472 Landin, John Manuel	1527 Mitchell, Eugene Owen
1364 Nolan, Marshall Edward	1420 Donovan, Robert Lawrence	1473 Howard, Preston Lavern	1528 Sutherland, Ben Herbert
1365 Stetson, Harvey Edwin	1421 Smith, Warren David	1474 Mcgann, Clarence Duke	1529 Roe, Harold Pitts
1366 Padilla, Angel Jose	1422 Coon, Darwin Evert	1475 Alarcon, Vincent Rodriquez	1530 Andrews, Isaiah
1367 Mcclelland, Hubert	1423 Jackson, Choyce Lee	1476 Anglin, John William	1531 Buckskin, Presley
1368 Coppola, Frank Richard	1424 Williams, William Gerald	1477 Johnson, James	1532 Nunez, Antonio Hernandez
1369 Burbank, Charles Robert	1425 Rosario-maldonado, Antonio	1478 Malek, Thomas Franklin	1533 Nunez, Gregory Hernandez
1370 Jackson, Deather	1426 Levine, Abraham	1479 Moon, Thomas Wright	1534 Quigley, Francis Thomas
1371 Jarrett, Billy Junior	1427 Gulovsen, Donald H.	1480 Townsend, Edwin Albert	1535 Barrett, Robert Baragas
1372 Johnston, William Reece	1428 Bulger, James Joseph, Jr. "Whitey"	1481 Hayes, Hiller Arthur	1536 Jones, Doyle
1373 Machibroda, John	1429 Harris, Henry, Jr.	1482 Patterson, Henry	1537 Williams, Felix
1374 Lupino, Rocco Salvatore	1430 Jones, Walter	1483 Johnson, Lee Roy	1538 Carpenter, Russell Wayne
1375 Iannelli, Donald Rick	1431 Sunday, Richard Benjamin	1484 Tatum, Ernest	1539 Reynolds, Winston Marion
1376 Mills, George Albert	1432 Pravato, Edward	1485 Anglin, Clarence	1540 Hunsaker, Jack Donald
1377 Kerner, Arthur Eugene	1433 Karabelas, Spiro Peter	1486 Marcella, Anthony Frank	1541 Robbins, Robert Joseph
1378 Riley, Fred Charles	1434 Deutschmann, Albert Edward	1487 Brown, Jess	1542 Mcdonald, Berl Estes
1379 Harvey, Elbert Dewitt	1435 Doyle, John Bernard	1488 Gilbert, George, Jr.	1543 Neal, James Raymond
1380 Soviero, Louis	1436 Romero-sandoval, Bernabe	1489 Atkins, Harold Jerome	1544 Santiago, Carlos Ruben
1381 Catalano, Charles	1437 Sanders, Charles Edward	1490 Mitchell, Robert (Nmi)	1545 Lurk, Benny
1382 Dulworth, Charles Mitchell	1438 Jefferson, Leroy	1491 Rogers, Rayford Daniel	1546 Johnson, David Graham
1383 Deveny, Michael John	1439 Talbot, L. Fred	1492 Williams, Thomas Laurence	1547 Lindsay, Thomas Norman
1384 Davidson, Taylor	1440 Seltenrich, Stanley Earl	1493 Spears, Robert Vernon	1548 Feeney, Martin Francis
1385 Amato, Vincent	1441 Morris, Frank Lee	1494 Cain, Richard Oliver	1549 Halliday, Russell Thomas
1386 Arquilla, Louis Arnold	1442 Mcnicholas, Martin Joseph	1495 Price, Carl Jerome	1550 Fuller, Leroy E. Alex
1387 Cagle, William, Jr.	1443 Kent, Thomas Augustine	1496 Case, Robert	1551 Teetzel, Bruce Harry
1388 Wacker, Carl Virgil	1444 Contreras, Daniel	1497 Tucker, Raymond Lee	1552 Mchenry, Edward Elmer
1389 Overman, Mark Lee	1445 Dellamura, Joseph	1498 Accardo, Anthony Michael	1553 Kent, Arthur Shelton
1390 Redden, Clifford Pierce	1446 Darland, Robert Leon	1499 Jones, James Edward	1554 Hernandez, Amadeo Brisano
1391 Heirman, John Leroy	1447 O'brien, John Joseph	1500 Linkenauger, David Ralph	1555 Rosenberg, Martin
1392 May, Glenn Leslie	1448 Mcgowan, William Laird	1501 Daoust, Louis Joseph	1556 Salter, Herman Clayton, Jr.
1393 Hubbard, Clifford Eugene	1449 Modock, Anthony (Nmi)	1502 Henson, Oliver, Jr.	1557 Scherk, Peter Stuyvesant
1394 Rosen, Carl	1450 Vinson, Orville Gene	1503 Semiean, Lonnit	1558 Tibbs, Harlan Allen
1395 Kritsky, Stephen	1451 Carlton, Matthew	1504 Beavers, Hugh Chester	1559 Gresham, Joseph Thomas, Jr.
1396 Scroggins, John Gewin	1452 Pependrea, Ronald Ralph	1505 Lessard, Albert Joseph	1560 Brous, Bernard Jerome
1397 Skiba, Walter E.	1453 Miller, Frederick Sibley	1506 Jones, Curtis Lee	1561 Paul, Benson
1398 Gomez, Gumersindo	1454 Armstrong, Henry Grady	1507 Groves, Lyle Mark, Jr.	1562 Fong, T. Wayne
1399 Hall, Willard Henry	1455 Askew, Charles Moran	1508 Tate, Mack Elroy	1563 Pummill, Walter Harold
1400 Cozzolino, Ralph Robert	1456 Crymes, Virgile Allen	1509 Harris, Nathaniel James	1564 Bearden, Leon Finifus
1401 Malone, John Raymond	1457 Sosa, Emilio Chavez	1510 Page, Clarence	1565 Henley, Melvin Eugene
1402 Maness, Daniel Duane	1458 Young, Raymond Douglas	1511 Pearce, Luther Dow	1566 Garris, David Wesley
1403 Scott, John Paul	1459 Quinn, Michael Patrick	1512 Milani, Joseph Harry	1567 Molless, Lincoln Joseph
1404 Hall, Johnnie Lamar	1460 Carter, Aubrey Randolph	1513 Ralph, John Edward	1568 Carbo, Paul John "Frankie"
1405 Moore, Melvin Eugene	1461 Gandara, Salvadore Mendoza	1514 Hess, Donald Kilsmuth	1569 Duval, Guy Auguste
1406 Mccraw, Carl Earnest	1462 House, Bernard G.	1515 Massie, James Robert	1570 Beardsley, Kenneth Ray
1407 Marcum, Charles Wilbur	1463 Reino-caballero, Angelo	1516 Gupton, Earl S.	1571 Flores, James Gallardo
1408 Splitt, Walter Carl	1464 Stein, Fred	1517 Battle, John Thomas	1572 Strickland, Adrill Clisby
1409 Hernandez, Henry Sanchez	1465 Thompson, Leon Warren	1518 Cohen, Meyer Harris "Mickey"	1573 Dickey, Robert Dean
1410 Hamilton, William Chester	1466 Caughorn, Lonas Ray	1519 Peterson, Charles Osborne	1574 Gill, Bobby Ray
1411 Lanosa, Henry	1467 James, William Carl	1520 Gainey, Woodrow Wilson, Jr.	1575 Hansen, Fred John
1412 Adams, Robert Thomas	1468 Rixinger, Henry George	1521 Reiley, Edward	1576 Weatherman, Frank Clay
1413 Parker, Darl Dee		1522 Crumpton, Volton	
1414 Sprenz, Frank Lawrence		1523 Oliver, Charles Lee	
1415 Boggs, William Adger			

Bibliography

NATIONAL ARCHIVE RECORDS

Administrative Files (NARA College Park, MD, and NARA's Center for Legislative Archives in Washington, DC): Pacific Branch United States Disciplinary Barracks, Alcatraz. Select Military Records, Annual Reports, and General Correspondence Files.

Administrative Files, Records of United States Penitentiary Alcatraz (NARA San Bruno, California): Extensive research included examination of materials relating to escapes, general prison grounds, buildings and other facilities; memorandums, blueprints, cell mechanism diagrams, contractor reports, budgetary planning documents, culinary, library reports, administration & correctional staff correspondence.

Comprehensive Case Files of Alcatraz Inmates: Extensive research included examination of multiple criminal history files, inmate correspondence, court records, medical records, Warden's notebook pages (1934–ca. 1963), visitation logs, and conduct reports.

REPORTS & SELECT PAPERS

Babyak, Jolene and Martini, John. *The Alcatraz Cellhouse Numbering Systems (Historic Structure Report Addendum).* California: Golden Gate National Recreation Area, 1999

Bergen, Philip R. *Letters and Hand Drawn Diagrams, special annotations to Alcatraz '46, and taped audio commentary discussing same, 1996–1999*

Bergen, Philip R. *Select Memorandums to Correctional Staff 1952–1953, as Captain of the Guards,* Compiled 2001

Bureau of Prisons. *Alcatraz. Washington,* D.C.: 1960

Campbell, Eileen, Rigsby, Michael and Dunham, Tacy. *Discover Alcatraz—A Tour of the Rock,* California: Golden Gate National Parks Association, 1996

Dunham, Tacy. *Discover Alcatraz Escapes—A Tour of the Attempts,* California: Golden Gate National Parks Association, 1997

Fish, Clifford. *Handwritten notes on the 1946 Escape Attempt, 2001*

Hart, Herbert M. *Old Forts of the Far West (Included in Report to S.F.)* Washington: Superior Publishing Company, Date of Publication Unknown

Hart, Herbert M.. *The U.S. Army on Alcatraz, A Report to the City of San Francisco.* Includes extensive source document enclosures on Alcatraz Military Period, 1969

Mack, Ellsworth, Lieutenant. *How to Search a Cell California* State Prison, San Quentin, 1949

Madigan, Paul J. *Institution Rules and Regulations, Alcatraz Federal Penitentiary,* 1959

Morrison, Neil W., Lieutenant, Alcatraz. *How to Search the Person of an Inmate (written by Morrison for Wisconsin State Prison Warden's Bulletin)* U.S Penitentiary, Alcatraz Island, California, 1949

Schaaf, Libby. *Discover Fortress Alcatraz,* California: Golden Gate National Parks Association, 2000

Slack, J. E., Major, Cavalry, (D.O.L.) *Adjutant. Post Regulations, Pacific Branch, U.S. Disciplinary Barracks, Alcatraz, California,* 1932

Staff Writer. *A Museum of Prison Life* (Eastern State Penitentiary) The Philadelphia Inquirer, 1999

Sundstrom, Carl. *Handwritten Summary of 1946 Escape Attempt, 1946*

Surgeon General's Office, War Department. *A Report on Barracks and Hospitals with Descriptions of Military Posts (Included within H.M. Hart's S.F. Report).* Government Printing Office, 1870

Surgeon General's Office, War Department. *Hygiene of the United States Army, with Descriptions of Military Reports (Included within H.M. Hart's S.F. Report).* Government Printing Office, 1875

NEWSPAPERS

Chicago Daily News, Dallas Times Herald, Houston Chronicle, Los Angeles Mirror, Los Angeles Times, Oakland Tribune, San Francisco Call Bulletin, San Francisco Chronicle, San Francisco Examiner, USA Today

BOOKS

Allsop, Kenneth. The Bootleggers: the Story of Chicago's Prohibition Era. *New York: Arlington House, 1968*

Audett, Blackie. Rap Sheet. *New York: Williams Sloan and Co., 1954*

Babyak, Jolene. Birdman—The Many Faces of Robert Stroud. *California: Ariel Vamp Press, 1994*

Babyak, Jolene. Breaking the Rock—The Great Escape from Alcatraz. *California: Ariel Vamp Press, 2001*

Babyak, Jolene. Eyewitness on Alcatraz. *California: Ariel Vamp Press, 1988*

Barnes, Bruce. Machine Gun Kelly: To Right A Wrong. A Factual Account of Machine Gun Kelley's Life. *California. Tipper Publications, 1991*

Barter, James. Alcatraz (Building History Series). *California: Lucent Books, 2000*

Bates, Sanford. Prisons and Beyond. *Macmillan, 1938.*

Beacher, Milton D. (edited by Dianne Beacher Perfit) Alcatraz Island—Memoirs of a Rock Doc. *New Jersey: Pelican Island Publishing, 2001*

Bean, Walton E. California—An Interpretive History. *McGraw-Hill Book Company, 1973*

Bennett, James V. I Chose Prison. *New York: Alfred A. Knopf, 1970*

Bergreen, Laurence. Capone—The Man and the Era. *New York: Simon & Schuster, 1994*

Beyeler, Ed & Lamb, Susan. Alcatraz—The Rock. *Arizona: Northland Press, 1988*

Bruce, J. Campbell. A Farewell to the Rock: Escape from Alcatraz. *New York: McGraw-Hill, 1963*

Cameron, Robert. Alcatraz—A Visual Essay. *California: Cameron & Company, 1974, 1983, 1987*

Chandler, Roy F. and Chandler, E.F. Alcatraz—The Hardest Years 1934–1938. *Iron Brigade Publishing, 1989*

Clauss, Francis. J. Alcatraz—Island of Many Mistakes. *California: Briarcliff Press, Inc., 1981*

Coon, Darwin E. Alcatraz: The True End of the Line. *California, August House Inc. 2002*

Costanso, Miguel. The Narrative of the Portola Expedition of 1769–1770. *California: University of California; Berkeley; 1910*

Cowdery, Ray R. Capone's Chicago. *South Dakota: NorthStar Maschek Books, 1987*

Delgado, James P. Alcatraz—Island of Change. *California: Golden Gate National Park Association, 1991*

Delgado, James P. Alcatraz Island—The Story Behind the Scenery. *Nevada: KC Publications, 1985*

DeNevi, Don and Bergen, Philip R. Alcatraz '46: The Anatomy of a Classic Prison Tragedy. *California: Leswing Press, 1977*

DeNevi, Don. Riddle of the Rock. The Only Successful Escape from Alcatraz. *New York: Prometheus Books, 1991*

Dowswell, Paul. Tales of Real Escapes. *New York: Scholastic, 1995*

Duffy, Clinton. The San Quentin Story. *New York: Doubleday, 1950*

Dunbar, Richard. Alcatraz. *California: Smith Novelty Company, 1999*

Eagle, Adam F. Alcatraz! Alcatraz! The Indian Occupation of 1969–1971. *Berkeley, CA, U.S.A.: Heyday Books, 1992*

Earle, Alice Morse, Curious Punishments of Bygone Days. *Public Domain Archive, 1896 (used extensive quotes from the Pillory reference)*

Eldredge, Zoeth S. The March of Portola' and the Discovery of the Bay of San Francisco / Includes Log Of The San Carlos & Other Original Documents. Transcribed and Annotated By E.J. Molera. *California: CA Promotion Committee 1909*

Freedman, Marlene. Alcatraz "No Good for Nobody." *California: Smith Novelty Company, 1974*

Friedman, Lawrence Meir. Crime and Punishment in American History. *New York: Basic Books, 1993*

Fuller, James, and Yumi, Gay. Alcatraz: Federal Penitentiary, 1934–1963. *California: Asteron Productions, 1985*

Gaddis, Thomas E. Birdman of Alcatraz, The Story of Robert Stroud. *New York: Random House, 1955*

Gaddis, Thomas E. Unknown Men Of Alcatraz. *Oregon: New Gate Publishing Company, 1977*

George, Linda. Alcatraz (Cornerstones of Freedom Series). *Connecticut: Children's Press, 1998*

Godwin, John. Alcatraz 1868–1963. *New York: Pocket Books, Inc. 1964*

Gordon, Dan. Murder In The First (The Story of Henri Young). *New York: St. Martin's Press, 1995*

Gregory, George H. Alcatraz Screw: My Years as a Guard in America's Most Notorious Prison. *Missouri: University of Missouri Press, 2002*

Gudde, Erwin G. California Place Names / The Origin And Etymology Of Current Geographical Names. *California: University of California; Berkeley Press; 1960–1962*

Hart, Eugene R. A Guide to the California Gold Rush. *California: Freewheel, 1993*

Heaney, Frank & Machado, Gay. Inside the Walls of Alcatraz. *California: Bull Publishing, 1987*

Howard, Clark. Six Against the Rock. *New York: The Dial Press, 1977*

Hurley, Donald J. Alcatraz Island: Maximum Security. *California: Fog Bell Enterprises, 1989*

Hurley, Donald. Alcatraz Island Memories. *California: Fog Bell Enterprises, 1987*

Johnston, James A. Alcatraz Prison and the Men Who Live There. *New York: Charles Scribner's Sons, 1949*

Johnston, James A. Prison Life is Different. *Boston: Houghton Mifflin Company, 1937*

Karpis, Alvin as told to Robert Livesey. On the Rock: Twenty-five Years in Alcatraz. *New York and Toronto: Beaufort, 1980*

Kemble, John Haskle. San Francisco Bay–A Pictorial Maritime History. *New York: Bonanza Books, 1957*

Kirkpatrick, Ernest E. Voices of Alcatraz. *Texas: The Naylor Company, 1947*

Kobler, John. Capone: The Life and World of Al Capone. *New York: Fawcett Crest, 1972*

Lageson, Ernest B. Alcatraz Justice—The Rock's Famous Murder Trial. *California: Creative Arts Book Company, 2002*

Lageson, Ernest B. Battle at Alcatraz, A Desperate Attempt to Escape the Rock. *Omaha, NE: Addicus Books, 1999*

Landesco, John. Organized Crime in Chicago. *Chicago: University of Chicago Press, 1968*

Martini, John A. Alcatraz at War. *California: Golden Gate National Recreation Area, San Francisco, 2002*

Martini, John A. Fortress Alcatraz—Guardian of the Golden Gate. *Hawaii: Pacific Monograph, 1990*

May, Antoinette. Haunted Houses of California. *California: Wide World Publishing, 1990, 1993*

Murray, George. The Legacy of Al Capone: Portraits and Annals of Chicago's Public Enemies. *New York: Putnam, 1975*

Needham, Ted, & Needham, Howard. Alcatraz. *California: Celestial Arts, 1976*

Ness, Eliot. The Untouchables. *New York: Messner, 1957*

Nichols, Nancy Ann. San Quentin—Inside the Walls. *California: San Quentin Museum Press, 1991*

Odier, Pierre. Rock: A History Of Alcatraz The Fort/The Prison. *California: L'Image Odier, 1982*

Presnall, Judith Janda. Life on Alcatraz (The Way People Live Series). *California: Lucent Books, 2001*

Quillen, Jim. Alcatraz from Inside, The Hard Years, 1942—1952. *California: Golden Gate National Recreation Area, San Francisco, 1991*

Redden, Clifford P. I Survived Alcatraz Twice: America's Notorious Flash Bandit. *Pennsylvania: [Self Published], 1995*

Ruth, David E. Inventing the Public Enemy: the Gangster in American Culture, 1918–1934. *Chicago: University of Chicago Press, 1996*

Schoenberg, Robert J. Mr. Capone: the Real—and Complete—Story of Al Capone. *New York: Morrow, 1992*

Sobell, Morton. *On Doing Time. New York: Charles Scribner's Sons, 1974*

Stanger, Frank M., and Brown, Alan K. Who Discovered the Golden Gate? *California: San Mateo Historical Association, 1969*

Stroud, Robert Franklin. Stroud's Digest on the Diseases of Birds

Stuller, Jay. Alcatraz—The Prison (*Essay originally printed in Smithsonian Magazine). California: Golden Gate National Parks Association, 1998*

Swisher, Carl Brent, Editor. Selected Papers of Homer Cummings, Attorney General of the United States, 1933–1939. *New York: Charles Scribner's Sons, 1939*

Thompson, Erwin N. The Rock: A History of Alcatraz Island, 1847–1972. *Denver: US Department of the Interior, 1979*

Thompson, Leon (Whitey). Last Train to Alcatraz (alternately titled Rock Hard). *New York: Simon & Schuster, 1988*

Trafzer, Clifford E. California Indians and the Gold Rush. *California: Sierra Oaks Publishing Company, 1989*

Williams, Nathan Glenn. From Alcatraz to the Whitehouse. *Washington: Willjoy Publishing, 1994*

Wlodarski, Robert and Anne; Kouri, Michael. Haunted Alcatraz. *California: Ghost Publishing, 1998*

MOTION PICTURES

Alcatraz Island, Warner Brothers, 1937

Alcatraz: The Whole Shocking Story, NBC-TV (Original Air Date: Nov. 5–6, 1980)

Birdman of Alcatraz, United Artists, 1962

Cell 2455, Death Row, Columbia Pictures, 1955

Chain Gang, Columbia Pictures, 1959

Duffy of San Quentin, Warner Brothers, 1954

Escape from Alcatraz, Paramount Pictures, 1979

Escape from San Quentin, Columbia Pictures, 1957

Murder in the First, Warner Brothers, 1995

Prison Train, Equity, 1938

Riot in Cell Block 11, Allied Artists, 1954

San Quentin, RKO, 1946 (Not a remake of the 1937 film)

San Quentin, Warner Brothers, 1937

Six Against the Rock, NBC-TV (Original Air Date: May 18, 1987)

MAGAZINES

Cummings, Homer. *Why Alcatraz is a Success*. Collier's Magazine, 1939

Esslinger, Michael. *Alcatraz—A Brief History*. Crime Magazine, 2000

Harper & Brothers. *San Francisco*. Harpers Monthly Magazine, 1883

Heroux, Harold. *Alcatraz Escape! Secrets of the Island's Most Baffling Mystery*. True Detective Mysteries, Vol 30. NO. 6, 1938

O'Neil, Paul. *Prodigious Intellect in Solitary (Story of Robert Stroud)*. Life Magazine—Reprinted in the Los Angeles Mirror, 1961

Parker, Gitta & Billy Woodfield (Photographer). *Children on Alcatraz*. Collier's Magazine, 1954

Secrist, W.G. & Kelliher, Dan T. *House of Living Hell. A True Picture of Alcatraz*. Liberty Magazine, 1936.

Staff Writer. *Inside Alcatraz: Visit "The Rock" Gold Star Graphic*, 1974

Stroud, Robert (As told to Joseph A. Duhamel with Michael Spivak) *My 53 Years in Jail!* Saga Magazine, 1963

Young, Henri (Assembled & Edited by W.A. Swanberg). *I Saw Hell Break Loose at Alcatraz*. Inside Detective Magazine, 1941

FILM DOCUMENTARIES

Al Capone—Scarface, A&E Biography. A&E Television Networks, 1995

Alcatraz—America's Toughest Prison, TMS WNT Independent Films, 1977. (MPI Release)

Alcatraz—The Big House Series, The History Channel. A&E Television Networks, 1998

Alcatraz—The Final Sentence, Huckleberry Films, 1988

Alcatraz Federal Penitentiary 1934—1963, Asteron Productions, 1986. Simitar Entertainment

Beneath Alcatraz. Michael Hoff Productions, A La Carte Communications, 2000

BreakOut. Michael Hoff Productions, A La Carte Communications, 1997

Dungeons of Alcatraz, Michael Hoff Productions. A La Carte Communications, 2002

Eastern State Penitentiary—The Big House Series, The History Channel. A&E Television Networks, 1997

Escapes from Alcatraz—The True Stories, Michael Hoff Productions. A La Carte Communications, 2000

Leavenworth—The Big House Series, The History Channel. A&E Television Networks, 1997

Public Enemies on the Rock, Michael Hoff Productions. A La Carte Communications, 1997

Return to Alcatraz—Secrets of the Rock, Acorn Media Publishing. A La Carte Communications, 1994

Secret Passages—Alcatraz, Jaffe Productions, The History Channel, June 17, 2002

Secrets of Alcatraz, Golden Gate National Park Association. A La Carte Communications, 1992

Secrets of the Gold Rush, Michael Hoff Productions. A La Carte Communications, 1994

Sing Sing Prison—The Big House Series, The History Channel. A&E Television Networks, 1998

INTERVIEWS / LECTURES / IN-PERSON PROGRAMS

ALCATRAZ FORMER INMATES:
Dale Stamphill, Morton Sobell, Tom Kent, John Dekker, Willie Radkay, Leon "Whitey" Thompson, Glenn Nathan Williams, Jim Quillen, Ben Rayborn, Darwin Coon, Herbert "Lucky" Juelich, and Jerie Bremmeyer.

CORRECTIONAL OFFICERS:
Philip R. Bergen, Clifford Fish, George DeVincenzi, Ned Ubben, Jerry Wheeler, John Robinson, Frank Heaney, John Hernon, Irving Levinson, Al Bloomquist, James Dukes, John McGoran, Joe Landers, Louis Nelson, Bill Long, Pat Mahoney, Larry Quilligan, Dale Cox, Orrin Maybee, Kingston Witchez, Robert E. Sutter, and Father Bernie Bush.

FORMER RESIDENTS AND CORRECTIONAL STAFF / INMATE RELATIVES:
Chuck Stucker, Bob Orr, Thomas Reeves, Bud Hart, Joyce Ritz, Herb Faulk, Don Bowden, John Brunner, Dick Fisher, Kathryn O'Brien, Larry Boyd, Jean Comerford, Harold Clark, Nancy Bertelsen, Ernest Lageson, Agnes Roberts, Phyllis Panter, Jerry Casey, Michael Walter, Cliff Mickleson, Betty Horvath, Ray Stewart, Stanley Stewart, Robert Stites, Jolene Babyak, Renee Keith, Nielen Dickens, and Dena Freeman.

Photography / Illustration Credits

tive Negative Collection, (bl) NARA – RG92, QMG General Correspondence, (br) AC; 49 (t) CSC, (b) SFC; 50 LCHABS, (Inset) AC; 51 (t) GGRNA, NARA – RG92, QMG General Correspondence; 52-53 Alcatraz Fights Program, 54 (t) NA (b) Joe Holt, 55 (t) AC, (cr) Alcatraz Fights Program, (bl) NA; 56 (tl)(tr) NA, (c) AC.

ALCATRAZ FEDERAL PENITENTIARY:

57 (tr)(c) SFPL, (b) LC; 58 PH, 59 (t) NA, (b) CSC; 60 (tl) MNHP/PDC, (center inset) AC, (b) NA; 61 (t) MNHP/PDC, (tc) NA, (tr) LCHABS, (bl) Andrea Pistolesi, The Image Bank, (br) Author; 62 (tl) NA, (tr) MNHP/PDC, (b) NA; 63 (tr) Author, (bc)(br) SFPL; 64 (c) MK, (bl) Author, (br) SFPL; 65 (tl) AC, (tr) MNHP/PDC, (bl)(br) AC; 66 (tl) AC, (tr) MNHP, (c) MNHP, (bl) NA; 67 (tl) AC, (tr) MNHP/DDC, (tc) MNHP/DDC, (bl) MNHP/DDC (bc) MNHP/PDC, (br) AC; 68 (tl) SFPL, (c) MNHP/FC, (b) SFPL; 69 (tl) GDV, (tr) MNHP, (cl) Author, (bl) MNHP/PDC, (br) MNHP/PDC; 70 (series) SFPL; 71 (tr) SFPL, (c) SQ, (b) Columbia Pictures; 72 (t) NA, (b) CSC; 73 (tl) CSC, (tr) NA, (cr)(bl)(br) CSC; 74 (tl)(inset) AC, (bl) MNHP/PDC, (br) MNHP/DDC; 75 (tl)(tr) MNHP/PDC, (c)(b) NA; 76-77 (series) NA; 78 (tl) NA, (tr) MNHP/PDC, (c) AP; 79 (series) SFPL; 80 (series) MNHP/DDC, 81 (tr) SFPL, (br) MNHP; 82 GGRNA – JM; 83 SFPL; 84 (bl) MNHP/PDC, (br) PARC; 85 Author; 86-87 NA; 88 (tr) SFPL (c)(b) NA; 89-90 NA; 92 (bl) SFPL, (br) AC; 93 (tl) MNHP/PDC (tr) PARC (JM Photo); 94 (series) NA; 95-97 NA; 98 (cl) SFPL, (inset) NA, (bl) CSC, (br) NA; 99 (series) Author; 100 (tl)(tc) AC, (cr)(bl)(br) NA; 101 (tl)(tr) AC, (bottom series) NA; 102 (t) CSC, (cl) CJA, (b) NA; 103 (documents) NA, (Photo) AC; 104 (tl) MNHP/DDC, (c) AC, (bottom series) SFPL; 105 (t) MNHP/PDC, (c) SFPL, (b) MNHP; 106 (series) MNHP/PDC, SFPL, NA; 107 (series) MNHP/FC, LC, SFPL; 108 (tl) Author, (c) SFPL, (bl) AC, (br) MNHP/PDC; 109 (series) Author; 110 (t) GGRNA, (bl) AC; 111 (tl) NA, (r) MNHP/PDC; 112 AC; 113 (t) SFPL, LC, (c) MNHP/DDC, (b)(c) SFPL; 114 (t) MNHP, (c) SFPL, (b) MNHP; 115 (tc) MNHP/PDC, (tr) NA, (cl) MNHP/DDC, (cr) AC, (b) MNHP/DDC; 116 (top series) MNHP/DDC, (c) SFPL, (bl) MNHP/PDC, (inset) AC, (br) NA; 117 (tl) GGNRA, (tr) AC, (c) CJA, (bl) NA, (br) MNHP/PDC; 118 (series) NA; 119 (t) GGRNA, (c) CJA, (b) CSC; 120 (t)(c) CSC, (b) Warner Brothers Pictures; 121 CSC; 122 (tl) MNHP/PDC, (bl)(br) GGRNA; 123 (t)(c)CWW-CSC, (b) GGNRA, Interpretative Negative Collection; 124 (t)(c) CWW-CSC, GGNRA, Interpretative Negative Collection; 125 (t)(c) CWW-CSC, (b) AC; 126 (left series) CWW-CSC, (br) CSC; 127 (top series) CSC, (br) GGRNA; 128 (tr)(tl) GDV, (lc) NA, Coast Guard, (cr) Herbert Hart, (bl) NA, (br) MNHP/PDC; 129 (t)(c) CSC, (b) NA; 130 (tl) NA, (c) ELC, (b) SFPL; 131 (t)(c)CWW-CSC, (b) AP; 132 (t) NA, (c)(b) BSC; 133 CWW-CSC, (tr) NA.

FAMOUS INMATES:

136 AC; 137 (bl) AC, (br) NA; 138 (t) JBC, (b) LC; 139 (t)(b) JBC; 140 (t) AC, (b) IV; 141 IV; 142 (t) NA, (bl)(br) IV; 143 ACM, (c)(b) NA; 144 (t) ESP, (c) NA, (b) ACM; 145 NA; 146 (t) AC, (b) NA; 147-153 NA; 154 ACM; 155 PP; 156 NA; 158 (t) BOP, (b) AP; 159; (t) NA, (c) BOP, (b) AC; 161-162 AC; 163 PP; 164 TFH; 165 (t) NA, (c)(b) TFH; 166 NA; 167 NA; 168 Author; 169 Random House; 170 NA; 171 MNHP/DDC; 173 NA; 174 Courtesy of Annette Tanner; 175-184 NA; 189 (t) NA (b) SFPL; 190 (tl)(tr) SFPL, (c) NA, (b) AC; 191 (t)(bl) SFPL, (cr) MNHP/DDC; 192 (t) NA, (c) MNHP/DDC, (b) NA; 193-197 NA; 198 (t) NA, (c)(b) Warner Brothers; 199-202 NA; 203 (t)(b) NA, (cr) MNHP/DDC; 204 SFPL; 205 (t) AP, (cr)(br) SFPL, (bl) NA; 206-207 NA; 208 (t)(cl) NA, (br) SFPL; 209-213 NA; 214 SFPL; 215 (c)(b) SFPL, (tr) AC; 216 SFPL.

THE ESCAPES:

217-218 PH; 219 NA; 221 SFPL; 222 (t) CSC, (b) NA; 223-227 NA, 228 SFPL, 229 AP; 230-233 NA; 235-240 SFPL; 241 NA; 242 (t) NA, (b) IV; 243-250 NA; 251 (t) NA, (b) MNHP/DDC; 252-253 NA; 254 (t) NA, (b) SFPL; 255 NA; 256-257 NA – J. Edgar Hoover Archive; 258-276 NA; 277 LCHABS; 278-292 NA; 293 (c) SFC, (b) NA; 294 (t) JM, (b) NA; 295-296 NA; 297 (t) NA, (b) MNHP/DDC; 298 (t) AC, (b) NA; 299 MNHP/DDC; 300-304 NA; 305 (t) MNHP/PDC (c) NA; 306-311 NA; 312 (tr) MNHP/PDC, (c)(b) NA; 313 NA, 315 (t) NA, (b) CSC; 316 MNHP/PDC; 317 (tl) GGRNA - Betty Wallar Collection, (ct) NA, (b) MNHP/DDC; 319 PH; 320 (t) Courtesy of Cliff Fish, (b) SFPL; 321 CSC; 324 (t) Author, (b) NA; 325 NA; 326 (t) (illustration) PH, (t)(b) MNHP/DDC; 327 NA; 328 AC; 330 CSC; 331 (t) NA, (b) CSC; 332 Julie Esslinger; 333 CSC; 334 (t) NA, (b) SFPL; 335 MNHP/DDC; 336-337 MNHP/DDC; 338 Courtesy of Ernest Lageson; 339 MNHP/DDC; 340 (t) SFPL, (c)(b) CSC; 341 (t) NA, (b) MNHP/DDC; 343 (t) P.R. Bergen, (b) MNHP/PDC; 344 CSC; 346 MNHP/DDC; 347 (br) MNHP/DDC, (bl) AP-Wire; 349 (series) SFPL; 350 (t) SFPL (b) AC; 353 (t)(c) SFPL, (b) CSC; 354 AC; 355 MNHP/DDC; 356 (t) NA, (b) MNHP/DDC; 357 (series) MNHP/DDC; 358 (series) MNHP/DDC; 359 NA; 361 (tl) MNHP/DDC, (tr)(c) NA, (b) SFPL; 362 NA; 363 SQ; 364 (t) Author, (c) AC; 366 (t) NA, (b) Author; 367-372 NA; 373 SFPL; 374-380 NA; 381 PP; 382-385; 386 (t) NA, (b) Author; 387 (t) NA, (b) Popular Mechanics; 388 NA; 389 (t) GGRNA, (c) Author, (b) NA; 390 NA; 391 (t) NA, (c) AC; 392 (tl)(tr) NA (bl)(br) Author; 393-412 NA.

THE CLOSING OF ALCATRAZ:

414 MNHP/DDC; 415 (t) J. F. K. Library, (b) NA; 416 NA; 417 (tr) GGRNA, (br) MNHP/DDC, (bl) NA; 418 (tl) SFPL; (tc) NA, (bl) ArtToday, Inc.; 419 NA; 430 (t) Warner Brothers; (b) SFPL; 421 (tl)(cl)(cr)(b) Author, (tr)(cr)(c) NA.

Index

Supplemental illustrations are italicized.

About the Author

Michael Esslinger is a historical researcher whose work has appeared in several major publications and film documentaries, including segments on the Discovery, National Geographic and History Channels, and a repeated guest on BBC Radio. He is the author of the forthcoming reference chronicling Mans' first expeditions to the moon titled: "APOLLO" - A Historical Chronicle of the Mercury, Gemini, and Apollo Lunar Expeditions. His research resulted in one of the most comprehensive assemblages of information on the Apollo Lunar Landing Program, derived from intensive archival research and in-depth one-on-one interviews, including the elusive Apollo 11 Astronauts Neil Armstrong, Michael Collins, and Buzz Aldrin. He is a contributing writer in the upcoming publication Chicken Soup for the Heroic Soul, part of the New York Times best-selling series, and he has also written historical pieces for the United States Naval Institute. In addition, he has worked as an emergency services professional in the ambulance industry for over 18 years, one of his many passions. He holds two advanced degrees in History from North Manhattan University, and is also a graduate from the former College of Recording Arts in San Francisco. He resides in California with his wife and two sons.